Tolley's Taxwise II
2010/11

Inheritance Tax
Taxation of Trusts and Estates

Authors:

Sue Jones CTA TEP ATT BSc (Hons)

Chris Jarman, Barrister, TEP

General Editor:

Rebecca Benneyworth FCA BSc (Hons)

Members of the LexisNexis Group worldwide

United Kingdom	LexisNexis, a Division of Reed Elsevier (UK) Ltd, Halsbury House, 35 Chancery Lane, London, WC2A 1EL, and London House, 20–22 East London Street, Edinburgh EH7 4BQ
Argentina	LexisNexis Argentina, Buenos Aires
Australia	LexisNexis Butterworths, Chatswood, New South Wales
Austria	LexisNexis Verlag ARD Orac GmbH & Co KG, Vienna
Benelux	LexisNexis Benelux, Amsterdam
Canada	LexisNexis Canada, Markham, Ontario
China	LexisNexis China, Beijing and Shanghai
France	LexisNexis SA, Paris
Germany	LexisNexis Deutschland GmbH, Munster
Hong Kong	LexisNexis Hong Kong, Hong Kong
India	LexisNexis India, New Delhi
Italy	Giuffrè Editore, Milan
Japan	LexisNexis Japan, Tokyo
Malaysia	Malayan Law Journal Sdn Bhd, Kuala Lumpur
New Zealand	LexisNexis NZ Ltd, Wellington
Poland	Wydawnictwo Prawnicze LexisNexis Sp, Warsaw
Singapore	LexisNexis Singapore, Singapore
South Africa	LexisNexis Butterworths, Durban
USA	LexisNexis, Dayton, Ohio

© Reed Elsevier (UK) Ltd 2010

Published by LexisNexis
This is a Tolley title

A CIP Catalogue record for this book is available from the British Library.

ISBN: 9 780754 539179

Printed in the UK by CPI William Clowes Beccles NR34 7TL

Visit LexisNexis at www.lexisnexis.co.uk

About this book

For over 27 years Tolley's Taxwise II has provided practitioners with a practical means of keeping up to date with changing legislation relating to inheritance tax and trusts. This is achieved by way of worked examples, which have been updated annually to illustrate the major changes introduced by Finance Act 2010 and Finance (No 2) Act 2010.

The publication is useful as a manual for staff, also acting as a training aid, as well as giving guidance as to the layout of computations. The examples are supplemented with explanatory notes explaining the law and practice relating to the issue illustrated.

The Taxwise publications are invaluable for students enabling them to apply their theoretical knowledge to practical examples of the types used by examiners in professional examinations.

COVERAGE

A selection of examples on inheritance tax, taxation of trusts and taxation of estates, based on the legislation current for 2010/11, complete with annotated solutions.

The examples are preceded by a summary on page (xiii) of the relevant provisions of Finance Act 2010, which received Royal Assent on 8 April 2010, and Finance (No 2) Act 2010, which received Royal Assent on 27 July 2010.

The book is not an exhaustive work of reference but it shows the treatment of the points that are most likely to be encountered.

The contents list starting on page (v) shows the broad coverage of each example. In addition, there is a general index at the back of the book to assist in the location of specific points.

All statutory references in the inheritance tax sections of the book are to the Inheritance Tax Act 1984 unless otherwise stated.

References to ITTOIA 2005 are to the Income Tax (Trading and Other Income) Act 2005.

THE AUTHORS

Sue Jones CTA TEP ATT BSc (Hons) is Technical Officer for the Low Incomes Tax Reform Group (LITRG); **Chris Jarman** TEP, is a barrister practising from Thirteen Old Square Chambers, Lincoln's Inn, before which he was a partner for 20 years in one of the leading solicitors' private client departments in London. His book *IHT Trusts 'Alignment': A Guide to the New Regime* was nominated for STEP Private Client Book of the Year in 2007. More recently he wrote the detailed section on Post-Death Reallocation of Property Devolving on Death in *Tolley's Tax-Efficient Will Drafting*. He is a regular and well-respected contributor to the Trusts Discussion Forum; General Editor: **Rebecca Benneyworth** FCA BSc (Hons); continuing the original work of Arnold Homer FCA CTA TEP, and Rita Burrows MBA ACIS CTA.

COMPANION PUBLICATION

Tolley's Taxwise I 2010/11 (covering Income Tax and National Insurance, Corporation Tax, Capital Gains Tax, Stamp Duty and VAT).

Contents

v

Contents

Abbreviations

AA 1870	Apportionment Act 1870
A & M trusts	Accumulation and maintenance trusts
art	Article
CAA	Capital Allowances Act
c/f	compare
CFC	Controlled Foreign Company
CGT	Capital Gains Tax
CGTA 1979	Capital Gains Tax Act 1979
CIR	Commissioners of Inland Revenue ('the Board')
CRCA	Commissioners for Revenue and Customs Act
CT	Corporation Tax
CTT	Capital Transfer Tax
CTTA 1984	Capital Transfer Act 1984
EC	European Communities
ECJ	European Court of Justice
EEC	European Economic Community
EU	European Union
Ex D	Exchequer Division
FA	Finance Act
FII	Franked Investment Income
FY	Financial Year
HC(I)	High Court (Ireland)
HL	House of Lords
HMRC	Her Majesty's Revenue and Customs
ICTA	Income and Corporation Taxes Act 1988
IHT	Inheritance tax
IHTA 1984	Inheritance Tax Act 1984
ITA	Income Tax Act 2007
ITEPA 2003	Income Tax (Earnings and Pensions) Act 2003
ITTOIA 2005	Income Tax (Trading and Other Income) Act 2005
NIC	National insurance contribution
pa	per annum
POA	Payments on account
NPDI	Net pre-death income
POCA 2002	Proceeds of Crime Act 2002

Abbreviations

NSB	National Savings Bank
s	Section
SA	Self-assessment
Sch	Schedule
SI	Statutory Instrument
SSCBA 1992	Social Security Contributions and Benefits Act 1992
SP	Revenue Statement of Practice
Sp C	Special Commissioners
TCGA 1992	Taxation of Chargeable Gains Act 1992
TMA 1970	Taxes Management Act 1970
TSI	Transitional serial interest
VAT	Value Added Tax
VATA 1994	Value Added Tax Act 1994
VE	Value of estate
VQTI	Vulnerable person's liability (see also Finance Act 2005 s 28)

CAPITAL TRANSFER TAX – RATES FROM 13 MARCH 1975 TO 14 MARCH 1988

Nil-rate threshold	From	To
£15,000	13.03.1975	26.10.1977
£25,000	27.10.1977	25.03.1980
£50,000	26.03.1980	08.03.1982
£55,000	09.03.1982	14.03.1983
£60,000	15.03.1983	12.03.1984
£64,000	13.03.1984	05.04.1985
£67,000	06.04.1985	17.03.1986
£71,000	18.03.1986	16.03.1987
£90,000	17.03.1987	14.03.1988

INHERITANCE TAX – RATES FROM 15 MARCH 1988

Since 15 March 1988 there has been a single rate of inheritance tax of 40% (halved for some lifetime transfers), applicable where the gross cumulative chargeable transfers exceed a stipulated threshold:

Threshold	Fixed by	Applicable to following transfers
110,000	FA 1988	Between 15 March 1988 and 5 April 1989
118,000	Statutory Instrument	Between 6 April 1989 and 5 April 1990
128,000	Statutory Instrument	Between 6 April 1990 and 5 April 1991
140,000	Statutory Instrument	Between 6 April 1991 and 9 March 1992
150,000	F (No 2) A 1992, FA 1993 and FA 1994	Between 10 March 1992 and 5 April 1995
154,000	Statutory Instrument	Between 6 April 1995 and 5 April 1996
200,000	FA 1996	Between 6 April 1996 and 5 April 1997
215,000	FA 1997	Between 6 April 1997 and 5 April 1998
223,000	Statutory Instrument	Between 6 April 1998 and 5 April 1999
231,000	Statutory Instrument	Between 6 April 1999 and 5 April 2000
234,000	Statutory Instrument	Between 6 April 2000 and 5 April 2001
242,000	Statutory Instrument	Between 6 April 2001 and 5 April 2002
250,000	FA 2002	Between 6 April 2002 and 5 April 2003
255,000	Statutory Instrument	Between 6 April 2003 and 5 April 2004
263,000	Statutory Instrument	Between 6 April 2004 and 5 April 2005
275,000	Finance Act 2005 s 98	Between 6 April 2005 and 5 April 2006
285,000	Finance Act 2005 s 98	Between 6 April 2006 and 5 April 2007
300,000	Finance Act 2005 s 98	Between 6 April 2007 and 5 April 2008
312,000	Finance Act 2006 s 155	Between 6 April 2008 and 5 April 2009
325,000	Finance Act 2006 s 155	Between 6 April 2009 and 5 April 2010
325,000	Finance Act 2010 s 8	Between 6 April 2010 and 5 April 2015

INCOME TAX RATES

Income tax rate bands have altered dramatically since 2007/08 with further changes to be made with effect from 2010/11.

Earnings, pensions, taxable state benefits, self-employed profits up to £37,400 are taxed at the rate of 20% (basic rate) except for a certain amount of income from savings.

Savings income (broadly, bank and building society interest) is regarded as the part of taxable income which is taxed next. The definition of income to be treated as savings income is contained in ITA 2007 s 18. FA 2008 s 5 introduced a 10% starting rate for savings income only, with a current limit of £2,440 subject to index-linking with a minimum increase of £10. If taxable non-savings income (ie earnings and pensions etc as mentioned above) is more than this limit, then the 10% savings rate will not be applicable and savings income will be taxed in full at 20%.

What this means is that if an individual has total income including savings of between £6,475 and £8,915 – the 10% rate will apply to at least part of their savings income. For people over 65 who are receiving the higher personal allowance or for those individuals claiming Blind Person's Allowance these limits will be increased.

However, if the personal allowance has been utilised against non-savings income (as explained above) but the remaining non-savings income is less than £2,440 – the balance of £2,440 against can be used to tax savings income at the 10% rate. Only the balance of savings income remaining is then chargeable at 20%.

Taxable income over £37,400 will be taxed at the 40% higher rate (apart from dividends) whether or not it is savings income up to a limit of £150,000.

From 2010/11 income over £150,000 is taxed at 50% and the personal allowance is withdrawn (gradually) for incomes in excess of £100,000. For every £2 of income above the £100,000 threshold, £1 of the personal allowance will be removed until the personal allowance is extinguished at an effective income level of £112,590. For income between £100,000 and £112,950 the effective marginal income tax rate is thus 60%.

There are changes to the taxation of dividends or distributions from unit trusts (but not interest) – they carry tax credits at the 10% rate and form the last tranche of income and so are taxed at the highest appropriate rate of tax. For an individual paying tax at 40% on their other taxable income they will pay tax at 32.50% on their dividends. For individuals paying tax at the 50% rate there is a new dividend rate for 2010/11 of 42.50%. (FA 2010 s 1, FA 2009 s 4 and 6.)

RATES FOR TRUSTS AND ESTATES

Special trust rates

The 'trust rate' (ITA 2007 s 9) applies to income of discretionary and accumulation trusts.

From 2010/11 the rate is 50% (FA 2009 s 6(4)(a)).The 2009/10 rate was 40%.

The 'dividend trust rate' (ITA 2007 s 9) applies to company dividends and other distributions (including share buy-backs) of discretionary and accumulation trusts. In addition it applies to some dividend income received by all trusts.

From 2010/11 the rate will be 42.50%. For 2009/10 and earlier years the rate was 32.50%.

The special trust rates do not apply to the first £1,000 of relevant income, instead that will be charged at the basic rate.

Trust income not liable at special rates and personal representatives

Trustees of other trusts and personal representatives of deceased's estates are charged at the dividend rate of 10% on dividend income, and the basic rate of 20% on savings income and non-savings income.

Trusts with vulnerable beneficiaries

Trusts with vulnerable beneficiaries are able to elect irrevocably for the income and gains of the trust to be taxed as if the income belonged to the vulnerable beneficiary. See Example 45.

CAPITAL GAINS TAX

From 23 June 2010, there will be two main rates of Capital Gains Tax (CGT), 18% and 28%, replacing the single rate of 18% for all gains. The rate paid by individuals will depend upon the amount of their total taxable income. (F (No 2) A 2010 Sch 1 s 2 amends TCGA 1992 s 4.)

Individuals who are taxed at the basic 20% rate on their total taxable income will be taxed at 18% on their capital gains falling within the basic rate band and those taxable at the higher rates of 40% and 50% will be liable at the 28% rate.

For individuals, where total taxable income and gains after all allowable deductions (including losses, personal allowances and the CGT annual exemption) are less than the upper limit of the basic rate income tax band (£37,400 for 2010/11), the rate of CGT is 18%. For gains (and any parts of gains) above that limit and arising on or after 23 June 2010 the rate will be 28%.

References below to the basic rate band refer to that band as extended by any reliefs eg gift aid or pension premiums. In the absence of such reliefs and of deductible expenses, for the tax year 2010/11 this will be £43,875.

To summarise:

(1)   If total taxable income is below that amount, gains up to the unused amount of the band are chargeable at 18%.

(2)   Any amounts that exceed any unused amount of the basic rate band are chargeable at 28%.

(3)   If total taxable income uses up the whole of the basic rate band all capital gains are charged at 28%.

Gains arising in 2010/11, but before 23 June 2010, will continue to be liable to CGT at 18% and will not be taken into account in determining the rate (or rates) at which gains of individuals arising on or after 23 June 2010 should be charged.

Certain CGT reliefs allow gains on disposal of an asset to be deferred until sometime after the disposal. For instance, a gain can be reinvested in shares under the Enterprise Investment Scheme (EIS) and, subject to conditions, can be deferred until the EIS shares are disposed of. The CGT rate(s) on a gain deferred in this way will be the rate(s) at the time the deferral ends and the gain becomes liable to tax. Gains on disposals before 23 June 2010 which are deferred until 23 June 2010 or later will therefore be liable to CGT at the 18 or 28% rates, in the same way as gains arising on disposals on or after that date.

Gains qualifying for entrepreneurs' relief will be taxed at a rate of 10%, and the lifetime limit of gains qualifying for entrepreneurs' relief will be raised to £5 million (F (No 2) A 2010 Sch 1 ss 4 and 5 amends TCGA 1992 s 169H and N) (from the previous figure of £2 million which applied from 6 April 2010 – the figure for 2009/10 being £1 million). This is discussed in more detail in Examples 36 and 40.

F (No 2) A 2010 *changes for UK resident trustees and personal representatives*

Personal representatives are entitled to the annual exemption, currently £10,100 for the tax year of death and the next two tax years. Gains not covered by the exemption are taxed at 28% for gains arising on 23 June 2010 and subsequently and at 18% before that date (F (No 2) A 2010 Sch 1 s 2 amends TCGA 1992 s 4).

For **trustees**, the CGT rate will be 28% for gains arising on 23 June 2010 and subsequently and at 18% before that date ((F (No 2) A 2010 Sch 1 s 2 amends TCGA 1992 s 4) except in certain cases where entrepreneurs' relief applies when the rate is 10%. For other trusts, the trustees are entitled to an annual exemption (AE) of £5,050 (2009/10 £5,050), divided equally between trusts created by the same settlor after 6 June 1978, subject to a minimum exemption of £1,010 for each trust (2009/10 £1,010).

SUMMARY OF PROVISIONS OF FINANCE ACT 2010 AND FINANCE (NO 2) ACT 2010 RELATING TO INHERITANCE TAX, INCOME TAX, CAPITAL GAINS TAX AND TAXATION OF TRUSTS AND ESTATES

Finance Act 2010 reference	*Tax rates and allowances*	*Example*
s 1	Section 1 imposes the income tax charge, sets the basic, higher and additional rates, sets the basic rate limit and starting rate limit for savings and sets the amounts of personal allowances for 2010/11.	
sub-s (1)	Subsection (1) imposes the income tax charge for 2010/11.	
sub-s (2)	Subsection (2) sets the basic rate at 20%, the higher rate at 40% and the additional rate at 50%.	

Rate bands

s 8	Section 8 provides for the limit of the inheritance tax nil-rate band to be set at £325,000 for the tax years 2010/11 to 2014/15 inclusive and maintains the tax rate at 40% for chargeable amounts in excess of this tax-free amount.	
sub-s (2)	Subsection (2) provides that s 4 of FA 2007 and the table of rates substituted by it will be omitted. Section 4 of FA 2007 previously provided for the limit of the inheritance tax nil-rate band to be set at £350,000 for the tax year 2010/11.	
sub-s (3)	Subsection (3) sets the nil-rate band for the tax year 2010/11 at £325,000 and disapplies indexation for tax years 2011/12 to 2014/15 inclusive.	

Reversionary interests of purchaser or settlor etc in relevant property

s 52	Section 52 provides that where a person transfers property into a trust in which they or their spouse or civil partner retains a future interest, or where a person purchases a future interest in a trust, then there will be inheritance tax (IHT) charges when that future interest comes to an end and they take their actual interest.	

Reversionary interests, as defined in IHTA s 47, are not generally treated as part of a person's IHT estate, but IHTA s 48(1) provides for certain exceptions to that rule.

IHT charges arise on relevant property at 20% on assets put into trust which exceed the IHT nil-rate band (with a further charge of up to 20% if the person dies within seven years of making the transfer); at 6% every ten years on the value of the trust assets over the nil-rate band (the 'periodic charge'); and an 'exit charge' when funds are taken out of trust between ten-year anniversaries at a rate based on the time since the last 'periodic charge'.

Section 52 provides that where certain reversionary interests that are treated as part of a person's estate come to an end and that person takes their actual interest in the relevant property trust then there is a deemed disposition for IHT purposes. This means that there is a transfer of value and IHT will be charged based on the value of the reversionary interest immediately before it came to an end. To prevent these charges being avoided by a person gifting their reversionary interest to another person, such a transfer will be an immediately chargeable IHT event.

These changes affect only reversionary interests in relevant property. They do not affect certain interests in possession which are not included as part of the relevant property regime (for example, a disabled person's interest).

sub-s (1)	Subsection (1) inserts new s 81A into the Inheritance Tax Act (IHTA) 1984:	

New s 81A(1) provides for there to be a disposition for IHT purposes where a reversionary interest (which is defined in IHTA s 47 as a future interest in a trust) in relevant property comes to an end and the person takes the actual interest where that person:

— purchased the reversionary interest; or

— where the person who is entitled to the reversionary interest is the settlor or the spouse or civil partner of the settlor of the trust.

New s 81A(2) provides that where a reversionary interest defined in new s 81A(1) is given away it will not be a potentially exempt transfer.

Subsection (2) provides for these changes to have effect for reversionary interests to which a person has become entitled in the circumstances specified in new s 81A on or after 9 December 2009.

s 53

Interests in possession

Section 53 provides that where an interest in possession in a trust is purchased then for inheritance tax (IHT) purposes it will be treated as part of the purchaser's estate.

An interest in possession is an interest in which a beneficiary has the right to any income arising on the property in a trust. Changes made to the trust rules in 2006 mean that most interests in possession are now included in the relevant property regime.

The section provides that where an interest has been purchased at full value then that interest will be treated as part of a person's estate. Where a person puts funds in to a trust in the normal course of events the normal IHT charges will apply, and the changes in new s 5(1B) will not apply. If a person purchases an interest in a trust other than at arm's length then s 10 of IHTA will not apply and there will be a transfer of value in the normal way.

Subsection (2) amends s 3A of IHTA 1984, which provides for certain transfers to individuals to be potentially exempt from IHT.

Subsection (2)(a) removes the reference to a charge under IHTA s 52 being treated as a potentially exempt transfer. (IHTA s 52 provides for there to be an IHT charge where an interest in a settlement that is treated as part of a person's estate comes to an end.)

Subsection (2)(b) inserts new subsection (6A) into IHTA s 3A. This reinstates the position that a transfer of value under s 52 will be potentially exempt, but provides for an exception to this where the section 52 charge arises in respect of an interest that is treated as part of a person's estate under new s IHTA s 5(1B). This means that, for example, where the trust comes to an end and the capital is paid out, the transfer of value will be immediately chargeable to IHT.

Subsection (3) amends IHTA s 5(1)(a)(ii) so that interests in possession defined in new s 5(1B) of IHTA will be excluded from the general provision that interests in possession are not treated as part of a person's estate.

Subsection (3)(b) inserts new subsection (1B) into IHTA s 5, so that it includes a new category of interests in possession that will be included as part of a person's estate. These are interests to which a UK domiciled person is entitled and which that person acquired in an arm's length transaction (as defined in IHTA s 10). Where new s 5(1B) applies to treat the interest as part of a person's estate the property in the trust will still be part of the relevant property regime.

Subsection (4) provides for consequential amendments to other provisions so that they include interests in possession as defined in new s IHTA s 5(1B).

Subsection (4)(a) provides that the person who has a section 5(1B) interest will be treated as being beneficially entitled to the property underlying that interest by virtue of IHTA s 49(1A). This means that, for example, on death, they will be treated as if they owned the property in which their interest subsisted.

Subsection (4)(b) amends IHTA s 51(1A), which provides that where a person disposes of an interest in possession, this is not a transfer of value, but IHT charges may arise under IHTA s 52. This provision applies only to certain categories of interest in possession, which are extended to include section 5(1B) interests.

Subsection (4)(c) amends IHTA ss 52(2A) and (3A) which provide for IHT charges when an interest in possession comes to an end during the beneficiary's lifetime. The charges only apply to certain interests in possession; these are extended to include section 5(1B) interests. This means, for example, that if a person gives their interest away or their interest comes to an end, then there is an IHT chargeable event.

Subsection (5) amends IHTA s 57A(1A), which provides for relief where an interest in possession is included as part of a person's IHT estate if within two years of their death the property in which they had their interest becomes held in a trust that has been approved as a heritage maintenance fund. The relief is extended to interests in possession that will be treated as part of a person's estate under s 5(1B).

Subsection (6) amends IHTA s 100(1A), which deems there to be a disposition for IHT purposes if there is a change in a close company's share capital (where an individual is entitled to certain categories of interests in possession.). This is extended to interests in possession that will be treated as part of a person's estate under s 5(1B).

Subsection (7) amends IHTA s 101(1A), which treats the participators of a close company as being entitled to an interest in possession in any settled property held by the company. This applies only to certain categories of interest in possession, which are extended to interests that will be treated as part of a person's estate under s 5(1B).

Subsection (8) amends FA 1986 s 102ZA(1)(b)(ii). This provides for the gifts with reservation rules to apply to a person with certain categories of interest in possession, which are extended to include interests that will be treated as part of a person's estate under s 5(1B).

Subsection (10) provides that these amendments will have effect only for interests in possession to which a person becomes entitled on or after 9 December 2009. Some interests in possession are already treated as part of a person's estate – for example, a disabled person's interest. This section does not affect any such interests.

Finance (No 2)
Act 2010 reference

Sch 1 para 2

Schedule 1 para 2 replaces s 4 of the Taxation of Chargeable Gains Act (TCGA) 1992, which previously provided that all gains were chargeable to CGT at a rate of 18%, and adds new s 4A.

Details of the revised s 4 and the new s 4A of TCGA

Subsection (1) of the revised s 4 provides for the section to prescribe the rates at which CGT is chargeable, and that the section is subject to s 169N of TCGA (which provides rules for charging CGT on gains qualifying for entrepreneurs' relief).

Subsections (2) to (4) provide that the rate of CGT is 18%, (subject to other provisions of the section), and that the gains of trustees and personal representatives, and individuals liable to income tax at higher rates, are to be charged at 28%.

Subsections (5) to (9) have the effect that where an individual's taxable income for a tax year is less than their basic rate limit, gains up to the amount of the unused portion of the basic rate band are charged at 18%. Gains above that limit are charged at 28%. Gains in respect of which entrepreneurs' relief is claimed, which are taxable at 10% are set against any unused amount of the basic rate band before other gains — the result being that other gains are more likely to attract the 28% rate.

TCGA 1992 s 4A

New s 4A supplements s 4 in cases where income tax liability is reduced by reason of certain reliefs in relation to life insurance policies, capital redemption policies and contracts for life annuities, or certain income of the estates of deceased persons.

It ensures that these reliefs are taken into account in determining any unused amount of the basic rate band. Section 4A has the same effect as the old TCGA 1992 s 6 which applied for tax years before 2008/09 when the rate of CGT was linked to income tax liability.

The revised s 4 and the new s 4A have effect for gains arising on or after 23 June 2010 (para 12).

TCGA 1992 s 4B

Schedule 1 para 3 inserts a new s 4B into the TCGA. This section provides that a person whose gains for a tax year are chargeable to CGT at more than one rate may deduct any allowable losses and the annual exempt amount for that year in the way that produces the lowest possible tax charge. Existing legislation that limits the way certain losses may be set off continues to apply. New s 4B has effect for the year 2010/11 and later years (para 13).

Paragraphs 4 to 8 amend the provisions of the TCGA that provide the rules for entrepreneurs' relief. Entrepreneurs' relief reduces the effective rate at which gains on disposals of certain assets are charged to CGT. There are two main changes.

First, from 23 June 2010 entrepreneurs' relief is given by charging qualifying gains at a reduced rate of 10%, whereas before that date the relief was given (with essentially the same effect) by reducing the amount of qualifying gains charged at the single rate of CGT prevailing at that time.

Second, the lifetime limit on the gains eligible for relief is increased from £2 million to £5 million. (It had been increased from £1 million to £2 million by FA 2010 s 4 from 6 April 2010; this further increase applies to disposals on or after 23 June 2010.)

Paragraph 4 amends the description of entrepreneurs' relief in the introductory s 169H, to reflect the change in the way the relief is given.

Paragraph 5 amends TCGA 1992 s 169N, providing the mechanism for giving entrepreneurs' relief. The effect of the changes is that from 23 June 2010 gains in respect of which entrepreneurs' relief is claimed are charged at 10%, up to an increased lifetime limit of gains of £5 million. Gains arising before 23 June 2010 that benefited from entrepreneurs' relief are taken into account in determining whether the lifetime limit has been reached.

Paragraphs 6 and 7 amend TCGA 1992 ss 169O and 169P, to remove references to the reduction of the gain made under the previous rules for entrepreneurs' relief.

The changes made by paras 4 to 7 of the Schedule have effect for disposals on or after 23 June 2010 (para 14).

Paragraph 8 substitutes a new s 169R in TCGA. That section applies where shares are exchanged for qualifying corporate bonds (QCBs) (for example, on the takeover of a company) and a gain on disposal of the shares could have qualified for entrepreneurs' relief. QCBs are exempt from CGT.

The main CGT legislation provides that the exchange is not treated as a disposal of the shares. Instead, a gain is calculated as though the exchange was a disposal, and comes into charge when there is a disposal of the QCBs.

Section 169R, as it stood before these changes, applied if a gain on the disposal of the shares at the time of the exchange could qualify for entrepreneurs' relief. It had the effect that, if a claim was made, then in computing the deferred gain that comes into charge on disposal of the QCBs, the deduction of 4/9 that gave the effective lower rate for entrepreneurs' relief should be taken into account, so that entrepreneurs' relief was effectively given.

The changes made by para 8 have the effect that, if entrepreneurs' relief would be available on a disposal of the shares at the time of the exchange for QCBs, an election can be made for the gain not to be deferred but instead brought into charge at that time and the relief claimed. If no election is made and the gain is therefore deferred, it is likely that in almost all cases the gain will not qualify for entrepreneurs' relief when it comes into charge at a later date.

The new rule has effect where the exchange of shares for QCBs takes place on or after 23 June 2010 (para 15).

Paragraph 9 applies where an individual's gain at the time of initial disposal could qualify for entrepreneurs' relief and could be deferred because the individual invests, within a specified time limit, in shares qualifying under the Enterprise Investment Scheme ('EIS shares').

The deferred gain comes back into charge on the occurrence of any of a number of 'chargeable events' (such as a disposal of the EIS shares). Under the entrepreneurs' relief rules as they stood before these changes, it was possible for a claim for entrepreneurs' relief to be made in respect of the gain at the time of the initial disposl, so that it was reduced by 4/9, and then for that reduced gain to be deferred against investment in EIS shares and come back into charge on the occurrence of a chargeable event.

Paragraph 9 modifies the rules for EIS relief following the change to the way in which entrepreneurs' relief is given. In future an individual may choose between claiming entrepreneurs' relief and paying tax on the gain at 10%, or deferring the gain under the EIS rules and paying tax at 18% or 28% when it later comes into charge.

Where a gain exceeds the £5 million lifetime limit for entrepreneurs' relief it will be possible to claim entrepreneurs' relief on the gain up to the limit and to defer the gain above the limit under the EIS rules. This change has effect where the gain arises on a disposal on or after 23 June 2010 (para 14).

When entrepreneurs' relief was introduced in FA 2008 there were a number of transitional provisions which enabled entrepreneurs' relief to be claimed in respect of certain deferred gains that arose before 6 April 2008.

In relation to both gains deferred as a result of an exchange of shares for loan notes, and gains deferred by investment in EIS shares or shares in a venture capital trust (VCT shares), it was possible to claim entrepreneurs' relief on the first occasion on or after 6 April 2008 when all or part of the deferred gain came into charge. Where such a claim was made, the deferred gain, which had not come in to charge before 6 April 2008 was reduced by 4/9.

Paragraphs 10 and 11 amend those transitional provisions following the change to the way in which entrepreneurs' relief is given, so that the new 10% rate and the new limit for it applies to these deferred gains. They have effect in cases where none of the gains deferred as at 6 April 2008 has come into charge between 6 April 2008 and 22 June 2010, so that no claim for entrepreneurs' relief can have been made in respect of those gains.

Paragraphs 12–17 cover commencement dates of the amended legislation.

Paragraphs 18 to 22 provide transitional rules for certain cases affected by the alteration in the rates of CGT part-way into the year 2010/11.

Paragraph 18 ensures that for 2010/11 gains arising before 23 June 2010 are charged at the single 18% rate that applied before that date, and are not taken into account in determining which gains arising on or after 23 June 2010 are set against any unused amount of the income tax basic rate band.

Paragraph 19 provides a rule in relation to TCGA 1992 s 10A. Section 10A provides that, where an individual ceases to be resident in the UK and then resumes residence within a specified time, certain gains that they realised during the period of non-residence are treated as arising in the year they again become resident. Where the resumption of residence is during 2010/11, all gains arising under s 10A are treated as arising before 23 June 2010, and are therefore chargeable at the single rate of 18%.

Paragraph 20 provides a rule for individuals who are taxed on the 're-mittance basis'. This basis is available to individuals who are resident in the UK but are not domiciled here. One aspect of the remittance basis is that gains on the disposal of assets situated outside the UK are charge-able only when they are remitted (brought into) the UK.

Paragraph 20(1) provides that for individuals taxed on the remittance basis for 2010/11, gains remitted to the UK are treated as arising at the time they are remitted (so that the time of remittance determines whether the gains are treated as arising before 23 June 2010 or on or after that date). The provision is subject to sub-paragraph (2).

Paragraph 20(2) addresses the case where ITA 2007 s 809J applies so that a remittance is not treated as a remittance of the actual income or gains being remitted, but instead is treated as a remittance of other in-come or gains in accordance with a special rule.

This can occur if an individual who elects for remittance basis has to pay a 'remittance basis charge' of £30,000. Any gains treated under s 809J as remitted during 2010/11 are deemed to arise before 23 June 2010, so that they are chargeable at the single rate of 18%.

Paragraph 21 relates to situations where TCGA 1992 s 86 applies. Sec-tion 86 applies in cases where the trustees of a settlement are not resi-dent in the UK, and the settlor of the settlement is resident and domi-ciled in the UK and has an interest in the settled property (within the extended meaning of that expression for the purpose of s 86). *51, explana-tory note 9*

The effect of s 86 is that the trustees' gains of the year (net of losses) are effectively charged on the settlor. Paragraph 21 has the effect that where s 86 applies for 2010/11, all the gains chargeable on the settlor by virtue of that section are treated as arising before 23 June 2010, so that they are chargeable at the single rate of 18%.

Paragraph 22 applies where trustees of a settlement are not resident in the UK and their gains are effectively charged on UK-resident beneficia-ries who receive capital payments from the trust under TCGA 1992 ss 87, 89 and Sch 4C. The amount of such a charge is determined by 'matching' capital payments received with trustees' gains (net of losses). *51*

Paragraph 22 has the effect that where the receipt of capital payments in 2010/11 results in gains being charged to beneficiaries for that year, the gains matched with each capital payment are treated as arising when the capital payment was received.

So gains matched with capital payments received between 6 April and 22 June 2010 will be chargeable at the single rate of 18%, while gains matched with capital payments received on or after 23 June 2010 will be chargeable at 18% or 28%, dependent upon how much of the beneficia-ry's income tax basic rate band is unused and subject to the order for setting off losses and the annual exemption under new TCGA 1992 s 4B (above).

Inheritance tax

Question

(i)   Outline the basic principles of inheritance tax.

(ii) 'Disposition', 'transfer of value', 'chargeable transfer', 'potentially exempt transfer' and 'relevant property' are primary terms which need to be considered when determining whether an inheritance tax liability arises on a transaction. Explain the meaning of each term, demonstrating how the terms are linked together.

(iii) Explain the term 'nil-rate band', when a transfer of the nil-rate band is available, and how it works in practice.

(iv) Explain how inheritance tax can become payable at death in respect of transfers of value already made in lifetime.

(v)   Outline the exemptions from inheritance tax.

(vi) Explain the 'grossing up' of a lifetime transfer.

Answer

(i) Basic principles of inheritance tax

Introduction of inheritance tax

Inheritance tax applies from 18 March 1986 having replaced capital transfer tax. As most of the capital transfer tax legislation was retained, the Capital Transfer Tax Act 1984 was renamed the Inheritance Tax Act (IHTA) 1984.

Transfers between spouses and civil partners

A husband and wife or civil partners are separate chargeable persons for inheritance tax, each being able to take advantage of any available reliefs and exemptions.

Chargeable transfers and potentially exempt transfers

Lifetime transfers of value may be completely exempt from inheritance tax (see **part (iv)**). If they are not exempt, they are divided between *chargeable transfers* and *potentially exempt transfers* (see **part (ii)**), the essence of inheritance tax being that chargeable gifts are accumulated for seven years. The tax cost of gifts depends upon whether or not the sum of the accumulated gifts plus the present chargeable transfer exceeds the threshold at which tax becomes payable on the scale applicable at the time of the chargeable transfer. The present nil-rate threshold is £325,000 and this will remain the same until the end of 2014/15, with tax being charged at 40% on the excess over that amount, or 20% for certain lifetime transfers (see below).

Position on death

On death, the chargeable estate is added to the chargeable transfers made in the previous seven years to determine the tax liability. In addition, transfers made in that seven year period that were potentially exempt now become chargeable because of the death. In charging those potentially exempt transfers, chargeable transfers made within seven years before each particular gift are taken into account even though the scale of tax used is that applicable at the date of *death*. Tax will only be payable to the extent that the total transfers less any unused annual exemption at the time of the gift (see **explanatory note 6**) exceed the nil threshold in force at the date of death and a taper relief is available as indicated in (iii) below.

If a donor survives a *potentially exempt transfer* by seven years, it will not attract inheritance tax unless the donor retains an interest in or benefits from the gifted property, in which case the seven year survivorship period only starts to run from the time the interest or benefit ceases.

Where the donor has avoided a pre-owned asset income tax charge by making an election under FA 2004 Sch 15 para 21 or para 22 then the asset is treated for inheritance tax as a gift with reservation and the seven year survivorship period starts from the time that the donor ceases to have any benefit or enjoyment from the property (see **Example 23**).

Chargeable lifetime transfers

Where a lifetime transfer (or deemed transfer) is *chargeable to inheritance tax when made*, the tax is calculated at one half of the then scale rates (see above), the rate applicable to each transfer being arrived at by aggregating it with accumulated chargeable transfers in the previous seven years. If the donor should die within seven years after the chargeable transfer, tax is recalculated at the full rate, but using the scale of rates in force at the date of death, and a taper relief is available as indicated in (iii) below.

Calculation of tax

Because the inheritance tax threshold is increased annually (unless Parliament decides otherwise — which it has for years up to and including 2014/15, see FA 2010 s 8(3)) and because tax rates may also change, it should be borne in mind that the correct starting point for calculating tax on a chargeable transfer is the cumulative chargeable transfers within the previous seven years. The tax on the transfer should then be calculated using a cumulative tax figure for the earlier transfers based on the *current* scale of rates (or the scale of rates at death, where tax or additional tax arises as a result of the donor's death within seven years). That cumulative tax figure will often not represent the tax that has actually been paid, but it is the simplest way to make the tax calculation (see the Example in **part (iii)**).

Trusts

Where property is held in trust, the inheritance tax treatment depends on the type of trust. The detailed provisions relating to trusts are dealt with in **Examples 42 to 65**.

From 22 March 2006 there are special rules for trusts that are created:

(1)   on death by a parent for a minor child who will be fully entitled to the assets in the trust at age 18 (or, with a slightly more onerous regime, by age 25), or

(2)   on death for the benefit of one life tenant in order of time only (more than one such interest may be created on death in respect of different items of property, or

(3)   either in the settlor's lifetime or on death for a disabled person.

The IHT treatment for trusts which do not satisfy these rules follows the mainstream IHT rules for 'relevant property' trusts, which, before 22 March 2006, had been broadly restricted to discretionary trusts. Relevant property is settled property in which there is no 'estate' interest in possession (IIP) (see **Example 52**).

A relevant property trust is any trust to the extent that the trust property is not one of the following categories (the list is not exhaustive):

(a)   excluded property, (see **Example 3**);

(b)   property held for charitable purposes only, whether for a limited time or otherwise;

(c)   property held on accumulation and maintenance terms, in the restricted (and transitional) scope of that concept from 6 April 2008 (only applicable to trusts which have qualified continuously from immediately before 22 March 2006);

(d)   property held on terms of a trust for bereaved minors (s 71A) or an age 18-to-25 trust (s 71D) (available only on the death of a parent of the beneficiary, except that an age 18-to-25 trust can apply from 6 April 2008 to a former accumulation and maintenance trust existing before 22 March 2006 where beneficiaries will become entitled to capital by age 25;

(e)   property held on trust for disabled people settled before 10 March 1981;

(f)   property held on terms of an approved maintenance funds for historic buildings;

(g)   property held in pension schemes (but not benefits which, having become payable under a fund or scheme, become comprised in a settlement);

(h)   property applied to pay a lump sum death benefit with FA 2004, s 168(1) (registered pension scheme lump sum death benefits) from the date of death of the scheme member to the date when the payment is made by the pension scheme;

(i)   property in which an IIP subsists which results in the beneficiary being treated as though he were beneficially entitled to the trust property itself. From 22 March 2006 this is restricted to the following categories of IIPs (for more details see **Example 52**);

  (i)   where the beneficiary has been beneficially entitled to the IIP since before 22 March 2006; or

  (ii)   an immediate post-death interest; or

  (iii)   a disabled person's interest; or

     (iv)   a transitional serial interest; or

     (v)   where the beneficiary became entitled to the IIP on or after 9 December 2009, at a time when he was domiciled in the UK, and did so under an arm's length transaction within s 10 (see 5(1B));

(j)   property in which a company has an IIP if the company purchased that interest at arm's length from an individual in whose hands it was an estate IIP and the company's business consists wholly or mainly of the acquisition of interests in settled property (s 59(2)).

Otherwise, IIP trusts are subject to the 'relevant property' rules.

A limited exception is given to Accumulation & Maintenance (A & M) trusts which allow the advance of capital to be delayed until the beneficiary is 25. It permits the relevant property rules to apply only when the beneficiary reaches the age of 18, so that the theoretical maximum exit charge will be 4.2% when the beneficiary turns 25. However, for trust property settled after 21 March 2006, this exception applies *only* where one of the beneficiary's parents has died and the funds come from the will of that parent or through a trust established under the Criminal Injuries Compensation Scheme.

For interest in possession (IIP) trusts which commenced before 22 March 2006 (see (i) above) the capital is to be treated as part of the life tenant's taxable estate. Interests in possession which commenced after 21 March 2006 will be subject to these rules only if they relate to either:

(a)   a bare trust; or

(b)   an immediate post-death interest; or

(c)   a disabled person's interest.

Otherwise, IIP trusts are subject to the 'relevant property' rules.

(ii) Dispositions, transfers of value, potentially exempt transfers and chargeable transfers

Chargeable transfers and transfers of value

IHTA 1984 part I incorporates a number of sections in arriving at the definition of a *chargeable transfer*:

s 1 Inheritance tax shall be charged on the value transferred by a *chargeable transfer*.

s 2(1) A *chargeable transfer* is any *transfer of value* made by an individual other than an exempt transfer. (It is provided in s 2(3), however, that references to chargeable transfers include references to occasions on which tax is payable by relevant property and other trusts under Part 3 Chapter 3.)

s 3(1) A *transfer of value* is any disposition made by a person (the transferor) as a result of which the value of his estate immediately after the disposition is less than it would be but for the disposition; and the amount by which it is less is the value transferred by the transfer. Unless otherwise provided, 'transfers of value' include events on which tax is chargeable (such as deemed transfers when someone with an interest in possession dies, or chargeable occasions in relation to relevant property trusts) (s 3(4)).

s 3(2) Any diminution in the value of the estate brought about by the disposition of 'excluded property' is ignored.

s 10 Furthermore any disposition which is not intended to confer any gratuitous benefit on any person and *either* was made at arm's length between unconnected persons *or* was such as might have been expected to be made in a transaction at arm's length between unconnected persons is *not* a transfer of value.

A *chargeable transfer of value* is therefore the difference between the value of the transferor's estate before and after the transfer less any exemptions and ignoring disposals of excluded property (as to which see **Example 3**).

A person's estate is defined by s 5(1) as the aggregate of all the property to which he is beneficially entitled, except that the estate of a person immediately before his death does not include excluded property. 'Property' includes rights or interests of any description, but does not include 'settlement powers', ie powers over, or exercisable directly or indirectly in relation to, settled property or a settlement (s 272).

Dispositions

The term *disposition* is not defined but case law has determined that the word has no special or technical meaning (*Ward v CIR* (1956)). It therefore covers any act by which a person deliberately divests himself of the beneficial ownership of his property. The legislation extends its meaning where there are associated operations (ss 268 and 272), deliberate failure to exercise a right (s 3(3)), and alterations of rights attaching to shares in a close company (s 98) (see **Example 22**). Certain dispositions are not transfers of value (see s 10 above and **Example 2**).

Potentially exempt transfers

The concept of a '*potentially exempt transfer*' is contained in s 3A, which was introduced by FA 1986 and extended by F (No 2) A 1987 (but restricted again by FA 2006). Any lifetime transfer of value which:

(1)   is made by an individual on or after 18 March 1986, and

(2)   would but for this provision be a chargeable transfer, and

(3)   is an gift to another individual (as defined – see below), or

(4)   arises because a life tenant with an interest in possession uses his own assets to buy a reversionary interest in the trust property,

is 'potentially exempt' from inheritance tax. It will therefore initially be treated as an *exempt transfer*. However if the transferor's death then occurs during the next *seven* years the transfer becomes a *chargeable transfer*. Any tax on the gift is paid by the transferee.

To come within the definition of a gift to an individual, the value transferred must be attributable to property that becomes part of the individual's estate, or as a result of which the individual's estate is increased. Since 22 March 2006, if the property is settled property immediately after the transfer (whether or not it was so immediately before the transfer) this condition can be fulfilled only if the property is then subject to a disabled person's interest.

Potentially exempt transfers which become chargeable transfers (because the transferor dies within the ensuring seven years) are charged to inheritance tax at their value at the time of the transfer, but using the rates applicable at the time of death. Where such transfers have occurred more than *three* years before death any tax due on that particular transfer (but not tax due on the transferor's estate at death is reduced by taper relief, as in (iii) below. Even though the potentially exempt transfers have become chargeable transfers, no tax is payable (and taper relief is not therefore relevant) if when added to the chargeable transfers in the previous seven years they do not exceed the nil threshold in force at the date of death. The nil-rate band available in respect of the death estate is, however, correspondingly reduced.

(iii) Transfer of the nil-rate band and nil-rate band archive

Nil-rate band archive since March 1975

For inheritance tax purposes the nil-rate band is the amount of the estate or lifetime gift on which there is no inheritance tax to pay. If the estate, including any assets held in trust and transfers of value made within seven years of death, is less than the nil-rate band, no inheritance tax will be due on it.

A simplified form of inheritance tax reporting is available for 'excepted estates' (see **Example 33** part (d)). One factor in determining whether the estate is an 'excepted estate' is its size relative to the nil-rate band or 'inheritance tax threshold'.

For an excepted estate from 6 April 2004, the inheritance tax (IHT) threshold means the amount above which IHT is payable. If the death was after 5 August and before 6 April in any one tax year or before 6 August but the grant of representation is applied for after 5 August of that year,, the threshold that applied at the date of death will be used.

If the deceased died after 5 April but before 6 August in any one tax year and the grant of representation is applied for before 6 August of that year, the threshold which applies for an excepted estate is the one from the tax year before that in which the deceased died.

The table below shows the different nil-rate bands in use for deaths up to 2014/15

From	To	Nil-rate band
13.03.1975	26.10.1977	£15,000
27.10.1977	25.03.1980	£25,000
26.03.1980	08.03.1982	£50,000
09.03.1982	14.03.1983	£55,000
15.03.1983	12.03.1984	£60,000
13.03.1984	05.04.1985	£64,000
06.04.1985	17.03.1986	£67,000
18.03.1986	16.03.1987	£71,000
17.03.1987	14.03.1988	£90,000
15.03.1988	05.04.1989	£110,000
06.04.1989	05.04.1990	£118,000
06.04.1990	05.04.1991	£128,000
06.04.1991	09.03.1992	£140,000
10.03.1992	05.04.1995	£150,000
06.04.1995	05.04.1996	£154,000
06.04.1996	05.04.1997	£200,000
06.04.1997	05.04.1998	£215,000
06.04.1998	05.04.1999	£223,000
06.04.1999	05.04.2000	£231,000
06.04.2000	05.04.2001	£234,000
06.04.2001	05.04.2002	£242,000
06.04.2002	05.04.2003	£250,000
06.04.2003	05.04.2004	£255,000
06.04.2004	05.04.2005	£263,000
06.04.2005	05.04.2006	£275,000
06.04.2006	05.04.2007	£285,000
06.04.2007	05.04.2008	£300,000
06.04.2008	05.04.2009	£312,000
06.04.2009	05.04.2015	£325,000

Transfer of the nil-rate band between spouses and civil partners

FA 2008 s 10 and Sch 4 (para 2 inserted a section 8A into IHTA) introduced legislation to allow a claim to be made to transfer any unused IHT nil-rate band on a person's death to the estate of their surviving spouse or civil partner who dies on or after 9 October 2007. This applies where the IHT nil-rate band of the first deceased spouse or civil partner was not fully used in calculating the IHT liability of their estate. When the surviving spouse or civil partner dies, the unused amount may be added to their own nil-rate band. The claim must be made within 24 months from the end of the month in which the surviving spouse or civil partner dies.

Death of first spouse or civil partner – records

The transferable allowance is available to all survivors of a marriage or civil partnership who die on or after 9 October 2007, whether the first spouse or civil partner's death occurred before or after that date.

The claim to transfer unused nil-rate band must be made by the personal representatives when the surviving spouse or civil partner dies and not when the first spouse or civil partner dies.

No specific action need be taken on the first death. The transfer of unused nil-rate band applies only on the death of the second spouse or civil partner, so there is no need to agree the amount that is transferable on the first death but it is necessary to preserve certain records that will be needed on the death of the second spouse or civil partner.

The information and documents to be kept comprise:

(i)   a copy of the HMRC return (form IHT205 or IHT400; in Scotland, forms C1 and C5);

(ii)   a copy of the deceased's will (if any);

(iii)   a copy of any documents, such as a Deed of Variation, executed after the death of the first spouse or civil partner, that change who benefits from their estate;

(iv)   any valuation(s) of assets that pass under will or intestacy other than to the surviving spouse or civil partner;

(v)   any evidence to support the availability of relief (such as agricultural or business relief) where the relievable assets pass to someone other than to the surviving spouse or civil partner.

But there can be other assets that are chargeable when someone dies such as:

(i)   assets owned jointly with another person;

(ii)   assets held in trust from which the first to die was entitled to benefit and which are treated as forming part of their estate on death;

(iii)   any lifetime gifts made by the first to die in the seven years before their death;

(iv)   any gifts made by the first to die where they did not give up possession and use of the assets, or where they retained a right to use the asset through an arrangement (a gift with reservation of benefit); and

(v)   where the first to die was over 75, any alternatively secured pension fund from which they received a pension.

If any of these apply to the estate of the first person to die, the personal representatives will need to pass on information about these assets as well, for Example:

•   details of the assets concerned and evidence of their values;

•   details about any exemptions and/or relief taken into account in arriving at the chargeable values.

The personal representatives of the survivor will be able to obtain copies of some of the documents required from public records bodies:

•   copies of grants of representation or confirmation and copies of wills are available from the Court Service (for England & Wales, www.hmcourts-service.gov.uk, for Scotland www.scotcourts.gov.uk, and for Northern Ireland www.courtsni.gov.uk); and

•   copies of death certificates and marriage certificates are available from the General Register Office (for England & Wales www.gro.gov.uk, for Scotland www.gro-scotland.gov.uk, and for Northern Ireland www-.groni.gov.uk).

These will give the value of the first estate that was declared for probate/confirmation and will also provide information about who inherited the assets that passed under the deceased's will or intestacy.

However, it will not provide any information about other assets that are chargeable when someone dies (list above).

The personal representatives will need to make enquiries of those who inherited the first estate to see if they can recall whether or not there may have been other assets that were chargeable on the first death. If values are known, they should be included on the claim form; if values are not known, the personal representatives should complete the claim form to the best of their ability and explain the position to HMRC when they make their claim. If there is no evidence that any other assets were chargeable, the personal representatives can make their claim based on the information they have from the documents already mentioned.

With regard to agreeing values of assets such as houses or household goods and whether a relief such as agricultural or business relief applies, it will only be necessary to agree values where such assets pass to chargeable beneficiaries on the first death (ie someone other than the surviving spouse or civil partner or charity). This will be done when the surviving spouse or civil partner dies, but only where it is necessary to do so because the amount of the unused nil-rate band may affect the amount of IHT to pay on the second death. Similarly, if a farm is left to, say, a son and the personal representatives of the first death consider that agricultural relief is due against the whole property, the extent to which the relief is due will be established, if it is necessary, on the second death.

Form IHT402

If the gross value of the estate of the second spouse or civil partner to die is below the IHT nil-rate band that applies when they die, no claim need be made for transfer of the unused nil-rate band.

If a claim is necessary to transfer the unused part of the nil-rate band of the first spouse or civil partner to die, because the gross value of the second estate is above the nil-rate band that applies on their death, the personal representatives will need to fill in form IHT400.

Under s 8B personal representatives dealing with the estate of the surviving spouse or civil partner can make a claim to transfer the unused nil-rate band from the estate of the first spouse or civil partner to die. They will need to fill in a claim form IHT402 available online, or from the helpline on 0845 30 20 900, and send it to HMRC together with the copy documents requested.

The form IHT402 is a request for information about the estate of the first spouse or civil partner to die and is necessary to calculate the amount of the nil-rate band that was unused. A calculation can then be made to determine the extent to which the nil-rate band available to the survivor may be increased and use that revised nil-rate band to calculate the inheritance tax payable on the survivor's estate.

The form should be sent to HMRC at the same time as form IHT400 for the estate of the survivor together with the documents requested (for Example, the death certificate of the first spouse or civil partner to die, a copy of their will and the marriage certificate).

Mechanics of the transfer (IHTA s 8 as amended by s 8A)

The increased nil-rate band does not replace the single nil-rate band available to the survivor that determines whether or not their estate is an excepted estate.

Where a valid claim to transfer unused nil-rate band is made, the nil-rate band that is available when the surviving spouse or civil partner dies will be increased by the proportion of the nil-rate band unused on the first death. For Example, if on the first death the chargeable estate is £162,500 and the nil-rate band is £325,000, 50% of the nil-rate band would be unused. If the nil-rate band when the survivor dies is £400,000, then that would be increased by 50% to £600,000.

The amount of the nil-rate band that can be transferred does not depend on the value of the first spouse or civil partner's estate. Whatever proportion of the nil-rate band is unused by chargeable transfers on the first death is available for transfer to the survivor.

Even if all the assets passing under the will are left to the surviving spouse or civil partner, there may be other components of the aggregate chargeable 'estate' on death for IHT purposes (such as assets in trust, or gifts to other people made within seven years of death). If present, these may use up some or all of the nil-rate band in the normal way, and so reduce the amount of unused nil-rate band that may be available for transfer.

The rules apply in the same way whether the first spouse or civil partner to die leaves a will or dies intestate.

The rules allow unused nil-rate band to be transferred from more than one deceased spouse or civil partner, up to a limit of one complete additional nil-rate band. Therefore, if someone has survived more than one spouse or civil partner, then on their death the personal representatives may be able to claim additional nil-rate band from more than one of the relevant estates. A separate claim form should be completed for each spouse or civil partner who died before the deceased.

However, the total additional nil-rate band accumulated for this purpose is limited to a maximum of the amount of the nil-rate band in force at the relevant time. This is set out in the Example of Martin below.

Existing wills

The rules do not change the effect of existing wills. So people who have, for Example, a nil-rate band trust written into their will do not have to take any action as a result of this measure. But if someone wants to change their will to take account of the rules by removing the nil-rate band trust, that change can usually be made by a codicil, rather than having to rewrite the will.

If the nil-rate band was fully used when the spouse or civil partner died and a nil-rate band discretionary trust was set up under their will and the remaining spouse or civil partner's estate exceeds the nil-rate band on death, they will have made full use of the two nil-rate bands that are available and no transfer will be possible.

If the spouse or civil partner died more than two years previously, there is nothing that can be done to terminate the trust. Any changes to the trust may give rise to a separate charge to inheritance tax on the trust itself.

If the spouse or civil partner died less than two years previously, an appointment of the trust assets in the remaining spouse or civil partner's favour (before the second anniversary of their death, but not within the three months immediately following the death) would normally be treated for IHT purposes as if the assets had simply been left to them outright (see **Example 63 explanatory note 5**). Ending the trust in this way would mean that the nil-rate band was not used on the first death, and so the amount available for eventual transfer to the remaining spouse or civil partner's estate would be increased appropriately.

If a surviving spouse/civil partner executed an Instrument of Variation to create a nil-rate band discretionary trust and use up the nil-rate band on the first death, the position is the same as above: if their spouse or civil partner died less than two years previously, an appointment of the trust assets in a remaining spouse or civil partner's favour (before the second anniversary of their death, but not within the three months immediately following the death) would normally be treated for IHT purposes as if the assets had simply been left to them outright. Ending the trust in this way would mean that the nil-rate band was not used on the first death. An appointment made in this way after the Instrument of Variation which created the trust is valid and will not be barred as a subsequent variation.

Where individuals leave assets on trust with a life interest for their surviving spouse or civil partner, with the remainder passing on their spouse or civil partner's death to someone else (for Example their children), there is no IHT to pay on the first death because spouse or civil partner exemption applies. So if the entire estate is left in trust to the surviving spouse or civil partner, the nil-rate band would be available for transfer to the estate of the survivor on their eventual death in the same way as if the estate had been left to them absolutely.

Any additional nil-rate band is only relevant in establishing whether or not any tax is payable on the estate of the survivor and whether any *additional* tax is payable by reason of the death on lifetime transfers within the preceding seven years – it does not replace the individual nil-rate band amount that determines the excepted estate limit for reporting purposes. If when the survivor dies, their gross estate exceeds the individual nil-rate band amount applicable at the time of their death, the estate cannot qualify as an excepted estate. The personal representatives will still need to deliver form IHT400 and make their claim for the transferable nil-rate band on the death of the survivor.

First death before 18 March 1986 (FA 2008 Sch 4 paras 10 and 11)

Inheritance tax was introduced with effect from 18 March 1986, but before this date other estate taxes (capital transfer tax (CTT) and estate duty) applied. Where a surviving spouse dies on or after 9 October 2007 and their spouse died before the introduction of the current inheritance tax provisions, a claim may still be made for the nil-rate band of the surviving spouse to be increased by reference to unused allowances of their spouse.

Where the first spouse died between 13 March 1975 and 18 March 1986 then the estate would have been subject to CTT. Any transfers to the spouse would have been exempt from tax in the same way as under the current rules. The transfer of nil-rate band provisions will operate in these cases in the same way as it works for inheritance tax. So that if on the death of the first spouse all their estate was transferred to their surviving spouse, then a claim may be made on the death of the surviving spouse to increase the nil-rate band by 100%.

For CTT, initially, all the gifts made during an individual's lifetime were to be taken into account when they died, although this was cut from an unlimited cumulation to a period of ten years in 1981 and then to seven years in 1986.

Before 13 March 1975 estate duty applied. Under estate duty there was no tax-free transfer permitted between spouses until 21 March 1972, when a tax-free transfer between spouses of up to £15,000 was introduced. For estate duty, settled property in which the deceased had a life interest was not always aggregated with the estate on death.

Where the first spouse died between 21 March 1972 and 13 March 1975 a claim to transfer the nil-rate band to the surviving spouse will be based on the amount of the tax-free band that was unused on the death of the first spouse. For Example, a husband died in 1973 and left an estate valued at £10,000, which was all transferred to his wife. As this was all within the spouse's exemption, the individual tax-free band was unused. In this case the full amount of that allowance may be transferred, and a claim may be made on the death of the surviving spouse to increase the nil-rate band by 100%.

Where any part of the first spouse's individual tax-free band was used then there will be a proportionate reduction in the amount by which the nil-rate band of the surviving spouse may be increased.

Similarly, where the first spouse died before 21 March 1972 the transfer of nil-rate band will be based on the proportion of the individual tax-free band that was unused on the death of the first spouse. However, as there was no relief from estate duty for transfers to spouses, any transfer made on the death of the first spouse will use up part of the tax-free band and so reduce the amount by which the nil-rate band of the surviving spouse may be increased.

Other issues

Lifetime gifts

Gifts and any other assets that are chargeable on the first death (eg assets in trust or assets owned jointly with a son or daughter) all utilise the nil-rate band in the normal way and reduce the amount that may be available for transfer.

The unused nil-rate band can only be transferred to be used against an estate when a person dies. If they were to die within seven years of making an immediately chargeable lifetime transfer, so that additional tax is payable on the gift as a result of their death, the transferred nil-rate band will be used in the normal way and may reduce any additional tax due as a result of the death – but the unused nil-rate band cannot be transferred against the tax due on a lifetime transfer at the time the transfer is made.

Low value estates

At present, the excepted estate rules remain as they are; so if the surviving spouse or civil partner's estate exceeds the single nil-rate band at their death (and assuming surviving spouse or civil partner exemption and charity exemption is not available), the estate cannot qualify as an excepted estate even though there may be no tax to pay because of transferred nil-rate band. So for the time being at least the surviving spouse or civil partner's personal representatives must deliver form IHT400 and make a claim to transfer the unused nil-rate band.

If the estates of both spouses or civil partners as at the time of the first death do not exceed one nil-rate band – the executors should still work out how much of the nil-rate band is available for transfer as the circumstances of the surviving spouse or civil partner may change before they die. But if, when they die, their estate remains below a single nil-rate band, there is no need for their personal representatives to make a claim to transfer unused nil-rate band. If by then they have remarried or entered into a new civil partnership, their personal representatives will however need to ensure that the records preserved from the first death remain available for reference on the eventual death of the new spouse/civil partner, since a referential claim at that time in respect of the original death could be made if advantageous.

Jointly owned assets

If all of the deceased's assets were jointly owned and so pass automatically to the surviving spouse or civil partner without the need to take out a grant of representation or confirmation (in Scotland) on the first death then provided there were no other assets chargeable to IHT on the deceased's death, the whole of the nil-rate band is unused and can be transferred to the surviving spouse or civil partner's estate. The personal representatives can make a claim to transfer the unused nil-rate band. Any other assets chargeable on death, such as gifts made within seven years of the death, will start to use up the nil-rate band.

It will be very important for the surviving spouse or civil partner to keep information about any assets (that they know about) that pass to others by survivorship, because the value of those assets will affect the proportion of nil-rate band that their personal representatives will be able to claim. The same applies to any other assets that are chargeable to IHT on the deceased's death such as gifts made within seven years that are not covered by one or other of the exemptions.

Consecutive deaths within a short period

If both parties to a marriage or civil partnership have died, one shortly after the other (even if the interval is just a matter of minutes), the appropriate forms to apply for a grant in the estate of the first person to die should be completed in the normal way. This will establish how much of the nil-rate band is unused on the first death. The extent of the second estate should then be computed by adding together the value of that person's own assets and any assets they inherited from the estate of the first spouse to die.

If this does not exceed the single nil-rate band available to the estate of the second spouse or civil partner to die, there is no need to transfer the unused nil-rate band from the first death. Provided the other conditions are satisfied, a grant as an excepted estate can be applied for.

If this does exceed the single nil-rate band, form IHT400 will need to be completed for the estate of the second spouse or civil partner to die. A provisional claim should also be made to transfer the unused nil-rate band which should be based on the information available at the time of the claim. The claim form should indicate that the value is an estimate and the personal representative should provide the final figure once it is known. The estimated amount of the nil-rate band that can be transferred can be used to work out the tax payable on the second death.

If husband and wife or civil partners die in circumstances where it is impossible to know which, if either, survived the other, for inheritance tax purposes they are deemed to have died simultaneously (s 4(2)). However, the interaction with English property law (Law of Property Act 1925 s 184) may mean that, unless negatived by provisions in the relevant will, the estate of the elder will pass through the estate of the younger, and in that event it would attract spouse exemption in the elder's estate. If that leaves any nil-rate band unused on death of the elder spouse or civil partner, it can be transferred to the estate of the younger, if required.

Remarriage and divorce

Assume that A and B are spouses or civil partners; that A dies; and that after A's death B remarries, or enters into another civil partnership, with C. The position on B's later death is:

- If C has also died in the meantime, while still married to or in civil partnership with B and without making full use of C's nil-rate band, B's personal representatives can if need be make a claim to transfer any unused nil-rate band from C's estate to B's estate, as well as from A's estate to C's estate, but subject to an overall maximum addition of 100% of B's own nil-rate band.

- If by then B and C have been divorced, or C is still living and the marriage/civil partnership is still subsisting – B's personal representatives can if necessary make a claim to transfer any unused nil-rate band from A's estate to B's estate.

- If C is still living at B's death and B did not fully use even B's own nil-rate band (so that a transfer of A's unused nil-rate band was not claimed), then on C's eventual death C's personal representatives can if necessary make a claim not only to transfer B's unused nil-rate band to C's estate, but also for that purpose to transfer A's unused nil-rate band to B's estate so that it is available for transfer to C's estate – but again subject to the overall maximum addition of 100% of C's own nil-rate band.

If on the other hand the marriage or civil partnership of A and B ended by divorce or its civil partnership equivalent, and A has since died, B's personal representatives cannot claim to transfer A's unused nil-rate band to B's estate, as the marriage must still have been in force at the date of the first death (see **Example 4** – Martin below).

Conditionally exempt property

This will depend on whether the surviving spouse or civil partner dies before the conditional exemption ceases. Where the conditional exemption ceases before the surviving spouse or civil partner dies, the charge on cessation of the exemption will apply in the usual way – and if this exhausts the nil-rate band, there will then be nothing left to transfer to the surviving spouse or civil partner.

If, however, the surviving spouse or civil partner dies first and their personal representatives transfer the unused nil-rate band, the amount transferred will not be available for use when the conditional exemption ceases. Nevertheless, if this is some considerable time after the surviving spouse or civil partner dies, the charge on cessation of the exemption will still reflect any increase in the nil-rate band that has occurred between death and cessation.

Examples of how the rules work

Example 1

Ben dies on 14 April 2009 with an estate of £400,000, which he leaves entirely to his spouse, Amanda.

Amanda dies on 17 June 2010 leaving an estate of £600,000 equally between her two children. When Amanda dies the nil-rate band is £325,000. As 100% of Ben's nil-rate band was unused, the nil-rate band on Amanda's death is doubled to £650,000. As her estate is £600,000 there is no IHT to pay on Amanda's death.

Example 2

Jane dies on 27 May 2008, with an estate of £312,000. She leaves legacies of £41,600 to each of her three children with the remainder to her spouse Keith. The nil-rate band when Jane dies is £312,000.

Keith dies on 15 September 2010 leaving his estate of £500,000 equally to his three children; the nil-rate band when Keith dies is £325,000.

Jane used up 40% ((41,600 × 3)/312,000 = 40%) of her nil-rate band when she died, which means 60% is available to transfer to Keith on his death. So Keith's nil-rate band of £325,000 is increased by 60% to £520,000. As Keith's estate is only £500,000 there is no IHT to pay on his death.

Example 3

Cassie dies on 14 April 2010 with an estate of £450,000, which she leaves entirely to her civil partner, Sally.

Sally dies on 17 June 2011 leaving an estate of £675,000 which she leaves equally between her two nieces. When Sally dies the nil-rate band is £325,000. As 100% of Cassie's nil-rate band was unused, the nil-rate band on Sally's death is doubled to £650,000. This leaves £25,000 chargeable to IHT on her death.

Example 4

Martin dies on 14 April 2008 with an estate of £250,000, leaving £124,800 to his son Thomas and the remainder to his spouse Pamela.

The nil-rate band when Martin dies is £312,000 so 60% of his nil-rate band is unused. Pamela later marries Will who dies on 14 May 2010 and also leaves 60% of his nil-rate band unused. Pamela dies on 14 June 2015 with an estate of £750,000 when the individual nil-rate band is £350,000.

Pamela's nil-rate band is increased to reflect the transfer from Martin and Will, but the amount of increase (ostensibly 60% + 60%) is limited to 100% of the nil-rate band in force at the time. So Pamela's nil-rate band is £700,000, leaving £50,000 chargeable to IHT on her death.

Nil-rate band transfer and Capital Gains Tax (FA 2008 Sch 4 para 8)

TCGA 1992 s 274 provides that where the value of an asset in a deceased person's estate has been ascertained for IHT purposes, that value also has effect for CGT purposes. The value of an asset transferred from a deceased's estate will not be determined for CGT purposes until a subsequent disposal of that asset. So generally, where the value of an asset needs to be ascertained for IHT purposes, this will occur on the death of the individual and so before the value of that asset is ascertained for CGT purposes.

In some cases the transfer of the nil-rate band will mean that, to calculate how much nil-rate band can be transferred from the first deceased spouse's estate, the value of assets in that estate will need to be determined when the second spouse dies.

In these circumstances, if the value of the asset differs from any already agreed for CGT purposes, TCGA 1992 s 274 would require CGT to be recalculated on the basis of the value agreed for IHT purposes.

Consequently, the requirement under TCGA 1992 s 274 to use the IHT valuation for CGT purposes will not have effect where the valuation of an asset does not have to be ascertained for IHT purposes on the death of an individual.

So, for Example, if the IHT valuation of an asset does not have to be ascertained until the death of the surviving spouse in order to establish the nil-rate band that may be transferred, then TCGA 1992 s 274 will not require that value to be used for any CGT calculation.

(iv) Tax chargeable on lifetime transfers following transferor's death

Apart from tax becoming payable because a transfer which was potentially exempt becomes chargeable, additional tax may be due on chargeable lifetime transfers made within seven years before death, on which tax is recalculated by reference to the full rate at death.

Four points have to be taken into account in calculating such tax:

(1)   If, because of a change in rate or for any other reason, the tax calculated at death is less than that calculated at the time of the gift, no repayment of tax is due.

(2)   Lifetime gifts which are reckoned at death are brought in at their value at the time of the gift, but using the later rates applicable at the time of death (although if the value of the gift has fallen before death, the death value may sometimes be substituted).

(3)   The taper relief reduces the tax on the gift, not the value of the gift, for the purpose of calculating the tax payable. So if the lifetime gift was below the nil-rate band at death, taper relief will be irrelevant. The percentages used for taper relief are as follows:

Years between gift and death	% reduction in tax payable
0 to 3	0
3+ to 4	20
4+ to 5	40
5+ to 6	60
6+ to 7	80

(IHTA 1984 s 7).

(4)   If business property relief or agricultural property relief was available to reduce the value transferred by the lifetime gift, certain conditions must be satisfied if the additional charge on death is to benefit from those reliefs (see **Example 25 part A(C)**).

Even though tax is only payable on most lifetime gifts if the donor does not survive them by *seven years*, it will still be necessary to keep records for inheritance tax purposes of lifetime transfers for up to 14 years.

Illustration

Edward, having used his available exemptions, makes a lifetime gift of £145,000 cash to a discretionary settlement on 31 May 1997. Although this is a chargeable transfer, no tax is payable since it is below the chargeable limit.

Edward makes a lifetime gift of £196,000 cash to Christopher on 30 April 2004. No tax is payable at that time since the first £6,000 of the gift is covered by two years' annual exemptions of £3,000 each, and the balance of £190,000 is a potentially exempt transfer.

Edward dies on 31 March 2011, leaving an estate at death of £248,000.

The tax arising at death is calculated as follows:

On £190,000 of the gift on 30.4.2004, which was within seven years before death

Having been a potentially exempt transfer, the gift of £190,000 is now chargeable by reference to the scale in force at 31 March 2011:

	£	Tax on scale at time of death £
Gift within previous seven years (31 May 1997)	145,000	–
Gift on 30 April 2004 (196,000 – 6,000 exempt, see **part (v)**)	190,000	4,000*
	335,000	4,000*

(* 335,000 – 325,000 = 10,000 @ 40%)

Tax on £190,000 potentially exempt transfer now chargeable	4,000
Less: taper relief (80% for surviving 6 years but not 7)	3,200
Tax payable by donee, Christopher	800

On estate at death 31 March 2011

	£	£
Gift within previous seven years (30 April 2004)	190,000	–
Estate at death	235,000	40,000*
	425,000	40,000*

(* 425,000 – 325,000 = 100,000 @ 40%)

Tax payable on estate at death	£40,000*

The gift of £145,000 to the discretionary settlement was made more than seven years before death (almost 14 years in fact), but because of the seven year accumulation period it has to be taken into account in calculating the tax on the gift to Christopher on 30 April 2004, since that gift was made within seven years after the gift to the trust and within seven years before Edward's death. The tax chargeable on the gift to Christopher is therefore calculated at the rates applicable to transfers between £145,000 and £335,000. (Had the gift of £145,000 been *potentially exempt*, it would have become totally exempt on 31 May 2004, and would not have been taken into account in calculating the tax on the potentially exempt transfer of £190,000 that became chargeable because of Edward's death.)

The gift to the discretionary settlement is excluded from the accumulation seven years after it was made, that is at 31 May 2004, so that it does not enter into the cumulative total at death on 31 March 2011. The tax on the death estate is calculated at the rates applicable to transfers between £190,000 and £425,000. Note that in the death estate calculation, the tax on the gift of £190,000 is shown as nil, whereas the tax actually chargeable, before taper relief, was £4,000. This is because the tax on the earlier cumulative transfers is a notional figure, based on the scale at death, in order to give the correct starting point for the calculation of tax on the death estate (see **part (i)**).

(v) Inheritance tax exempt transfers

Most lifetime transfers of value made by an individual other than into trust are *potentially exempt*, only becoming chargeable if the donor dies within seven years after the gift (s 3A).

There are however some transfers which are *completely exempt; some of these exemptions apply only in lifetime, others in lifetime and on death*:

(a)   *Transfers between spouses and civil partners (s 18)*.

This applies to all lifetime and death transfers between spouses except where the transferee spouse is foreign domiciled and the transferor spouse is UK domiciled, when transfers are only exempt to a cumulative total of £55,000. See **Example 3(c)** for more detailed information on this point.

Where the transfer results in property being held in trust, with the transferor's spouse or civil partner having an interest in possession or deemed interest in possession (see **Example 52**), the exemption will apply on death. In lifetime, it will only apply if the transferee spouse or civil partner is a disabled person so that the interest in possession (or deemed interest in possession) is a disabled person's interest; otherwise the trust will be a relevant property trust and the transfer will be a chargeable transfer.

The definition of spouse includes civil partners. This enables same sex couples who have performed a civil ceremony to have the same tax position as a married couple (FA 2005 s 103). In the case of *Burden v UK* (Application no. 13378/05) it was decided that sisters in their eighties who had lived together all their lives did not qualify for the exemption.

(b)   *Small gifts to same person* (s 20).

Any outright lifetime gifts to any one person in any one tax year are exempt up to the value of £250.

(c)   *Normal expenditure out of income* (s 21).

To obtain exemption the gift must be made in lifetime and:

(1)   part of the donor's normal expenditure.

(2)   Made out of income (taking one year with another).

(3)   Such as will not reduce the donor's available net income (after all other similar transfers) below that required to maintain his usual standard of living.

An Example would be payment of a life insurance or stakeholder pension premium for the benefit of another. HMRC will normally look for a pattern of giving in relation to this exemption.

(d)   *Gifts in consideration of marriage* (ss 22 and 57).

A gift of up to £5,000 by a parent of a party to a marriage; of £2,500 by a lineal ancestor; of £2,500 by one party to the marriage to the other; or of £1,000 by any other person is exempt providing it is a lifetime gift made in consideration of the marriage. If it is a marriage settlement it must be primarily for the benefit of the parties to the marriage, their issue or the spouses of such issue. The limit applies to gifts by any one donor for any one marriage. For this exemption 'children' include step-children, adopted and illegitimate children.

A civil partnership is deemed, for taxation, to be the equivalent of a marriage and therefore gifts in consideration of a civil ceremony, to the limits set out above, will be exempt transfers.

(e)   *All gifts to charities or registered community amateur sports clubs, either outright or held on trust for charitable purposes only or, in the case of a sports club, held for the purposes of the club or another registered club or an eligible sports governing body or a charity (s 23 and FA 2002 Sch 18 para 9).*

All such gifts are exempt whether in lifetime or on death.

(f)   *Gifts to political parties* (s 24).

Gifts to a qualifying political party, whether in lifetime or on death, are wholly exempt.

(g)   *Gifts for national purposes* (s 25 and Sch 3).

All such qualifying gifts are exempt whether in lifetime or on death.

(h)   *Maintenance funds for heritage property* (s 27 and Sch 4).

On a claim being made, transfers into a settlement established for the maintenance, repair or preservation of heritage property are exempt providing a Treasury direction is made in respect of the property under Sch 4. The exemption applies in lifetime or on death. A claim must be made within two years of the date of transfer or such longer period as HMRC may allow.

(i)   *Gifts to housing associations* (s 24A).

Gifts of land to a registered housing association are exempt whether in lifetime or on death.

(j)   *Employee trusts* (s 28).

Transfers by individuals of shares or securities in a company to a trust for the benefit of employees of the company are exempt, providing detailed conditions are satisfied.

HMRC concession F20 exempts certain compensation payments made to World War 2 survivors or their estates — see **Example 3 part (a)**. As indicated in (ii) above, certain property that is not exempt is nonetheless left out of account because it is 'excluded property'. Details of excluded property are also in **Example 3 part (a)**.

Where an exempt beneficiary settles a claim against a deceased's estate out of his own resources the exemption is abated. This could occur, for Example, where a claim is made for financial provision against an estate by a non-exempt beneficiary (eg a child or mistress of the deceased). If, instead of the estate meeting the claim, an exempt beneficiary met the liability (eg spouse, charity etc) then tax would be avoided, since that part of the estate passing to the exempt beneficiary rather than to the non-exempt beneficiary would not have attracted tax. Section 29A provides that any such value transferred by the exempt beneficiary is treated as a chargeable part of the deceased's estate.

Annual exemption (s 19)

For those *lifetime transfers* which are not completely exempt there is an annual exemption.

The first £3,000 of transfers in any tax year are exempt provided they are completed in the lifetime of the individual. Any unused portion of the exemption may be carried forward for one year only, for use in the following tax year after the exemption for that following year has been completely used.

The annual exemption is applied to lifetime transfers that are not completely exempt in strict chronological order. In the case of a lifetime transfer which does not give rise to an immediate charge, it is only the balance over and above any available exemptions, including any annual exemptions, which is a potentially exempt transfer, as illustrated in **part (iii)** above in relation to the gift by Edward.

Availability of exemptions to trusts

With the exception of (b), (c) and (j), the above exemptions are available to transfers out of interest in possession trusts, subject in the case of the annual and marriage exemptions to certain conditions (s 57 — see **Example 55 explanatory note 3**).

The exemptions are not available on distributions out of relevant property trusts since those are not transfers of value'; but equivalent exemptions are provided in the case of distributions to employee trusts or charitable trusts — see **Example 59 explanatory note 11**).

Conditional exemption for heritage property (s 30).

On a claim being made within two years of the event, exemption is granted, subject to conditions, for the transfer of property that is designated by the Treasury as of pre-eminent national, scientific, historic, artistic or scenic interest (eg works of art and historic buildings). This applies to transfers on death and to lifetime transfers where the property has been owned for six years or more by the transferor and/or his spouse, or where it passed to the transferor on the death of another. Tax may be chargeable if the conditions are no longer satisfied — see **explanatory note 4**.

(vi) 'Grossing up' of a lifetime transfer

'Grossing up' is a term that applies where the donor pays the inheritance tax arising on the making of a chargeable transfer. The donor is therefore effectively making two dispositions, one directly to the transferee and the second to HMRC in respect of a liability arising on the first disposition. The value of the donor's estate is reduced on each occasion and the inheritance tax is calculated by reference to the reduction in the value of the donor's estate.

Illustration

Mr Smith has already made chargeable transfers of £325,000 and has used up all his available exemptions. He makes a chargeable transfer of £8,000 to a discretionary settlement on 1 May 2010 and agrees to pay the inheritance tax. The rate of tax on lifetime gifts over £325,000 is one half of 40%, ie 20% so that the £8,000 received into the settlement must represent 80% of the gross gift, so the gross gift is 100/80ths of the net gift = £10,000.

The calculation is as follows:

		Gross £	*Tax* £	*Net* £
Cumulative chargeable transfers to date		325,000	–	325,000
1 May 2010	Gift to discretionary settlement			
	Net			8,000
	Grossed up			
$\frac{100}{80} \times 8,000$		10,000	2,000	
Cumulative chargeable transfers carried forward		335,000	2,000*	333,000

(*335,000 – 325,000 = 10,000 @ 20%)

If Mr Smith's previous transfers had been £319,000 instead of £325,000, the position would have been:

		Gross £	*Tax* £	*Net* £
Cumulative chargeable transfers to date		319,000	–	319,000
1 May 2010	Gift to settlement within nil band	6,000	–	6,000
	Remaining net gift			2,000
	Grossed up			
$\frac{100}{80} \times 2,000$		2,500	500	
Cumulative chargeable transfers carried forward		327,500	500*	327,000

(*327,500 – 325,000 = 2,500 @ 20%)

A potentially exempt transfer never has to be grossed up. This is because the transferor is never personally liable for the tax. If tax is payable it is because of the death of the transferor within the next seven years. In that event the donee is primarily responsible for the tax.

Explanatory Notes

Normal expenditure out of income

(1)   'Normal expenditure out of income' was considered in the case of *Bennett and Others v CIR* (1994), where it was held that there was no fixed minimum period during which the expenditure must be incurred. All that was required was for the pattern of actual or intended payments to have been established, and for the pattern of payments to be intended to remain in place for a sufficient period to be regarded as a regular feature of the transferor's annual expenditure, and that the item in question conformed with that pattern.

Gifts in consideration of marriage or civil ceremony

(2)   Whether a gift is in consideration of a marriage or civil ceremony is a question of fact. A gift made on the occasion of a marriage or civil ceremony or one made conditionally upon the marriage/civil ceremony taking place, whilst usually qualifying, is not automatically in consideration of marriage/ civil ceremony. This is an involved legal point and reference to appropriate judicial decisions should be made if the point requires consideration in greater depth.

Gifts to political parties

(3)   Exemption is not given for gifts to all political parties, but only to those where, at the last general election preceding the transfer:

(a)   Two members of that party were elected to the House of Commons, or

(b)   One member of that party was elected to the House of Commons and no fewer than 150,000 votes were given to candidates of that party (s 24(2)).

Heritage property

(4)   The conditions under which exemption is available for heritage property and the circumstances in which inheritance tax becomes payable are dealt with in **Example 29**.

Gifts to housing associations

(5)   Land is not defined for the purpose of the s 24A exemption on gifts to housing associations. It would appear therefore that buildings are included, since they are within the definition of land in the Interpretation Act 1978 Sch 1.

Annual exemption

(6)   The treatment of the annual exemption outlined in **part (v)** of the Example appears to conflict with s 19(3A), which provides that if a potentially exempt transfer becomes a chargeable transfer because of the donor's death within seven years, any annual exemption which has not been used then becomes available, and is given against the earliest transfer if there is more than one. An annual exemption which has already been given on chargeable transfers in the same year is not to be disturbed, even if some or all of the potentially exempt transfers that have become chargeable were made before the transfers against which the annual exemption had been utilised. But potentially exempt transfers that become chargeable take priority over chargeable transfers in a *later* tax year, so that where an unused annual exemption had been carried forward and used in the following tax year, the exemption is to be given instead against the potentially exempt transfers, and the tax on the transfers which originally used it has to be recomputed.

The provisions of s 19(3A) are, however, redundant when considered in the light of the definition of 'potentially exempt transfer' in s 3A, namely that a potentially exempt transfer is a transfer that would be a chargeable transfer but for s 3A. Any part of a transfer covered by the annual exemption is an exempt transfer, and therefore would not be a chargeable transfer apart from s 3A. It follows that if a potentially exempt transfer becomes chargeable there cannot possibly be any available annual exemption to use against it. Despite the fact that a drafting error makes s 19(3A) meaningless, no action has been taken to correct it.

The capital gains tax gifts holdover relief provisions of TCGA 1992 s 260 are available against a lifetime gift that is to any extent a chargeable transfer, even if a slice of it is covered by the inheritance tax annual exemption. Capital gains tax gifts relief is dealt with in the companion to this book, **Tolley's Taxwise I 2010/11**. See **Example 25 part A (c)** for the interaction between the annual exemption and business and agricultural property relief.

Voidable transfers

(7)   A transfer which is set aside by enactment or rule of law (eg bankruptcy) is not counted as a transfer for inheritance tax purposes, and neither is the transfer back (s 150 — voidable transfers).

Dispositions that are not transfers of value

(8)   This Example deals with transfers of value that are wholly or partly exempt. **Example 2** at **part (a)** illustrates that there are certain dispositions which are not treated as transfers of value at all.

Taper relief

(9)   It should be noted that even though transfers may immediately or subsequently be chargeable transfers, no tax is payable until the cumulative total exceeds the nil threshold. Any transfers within that nil rate slice do not attract any tax, later transfers above the threshold bearing the whole of the tax payable (subject to taper relief if available). Since the transfers within the nil rate slice never attract any tax, the taper relief that applies when a donor survives a gift by more than three years but less than seven is irrelevant on those transfers.

Illustration

A wealthy married couple who have made no previous gifts want to know how much cash they could give away on 4 April 2011 without any possibility of inheritance tax ever being payable on the gifts. (No specific exemptions are available.)

Each spouse could give £331,000, making a total of £662,000. £6,000 each would be covered by the current and previous years' annual exemptions, leaving potentially exempt transfers of £325,000 each. If they both then died the next day, the potentially exempt gifts would become chargeable, but they would be covered by the nil threshold. Tax at 40% would be payable on each of their chargeable estates at death, since the nil threshold would have been used up by the lifetime gifts.

If they survived for seven years, they could in the meantime each make annual gifts amounting to the £3,000 annual exemption plus any annual increase in the nil threshold and after the seven years they could then make further gifts equal to the then nil threshold each, because their initial potentially exempt gifts would become completely exempt at that point. Taper relief would not be relevant no matter how long they survived, since all gifts would be either exempt or covered by the nil threshold. Again tax at the full rate would be paid on the whole of their chargeable death estates, since the nil threshold would have been fully used against lifetime gifts.

Failure to exercise a right

(10)   As indicated in **part (ii)** of the Example, the failure to exercise a right is a disposition for inheritance tax under s 3(3). Such a disposition is treated as made at the latest time that the right could have been exercised. On the other hand, s 10 provides that any disposition that is not intended to confer a gratuitous benefit is not a transfer of value.

Where an employee dies in service after the earliest age at which he could have retired, and a lump sum death benefit is held in trust for his dependants, the employee could be regarded as having failed to exercise his right to take the pension. HMRC had stated that they will not take this point in genuine cases of deferred retirement, and will only do so where there is evidence that the intention of deferring benefits was to increase the estate of someone else. However, the recent decision in Fryer and others (PRs of Arnold) v HMRC (2010) demonstrates that other motives such as minimising income tax and non-requirement of income will not displace an intention of benefiting others ascertained from an earlier assignment of death benefits.

Similar provisions apply in respect of Registered Pension Schemes from 6 April 2006. The legislation is to be found in FA 2006, Sch 22.

An IHT charge can arise in a scheme member's lifetime under IHTA 1984 s 3(3), if they do not exercise their right to take pension benefits. The charge applies at the latest time when the right could be exercised i.e. immediately before death. For Example, if a scheme member did not take their pension when their life expectancy was seriously impaired, and this resulted in an enhanced death benefit being paid to their beneficiaries, then IHT could apply.

Currently, by concession, IHT is not charged in respect of these enhanced death benefits where the beneficiary is a spouse, civil partner or person who is financially dependant on the scheme member. In addition, payments arising in these circumstances which are made to charity will also be exempted from IHT. Nor is IHT applied where a scheme member chooses not to exercise a right at a time when this choice does not trigger a charge (for Example, choosing not to take a pension when they are in good health) and does not subsequently vary that choice, even when a reduction in their life expectancy would in strictness trigger an IHT charge.

Fall in value of gift before donor's death

(11) For detailed notes on the relief where the value of a gift has fallen before the donor's death see **Example 12**.

Question

(a)   Consider whether the following are 'transfers of value':

    (i)   School fees paid for the education of the transferor's son.

    (ii)   School fees paid for the education of the transferor's grandson.

    (iii)   Sums paid to a sister of the transferor for her maintenance.

    (iv)   An entitlement to a bonus as sales director of a family company, and to a dividend on a holding of shares therein, both of which have been waived.

    (v)   Payment by a sole trader of £30,000 compensation for loss of office to a former employee.

    (vi)   A loan of £50,000 to a friend.

(b)   Charles, a widower, made the following gifts (after all exemptions other than the annual exemption):

    (i)   10 July 1996: £66,000 to grandson

    (ii)   20 May 2000: £242,000 to a discretionary settlement — on condition that the trustees paid the inheritance tax due

    (iii)   12 June 2001: £37,000 to nephew

    (iv)   20 October 2003: £198,000 to a discretionary settlement — on condition that the trustees paid the inheritance tax due

    (v)   1 January 2005: £270,000 to an accumulation and maintenance settlement for his grandchildren

On 8 August 2010 Charles died leaving an estate of £400,000. By his will he left £200,000 to the Save the Children Fund and the balance to his daughter absolutely.

Calculate the inheritance tax payable on each of the gifts in lifetime and on death, and on the death estate.

Answer

(a) Dispositions that are not transfers of value

Certain dispositions are not transfers of value:

(1) Dispositions which are not intended to confer any gratuitous benefit and made on arm's length terms (s 10).

(2) Expenditure on family maintenance (s 11). This covers dispositions:

> (a) For the maintenance of the transferor's spouse, or former spouse if made on dissolution or annulment of the marriage (s 11(1) and (6)) (the same rules now apply to civil partnerships), or
>
> (b) For the maintenance, education or training of a child for a period ending not later than the tax year in which the child becomes 18 years of age or, after attaining that age, ceases to undergo full-time education or training.
>
> > For this purpose 'child' includes:
> >
> > (i) A child of the transferor by marriage or previous marriage (s 11(1) (6)).
> >
> > (ii) An illegitimate child of the transferor (s 11(4)).
> >
> > (iii) A child who is not in the care of a parent (but dispositions to such a child for a period ending after the year in which he reaches age 18 will not be exempt unless the child was in the care of the transferor for substantial periods before he became 18) (s 11(2)).
>
> or
>
> (c) Made for the reasonable care and maintenance of a dependent relative (s 11(3)). The term 'dependent relative' is defined in s 11(6).

(3) A waiver or repayment of remuneration (s 14), and a waiver of dividends made within twelve months before any right to the dividend has accrued (s 15).

(4) Expenditure which is allowable as a deduction in computing a person's profits or gains for income or corporation tax (s 12).

(5) Transfers to employee trusts by close companies (s 13).

(6) A grant of an agricultural tenancy for full consideration (s 16).

(7) Deeds of variation within s 142 and certain other post-death adjustments (s 17).

The position in the six situations given is therefore:

(i) *School fees for education of transferor's son*

> Leaving aside the possibility that the school fees were paid out of income and therefore may be exempt as annual expenditure out of income, school fees paid for the education of the transferor's son will not be a transfer of value providing the son is under 18 or still in full-time education or training.

(ii) *School fees for education of transferor's grandson*

> If the school fees for the grandson were not paid out of income then they will be a transfer of value unless the grandson is under 18 and is not in the care of one of his parents; or the grandson is over 18 and is not in the care of one of his parents *and* was in the care of his grandparent for substantial periods before reaching the age of 18.

(iii) *Gifts for maintenance of sister*

Again leaving aside the question of exempt normal payments out of income, gifts to the transferor's sister for her maintenance would be a transfer of value unless the sister was a dependent relative by reason of old age or infirmity *and* the amounts were reasonable for her care and maintenance, or unless she was not in the care of a parent and was either under 18 years of age or if over 18, had been in the care of the transferor for substantial periods before reaching age 18 and in that event was still in full time education or training.

(iv) *Waiver of remuneration and dividends*

The waiver of remuneration is not a transfer of value, nor is the dividend waiver if waived within twelve months before any right to it has accrued.

(v) *Compensation for loss of office*

So long as the compensation payment is allowed in computing profits, it will not be a transfer of value.

(vi) *Loan to a friend*

If someone lends money or property for a prolonged period, or denies himself the opportunity to recall the money or property, the property is then worth less in the owner's hands than it was before. Thus if the £50,000 is lent free of interest for a fixed term of ten years and after making the loan the lender requires the cash, the only way to obtain it is to assign the debt to someone else. But for how much? Not £50,000, because the assignee will want a commercial return, which he will obtain by paying sufficiently below £50,000 to compensate for having to wait for the remainder of the ten years before the capital sum becomes repayable. A transfer of value will thus arise on the difference between the amount lent and the discounted present value of the future right to repayment.

If however the loan is repayable on demand or on reasonable notice, especially but not necessarily if it is at a commercial rate of interest, and there is no question over the borrower's ability to repay it, then there will be no diminution in its value, and a transfer of value will not arise.

If the various conditions stated above were not satisfied, the payments would be transfers of value, against which the current and previous years' annual exemptions could be used if available.

To the extent that the amounts in (iii) and (v) were not covered by the annual exemption, they would be potentially exempt transfers and therefore only brought into account if the donor died within the next seven years.

If the school fees under (i) and (ii) are not within the 'family maintenance' exemption and are not by way of settlement, it is possible that the transfers could be regarded as chargeable transfers of value (subject to any other available exemptions) rather than potentially exempt transfers because for a transfer to an individual to be potentially exempt, the transferee's estate must be increased by the transfer, which would not directly apply in these two instances. Similarly, any transfer of value arising out of the loan at (vi) would be a chargeable transfer rather than a potentially exempt transfer unless the estate of the borrower could be regarded as increased by the value of the right to have the loan on favourable terms. If this represents a risk it can be avoided by paying the money in the first instance to, or to a bare trustee for, the person whose education is being funded, with a view to that person then actually paying the school fees.

(b) Charles — inheritance tax position on lifetime gifts and on estate at death

Tax payable in lifetime

				Gross accumulation £	Tax £
10 July 1996 —	gift to grandson			66,000	
	Less: Annual exemptions	1996/97	3,000		
		1995/96	3,000	6,000	
Potentially exempt transfer				60,000	
20 May 2000 —	gift to discretionary settlement			242,000	
	Less: Annual exemptions	2000/01	3,000		
		1999/00	3,000	6,000	
Lifetime chargeable transfer (one half rates)				236,000	400*

(* 236,000 – 2000/01 threshold 234,000 = 2,000 @ 20%)
Inheritance tax payable by trustees £400.

				Gross accumulation £	Tax £
12 June 2001 —	gift to nephew			37,000	
	Less: Annual exemption	2001/02		3,000	
Potentially exempt transfer				34,000	

					Tax on 2003/04 scale
				236,000	–
20 Oct 2003 —	gift to discretionary settlement		198,000		
	Less: Annual exemptions	2003/04	3,000		
		2002/03	3,000	6,000	
Lifetime chargeable transfer (one half rates)				192,000	34,600*
				428,000	34,600*

(* 428,000 – 2003/04 threshold 255,000 = 173,000 @ 20%)
Inheritance tax payable by trustees £34,600.

			Gross accumulation £	
1 Jan 2005 —	gift to accumulation and maintenance settlement		270,000	
	Less: Annual exemption	2004/05	3,000	
Potentially exempt transfer			267,000	
20 May 2007 —	exclude transfer seven years earlier		(236,000)	
			192,000	

On death of Charles — 8 August 2010

	Gross £	Tax (using 2010/11 rates) £

Transfers within seven years before death i.e.
    9 August 2003 to 8 August 2010:
    20 October 2003 — gift to discretionary settlement

		Gross £	Tax (using 2010/11 rates) £
Cumulative *chargeable* transfers within previous seven years			
(ie 21 October 1996 – 20 October 2003 — see **explanatory note 3**)		236,000	
Chargeable transfer (full rates)		192,000	41,200*
		428,000	41,200*

(* 428,000 – 325,000 = 103,000 @ 40%)

1 January 2005 — gift to accumulation and maintenance settlement

		Gross £	Tax £
Cumulative *chargeable* transfers within previous seven years			
(ie 2 January 2000 – 1 January 2005)		428,000	41,200
Chargeable transfer		267,000	106,800
		695,000	148,000*

(* 695,000 – 325,000 = 370,000 @ 40%)

8 August 2010 – date of death

		Gross £	Tax £
Cumulative chargeable transfers within previous seven years			
(192,000 + 267,000) (ie 9 August 2003 – 8 August 2010)		459,000	53,600*
Estate on death	400,000		
Less: Exempt – Legacy to charity	200,000	200,000	80,000
		659,000	133,600**

(* 459,000 – 325,000 = 134,000 @ 40%)
(** 659,000 – 325,000 = 334,000 @ 40%)

Inheritance tax payable — lifetime

		£
(i)	Grandson	nil
(ii)	trustees of 2000 discretionary settlement	400
(iii)	Nephew	nil
(iv)	trustees of 2003 discretionary settlement	34,600
(v)	trustees of accumulation and maintenance settlement	nil

Inheritance tax payable — death

		£	£
By grandson, trustees of 2000 discretionary settlement and nephew (excluded as gifts were made more than seven years before death)			
By trustees of 2003 discretionary settlement			
Tax due on death scale		41,200	
Less: Taper relief 80% (6–7 years)		32,960	
		8,240	
Less: Paid on lifetime transfer		34,600	nil
(No repayment will be made to the trustees)			
By trustees of accumulation and maintenance settlement			
Tax due on death		106,800	
Less: Taper relief 20% (3–4 years)		21,360	85,440
By personal representatives			80,000
			165,440

Explanatory Notes

Dispositions for family maintenance

(1) The distinction between school fees paid for the education of the transferor's son and his grandson illustrates how carefully the wording of a section has to be considered, particularly since the heading of a section is often widely descriptive, in this case being 'disposition for maintenance of family' (s 11). Broadly speaking, transfers for the maintenance of one's own children are not chargeable if the child is either under 18 or still in full time education. Transfers for the maintenance of other persons are chargeable (in the absence of other exemptions) unless the child is *not* in the care of a parent and if over 18, was in the care of the transferor for substantial periods before reaching age 18 and is still in full time education or training.

Potentially exempt transfers to grandson and nephew

(2) The gifts to grandson and nephew in **part (b)** are made after 17 March 1986 and are outright gifts by an individual to another individual, and are therefore potentially exempt transfers in so far as they exceed the available annual exemptions.

Since the transferor did not die within seven years after the gifts, the potentially exempt transfers become exempt transfers, so there is no inheritance tax liability on them and they are not taken into account in the figure of cumulative chargeable transfers. For more detailed notes see **Example 4 explanatory note 6**.

Cumulation of transfers

(3) When calculating the tax on a transfer, the tax on the brought forward figure is always recalculated on the current scale, and it may, or may not, represent the tax that was actually paid on the earlier transfers. This gives the correct starting point to calculate the tax on the current transfer. Now that there is only one rate of tax, this will only be relevant where the cumulative transfers are below the nil threshold applicable at the date of the current transfer, because later lifetime transfers will be at 20% and death transfers at 40%.

(4) In the Example the cumulative chargeable transfers within seven years before 20 October 2003 exclude the 10 July 1996 and 12 June 2001 transfers (as potentially exempt transfers that became exempt transfers after seven years), but include the 20 May 2000 transfer, whereas the total as at 1 January 2005 includes both the 20 May 2000 and 20 October 2003 transfers. On death the 20 October 2003 chargeable transfer and the 1 January 2005 potentially exempt, now chargeable, transfer are included.

Question

In connection with inheritance tax:

(a)   Explain the meaning and inheritance tax treatment of excluded property for both domiciled and non-domiciled individuals.

(b)   Briefly describe the circumstances in which a charge to tax may arise on property comprised in a settlement.

(c)   Discuss the basic overseas aspects of IHT.

(d)   Explain the non-domiciled spouse exemption.

Answer

(a) Excluded property

'Excluded property' is defined in IHTA 1984 ss 6 and 48.

If a person is not domiciled in the UK, the following types of asset may be treated as excluded property and no inheritance tax is chargeable:

(i)   Foreign property owned by individuals domiciled outside the UK (s 6(1)).

(ii)   Settled property – situated outside the UK is excluded property if the settlor was domiciled outside the UK at the time the property was settled (s 48(3)).

(iii)   Holdings in Authorised unit trusts (AUTs) and Open-ended investment companies (OEICs) are excluded property if held:

  •   by an individual domiciled outside the UK (s 61(A)), or

  •   in a trust made by a settlor domiciled outside the UK at the time the property was settled (s 48(3A)).

(iv)   Reversionary interests in settled property (other than deemed settlement arising from a lease for life, see (**explanatory note 3** and **Example 63 explanatory note 3**) are also generally excluded property (s 48(1)–(2)). The exceptions are:

  •   where the interest has ever been owned by the settlor of the settled property or his spouse or civil partner (but not where the settlement was made before 16 April 1976, or where the current owner acquired the interest before 10 March 1981); and

  •   where the interest has ever been owned by someone who acquired it for consideration in money or money's worth;

        but even those exceptions do not apply, to the extent that the settled property is situated outside the UK or comprises holdings in AUTs or OEICs, so long as the owner of the reversionary interest is domiciled outside the UK and no UK domiciled individual has owned an interest in possession which was acquired on or after 9 December 2005 for consideration in money or money's worth (s 48(3)–(3B)).

(v)   Visiting armed forces – emoluments and tangible movable property of members of visiting forces (other than British citizens, British overseas territories citizens or British overseas citizens or British Nationals (overseas)) and certain staff of allied headquarters are excluded property. For inheritance tax purposes, HMRC will not take periods spent on duty in the UK into account in deciding whether a transferor is resident, domiciled or deemed to be domiciled here (ss 6(4) and 155(1)).

(vi)   Former employees of ex-colonial governments – there are special rules about pensions paid to former employees of former colonial governments. On the death of a former employee any pension payable under the Government of India Act 1935 s 273, or an equivalent scheme under the Overseas Pensions Act 1973 s 2, is exempt.

(vii)   Pension payments and gratuities – certain other pension payments and gratuities are treated as being paid abroad and there is no inheritance tax due on such pensions on the estate of a deceased pensioner who dies whilst domiciled abroad.

(viii) National Savings Certificates and small savings – if an individual is domiciled in the Channel Islands or the Isle of Man and holds National Savings Certificates and certain other forms of small savings, they are excluded property. The deemed domicile provisions do not apply (s 6(3)).

(ix)   Non-sterling accounts with a bank – balances on non-sterling accounts with a bank are excluded from inheritance tax on death if they are held by:

- an individual not domiciled, resident or ordinarily resident in the UK, or

- as settled property where such an individual has an interest in possession, if the trustees are not domiciled, resident or ordinarily resident in the UK and the settlor was not domiciled in the UK when the settlement was made. (The interest in possession need not be an estate in possession – see **Example 52** for this purpose.

(x)   FOTRA securities first issued before 30 April 1996 are exempt from tax if a person is neither domiciled nor ordinarily resident in the UK (s 6(2)).

(xi)   For FOTRA securities first issued after 29 April 1996 new conditions apply which mean that domicile is not relevant. An individual needs to be not ordinarily resident in the UK to benefit from the exemption. From 6 April 1998 the new conditions apply to all British Government Securities, except 3½% War Loan 1952 or later.

By HMRC concession F19, a decoration awarded for valour or gallant conduct is to be treated for inheritance tax as excluded property if it is shown never to have been transferred for consideration in money or money's worth.

By HMRC concession F20, ex gratia compensation payments of up to £10,000 made by the Government to British survivors of Japanese imprisonment or their spouses, and various other modest amounts paid by European bodies to slave labourers and other World War 2 victims or their spouses, or payments of such compensation made to the person's personal representatives, are left out of account in calculating the value of the person's estate for inheritance tax.

Excluded property is generally outside the scope of inheritance tax, because inheritance tax is not charged on the lifetime disposal of such property nor on such property passing at death (ss 3(2) and 5(1)). A charge to tax in respect of a lifetime transfer of non-excluded property can, however, be affected by excluded property, because excluded property is taken into account when measuring the value of the estate before and after the transfer of non-excluded property. If, for Example, someone owned shares in a company in their own right, and had an interest in possession in shares in the company under a settlement made by a non-UK domiciled settlor, the two holdings together constituting a controlling interest, and a transfer was made of the shares held directly which reduced the combined holding to a minority holding, the loss to the donor's estate would reflect the fall in value of the combined holding.

Excluded property held in a settlement can also affect the calculation of relevant property exit charges in the first ten years after the commencement of the settlement (see Example 60 explanatory note 6), because it is not left out of account in establishing the value of the settled property immediately after it became comprised in the settlement.

Apart from the points made in the above two paragraphs, excluded property is treated in the same way as property that is exempt.

Certain other property, although not within the definition of 'excluded property', is also outside the scope of inheritance tax as follows:

Cash options under approved annuity schemes (s 152);

Overseas pensions, in valuing an estate at death (s 153);

Property passing as a result of death on active military service (s 154).

Foreign currency bank accounts, on the death of an individual not domiciled, resident or ordinarily resident in the UK (s 157).

Works of art, normally kept overseas, physically present in the UK on the death of a foreign owner are excluded if brought into the UK solely for public exhibition, cleaning or restoration (s 5(1)(b) as amended by SI 2009/730).

(b) Charge to tax on property comprised in a settlement

The charge to tax on property comprised in a settlement depends upon the type of settlement.

(i)   If the settlement has an *interest in possession* (see **Example 52**, broadly where one or more persons are entitled to the income), and it is an estate IIP (again see **Example 52**) the property in the settlement is deemed to belong to the person who is entitled to that interest and any liability will arise when that person's interest in the property comes to an end, for Example, if he makes a sale or gift of his interest, or his interest ceases by reason of a death, marriage, appointment or other reason. Like any other transfer in lifetime, however, the cessation of the life interest may be potentially exempt. This will apply where the trust property is transferred to an individual, or to a disabled trust. The transfer will only become a chargeable transfer if the life tenant who has given up his interest dies within the next seven years, the tax being computed by taking into account transfers within the seven years before the now chargeable transfer and calculating tax on the death scale.

(ii)   In most other cases – which includes many interest in possession trusts since 22 March 2006 – the trust property will be subject to the relevant property regime, in which case a charge to tax will occur on the tenth anniversary of the creation of the trust and at ten yearly intervals thereafter. The tax is charged on the value of the 'relevant property' in the trust at 30% of the effective rate (called the 'principal charge').

The lifetime rate of tax is used to calculate the effective rate, and the maximum possible charge is 30% of 20%, ie 6%.

As it would otherwise be possible to avoid the forthcoming principal charge to tax on a discretionary settlement by distributing assets between ten-year anniversaries, an 'exit charge' arises when property ceases to be relevant property. The tax on the amount leaving the settlement is charged at the appropriate fraction of 30% of the effective rate, the appropriate fraction depending on the number of complete quarters that have elapsed since the creation of the trust or the last ten year anniversary as the case may be. For more details see **Examples 59** to **62**.

(iii)   Special charging regimes are imposed for certain other more specialised circumstances or types of trust. Many of these involve a rate which does not depend on the value of the property involved but escalates according to the length of time the trust has been within that regime. Age 18-to-25 trusts where the beneficiary has passes age 18, on the other hand, are subject to a more lenient version of relevant property exit charges occurring before the first ten-year annive

(c) Basic overseas aspects of inheritance tax

Effects of domicile on inheritance tax

Domicile means the legal system with which a person is most closely connected. This will normally be a country, but it may be a State within a country if it has its own legal system. Such countries include the United States, Canada and Australia; even the UK has three separate jurisdictions for domicile purposes (England and Wales; Scotland; and Northern Ireland).

HMRC explain domicile as follows:

'Domicile is not the same as nationality or residence. Broadly speaking, you have your domicile in the country that is your "real" or permanent home. Everyone acquires a domicile of origin at birth. This is generally the country that your father considered to be his 'home country' at the date of your birth. If you have a domicile of origin outside the UK, then this is likely still to apply unless you have chosen to remain in the UK permanently or indefinitely. In most cases an individual's domicile is obvious.'

So domicile can be loosely thought of as the place to which someone will ultimately return even though they may be absent from it from time to time, or even for a very long time.

Whether a disposition by a person gives rise to a liability or potential liability to UK inheritance tax may depend on whether the person is domiciled, or deemed to be domiciled, in the UK at the time they make it.

Domicile of origin

A 'domicile of origin' is the domicile of the person on whom the child is legally dependent (the father, if the parents were married) at the time when the child is born. This may not necessarily be the actual country of birth. For Example, if Jack is born in Germany while his father is working there, but the father's permanent home is in the UK, Jack's domicile of origin is the UK.

Domicile of dependency

Until a person can legally change it by acquiring a domicile of choice, their domicile will be the same as that of the person on whom they are legally dependent. If that person's domicile changes, the dependant automatically acquire the same domicile in place of their domicile of origin. This is known as a domicile of dependency.

Until 1 January 1974 a wife's domicile automatically followed that of her husband, again as a domicile of dependency. When this rule was abolished on that date, those already married retained the previous domicile of dependency for the time being as though it was a domicile of choice, but became capable of changing their domicile like any other independent adult.

Deemed domicile

There is a concept of 'deemed domicile' for inheritance tax. Even if a person is not domiciled in the UK under general law they will be treated as if they are domiciled in the UK at the time of a transfer if:

- they were domiciled in the UK at any time within the three years immediately before the transfer, or

- they were resident in the UK in at least 17 of the 20 tax years ending with the year in which they make the transfer. This rule can therefore sometimes bite little more than 15 years after the person first became UK resident, if that was late in a tax year.

Generally, if an individual is domiciled, or deemed to be domiciled, in the UK, inheritance tax applies to their assets wherever they are situated. Similarly, inheritance tax applies to settled property in the UK. It does not apply to settled property outside the UK, unless the settlor was domiciled, or deemed to be domiciled, in the UK when the property was settled.

The deemed domicile rules do not apply to the various forms of UK government investment whose IHT status turns (or used to turn) on the owner's domicile (see items (viii) and (x) in **part (a)**). Otherwise, a person will only count for inheritance tax as domiciled outside the UK if he does not have a UK domicile under either the general law or the deemed domicile rules.

Location of assets

If a person is domiciled abroad, inheritance tax applies only to their assets located in the UK; their property located abroad will be excluded property, as will some specific items even though they are located in the UK (see **part (a)**).

The location of assets is subject to general law as amended by any special provisions in a double taxation agreement. The normal UK rules for the more common types of asset are that:

- rights or interests in or over immovable property and chattels are situated where the property is located;

- registered shares or securities are situated where they are registered;

- coins and bank notes are situated wherever they happen to be at the time of the transfer;

- bearer securities are situated where the certificate of title is located at the time of the transfer;

- goodwill is situated where the business, to which it is attached, is carried on;

- an interest in a partnership is situated in the country whose law governs the partnership agreement;

- debts are situated where the debtor resides;

- bank accounts are situated at the branch where the account is kept.

Domicile of choice

A person can legally acquire a new domicile, a domicile of choice, from the age of 16. To do so, they must leave the country in which they are now domiciled and settle in another country, and in addition provide irrefutable evidence that they intend to live there permanently or indefinitely.

The fact of living in another country for a long time, although an important factor, does not prove an individual has acquired a new domicile and as might be expected, there is a substantial body of case law on this topic.

Double taxation treaties and IHT

The UK has a number of bilateral treaties for taxes on estates, gifts and inheritances.

For the purpose of the agreement, the treaties permit:

- The country in which the transferor is (or in the case of a death, was) domiciled to tax all property wherever it is, and the other country to tax only specified types of property, such as immovable property, in its territory. The treaty in question will contain provisions to explain what is meant by "domiciled" under each country's domestic law and which is to be treated as the country of domicile if for the purpose of the treaty if both countries regard the individual as domiciled there under their respective domestic laws.

- Where the person is doubly taxed there are rules for deciding which country gives credit for the other's tax. Where, exceptionally, the relief given by a treaty would be less than that given by unilateral relief the person receives the benefit of unilateral relief.

If there is no treaty and the transfer is liable to inheritance tax and also to a similar tax imposed by another country with which the UK does not have an agreement, an individual may be able to get relief under unilateral relief provisions.

Credit is given against inheritance tax for the tax charged by another country on assets situated in that country. For this purpose, UK law determines the location of the asset. If the tax that is charged on the asset by the other country exceeds inheritance tax on that asset, the credit is limited to the amount of inheritance tax.

Credit is also given where both the UK and another country impose tax on assets that are situated:

- in a third country, or

- both in the UK under UK law and in the other country under that country's law.

In these cases the credit is a proportion of the tax. The proportionate credit is computed by the formula:

$$\frac{A}{(A+B)} \times C$$

A is the inheritance tax, B is the overseas tax and C is whichever of A or B is the lesser.

If the UK and two or more other countries charge the same asset to tax – the above applies but with modifications.

Example 1

Kirsty is domiciled in Xanadu, but is also treated as domiciled in the UK. She makes a gift of property situated in Shangrila.

UK inheritance tax (A) £1,500,

Xanadu inheritance tax (B) £500,

C is the smaller of A and B £500,

The amount to be set against UK inheritance tax is:

$$\frac{£1,500}{(£1,500 + £500)} \times £500 = £375$$

Balance of UK tax due is £1,125.

Example 2

Jamie is domiciled in Shangrila but holds shares in a Xanadu company, which maintains a duplicate share register in the UK. Under UK law the shares are regarded as situated in the UK, but Xanadu law regards them as situated in Xanadu. Jamie dies (but his estate is not liable to Shangrilan tax).

UK inheritance tax (A) £500,

Xanadu inheritance tax (B) £2,000,

C is the smaller of A and B £500,

The amount to be set against UK inheritance tax is:

$$\frac{£500}{(£500 + £2,000)} \times £1,000 = £200$$

Balance of UK tax due is £300.

(d) Transfers to a spouse or civil partner not domiciled in the UK

Spouse or civil partner exemption on transfers on death and life is restricted to a total of £55,000:

- where the deceased/donor is domiciled in the UK, and

- the transferee spouse or civil partner is not domiciled in the UK,

and, for the purpose of the exemption, domicile includes domicile (s 18(2)).

As regards the transfer of the nil-rate band – this restriction may mean that bequests to the surviving spouse or civil partner will use up some of the nil-rate band available on the non-domiciled individual's death; but anything unused remains available for transfer and can be claimed by the personal representatives of the surviving spouse or civil partner when they die.

For Example, Mr and Mrs Hill live in the UK. Mr Hill is UK domiciled but his wife is domiciled in Fiji. Mr Hill owns a house in Cornwall – an area his wife likes particularly so he decides to gift the house to her as a birthday present. The property is worth £375,000 at the time of the gift. Had Mrs Hill been UK domiciled the whole gift would have been an exempt transfer, but under s 18(2) only £55,000 of the gift remains exempt and the remaining £320,000 becomes a potentially exempt transfer. Mr Hill will need to live for a further seven years if the gift is to become exempt from IHT.

In 2003, Mr Cliff, who was domiciled in the UK, transferred £200,000 to Mrs Cliff, who was not domiciled in the UK. Of this transfer, £55,000 is exempt under s 18(2), and £145,000 is a potentially exempt transfer and assumed to be exempt. Mr Cliff dies in 2011 and leaves all his property to Mrs Cliff, who remains domiciled outside the UK. Even though Mr Cliff has survived for seven years after making the transfer, the limited exemption under s 18(2) has all been used and is not available on Mr Cliff's death.

In 2003 Mr Brink transfers a UK property worth £500,000 to Mrs Brink. Both are domiciled outside the UK. Exemption under s 18(1) is available in full. In 2011 Mr Brink is deemed to be domiciled in the UK and a year later gives £100,000 to Mrs Brink who remains domiciled outside the UK. The limited exemption under s 18(2) is not then available because the amount of exemption already conferred under s 18 as a whole exceeds £55,000.

Explanatory Notes

Reversionary interest

(1)   'Reversionary interest' is defined in s 47 as a future interest under a settlement, whether vested or contingent. Where, for Example, property is settled on A for life, then to B absolutely, B (sometimes called the remainderman) has a reversionary interest in the settled property.

If a reversionary interest in settled property has been purchased, or is owned by the settlor or the spouse or civil partner of the settlor, then it will not be excluded property (see item (iv) in **part (a)** of the Example); but from 9 December 2009 an additional anti-avoidance rule is introduced in cases where the reversionary interest is owned by such a person (relevant reversioner), whereby, if the settled property is relevant property and the reversionary interest comes to an end by reason of the relevant reversioner becoming entitled to an interest in possession in it, then the relevant reversioner is deemed to have made a disposition of the reversionary interest at that time. The resultant transfer of value cannot be a potentially exempt transfer (s 81A). It is unclear whether this rule will be interpreted as catching the more usual case where the reversionary interest does not come to an end but merely ceases to be reversionary.

Deemed UK domicile

(2) See **part (c)** of the Example for a detailed explanation of deemed domicile.

For related points and the treatment of foreign currency bank accounts see **Example 27**. **Example 27** also illustrates excluded property held by a non-UK domiciled person. For the treatment of reversionary interests see **Example 58**.

Meaning of 'settlement'

(3) For inheritance tax purposes a settlement is defined as any disposition or dispositions of property whereby the property is for the time being:

(a) held in trust for persons in succession, or for any person subject to a contingency (s 43(2)(a))

(b) held by trustees on trust to accumulate the whole or any part of any income of the property, or with power to make payments out of that income at the discretion of the trustees or some other person, with or without the power to accumulate surplus income (s 43(2)(b))

(c) charged or burdened (otherwise than for full consideration in money or money's worth) with the payment of any annuity or other periodical payment for a life or any other limited or terminable period (s 43(2)(c)).

A bare trust – for an individual absolutely entitled, even if presently a minor – is not a settlement.

Also treated as a settlement is a lease of property for the duration of a person's life or persons' lives (or for a period ascertainable, through the giving of notice or otherwise, only by reference to a death), unless the lease was granted for full consideration in money or money's worth.

The words 'settlement' and 'trust' are usually regarded as being interchangeable, although as can be seen from the definition, 'settlement' has a wider coverage. Any reference in IHTA 1984 to a trustee, in relation to a settlement where there would otherwise be no trustees, is to any person in whom the settled property or its management is vested (s 45).

Classes of settlement

(4) For inheritance tax purposes settlements may be considered to fall into four main classes:

(a) Settlements with an estate interest in possession (see **Example 52**).

(b) Relevant property settlements (whether or not an interest in possession subsists, if it is not an estate IIP or held by a reversionary interest company (see **Example 63 Explanatory note 2**).

(c) Privileged trusts for children and young persons, in the restricted circumstances to which such privileges are not applicable (see **Example 52 Explanatory note 1**), being bereaved minors' trusts, age 18-to-25 trusts, and any pre-2006 accumulation and maintenance trusts remaining as such (with beneficiaries due to become absolutely entitled by age 18) since 6 Apr 2008.

(d) Certain other special types of settlement, eg trusts for the benefit of employees, protective trusts and charitable trusts.

The distinction between settlements in which there is an estate interest in possession and relevant property trusts is fundamental to an understanding of the inheritance tax legislation. The position is dealt with in detail in the section of this book dealing with settlements and trusts **Examples 52 ff**.

The inheritance tax settlement provisions do not apply to registered pension schemes.

Adding property to a settlement

(5) With regard to points (ii), (iii) and presumably (ix) in **part (a)** of the Example, HMRC take the view that a separate settlement is made when property is put into an existing settlement, so that even if a settlement of foreign property was made when the settlor was not UK domiciled, foreign property derived from any further property added to the settlement at a time when the settlor was UK domiciled would not be excluded property (Tax Bulletin February 1997).

Question

Mr C T Tax made the following lifetime gifts:

20 November 2003	£267,000 to a discretionary trust
11 January 2005	£65,000 to his sister, Ann
3 May 2007	£86,000 to his daughter, Joan
4 April 2008	£90,000 to his son, Ben.

Mr C T Tax died on 2 April 2011 leaving an estate of £628,000 equally to Ben and Joan.

(i)   Compute the tax payable by reason of the death of Mr C T Tax.

(ii)   Would the tax payable be different if Mr C T Tax had not made gifts to his children in 2007 and 2008 totalling £176,000 but had left an estate of £804,000 instead of £628,000?

(iii)   Show the tax payable in lifetime and on death if the circumstances were as in (i) except that instead of giving £90,000 to Ben on 4 April 2008, Mr C T Tax transferred £90,000 to a discretionary trust (the trustees paying the tax) on:

(a)   4 March 2008; or

(b)   6 April 2009.

Answer

(i) Inheritance tax position of Mr C T Tax

Tax payable in lifetime

			£	£
20 Nov 2003	gift to discretionary trust			267,000
	Less: Annual exemptions	2003/04	3,000	
		2002/03	3,000	6,000
	Chargeable transfer			261,000
	Tax payable by trustees (on 2003/04			
	scale) 261,000 – 255,000 = 6,000 @ 20%	£1,200		
11 Jan 2005	gift to Ann			65,000
	Less: Annual exemption	2004/05		3,000
	Potentially exempt transfer			62,000
3 May 2007	gift to Joan			86,000
	Less: Annual exemptions	2007/08	3,000	
		2006/07	3,000	6,000
	Potentially exempt transfer			80,000
4 April 2008	gift to Ben – potentially exempt transfer			90,000

On death of Mr C T Tax 2 April 2011

Potentially exempt transfers since 3 April 2004 now become chargeable transfers:

	Gross	Tax (using rates at 2 April 2011)
	£	£
Cumulative transfers in seven years before gift to Ann		
20 November 2003 — discretionary trust	261,000	–
11 January 2005 — gift to Ann	62,000	–
	323,000	–
3 May 2007— gift to Joan	80,000	31,200*
	403,000	31,200*
(*403,000 – 325,000 = 78,000 @ 40%)		
4 April 2008 — gift to Ben	90,000	36,000
	493,000	67,200
20 November 2010		
Deduct transfer made more than seven years previously		
(ie prior to 21 November 2003)	261,000	
Cumulative transfers in seven years before death	232,000	–
Estate chargeable on death	628,000	214,000*
	860,000	214,000*

(* 860,000 – 325,000 = 535,000 @ 40%)

	£
Inheritance tax payable:	
By Ann on gift made 11 January 2005:	nil
By Joan on gift made 3 May 2007:	
As gift is made more than 3 but not more than 4 years	
before death tax payable is 80% × £31,200 =	24,960
By Ben on gift made 4 April 2008:	
As gift is within 3 years of death there is no reduction	
in the tax payable	36,000
By Estate	214,000
Tax payable by reason of death of Mr C T Tax	274,960

(ii) If no lifetime gifts made to children — position on death of Mr C T Tax 2 April 2011

	Gross £	Tax £
Cumulative transfers in seven years before death		
(ie 3 April 2004 – 2 April 2011)		
11 January 2005	62,000	–
Estate chargeable on death	804,000	216,400*
	866,000	216,400*
(* 866,000 – 325,000 = 541,000 @ 40%)		
Tax with gifts to children (**part (i)**)		274,960
Tax without gifts to children — estate	216,400	
Tax on gift to Ann — as above	nil	216,400
Additional tax because of chargeable transfers made within		
seven years before lifetime gifts to children		£58,560

(iii) Inheritance tax position of Mr C T Tax with gift to discretionary trust instead of to Ben

(a) *Gift to discretionary trust on 4 March 2008*

Tax payable in lifetime

		Gross £	Tax on 2003/04 scale £
20 November 2003 —	chargeable transfer	261,000	1,200
11 January 2005	potentially exempt transfers		
and 3 May 2007 —	£62,000 and £80,000 as before		

		Tax on 2007/08 Scale £
Cumulative transfers before gift to discretionary trust on 4 March 2008	261,000	–
4 March 2008 — gift to discretionary trust	90,000	10,200*
	351,000	10,200*

(* 351,000 – 300,000 (using 2007/08 scale) = 51,000 @ 20%)

Tax payable by trustees   £10,200

On death of Mr C T Tax 2 April 2011

	Gross £	Tax (using rates at 2 April 2011) £
Cumulative transfers in seven years prior to gift to Ann	261,000	–
11 January 2005 — gift to Ann	62,000	–
	323,000	–
3 May 2007 — gift to Joan	80,000	31,200*
	403,000	31,200*

(* 403,000 – 325,000 = 78,000 % 40%)

	Gross £	Tax £
4 March 2008 — gift to discretionary trust	90,000	36,000
	493,000	67,200

Inheritance tax payable by Ann on gift made 11 January 2005		nil
Inheritance tax payable by Joan on gift made 3 May 2007		
80% × £31,200 (taper relief as before)		24,960
Additional inheritance tax payable by trustees — as gift is made more than 3 but not more than 4 years before death tax payable is:		
Tax on death scale	36,000	
Less 20% taper relief	7,200	
	28,800	
Less paid in lifetime	10,200	18,600
Tax on estate:		
Cumulative transfers as above	493,000	
Deduct transfer made more than seven years previously	261,000	
	232,000	
Estate chargeable on death	628,000	
	860,000	
Tax payable (860,000 – 325,000 = 535,000 @ 40%)		214,000
		£257,560

(b)   *Gift to discretionary trust on 6 April 2009*

Tax payable in lifetime

			Gross £	Tax on 2003/04 scale £
20 November 2003 —	chargeable transfer		261,000	1,200
11 January 2005	potentially exempt transfers			
and 3 May 2007 —	£62,000 and £80,000 as before			
Cumulative transfers before gift to				
discretionary trust on 6 April 2009 (c/f)			261,000	

			Gross £	Tax on 2009/10 scale £
Cumulative transfers before gift to				
discretionary trust on 6 April 2009 (b/f)			261,000	–
6 April 2009 — gift to discretionary trust		90,000		
Less: Annual exemptions	2009/10	(3,000)		
	2008/09	(3,000)	84,000	4,000*
			345,000	4,000*

(* 345,000 – 325,000 (using 2009/10 scale) = 20,000 @ 20%)
Tax payable by trustees   £4,000

On death of Mr C T Tax 2 April 2011

	Gross £	Tax (using rates at 2 April 2011) £
Cumulative transfers in seven years prior to		
gift to Ann (as above)	261,000	–
11 January 2005 — gift to Ann	62,000	–
	323,000	–
3 May 2007 — gift to Joan	80,000	31,200*
	403,000	31,200*
(* 403,000 – 325,000 = 78,000 @ 40%)		
6 April 2009 — gift to discretionary settlement	84,000	33,600
	487,000	64,800
20 November 2010		
Deduct transfer more than seven years previously		
(ie prior to 21 November 2003)	261,000	
Cumulative transfers in seven years before death	226,000	–
Estate chargeable on death	628,000	211,600*

	854,000	211,600*

(* 854,000 − 325,000 = 529,000 @ 40%)

Inheritance tax payable by Ann on gift made 11 January 2005	nil
Inheritance tax payable by Joan on gift made 3 May 2007	
80% × £31,200 (taper relief as before)	24,960
Additional inheritance tax payable by trustees on gift made 6 April 2009	
(no taper relief because within 3 years before death):	

Tax on death scale	33,600	
Less paid in lifetime	4,000	29,600
Tax payable by estate		211,600
		£266,160

The total tax payable is £2,400 more than in iii(a):

	(a) £	(b) £
Ann	–	–
Joan	24,960	24,960
Trustees	28,800	33,600
Estate	214,000	211,600
Total tax payable	267,760	270,160
Paid in lifetime by trustees	10,200	4,000
Due on death	257,560	266,160

The increase in the tax payable arises as follows:

Loss of taper relief on transfer to trust, since gift now less than three years before death (36,000 @ 20%)	7,200
Less: Reduction of trust transfer by 2009/10 and 2008/09	
exemptions, saving 6,000 @ 40%	(2,400)
Consequential reduction in cumulative transfers	
at death, saving a further 6,000 @ 40%	(2,400)
	£2,400

The inheritance tax liability can therefore vary depending on the timing and amounts of lifetime gifts. C T Tax had the same value of assets in each of the above Examples. The total tax payable by the first discretionary trust remains constant at £1,200, being a lifetime gift made more than seven years before death. The tax payable on death plus gifts made within seven years before death is:

(i)	(ii)	(iii)(a)	(iii)(b)
£274,960	£216,400	£267,760	£270,160

The reduction of £58,560 in (ii) is due to non-aggregation of the gift to the first discretionary trust with other lifetime gifts (see **explanatory note 6**). The reduction of £7,200 in (iii)(a) compared with (i) is because the chargeable gift to the trust of £90,000 on 4 March 2008 was more than three years before death, thus giving rise to taper relief of £7,200. The difference in tax payable in (iii)(a) and (iii)(b) is explained above.

Explanatory Notes

Potentially exempt transfers to sister and children

(1) As the transfers to the sister and to the children are gifts by one individual to another they are potentially exempt, after deducting available annual exemptions from the earliest gift in any tax year. Accordingly no tax is payable at the time.

Inheritance tax liability arising on death

(2) On the death of Mr C T Tax a liability arises both on his estate at death and also on transfers made within seven years before death.

The additional charge on death is the tax due using the scale in force on the date of death less any tax paid on that gift during lifetime. If the tax already paid exceeds that now due no refund will arise. Any tax due is payable primarily by the donee (see **Example 5**).

Taper relief on lifetime transfers

(3) Transfers which were potentially exempt in lifetime become chargeable if the donor dies within seven years after the lifetime transfer. They are chargeable on their value when made, but at the full scale rate at the time of death (assuming this is more lenient than the scale at the date of the gift). Where the period between the gift and death exceeds three years then the tax calculated on the full scale rate is reduced as follows:

Years between transfer and death	Percentage reduction	Percentage of full rate tax due
3 to 4	20	80
4+ to 5	40	60
5+ to 6	60	40
6+ to 7	80	20

Thus, in **part (i)** of the Example Ann's gift would attract an 80% reduction as the gift is made more than six but less than seven years before death. In fact no tax is payable on the gift and therefore the taper relief is lost. Joan can claim a 20% reduction as her gift was more than three but less than four years before death, but Ben cannot claim any reduction as his gift was within three years of death.

Calculating tax on potentially exempt transfers that become chargeable

(4) When computing the tax on potentially exempt transfers which have become chargeable it is necessary to take into account other *chargeable* transfers made within *seven years before those transfers* even though those transfers themselves may not be subject to any uplift on death because they were made more than seven years before the date of death. Thus when computing any tax on the gifts in January 2005, May 2007 and April 2008 the cumulative chargeable transfers include the gift into settlement in November 2003. However when computing the tax due on the estate at death, the November 2003 chargeable transfer is excluded since it was made more than seven years prior to death. Even if it had exceeded the nil threshold at death, the November 2003 transfer could not have attracted additional tax, since Mr C T Tax survived it by seven years.

Interaction of annual exemption with chargeable/potentially exempt transfers

(5) **part (iii)** of the Example illustrates the provisions relating to the annual exemption where there are both chargeable lifetime transfers and potentially exempt transfers within the same year. The detailed notes are in **Example 1**. The annual exemption is given against transfers in strict chronological order, thus the gift to Joan on 3 May 2007 (which is otherwise potentially exempt) receives the benefit of the annual exemptions, even though no tax would be payable if C T Tax survived for more than seven years. No exemptions are accordingly available to reduce the chargeable lifetime transfer on 4 March 2008 in **part (iii) (a)** and tax of £10,200 is immediately payable by the trustees. Note that if the gifts in (iii) (a) to Joan on 3 May 2007 and to the discretionary trust on 4 March 2008 had occurred in reverse order then the annual exemptions of

£6,000 would reduce the chargeable transfer to the trust to £84,000 and the tax immediately payable to £11,000. This benefit would have been retained if C T Tax had lived for more than seven years. In fact death occurs within that period, so that the annual exemptions reduce the transfer on which Joan is chargeable and have not been wasted by being used against a potentially exempt transfer that never became chargeable.

Cumulation with earlier chargeable transfers

(6)   It is not always appreciated that making gifts within seven years before death rather than leaving a correspondingly greater amount at death can increase the overall tax liability. This occurs because of the need, in calculating the tax payable on a potentially exempt transfer which becomes chargeable, to include *chargeable* transfers made within the seven years before the gift. (Potentially exempt transfers are never taken into account unless the donor dies within seven years after making them, in which case they become chargeable transfers.) Thus a period of up to fourteen years might need to be taken into account to calculate the inheritance tax liability arising on a death. The earlier transfers (ie years 8–14 before death) are eliminated after seven years and are therefore not included in calculating the liability on the estate at the date of death. The additional charge is often mitigated by the taper provisions set out at note 3 above and the amount chargeable is reduced by use of lifetime exemptions. However, as shown in parts (i) and (ii) of this Example those provisions are insufficient to cover the additional charge arising through having to include the earlier gifts in calculating the tax payable on the potentially exempt transfers, the additional tax payable by reason of the lifetime transfers to the children being as follows:

	£
Savings:	
Reduction in chargeable estate because of lifetime gift to Joan	
Annual exemptions 2007/08 and 2006/07 (6,000 @ 40%)	2,400
Taper relief on Joan's gift (31,200 – 24,960)	6,240
	8,640
Additional liability:	
Gift of £261,000 20 November 2003 accumulated with gifts made	
11 January 2005, 3 May 2007 and 4 April 2008 but not with estate,	
Causing lifetime gifts to Joan and Ben to exceed nil threshold (78,000 +	
90,000) = £168,000 @ 40%	67,200
Net additional liability as in **part (ii)** *of the Example*	£58,560

This problem only arises when transfers that were immediately chargeable in lifetime are taken into account in calculating the tax on potentially exempt transfers that become chargeable. If, for Example, C T Tax's transfer on 20 November 2003 had been a potentially exempt transfer, the transfers to Ann, Joan and Ben would still have become chargeable transfers, but the potentially exempt transfer on 20 November 2003, more than seven years before C T Tax's death, would then be totally exempt and would not enter into the cumulative total.

Interaction with capital gains tax

(7)   Where a gifted asset is a chargeable asset for capital gains tax, that tax needs to be considered in addition to inheritance tax. Capital gains tax is not payable on death, and there is normally an automatic uplift of base values to the probate value, unless the probate value of the asset has not been *ascertained* for inheritance tax (which would be the case, for Example, if no inheritance tax was payable on the estate) (TCGA 1992 s 274). In that event the acquisition value for capital gains tax is the open market value at the date of death (TCGA 1992 s 272 — see **Example 38 explanatory note 1**). If an election has been made to avoid a pre-owned asset income tax charge then the asset is included within the estate at death for inheritance tax. However that election does not apply for capital gains tax and the value will remain at the capital gains tax value at the time of transfer (normally open market value at date of original gift) (TCGA 1992 s 18 see **Example 23 explanatory note 13**).

On gifts made in lifetime, capital gains tax may be payable unless the gain is deferred under the gifts holdover relief provisions — either the business gifts relief of TCGA 1992 s 165 or the relief under TCGA 1992 s 260 for gifts that are *immediately* liable to inheritance tax (such as gifts to discretionary trusts). Consequently, capital gains tax may be paid on a potentially exempt transfer, and if the donor dies within seven years the gift will also be liable to inheritance tax (unless covered by reliefs or exemptions). There is no direct relief against inheritance tax for the capital gains tax paid, although the chargeable estate at death will have been reduced by the capital gains tax paid or owing.

If the capital gains tax gifts holdover relief *is* available, and the potentially exempt transfer becomes liable to inheritance tax, any inheritance tax payable is deducted in computing the donee's gain when he eventually disposes of the asset (TCGA 1992 s 165(10)). The same applies in relation to the inheritance tax on a gift to which capital gains holdover relief under TCGA 1992 s 260 applied because the gift was immediately chargeable to inheritance tax (s 260(7)). The inheritance tax taken into account in each case to reduce the capital gain is the amount finally payable, after any adjustments following death.

For detailed coverage on capital gains tax see the companion to this book, **Tolley's Taxwise I 2010/11**.

Question

(a)   When is inheritance tax due to be paid:

    (i)   on chargeable lifetime transfers?

    (ii)   when it arises because of death?

(b)   Who is accountable for the inheritance tax arising on:

    (i)   chargeable lifetime transfers?

    (ii)   potentially exempt transfers which become chargeable at death?

    (iii)   the estate at death?

    (iv)   settled property in which the deceased enjoyed a life interest?

(c)   What penalties can be charged for late filing, late payment, incorrect returns and understatement of IHT due?

(d)   What are the time limits for making assessments and claims?

Answer

(a) Due date of payment of inheritance tax

Payment of inheritance tax may sometimes be made by instalments, but otherwise the due date is as follows (s 226):

(i)	Lifetime chargeable transfers between 6 April and 30 September	30 April in following year
	Lifetime chargeable transfers between 1 October and 5 April	6 months after end of month in which transfer was made
(ii)	Death, including tax on what were previously potentially exempt transfers and additional tax on chargeable lifetime transfers	6 months after end of month in which death occurred

The personal representatives must, however, pay any tax for which they are liable when they deliver their account in connection with their application for a grant of probate or administration, even if this is earlier than the due date shown above. This will be before they have access to the funds. However certain financial institutions may be prepared to release the funds of the deceased before probate is granted by way of an electronic transfer to HMRC against an inheritance tax reference (see **explanatory note 13**).

The same rules apply to charges in relation to settled property other than on the death of a beneficiary with an estate interest in possession, which count as chargeable transfers under s 2(3).

Interest on unpaid inheritance tax is charged at the rate of 3% from 29 September 2009 (see also **explanatory note 1**).

(b) Liability for payment of inheritance tax

(i) *Chargeable lifetime transfers*

On chargeable lifetime transfers of property not already comprised in a settlement, primary liability for payment of tax rests with the *donor* except in the case of any extra tax payable on death which is primarily the responsibility of the *donee*. The personal representatives are only liable if the additional tax exceeds the value of the asset in the hands of the recipient, or if the tax is not paid by the recipient (s 204).

The donor and donee may, however, agree between them who is to pay the tax, and if the donor is to pay the tax the transfer has to be grossed up, because the extent to which the donor's estate is depleted is the transfer to the donee plus the tax paid. If the donee pays the tax grossing up is not necessary.

Grossing up does not apply on a potentially exempt transfer since tax is not payable in the donor's lifetime.

A return for inheritance tax because of a chargeable transfer in lifetime has to indicate who is to pay the tax.

In the case of lifetime transfers of property comprised in a settlement, the primary liability is that of the trustees.

(ii) *Potentially exempt transfers which become chargeable*

The liability on potentially exempt transfers which become chargeable at death is primarily that of the donees. The donee is also primarily responsible where property subject to reservation of an interest by the deceased becomes liable to tax on death.

(iii)   *Estate at death*

The personal representatives are liable to pay the tax on property which is not immediately before death included in a settlement, or owned jointly by the deceased and others as joint tenants (usually called the 'free estate').

They are also liable to pay the tax on UK land which is included in a settlement but which devolves on them in their capacity as personal representatives.

In England and Wales this is limited to settlements governed by the Settled Land Act 1925 when the settlement comes to an end on the death of the tenant for life.

Property owned by the deceased and others as joint tenants is not dealt with by the personal representatives because it becomes the property of the other owner(s) and any tax attributable to the value of that property is payable by the person(s) in whom it is vested (s 200(1)(c)).

See **explanatory note 10** as to who bears the tax.

(iv)   *Settled property in which deceased had interest in possession*

In all cases of inheritance tax charges on settled property other than the special situation in (iii) above, the liability rests with the trustees of the settlement. Whether an inheritance tax charge arises on the death of the interest in possession beneficiary, however, depends on whether:

- his interest is an estate interest in possession (see **Example 52**), in which case the trust fund will be aggregated with his estate and charged on his death; or

- the trust fund is relevant property, in which case an exit charge under s 65 will only arise if the death brings the settlement to an end or (exceptionally) an interest in possession arises for a person who was a disabled person when the property was originally settled (see **Examples 59** and **Example 60**, and again **Example 52**); or

- the trust fund is within the age 18-to-25 trusts regime (s 71D) and the beneficiary is over age 18 (but by definition under age 25), in which case there is an exit charge under s 71E; or

- the beneficiary had an interest in possession despite being still under age 18 and the trust fund is (wholly exceptionally) within the bereaved minors' trusts regime (s 71A), the age 18-to-25 trusts regime (s 71D) or the much-restricted A & M trusts regime for pre-2006 A & M trusts (s 71), in which case no charge will arise.

Other persons liable for payment

In addition to the persons mentioned above, certain other people may be liable to pay inheritance tax in respect of a lifetime transfer, but usually only where tax remains unpaid after the due date.

This is because of s 199, which is headed 'Dispositions by transferor' and imposes a liability on:

(1) The transferor

(2) Any person whose estate is increased by the transfer

(3) In respect of tax attributable to the value of any property, any person in whom the property is vested, whether beneficially or otherwise, at any time after the transfer or who is beneficially entitled to an interest in possession in the property

(4) Where property has become settled property, any person for whose benefit any of the property or income from it is applied.

Where more than one person is liable for the same tax then each of them may be called upon for the whole amount (s 205).

Section 199 poses a problem for personal representatives, because the deceased's estate is liable for tax on potentially exempt transfers in the seven years before death (even though the liability would not arise if the tax was paid, as it ought to be, by the donee), and the personal representatives may not be able to trace all such transfers. HMRC have, however, stated that they would not usually pursue the personal representatives for any such unpaid tax if, after making full enquiries and doing all in their power to disclose all lifetime transfers to HMRC, the personal representatives had obtained a certificate of discharge and distributed the estate before a chargeable lifetime transfer came to light (Law Society's Gazette 13 March 1991).

Similarly wide extensions to liability, mirroring broadly points (3) and (4) above, are contained in s 200 relating to a person's estate on death and s 201 relating to other charges on settled property.

(c) Penalties

Any person for inheritance tax purposes who understates their tax liability, whether deliberately or by failing to take reasonable care in completing returns, will be subject to the penalty regime introduced in FA 2008 s 122, s 123 and Sch 40. This legislation extended the provisions enacted in FA 2007 Sch 24. The penalty will be determined by the amount of tax understated, the nature of the behaviour giving rise to the understatement and the extent of disclosure by the taxpayer.

Penalties for failure to notify have effect for failure to meet notification obligations that arise on or after 1 April 2009.

For incorrect returns, the rules apply for return periods which commenced on or after 1 April 2009 where the return filing date is on or after 1 April 2010.

HMRC have now set out their guidance on the above provisions. There is now one penalty regime for inaccuracies in tax returns and other tax documents for most taxes. Consequently, if the liable person takes 'reasonable care' they will not suffer a penalty, even if they do make a mistake. Finance Act 2008, Sch 40 contained provisions to extend this regime to inheritance tax.

The commencement order for Sch 40 has been published and the revised penalty regime applies to inheritance tax for all chargeable events that occur on or after 1 April 2009. The provisions of IHTA 1984 ss 247(1) and (2) will continue to apply to events before that date.

So, for events on or after this date, the liable person(s) may be charged a penalty if they do not take 'reasonable care' in preparing their inheritance tax account or excepted estate return. There may also be a penalty if the liable person(s) subsequently discovers an inaccuracy but does not take reasonable steps to notify HMRC.

The test is now of 'reasonable care' rather than 'negligence'. HMRC considers the personal representatives will have taken reasonable care where they:

- follow the guidance provided about filling in forms such as the IHT400 and IHT205/207/C5;

- make suitable enquiries of asset holders and other people (as suggested in the guidance) to establish the extent of the deceased's estate;

- ensure correct instructions are given to valuers when valuing assets;

- seek advice about anything they are unsure of;

- follow up inconsistencies in information they receive from asset holders, valuers and other people;

- identify any estimated values included on the form.

Where the personal representatives leave all this in the hands of an agent, HMRC expects them to check through the form before signing it and to question anything that does not accord with what they know about the deceased. Simply signing an account completed by an agent is not taking reasonable care.

Where inheritance tax is payable other than on death, HMRC expects the transferor (or trustees) to deliver a full and complete return of the transaction concerned, and to have sought professional advice as necessary. Again, simply signing an account completed by an agent is not taking reasonable care.

The penalty regime identifies three levels of behaviour that give rise to an inaccuracy in an account or return that may give rise to a penalty. These behaviours are:

*   careless;

*   deliberate;

*   deliberate and concealed.

The less serious the reason for the inaccuracy, the smaller the penalty.

In addition, HMRC will have regard to the nature of disclosure of the inaccuracy – whether it was prompted or unprompted. The legislation sets out a minimum penalty for each combination of behaviours.

Behaviour	Disclosure	Minimum penalty	Maximum penalty
Careless	Unprompted	0%	30%
	Prompted	15%	30%
Deliberate	Unprompted	20%	70%
	Prompted	35%	70%
Deliberate and concealed	Unprompted	30%	100%
	Prompted	50%	100%

There is the potential for a penalty to be charged where a document given to HMRC contains an inaccuracy in connection with a deduction, exemption or relief taken against the estate or transfer. This includes the information given on the relevant supplementary pages to the account and makes explicit what was implicit in the inheritance tax legislation.

The legislation also permits a penalty to be charged where an inaccuracy in the liable person's document was attributable to another person. This is particularly relevant to inheritance tax where the personal representatives will inevitably be relying on other people to provide them with information about the deceased's estate.

Where it can be shown that the other person deliberately withheld information or supplied false information to the liable person, with the intention that the inheritance tax account or return would contain an inaccuracy, a penalty may be charged on that other person. But that will not necessarily mean that the personal representative themselves may not also be chargeable to a penalty. If the withheld or false information gives rise to inconsistencies in the information they have received about the estate and they do not question those inconsistencies, the liable person may still be charged a penalty for failing to take reasonable care as well.

If after discussion with the taxpayer, HMRC is unable to agree that a penalty should be charged, or the amount of a reduction, a penalty assessment will be issued. It is this document against which the liable person can appeal, and they will then be subject to processes that apply (also from 1 April 2009) within the tribunal system (see **explanatory note 14**).

In addition FA 2008 Sch 36 para 39 applies to a person who fails to comply with an information notice or deliberately obstructs an officer during an inspection authorised by a first tier tribunal – the penalty is £300 and continues at £60 per day (para 40) for each day on which the failure or obstruction continues.

Penalties for late filing of returns – Introduction

The revised regime means late filing penalties where the obligation to file the return is annual or occasional which includes:

*   a £100 penalty immediately after the due date for filing (whether or not the tax has been paid);

*   daily penalties of £10 per day (annual obligations only) for returns that are more than three months late, running for a maximum of 90 days;

*   penalties of 5% of tax due for the return period for prolonged failures (over six months and again at twelve months); and

- higher penalties of 70% of the tax due where a person fails to submit a return for over twelve months and has deliberately withheld information necessary for HMRC to assess the tax due (100% penalty if deliberate with concealment).

The revised rules

FA 2009 s 106 and Sch 55 introduced a revised penalty regime for late filing of tax returns for income tax and inheritance tax. Taxpayers have a right of appeal against all penalties and no penalty can be charged if a taxpayer has a reasonable excuse for their failure.

The Schedule details the returns to which an annual or occasional penalty applies and provides that a failure to submit a return listed in the Schedule will result in a penalty of £100 (para 3).

Schedule 55 also sets out the conditions for charging daily penalties where the delay in filing a return is prolonged. These are:

- a penalty will be payable of £10 for each day that the failure to submit a return continues for a period of up to 90 days beginning with the date specified in the notice (para 4(2));

- a penalty will be payable if a return is still outstanding six months after the filing date and there would have been a liability to tax shown in the return (para 5(1));

- such penalty will be the greater of £300 or 5% of the liability to tax shown in the return (para 5(2));

- a penalty will be payable if a return is still outstanding twelve months after the filing date and there would have been a liability to tax shown in the return (para 6(1));

- a penalty will be payable where, by failing to make the return, a person withholds information which would enable or assist HMRC to assess the person's liability to tax (para 6(2));

- in any other case, the penalty is to be the greater of £300 or 5% of the liability shown in the return (para 6(3)).

Reductions for disclosure (paras 14 and 15)

Where there has been information withheld by failure to make a return, there may be reductions for disclosure in certain penalties where the taxpayer discloses relevant information.

Schedule 55 defines what is meant by disclosure of relevant information. It sets out three distinct elements, all of which are required for the maximum reduction:

(1) admission – telling HMRC that information has been withheld;

(2) taking active steps – giving HMRC reasonable help in assessing any tax unpaid as a result of the information being withheld; and

(3) access – allowing HMRC access to records to check the extent of any liability.

There are two types of disclosure:

- unprompted – where the taxpayer has no reason to believe that HMRC have discovered or are about to discover the relevant information;

- prompted – all other disclosures.

Schedule 55 provides definitions regarding:

- quality of disclosure in terms of timing (how promptly the disclosure was made);

- nature (the level of evidence provided and degree of access to test the disclosure); and

- extent (how complete the disclosure may be).

HMRC cannot reduce the penalty under this paragraph to below the minimum amount set under Sch 55 para 14.

Special reduction (para 16(1))

Paragraph 16(1) gives HMRC a power to reduce any penalty under Sch 55 including the minimum amount penalty where they think it right because of special circumstances.

Interaction with other penalties and late payment surcharges (para 17)

Schedule 55 sets out which penalties HMRC should charge if a taxpayer is liable to more than one penalty which is determined by reference to the same tax liability (which could, for Example, include late payment surcharges, penalties for incorrect returns etc), subject to some exclusions. Tax-geared penalties under this Schedule cannot exceed 100% of the relevant liability to tax.

All penalties must be paid before the end of the period of 30 days beginning with the day on which the notification of the penalty is issued.

The assessment of any penalty must be made on or before the later of two dates:

- the first date is the last day of the two-year period beginning with the filing date;

- the second date is the last day of the period of twelve months beginning with the end of the appeal period for the assessment of the amount of tax shown on the return, or, where there is no such assessment, the date on which the amount of tax is ascertained.

Appeals

Schedule 55 gives appeal rights against decisions by HMRC to impose a penalty and of the amount of the penalty (para 20).

A person is not required to pay a penalty before an appeal against the assessment of the penalty is determined (para 21(2)).

Reasonable excuse (para 23)

No penalty arises in relation to any failure if the person satisfies HMRC or (on appeal) the tribunal that there is a reasonable excuse for the failure (para 23(1)).

Schedule 55 para 23(2) contains provisions about what is precluded from being a reasonable excuse.

Penalty for failure to pay tax – Introduction

Penalties for late payment where the obligation to make payment is annual or occasional include:

- penalties of 5% of the amount of tax unpaid, generally one month after the payment due date (or at the filing date of the relevant return for CT and IHT);

- further penalties of 5% of any amounts of tax still unpaid at six and twelve months; and

- suspension of late payment penalties where the taxpayer agrees a time to pay arrangement (where a tax debt is paid over time) with HMRC.

The revised rules

Finance Act 2009 s 107 and Sch 56 introduced a revised penalty regime for most taxes including late payment of income tax and inheritance tax.

Taxpayers have a right of appeal against all penalties and no penalty can be charged if a taxpayer has a reasonable excuse for their failure.

Schedule 56 which will be bought into force by Treasury order, provides that if a taxpayer enters into a time to pay arrangement with HMRC, any late payment penalties that they would become liable to after the agreement is reached will be removed if the taxpayer meets the terms of the agreement.

The penalties to be charged are:

- A penalty of 5% of the amount of tax unpaid. This penalty is incurred if a taxpayer fails to pay the tax in full by the due date This date is normally 30 days after the due date for the tax (para 3(2)).

- Where tax is unpaid five months after the penalty date, an additional penalty of 5% of the remaining unpaid tax (para 3(3)).

- Where tax is unpaid eleven months after the penalty date, an additional penalty of 5% of the remaining unpaid tax (para 3(4)).

Schedule 56 provides for a reduction in penalty where there are special circumstances (para 9(1)).

This will occur when:

(a) the taxpayer fails to pay an amount of tax;

(b) before the date before the taxpayer becomes liable to any penalty under the Schedule, they make a request to HMRC that the amount of tax be deferred (commonly referred to as a time-to-pay arrangement); and

(c) HMRC agrees to defer that payment (even if the agreement comes after the penalty is incurred).

If the taxpayer breaks the agreement and HMRC serves a notice specifying to which penalties they would become liable, they become liable to that penalty from the date of the notice. This provision effectively enables HMRC on issue of a notice to reinstate a liability.

Appeals (para 13)

Schedule 56 para 13 gives appeal rights against decisions by HMRC to impose a penalty and of the amount of the penalty.

Reasonable excuse (para 16)

No penalty arises in relation to any failure under Sch 56 if the person satisfied HMRC or (on appeal) tribunal that there is a reasonable excuse for the failure. The Schedule contains provisions about what is precluded from being a reasonable excuse.

Suspension of penalties

Under FA 2009 s 108 taxpayers who enter into agreements with HMRC to defer payment of taxes are not liable to certain surcharges or penalties that would otherwise be due because of late payment. Section 108 includes a power to impose the surcharge or penalty if the taxpayer does not keep to the terms of the agreement. The change becomes effective for deferral agreements reached on or after 24 November 2008.

(d) Time limits for making assessments and claims

Introduction

At present the time limit for making claims for IHT varies but under legislation brought in by Finance Act 2009 s 99 and Sch 51 the time limit will become four years.

For cases where fraud, default or neglect are involved the time limit is currently six years from the date when the (last) payment of tax was made, or the date when fraud, default or neglect comes to HMRC's knowledge.

The time limits are to be amended to:

Mistake	4 years
Careless error	6 years
Deliberate error	20 years

The new rules will take effect from 1 April 2011, with a transitional saving for proceedings by HMRC in the case of a loss of tax brought about deliberately where the chargeable transfer in question took place on or before 31 March 2011 (SI 2010/867).

The revised rules

FA 2009 s 99 and Sch 51 amend IHTA 1984 by introducing changes to time limits that apply to inheritance tax claims and assessments.

Schedule 51 para 6 inserts s 131(2ZA) into IHTA. It introduces a new time limit of four years from the transferor's death for a claim under s 131(2)(b) of IHTA.

Schedule 51 para 11(2) amends s 240(2) of IHTA. This reduces the period allowed for HMRC to bring proceedings to recover additional tax under s 240(2) of IHTA (ie in a case where an account has been delivered) from six to four years.

Section 240(3) of IHTA is also amended by Sch 51 para 11(3) with subsections (3) to (8):

- It confirms that the time limit remains at six years where the underpayment has been brought about carelessly (s 4).

- The time limit is increased to 20 years where the loss of tax is brought about deliberately (s 5) and the time limit applies in cases where no account has been delivered, and there is no deliberate loss of tax (s 6).

- There is a 20-year time limit on proceedings to recover additional tax in such cases (s 7). The rules include settlors of trusts in certain cases (s 8).

Section 240A is inserted into IHTA by Sch 51 para 12:

- The section supplements the revised time limits in s 240 of IHTA (s 1).

- Section 240A provides that a loss of tax is brought about carelessly by any person if the person fails to take reasonable care to avoid bringing about that loss (s 2). This corresponds with the definition of careless at FA 2007 Sch 24 para 3(1)(a).

- Where information is provided to HMRC by someone who later discovers that the information was inaccurate but does not take reasonable steps to inform HMRC, any loss of tax brought about by this is to be treated as having been brought about carelessly (s 3). This corresponds with the definition in FA 2007 Sch 24 para 3(2).

- Under s 240A, where a loss of tax is brought about by a deliberate inaccuracy in a document, it is to be treated as brought about deliberately. This is to ensure that in cases where a penalty is due for deliberate inaccuracy under FA 2007 Sch 24 para 3, the corresponding increase in time limit also occurs.

IHTA s 241(1) is also amended by Sch 51 para 13 by reducing the period in which repayment of an excess tax payment may be claimed from six to four years.

Explanatory Notes

Rates of interest on unpaid and overpaid inheritance tax

(1)   As stated in **part (a)** of the Example, the current rate of interest on unpaid inheritance tax is 3%.

Previous interest rates from 6 January 2008 were:

6.1.08 to 5.11.08	6.11.08 to 5.1.09	6/01/09 to 26/01/09	27/01/09 to 23/03/09	From 24/03/09 to 28 /09/09
4%	3%	2%	1%	0%
				From 29/09/09 3%

Where tax is overpaid, the overpayment used until 28 September 2009 to carry interest in favour of the taxpayer from the date on which the payment was made at the same rate as overdue tax carries interest (s 235). From 29 September 2009 interest on repayments of inheritance tax is at 0.5%.

In making interest calculations, IR Capital Taxes use a denominator of 366 for interest on overdue tax and 365 for interest on overpaid tax, whether or not a leap year is involved (March 1997 CTO Newsletter). In both cases this gives a slight advantage to the taxpayer.

Official rate of interest on pre owned assets

The rate decreased from 4.75% to 4% on 6 April 2010.

Rates of interest – Finance Act 2009 changes

(2)   Finance Act 2009 s 103 established a single rate of interest applied by HMRC on overpayments across all taxes, duties and penalties. The regulations would also provide for a single rate of interest to apply late payments across all taxes, duties and penalties.

Section 103 also provides the power to arrive at the prevailing rates of interest using formulae. The proposal is for HMRC to calculate interest by reference to the Bank of England base rate.

The legislation includes the power for regulations to be made that set different rates for different taxes, if appropriate.

The most recent interest rates detailed in **explanatory note 1** above reflect these new rules.

Treatment of interest on overdue and overpaid tax

(3)   Interest charged on overdue tax does not qualify for tax relief, nor is interest received on an overpayment taxable (ss 233(3) and 235). HMRC have issued a statement of practice (SP 6/95) indicating that they do not automatically initiate an assessment that would lead to a repayment of tax if the amount involved is £25 or less, although the repayment will be made if claimed.

Where payments are made before IR Capital Taxes notify the amount due, if their calculation shows a balance of tax due of less than £20 it will not be collected and if less than £10 is overpaid it will not be repaid unless claimed by the taxpayer (HMRC Inheritance Tax: Customer Guide (online version only)). Payments in advance do not attract interest, which only runs from the date that tax is due for payment (see **Example 28** for an illustration).

Late payment interest on sums due to HMRC – FA 2009 changes

(4) Finance Act 2009 s 101 introduced the rules for applying late payment interest to any sum due to HMRC but paid late. Schedule 53 sets out the special provisions concerning the amounts, start date and end dates for charging late payment interest as well as further provisions to clarify the effect of interest on certain reliefs.

Section 101 is intended to apply a simple and consistent interest charge to late payments across all taxes and duties. Late payment interest will apply, for the majority of payments due to HMRC and made late, from the payment due date until the date that payment is received. The interest charged will be simple interest, and will not generally be deductible in computing profits or income.

Section 101 sets out the method for applying late payment interest to any sum due to HMRC but paid late. The formulae follow FA 2008 s 127(1), which was designed to facilitate recovery action for sums owed to HMRC.

Repayment interest payable by HMRC – FA 2009 changes

Finance Act 2009 s 102 and Sch 54 sets out the general rules for applying repayment interest on sums to be repaid by HMRC. HMRC will pay interest on repayments from the date the tax was due to be paid or, if later, the date the payment was actually received, to the date the repayment is made.

Schedule 54 also includes the exceptions to the general rules set out in s 102 regarding repayment interest and covers how repayment interest will operate in particular situations.

Conditionally exempt transfers

(5) Where tax has not been paid because a transfer was conditionally exempt (works of art and historic buildings etc), or because of the deferral relief for woodlands, and it later becomes payable on those objects, buildings or woodlands, the due date is six months after the end of the month in which the event by reason of which it is chargeable occurs (s 226(4)), following which interest then runs (s 233).

Different payment dates re one transaction

(6) It should be noted that tax can be due at different times in respect of one transaction. If, for Example, a chargeable transfer was made to a discretionary trust on 1 May 2010, the tax would be payable on the lifetime transfer on 30 April 2011. Any additional tax payable as a result of the subsequent death of the donor would be due six months after the end of the month in which the donor died. Therefore if the donor died on 21 May 2010 the additional tax would be payable on 30 November 2010, some five months before the date for payment of the original liability.

Payment by instalments

(7) Tax may be paid by equal yearly instalments over ten years on qualifying assets in respect of transfers on death; chargeable lifetime transfers if the donee pays the tax; and transfers of settled property where the property concerned continues to be comprised in the settlement (eg termination of an estate interest in possession without the property leaving the settlement; or ten yearly charges on relevant property trusts) (s 227). The first instalment is due for payment on death transfers and on additional liabilities arising because of the death of the donor six months after the end of the month in which the death occurred. The first instalment on lifetime chargeable transfers is due on the normal due date as indicated in **part (a)(i)** of the Example.

The instalment option applies to the following assets:

(a) Land of any description, wherever situated.

(b) Shares which gave the transferor control immediately prior to the transfer.

(c) Unquoted shares and securities (unquoted being defined as not listed on a recognised stock exchange (ss 227(1AA) and 228(5)):

    (i) where tax cannot be paid without undue hardship (s 228(1)(c)); or

(ii)   for shares only, where they are valued in excess of £20,000 and either the nominal value of the shares is not less than 10% of the nominal value of all the shares of the company at that time or, if the shares are ordinary shares, their nominal value is not less than 10% of the nominal value of all ordinary shares in the company at that time (s 228(3)); or

(iii)   where the tax payable on the shares or securities, together with the tax on the other instalment assets, amounts to 20% or more of the tax payable by the same person on the same transfer (s 228(2)). This applies only to transfers on death.

(d)   A business or an interest in a business.

(e)   Timber, when a chargeable transfer is made following its being left out of account on a previous death (s 229).

The facility to pay by instalments is only available on potentially exempt transfers which become chargeable transfers if the transferee still owns the qualifying property at the time of the transferor's death, (or, for transfers of property qualifying for business or agricultural relief, replacement property).

The instalment option on unquoted shares is not available for tax payable in consequence of the donor's death, unless the shares are still unquoted when the donor dies (or if earlier, when the donee dies) (s 228(3A)). This applies to both controlling and non-controlling holdings.

Unquoted shares include those dealt in on the Alternative Investment Market.

See **Example 59 explanatory note 11**, in relation to the instalment option and the ten yearly charge on a relevant property settlement.

(8)   In the case of land, except land that forms part of a business (as distinct from land owned by partners or directors and occupied by their business) or land that qualifies for agricultural property relief, interest is charged on the *total* amount of tax for the time being remaining unpaid, the interest being added to each instalment as it falls due. Interest is also charged on any instalment that is paid late.

In the case of land that forms part of a business, land qualifying for agricultural property relief and all other assets in (b) to (e) of **explanatory note 7** above (excluding shares in an investment company) interest is not charged unless an instalment is paid late, in which case the interest is charged only on the late instalment and not on the full amount of the deferred tax (s 234).

Sale of instalment property

(9)   If instalment property is sold, the outstanding tax becomes payable immediately (s 227(4)). This explains why a lifetime transferor cannot pay tax on his chargeable transfer by instalments, because he cannot direct the actions of the transferee. If instalment property was comprised in a potentially exempt transfer and then disposed of by the donee, the instalment option would not be available to the donee if a charge to inheritance tax subsequently arose because of the donor's death within seven years.

Incidence of tax

(10)   The question of who is liable to pay inheritance tax is complex and is dealt with in IHTA 1984 ss 199 to 214. HMRC have powers to collect tax from a wide range of persons, but in most cases tax would be paid by the persons indicated in **part (b)** of the Example.

Where tax is unpaid there is normally a HMRC charge on the property concerned, however, this cannot take priority over an existing valid charge (s 237). No HMRC charge may be imposed on personal or movable property vested in personal representatives (other than settled property in which the deceased had an estate interest in possession). The HMRC charge can also apply in relation to outstanding tax and interest on assets from which heritage reliefs have been withdrawn.

The person who is liable to pay inheritance tax because of death is not necessarily the person who ultimately bears the tax. Tax on death is borne as follows:

Tax relating to an estate interest in possession of the deceased in settled property is borne by the trust funds and thus reduces the value of the funds for the person who becomes entitled to them, or to an interest in them.

Tax relating to property nominated to others during the lifetime of the deceased or held jointly by the deceased and others as joint tenants, is payable out of that property, and hence borne by the nominees or joint tenants.

Tax (and interest on it) on all other property in the UK (both real and personal) that vests in the deceased's personal representatives, other than property which was comprised in a settlement immediately before the death, is a testamentary expense and, in the absence of specific provisions in the will, payable out of the residue of the estate and thus borne by the residuary legatees (s 211). This is most important in relation to the drafting of wills and if it is intended that any particular asset should bear its own tax, this should be expressly provided in the terms of the will.

The tax on property situated abroad is a charge on that property.

Where the personal representatives are liable for and pay tax (and interest) which is not a testamentary expense under the above rule, the amount paid is, where occasion requires, to be repaid to them by the person in whom is vested the property to whose value the tax was attributable (s 211(3)).

Income tax relief re loan to pay inheritance tax

(11) Income tax relief is available in respect of interest paid for a period of up to one year on a loan raised by personal representatives to pay inheritance tax on personalty (ie all property other than freehold land and buildings) in order to obtain probate. Any excess interest over income of the estate in the tax year of payment may be carried back against the income of the estate in the preceding tax year(s) and any remaining excess is carried forward against future income of the estate (ITA 2007 s 405).

Obtaining an IHT reference number

(12) Before a personal representative can make the first payment of inheritance tax they must obtain an inheritance tax reference number and payslip. They can do this by applying for an IHT reference online or by using the Form IHT422 application for an inheritance tax reference. The application for a reference should be made at least three weeks before the expected date of any payment.

HMRC will send a note of the reference number and a pre-referenced payslip by post which should be used to pay the tax. The payslip can be used only for payments regarding a particular estate.

Electronic transfer of inheritance tax from participating financial institutions

(13) Most banks and building societies are able to accept instructions from personal representatives to make a payment of inheritance tax, by electronic transfer, before probate is obtained. They will need to complete Form IHT423 for each bank or building society making the transfer of funds.

If a personal representative wishes to use this facility they must contact HMRC at IR Capital Taxes, Ferrers House, PO Box 38, Castle Meadow Road, Nottingham NG2 1BB or telephone 0845 30 20 900 or fax 0115 974 2526.

HMRC will then allocate an IHT reference number to the estate. When the personal representative is ready to apply for probate (or letters of administration) they will send the form of authority (included with the probate pack) to the bank/building society. They in turn will transfer funds to HMRC electronically. HMRC will provide the personal representative with a receipt which must be presented to the Court Service to obtain the grant.

Reviews of HMRC decisions and appeals

(14) The system of tax appeals changed fundamentally from 1 April 2009, and was accompanied by (optional) statutory provisions for a review by HMRC of their decisions prior to an appeal being taken forward. The

legislation for inheritance tax is in ss 222–224 as amended (including new ss 223A–223I). For details see **Example 33 explanatory notes 6** and **7**.

Question

You have been asked by the chairman of your company for advice on the inheritance tax position on the death of his father.

The following information is available:

(1)   The chairman's father died on 1 March 2011.

(2)   His estate comprised:

   (a)   Freehold house and land valued for probate at £500,000. This property was owned jointly by the deceased and his wife (who survived him) as joint tenants.

   (b)   Stocks and shares:

      (i)   £100,000 6% bonds valued @ 92–96.

            Interest is payable half-yearly on 30 June and 31 December.

      (ii)   £20,000 5% stock valued @ 86–88 ex dividend.

             Interest is payable half-yearly on 31 March and 30 September.

(c)	Bank deposit account	£23,305
	Accrued interest (net of 20% tax)	£1,000
(d)	Proceeds of an insurance policy	£27,990
(e)	Personal chattels	£20,000

(3)   He had for the past ten years been life tenant of a trust fund, the assets of which amounted to £216,000, including gross accrued non-dividend savings income to 1 March 2011 of £1,000 (taxable at 20%). The trust funds are payable to the chairman on the death of his father.

(4)   Debts and funeral expenses amounted to £2,675.

(5)   By his will the deceased bequeathed legacies of £5,000 to each of two grandchildren, a legacy of £5,000 and the personal chattels to his widow and the residue to your chairman.

(6)   There had been no lifetime transfers.

Prepare a statement showing the amount of inheritance tax payable, who is accountable for the payment, and upon whom the burden falls.

Answer

Estate of Chairman's Father

	Date of death 1 March 2011		
	£	£	£
Property jointly owned with spouse			
Freehold house – half share		250,000	
Less: devolving on widow by survivorship		250,000	–
Free estate			
£100,000 6% bonds @ 93		93,000	
£20,000 5% stock @ 86½% ex dividend	17,300		
Add: net interest 31 March 2011 (£1,000 less 20%)	800	18,100	
Bank deposit account, including accrued interest (net of income tax)		24,305	
Proceeds of insurance policy		27,990	
Personal chattels		20,000	
Accrued income from trust fund to 1 March 2011 (£1,000 less 20%)		800	
		184,195	
Less: debts and funeral expenses		2,675	
		181,520	
Less: spouse exemption			
Legacy	5,000		
personal chattels	20,000	25,000	156,520
Settled property			
Trust fund		216,000	
Less: gross accrued income		1,000	215,000
			371,520

Inheritance tax due on death (2010/11 scale)

Inheritance tax payable on (371,520 – 325,000) = 46,520 @ 40%   £18,608

$$\text{Estate rate} = \frac{18,608}{371,520} \times 100 = 5.0086\%$$

Payable by executors	156,520	@ 5.0086%	7,839
Payable by trustees of trust fund	215,000	@ 5.0086%	10,769
	£371,520		£18,608

The tax payable by the executors will fall on the residue of the estate, so that the two grandchildren will receive their £5,000 legacies in full, with the chairman receiving the balance of residue after legacies and inheritance tax.

The tax payable by the trustees will reduce the trust fund remaining for the chairman.

Explanatory Notes

Quoted securities — valuation, sale within twelve months of death

(1)   Quoted securities are valued cum div at a price one-quarter up on the buying and selling quoted market prices. Thus the 6% bonds at 92–96 are valued at 92 + (¼ × (96 − 92)) = 93. If the midpoint between the highest and lowest recorded bargains gives a basic figure, then this is used instead (TCGA 1992 s 272(3)).

Where securities are quoted ex div then it is necessary to add the full amount of impending dividend or interest less lower rate tax to the above valuation.

Relief may be claimed if quoted securities are sold for less than the death valuation within twelve months after death. All securities sold have to be aggregated to determine whether there is any relief. In arriving at the aggregate sale proceeds the sale values are taken *before* deducting any expenses of sale. The relief is restricted if any purchase of quoted securities takes place in the period beginning at the date of death and ending two months after the date of the last sale within the twelve months period after death (ss 178–189). See **Example 11** for a detailed illustration. Strictly the same is true of dividends and the dividend normal rate; but in practice UK dividends are declared on a net basis and the tax credit is only notional, so the amount added is simply the dividend as declared.

Life interest in settlement — accrued income

(2)   Accrued income of a life interest in a trust fund forms part of the free estate of the deceased life tenant and not part of the settled property, the trustees having a liability to pay the accrued income less the appropriate rate of tax to the estate of the deceased life tenant (the appropriate rate being the rate of 10% on dividend income (covered by the tax credits), the lower rate on other savings income and the basic rate on non-savings income). This applies whether or not the life interest is an estate interest in possession (see **Example 52**); in the present case it was, because the father had been entitled to it since before March 2006.

Joint tenancy and tenancy in common

(3)   Assets held jointly by husband and wife (or civil partners) are deemed to be held on a joint tenancy unless this has been specifically rebutted.

The characteristic of a joint tenancy is that there are no separate shares which can be disposed of, so that on the death of a joint tenant his share automatically merges with that of the survivor. It therefore follows that the intestacy rules do not apply to the distribution of such assets, nor do they pass under the deceased's will nor vest in his personal representatives.

There can be a joint tenancy between persons who are not husband and wife or civil partners, but this has to be specifically created (whereas with husband and wife and civil partners it is implied).

If husband and wife (or civil partners) have specifically rebutted the joint tenancy and in other cases of joint ownership where a joint tenancy has not been specifically created, the ownership is on the basis of a tenancy in common. This means that there are separate shares which do not merge on death and which can therefore be independently dealt with by will or under an intestacy.

Had the chairman's father and mother owned the house in this Example as tenants in common, his will would have covered the disposition of his share, and for it to have been exempt it would have had to be devised to his widow as distinct from accruing to her by survivorship in the circumstances of the joint tenancy indicated in the Example.

(4)   Had the house been owned by say the chairman's father and his uncle, the position would have been:

(a)   If held as tenants in common (which is presumed unless specifically rebutted) the will would cover the disposition of the share and it does not automatically go to the survivor.

The share would be exempt if devised/bequeathed to a spouse or a charity but otherwise would be chargeable.

(b)   If held under a specifically created joint tenancy the share of the deceased would automatically merge with the survivor's share. The share would accordingly be chargeable on the death of the chairman's father since clearly its devolution to the uncle would not be exempt.

In both cases, however, the value of the share in the property would be affected by the joint ownership in that the difficulty of dealing with the share would be taken into account in making the valuation.

(5)   Where the property is held jointly by husband and wife or civil partners, whether as joint tenants or tenants in common, the related property provisions do not permit any such reduction in value, because the legislation provides that the whole is first valued and then divided pro rata between the part owners. For the detailed provisions see **Example 10**.

(6)   As indicated in note 4 property held jointly may or may not be liable to inheritance tax.

Further, it may or may not form part of the estate for the purposes of applying for a grant of probate or administration and in administering the estate.

If it is held under joint tenancy with accrual to the survivor it does not technically form part of the estate (although it may be liable to tax, depending on who the other joint tenant is) and is not therefore comprised in the probate summary in the HMRC account.

This is one reason why the value of published estates often does not accord with what the public expects to see in that the value of assets held as a joint tenant will not be included in the total. Similarly settled property will not generally vest in the personal representatives (but see **Example 4 part (B)(III)** and will not be included in the published value of an estate.

(7)   In the administration of the estate all that is required in relation to assets held on a joint tenancy is the registration of the death, for Example by a building society or bank in the case of joint accounts, or the placing of a death certificate with the title deeds (or production of it to the Land Registry) in the case of properties, the share in the asset itself having accrued by survivorship.

A share of an asset held as a tenant in common does form part of the estate, will appear in the probate summary in the HMRC account and will require dealing with by the personal representative as distinct from accruing by survivorship.

Position of surviving spouse where private residence owned as tenants in common

(8)   As indicated in **explanatory note 3**, where the home is held by husband and wife or civil partners as tenants in common, the will of the deceased will deal with that person's share, and in order to avoid wasting the inheritance tax nil-rate band of the first to die, the share may be left other than to the survivor. In order to protect the survivor's right to remain in the home, however, it used to be common for wills to provide for the surviving partner to be allowed to remain in the property free of charge, the share then passing, say, to the children. Such a provision was held in *CIR v Lloyd's Private Banking Ltd* to create an interest in possession in favour of the survivor, so that the whole property is chargeable on the second death, the former disadvantages of this result were largely eliminated by the introduction of the transferable nil-rate band in October 2007 (see **Example 1 part (III)**).

Position of co-habitees

(9)   Care needs to be taken where unmarried couples share a house that was purchased in the name of only one of them. If it is intended that the ownership of the property is to be regarded as shared, the purchaser could make a written declaration that the property was held on trust for himself and the co-habitee as joint tenants in equal beneficial shares, and the treatment would then be as indicated in **note 4** above, so that on the first death the survivor would acquire the deceased's share. Such a declaration would not represent a transfer of value by the purchaser to the extent that the other had contributed to the cost. Any amount not so covered would be a potentially exempt transfer.

In the absence of such a declaration the legal position is complex and HMRC may argue that, even if the co-habitee has made substantial direct or indirect contributions to the cost of the property (for Example by sharing mortgage payments, cost of alterations and household bills generally), the whole property is chargeable on the death of the legal owner (see also **Example 10 part a** re valuing the share of a co-habitee). The position is no less fraught following the decision of the House of Lords in Stack v Dowden (2007).

Calculation of inheritance tax

(10)   In the Example, the specific gifts to the widow (cash and chattels) is exempt under s 18 and is therefore deducted from the free estate before the inheritance tax calculation is made.

(11)   As no lifetime transfers had been made the scale rates apply to the taxable value of the estate without aggregation with any earlier transfers, giving an estate rate of 5.0086%. The tax is then payable by the executors and by the trustees of the settled property on presentation of the probate papers. Interest is payable from 30 September 2010, being six months after the end of the month in which the death occurred (s 226(2) and s 233(1)).

(12)   Had the trust funds in which the chairman's father had a life interest devolved on his death to his widow, either for her lifetime (as a transitional serial interest under s 49D, the chairman's interest dating from before 22 March 2006) or absolutely, they would have been left out of the inheritance tax calculation because of the surviving spouse exemption. There would then have been no tax payable on the death, since the £156,520 free estate would have been below the £325,000 threshold.

Question

Christopher died on 20 March 2011 at which date his assets were valued at:

Quoted investments	£156,000
Cash at bank	£5,312
Life policies on his own life, producing	£47,500

Outstanding liabilities at 20 March 2011 were £4,464 and the funeral expenses amounted to £1,748. The quoted investments were sold by the executors on 28 September 2011 for £150,000, less expenses of sale of £2,500 giving net proceeds of £147,500.

By his will Christopher gave the residue of his estate to his daughter absolutely.

Christopher had not made any chargeable transfers before 5 April 2005 but since then he had made the following cash gifts:

2005	26	April	Recognised charity	£110,000
2006	2	June	Discretionary trust	£293,000
2007	24	December	Daughter	£63,000
2008	20	February	Godson (on the occasion of his marriage)	£1,600
2009	24	December	Daughter	£90,000
2010	2	June	Discretionary trust	£77,500

Christopher had agreed to pay any tax due on the lifetime gifts.

Compute:

(a)   The original amounts of tax payable on the lifetime gifts, stating the due dates for payment.

(b)   The additional amount of tax payable on the gifts following Christopher's death, showing who is liable for the tax, and stating the due date for payment.

(c)   The amount of inheritance tax payable by the executors, stating the due date for payment.

Answer

Inheritance tax payable in Christopher's lifetime

		£	Gross £	Tax on 2007/08 scale £	Net £
26 April 2005					
Gift to charity			110,000		
Less: Exempt transfer (s 23)			110,000	–	–
2 June 2006 (explanatory note 1)					
Settlement on discretionary trust			293,000		
Less: Annual exemptions					
2006/07	3,000				
2005/06	3,000	6,000			
Net transfer, grossed up			287,000	287,500	500	287,000
24 December 2007					
Gift to daughter —			63,000		
Less: Annual exemption 2007/08			3,000		
			60,000		
20 February 2008					
Gift to godson			1,600		
Less: Marriage exemption (s 22)			1,000		
Potentially exempt transfer			600		
24 December 2009					
Gift to daughter			90,000		
Less: Annual exemptions					
2009/10	3,000				
2008/09	3,000	6,000			
Potentially exempt transfer			84,000		

		£	Gross £	Tax on 2010/11 scale £	Net £
2 June 2010 (explanatory note 1)					
Chargeable transfers within previous seven years				287,500	–	287,500
Settlement on discretionary trust			77,500		
Less: Annual exemption 2010/11			3,000		
			74,500		
Net transfer, grossed up					
(*371,250 – 325,000 = 46,250 @ 20%)				83,750	9,250	74,500
				371,250	9,250	362,000

On Christopher's death – 20 March 2011

	Gross	Tax on 2010/11 scale
	£	£
Gifts within seven years before death:		
Accumulation before first such gift	–	–
2 June 2006		
Settlement on discretionary trust	287,000	–
24 December 2007		
Gift to daughter	60,000	9,000
(*347,500 – 325,000 = 22,500 @ 40%)		
	347,500	9,000
20 February 2008		
Gift to godson	600	240
24 December 2009	348,100	9,240
Gift to daughter	84,000	33,600
2 June 2010	432,100	42,840
Settlement on discretionary trust	83,750	33,500
Cumulative transfers in seven years prior to death	515,850	76,340

Estate of Christopher deceased

	Date of death 20 March 2011	
	£	£
Quoted investments		156,000
Cash at bank		5,312
Life policies		47,500
		208,812
Less: Liabilities	4,464	
Funeral expenses	1,748	
Inheritance tax re settlement 2 June 2010	9,250	15,462
Value on death		193,350
Less: Loss on sale of quoted securities		
Probate value	156,000	
Proceeds (before expenses)	150,000	6,000
Chargeable to inheritance tax on death		187,350
Cumulative transfers in seven years before death	515,850	76,340
Chargeable estate and tax thereon	187,350	74,940
	703,200	151,280

Summary

(a)   The original amounts of inheritance tax payable on chargeable lifetime gifts were as follows:

Gift	Tax payable	Due date
2 June 2006	£500	30 April 2007
2 June 2010	£9,250	30 April 2011

(b)   The additional amounts of inheritance tax payable by reason of the death of Christopher are:

By discretionary trust

Amounts payable by trustees re transfers to discretionary trust made on:

2 June 2006 —	On death	–	
	Paid on original transfer	500	–
(No amount repayable)			–
			–
2 June 2010 —	On death	33,500	
	Payable on original transfer	9,250	24,250
By daughter			£24,250
24 December 2007	Gift	9,000	
Less: taper relief as gift is made more than 3 but not more than 4 years before death – 20%		1,800	7,200
24 December 2009	Gift		33,600
			£40,800
By godson			
20 February 2008	Gift	240	
Less: taper relief as above — 20%		48	£192

The tax is payable in each case on 30 September 2011.

(c)   The amount of inheritance tax payable by the executors is £74,940. It is payable on 30 September 2011 (ie six months after the end of the month in which the death occurred), or if earlier, upon the application for a grant of probate.

Interest runs from 30 September 2011 (ie six months after the end of the month in which the death occurred).

If tax had been paid on the estate before relief was claimed for the shares sold at a loss (amounting to £6,000 @ 40% = £2,400), the amount paid would have been £77,340 and the £2,400 reduction due to the fall in value of the shares would be repaid with interest from 30 September 2011 (or the date of payment if later) once the claim for fall in value was made.

Explanatory Notes

Grossing up lifetime gifts to discretionary trust

(1)   The gift to the discretionary trust on 2 June 2006 is a chargeable lifetime transfer liable to inheritance tax at one half of the full rate. As Christopher has agreed to pay the tax on the transfer the net chargeable gift must be grossed up using the 2006/07 lifetime table. The net transfer of £287,000 exceeds the nil band of £285,000 by £2,000, which is grossed up using the 20% lifetime rate. The calculation is therefore:

	Net £	Gross £
Nil band	285,000	285,000
Net amount within 20% rate band is	2,000	
Grossed up		
$2000 \times \dfrac{100}{80}$		2,500
	287,000	287,500

The second transfer to the discretionary trust on 2 June 2010 must also be grossed up. Tax on the cumulative transfers brought forward is recomputed on the 2010/11 scale to give the starting point for later transfers. As the cumulative total of £287,500 falls short of the 2010/11 nil threshold of £325,000, the second transfer to the discretionary trust of £74,500 falls within the 20% band to the extent of £37,000, the gross equivalent of which is:

	Net £	Gross £
Nil band	325,000	325,000
Net amount within 20% rate band	37,000	
Grossed up		
$37,000 \times \dfrac{100}{80}$		46,250
	362,000	371,250

The gross chargeable transfer is therefore (37,500 + 46,250 =) £83,750.

Potentially exempt transfers

(2)   The other gifts are all potentially exempt transfers. They are reduced by the marriage exemption on the gift to the godson and the annual exemptions on the gift to the daughter on 24 December 2009 for the purposes of any future charge to inheritance tax.

Recomputation of tax following Christopher's death

(3)   On the taxpayer's death, gifts within seven years before death must be reconsidered and the tax recomputed using the scale applicable at the date of death (s 7). If the original gift required grossing up, the originally calculated grossed up gift is used in the second calculation. The tax payable is the difference between that now calculated and the amount previously paid (Sch 2.2). If the amount paid exceeds the revised amount due on the new scale no refund of tax is made.

Quoted securities

(4)   Quoted securities sold within the twelve months following death by the person liable to account for the inheritance tax thereon must be aggregated and if the resulting sale proceeds are lower than the probate value of those securities a claim may be made for the loss to be deducted from the probate value (ss 178–189). For this purpose proceeds means sale value *before* deducting any expenses of sale. For detailed notes see **Example 8**.

Due date of payment of tax

(5)   Inheritance tax is payable on lifetime transfers six months after the end of the month in which the transfer was made, or at the end of April in the following tax year if this is later (s 226).

Inheritance tax on the estate at death (other than tax payable by instalments, as to which see **Example 9**) is payable on the delivery of the HMRC account. The account is submitted in conjunction with the application for a grant of probate or administration, which is usually made within twelve months after death. Interest runs from six months after the end of the month in which death occurred (s 226(2)(3)).

Inheritance tax on potentially exempt transfers that become chargeable and the additional inheritance tax on chargeable lifetime transfers made within seven years before death is payable by the transferee six months after the end of the month in which the death occurred (s 226).

Question

(a)   On 31 May 2010 X died leaving a net estate included in the application for probate at £364,250. Application for probate was made on 2 March 2011 and inheritance tax of £15,700 was paid on that date. Interest of £116 was also paid.

(b)   The executors subsequently became aware that certain assets valued at £12,500 had been omitted from the Inland Revenue Account.

(c)   Before his death the deceased had contracted for certain alterations to be made to the house in which he resided. The work was completed on 10 June 2010 and the valuation for probate which was subsequently made had taken the improved condition of the house into account. The contractors were now requesting payment of their final account amounting to £9,500, which had not been deducted from the value of the estate for probate purposes, since it was not clear at that time whether all alterations had been paid for by progress payments.

(d)   Prior to his death the deceased had made an unsecured loan of £8,000 to the company XZ Ltd, which loan had been included in the value of the estate for probate at its face value. On 1 May 2010 the company had gone into liquidation and it was now clear that nothing would be available for the unsecured creditors.

(e)   In order to pay the cash legacies the executors had to sell all the deceased's quoted securities. They did this on 1 April 2011 as follows:

   (i)   2,000 £1 shares in CD plc, quoted at death at 219p–223p with recorded bargains of 219p, 220p and 222p, were sold at 190p.

   (ii)   4,000 £1 shares in DE plc, quoted at death at 109p–116p with recorded bargains of 109p, 109½p and 111p, were sold at 87½p.

   (iii) 12,000 6% preference shares in DE plc, quoted at death at 53p–61p with no recorded bargains, were sold at 60p.

Advise the executors how they should proceed, and calculate the inheritance tax and interest payable or repayable if the position were finalised on 2 September 2010, assuming that the present rates of interest on underpaid and overpaid inheritance tax, effective since 29 September 2009, remain in force throughout, namely 3.0% and 0.5% respectively.

Answer

The executors should submit a corrective account which should include the omitted assets and other amendments (s 217).

Quoted securities (see **explanatory note 1**)

Where quoted securities are sold by the persons liable to account for the inheritance tax thereon within twelve months after death at an aggregate value that is lower than probate value, relief may be claimed for the loss. In arriving at the aggregate value the sale values taken into account are the gross proceeds *before* deducting selling expenses. In this case the position is:

	Death Value		Realised Value	
2,000 shares in CD plc	@ 220p	4,400	@ 190p	3,800
4,000 shares in DE plc	@ 110p	4,400	@ 87½p	3,500
12,000 6% preference shares in DE plc	@ 55p	6,600	@ 60p	7,200
		£15,400		£14,500

A reduction of £900 (£15,400 – £14,500) is available on a claim being made (ss 178–189).

Alterations to the house

The deceased had placed the contract for the work to be done and therefore he or his estate is liable for the cost, the value of his house having reflected the work done or to be done in performance of the contract and that increased value being included in the net estate.

Unsecured loan to XZ Ltd

The loan must be valued at the price it would have realised on a sale on the open market at the time of death (s 160). The market value at the date of death in the circumstances outlined would be nil. Since the value included in the net estate was £8,000, a reduction of £8,000 will be made. The valuation is not affected by an event *after* death. Here the liquidation had commenced *before* death but the proper value *as at death* has been ascertained later.

After making the appropriate adjustments the revised inheritance tax will be:

Value per account submitted at the time of the application for probate			364,250
Omitted assets			12,500
			376,750
Less: Loss on quoted securities		900	
Additional debt		9,500	
Reduction in value of loan to XZ Ltd		8,000	18,400
Adjusted estate			£358,350
Inheritance tax on 2010/11 death scale			
(358,350 – 325,000 = 33,350 @ 40%)			13,340
Amount paid			15,700
Repayment due			£2,360
Interest overpaid 1 December 2010 to 1 March 2011			
90 days @ 3% × £2,360			£17

Inheritance tax overpaid	2,360
Interest overpaid	17
	2,377
Interest thereon (185 days @ 0.5% 2 March 2011 to 2 September 2011)	6
Total repayable	£2,383

Explanatory Notes

Valuation of quoted securities

(1) Quoted securities are valued at cum div prices at the lower of:

  (a) ¼ up from the lower of the closing prices

  (b) The midpoint of recorded bargains.

  X's estate therefore included the following values:

					Lower
Value of CD plc shares					
(a) ¼ (223 – 219) = 1	+ 219	=	220	)	220p
(b) ½ (219 + 222)		=	220.5	)	
Value of DE plc shares					
(a) ¼ (116 – 109) = 1.75	+ 109	=	110.75	)	110p
(b) ½ (109 + 111)		=	110	)	
Value of DE plc preference shares					
(a) ¼ (61 – 53) = 2	+ 53	=			55p
(b) N/A					

Relief for a fall in value of quoted securities

(2) The relief for a fall in value of quoted securities sold in the twelve months following death is not available if the person who claimed the relief purchases further quoted securities of a value equal to or greater than the proceeds of sale within the period beginning with the date of death and ending two months after the date of the last sale in that twelve months. If the reinvestment does not amount to the whole of the sale proceeds the relief is withdrawn proportionately (s 180). For an illustration see **Example 11**.

(3) *All* sales of quoted securities, whether at a loss or at a profit, which take place in the period of twelve months following the death must be included in the computation for relief (s 179).

(4) The provisions giving relief where securities are sold at a loss within twelve months after death also apply to securities for which the quotation is suspended, or which are cancelled, within that period. For details see **Example 11**.

Interest on overpaid tax

(5) The repayment of inheritance tax, including the interest overpaid (calculating the overpayment at the late payment rate(s) used to calculate the original interest charge in favour of HMRC), carries interest against HMRC from the due date (or the date of payment if later) to that of repayment, at the repayment rate(s) (s 235 as amended by FA 2009, and see FA 1989 s 187 and SI 2010/1879 (see **Example 5 explanatory note 1**).

(6) The original tax and interest will have been calculated as follows:

Net estate per original grant application	£351,250
Tax on (364,250 − 325,000) = £39,250 @ 40%	£15,700
Interest at 3% pa from 1 December 2010 to 1 March 2011 (90 days)	£116

Provisional figures in HMRC Account

(7) Personal representatives need to take care when including provisional figures in the HMRC Account, because HMRC are taking a harsher attitude to penalties where asset values are understated — see **Example 33 explanatory note 10.**

Question

Smith, who had been in partnership with his son for many years, died on 5 April 2011. He had made a lifetime gift on 12 November 2005 of £182,000. He had subsequently made gifts to use his annual exemptions but had made no other transfers of value.

The value of his estate at the date of his death was agreed as follows:

	£
Stocks and shares	10,000
Cash at bank	2,000
Furniture and effects	4,000
Interest as a partner in partnership of Smith & Son	200,000
His house, 5 Side Street	363,000
Let agricultural land (owned and let on same lease for 20 years)	173,000
His outstanding debts were:	
General household bills	7,250
Income tax and capital gains tax	11,000

His funeral expenses amounted to £2,750.

Under his will his whole estate passed to his son absolutely.

Where possible the inheritance tax in connection with his death is being paid by instalments. The first instalment and the inheritance tax not payable by instalments was paid on 1 January 2012. The second instalment was paid on 1 January 2013.

Calculate the inheritance tax and interest payable on those two dates, assuming that the present rate of interest on underpaid inheritance tax, namely 3.0% effective since 29 September 2009, remains in force throughout.

Answer

Estate of Smith deceased

Date of death 5 April 2011
£

Non-instalment option property

Stocks and shares			10,000
Cash at bank			2,000
Furniture and effects			4,000
			16,000

Less:	Funeral expenses	2,750	
	General household bills	7,250	
	Income tax and capital gains tax	11,000	21,000
Amount to be deducted from instalment option personalty			(5,000)

Instalment option property

Freehold house			363,000
Let agricultural land		173,000	
Less:	agricultural property relief 50%	86,500	86,500
Personalty – Interest as a partner in partnership of Smith & Son		200,000	
Less:	balance of debts as above		
(see **explanatory notes 3 and 4**)		(5,000)	
		195,000	
Less:	business property relief 100%	195,000	–
Chargeable to inheritance tax at death			449,500

					Tax on 2010/11 scale
				£	£
November 2005 — Gift			182,000		
Less: Annual exemptions	2005/06	3,000			
	2004/05	3,000	6,000	176,000	
Chargeable estate				449,500	120,200*
				625,500	120,200*

(* 625,500 – 325,000 = 300,500 @ 40%)

Tax on estate at death is therefore:	£120,200

Part attributable to house

$$\frac{363,000}{449,500} \times 120,200 \qquad\qquad 97,069$$

Part attributable to agricultural land

$$\frac{86,500}{449,500} \times 120,200 \qquad\qquad 23,131$$

£120,200

The tax may be paid by ten equal annual instalments in each case. Interest on the tax relating to the house is charged on the *total* amount for the time being remaining unpaid, the interest being added to each instalment as it falls due, and interest is also charged on the instalment if it is paid late. In respect of land qualifying for agricultural relief, interest is payable only on the amount of the instalment if it is paid late.

The amounts of tax and interest payable are therefore:

	£	£
On 1 January 2012		
Re agricultural land:		
Instalment due 31 October 2011	2,313	
Interest thereon from 31 October 2011 to 31 December 2011		
£2,313 × 3% × 62/365	12	2,325
Re house:		
Instalment due 31 October 2011	9,707	
Interest thereon from 31 October 2011 to 31 December 2011		
£9,707 × 3% × 62/365	49	9,756
Total tax and interest due		12,081
On 1 January 2013		
Re agricultural land:		
Instalment due 31 October 2012	2,313	
Interest thereon from 31 October 2012 to 31 December 2012		
£2,313 × 3% × 62/365	12	2,325
Re house:		
Instalment due 31 October 2011	9,707	
Interest thereon from 31 October 2011 to 31 December 2011		
£9,707 × 3% × 62/365	49	
Interest on unpaid tax of (£97,069 less 1st instalment of £9,707)		
from 31 October 2011 to 31 October 2012		
£86,362 × 3% × 1 year	2,621	12,377
Total tax and interest due		14,702

Explanatory Notes

Recomputation of tax following donor's death

(1)   Where gifts are made within seven years before the donor's death, tax has to be recomputed (or, in the case of potentially exempt transfers, computed) on the death scale in force at the date of death and any additional tax arising is payable by the donee (but no tax is repayable should the tax on the current scale be less than the lifetime tax originally paid).

Payment by instalments

(2)   Tax may be paid by equal yearly instalments over ten years on certain assets where they are transferred on death. The instalment facility is also available for chargeable lifetime transfers where the donee pays the tax, and, so long as the assets are still owned by the donee, in respect of additional tax or tax on potentially exempt transfers that becomes payable on death. The detailed notes on the assets qualifying for this treatment are in **Example 5 explanatory note 7**. Smith's instalment assets are his freehold house and agricultural land. His partnership interest would also have qualified but as it attracts 100% business property relief no tax is payable in respect of that asset.

Debts payable out of estate

(3) Debts payable out of a deceased's estate are payable primarily from personalty (ie property other than freehold land and buildings) unless charged against specific property, in which case the deduction is against that property (s 162(4)). It could be argued that the liabilities are to be deducted pro-rata against the non-instalment personalty (£16,000 in this Example) and the instalment personalty (£200,000 in this Example). Since the instalment personalty in the Example qualifies for 100% business property relief, the effect would be to increase the chargeable estate by the proportion of the debts set against that property. It is understood that in practice it is accepted that the debts reduce non-instalment option personalty before instalment option personalty.

Business property relief

(4) Business property relief is given at the rate of 100% or 50% on relevant business property (for detailed notes see **Example 25**). In the case of a business or an interest in a business the value is defined as the value of the assets used in the business (including goodwill) reduced by the liabilities incurred for the purpose of the business (s 110). Even if any of the taxation liabilities in this Example relate to the business they were not incurred for the purpose of the business and do not affect the business property relief. Section 104 provides, however, that business property relief is given on such part of the value transferred as is attributable to relevant business property. In this Example the excess of liabilities over non-instalment option personalty reduces the value transferred in respect of the partnership interest. The excess of £5,000 therefore reduces the amount on which 100% business property relief is given.

Agricultural property relief

(5) Agricultural property relief on agricultural property let before 1 September 1995 is at the rate of 50% (subject to special transitional provisions for certain property owned since before 10 March 1981 and let within a farming family). See **Example 25** for details.

Interest on overdue tax

(6) Where tax is not paid on the due date, interest is payable thereon, currently at 3% (from 29 September 2009), in respect of transfers made on death and on the tax or additional tax payable on gifts within the seven previous years. The detailed provisions and previous rates of interest are in **Example 5**. HMRC use a denominator of 366 when calculating interest on overdue tax, as shown in the Example (and a denominator of 365 when calculating interest on overpaid tax) — see **Example 5 explanatory notes 1 and 2**.

(7) Although land is one of the assets qualifying for the instalment treatment as indicated in note 2 above, interest is charged not only on the amount of any instalment paid late but also on the *total* amount of tax remaining unpaid, the interest being added to each instalment as it falls due (s 227(3)). (This does not apply to land that forms part of a business or qualifies for agricultural property relief.) Thus in the Example, interest arises re the freehold house on the balance of tax outstanding after deducting the first instalment, in addition to the interest that is due on the overdue instalment. The amount on which interest will be calculated at 31 October 2013 is £76,655, being the previous balance of £86,362 less the second instalment of £9,707. Further interest will arise if the third instalment is paid late, and so on.

Question

A.

Inheritance tax is charged on the value transferred by a chargeable transfer.

How is property valued for this purpose, and how is the value affected if the property is 'related property'?

Comment upon the basis applicable to the following property:

(a)   Unquoted securities

(b)   Farm cottages and farmhouses

and the effect on that valuation of

(i)   A special purchaser

(ii)   Capital gains tax.

B.

A testator who was a widower died in November 2010 leaving a freehold property, Blackacre. The value as at the date of his death is agreed by the executors with HMRC as being £700,000 and inheritance tax is paid on that basis.

What effect will there be, if any, on the inheritance tax payable in respect of Blackacre if eighteen months after his death the executors sell Blackacre for (i) £650,000 or (ii) £750,000?

Answer

A. Valuation of property

The amount on which inheritance tax is charged on a lifetime chargeable transfer of value is the difference between the value of the transferor's estate before and after the transfer less any exemptions and ignoring disposals of excluded property (s 3). On death the value transferred is the value of the deceased's estate (other than excluded property) immediately before his death (ss 4, 5(1)(b)).

The value of property is the price which it ought reasonably to be expected to fetch if sold on the open market at the time. The value is not, however, to be reduced on the ground that the whole property is to be placed on the market at one time (s 160).

With regard to open market value, it has been held by the Land Tribunal in the case of Walton (exor of Walton decd) v CIR (1994), that the interest of a partner in a non-assignable agricultural tenancy should be valued according to the extent to which the partnership profits were enhanced as a result of not paying a full market rent, rather than by reference to the vacant possession value compared with the tenanted value.

Valuation on death

The valuation of property on death is dealt with in ss 171–177. These sections provide that the value shall be that immediately prior to death, but taking into account changes in the value of the estate resulting from the death (other than changes relating to life interests or property passing by survivorship). However, allowances are to be made for reasonable funeral expenses (s 172) and for expenses incurred in administering or realising property situated outside the United Kingdom not exceeding five per cent of the value of that property, where the expense is incurred because of the situation of the property (s 173). Thus the deduction is limited to the additional cost of administering the property because it is situated outside the United Kingdom.

In some circumstances where the value of property has fallen between the date of a gift and the donor's death, the lower value may be taken into account to compute the tax or additional tax payable by the donee. The value in the accumulation for later transfers, including that on death, is not, however, altered.

Where a death estate includes quoted securities and they are sold, cancelled or the quotation is suspended within twelve months after the date of death, then a claim may be made for relief for the fall in value under ss 178–189. Similarly if the estate includes land which is sold within four years after death, ss 190–198 apply as detailed in part B below.

When valuing assets in a deceased's estate, care must be taken to ensure that all parts of an asset included in the estate are aggregated when considering its value, eg if the deceased owned a half share of a house personally and had a life interest in the other half then the value to be used will be that of the whole, allocated equally between the free estate and the settled property.

By comparison, if the deceased owned a half share of a house personally and the other half is owned by a co-habitee then the value of the deceased's share should be reduced by a discount, typically 15%, to reflect the fact that any purchaser would have to share the house with the co-habitee (Wright & Another v CIR (1982)). See **Example 6 explanatory note 9** re establishing that co-habitees do actually share the ownership of the property.

Valuation of lifetime transfers

Similar valuation rules apply in relation to lifetime transfers, except where the transfer is of settled property in which the transferor had an estate interest in possession (see **Example 52**). In that event s 52(1) provides that the value transferred is treated as being equal to the value of the property in which the life interest subsisted. Where a life tenant also owns property of a similar kind (eg shares in the same company) in his own right, the value of the life interest is valued independently. If therefore someone owned shares both directly and as a life tenant, and the combined holding gave a controlling interest, a gift of the shares owned directly that reduced the combined holding to a minority holding would be valued so as to reflect the loss of control, whereas a transfer of the life interest would be valued only in terms of the life interest shares, even though the life tenant's estate had fallen in value by a greater amount.

Related property

Special rules apply to calculate the value of an asset to which the related property rules apply (s 161). These rules do not apply if the asset is sold within three years after death and relief is claimed under s 176 (see **explanatory note 4**).

The related property rules provide that property is related to the property in a person's estate if it is:

(a)   Property belonging to his spouse.

(b)   Property which was the subject of an exempt transfer by the taxpayer or his spouse to a charity, political party, national heritage body or housing association after 15 April 1976 and which is owned by that body or has been owned by that body at any time in the previous five years.

If it produces a higher value than its unrelated value, the value of the property in the transferor's estate will be:

$$\frac{\text{Value of that property at unrelated value}}{\text{Value of that property and the related property at unrelated value}} \times \text{Related value of total}$$

In arriving at this proportion for shares or debentures etc of the same class, the respective unrelated values are deemed to be equivalent to the number of shares held (s 161).

For Example, the shareholders of Related Ltd are Mr R 40%, Mrs R 25%, Discretionary trust created by Mr R in 1970 15%, Others 20%.

An 80% shareholding is valued at £80,000

A 65% shareholding is valued at £58,500

A 40% shareholding is valued at £24,000

A 25% shareholding is valued at £15,000

A 15% shareholding is valued at £ 4,500

The inheritance tax values of the shares held by Mr & Mrs R would be:

$$\text{Mr R} \ \frac{40}{65} \times £58,500 \text{ for a 65 \% holding} = £36,000$$

$$\text{Mrs R} \ \frac{25}{65} \times £58,500 \text{ for a 65 \% holding} = £22,500$$

since these are higher than £24,000 (for a 40% holding) and £15,000 (for a 25% holding) respectively.

Unquoted securities

Section 168 refers to *unquoted shares and securities* and states that the valuation is to be made on the basis that the prospective purchaser has available all the information which a prudent purchaser might reasonably require in an arm's length transaction.

Farm cottages and farmhouses

Section 169 deals with *farm cottages* occupied by agricultural employees. In valuing such agricultural property no account is to be taken of any value attributable to the fact that the cottages are suitable for residential purposes of any other persons. If the cottage is occupied by a retired employee or the retired employee's widow(er) it is deemed to be occupied by an employee provided it is occupied under a statutorily protected tenancy or under a lease granted to the employee (and surviving spouse) for life as part of his contract of employment.

In a Lands Tribunal decision in the Antrobus case it has been decided that only the agricultural value of a farmhouse qualifies for agricultural property relief, not its full market value, which will often be much higher.

A special purchaser

A problem arises when the property to be valued could be the subject of a bid by a *special purchaser*. For Example, a piece of land with a normal value of £100,000 might be worth more to an adjoining landowner for the value that it would add to his own holding. Although he might be prepared to bid up to, say £170,000, he would, in fact, only usually make the bid necessary to obtain the land. That might well be very little more than its normal market value. The value of such property will therefore be between its normal value and the highest price that a special purchaser would pay.

Capital gains tax

If the asset to be transferred will give rise to a liability to *capital gains tax* and the *donee* bears that tax, then the value transferred is reduced by the tax paid (s 165). Capital gains tax may be held over on the disposal of certain property otherwise than under a bargain at arm's length if a claim is made under the provisions of TCGA 1992 s 165 or s 260. In this event the inheritance tax value is not altered, and any inheritance tax payable, either immediately or as a result of the donor's death within seven years, is deducted in computing the chargeable gain arising when the donee eventually disposes of the asset (but not so as to create or increase a loss).

B. Blackacre — sale after death above or below probate value of £700,000

Sale below probate value

If Blackacre is the only sale of land involved, then relief is available under s 191 for the reduction in value. This is given by comparing the value at death with the gross sale value of all land sold within three years after death, and with land sold at a loss within the fourth year after death.

If the result of a disposal is a net adjustment which is less than £1,000 (or 5% of the value at death if lower) then no adjustment will be made for that disposal (s 191(2)).

The relief can only be claimed if the land was sold to an unconnected person by the 'appropriate person', ie the person liable to pay the inheritance tax on the land at death (eg personal representative or trustee of settlement).

In arriving at the *sale value* there are provisions to substitute for the *sale price*, the best consideration which could reasonably have been obtained at the time of sale.

If a claim for relief is made, all sales within the *three* year period (except those covered by the de minimis rule above) must be taken into account, ie including sales at a profit. Sales at a profit in the *fourth* year are not taken into account.

Sale above probate value

If the property increases in value no additional inheritance tax is payable on the increase providing no claim for a reduction in value of other properties has been made (but capital gains tax at 18% or 28% as appropriate (see **Example 64 part B paragraph (4)**)*is* payable subject to any exemptions and reliefs available to the executors). Such a sale may, however, influence the agreement of a value on death. (See also **explanatory note 7**.)

Therefore if the executors sell Blackacre for £650,000 on the open market eighteen months after the date of death, and the estate does not sell any other land, a claim under s 191 should be made, reducing the value of the estate by £50,000. If the property were sold in similar circumstances for £750,000 the executors would be liable for capital gains tax on a gross gain of £50,000, reduced by the capital gains tax annual exemption.

Explanatory Notes

Open market value

(1)   The 'open market value' rule is the general valuation rule applicable to both lifetime and death transfers. There are, however, a number of special rules relating to particular assets, some of which are dealt with in the Example.

The special rules relating to valuation of quoted securities on death are dealt with in Examples 6, 8 and 11. The provisions for claiming relief for a fall in value of a gift before the donor's death are dealt with in **Example 12**. See also **Example 38 explanatory note 1** for differences in valuation for capital gains tax and inheritance tax purposes.

Valuation of life policies

(2)   The usual market value rule applies to the valuation of life policies (whether on the life of the transferor or of someone else) and for this purpose it will be necessary to consider not only the surrender value of the policy (if applicable) but also the actuarial value in the sense of what sum the policy will produce and how long (taking account of the life expectancy, health etc of the life assured) a putative buyer would have to wait to receive that sum. However, two other points may be relevant:

(a)   Except for transfers on death (or transfers where the policy does not leave the transferor's estate) the sum of the premiums paid to date must in many cases be substituted if it is higher than the market value on the above principles (s 167). This does not however apply to term policies or survivorship policies, provided (in broad terms) that in the case of policies for a term of more than three years (whether initially or by exercise of a policy option) premiums are payable at least annually and in regular amounts and for at least two thirds of the term of the policy.

(b)   In the case of a transfer on death, if the death results in the policy maturing and the proceeds being payable, the value to be taken will be the amount of the proceeds, as being one instance of a change in value resulting from the death (s 171).

Associated operations

(3)   The valuation to be placed on a particular asset will be affected if it is disposed of as part of a series of associated transactions (see **Example 22**).

Related property

(4)   Where property in a death estate has been valued under the related property rules, and the property is sold within three years after the death, a claim may be made under s 176 for the value of the property immediately before the death to be redetermined as if the related property rules did not apply. This does *not* mean substituting the *sale proceeds* for the probate value.

A claim may only be made if:

(a)   The property is sold either by the personal representatives or the person in whom the property is vested.

(b)   The sale is at arm's length for a freely negotiated price and not made in conjunction with a sale of any of the related property.

(c)   The vendor and purchaser are totally unconnected.

(d)   The vendor does not have a right to reacquire the property.

Valuation at death

(5)   Although the value of property at death is deemed to be its value immediately prior to death, the valuation may anticipate the effect of the death, but not the effect of the sale of the assets. For Example, the value of

unquoted shares in a company would be affected by the death of the sole director who ran the business and this could be taken into account. But if someone had a large holding of shares, the availability of which affected the market and caused the price to drop, the drop in price could not be taken into account in arriving at the death valuation, since the drop would be attributable to the *sale* not to the *death*.

(6) Where an estate at death includes a building society account on which demutualisation profits in the form of a cash bonus and/or shares will arise, but the date when the benefits will be received is not determined at the date of death, the value of the rights in the demutualisation will be taken into account in the death valuation, but it will be discounted to reflect the degree of uncertainty or delay at the time of death.

Sale of land after death

(7) Valuation adjustments have to be made where the legal interest in land sold within four years after death is not the same as that held at death, and in connection with leases, exchanges and compulsory purchase (ss 192–198).

In order to qualify for relief under s 191, the sale of the land must actually take place. In the case of Jones v CIR (1997), contracts had been exchanged within the (then) three year period, but the sale did not take place and the intended purchaser forfeited his deposit. It was held that s 191 relief was not available.

HMRC Capital Taxes will not consider a claim under s 191 when there is not a chargeable transfer and as a consequence there is no appropriate person. This would arise where, for instance, 100% agricultural property relief would be due. This was confirmed in the case of Stonor & Mills (Dickinson's Executors) v CIR (SpC 288, 2001), where the executors sold land within three years of death at figures considerably in excess of the probate values. This did not increase the inheritance tax, because the value of the estate was covered by exemptions and the nil band, so no tax was payable. The executors' attempt to have the values revised under s 191 failed because the Special Commissioners upheld the Revenue's view that there was no 'appropriate person' who could make a claim.

Interaction of inheritance tax and capital gains tax gifts holdover relief

(8) If an asset is transferred in lifetime and a holdover election for capital gains tax is made under TCGA 1992 s 165 or s 260, any inheritance tax paid is allowed as a deduction in computing the chargeable gain when the donee disposes of the asset. This will also apply if the transfer is a potentially exempt transfer for inheritance tax purposes and a death occurs within seven years, causing inheritance tax then to be payable. But the inclusion of inheritance tax as an allowable cost cannot have the effect of creating an allowable loss. Where a potentially exempt transfer is made on which capital gains holdover relief is not available so that capital gains tax is payable, there is no set-off against inheritance tax should the potentially exempt transfer become chargeable on the donor's death. See **Example 4 explanatory note 7** for further details (full details of when a chargeable capital gain may be held over under TCGA 1992 s 165 or s 260 are in companion book **Tolley's Taxwise I 2010/11**).

Question

When X, a widower, died on 7 April 2010 his own assets included a policy on his own life which produced £21,600. As soon as the proceeds of the policy were available his executors invested the whole sum in a new issue of 28,000 shares in AB plc, doing so in July 2010.

He owned at death:

5,000	50p	ords in AB plc quoted at 75–79 with bargains done at 75, 75½ and 78
5,000	£1	ords in CD plc quoted at 121–129 with bargains done at 121 and 123
20,000	£1	ords in EF plc quoted at 240–242 but with no recorded bargains
15,000	£1	ords in GH plc quoted at 252–256 with a single bargain at 252
10,000	£1	ords in IJ plc quoted at 4–6 with no recorded bargains
1,000	50p	ords in KL plc quoted at 92–96 with bargains at 93 and 95

His executors made the following sales:

1 February 2011:	5,000	shares in CD plc sold for £7,500 gross
3 March 2011:	20,000	shares in EF plc sold for £40,550 gross
23 March 2011:	15,000	shares in GH plc sold to the residuary beneficiary Y for £37,000 gross
12 April 2011:	33,000	shares in AB plc sold for £26,400 gross

X had also been entitled to receive equally with his brother the income from a settled fund set up under the will of his father in 2001. The trust assets at the date of X's death were:

8,000	50p	ords in AB plc
12,000	£1	ords in EF plc
20,000	£1	ords in MN plc quoted at 251–256 with bargains done at 251, 251½ and 253

On 5 May 2010 the trustees sold half the shares in EF plc (6,000 shares) for £13,800 gross which they used to pay the inheritance tax in respect of half the trust fund in connection with X's death. They then retired and appointed new trustees. There was a dispute about the devolution of X's half share of the trust fund and the new trustees sold half the shares in AB plc on 24 February 2011 (4,000 shares) for £3,120 gross which they used to pay the cost of Counsel's Opinions etc. It is agreed that X's son S is entitled to X's half share of the trust fund absolutely and the new trustees accordingly transferred to him half of the shares in MN plc plus the remaining cash capital in hand. On 15 March 2011 S sold for £27,000 gross, the 10,000 shares in MN plc which were transferred to him.

In each sale or purchase, the expenses incidental to that sale or purchase may be taken to be equal to 1% of the gross sale or purchase price.

On 23 November 2010 IJ plc went into liquidation and the shares were subsequently cancelled without payment of dividend.

The Stock Exchange suspended the shares in KL plc on 5 March 2011, the market value of the 1,000 shares on 7 April 2011 being £400.

Appropriate claims for relief are made.

HMRC point out that at the time of the sale by the executors of the 15,000 shares in GH plc to the residuary beneficiary, such shares were quoted at 253–256, with a single recorded bargain at 253.

Calculate the original and revised values for taxation purposes placed on each holding of shares as at the date of death of X.

Answer

(1) Valuation of X's own shares

Date of death 7 April 2010

				£	£
5,000	50p	ord in AB plc	@ 76	3,800	
5,000	£1	ord in CD plc	@ 122	6,100	
20,000	£1	ord in EF plc	@ 240½	48,100	
15,000	£1	ord in GH plc	@ 252	37,800	
10,000	£1	ord in IJ plc	@ 4½	450	
1,000	50p	ord in KL plc	@ 93	930	97,180

Less relief for loss on shares sold, cancelled or suspended within one year after death:

		£	£	
AB plc —	Sold more than one year after death (12 April 2011)		–	
CD plc —	Sale price (1 February 2011)	7,500		
	Probate value	6,100	1,400	
EF plc —	Sale price (3 March 2011)	40,550		
	Probate value	48,100	(7,550)	
GH plc —	'Best price' (23 March 2011)	37,950		
	Probate value	37,800	150	
KL plc —	Suspended security — market value	400		
	Probate value	930	(530)	
Reduction in value			£(6,530)	
Acquisition of 'qualifying investments' —			£	
	Shares in AB plc purchased by executors		21,600	
Total value of disposals within year —				
	(£7,500 + £40,550 + £37,950 + £400)		86,400	
Reduction in value on death is therefore restricted by				
		$\dfrac{21,600}{86,400}$		ie ¼

	£
Claim for reduction in probate value ¾ × 6,530	4,898
	92,282

The value of each holding on death then becomes:

Shares in		£
	AB plc	3,800
	CD plc (£ 6,100 + ¾ of £1,400)	7,150
	EF plc (£48,100 − ¾ of £7,550)	42,438
	GH plc (£37,800 + ¾ of £150)	37,912
	IJ plc	450
	(see**explanatory note 4**)	
	KL plc (£930 − ¾ of £530)	532
		£92,282

(2) Valuation of Trust Fund (in which X has a one half interest)

Date of death 7 April 2010				£	£
8,000 50p		ord in AB plc	@ 76	6,080	
12,000	£1	ord in EF plc	@ 240½	28,860	
20,000	£1	ord in MN plc	@ 252	50,400	£85,340

Relief for loss on shares sold within one year after death:

			£	£	
EF plc	Sale price (5 May 2010)		13,800		
	Probate value				
	6,000 @ 240½		14,430	(630)	
AB plc	Sale price (24 February 2011)		3,120		
	Probate value				
	4,000 @ 76		3,040	80	
MN plc	Sale by beneficiary cannot affect position			–	
Reduction in value				(550)	
Value of shares taxable on death of X					
	½ of £85,340				42,670
Less:	Reduction in value				
	½ of £550				275
					£42,395

The value of each holding on death then becomes:

Shares in	AB plc	½ of (£6,080 + £80)	3,080
	EF plc	½ of (£28,860 – £630)	14,115
	MN plc	½ of £50,400	25,200
			£42,395

Explanatory Notes

Quoted securities

(1) The notes to **Examples 6 and 8** relating to shares sold within twelve months after death apply also to this Example, but the problems of partial reinvestment and a partial interest in trust property are also considered here.

(2) Listed shares and securities are valued at the lower of:

(a) The lower closing price plus one-quarter of the difference between the lower and higher closing prices; or

(b) Half way between the highest and lowest recorded bargains for the day of valuation.

(c) The respective valuations are therefore:

Own Shares	Closing Prices	Bargains	Lower
AB plc	$75 + \frac{1}{4}(79 - 75) = 76$		
	$\dfrac{75 + 78}{2}$	$= 76\frac{1}{2}$	76
CD plc	$121 + \frac{1}{4}(129 - 121) = 123$		
	$\dfrac{121 + 123}{2}$	$= 122$	122
EF plc	$240 + \frac{1}{4}(242 - 240) = 240\frac{1}{2}$	None	$240\frac{1}{2}$
GH plc	$252 + \frac{1}{4}(256 - 252) = 253$	252	252
IJ plc	$4 + \frac{1}{4}(6 - 4) = 4\frac{1}{2}$	None	$4\frac{1}{2}$
KL plc	$92 + \frac{1}{4}(96 - 92) = 93$		
	$\dfrac{93 + 95}{2}$	$= 94$	93

Trust Shares

MN plc	$251 + \frac{1}{4}(256 - 251) = 252\frac{1}{4}$		
$\dfrac{251 + 253}{2}$		$= 252$	252

Where a death occurs on a Sunday or other day for which no prices are available, the price of each individual item may be taken for either the first day before or after the death for which prices are available. Units in an approved unit trust are valued at the manager's buying price (ie the lower of the two prices quoted). If no price was published on the date of death the last published price before death should be used.

Sales within twelve months after death

(3)   When qualifying securities are sold at an overall loss within twelve months after death, s 179 enables the 'appropriate person', ie the personal representatives or trustees accounting for the tax, to claim a reduction in the value of those securities at the time of death. 'Qualifying securities' means quoted securities or holdings in authorised unit trusts. 'Quoted securities' means securities listed on a recognised stock exchange (ss 178(1) & 272). Securities on the Alternative Investment Market (AIM) are unquoted.

To compute the reduction, if any, *all* qualifying securities sold within one year after death by the appropriate person are taken into account (s 179(1)(a)). The total sale proceeds, or if higher, the best consideration which could reasonably have been obtained for them at the time of sale, are substituted for probate value at death (s 179(1)(b)). No allowance is made for expenses (s 178(5)).

Thus the sale of shares in AB plc by the executors is ignored as it occurred more than twelve months after death.

Actual selling prices before expenses are substituted for probate value for the holdings by the deceased in CD plc and EF plc (subject to **explanatory notes 5 and 6**).

The shares in GH plc were sold to the residuary beneficiary for £37,000 but if they had been sold on the Stock Exchange they would probably have made $15,000 \times 253 = £37,950$.

HMRC would normally use the same valuation rules as for date of death ie the lower of

Closing Prices	*Bargains*	*Lower*
$253 + \frac{1}{4}(256 - 253) = 253\frac{3}{4}$	253	253

A claim cannot be restricted to disposals with losses; all disposals must be included in the computation.

Shares cancelled or in which dealings suspended

(4)   If dealings in quoted shares are suspended as at the first anniversary of death, and the then market value is lower than the value at death, the security may be deemed to have been sold at its market value twelve months after death (s 186B). The shares in KL plc are therefore deemed to have given rise to a notional loss of £530. In practice it will be difficult to arrive at a market value of shares, in which dealings are suspended. No guidance has been given as to how such a market value is to be arrived at.

Under s 186A, if a qualifying security is cancelled within twelve months after death, it may be treated as sold twelve months after death for £1. Shares are sometimes cancelled in company reorganisations, but the apparent intention of s 186A is to deal with company liquidations. Cancellation does not, however, take place when liquidation commences, but at the time the liquidation is completed. It would be rare for a company whose shares had a significant value on death to go into liquidation and for the liquidation to be completed within the required twelve month period. It appears, therefore, that s 186A does not meet its objective. One possible solution where shares have a significant value at death but then become worthless is to undertake a deed of variation to direct the shares to an exempt beneficiary, such as a charity. The value would not then be included in the chargeable estate.

It has been assumed that the liquidation of IJ plc in the Example was not completed before 7 April 2011.

Sales followed by reinvestment

(5)   To prevent the appropriate person selling investments and reacquiring them shortly afterwards s 180 provides that, if any qualifying investments are acquired in the same capacity within a period beginning on the date of death and ending two months after the date of the last sale (or deemed sale), then the claim shall be reduced by the proportion which the purchase prices of all such qualifying purchases bears to the aggregate sale prices used in the claim.

In this Example the executors had invested £21,600 in quoted securities during the relevant period. The total relief is therefore reduced by the proportion which that investment bears to the sale values of securities disposed of or deemed to be disposed of within twelve months after death (ie CD plc + EF plc + GH plc + KL plc = £86,400) giving actual relief of

$$£6,530 - \left(\frac{21,600}{86,400} \times 6,350\right) = £4,898$$

The purchase does not have to be made out of the proceeds of sale of the securities sold. Any purchase of qualifying shares made during the period commencing with the date of death and ending two months after the date of the last sale, whether before or after the sale, and irrespective of the source of the purchase money, reduces the amount of relief available.

(6)   The relevant proportion of gain or loss is then added to or subtracted from probate value at death of each security included in the claim for reduction in value to give the revised value for inheritance tax. That revised value is also deemed to be market value at date of death for capital gains tax (s 187).

Thus the value of the shares in AB plc is unaltered because they are not sold within twelve months after death and therefore not included in the s 179 claim;

The value of the shares in CD plc is increased by ¾ of the gain on sale, £1,400;

The value of the shares in EF plc is reduced by ¾ of the loss on sale, £7,550;

The value of the shares in GH plc is increased by ¾ of the notional gain of £150 on disposal, notwithstanding the fact that the actual proceeds showed a loss;

The value of the shares in IJ plc remains unaltered because they were not cancelled within twelve months after death;

The value of the shares in KL plc is reduced by ¾ of the notional loss on suspension, £530.

Shares forming trust property in which deceased had a part interest

(7)   As the trust assets have not been appropriated into separate funds for X and his brother, the entirety of the trust fund has to be calculated at the death of X (s 186) but only the one half proportion representing his life interest is included in the computation of tax due. This has the effect of treating a part of the securities disposed of as belonging to the non taxable part of the trust and therefore restricts the relief claimable. In this Example one half of the trust fund is taxable and therefore only one half of the computed reduction in value is claimable.

(8)   The trustees of a settled fund are treated as a single and continuing body (s 178(4)) and therefore the computation includes the sales of shares by the old and new trustees.

However the beneficiary is not the same person as the trustees and was not himself accountable for the tax on the death even though he ultimately bore the burden of its payment by receiving less funds from the trust and therefore the disposal by S as beneficiary of shares in MN plc transferred to him by the trustees is not included in the calculation of relief.

Investments not found until more than twelve months after death

(9)   The relevant sale must take place within twelve months of the date of death for relief for loss to be available. In the case of *Exors of CE Lee v IRC* (SpC 349 2002) the documents relating to the investment were not found until more than twelve months after death. The shares had lost value. The value for inheritance tax was market value at date of death. Relief for loss in value was not available.

Question

Pilling, who had been a widower since 1990, died on 3 May 2010. He was survived by a son and daughter – twins born in 1953. Mrs Pilling had an estate of £175,000 and there is no available nil-rate band to carry forward to be utilised on Pilling's death.

For many years up to 5 April 2003, Pilling had made regular gifts, fully using the annual exemption for inheritance tax, but he had not made any chargeable transfers.

Pilling had made the following gifts after 5 April 2003:

15 June 2004	To nephew £216,400 in securities.
15 April 2005	10,000 £1 shares in Black plc, a listed company, to his niece. The shares were worth £13.00 each at the date of the gift. On 3 December 2005 Black plc was taken over by White plc and in exchange for her Black plc shares, Pilling's niece was given 15,000 White plc shares of 25p each, those shares being worth £7.00. At Pilling's death they were worth £2.80 each.
25 December 2005	Motor car worth £12,600 to his nephew. Two days before Pilling's death the car was totally destroyed by fire. The insurance compensation was £5,000.
4 July 2007	Cash gift of £63,000 to his grandson in consideration of his marriage, which took place on that date.

At the time of his death Pilling owned 3,200 ordinary shares in Briggs and Pilling Ltd; he had subscribed for these shares when the company was formed in 1957 and they were valued at £55 per share on his death. The company has an issued capital of 5,000 ordinary shares and is engaged in demolition contracting.

His other assets comprised quoted investments and personal chattels with a total value of £240,700. He had a bank overdraft of £33,100 and his funeral expenses were £1,100.

By his will, which was made immediately after the death of his wife in 1990, Pilling left his shares in Briggs and Pilling Ltd to his son, with the residue of his estate divided equally between his son and his daughter.

Pilling's son accepts that because he will receive the legacy of the shares in Briggs and Pilling Ltd, his sister or her family should have a larger share in the residue of the estate. In September 2010 they ask you for advice on dealing with their father's estate in the most efficient way in relation to inheritance tax. The son is married with two children whose ages are 13 and 10; the daughter is a widow whose only child is Pilling's grandson who was married in July 2007.

(a)   Calculate the inheritance tax payable as a result of Pilling's death, stating the due date of payment.

(b)   List the points that you would bring to the attention of Pilling's son and daughter in connection with altering the terms of Pilling's will.

Answer

(a) Inheritance tax payable as a result of Pilling's death on 3 May 2010

Lifetime transfers

			Gross		Tax on 2010/11 scale
	Potentially exempt transfers now chargeable:		£	£	£
June 2004	Nephew — securities		216,400		
	Less: Annual exemptions 2004/05		(3,000)		
	2003/04		(3,000)	210,400	–
April 2005	Niece — shares		130,000		
	Less: Annual exemption 2005/06		(3,000)	127,000	4,960*
	(337,400 – 325,000 = 12,400 @ 40% = £4,960)			337,400	4,960
December 2005	Nephew — car			12,600	5,040**
July 2007	Grandson		63,000		
	Less: Marriage exemption		(2,500)		
	Annual exemptions 2007/08		(3,000)		
	2006/07		(3,000)	54,500	21,800
				404,500	

*On a claim by the niece, tax on her gift may be recomputed as follows:

Value of gift	130,000
Value on death (15,000 @ £2.80)	42,000
Reduce transfer by	£88,000
Giving chargeable transfer of (117,000 – 88,000) = £29,000	

When this is added to the chargeable transfers brought forward of £210,400, the total is £239,400, which is below the nil threshold, so that the inheritance tax payable by the niece is reduced to nil.

**Taper relief of 40% will be available to the nephew on the gift on 25 December 2005, because it was made between four and five years before death. Inheritance tax payable will be 60% × £5,040 = £3,024.

		£	Due date
Tax payable on PETs which became chargeable because of Pilling's death within 7 years:			
15 June 2004	By nephew	nil	
15 April 2005	By niece (after claim re fall in value)	nil	
25 December 2005	By nephew (after taper relief)	3,024	30 November 2010
4 July 2007	By grandson	21,800	

Pilling's estate at death

| | Date of death 3 May 2010 | |
	£	£
Shares in Briggs and Pilling Ltd 3,200 @ £55	176,000	
Less: 100% business property relief	176,000	–
Quoted investments and personal chattels		240,700
		240,700
Less: Debts and funeral expenses (33,100 + 1,100)		34,200
Chargeable estate at death		206,500

Since the lifetime transfers exceed the nil threshold, the tax payable by the personal representatives is £206,500 @ 40%, ie £82,600. The due date of payment is 30 November 2010, or when they deliver their account with their application for probate if earlier.

(b) Points to be brought to attention of Pilling's son and daughter in connection with altering the terms of Pilling's will

(1)   Pilling's son and daughter may vary the way in which the estate is distributed, providing they do so within two years after the date of his death. The son must sign the instrument of variation; signature by the daughter is not necessary if she is not giving up any of her existing entitlement. The personal representatives will not be required to sign, since the variation will not result in any additional tax being payable by them. The variation will be treated for inheritance tax as if it had applied at the date of death (see **explanatory note 7**).

(2)   The variation is also effective for capital gains tax purposes (providing a statement to that effect is included within the deed – TCGA 1992 s 62(6) and (7)), so that the ultimate beneficiaries who receive any chargeable assets directly will be treated as having acquired them at market value at the date of Pilling's death.

(3)   For income tax purposes, any income arising on the assets before the variation which was taxable on the original beneficiary apart from the variation is still treated as belonging to him and taxed at his/her tax rates. If that person is assessed to higher rate tax on the income, it may be thought appropriate for the tax to be paid by whoever receives the income; this needs careful drafting to avoid the payment being treated as inadmissable consideration which disqualifies the variation from relief.

(4)   If Pilling's son and daughter already have adequate income, they may wish to provide in the instrument of variation that some or all of Pilling's estate is transferred direct to their children. In the case of Pilling's son's infant children the funds would be held in trust until they reached age 18 or married before that time. If, however, Pilling's son gives up some or all of his entitlement in favour of his own infant children this would be treated as a parental settlement and the income arising from the assets would be treated as Pilling's son's income so long as his children were infant and unmarried, unless the funds were transferred by way of settlement providing for the income to be accumulated. There would be no problem in relation to Pilling's daughter, since her son is married, nor in relation to any transfer by Pilling's son to his nephew.

Explanatory Notes

Fall in value of gift before death

(1)   If the value of a gift has fallen between the date of gift and the date of death, a claim may be made for the tax to be computed as if the value transferred were reduced by the reduction in value of the asset. The recomputation does not affect the amount of the chargeable transfer taken into account in the figure of cumulative transfers for the purpose of computing the tax on any later chargeable transfers or on death. The

relief does not apply to wasting chattels and hence the car value is not reduced in this Example (s 131). If the asset is shares and there is a reorganisation or takeover prior to death, the original shares and the new holding are treated as the same property (s 135).

(2)   A claim for the relief must be made by the person liable to pay the tax. So, following a claim by Pilling's niece, the value of the shares given to her is reduced by £88,000 in computing the tax payable.

(3)   These provisions also apply where the asset has been sold prior to death by the transferee or his spouse, providing it was a bona fide sale at arm's length to an unconnected person (s 131(3)). In this case the relief applies to the difference between the value transferred and the sale proceeds.

(4)   If the property to which the claim for reduction of value relates qualified for business property relief (or agricultural property relief) then that relief is also reduced proportionately. This will only be relevant where the relief is less than 100%.

(5)   If the original gift was a chargeable lifetime transfer on which the donor paid the tax, the *original* amount of tax would be added to the recomputed transfer.

Cumulative transfers exceed nil threshold

	Gross £	Tax £	Net £
Net gift of 10,000 shares worth £4 each to discretionary trust			40,000
Grossed up $\left(\times\dfrac{100}{80}\right)$	50,000	10,000	
		(½ rate)	
Shares worth £3 each on death within seven years			
Recomputed gift 10,000 @ £3	30,000		
Add tax on original gift	10,000	40,000	16,000
		(full rate)	

Additional tax payable because of death within seven years after the gift is £6,000 (£16,000 – £10,000), subject to any available taper relief.

Increase in value of gift before death

(6)   If the value of a gift has *increased* between the date of gift and the date of death, the death scale is nonetheless only applied to the original chargeable transfer.

Deeds of variation

(7)   Deeds of variation do not have to be sent to HMRC Capital Taxes unless the variation results in additional tax becoming payable then the beneficiaries and personal representatives must send a copy of the variation to HMRC Capital Taxes within six months and notify them of the amount of additional tax payable (IHTA 1984 s 218A). See **Example 34** for further details, in particular **explanatory note 5**.

Cross references

(8)   For further notes on exemptions, see **Example 1**; business property relief, see **Example 25**; dates of payment, see **Example 5** and the treatment of liabilities in relation to the instalment option and business property relief, see **Example 9**.

Question

Hartford, who had never married, owned and operated a farm in Cheshire until his death on 31 May 2010.

Hartford had made two lifetime gifts as follows. On 14 October 1995 he gave £112,700 to his sister Providence. On 25 September 2002 he gave £148,500 to his cousin Lansing in consideration of Lansing's marriage, which took place on that date.

The assets owned by Hartford at the time of his death were valued for probate as follows:

	£
Freehold farm in Cheshire (agricultural value £640,000)	780,000
Quoted investments, personal possessions and bank balances	335,500

Debts due at death and funeral expenses (all allowable in calculating inheritance tax) totalled £7,280.

Hartford was also life tenant of a family trust in which his interest had commenced on the death of a brother on 25 November 2004, when the value of the trust fund was £83,800, out of which inheritance tax of £18,500 was paid as a result of the brother's death. On 31 May 2010 the trust fund consisted of quoted investments valued at £153,850 (including accrued income £2,410) and there was also undistributed income due to Hartford amounting to £3,730.

By his will, which was made in February 2001, Hartford made charitable bequests totalling £87,000 and also left £30,000 to a qualifying political party. The farm was left absolutely to his cousin Lansing and the residue was to be held in trust for Sally (born 2000) the infant child of his deceased sister Augusta, on Sally's attaining age 25 with power to accumulate income up to that age. Hartford was Sally's legal guardian at the time of his death.

(a) State the points relating to taxation that should have been taken into consideration if Hartford had, a year before he died, requested advice on the terms of the trust created by Hartford's will for his sister's infant child.

(b) Calculate the inheritance tax payable as a result of Hartford's death, stating the persons responsible for payment of the tax and the amount payable by each.

(c) State what difference, if any, it would have made to the calculations in (b) if the gifts to Providence and Lansing had been made one year later, ie 14 October 1996 and 25 September 2003 respectively.

(d) State the rate of inheritance tax that will be charged when Sally becomes absolutely entitled to Hartford's residuary estate at age 25, assuming present statutory inheritance tax rates remain unchanged; and how this would be affected if lifetime gifts had been timed as in (c).

Answer

(a) Hartford – Tax points in relation to the trust for Sally

Hartford's will was drafted before the substantial changes to the inheritance tax treatment of trusts wrought by the Finance Act 2006. When it was prepared the anticipation was that the trust for Sally would qualify as an accumulation and maintenance settlement under s 71 as then applicable, and that the trust would carry no inheritance tax implications (so long as the trustees did not carry out depreciatory transactions) when Sally either became entitled to the capital by age 25 or died under that age (nor in the meantime). If the trust had not deferred Sally's entitlement to income until the same age at which she would receive the capital, she would have become entitled to an interest in possession at age 18 and (under the pre-2006 regime) the fund would have been exposed to inheritance tax in the event of her death between then and age 25.

A trust created by the will of someone who dies on or after 22 March 2006 will be subject to the relevant property regime unless:

(i)   it is for the benefit of someone to whom the testator was a parent, and satisfies the conditions for treatment as either,

     (A)   a bereaved minor's trust within s 71A; or

     (B)   an age 18-to-25 trust within s 71D; or

(ii)   it confers an interest in possession taking effect immediately on the testator's death (which will be either an immediate post-death interest under s 49A or a disabled person's interest under s 89B(1)(c), depending on whether the beneficiary is a disabled person at the date of the testator's death); or

(iii)   the beneficiary is a disabled person and, though not having an interest in possession, the trust meets the conditions for a disabled person's interest under s 89(1) that is treated for inheritance tax purposes as an interest in possession.

Hartford would have been advised that the relevant property regime would be relatively disadvantageous and that, since he is within the extended definition of "parent" for the purpose of (I) because he is Sally's legal guardian (s 71H), options (I)(A), (I)(B) and (II) were all open to him for avoiding the relevant property regime. The trust incorporated in the will would in principle be within (I)(B) as an age 18-to-25 trust since Sally is to become entitled to the trust capital by age 25 (and would have been in principle within (I)(A) as a bereaved minor's trust if the will had specified instead that she should receive capital by age 18).

There are several conditions that must be satisfied in either case (which are in practice likely to be met satisfactorily by a trust in the straightforward terms indicated): while Sally is living and under the specified age (25 or 18 as the case may be),

•   she must either have an interest in possession in the income, or no income may be applied for the benefit of anyone other than Sally,

•   the capital must also not be capable of being applied for benefit of anyone other than Sally, and

•   her entitlement at the specified age must include not just the capital and future income but all undistributed or accumulated income.

The statutory power of advancement, or express powers to similar effect, will not offend these conditions (even if not limited to half the beneficiary's interest as is the statutory power itself).

If the will were, unusually, to confer an interest in possession immediately (as opposed to once Sally has reached majority, given that she is under 18 at Hartford's death), and the above conditions were satisfied, then the inheritance tax effect would differ according to whether her capital entitlement was to arise by age 18 or by age 25. In the former case the trust would be a bereaved minor's trust notwithstanding the interest in possession; in the latter case the interest in possession would be an immediate post-death interest and the trust would not be an age 18-to-25 trust. (On the other hand if it is an age 18-to-25 trust to start with, and an interest in possession were then to arise in Sally's favour on her attaining majority, the trust would remain within the age 18-to-25 trust regime.)

Inheritance tax treatment of bereaved minors' trusts

A bereaved minor's trust benefits from broadly the same inheritance tax privileges as the former accumulation and maintenance trusts: no charge will arise:

(i)   on Sally becoming absolutely entitled to the settled property on or before attaining the specified age of 18 years; or

(ii)   on Sally's death before her attaining the specified age of 18 years;

(iii)   on funds being paid or applied for Sally's advancement or benefit; or

(iv)   on the payment of costs or expenses attributable to the trust property.

Inheritance tax treatment of age 18-to-25 trusts

While the beneficiary of an age 18-to-25 trust is still under age 18 the inheritance tax treatment of it is essentially the same as with a bereaved minor's trust: none of the events in (i) to (iv) above will give rise to a charge. Once the beneficiary has passed age 18, the position changes. Payments of costs or expenses are still exempt, but the other three events will give rise to an inheritance tax charge under the special regime in s 71F.

This regime is not dissimilar to that which applies to exit charges under the relevant property regime in the first ten years of a trust's existence (see **Example 60 explanatory note 6**). A notional chargeable transfer is supposed, based on the settlor's cumulative total of chargeable transfers in the seven years leading up to the formation of the trust (in this case Hartford's death) and the value of the trust property in the trustees' hands immediately after its formation (plus where relevant the initial value of property in any related settlement and of any further property added to the age 18-to-25 trust after its formation). The effective rate of inheritance tax on that notional transfer is calculated using the lifetime rate (half the death rate), and the rate that applies to the s 71F charge is the relevant fraction of that effective rate. The relevant fraction is

$$3/10 \times N/40$$

where N is the number of completed quarters since the beneficiary's 18th birthday (or if later the date when the age 18-to-25 trust came into effect).

The amount to which this rate is applied is the amount by which the value of the settled property in the age 18-to-25 trust is reduced as a result of the event giving rise to the charge.

Interaction with capital gains tax

On the beneficiary (or someone else on his death under the specified age) becoming absolutely entitled to the trust property under a bereaved minor's trust or an age 18-to-25 trust, such that a deemed disposal for capital gains tax purposes occurs (see **Example 50**), hold-over relief under TCGA 1992 s 260 will be available whether or not the circumstances are such that an inheritance tax charge arises under the special regime in s 71F.

Depreciatory transactions

As with the former accumulation and maintenance trusts, a charge would arise, under either of the regimes just discussed, if the trustees were to effect a depreciatory transaction, or if something were to happen which took the trust outside the bereaved minor's trust rules (or the age 18-to-25 trust rules, as the case may be) which was not within (i) to (iv) above. (The latter would almost certainly not arise except as a result of a deliberate act, such as an exercise of a power of advancement which deferred the vesting of capital beyond the specified age.) The rate on such a charge – set by s 70(6)–(9) which is applied referentially – does not depend on the value of the property concerned, but purely on the length of time the trust has been within the bereaved minor's trust regime. The rate charged is again reduced if any of the property is, or was, excluded property.

(b) Inheritance tax payable as a result of Hartford's death on 31 May 2010

				£
Estate at death was as follows:				
Freehold farm in Cheshire			780,000	
Less: Agricultural property relief 100% × 640,000	640,000			
business property relief 100% × 140,000	140,000	780,000		–
Quoted investments, personal possessions and bank balances				335,500
Accrued income from trust fund*				2,410
Undistributed income due from trust fund*				3,730
(* Assumed to be net of income tax)				
				341,640
Less: debts and funeral expenses				7,280
				334,360
Less: charitable bequests			87,000	
qualifying political party bequest			30,000	117,000
				217,360
Settled property (153,850 – 2,410)				151,440
				368,800

The only lifetime transfers made by Hartford were the potentially exempt transfer to Providence on 14 October 1995, which became completely exempt on 14 October 2002, and the potentially exempt transfer to Lansing on 25 September 2002, which became completely exempt on 25 September 2009.

The tax payable on the death estate is therefore:

368,800 – 325,000 = 43,800 @ 40%   17,520

$$\text{Less: quick succession relief} \quad 20\% \times 18,500 \times \frac{65,300}{83,800} \qquad 2,883 \qquad \pounds14,637$$

$$\text{Payable as to} \quad \frac{217,360}{368,800} \times 14,637 = \pounds8,627 \qquad \text{by Hartford's personal representatives}$$

$$\text{and as to} \quad \frac{151,440}{368,800} \times 14,637 = \pounds6,010 \qquad \text{by trustees of settled property}$$

(c)

If the transfers to Providence and Lansing had been made a year later, there would be no difference in relation to the transfer to Providence – the potentially exempt transfer would have become completely exempt on 14 October 2003. The transfer to Lansing would have been within seven years before Hartford's death and would thus become a chargeable transfer. The position would therefore be:

Cumulative transfers at Hartford's death:				*Gross*	*Tax*
				£	£
25 September 2003	Gift to Lansing		148,500		
	Less:	Marriage exemption	(1,000)		
		Annual exemptions			
		2003/04	(3,000)		
		2002/03	(3,000)		
	PET now chargeable		141,500		–
Estate at death				368,800	74,120
				510,300	74,120**

(** 510,300 – 325,000 = 185,300 @ 40%)

Tax on estate at death		74,120	
Less: quick succession relief	$20\% \times 18,500 \times \dfrac{65,300}{83,800}$	2,883	£71,237

Payable as to $\dfrac{217,360}{368,800} \times 71,237 = £41,985$ by Hartford's personal representatives

and as to $\dfrac{151,440}{368,800} \times 71,237 = £29,252$ by trustees of settled property

Thus the transfer to Lansing would not itself attract tax, since it was below the nil threshold, and the taper relief of 80% for transfers within six and seven years before death would not therefore be relevant, but the transfer would take up £141,500 of the nil band otherwise available to the death estate. The tax on the death estate would accordingly increase by £141,500 @ 40% = £56,600 (ie 71,237 – 14,637).

(d) Inheritance tax rate on Sally's entitlement at age 25

One feature of the special charging regime for age 18-to-25 trusts under s 71F is that it is possible, right from the outset, to calculate the rate of tax that will be charged when the beneficiary becomes entitled at the specified age, subject only to changes in the statutory scale of rates and to the effect of any later additions to the trust. This is because the only variables (the settlor's cumulative total and the value of the trust property (and of the property in any related settlement) immediately after the trust commences can be quantified from the start. The rate of the charge is unaffected by any changes in value of the trust property – the same rate will apply even if the fund has increased in value tenfold in the meantime.

The initial value of the trust fund for Sally – being Hartford's free estate other than the farm left to Lansing, net of debts, funeral expenses and bequests to charities and the political party – was £217,360 as in (b) above. With this information the rate chargeable under s 71F when Sally becomes absolutely entitled at age 25 (28 quarters after her 18th birthday) is calculated as follows:

(i) Timing of Hartford's lifetime gifts as in main example

	Gross	*Tax on 2010/11 scale*
Notional chargeable transfer		
Cumulative total (Hartford's cumulative total at death)	–	–
Value transferred (initial value of trust fund)	217,360	–
Total transfers (within nil rate band)	217,360	–

Effective rate on notional transfer

$$\frac{0}{217,360} = 0\%$$

Therefore rate chargeable on entitlement at age 25 = 0%

(ii) Timing of Hartford's lifetime gifts as in question (c)

	Gross	Tax on 2010/11 scale
Notional chargeable transfer		
Cumulative total (Hartford's cumulative total at death)	141,500	–
Value transferred (initial value of trust fund)	217,360	13,544*
Total transfers	358,860	13,544*

(* 358,860 – 325,000 = 33,860 @ 40%)

Effective rate on notional transfer

$$\frac{13,544}{217,360} = 6.231\%$$

Rate chargeable on entitlement at age 25:

$$6.231\% \ \times \frac{3}{10} \times \frac{28}{40} = 1.308\%$$

Explanatory Notes

Will trusts

(1)   When property is left by a will into a trust the normal rules for settlements apply (see **Examples 52 to 63**). Accordingly if the will conferred an interest in possession (which since 22 March 2006 would be an estate interest in possession as an immediate post-death interest or a disabled person's interest, unless the conditions for bereaved minor's trust status were fulfilled) then the trust fund would be deemed to be part of the estate of the person with that interest, as in the case of Hartford under his brother's will trust in this Example. However, when the beneficiaries are minors it is usual to retain a degree of discretion over the income of the settlement and where that is done then, unless the trust qualifies as a bereaved minor's trust or an age 18-to-25 trust, the rules relating to discretionary settlements apply (see **Example 60**).

Transfer to Providence

(2)   Providence would have no liability as a result of Hartford's death whether her gift had been made on 14 October 1995 or 14 October 1996. As a potentially exempt transfer the gift becomes completely exempt after seven years. In computing the liability on the gift to Lansing, if it had been made on 25 September 2003, only chargeable transfers in the previous seven years would be taken to form the opening figures. The gift to Providence, being potentially exempt, and subsequently completely exempt, is not taken into account.

Cross references

(3)   For notes on agricultural property relief and business property relief, see **Example 25**; for notes on exemptions, see **Example 1**; and quick succession relief, see **Example 21**.

Question

Thomas died on 20 December 2010.

He left an estate valued at £400,000 after payment of all debts and funeral expenses.

By his will he gave a pecuniary legacy of £206,000 to his son Dick, with the residue of his estate to his wife.

He had on 31 December 2007 made a gift of £230,000 to Dick. This was the only gift made by Thomas since 2002.

Calculate the inheritance tax payable in consequence of Thomas's death.

Answer

Lifetime transfer

			£
31 December 2007			
Gift to Dick			230,000
Less: Annual exemptions	2007/08	3,000	
	2006/07	3,000	6,000
Potentially exempt transfer			224,000

Inheritance tax payable on death of Thomas 20 December 2010

	Gross	Tax on 2010/11 scale
	£	£
By Dick		
31 December 2007		
Gift — potentially exempt transfer now chargeable	224,000	–

By Estate

Tax is payable on the grossed up equivalent of the £206,000 legacy to Dick when added to an inheritance tax accumulation of £224,000 using the 2010/11 scale:

	Gross	Tax	Net
	£	£	£
Before death	224,000	–	224,000
Pecuniary legacy (see working note)	276,000	70,000	206,000
	500,000	70,000	430,000
Tax payable by estate (£500,000 – 325,000 @ 40%) = £175,000 @ 40%		£70,000	

The estate will accordingly be divided as follows:

	£	£
Gross estate		400,000
To HMRC — payment of inheritance tax		70,000
To Dick		206,000
To Wife (exempt transfer)		
(ie) £400,000 estate – £206,000 to Dick	194,000	
Less: Tax on Dick's legacy	70,000	124,000
		400,000

Working Note

As cumulative net transfers of £430,000 exceed £325,000 the 40% rate of tax applies to the excess of £105,000, giving a gross equivalent for that part of the legacy of:

$$\frac{100}{60} \times £105,000 = £175,000$$

with tax payable of £70,000.

Explanatory Notes

Potentially exempt transfer on 31 December 2007

(1)   The gift made on 31 December 2007, in so far as it exceeded the available annual exemptions, was a potentially exempt transfer that became a chargeable transfer on the death of Thomas (s 19). It is then chargeable using the rates applicable at death. The lifetime gift attracts the nil rate band before the estate at death and accordingly no tax is due on that gift. If a liability had arisen it would be payable by the transferee.

Pecuniary legacies

(2)   On death, the residue left to the wife is exempt (s 18) but it cannot be ascertained until the tax payable by the estate has been calculated. Tax is payable on the pecuniary legacy and since the legatee receives the actual amount of the legacy, the tax payable is found by grossing it up (ss 36–42).

(3)   The amount received by the widow is much less than she at first sight appears entitled to:

Estate	400,000
Dick's legacy	206,000
Apparent entitlement	£194,000

but in fact she gets:

Estate		400,000
Dick's legacy	206,000	
after tax of	70,000	276,000
		£124,000

(4)   Contrast the above with the position if the will had left a legacy of £206,000 to the widow and the residue (£194,000) to Dick. Then the taxable estate would be:

Value on death at 20 December 2010	400,000
Less: Exempt legacy – wife	206,000
Chargeable to inheritance tax on death	£194,000

Inheritance tax due on death

	£	2010/11 scale £
Chargeable transfers accumulation at death	224,000	–
Chargeable estate	194,000	37,200*
	418,000	37,200*

(* 418,000 – 325,000 = 93,000 @ 40%)

The estate would then be divided:

	£	£
Gross estate		400,000
To HMRC – payment of inheritance tax		37,200
To Wife		206,000
To Dick	194,000	
Less: Tax on residue	37,200	156,800
		400,000

The widow is better off by more than Dick is worse off, HMRC being the loser:

	Legacy to Dick	Legacy to widow	Difference
	Residue to widow	*Residue to Dick*	£
Dick	206,000	156,800	(49,200)
Widow	124,000	206,000	82,000
HMRC	70,000	37,200	(32,800)
	£400,000	£400,000	

There is nothing to prevent the widow making a personal gift to Dick from her own resources, covered in part by available exemptions and the amount reckonable being a potentially exempt transfer. If, however, a claim was made by Dick against the estate for an increased share of the estate and that claim was settled by Thomas's widow out of her own assets rather than out of assets from the estate, then s 29A would operate to treat that amount as being a payment out of the estate, reducing accordingly the exempt amount to the widow (claims under the Inheritance (Provision for Family and Dependants) Act 1975 that are settled out of the estate are already treated as if they were effected by the will (s 146)).

Question

Samuel Smith died on 31 March 2011 leaving net estate valued as follows:

	£
His half share in the business of S and D Smith carried on in partnership for many years (his brother, David Smith, owning the other half share)	400,000
An office building occupied by S and D Smith	430,000
Bank and building society accounts	34,600
Quoted securities	95,300
Half share in the matrimonial home and contents, valued at £545,000, being held by himself and Mrs Smith (who survived him) as joint tenants	272,500
Life assurance policies on his own life — amount receivable	132,400
A house in France (there are no additional costs of administration because of the situation overseas)	140,800

He made bequests of £100 to each of three grandchildren and £5,000 to his daughter on her reaching the age of twenty-five or her earlier marriage.

He left £18,000 to charities and £100 to a political party.

He left his widow a legacy of £150,000.

The house in France was left to his daughter with the stipulation that she bore any inheritance tax applicable to it.

His share in the partnership business together with the office building occupied by the partnership was left to his son with the stipulation that he bore any tax thereon.

The residue of the estate was left equally to his son and daughter. He had made no lifetime transfers.

(a)   Calculate the inheritance tax payable and show by whom it would be borne.

(b)   Explain the position regarding capital gains tax on the assets comprised in the estate.

Answer

(a) S Smith deceased

		Date of death 31 March 2011	
	£	£	£
Share in matrimonial home and contents		272,500	
Less: Exempt because of devolution on widow		272,500	–
House in France (see **explanatory notes 4 and 5**)			140,800
Half share in S and D Smith		400,000	
Less: 100% business property relief		400,000	–
Office building occupied by S and D Smith		430,000	
Less: 50% business property relief		215,000	215,000
Residuary estate			
Bank and building society accounts		34,600	
Quoted securities		95,300	
Life assurance policy proceeds		132,400	
		262,300	
Less: Exempt legacies			
Gifts to charities	18,000		
Gift to political party	100		
Legacy to widow	150,000	168,100	94,200
Total estate on which inheritance tax is payable			450,000

Comprising:

Estate before reliefs and exemptions (*after* jointly owned assets which pass directly to widow)	1,233,100
Less: Business property relief	615,000
	618,100
Less: Exempt legacies	168,100
	£450,000
Tax payable on estate (450,000 – 325,000) = £125,000 @ 40%	£50,000

Which would be borne as follows:	*Tax*	*Borne by*
Matrimonial home	–	
House in France $\dfrac{140,800}{450,000} \times 50,000$	15,644	Daughter
Office Building $\dfrac{215,000}{450,000} \times 50,000$	23,889	Son

Residue	$\dfrac{94{,}200}{450{,}000} \times 50{,}000$	10,467	Son and daughter out of residue

$$\underline{\underline{\text{£}50{,}000}}$$

The tax on the house in France and on the office building could be paid by instalments over ten years so long as the daughter and son retained the assets, but subject to payment of interest on the outstanding tax for the time being – even in the case of the business premises, which are not covered by the interest-free rule in s 234(1).

(b) Capital gains tax position on death

There is no capital gains tax charge on death (but note the income tax charge, referential to the capital gains tax rules, on any offshore income gains under SI 2009/3001 made under FA 2008 ss 41, 42 (see now Taxation (International and Other Provisions) Act 2010 ss 354–363). The legatees or devisees who receive chargeable assets acquire them for capital gains tax purposes at the probate value, so that the increase in value during the ownership of the deceased escapes capital gains tax.

Explanatory Notes

Joint tenancies and tenancies in common

(1)   For details of joint tenancies (and tenancies in common), see the explanatory notes to **Example 6**. Since Smith's matrimonial residence and contents are jointly owned with his wife as joint tenants, they automatically accrue to his widow who survived him, and are thus left out of the calculation of the chargeable estate for inheritance tax because of the spouse exemption.

Had the house been held under a tenancy in common, then husband and wife would each be entitled to a separate share, which would have formed part of the residue of the estate which devolved on the son and daughter, Smith's one half share of the value then being included in the calculation of the chargeable estate.

Life insurance

(2)   The Example illustrates that life insurance on one's own life swells the chargeable estate where the proceeds are payable to the estate. A preferable alternative is where the policy is taken out by the taxpayer on his own life but a trust is created in favour of his children, so that the proceeds of the policy eventually fall into the trust fund as distinct from the estate.

Any gifts will have occurred yearly as the taxpayer has maintained the policy by paying the premiums. They will usually be exempt as payments out of the donor's income. The proceeds are payable to the trustees; if it is a bare trust, the money is passed on to the beneficiaries without any inheritance tax liability, since the beneficiaries have always had a right to the capital of the trust fund (which has now become cash instead of a life policy). If it is a different form of trust the relevant inheritance tax rules will apply.

Alternatively the children of a taxpayer could themselves take out and maintain a policy on the life of their parent on a 'life of another' basis with the same inheritance tax advantages.

(3)   Another advantage of life policies not belonging to the estate is that the beneficiaries have cash without waiting for the grant of probate. The policy monies do not belong to the deceased and their receipt does not depend upon the grant of probate. They are paid upon proof of death — the death certificate. This is often a useful way of putting the dependants in funds for family necessities, or to pay inheritance tax, as well as mitigating the inheritance tax charge.

Foreign property and domicile

(4)   Property situated abroad does not escape inheritance tax unless the taxpayer is also domiciled abroad. Domicile is a complex legal concept and differs from nationality or residence; but it also has a specially extended meaning for inheritance tax (see **Example 3 part (C)**).

(5)   Where property is situated abroad, an allowance of up to a maximum of 5% of the value of the property may be claimed in respect of the additional expenses incurred in administering or realising that property because it is situated overseas (s 173).

Treatment of specific gifts and gifts of residue where there are exempt beneficiaries

(6)   Detailed notes on business and agricultural property relief are in **Example 25**.

In this Example the interests in the partnership business and related office building were left specifically to the son and thus did not attract any exemption from inheritance tax, as they would have done if left to a surviving spouse or to a charity. There are various ways in which a deceased may have dealt with business or agricultural property in his will, and the effect is as follows (s 39A):

(a)	Business or agricultural property left specifically to a non-exempt beneficiary (as it was to the son in this Example)	BPR/APR reduces the value of the business/agricultural property, reducing the tax accordingly, and it is not affected by any exempt legacies.
(b)	Business or agricultural property left specifically to an exempt beneficiary, such as to a spouse (or as part of residue to an exempt beneficiary)	BPR/APR wasted, since no tax payable on the property in any event.
(c)	Business or agricultural property left as part of residue that goes wholly to a non-exempt beneficiary, where there are no pecuniary or other specific gifts to exempt beneficiaries	BPR/APR reduces the value of the residue, reducing the tax accordingly.
(d)	Business or agricultural property left as part of residue to a non-exempt beneficiary where there are pecuniary or other specific gifts to exempt beneficiaries, or where the residue is left partly to an exempt beneficiary (eg half to son, half to spouse)	BPR/APR is applied rateably to the exempt and non-exempt parts of the estate, and is thus wasted to the extent that it is attributed to exempt legacies or exempt residue.

For the technical way in which this is expressed in the legislation and the complications where part of the residue is exempt from tax and part is chargeable, see **Example 17**.

(7)   The exempt legacies in this Example, which are pecuniary legacies rather than legacies of specific property but are still specific gifts for inheritance tax purposes, are paid out of assets not subject to business property relief and the business property relief is therefore fully available.

If the will had merely left the legacies as stated with the residue to the son and daughter, without specifically leaving the partnership share and office building to the son, then the relief for business property would be spread rateably between the exempt and non-exempt parts of the estate, that relating to the exempt part then being wasted as follows:

$$\text{Maximum business property relief } 615,000 \times \frac{\text{Exempt estate } 168,100}{\text{Total estate } 1,233,100} = £83,839$$

The full business property relief would still be deducted from the business property in ascertaining what tax relates to that property from an instalment option point of view (see **note 10**), the reduction in relief being regarded as reducing the exempt legacies. The estate liable to inheritance tax would become:

Estate before reliefs and exemptions as before   1,233,100

Less:	Business property relief			615,000
				618,100
Less:	Exempt legacies		168,100	
	Restricted by reference to business property relief		83,839	84,261
				£533,839
Comprising:				
	House in France			140,800
	Residue as before		262,300	
	Business property	830,000		
	Less: 100%/50% business property relief	615,000	215,000	
			477,300	
Less:	Exempt legacies		84,261	393,039
				£533,839
	Tax payable would be (533,839 – 325,000) = £208,839 @ 40%			£83,536

Which would be borne as follows:

Daughter

$$\frac{140,800}{533,839} \times 83,536 \qquad 22,033$$

Residuary legatees

$$\frac{393,039}{533,839} \times 83,536 \qquad 61,503$$

$$£83,536$$

(8)   Similarly if the partnership share and office building formed part of the residue and the matrimonial home had been held as tenants in common in equally shares rather than beneficial joint tenancy, but Samuel Smith's half share had been left as a specific gift to the widow, the position would be:

Estate before exemptions and reliefs as before	1,233,100
Add matrimonial home half share	272,500
	£1,505,600

Maximum business property relief is restricted by

$$615,000 \times \frac{\text{Exempt estate}(168,100 + 272,500)}{\text{Total estate}} = \frac{440,600}{1,505,600} = £179,974$$

The estate liable to inheritance tax becomes:

Estate			1,505,600
Less:	Business property relief		615,000
			890,600
Less:	Exempt legacies	440,600	
	Restricted by reference to business property relief	179,974	260,626
			£629,974

Comprising:

House in France					140,800
Matrimonial home				272,500	
Residue as before			262,300		
Business property		830,000			
Less: 100%/50% business property relief	615,000	215,000			
		————	477,300		
Less: Exempt legacies		260,626	216,674	489,174	
				£629,974	
				£121,990	

Tax payable would be (629,974 – 325,000) = £304,974 @ 40%

Which would be borne as follows:

Daughter

$$\frac{140,800}{629,974} \times 121,990 \qquad\qquad 27,265$$

Residuary legatees

$$\frac{489,174}{629,974} \times 121,990 \qquad\qquad 94,725$$

$$£121,990$$

(9)   The above shows that on S Smith's estate the increase in the inheritance tax payable if the business property is part of the residue is as follows:

	If exempt legacies were £168,100	If exempt legacies were £440,600
Tax payable	83,536	121,990
Compared with tax payable as per **part (a)** of Example	50,000	50,000
	£33,536	£71,990

Although the exempt legacies are the *cause* of the higher tax, they do not themselves *bear* any of it. It is borne rateably by the residuary estate and by the specific legacies that bear their own tax under the terms of the will, as shown in **notes 7 and 8**

(10)   In **note 7**, the tax of £61,503 borne by the residuary legatees would relate to the respective parts of residue as follows:

Business property

$$\frac{215,000}{477,300} \times 61,503 \qquad\qquad 42,669$$

Remainder of residue

$$\frac{262{,}300}{477{,}300} \times 61{,}503 \qquad\qquad 52{,}056$$

$$\underline{\underline{£94{,}725}}$$

In **note 8**, the tax of £94,725 borne by the residuary legatees would relate to the respective parts of residue as follows:

Business property

$$\frac{215{,}000}{477{,}300} \times 94{,}725 \qquad\qquad 27{,}704$$

Remainder of residue

$$\frac{262{,}300}{477{,}300} \times 94{,}725 \qquad\qquad 33{,}799$$

$$\underline{\underline{£61{,}503}}$$

The tax relating to the business property could be paid by instalments if the conditions were satisfied, but see the note as to interest at the end of **part (A)** of the example (see **Example 5 explanatory note 9**).

Question

Mr Algernon died on 3 May 2010. His estate contained the following:

	Value at date of death £
Main residence	725,000
Proceeds from insurance policy	300,000
Quoted shares	775,000
Bank account	185,000
Other possessions	40,000
Mortgage on main residence	(12,000)

Mr Algernon's will which was executed in 2006 required that:

(1)   his daughter receive £337,000 free of all taxes;

(2)   his son John receive £400,000 bearing its own taxes;

(3)   his wife receive one-half of the residue, the other half to pass into a trust for his grandchildren, and the division into equal shares to be made before deduction of inheritance tax thereon.

Mr Algernon had made no lifetime transfers.

Advise the trustees as to the amount of funds they can expect from Mr Algernon's estate.

Answer

Death of Mr Algernon 3 May 2010 — calculation of inheritance tax

	£	£
His estate on death amounted to:		
Main residence	725,000	
Less: Mortgage thereon	12,000	713,000
Insurance policy		300,000
Quoted shares		775,000
Bank account		185,000
Other possessions		40,000
Gross estate		2,013,000

Stage 1

Gross up specific gifts which do not bear their own tax as though they alone were chargeable to inheritance tax on death:

	£
Legacy to daughter (see **explanatory note 5**)	337,000
Tax thereon	8,000
Gross gift	345,000

Stage 2

Using gross gift as calculated in Stage 1, divide the estate between exempt and non-exempt parts:

	Exempt	Non-Exempt	
	£	£	£
Gross estate			2,013,000
Gross legacy to daughter		345,000	
Legacy to John bearing its own tax		400,000	
Residue (£1,268,000)			
Wife	634,000		
Trust		634,000	
	634,000	1,379,000	2,013,000

Stage 3

Calculate the inheritance tax on the non-exempt estate at Stage 2:

1,379,000 – 325,000 = £1,054,000 @ 40% = £421,600

Stage 4

Using the tax computed at Stage 3, recompute the grossing up of specific gifts not bearing their own tax:

$$\text{Legacy to daughter } 337,000 \times \frac{1,379,000}{1,379,000 - 421,600} = £485,401$$

Stage 5

Using the revised gross gifts from Stage 4, re-divide the estate between exempt and non-exempt parts:

	Exempt £	Non-Exempt £	£
Gross estate			2,013,000
Legacy to daughter as in Stage 4		485,401	
Legacy to John		400,000	
Residue (£1,127,599)			
Wife	563,800		
Trust		563,799	
	563,800	1,449,200	2,013,000

Stage 6

Calculate the inheritance tax on the revised non-exempt part of the estate and calculate the effective rate of tax:

1,449,200 − 325,000 = £1,124,200 @ 40% = £449,680

$$\frac{449,680}{1,449,200} \times 100 = 31.0295\% \text{ effective rate}$$

Stage 7

The residue of the estate is therefore as follows:	£	£	£
Gross estate			2,013,000
Less: Inheritance tax payable			449,680
			1,563,320
Less: Legacy to daughter		337,000	
Legacy to John	400,000		
Less IHT thereon at 31.0295%	124,118	275,882	612,882
Residue			950,438

However none of the charge to inheritance tax is to fall on the exempt part due to the spouse.

The estate is therefore distributed as follows:	£	£	£
Daughter			337,000
John			275,882
			612,882
Tax on legacies at 31.0295% (per Stage 6) at grossed up value (per Stage 4) 485,401+ 400,000 = £885,401 × 31.0295%		274,735	
Residue before tax (2,013,000 − (612,882 + 274,735))	1,125,383		
Half to widow			562,691
Half to A & M Trust	562,692		

Less: Tax @ 31.0295% on £563,799 (per Stage 5)	174,944	174,944	
	387,748		387,748
Inheritance tax		449,679	449,679
Gross estate			2,013,000

The trustees may therefore expect to receive £387,748.

Explanatory Notes

Incidence of tax on deceased's estate

(1)   The calculation of the inheritance tax and the distribution of the estate is not straightforward where on a person's death part of the estate is the subject of an exempt transfer (for example, to the surviving spouse) and part is chargeable.

(2)   The ultimate incidence of tax on a deceased's estate is as follows:

Tax relating to an estate interest in possession of the deceased in settled property (including where the settlement ends on the death) is payable out of the trust funds.

Tax relating to nominated and jointly held property of the deceased, and property subject to a reservation, is payable out of that property.

The tax on property situated abroad is a charge on that property.

In the absence of specific provisions in the will, tax on all other property, both real and personal, wherever situated in the UK, is a testamentary expense payable out of the residue of the estate.

However, under s 200 the deceased's personal representatives are liable for all the inheritance tax chargeable on the death transfer with the exception of property that was comprised in a settlement immediately before the death (but including land in the UK which, even though so comprised, devolves on or vests in the personal representatives on the death), and – subject to the instalment option – they are obliged to pay that tax on delivering their inheritance tax account (s 226(2)). To the extent that the tax is not a testamentary expense, the personal representatives then have a statutory right to recover it from the persons in whom the property in question is vested (s 211, and see **Example 5 explanatory note 10**).

Partially exempt legacies

(3)   Thus, although the widow's share of the estate is exempt, the tax on specific legacies must come out of the residue (unless the will specifically provides that the legacy is to bear its own tax).

If the residue then remaining is left partly to the widow and partly by way of chargeable transfer, the tax on the residue must be borne in accordance with the will. This is subject to s 41, which provides that, notwithstanding the terms of the will, none of the tax on a particular gift (whether specific or residuary) is to fall on that gift if the gift is exempt.

Re Benham

In the case of *Re Benham's Will Trusts* (1995) it was held that the plain intention of the deceased's will was that each beneficiary should *receive* the *same amount* and that this was not inconsistent with s 41. Consequently the non-exempt shares of residue had to be grossed up so that the after tax amounts were equal. This had the effect of increasing both the tax charged on the estate and the shares of non-exempt residuary beneficiaries at the expense of exempt beneficiaries, which was contrary to the accepted practice and was not the view taken by the Capital Taxes Office. In 1999 a different High Court judge came to the opposite conclusion in the case of *Re Ratcliffe (deceased)*. He referred to the *Benham* approach as the 'net division' approach and the previously accepted approach as the 'gross division' approach, and held that the 'gross division' approach was correct on the facts of the case. The case has not been taken to appeal, but is generally regarded as overriding the *Benham* decision except on facts very close to those arising in *Benham*. Even so, it would be sensible to review the wording of wills where there is partly exempt residue, to ensure that it is clear whether the division of residue is to take place before or after deducting the tax on the residue.

Stages in tax calculation

(4)   Unless the cumulative lifetime transfers exceed the nil threshold the method of calculation is complex (ss 36 to 42). The procedure is straightforward where lifetime transfers exceed the nil threshold, because all grossing calculations are at the same rate, ie 100/60 (see **explanatory note 7**).

Where, as in this example, the lifetime transfers are less than the nil threshold, there are seven stages in the calculation, the first six of which are notional calculations used in order to ascertain the effective rate of inheritance tax on the estate.

The stages are as follows:

(1)   Gross up specific gifts which do not bear their own tax as though they were the only chargeable transfers made at death (s 38(1) and (3)).

(2)   Using the grossed up gifts arrived at in (1) divide the estate between exempt and non-exempt parts.

(3)   Compute tax on the *notional* non-exempt part of the estate.

(4)   Once again gross up specific gifts which do not bear their own tax but using the tax arrived at in (3) (s 38(4) and (5)). This replaces Stage 1.

(5)   Using the revised gross gifts in (4) re-divide the estate between exempt and non-exempt parts.

(6)   Compute tax on the non-exempt part and calculate the effective rate of tax (s 38(1)).

(7)   Distribute the estate in such a way that the tax, if any, on the gifts in the will not bearing their own tax comes out of the whole of the residue, and the tax on the residue falls on the part of the residue that is not exempt (s 41).

(5)   The grossing up calculation in Stage 1 of the example on the legacy to the daughter is as follows:

Cumulative net transfers of £337,000 exceed £325,000 by £12,000. This is grossed up using the 40% tax rate.

	Gross £	Tax £	Net £
	325,000	–	325,000
Gross equivalent $\dfrac{100}{60} \times 12,000$	20,000		12,000
and tax thereon		8,000	
	345,000	8,000	337,000

(6)   The calculation of tax on the trustees' share of the residue is based upon their notional share of residue ie £563,800 per Stage 5 not their actual share of £562,692 at Stage 7. This method is used by HMRC Inheritance Tax. Views have been expressed that the tax should be based upon the actual share of residue (ie £562,692 @ 31. 0295% = £174,600 compared with £174,944 as computed). This does not appear to follow the requirement that none of the tax as computed is to fall on the spouse or other exempt transfers. Instead it recomputes the tax yet again.

Calculation if lifetime transfers exceed nil band

(7)   If Mr Algernon had made cumulative lifetime transfers of £325,000, the seven stage calculation would not be necessary and the position would be as follows:

	Gross £	Tax £	Net £
Inheritance tax accumulation at death on 2010/11 scale	325,000	–	325,000
Legacy to daughter grossed up 337,000 × 100/60	561,667	224,667	337,000
Legacy to John	400,000	160,000	240,000
Leaving residue of 2,013,000 − (561,667 + 400,000) = £1,051,333, of which half, ie £525,666, is exempt, so that non-exempt residue is	525,667	210,267	315,400
	1,812,334	594,934	1,217,400

The estate would therefore be distributed as follows:

Daughter — legacy			337,000
John — legacy			240,000
Widow's share of residue			525,666
Trust's share of residue		525,667	
Less tax @ 40%		210,267	315,400
Inheritance tax:			
On legacies — daughter		224,667	
John		160,000	
On Trust's share of residue		210,267	594,934
			£2,013,000

The same procedure would apply if the lifetime transfers had been any amount in excess of £325,000.

Further examples

(8)   For further illustrations of the treatment of partially exempt legacies, including the provisions in relation to settled property, business and agricultural relief and intestacy, see **Examples 17 and 18**.

Grandchildren's trust

(9)   If the will was executed in 2005, it is likely that the grandchildren's trust would have been an accumulation and maintenance settlement in accordance with IHTA 1984 s 71. Had Mr Algernon died before 22 March 2006, this would have allowed the income to have been accumulated without the trust fund becoming relevant property (and so subject to the ten-yearly and exit charges regime).

However, since Mr Algernon died after 21 March 2006, any trust for his grandchildren would constitute relevant property except so far as it conferred an immediate post-death interest in possession within s 49A or a disabled person's interest within s 89B.

Question

On 1 January 2006 X, who had made no previous lifetime transfers, gave £123,000 to his daughter D and on 1 November 2006, £81,500 each to his daughter E and his son S.

On 1 June 2010 X died leaving an estate which, after payment of all debts and funeral expenses, was valued at £300,000, after deduction of business property relief of £150,000.

By his will he left business property valued at £120,000 (before business property relief of £60,000) equally to his daughter E and his wife W free of tax, £25,000 to a charity, a pecuniary legacy of £40,000 to his son S and the residue of his estate equally (before inheritance tax thereon) to W and three children D, S and E.

X was entitled for life to the income of the residuary estate of his father (and had been so since his father's death in 1993) with remainder to his son S. The assets of that settlement were valued at £100,000 on 1 June 2010.

Calculate the inheritance tax payable on X's death.

Answer

X — inheritance tax accumulation

		£
1 January 2006		
Gift to D		123,000
Less: Annual exemptions 2005/06	3,000	
2004/05	3,000	6,000
Potentially exempt transfer		117,000
1 November 2006		
Gift to E		81,500
Gift to S		81,500
		163,000
Less: Annual exemption 2006/07 (split equally)		3,000
Potentially exempt transfers		160,000

On death of X — 1 June 2010

	Gross	Tax on 2010/11 scale
	£	£
PET to D — 1 January 2006	117,000	–
PETs to E and S — 1 November 2006	160,000	–
Inheritance tax accumulation at death	277,000	–

No tax payable on lifetime transfers since below nil threshold (but correspondingly no tapering relief).

Estate on Death

Free estate	450,000	
Less: Business property relief	150,000	300,000
Settled property		100,000
		£400,000

Preliminary Stage: Allocation of business property relief to specific gifts, and residue, for grossing calculations

	Before BPR	After BPR
Total free estate	450,000	300,000
First allocate BPR on specific gifts		
of business property to that property		
Business property to wife – W	60,000	30,000
Business property to daughter – E	60,000	30,000

			120,000	60,000
Remainder of estate			330,000	240,000

Then allocate a pro rata share of
remaining BPR (net/gross – × 240,000 / 330,000) to other specific gifts

Pecuniary legacy to charity	$\text{gross} \times \dfrac{240,000}{330,000}$		25,000	18,182
Pecuniary legacy to son — S			40,000	29,091
			65,000	47,273

Summary of specific gifts and allocation of BPR

	Before BPR		After BPR	
Total free estate		450,000		300,000
Specific gifts from free estate				
Business property to wife – W	60,000		30,000	
Business property to daughter – E	60,000		30,000	
Pecuniary legacy to charity	25,000		18,182	
Pecuniary legacy to son – S	40,000		29,091	
Total specific gifts		185,000		107,273
Residue of free estate (receives balance of BPR)		265,000		192,727
		450,000		300,000

Division of estate to compute exempt transfers

Stage 1

Gross up non-exempt specific gifts that do not bear their own tax, at net of BPR values, as though they alone were chargeable to IHT on death:

Half of business property (after BPR) to E			30,000
Legacy to S (after BPR)			29,091
			£59,091

	Gross	Tax	Net
	£	£	£
Inheritance tax accumulation at death	277,000	–	277,000
Specific gifts	66,485	7,394	59,091
	343,485	7,394	336,091*

* Grossed up

	Net		Gross
	325,000		325,000
	11,091	× 100/60	18,485
	£336,091		£343,485

Stage 2

Using notional gross gift as calculated in Stage 1, divide estate, net of business property relief, between exempt and non-exempt parts:

		Exempt £	Non-exempt £	Total £
Business property to wife W	(as prelim. stage)	30,000		30,000
Business property to E	$\dfrac{30,000}{59,091} \times 66,485$		33,754	33,754
Legacy to S	$\dfrac{29,091}{59,091} \times 66,485$		32,731	32,731
Legacy to charity	(as prelim. stage)	18,182		18,182
Total specific gifts		48,182	66,485	114,667
Residue —	Balance			185,333
	Wife (¼)	46,333		
	Children (¾)		139,000	
		94,515	205,485	300,000

Stage 3

Calculate the notional inheritance tax payable on non-exempt estate at Stage 2:

	Gross £	Tax £
Accumulation at death	277,000	–
Non-exempt estate	205,485	62,994*
	482,485	62,994*

(* 482,485 – 325,000 = 157,485 @ 40%)

Stage 4

Using the tax computed at Stage 3, recompute the grossing up of specific gifts not bearing their own tax:

$$£59,091 \times \frac{205,485}{(205,485 - 62,994)} = £85,215$$

Stage 5

Using the revised gross gifts from Stage 4, re-divide the estate between exempt and non-exempt parts:

		Exempt £	Non-exempt £	Total £
Business property				
to wife W	Specific gift after BPR	30,000		30,000
to daughter E	$\dfrac{30,000}{59,091} \times 85,215$		43,263	43,263

Pecuniary legacies

to son S	$\dfrac{29,091}{59,091} \times 85,215$		41,952	41,952
to charity	specific gift after BPR	18,182		18,182
				133,397
Residue				166,603
	Wife (¼)	41,651		
	Children (¾)		124,952	
		89,833	210,167	300,000

Stage 6

Calculate the inheritance tax on the revised non-exempt part of the estate and calculate the effective rate of tax:

		Gross	*Tax*
		£	£
Accumulation at death		277,000	–
Non-exempt estate as stage 5	210,167		
Settled property	100,000	310,167	104,867*
		587,167	104,867*

(* 587,167 – 325,000 = 262,167 @ 40%)

Effective rate $\qquad \dfrac{104,867}{310,167} \times 100 = 33.81\%$

Inheritance tax payable by

Personal representatives	210,167	× 33.81% =	71,057
Trustees of settled property	100,000	× 33.81% =	33,810
	£310,167		£104,867

Stage 7

Distribution of free estate:

Estate at death				450,000
Less:	Inheritance tax			71,057
				378,943
Less:	Exempt specific gifts			
	To	wife	60,000	
		charity	25,000	85,000
				293,943
Less:	Non-exempt specific gifts (not bearing their own tax)			
	To	E	60,000	
		S	40,000	100,000
Net residue				£193,943

Distribution of net residue so that no inheritance tax relates to widow

Legacies to E and S (at grossed up value stages 4 and 5) at final effective rate of 33.81%

Distribution of net residue so that no inheritance tax relates to widow

Legacies to E and S (at grossed up value stages 4 and 5) at final effective rate of 33.81%

Tax thereon = £85,215 × 33.81% =		£28,811	
Estate on death			450,000
Exempt legacies	— wife	60,000	
	— charity	25,000	
Legacies not bearing own tax			
	— E	60,000	
	— S	40,000	
	— tax thereon	28,811	213,811
Residue before tax			£236,189
Net residue as at stage (7) above			193,943
One quarter of residue before tax to widow ½ × 236,189			59,047
Balance equally to children:			£134,896
	D		£44,965
	S		£44,965
	E		£44,966

Summary of division of estate and trust funds

		£	£
To Son S from trustees of settled property		100,000	
Less:	Inheritance tax thereon	33,810	66,190
To charity	legacy		25,000
To E	specific gift of business property	60,000	
	share of residue	44,966	104,966
To S	legacy	40,000	
	share of residue	44,965	84,965
To D	share of residue		44,965
To wife	specific gift of business property	60,000	
	share of residue	59,047	119,047
Inheritance tax (including that on settled property)			104,867
			£550,000

Explanatory Notes

Same-day transfers

(1)   The first step is to compute the inheritance tax accumulation at death.

(2)   Where two or more transfers are made on the same day they are treated except in certain special circumstances as one transfer and the effective rate of tax on the total transfer is applied to the individual transfers (s 266(2)).

Interest in possession in settled property

(3)   Settled property in which the donor had an estate interest in possession is treated as belonging to the donor absolutely for inheritance tax purposes, although the tax relating to the settlement is payable by the trustees of the settlement (ss 49 and 200(1)(b)). An interest in possession to which the beneficiary had been entitled since before 22 March 2006 continues to be treated in this way despite the changes wrought by FA 2006.

Partially exempt legacies and business and agricultural property relief

(4)   In order to compute the tax payable on death the rules for partially exempt transfers must be applied (ss 36–42). These are detailed in **Example 16**.

Where an estate is entitled to business property or agricultural property relief and there are specific gifts then special rules apply in computing the inheritance tax payable, as follows:

(a)   Specific gifts of relevant business or agricultural property are taken at their value reduced by BPR or APR.

(b)   Specific gifts other than in (a) above are taken at the appropriate fraction of their value (s 39A), that is:

$$\text{Specific gift} \times \frac{\text{Assets transferred (net of BPR/APR) less specific gifts of business/agricultural property (net of BPR/APR)}}{\text{Assets transferred (before BPR/APR) less specific gifts of business/agricultural property (before BPR/APR)}}$$

A specific gift is any gift other than a gift of residue or of a share in residue (s 42). It therefore covers both specific legacies of particular property and general (ie pecuniary) legacies. It would also cover settled property which devolves under the terms of the settlement (and not under the terms of the life tenant's will by way of general power of appointment, which would be unusual).

Where specific gifts are tax-free then the grossing up rules are applied to the value so reduced, as shown at Stage 1.

Gifts out of different funds

(5)   Section 40 provides that where gifts take effect separately out of different funds (for Example where a deceased has a free estate and a life interest in a settlement, and gifts are made out of the free estate), the partial exemption rules in ss 36–39A are to be applied separately to the gifts taking effect out of each of those funds. The rate of tax used to gross up the gifts is arrived at by looking at each fund separately and in isolation. In the Example, therefore, the tax on the non-exempt estate at stage (3) that is used to re-gross the specific gifts is arrived at by taking into account only the free estate and not the settled property.

Pecuniary legacies

(6)   Where a will provides a pecuniary legacy (a gift of cash like the legacy of £40,000 to S), then the legatee receives the amount stated and any inheritance tax relating to that legacy is borne by the residue of the estate unless the will provides that the legatee is to bear the tax (s 211). For further notes on this point see **Example 5 explanatory note 10**.

Re Benham and Re Ratcliffe

(7)   Where a will provides that the residuary shares are computed on the residue after deduction of inheritance tax, there were conflicting views in *Re Benham* and *Re Ratcliffe* on how the shares of residue should be calculated. It is now generally regarded as settled that the established approach in dealing with partly exempt estates is correct unless the will is very clear in specifying that the shares are fixed *after* deducting IHT — see **Example 16 explanatory note 3**.

Question

Jones, who was domiciled in England and Wales, died intestate on 10 June 2010 and was survived by his wife and two children.

He had made no chargeable lifetime transfers.

His estate according to the account accompanying the application for a grant of administration consisted of:

5,000	£1 shares in A plc quoted at 1088–1092 with recorded bargains at 1088, 1089, 1090 and 1091
10,000	£1 shares in B plc quoted at 295–297 with a sole recorded bargain at 295
8,000	50p shares in C plc quoted at 60–69 with bargains at 61, 61½, 62 and 63
10,000	shares in the Hong Kong Bank valued at £70,000

	£
Cash at bank	87,569
Policy on his life, insuring	270,000
Salary accrued due to date of death (net)	2,275
Rents from his father's will trust (net of basic rate income tax)	
accrued due	645
apportionment to date of death	621
Furniture and effects	10,500

His debts were shown as:

	£
Funeral expenses	1,650
General household bills (electricity, gas, etc)	220
Daughter, under a deed of covenant dated 1 January 1992	
binding his legal personal representatives to pay her on his death	5,000

Under the will of his father who had died in 1985 he also had a life interest in a house, No 12 High Street, valued at £200,000, which passed on his death to his children equally. The rent due to Jones at death is indicated above.

A grant of administration was obtained on 15 March 2011 when inheritance tax amounting to £2,630 and £16 interest was paid by the intended administrators on the basis of the above information.

The administrators subsequently discover:

(1) Jones is entitled to a pecuniary legacy of £10,000 free of tax under the will of his brother who died on 4 August 2009. Inheritance tax amounting to £13,000 had been paid on the brother's (fully taxable) estate valued at £100,000.

(2) There was an outstanding income tax liability of £750.

(3) There were bonuses totalling £47,250 attaching to the life policy.

(4) The value of the shares in the Hong Kong Bank is agreed at £70,000, but death duties amounting to the sterling equivalent of £7,000 and £420 interest had to be paid locally because the shares were registered there. The additional cost of employing a local agent to make title to the shares, including agreeing the value with the local fiscal authorities, amounted to a sterling equivalent of £4,150.

(5) The remaining values were agreed with HMRC.

A corrective account is lodged and the final adjustment to the inheritance tax payable is made on 5 November 2010, the trustees also paying any tax and interest attributable to the trust funds on that day.

Given that the 'statutory legacy' payable to the spouse on an intestacy when the intestate leaves issue is £250,000 with the spouse also taking the personal chattels and a life interest in one half of the residue, whilst the other half of the residue devolves on the issue:

(a)   Calculate the inheritance tax and interest paid by or repaid to the administrators on 5 November 2010.

(b)   Show the distribution of the free estate and trust funds upon Jones's death and the allocation of the tax payable.

The rate of interest on tax overdue or repayable was 0% from 23 March 2009 until 29 September 2009. Thereafter the rate chargeable on tax overdue has been 3.0%, and the rate payable on tax refunded has been 0.5%; assume that these rates remain in force.

Answer

(a) Estate of Jones (after submission of corrective account)

		Date of Death 10 June 2010	
Free estate		£	£
Quoted shares:			
5,000 £1 shares in A plc	@ 1089	54,450	
10,000 £1 shares in B plc	@ 295	29,500	
8,000 50p shares in C plc	@ 62	4,960	88,910
Cash at bank			87,569
Policy on life		270,000	
Bonuses thereon		47,250	317,250
Salary due			2,275
Rents accrued due to date of death			
(after basic rate income tax) (645 + 621)			1,266
Furniture and effects			10,500
Legacy due from unadministered estate of brother			10,000
Property abroad			
10,000 shares in the Hong Kong Bank		70,000	
Less: Costs of administration (£4,150 but restricted to maximum 5%)		3,500	66,500
			584,270
Less: Funeral expenses		1,650	
General household debts		220	
Income tax		750	
Covenanted debt — no deduction possible since no consideration was given		–	2,620
			581,650
Settled property			
Father's will trust			200,000
Total estate for inheritance tax			781,650

The statutory legacy of £250,000 plus furniture and effects £10,500 and one half of the residue in trust for the widow are exempt transfers. To determine the amount deemed to be transferred to the trust for the widow it is technically necessary to apply the 'double grossing up' rules that apply to partially exempt residue (though on the figures this has no practical impact).

Division of estate to compute exempt transfer

(1)   Gross up specific gifts not bearing own tax:

Covenanted gift to daughter D	£5,000
As there were no lifetime transfers and value is below £325,000, its grossed up value is	£5,000

(2)   Divide estate between exempt and non-exempt parts, using notional gross gifts:

		Exempt	Non-exempt	Total
Specific gift			5,000	5,000
To Wife	Statutory legacy	250,000		250,000
	Furniture etc	10,500		10,500
	½ of residue (life interest)	158,075		
To Children	½ of residue		158,075	316,150
		£418,575	£163,075	£581,650

(3)   Inheritance tax payable on non-exempt estate:

	Gross	Tax
Inheritance tax accumulation at death	–	–
Non-exempt free estate	£163,075	£–

As the value of the non-exempt free estate (ie excluding settled property) is less than £325,000, it is not necessary to re-gross up the specific gift, or to re-divide the free estate. The inheritance tax payable is therefore:

		Gross	Tax
Non-exempt free estate	163,075		
Settled property	200,000	£363,075	£15,230*

(* 363,075 – 325,000 = 38,075 @ 40%)

	£
Inheritance tax on chargeable estate	15,230
Less: Quick succession relief	1,300

$$100\% \text{ of } \frac{10,000}{100,000} \times £13,000$$

	13,930

Less: Relief for overseas tax — re Hong Kong)
Bank shares. Amount paid £7,000 but)
restricted to inheritance tax attributable to)
that property)

	1,185

$$\frac{66,500}{781,650} \times 13,930$$

	12,745

Tax payable by administrators

$$\frac{163,075}{363,075} \times 13,930 = 6,257 - 1,185$$

	5,072

Less: already paid on 15.3.2011		2,630
Additional tax payable		2,442
Interest on £5,072 at 3.0% from 1.1.2011 to 15.3.2011 = 74 days	31	
Interest on £2,442 at 3.0% from 15.3.2011 to 5.11.2011 = 236 days	47	
	78	
Less interest paid at time of grant	(16)	62
Total payable by the administrators 5.11.2011		2,504

Tax payable by the trustees of father's will trust

$$\frac{200,000}{363,075} \times 13,930 =$$

7,673

Interest at 3.0% from 1.1.2011 to 5.11.2011 = 309 days

195

Total payable by the trustees 5.11.2011

£7,868

(b) Distribution of funds and allocation of tax payable

		£	£
Daughter —	specific gift (covenanted payment)		5,000
Widow —	Cash (statutory legacy)	250,000	
	Chattels	10,500	260,500
Life interest trust for widow —	½ of residue as at (a) (2)		158,075
Children —	½ of residue as at (a) (2)	158,075	
	Less: inheritance tax payable	5,072	153,003
Inheritance tax payable by administrators			5,072
			581,650
Inheritance tax payable by trustees of father's will trust			7,868

The interest payable on overdue tax will be dealt with through the income accounts of the estate and the trust.

Explanatory Notes

Partially exempt legacies — intestacy

(1)   The notes to **Examples 16** and **17** also apply to this Example. The Example highlights the fact that an intestacy will often create partially exempt residue, though there will only rarely be specific non-exempt gifts payable out of the free estate. The impact would be greater here if lifetime chargeable transfers had exceeded the available nil rate band. See in particular **Example 17 note 5** regarding the treatment to be adopted where a partly exempt estate consists of free estate and an interest in settled property. The rules relating to distribution on intestacy in England and Wales are set out at **explanatory note 6** below.

For further details on:

Corrective and supplementary accounts	see **Example 8**
Administration of foreign assets	see **Example 15**
Quick succession relief	see **Example 21**
Double taxation relief	see **Example 28** and **Example 3(c)**

Valuation of quoted shares

(2)   Quoted shares are valued at the lower of

(a)   One quarter up on lower quoted closing price

(b)   Midpoint of bargain prices, thus:

	Closing Price		Bargains	Lower
Shares in A plc	$1088 + ¼ (1092 - 1088) = 1089$			
	$\dfrac{1088 + 1091}{2} = 1089½$			1089
B plc	$295 + ¼ (297 - 295) = 295½$		295	295
C plc	$60 + ¼ (69 - 60) = 62¼$			
		$\dfrac{61 + 63}{2} = 62$		62

Covenanted gift

(3)   The non-deductible covenanted sum is treated as a specific gift (s 38(6)) and thus does not bear its own tax.

Double tax relief

(4)   Double tax relief is available where tax is charged both abroad and in the UK. For detailed notes see **Example 28 explanatory note 6**. The relief is given as a reduction of the tax on the relevant property (s 159). In this Example therefore the relief reduces the tax on the non-settled part of the estate.

The additional costs of administering or realising assets abroad may be deducted if shown to be attributable to the situation of the property, up to a maximum of 5% of the value of the property (s 173).

Intestacy rules for dividing estates

(5)   When a person dies without leaving a will, or leaves a will that does not fully dispose of his estate, then the rules of intestacy apply to the estate not disposed of by will. These rules determine to whom the estate is to be distributed. The inheritance tax rules then determine the amount of tax to be paid, with the amounts allocated to the spouse being exempt transfers. Section 211 provides that the tax payable is to be borne by the residue of the estate as a general testamentary expense. This is subject to s 41, which provides that none of the tax on residue is to fall on any part of the residue that is exempt. Thus, in this Example, although the widow's share of the estate is exempt, the tax, if any, on specific legacies must come out of residue and the tax on the residue must be borne wholly by the chargeable part of the estate. The rules for calculating the tax are set out in ss 38 to 42.

(6)   The rules of intestacy for England and Wales are to be found in Administration of Estates Act 1925 ss 46–47, as amended by Family Provision Act 1966 and Civil Partnership Act 2004. The fixed sums payable to the surviving spouse in the table below are provided for by Family Provision (Intestate Succession) Order 2009 (SI 2009/135) in respect of deaths on or after 1 February 2009. The rules provide that the estate is to be distributed as set out below.

Those surviving	*Those entitled to the estate*
Spouse/civil partner — no issue, parent, brother, sister or issue thereof	Spouse/civil partner absolutely
Spouse/civil partner and issue	Spouse/civil partner takes: (i) Personal chattels (ii) £250,000 (iii) Life interest in ½ of residue Issue share other ½ of residue (on statutory trust to 18) and take spouse's/civil partner's life interest share on his (her) death.
Spouse/civil partner, no issue but parent(s)	Spouse/civil partner takes: (i) Personal chattels (ii) £450,000

Those surviving	*Those entitled to the estate*
	(iii) ½ of residue absolutely
	Parent(s) share ½ of residue absolutely.
Spouse/civil partner, no issue or parents but brothers or sisters of the whole blood (or issue thereof)	Spouse/civil partner takes:
	(i) Personal chattels
	(ii) £450,000
	(iii) ½ of residue absolutely
	Brothers and sisters (or their issue) share ½ of residue absolutely
No spouse/civil partner but issue	Issue take all absolutely
	(held on statutory trust if under 18)
No spouse/civil partner or issue but	
Parent(s)	Take absolutely
Brothers and sisters of the whole blood	Take absolutely
Brothers and sisters of the half blood	Take absolutely
Grandparents	Take absolutely
Uncles and aunts (whole blood)	Take absolutely
Uncles and aunts (half blood)	Take absolutely

(Each category takes the whole estate to the exclusion of any later category.)

No relatives mentioned above	The Crown

'Issue' means children, grandchildren, great grandchildren etc. Where someone entitled to a share is deceased but has surviving children, the children will take the deceased's parent's share (and so on for grandchildren etc).

From 1 January 1996 a spouse (and since 5 December 2005, a civil partner) does not inherit under the intestacy rules unless he/she survives the deceased by at least 28 days.

(7) The rules of intestacy applying to the distribution of an estate in Scotland are as follows:

1. Prior rights

After debts and other liabilities have been met, a widow, widower or a surviving civil partner has a certain 'prior rights of a surviving spouse or civil partner' in the deceased person's estate, where no will has been left.

He or she is entitled to the dwelling house of the deceased in which the surviving spouse or civil partner was resident at the time of the deceased's death, plus up to the value of £24,000 any furnishings and furniture of that house. (In certain cases, eg where the house is a farmhouse or part of a shop, or where the house is worth more than £300,000 the entitlement is not to the house itself, but to its value up to £300,000).

The surviving spouse or civil partner is also entitled to the first £42,000 out of the estate if the deceased left children or descendants of children or to the first £75,000 if the deceased left no children or descendants.

Prior rights are a first claim on the estate, before legal rights (see below).

2. Legal rights

A surviving spouse or civil partner and children are entitled to certain 'legal right' out of the deceased person's moveable estate. In Scots law, heritable property means land and buildings, while moveable property includes such things as money, shares, cars, furniture and jewellery.

The surviving spouse or civil partner is entitled to *one-third* of the deceased's moveable estate if the deceased left children or descendants of children, or to *one-half* of it if the deceased left no such children or descendants.

The children are collectively entitled to *one-third* of the deceased's moveable estate if the deceased left a spouse or civil partner, or to *one-half* of it if the deceased left no spouse or civil partner. Each child has an equal claim. Where a child would have had a claim had he (she) not died before his (her) parent, his (her) descendants may claim his (her) share by the principle known as representation.

3. Other rights on intestacy

After any prior rights and legal rights have been satisfied, the remainder of the intestate estate, both heritable and moveable, devolves (without distinction between heritable and moveable estate) in the following order, any surviving relative in an earlier group taking precedence, thereby precluding any surviving relatives in a later group from succeeding to any part of the estate, *viz*:

(a)   Children take the whole.

(b)   Either or both parents and brothers and sisters – half to parent or parents and half to brothers and sisters.

(c)   Brothers and sisters take the whole.

(d)   Either or both parents take the whole.

(e)   Husband or wife or civil partner – surviving spouse or civil partner takes the whole.

(f)   Uncles or aunts (on either parent's side) take the whole.

(g)   Grandparent or grandparents (on either side) take the whole.

(h)   Brothers and sisters of any grandparents (on either side) take the whole.

(i)   Ancestors of intestate remoter than grandparents, on both paternal and maternal sides generation by generation successively take the whole, but if no ancestors survive in any generation their brothers and sisters come before ancestors of the next more remote generation.

(j)   Finally, the Crown, failing any relatives in the foregoing categories, takes the whole.

The application of the foregoing order of succession is subject to three general principles:

(i)   There is no preference for male persons, or in regard to age. For instance, brothers do not rank before sisters, or elder brothers before younger (except in relation to succession to such things as titles and coats of arms).

(ii)   There is representation in all branches of succession, ie where any relative who would, if alive, have been entitled to succeed to the whole or any part of the intestate estate has predeceased leaving children, such children take equally among them the share which their deceased parent would have received if in life. If, however, the persons taking by representation are all in the same degree of relationship to the deceased, each individual takes an equal share.

(iii)   In the case of collaterals, ie brothers and sisters of the deceased or of an ancestor of the deceased, both those of the full blood and those of the half blood are entitled to succeed, but collaterals of the full blood have preference: if there are no collaterals of the full blood, the collaterals of the half blood rank without distinction as between those related through the father or mother.

4. Adopted children

The position of adopted children is the same as that of natural children for the purposes of succession. Thus an adopted child has the same rights of succession in relation to its adoptive parent's estate as a natural child, and adoptive parents have the same rights of succession that they would have, had they been natural parents of the child.

Question

I B Smart, aged 62 and in poor health, and his wife aged 55 and in excellent health, were worried about their potential inheritance tax liability on death. They had not made any chargeable transfers. They had two children, John aged 22 who is a director of the family trading company, Smart & Co Ltd, and Jill aged 24, who is married with one child aged 6 months.

Their estates consisted of:

	I B Smart	Mrs Smart
Shares in Smart & Co Ltd	49 shares	49 shares
Freehold offices rented at £10,600 pa to Smart & Co Ltd	£130,000	–
Villa in Spain valued at	£176,000	–

They also owned as joint tenants their private residence, valued at £317,000, and had joint accounts at building societies totalling £196,000.

Mr Smart had recently retired from the family company and was drawing a pension of £40,000 pa. This pension would increase by 3% pa and on his death a 2/3rds pension would be payable to Mrs Smart.

The estimated value of the shares in Smart & Co Ltd is:

100% holding	£1,230 per share
98% holding	£1,224 per share
51% holding	£1,200 per share
49% holding	£1,000 per share
2% holding	£100 per share

There are 100 shares in issue.

No dividends have been declared.

Mr and Mrs Smart wished to continue to live in their main residence but to spend four weeks per year in Spain. They believed that their personal expenditure would require the whole of the rent on the offices as well as the pension but were prepared to forgo the rent on the overseas property of £5,000 pa (rent £500 per week in season). They did not wish to give away any cash.

The wills of Mr and Mrs Smart each provide for the whole of their estates to be left to the surviving spouse for life and on the death of the survivor to be divided equally between the children.

After talking informally to an acquaintance who is a personal finance consultant they attempted to mitigate their liability by Mr Smart giving all of his shares in Smart & Co Ltd to John and the holiday home to Jill, reserving the right to use it rent free when they wished. Both gifts were made on the same day. They did not alter their wills.

Nine months after effecting the above Mr and Mrs Smart were involved in a boating accident in Spain. Mrs Smart died immediately and Mr Smart six weeks later. The gifted assets were still owned by the respective donees.

Assuming that:

(1)   all values are unaltered;

(2)   the current legislation remains throughout;

(3)   2010/11 rates apply throughout; and

(4)   the personal representatives of Mr and Mrs Smart neglect to elect to take advantage of the provisions under IHTA 1984 s 8A (transfer of nil-rate band between spouses – see **Example 1 section (iii)**):

(a)   Set out the inheritance tax liabilities on the assumption that Mr Smart had not undertaken the above proposals.

(b)   Set out the inheritance tax liabilities which do arise following his actually having effected the proposals in May 2010.

(c)   Compute the tax liabilities on the assumptions that the following proposals had instead been adopted:

(i)   Mr Smart to give the Spanish property to Jill.

(ii)   Mrs Smart to give a 47% interest in Smart & Co Ltd to John.

(iii)   The freehold office premises to be transferred to Mrs Smart.

(iv)   The building society accounts to be transferred into Mrs Smart's sole ownership.

(v)   Mr and Mrs Smart to pay open market rent of £500 per week when they visit the Spanish property.

(vi)   Each of their wills to provide that on death a discretionary trust should be created for the benefit of the surviving spouse, children and grandchildren, with specific bequests to the trustees of the business property, shares and residue of the estate (the house passing to the spouse by survivorship).

(d)   Compare the tax liabilities in the three situations had the deaths occurred nine years later rather than nine months, all values and tax rates remaining the same.

Answer

I B Smart — gifts with reservation

(a) *If proposals had not been implemented*

Death of Mrs Smart

	£	£
Estate:		
Shares in Smart & Co Ltd (**explanatory note 3**)		
49 × £1,224	59,976	
Less: 100% business property relief	59,976	–
½ share of jointly owned assets:		
Freehold house	158,500	
Building society accounts	98,000	256,500
Not chargeable because of spouse/civil partner exemption – no inheritance tax payable		256,500

Death of Mr Smart

	£	£	£
Estate:			
Freehold house		317,000	
Property in Spain		176,000	
Freehold offices	130,000		
Less: 50% business property relief	65,000	65,000	558,000
Shares in Smart & Co Ltd			
98 × £1,224 (one half owned by Mr Smart and			
one half life interest from Mrs Smart)		119,952	
Less: 100% business property relief		119,952	–
Building society accounts			196,000
Estate chargeable to inheritance tax			754,000
Tax payable (at 2010/11 rates) (754,000 − 325,000 = 429,000 @ 40%)			171,600

(b) *If proposals were implemented in May 2010*

Death of Mrs Smart

Exempt as before — all to Mr Smart for life or absolutely as the surviving joint tenant (but Mrs Smart's shares were valued in their own right as a 49% holding since Mr Smart's shares had been given to John and were no longer related property).

Death of Mr Smart

(1) *Charging gift with reservation in death estate and ignoring the gift to Jill*

	£	£
Freehold house	317,000	
Property in Spain (gift with reservation)	176,000	
Freehold offices (no BPR as no control)	130,000	623,000
Shares in Smart & Co Ltd		
49 × £1,000 (life interest from Mrs Smart)	49,000	
Less: 100% business property relief	49,000	–
Building society accounts		196,000
		819,000

Tax on gifts made within seven years before death

Shares to John

before transfer $\dfrac{49}{98} \times (98 \times £1,224) =$ 59,976

after transfer — no shares held	nil
	59,976
Less: 100% business property relief	59,976
	nil

As the shares still qualify for business property relief at 100% no amount is chargeable on death in respect of the gift, and it does not cumulate.

Inheritance tax payable on death

	Gross £	Tax £
Cumulative transfers within seven years before death	–	–
Estate on death	819,000	197,600*
	819,000	197,600*

(* 819,000 – 325,000 = 494,000 @ 40%)

Tax payable on estate at death (which is the total tax payable as a result of Mr Smart's death, since no tax was payable on gifts within previous seven years)   £197,600

(2) *Charging gift to Jill and ignoring the value of the gift in the death estate*

Death estate as above	819,000
Less: property in Spain	176,000
	£643,000

Tax on gifts made within seven years before death

Shares to John as above	–
Property in Spain to Jill	176,000

			176,000
Less: Annual exemptions			
2010/11		3,000	
2009/10		3,000	6,000
PETs now chargeable			£170,000

No tax payable on death within 7 years since 2010/11 threshold is not exceeded.

Inheritance tax payable on death

	Gross	Tax
	£	£
Cumulative transfers within seven years before death	170,000	–
Estate on death	643,000	195,200*
	813,000	195,200*
(× 813,000 – 325,000 = 488,000 @ 40%)		
Tax payable on estate at death		195,200
Add tax on gifts within previous seven years		–
Total tax payable as a result of Mr Smart's death		£195,200

As the first calculation is greater than the second, that is deemed to be the one that determines the tax liabilities. The effect is that the whole of the tax will be payable out of Mr Smart's estate, and borne equally between John and Jill.

(c) *If alternative proposals had been adopted*

Death of Mrs Smart

Estate:	£	£
Business property	130,000	
Less: 50% business property relief	65,000	65,000
Freehold house – ½	158,500	
Less: Exempt on devolution to spouse	158,500	–
Shares in Smart & Co Ltd		
2 × £1,200 (related property × 51%)	2,400	
Less: 100% business property relief	2,400	–
Building society accounts		196,000
Chargeable to inheritance tax		261,000

Gifts within seven years before death

			Gross £	Tax £
Shares to John				
before transfer	$\frac{49}{98} \times (98 \times £1{,}224) =$	59,976		
after transfer	$\frac{2}{51} \times (51 \times £1{,}200) =$	2,400		
		57,576		
Less: 100% business property relief		57,576		
		nil		
Cumulative transfers within seven years before death			–	
Estate on death			261,000	–
No tax payable since threshold is not exceeded			261,000	–

Death of Mr Smart

Estate:		
Freehold house		317,000
Shares in Smart & Co Ltd		
49 shares @ £1,000	49,000	
Less: 100% business property relief	49,000	–
		317,000

Gifts within seven years before death

				Gross £	Tax £
To Jill					
Spanish property			176,000		
Less: Annual exemptions	2010/11	3,000			
	2009/10	3,000	6,000	170,000	–
Cumulative transfers within seven years before death				170,000	–
Estate on death				317,000	64,800*
				487,000	64,800*

(* 487,000 – 325,000 = 162,000 @ 40%)

Tax payable on estate at death   £64,800

(d) *Comparative tax liabilities if deaths had occurred nine years later*

   (a)   *No change — as above*

                                             £171,600

(b) *Original proposals*

If the donor survived the gifts (including the gift with reservation) by more than seven years, there would be no charge to tax on the gifts and therefore the double charges regulations would not apply. The Spanish property would, however, still be included in Mr Smart's estate, so the position (as in option (1) under the double charges regulations, as illustrated) would be:

	Gross £	Tax £
Cumulative transfers within previous seven years	–	–
Estate on death (including Spanish property)	819,000	197,600*

* (819,000 – 325,000 = 494,000 @ 40%)

(c) *Revised proposals*

Mrs Smart

	Gross £	Tax £
Cumulative transfers within previous seven years	–	–
Estate on death	261,000	–

Mr Smart

	Gross £	Tax £
Cumulative transfers within previous seven years	–	–
Estate on death (within nil rate)	317,000	–

Explanatory Notes

Effect of different scenarios on tax liabilities

(1) This Example illustrates that it is possible to increase the liability to inheritance tax by making gifts without considering their tax implications.

The tax liability on the second death if none of the proposals were adopted would amount to £171,600 (nil liability on first death).

If the first proposals were adopted then following the earlier death of Mrs Smart the tax liability on the death of Mr Smart would be increased by £26,000 to £197,600.

Whereas if the second proposals had been adopted then on the first death (Mrs Smart) no tax would be payable and on the second death (Mr Smart) £64,800 would be payable. An overall reduction of £106,800 would arise.

If Mr Smart had predeceased his wife then the tax liabilities under the proposals at (c) would have become:

Mr Smart

	£	£
Gifts within seven years before death		
— property to Jill (176,000 – 6,000 annual exemptions)		170,000
Estate on death:		
Shares in Smart & Co Ltd		

	£	£
49 shares @ £1,200 (related property 51%)	58,800	
Less: 100% business property relief	58,800	–
Freehold house —	158,500	
Exempt since devolving on Mrs Smart	158,500	–
		170,000

No tax is payable since threshold is not exceeded.

		£	£
Mrs Smart			
Gifts within seven years before death (as before with BPR)			–
Estate on death:			
Freehold house		317,000	
Office premises (no BPR, only 2% of shares held)		130,000	
Shares in Smart & Co Ltd			
2 × £100	200		
Less: 50% business property relief	100	100	
Building society accounts		196,000	643,100
			643,100

Tax payable (643,100 – 325,000 = 318,100 @ 40%)   £127,240

Taking both deaths together the tax is £127,240.

Thus the reduction from £171,600 would be £44,360.

In considering how best to mitigate inheritance tax liabilities, one has to remember the continuing need for the income from the business property, and that the personal residence cannot be transferred (except to each other) whilst the Smarts remain in residence (such a transfer would be a gift with reservation and therefore ineffective). However the second proposals would mitigate the potential liabilities regardless of who died first. (The transfer of the office premises to Mrs Smart is not caught by the gifts with reservation provisions because of the spouse exemption, see **note 4** below.) Furthermore after the earlier death of Mr Smart, Mrs Smart could possibly start to make use of the annual exemption by making gifts to her children or grandchildren if her capital was likely to increase by unspent income.

Transfers to discretionary trust

(2) The amounts transferred to the discretionary trust on the death of Mrs Smart would be potentially liable to further inheritance tax charges, as although she had made no transfers in the seven years before her death, the initial value of the property comprised in the settlement (being the values *before* business property relief) is above the inheritance tax threshold of £325,000, ie:

Business property	130,000
Shares in Smart & Co Ltd	2,400
Building society accounts	196,000
	£328,400

A liability will arise if there are any exits from the settlement within ten years. The initial rate applicable to such exits would be +arrived at as follows:

(328,400 – 325,000) @ 20% = £680, which is an effective rate on £328,400 of 0.00207%. The actual rate is 30% of the effective rate, ie 30% of 0.021% = 0.000621%.

$$\text{The initial rate would be} \quad 0.000621 \% \times \frac{X}{40}$$

where x is the number of complete quarters since the creation of the settlement.

A liability at or after ten years would only occur if the assets increased in value to the extent that after business property relief their value exceeded the then threshold (which is usually increased annually by at least the rate of inflation). For detailed notes on discretionary trusts see **Examples 59 to 63**, particularly **Example 62 explanatory note 5**.

In the event that the property was appointed absolutely to the beneficiaries within two years after death (following the later death of Mr Smart) it will be deemed to have been transferred by Mrs Smart under her will (s 144) and no further tax would be payable. See **Example 63 explanatory note 5**.

Related property; valuations for capital gains tax

(3)   The related property rules (s 161) apply to the shares in Smart & Co Ltd and accordingly it is necessary to look at the appropriate proportion of the value of the combined holdings of Mr and Mrs Smart before and after the transfer. Furthermore the entitlement to business property relief depends on the total related shares held by Mr and Mrs Smart (but not the discretionary settlement). Business property relief is not available on the office premises if the combined holding drops below 51%. See **Examples 10, 22** and **26** for the related property rules and **Example 25** for the rules relating to business property relief.

The related property provisions are not relevant for capital gains tax. For capital gains tax purposes, the value of an asset in the hands of a beneficiary is its open market value at the date of death (TCGA 1992 s 62). It is, however, provided by TCGA 1992 s 274 that if the value of an asset has been *ascertained* for inheritance tax, the same value applies for capital gains tax. But if shares qualify for 100% business property relief, or attract spouse relief, their value will not require to be ascertained for inheritance tax, so that the normal open market value rule will apply for capital gains tax. The beneficiary's acquisition value may thus be lower than the inheritance tax value, since it will be based on the number of shares held by the beneficiary in isolation. See **Example 38 explanatory note 1** for further comments on this point.

Gifts with reservation

(4)   FA 1986 s 102 and Sch 20 provide in respect of gifts on or after 18 March 1986 that if an asset is transferred and

   (a)   possession and enjoyment of the property is not bona fide assumed by the donee at or before the beginning of the relevant period, (ie the period beginning seven years before the donor's death or on the date of the gift if later) or

   (b)   at any time in the relevant period the property is not enjoyed to the entire exclusion, or virtually to the entire exclusion, of the donor and of any benefit to him by contract or otherwise,

then the gift is treated as property within the donor's estate as at the date of death.

The gifts with reservation provisions do not apply if or to the extent that the transfer is covered by one of the following inheritance tax exemptions (as to which see **Example 1**):

—   transfers between spouses/civil partners (s 18) (but see * below)

—   small gifts (s 20)

—   gifts in consideration of marriage or registration of a civil partnership (s 22)

—   gifts to charities (s 23)

- — gifts to political parties (s 24)

- — gifts to housing associations (s 24A)

- — gifts for national purposes etc (s 25)

- — maintenance funds for historic buildings (s 17)

- — employee trusts (s 28).

* Note that reliance on the spouse exemption to protect from the gifts with reservation rules was restricted from 20 June 2003 in cases where the property became settled property as a result of the gift (with an interest in possession for the donor's spouse): FA 1986, s 102(5A)–(5B). This rule still applies after the changes to the settled property rules made by FA 2006, but will in practice now be of potential application only where the spousal interest in possession is a disabled person's interest.

If it can be shown that the property ceased to be subject to a reservation prior to death then the donor is treated as making a potentially exempt transfer of the property at the time that the reservation ceased (FA 1986 s 102(4)). Such a transfer could not be reduced by annual exemptions.

The initial gift is still a transfer of value, although it may be potentially exempt (after deducting available annual exemptions). If it is potentially exempt then it will not be charged to tax if the donor survives seven years.

These provisions are illustrated in the Example. The proposed gift of the Spanish property to Jill will not remove the property from Mr Smart's chargeable estate if Mr and Mrs Smart continue to use the property rent free. If, however, the gift was made nine years before Mr Smart's death as in **part (d)** of the Example, the gift would escape tax, but the value of the property would be brought into his estate if the reservation was not released. If say he had released the reservation between three and four years before his death he would be treated as making a further potentially exempt transfer to Jill equal to the value of the property at that time (not reduced by any annual exemptions) and following his death tax would be charged, subject to tapering relief of 20%, but the value of the property would be excluded from his estate.

An exception to the gifts with reservation rules is made when either

(i)   full consideration is given for any right of occupation or enjoyment retained or assumed by the donor and the property is land or chattels, or

(ii)   in the case of land, the donor later occupies the property as a result of a change of circumstances that was unforeseen at the time of the original gift and the benefit provided by the donee to the donor only represents reasonable provision for the care and maintenance of an elderly or infirm relative.

Thus the occupation by Mr and Mrs Smart of the Spanish property at full rent would be sufficient to nullify the reservation of benefit arising from actual use of the property (but would not negate any reservation arising from retention of a binding right to occupy it for less); the second exception might apply, depending on the circumstances, to any occupation rent free by Mr Smart after the boating accident.

Continuing gifts made under the terms of a regular premium insurance policy effected before 18 March 1986 are not caught by the gifts with reservation rules, unless the policy is altered after that date.

There are special rules to provide for the benefits reserved to be followed through when the original property is substituted by replacement property, with appropriate adjustments if the donee provides consideration.

(5)   The gifts with reservation legislation was strengthened following the decision in *Ingram v CIR (1999)*. The House of Lords held that the rules did not apply to Lady Ingram, who created a rent-free lease for herself of her freehold property and then gave away the freehold.

Under FA 1986 ss 102A, 102B and 102C, gifts of interests in land or shares of interests in land made on or after 9 March 1999 will be treated as gifts with reservation if there is some significant interest, right or arrangement which enables or entitles the donor to occupy the land to a material degree without paying full consideration.

(6)   The provisions do not apply where the gift is covered by one of the inheritance tax exemptions listed in note 4, nor where exception (i) or (ii) in note 4 applies. Nor do they apply where, despite some negligible benefit retained, the donor is virtually excluded from any enjoyment of the land, or to gifts made more than seven years after the interest etc was created, or where the donor cannot occupy or enjoy the land until the interest given away expires (for Example when a lease terminates).

(7)   Where there is a gift of an undivided share of an interest in land, the donor and donee may both occupy the land providing the donor receives no other benefit at the donee's expense in connection with the gift (ie the donee pays no more than his fair share of the outgoings) (s 102B(4), giving effect to existing Revenue practice as stated in their letter of 18 May 1987 to the Law Society Gazette following a ministerial statement in Standing Committee G on 10 June 1986).

(8)   For further comments on gifts with reservation relating to land see **Example 23**. For the interaction of the gifts with reservation provisions and business and agricultural property relief, see **Example 25 explanatory note 9**.

(9)   Under FA 1986 s 102ZA the termination of a pre-22 March 2006 interest in possession or of an IPDI, a disabled person's interest or a transitional serial interest during the lifetime of the beneficiary is treated as a gift of the property in which the interest subsists. If the beneficiary continues to benefit the property will now be subject to the gifts with reservation rules.

Pre-owned assets

(10)   Since 6 April 2005 where a potential inheritance tax liability does not arise under the gifts with reservation provisions a free-standing income tax charge will apply to the benefit of using an asset that was formerly owned by the taxpayer. A similar charge will apply to the use of assets at low cost or to the use of assets purchased with funds provided by the taxpayer. The charge applies to tangible and intangible assets. For details see **Example 23**.

Relief for double charges

(11)   Making a gift with reservation as outlined in **notes 4 and 5** is one of the occasions within the inheritance tax legislation where it is possible to get a double charge to tax. There are regulations to eliminate such double charges (SI 1987/1130). The operation of the regulations for gifts with reservation where the original gift was potentially exempt is illustrated in the Example. See **Example 20** for the other occasions when double charges arise and the detailed provisions of the regulations and **Example 23** for interaction with the pre-owned assets provisions.

More than one double charge

(12)   When most lifetime transfers were potentially exempt, there were few occasions in practice where the double charges regulations could come into effect. Following FA 2006, many more gifts are not potentially exempt and the occasions on which the double charges regulations will apply are increased. The regulations are very complex, and even so they do not cover the possibility of a single donor being affected by more than one occasion of double charge, such as for Example if Mr Smart had made a cash gift to his daughter, in addition to the gift with reservation, and the daughter had then made a loan back to Mr Smart. No guidance has been given on the procedure to be followed in such a case.

Same day transfers

(13)   Where transfers that are or become chargeable transfers are made on the same day, the annual exemption is apportioned between them (s 19(3)(b)) even if one of the transfers was chargeable immediately and the other was potentially exempt. For detailed notes on this point, see **Example 24 explanatory note 1**.

Capital gains implication of gifts with reservation

(14)   Where there are gifts with reservation, not only is the inheritance tax chargeable on the higher of the two bases as indicated in the Example, but for capital gains tax the tax-free uplift to market value on death does

not apply. Instead the donee's capital gains tax cost will be the market value at the date of the gift (subject to any available holdover relief claims).

Question

(a) Albert, a bachelor aged 70, sold his business for cash in the 1990s and subsequently carried out the following:

May 2004   Gave his younger sister Beryl cash of £142,000 (no previous gifts having been made)

June 2004   Created a discretionary trust with cash of £267,500, the trustees paying any tax due. The potential beneficiaries of the trust were his brothers and sisters and their children.

In June 2005 Beryl died. During her lifetime she had made an unsecured interest-free loan of £136,000 to her son's business. On her death she left to Albert the debt due from her son.

In July 2010 Albert died, leaving an estate of £329,000, including the £136,000 debt due from his nephew's business.

Calculate the tax payable as a result of Albert's death.

(b) In July 2010 Andrew died, aged 87. He had been a widower for many years and had supported his only grandson Barry in his business ventures. In May 2006 Andrew had made a gift of £166,000 to Barry to help launch a new product in his business.

In June 2006 Andrew had created a discretionary trust with cash of £306,000, including as beneficiaries his only daughter Clarice, her children and Barry's children. The trustees paid any tax due.

In June 2007 Andrew was taken ill and had to move into a nursing home. He sold his house and received a loan from Barry of £100,000 to help fund the fees.

In July 2010 the value of Andrew's estate was £50,000, excluding the debt of £100,000 to Barry.

Calculate the tax payable as a result of Andrew's death.

Answer

Double charges regulations

(a)   *Tax payable as a result of Albert's death*

Lifetime gifts

			£	£
May 2004	Gift to Beryl			142,000
Less:	Annual exemptions	2004/05	3,000	
		2003/04	3,000	6,000
Potentially exempt transfer				136,000

		Gross	Tax on 2004/05 scale
		£	£
June 2004	Gift to discretionary trust	267,500	900*

(* 267,500 – 263,000 = 4,500 @ 20%)

Tax payable by trustees			£900

On death of Albert — July 2010

(1)   *Including loan inherited from Beryl in Albert's estate and ignoring gift to Beryl in May 2004*

		Gross	Tax on 2010/11 scale
		£	£
June 2004	Gift to trust (within nil band)	267,500	–
July 2010	Estate on death	329,000	108,600*
		596,500	108,600*

(* 596,500 – 325,000 = 271,500 @ 40%)

Tax payable by trust		–
(No repayment of tax of £900 paid at time of gift)		
Tax payable by estate		108,600
Total tax payable		£108,600

(Note that if Albert had died earlier than June 2010, ie less than five years after Beryl's death, quick succession relief would have been available by reference to the tax paid in Beryl's estate on the £136,000 left to him by Beryl — see **Example 21**.)

(2)   *Including gift to Beryl in May 2004 and ignoring value of gift back in Albert's estate*

		Gross	Tax on 2010/11 scale
		£	£
May 2004	Gift to Beryl	136,000	–
June 2004	Gift to trust	267,500	31,400*
		403,500	
July 2010	Estate at death (excluding £136,000 loan)	193,000	77,200
		596,500	108,600

(* 403,500 – 325,000 = 78,500 @ 40%)

	Gross	Tax on 2010/11 scale
	£	£
Tax payable by Beryl's estate on gift from Albert (within nil band)		–
Tax payable by trust	31,400	
Less: taper relief 80% (6 to 7 yrs)	25,120	
	6,280	
Less: tax already paid at time of gift	900	5,380
Tax payable by Albert's estate		77,200
Total tax payable as a result of Albert's death		£82,580

As (1) shows the higher amount of tax payable, that calculation is used to calculate the tax liabilities (see **explanatory note 4**).

(b)   *Tax payable as a result of Andrew's death*

Lifetime gifts

		£	£
			166,000
May 2006 — Gift to Barry			
Less: Annual exemptions	2006/07	3,000	
	2005/06	3,000	6,000
Potentially exempt transfer			160,000

		Gross	Tax on 2006/07 scale
		£	£
June 2006	Gift to discretionary trust	306,000	4,200*

(* 306,000 – 285,000 = 21,000 @ 20%)

Tax payable by trustees	£4,200

On death of Andrew — July 2010

(1)   *Excluding £100,000 of May 2006 gift and not deducting debt in Andrew's death estate*

		Gross	Tax on 2010/11 scale
		£	£
May 2006	Gift to Barry (within nil band)	160,000	
Less:	amount subsequently lent back	100,000	
		60,000	
June 2006	Gift to trust	306,000	16,400*
		366,000	
July 2010	Estate at death	50,000	20,000
		416,000	36,400

(* 366,000 – 325,000 = 41,000 @ 40%)

Tax payable by trust		16,400	
Less:	taper relief 40% (4 to 5 yrs)	6,560	
		9,840	
Less:	tax already paid at time of gift	4,200	5,640
Tax payable by estate			20,000
Total tax payable as a result of Andrew's death			£25,640

(2) *Charging full gift in May 2006 and allowing debt as a deduction in Andrew's death estate*

		Gross	Tax on 2010/11 scale
		£	£
May 2006	Gift to Barry (within nil band)	160,000	–
June 2006	Gift to trust	306,000	56,400*
July 2010	Estate at death (50,000 – 100,000, see **note 7**)	–	–
		466,000	56,400

(* 466,000 – 325,000 = 141,000 @ 40%)

Tax payable by trust		56,400	
Less:	taper relief 40% (4 to 5 yrs)	22,560	
		33,840	
Less:	tax already paid at time of gift	4,200	29,640
Total tax payable as a result of Andrew's death			29,640

The second calculation shows the higher amount of tax payable, therefore that is the calculation used to compute the tax liability.

Explanatory Notes

Relief for double charges

(1) There are several occasions within the inheritance tax legislation where it is possible to get a double charge to tax. Double charges occur where there are gifts with reservation, under the pre-owned asset rules, where there are 'mutual transfers' (ie where a gift is made and the donee makes a gift back), and where a gift is made and the donee then lends money to the donor. The debt is disallowed in the donor's estate at death.

A debt is only deductible from an estate if

(i)   it was incurred for full consideration (s 5(5)) and without a realistically enforceable right of reimbursement, and

(ii)   it is not connected with any gifts received directly or indirectly by the lender from the deceased. (However this restriction does not apply if it can be shown that the loan was not made out of the property derived from the deceased and was not facilitated by the deceased's gifts.)

If a borrower repays a loan which would otherwise not be a deductible loan he is treated as making a potentially exempt transfer of the amount repaid at the time of repayment (FA 1986 s 103).

(2)   Regulations have been made under the authority of FA 1986 s 104, by SI 1987/1130, SI 2005/724 and SI 2005/3441 to eliminate double charges. In each case two calculations are made, and the calculation that produces the higher amount of tax is the one used. If both produce the same amount of tax, the first calculation stipulated in the regulations is treated as producing the higher amount and is thus the calculation used to determine the liabilities. Whether or not the total amount of tax works out the same, the burden of the tax may fall on different people (see **note 4** below).

Double charges relief for gifts with reservation

(3)   A lifetime gift with reservation may be either potentially exempt, for Example the gift of a house while reserving the right to live in it, or immediately chargeable, for Example where a gift is made to a discretionary trust in which the donor is a beneficiary. The method laid down in the 1987 double charges regulations for gifts with reservation (regulation 5) is firstly to charge the gift with reservation in the deceased's estate and ignore the lifetime transfer. The second calculation is to charge the lifetime transfer and leave the gift with reservation out of the deceased's estate. If the gift was a chargeable transfer on which inheritance tax had been paid when it was made, and the first calculation produces the higher figure, the tax paid in lifetime is deducted from the tax payable on death (but not exceeding the part of the death tax payable that relates to that transfer).

The rules are illustrated in **Examples 19, 24** and **32.**

Double charges relief for pre-owned assets

(4)   Where a taxpayer has a liability to income tax under the pre-owned assets rules following a transfer of value (see **Example 23** and **Tolley's Taxwise I 2010/11**) and elects to eliminate that charge by deeming the gifts with reservation provisions for inheritance tax to apply, then a double charge to inheritance tax could arise. This would occur if the taxpayer died within seven years of the original gift. Tax would arise on the original gift, and also on the property subject to the reservation. As in note 3 two calculations are made. The first is to charge the gift with reservation in the deceased estate and ignore the lifetime transfer. The second calculation charges the lifetime gift and excludes the value of the reservation. The higher tax liability applies.

These provisions (SI 2005/724 regulation 6) only apply where both the lifetime gift and the reservation relate to the same individual. Therefore, where in certain schemes, such as 'Eversden', one spouse or civil partner makes the lifetime gift, but the election under the pre-owned asset rules places the property in the estate of the other spouse or civil partner, no double charge relief is available.

(5)   A different form of potential double charge is relieved by SI 2005/3441, which responds to one means of unscrambling certain types of scheme that were attacked by the pre-owned assets legislation. A taxpayer might have sold his house to trustees of an interest in possession trust for himself on a basis that the price was left outstanding, giving rise to a debt owed by the trustees to the taxpayer. (The property itself, subject to the debt, would thus have remained within his estate for inheritance tax purposes, prior to 2006.) He might then have given away the benefit of that debt by way of a potentially exempt transfer; the value remaining in his estate, if he survived for seven years thereafter, would be the value of the property from time to time less the amount of the debt.

Arrangements of this sort were often found unattractive following the introduction of the pre-owned assets legislation, and as an alternative to making the election referred to in **explanatory note 4** it might have been wished to unscramble the scheme by placing the debt in the hands of a party who could (without breach of trust) write it off.

Double charges relief for gift and gift back

(6)   With regard to a gift and gift back where the first gift was initially potentially exempt but then becomes chargeable, the 1987 regulations (regulation 4) provide for the first calculation to include the gift back in the estate of the original donor and ignore the potentially exempt gift, and the second calculation to charge the potentially exempt gift and ignore the value of the gift back in the hands of the original donor.

This is illustrated in **part (a)** of the Example in relation to the gift by Albert to Beryl and her bequest to him of the debt owing from her son. The first calculation showed the higher amount of tax payable, so that calculation was used to calculate the tax liabilities.

Note how the incidence of tax may vary:

	Calculation 1 £	Calculation 2 £	Saving/(Loss) £
Payable by trust	–	5,380	5,380
Payable by estate	108,600	77,200	(31,400)

Double charges relief for gift and loan back

(7)   Where a gift is made, followed by a loan to the donor by the donee, with the donor dying within seven years when the debt is still outstanding, the first calculation under the 1987 regulations (regulation 6) is to ignore the debt and the part of the gift equal to the loan. The second is to charge the gift and also allow the debt. This is illustrated in **part (b)** of the Example, where the second calculation (charging the full gift to Barry and allowing the debt to Barry as a deduction in Andrew's estate) showed the higher amount of tax payable and was thus used to calculate the tax liabilities. Where the first calculation shows the higher amount, credit may be due for all or part of any tax paid on the gift in lifetime.

(8)   Normally Andrew's estate would be considered to be insolvent as the debt to Barry exceeds the available assets. This does not prevent a liability to inheritance tax arising on earlier gifts as that charge is made on the donees. The rules relating to gifts followed by subsequent loanbacks are designed to prevent avoidance of tax by the making of potentially exempt transfers at a time when death is very unlikely within seven years (and therefore term assurance is very cheap) followed by a loan of a similar amount thus removing assets from the tax computation whilst retaining effective control of both the capital and the income arising therefrom.

More than one double charge

(9)   The double charges regulations do not cover the possibility of a single donor being affected by more than one double charge, and no guidance has been given as to the procedure to be followed.

Transfers to trusts

(10)   Where transfers are made to most trusts (before 22 March 2006, confined primarily to discretionary trusts), tax liabilities may arise within the trust if there are any exits from the trust within ten years. For details see **Examples 59 to 63**. There will be no such liabilities in this Example, since the transfers in both parts (a) and (b) were of cash and were below the nil threshold at the death of the donor; but a charge could apply at the tenth anniversary of the gifts to the respective trusts (and on subsequent occasions), depending on the relation between the then value of the trust investments and the then nil rate band.

Question

On 6 April 2004 Basil made gifts to his brothers Simon and Charles of £149,000 each.

Basil died on 26 November 2006 leaving an estate of £200,000.

By his will he provided for a legacy to Charles of £90,000 (free of tax) with the residue to Simon.

On 12 March 2007 Simon died. His estate was valued at £322,000 including the residuary legacy from Basil. He left the whole of his estate to his surviving brother Charles.

Charles died on 10 May 2010 when his estate was worth £482,000.

Compute the tax payable by the personal representatives of each of the brothers on the assumption that none of the brothers had made any lifetime transfers other than those stated, and that no inheritance tax exemption applies on Charles's death.

Answer

Death of Basil — 26 November 2006

Tax on gifts made within seven years before death:

			Gross	Tax on 2006/07 scale
			£	£
6 April 2004	Gift to Simon		149,000	
	Gift to Charles		149,000	
			298,000	
	Less: Annual exemptions			
	2004/05	3,000		
	2003/04	3,000	6,000	
PETs now chargeable			292,000	2,800*

(* 292,000 – 285,000 = 7,000 @ 40%)

The £2,800 is not reduced by taper relief since the gifts are within three years before death.

		£
Tax payable —	Simon	1,400
	Charles	1,400
		2,800

Inheritance tax on Basil's Estate

	Gross	Tax
	£	£
Cumulative transfers within seven years before death	292,000	2,800
Estate on death	200,000	80,000
	492,000	82,800

Division of Estate

	£
Pecuniary legacy to Charles free of tax	90,000
Inheritance tax (see **explanatory note 3**)	80,000
Residue to Simon	30,000
	200,000

Death of Simon — 12 March 2007

Inheritance tax on death

	Gross	Tax on 2006/07 scale
	£	£
Cumulative transfers within seven years before death	–	–
Estate on death	322,000	14,800*
(* 322,000 – 285,000 = 37,000 @ 40%)		

Inheritance tax payable:

	£	£
Due on estate before QSR		14,800
Less: Quick succession relief		
Gift from Basil 6 April 2004 (£149,000 less £3,000 exempt, tax £1,400)		
2+ to 3 years before $60\% \times \dfrac{146,000 - 1,400}{146,000} \times 1,400$	832	
Residuary gift from Basil's estate 26 November 2006		
less than 1 year before $100\% \times \dfrac{30,000}{30,000 + 20,000} \times 20,000$	12,000	12,832
Inheritance tax payable by personal representatives of Simon		1,968

The estate passing to Charles is:

	£
Estate	322,000
Less: Inheritance tax	1,968
	320,032

Death of Charles — 10 May 2010

Inheritance tax on death

	Gross	Tax on 2010/11 scale
	£	£
Cumulative transfers within seven years before death	–	–
Estate on death	482,000	62,800*
(* 482,000 – 325,000 = 157,000 @ 40%)		

Inheritance tax payable:

	£	£
Due on estate before QSR		62,800

Less: Quick succession relief
Gift from Basil 6 April 2004
Over five years before Charles's death —
Legacy from Basil's estate 26 November 2006
3+ to 4 years before

$$40\% \times \frac{90,000}{90,000 + 60,000} \times 60,000 \qquad 14,400$$

Residuary gift from Simon's estate 12 March 2007

$$40\% \times \frac{320,032}{322,000} \times 1,968$$

3+ to 4 years before $\qquad\qquad\qquad$ 782 $\qquad$ 15,182

Inheritance tax payable by personal representatives of Charles $\qquad$ 47,618

Explanatory Notes

Quick succession relief

(1) Where a person dies shortly after receiving a chargeable transfer, the transfer has increased the estate at death and therefore attracts tax in the deceased's estate, as well as having been taxed at the time of the transfer. Relief is provided where the *death occurs* within five years after the chargeable transfer, known as quick succession relief (s 141). There is no requirement to retain the asset obtained by that transfer.

(2) The first step is to calculate the tax payable on the original transfer. A potentially exempt transfer becomes a chargeable transfer on the death of the donor within seven years. Although the tax is calculated using the rates applicable at the time of death, the date of transfer is relevant in calculating quick succession relief. The part of the transfer covered by the annual (or any other) exemption is not a chargeable transfer and is therefore excluded from the QSR calculation. As the donee is responsible for the tax on a PET, grossing up is not required.

(3) The inheritance tax payable on the death of Basil is a charge on the residue (see **Example 5 explanatory note 10**). Thus the amount receivable by Simon is the net £30,000. The estate rate is 40% so that the figures to use in the calculation of quick succession relief are a gross legacy of £50,000 (£30,000 × 10/6) with tax paid of £20,000. Put another way (in the terms of s 141) the tax of £80,000 on Basil's estate was attributable to the net gifts of £90,000 to Charles and £30,000 to Simon, so the parts of it attributable to those gifts were respectively:

$$80,000 \times \frac{90,000}{30,000 + 90,000} = 60,000$$

and

$$80,000 \times \frac{30,000}{30,000 + 90,000} = 20,000$$

(4) The total tax on the deceased's estate is reduced by the quick succession relief. Thus if his estate for inheritance tax includes assets outside his free estate, such as joint property or settled property in which he had an estate interest in possession, each fund benefits proportionally from the relief. This typically means a partial loss of relief to the fund which is suffering a second tax charge on the same value. See also **note 7** and **Example 53**.

(5)   Where death occurs within one year of the transfer the relief is 100% of the *tax paid on the previous transfer*, reduced in the proportion of net value transferred to the deceased over the gross chargeable transfer.

Where the period between transfer and death is over one year, the percentage becomes:

1+ to 2 years	80%
2+ to 3 years	60%
3+ to 4 years	40%
4+ to 5 years	20%

Donee dying before donor

(6)   If the donee dies before the donor then the original gift will continue to be a potentially exempt transfer at that time. Tax will be charged on the estate of the donee (including the gift) without relief. If the donor subsequently dies within seven years of the original gift then the original gift becomes a chargeable transfer, with the tax payable being a liability of the executors of the donee. The inheritance tax due on the death of the donee then needs to be recomputed, and quick succession relief may become available in the process. See **Example 55** for an illustration of this point.

Quick succession relief on trust property

(7)   Quick succession relief is also available where there are successive charges within five years on trust property in which there is an interest in possession. The rates of relief are the same as those in **note 5** above, with the percentage relief depending on the period between the successive charges (s 141). For a more complex Example of quick succession relief, showing the treatment of settled property and giving further detailed notes, see **Example 53**.

Other double charges reliefs

(8)   Quick succession relief applies where as in this Example successive transfers are charged in relation to different donors. There are other occasions under the inheritance tax rules where property can be charged twice in relation to the same donor. Regulations made under the authority of FA 1986 s 104 provide relief against double charges to tax in those circumstances (SI 1987/1130). This will normally be where there are gifts with reservation, pre-owned assets or non-deductible debts (see **Examples 19, 20** and **23**).

Question

In order to reduce the potential liability to inheritance tax on his accumulated wealth, Henry, aged 80, proposes the following:

(a)   To sell one of a pair of antique objects to his daughter at its market value of £40,000, and then in a year's time to give her the other of equal value.

The value of the pair is £130,000.

(b)   To sell 2% of his holding of 51% of the shares of Henry Ltd, a property investment company, to John, an unconnected friend, for its market value, then to give the remaining 49% of the shares to his son, Simon, who already holds 35% of the shares.

The market value of the shares in Henry Ltd is:

51%	holding	£800,000
49%	holding	£500,000
15–20%	holding	£100,000
2%	holding	£5,000

(c)   If the scheme in (b) above is unsuitable, Henry proposes giving 2% of his shares to 'Age UK', a recognised charity, then to give the remaining 49% of the shares to Simon.

(d)   A further suggestion is that next winter while Henry is on a cruise around the world Henry Ltd should make a rights issue of four shares for every one share held. Henry will not be back until after the issue has been made and will not be able to take up his entitlement.

Henry has made cash gifts every year to use up his annual exemption.

Advise him of the inheritance tax effect of each of the above proposals.

Answer

(a) Pair of antiques — sale followed by gift to daughter

There are two problems in relation to Henry's proposed sale and gift of the two antique objects.

The first is whether the sale at full value to his daughter will itself escape being treated as a transfer of value at that time, since although she would be paying full price for the object, his estate would actually fall by £50,000 (£130,000 – cash received £40,000 and value of remaining object £40,000). A sale at full value is not a transfer of value if it was not intended to confer a gratuitous benefit on anyone and was either made at arm's length (which this transaction is not) or was such as might be expected to have been made at arm's length (s 10). Since the daughter would be paying the full market price, which is the same amount as a stranger would have paid, the transaction will probably not be treated as a transfer of value at that time.

But when Henry gives his daughter the other object HMRC may use the associated operations rules of s 268 to treat the two events as one. There would then be a potentially exempt transfer on the second occasion of £90,000 (£130,000 – £40,000 cash received) which would become a chargeable transfer if Henry dies within seven years of the gift of the second object.

It would have been better for Henry to sell the pair of objects to his daughter for £40,000 in the first place, because the potentially exempt transfer of £90,000 would then be made one year earlier and the seven year survivorship period would start at that time.

(b) Shares – sale followed by gift to son

Again HMRC may use s 268 in determining the inheritance tax position on the gift of shares to Simon. The reason they might do so is that no inheritance tax implications would arise on the sale of shares to John, because in isolation this is a commercial transaction at arm's length and not a transfer of value and on the gift of shares to Simon inheritance tax would ordinarily be payable on death within seven years on a transfer of £500,000 (the value of a 49% holding), whereas but for the earlier sale the transfer would have been valued at the difference between a 51% holding (£800,000) and a 2% holding (£5,000), ie at £795,000. HMRC can be expected to look inter alia for any evidence that the gift was conceived before the sale had been completed.

If HMRC applied s 268 the value transferred to Simon would be as follows:

	£
Value of 51% before first of associated operations	800,000
Value of 0% after second of associated operations	–
	800,000
Less: Cash received (on the sale of the 2% holding)	5,000
Value transferred (potentially exempt transfer)	795,000

(c) Shares — gift to charity followed by gift to son

If Henry adopts the alternative of giving 2% of the shares to 'Age UK' the related property rules will be applied. These are contained in s 161. The rules provide (inter alia) that where property is transferred to a charity, political party etc by the taxpayer or his spouse/civil partner, such property is related to any other property of the taxpayer and his spouse/civil partner.

The property will continue to be related until five years after it is disposed of by the charity etc.

The value of appropriate parts of the related property is proportionate to the value of all related property, if this produces a higher value than the value of the appropriate part on its own.

Consequently the value transferred by Henry will be:

2% to charity — exempt transfer
49% to son — value before transfer

Own holding		49%	
Related holding		2%	
Value of	51%	=	£800,000

Henry's 49% holding is therefore worth $\frac{49}{51} \times £800,000 =$ 768,627

Value of Henry's holding after transfer   nil
Value of transfer (which is a potentially exempt transfer)   £768,627

The above computation would apply unless Henry deferred the gift of shares to Simon until five years after 'Age UK' had disposed of their shares. If the transfer took place after that time the potentially exempt transfer would be:

Value transferred (49% holding — assuming no change in values)   £500,000

Care would need to be taken over any pre-emption rights in Henry Limited's Articles of Association, if 'Age UK' seeks to dispose of the shares given to it. Any failure by Henry (or for that matter Simon) to exercise pre-emption rights given to other shareholders by the Articles could itself give rise to a disposition by them under s 3(3) (see (D) BELOW), and any such disposition by Henry may well be taken with his original gift to 'Age UK' as associated operations. Any resultant loss to his estate would then itself constitute a transfer of value by him.

(d) Failure to take up rights shares

Henry's proposal concerning the rights issue is covered by s 3(3), which provides that the deliberate omission to exercise a right is a transfer of value.

The issue of rights shares in the circumstances outlined would be caught by this subsection.

The value transferred would be:

	£
Value before transfer (51%)	800,000

Value after transfer:

	Original Shares	Rights Shares	Total
Henry	51	–	51
Son	35	140	175
Others	14	56	70
	100	196	296

Value of

$$\frac{51}{296} = 17.23\% \; holding$$

	100,000
Value transferred (potentially exempt transfer)	700,000

Because s 3(3) treats the deliberate omission as a disposition such an act would constitute an actual transfer of value and s 3A would apply treating the transfer as potentially exempt.

There would also be a CGT liability.

Explanatory Notes

Associated operations

(1)   The associated operations rules are contained in IHTA 1984 s 268. Certain associated operations are specifically covered by other legislation, viz:

Related property — s 161 (see **note 5**)

Omission to exercise a right — s 3(3) (see **part (d)** of the Example)

Alteration of capital — s 98 (see **note 7**)

(2)   One cannot be certain whether the Revenue will seek to use the associated operations rules in any particular case, but IHTA 1984 s 268 covers:

(i)   Two or more operations of any kind affecting the same property or property which represents whether directly or indirectly that property, or income arising from that property, or property representing accumulations of such income (s 268(1)(a)).

(ii)   Any two operations of which one is effected with reference to the other, or with a view to enabling the other to be effected, or facilitating its being effected and any further operation having a like relation to any of those two and so on (s 268(1)(b)).

The operations might be effected by the same person or different persons and might or might not be simultaneous (s 268(1)).

'Operation' includes an omission (s 268(1)).

(3)   Where a transfer of value is made by associated operations carried out at different times, it is treated as made at the time of the last of them (s 268(3)). But where one or more of the earlier operations also constitutes a transfer of value made by the same transferor, the value transferred by the earlier operations is treated as reducing the value transferred by all the operations taken together, except to the extent that the earlier operations were exempt because of the spouse transfer rules (s 18) but all operations taken together were not so exempt (s 268).

Series of settlements

(4)   The taxpayer was successful in the Court of Appeal, in the case of *Rysaffe Trustee Co (CI) Ltd v IRC* (2003) in contending that the associated operations provisions did not apply where five separate identical settlements were created on five separate dates within the same month (see **Example 62 explanatory note 12**). A subsequent decision of a Special Commissioner (*Smith v IRC* (2007)) distinguished the *Rysaffe* decision where three annuities and three life assurance policies were issued on the same date: in that case the associated operations provisions did apply.

Interaction of associated operations and related property provisions

(5)   HMRC Inheritance Tax have indicated (in correspondence with Butterworths Tolley – see Taxation 15 February 1996) how the related property and associated operations provisions would interact where assets were transferred in stages, with some being routed via a spouse (or, now, a civil partner). The Example illustrated is of a set of four antique chairs, of which two are given by husband to wife, and each then gives one to their son in successive years. The related property rules would value each of the first transfers to the son at half of the value of the set of four less half the value of a set of two, and the second transfers at half the value of a set of two, thus bringing into account the whole of the value of the set of four, half being a transfer by the husband and the other half a transfer by the wife.

If the associated operations rules were invoked at the time the son became the owner of the set, the transfers by the wife would be treated as made by the husband (and so would not be taken into account in her own inheritance tax calculations). The overall effect would be the same in terms of the value transferred, but the whole of the transfer would affect the husband's estate.

See **Example 23** for other illustrations of associated operations.

Grant of a lease

(6)   The granting of a lease for full consideration in money or money's worth is not associated with any operation effected more than three years after the grant (s 268(2)).

By granting a lease, even for full value, a property owner restricts his rights over that property. If he were then to make a gift of those rights (ie the right to receive the rent under the lease and the freehold reversion) the full value of both rights might be less than that of the unencumbered freehold. He might therefore first grant a lease followed by a gift, instead of giving the freehold out of which the donee could grant the lease.

The associated operations rules will not apply if the gift is more than three years after the grant of the lease.

Alteration of rights re shares

(7)   If, instead of a rights issue being made that is available equally to all shareholders, the unquoted share or loan capital of a close company is altered (or there is any alteration in the rights attaching to such shares or debentures) then s 98 applies. This provides that such a change is to be treated as a disposition made by the participators. Such a transfer cannot be a potentially exempt transfer (s 98(3)).

Where there are deferred shares, an alteration of rights within s 98(1)(b) takes place when the deferred shares come to rank equally, or become merged, with shares of another class.

Business property relief

(8)   Business property relief is not available on the shares in Henry Ltd because it is a company that invests in land and buildings (s 105(3)).

Gifts with reservation etc

(9)   In addition to the associated operations legislation donors must also be fully aware of the rules relating to gifts with reservation and the treatment of certain debts. These are illustrated in **Examples 19, 20** and **23**.

Question

A.

Lucton, a widower aged 80, lives with his unmarried and only daughter Frances at Hayseeds, a bungalow currently valued at £250,000.

His only other asset of significance is £300,000 invested in a building society account.

He has already made a transfer of £80,000 in the last but one tax year, £6,000 of which was covered by annual exemptions and the balance of £74,000 was a potentially exempt transfer.

He is conscious that the value of the bungalow is likely to increase, thus worsening the potential inheritance tax position upon his death, when the bungalow is to devolve upon Frances.

Three schemes have been suggested to him for the mitigation of inheritance tax:

(a)   That the bungalow is given to Frances now, but that he continues to live in it with her, since at least this would ensure that whilst the gift less the annual exemption would be a chargeable transfer if he died within seven years, future growth would be in the hands of Frances and not his own.

(b)   That the bungalow is sold to Frances for its current market value but that the purchase price would be left on loan to her. Lucton would then waive £3,000 of the loan each year, the waiver being covered by his annual exemption for inheritance tax.

(c)   That the bungalow is retained by Lucton and instead £300,000 in cash is given to Frances. As Lucton would then have no liquid assets, Frances would each year lend £20,000 to Lucton to enable him to maintain his present lifestyle.

Discuss whether any of these schemes will be successful in mitigating inheritance tax.

B.

A wealthy client, Mr Douglas, who is *not* a farmer, has been involved in the following transactions during the current tax year. All land has been owned by Mr Douglas for more than ten years.

(a)   He divided his land at Ambridge into Upper and Lower Ambridge. He gave Lower Ambridge to his son Kirk and he and Kirk commenced to use the two properties in partnership. None of the land is partnership property.

(b)   He granted a lease of Green Gables at a nominal rent to his wife and himself as tenants in common; he then gave the freehold reversion to his daughter Anne. Thereafter he occupied Green Gables with his wife.

(c)   He granted a landlord's repairing lease of Blackacre at a commercial rent to his wife and himself. He then gave the freehold reversion to Anne.

Explain, with references to statute and case law as appropriate, whether any of these transactions are likely to constitute a gift with reservation for inheritance tax purposes.

C.

Mrs Jones, a wealthy widow, wished to reduce her estate's liability to inheritance tax. In order to do so she gave Catherine, her only daughter, £500,000 in cash in May 2007. Her daughter then bought a property in Cornwall in February 2008 for £700,000. Catherine had invested the £500,000 in the stock market, realising those investments for just £420,000 in January 2008 in order to help pay for the property. Mrs Jones looked round this property with Catherine but did not stay there; however in early 2010 she decided that she would like to live there each summer, and with Catherine's agreement she took up residence on 6 April 2010. For the remainder of the year Mrs Jones continues to live in her London residence. Although Mrs Jones is aged 72 she is in good health and would be expected to live for another 15+ years. She is a 40% income taxpayer. For 2010/11 the annual rental value of the Cornwall property would be £36,000 pa and its open market value on 6 April 2010 is £900,000. Mrs Jones has no legal obligation to contribute towards the costs of that property.

(a)   Explain why an income tax charge might arise, and set out how long Mrs Jones could spend at the Cornwall property before a computation needs to be carried out.

(b)

    (i)   Compute the 2010/11 income tax liability arising for a full year's occupation based upon the above facts,

    (ii)   set out how long Mrs Jones could occupy the property in the coming years without in fact incurring an income tax charge, and

    (iii)   state how soon this aspect would need to be reconsidered.

(c)   Set out any available election to mitigate that charge (assuming that inheritance tax rates and rules remain unchanged).

Answer

A. Lucton — proposals to mitigate inheritance tax

(a) Gift of property while continuing to live in it

By continuing to live in the bungalow with Frances, Lucton will be retaining a benefit from the gift.

In order to make an effective transfer it is necessary to show that the subject matter of the gift is enjoyed to the entire or virtually the entire exclusion of the donor and of any benefit to him by contract or otherwise. The transfer of ownership to Frances, with Lucton continuing to live there, would not, therefore, be a viable way of mitigating the inheritance tax position, since in the case of land or a chattel the actual occupation or possession is only disregarded if it is made for full consideration.

In this case no consideration is proposed. If a full rent was paid by Lucton for his occupation of the bungalow this could give rise to a charge to income tax on Frances (subject to any 'rent a room' relief) and could also affect her capital gains exemption in respect of owner occupation of the bungalow.

Occupation of land is also disregarded where the occupation by the donor results from a change of circumstances arising since the time of the gift, being a change which was unforeseen at that time and was not brought about by the donor to save inheritance tax. Furthermore the occupation must occur at a time when the donor has become unable to maintain himself through old age or infirmity and must represent a reasonable provision by a donee who is a relative for the care and maintenance of the donor. Clearly Lucton would not qualify under this heading as he already occupies the bungalow and will continue to live there.

The original transfer to Frances, less the current and previous years' annual exemptions, will be a potentially exempt transfer, becoming chargeable if Lucton dies within seven years. As a gift with reservation the property will, however, continue to form part of Lucton's estate for the purpose of the inheritance tax charge on his death. The value of the property will only be taken out of Lucton's estate if it ceases to be property subject to a reservation. In that event Lucton would be deemed to make a potentially exempt transfer to Frances equal to the value of the property at that time, in addition to the potentially exempt transfer made when he gave her the property (and without the benefit of any annual exemptions). There are regulations to eliminate any double tax charge (see **Example 20**).

If Lucton made a gift of an *undivided share of the bungalow* to Frances and both she and Lucton continue to live at Hayseeds then the reservation of benefit rules will not apply provided the gift is unconditional and there is no collateral benefit to Lucton (see **Example 19 explanatory note 7**). The payment by Frances of Lucton's share of the running costs (which where appropriate might be proportional to use rather than just to ownership) would be such a benefit. The protection of this provision would however not apply if Frances later ceased to occupy the property, or died.

(b) Sale of property with purchase price left on loan

If the bungalow were sold to Frances at its current market value, the purchase price being left on loan to her and then waived at £3,000 per annum (as to which see **explanatory note 3**), HMRC would probably argue that the associated operations rules should apply. They may also take that view if, instead of waiving parts of the debt, Lucton were to make periodic cash gifts to Frances to use his annual exemptions; but it is less easy to accept that the associated operations rule could apply in that event so long as Frances is not seen to make corresponding repayments of the loan.

If later gifts of either sort are properly treated as associated operations with the sale, the value of the bungalow at the time of the last waiver would have to be ascertained, and any excess of that value over its value at the time of the sale would be treated as a potentially exempt transfer at the time of the last of the waivers.

Thus, the mitigation of the potential inheritance tax liability by disposing of an appreciating asset for its present value in consideration for a non-appreciating loan debtor would be negated. The annual exemptions will, however, have been used against any waivers, avoiding them being wasted if there was no other facility for using them, and effectively limiting the potential chargeable transfer to the increase in value between the time of the last waiver and that of the actual transfer (the amount of the debt not waived at the time of death would itself form part of the estate). However in view of Lucton's age, it is probable that most of the value will fall to be charged to inheritance tax on death.

The fact that interest on the loan was or was not charged does not apparently affect HMRC's attitude.

(c) Cash gift followed by loans back

The gift of £300,000 cash by Lucton to Frances, less the current and previous years' annual exemptions totalling £6,000, would be a potentially exempt transfer provided possession and enjoyment is fully assumed by Frances. This means that there would be no immediate liability to tax. If Lucton died within seven years of his earlier potentially exempt transfer of £74,000, tax would be payable on the gift to Frances, unless the nil threshold had in the meantime increased above £368,000 (ie £294,000 + £74,000). Taper relief would reduce any tax payable if Lucton survived the gift to Frances by three years, and after seven years the gift would cease to be potentially liable to tax.

However, if Lucton retains a benefit by way of contract or otherwise the gift is negated. If the amount repaid to Lucton is by way of loan then this will also affect the position, as any debt incurred after 17 March 1986 that arises from a disposition made by the borrower will not be a deductible debt on death. (But if, as is implied, Lucton uses the £20,000 cash each year to support his lifestyle, he will not have accumulated that money as savings upon which inheritance tax could be levied.) Furthermore any repayment of that debt by Lucton will be a further transfer, albeit potentially exempt.

If the amounts paid to him by Frances after his gift to her could be treated as a disposition made in favour of a dependent relative for his reasonable care and maintenance they would not be a transfer of value by Frances (s 11(3)), and may not be regarded by HMRC as a reservation of benefit to Lucton if at the time of the original gift by him there was genuinely no expectation that they would be paid. On the facts given, it might be hard to resist a suggestion of reservation; but if Lucton had limited his cash gift to say £170,000 (retaining £130,000 to cover his expenses over the next few years by which time he would be in his mid to late 80s) it would be harder for HMRC to make that link.

B. Douglas — land transactions

(a) Gift of land subsequently used by partnership of donor and donee

Unless the use of Lower Ambridge by Mr Douglas (through the partnership) is for full consideration then the transfer would appear to be a gift with reservation, as the property is not enjoyed to the entire (or virtually entire) exclusion of the donor (FA 1986 s 102). If, however, the two properties are of similar value and profit sharing and capital sharing ratios are equal, then full consideration would appear to be given and the gifts with reservation rules and pre-owned asset provisions would not apply (FA 1986 Sch 20 para 6).

All of the relevant circumstances would have to be taken into account to determine full consideration. These would include profit shares, values, actual input to the partnership and any actual rent paid.

(b) Division of asset followed by gift of part

Where a donor splits an asset into parts and then makes a gift of the whole of a part without retaining an interest in that part then the gifts with reservation rules are in principle avoided, though the rules were tightened in 1999 insofar as landed property is concerned. In this Example Mr Douglas has divided Green Gables into a leasehold interest and a freehold reversion and then given the freehold reversion to his daughter Anne. Mr Douglas and his wife continue to occupy Green Gables under the leasehold interest.

Until FA 1999 this would have been outside the rules for gifts with reservation, although unless the grant of the lease and the subsequent gift of the freehold reversion were independent transactions, HMRC might have sought to use the associated operations rules of s 268 to say that the grant of the lease and the gift of the freehold reversion were a single transaction occurring at the time of the gift of the freehold, so that the lease at a nominal rent would be a benefit retained by Mr Douglas. Under FA 1986 s 102A, from 9 March 1999 it is no longer possible to avoid the gifts with reservation rules by taking a leasehold interest and giving away the freehold (see **explanatory note 6**). Mr Douglas's gift of the freehold of Green Gables to Anne will therefore be treated as a gift with reservation.

(c) Grant of lease followed by gift of freehold

In giving away a freehold reversion Douglas must not reserve a benefit in that gift. In the case of *Nichols v CIR 1975* it was held that where a gift was made of freehold land, subject to an obligation on the donee to grant an immediate lease back and to keep the property in full repair, this amounted to a gift with reservation. But in Mr Douglas's case (i) the lease was created before the gift of the freehold, rather than reserved out of it, and (ii) he is paying a full commercial rent, so it is considered that the daughter's obligation to repair the property would be reflected in the rent and that no benefit would be regarded as having been reserved. FA 1986, s 102A (introduced by FA 1999 as referred to in (b) above) does not apply where the donor's right to occupy the land to the exclusion of the donee depends on full consideration.

C. Mrs Jones – pre-owned assets

(a) Attribution of cash gift towards property now occupied

A charge to income tax arises in principle because Mrs Jones has contributed towards a property she now occupies.

An absolute gift of cash is not normally subject to the inheritance tax gifts with reservation provisions. However under the pre-owned asset income tax rules a charge will apply where it is reasonable to attribute the gift as a contribution directly or indirectly, towards the acquisition of the property now occupied. This does not apply if the outright gift of money was made at least seven years before the taxpayer first occupied the premises. For Mrs Jones the period is only 2 years 10 months.

Occupation is a very wide term and could even include usage for storage or sole possession of the means of access linked with occasional use of the property. Incidental usage is not considered to be occupation. This could include:

- Stays not exceeding two weeks each year (one month if the owner is present and it is the owner's residence).

- Social visits that do not include overnight stays.

- Domestic visits eg babysitting the owner's children.

- Temporary stays eg for convalescence after medical treatment or to look after the owner whilst they are convalescing.

However if the property is a holiday home which is only used on an occasional basis by the owner then even occasional visits by the donor could be deemed to be occupational.

It would appear that Mrs Jones wishes to use the Cornwall property for a number of weeks each year. Unless she pays full market rent for that occupation (which would be liable to income tax in the hands of her daughter) she will be liable to a pre-owned asset income tax charge. If she keeps her possessions at the property, and even more so if she retains a key to it, for the rest of the year then there is a risk she will be regarded as occupying it for the whole year not just for the weeks she physically spends there; the remainder of this Example assumes that she does not fall foul of this and that we are concerned only with the time she actually spends there.

If her occupation was for less than one month per year no charge would arise provided her daughter lived in the property as her residence and was present, otherwise occupation could cause the charge to occur.

In practice it would be advisable to pay full market rent for limited occupation of holiday accommodation.

(b) Income tax liability on pre-owned asset

(i) 2010/11 with occupation for whole year

To apply the pre-owned assets rules in the case of a property contributed to (rather than disposed of) by the taxpayer, it is necessary to ascertain the part of the property's value, at the valuation date (6 April 2010 on the facts given), that can reasonably be attributed to the consideration provided by the taxpayer.

On the facts, Mrs Jones' contribution to the £700,000 price of the Cornwall property she now occupies was not the full £500,000 original gift but the £420,000 into which it can clearly be traced; so the proportion of the purchase price attributable to her contribution was:

$$\frac{420,000}{700,000} = 60\%$$

(Equally, if Catherine's investments had gone up rather than down in value this increased value would be taken into account where traceable into the purchase,)

The appropriate rental value for (in effect) the first five tax years in which Mrs Jones occupies the property is thus:

$$£36,000 \times \frac{60\% \times 900,000}{900,000} = £21,600$$

which gives an income tax liability for 2010/11, based on a full tax year of occupation, of: £21,600 @ 40% = £8,640.

Depending on the level of Mrs Jones' taxable income within the 40% bracket (£37,401 to £150,000), the extra £21,600 of income could in practice lead to a greater increase in her tax liability than the basic £8,640, through loss of part or all of her personal allowance. This would arise if her income before the pre-owned assets charge was between £78,400 and £112,950 (at which latter level the personal allowance would already have been fully extinguished). If her income apart from the pre-owned assets rules was over £108,400 (£130,000 – £21,600) and she or an employer was contributing to a pension scheme for her, the pre-owned assets income would also give rise to a need to value those pension contributions to ascertain how far they then led to a supplementary income tax so as in effect to restrict pension relief to the basic rate.

(ii) Occupation for only part of tax year

This full-year income figure of £21,600 would be scaled down according to the part of the tax year for which Mrs Jones is to be regarded as being in occupation (as to which see **(a) above**). Therefore if her occupation is for no more than 84 days in the tax year (and there were no other pre-owned assets income to take into account), her 2010/11 liability would be nil because the de minimis level of £5,000 of pre-owned assets income is not exceeded:

$$\frac{84}{365} \times £21,600 = £4,970$$

Because this de minimis provision creates a full exemption from the pre-owned assets rules, there is in that situation no additional income to be taken into account in connection with the restriction of the personal allowance or of pension relief.

(iii) When must the figures be reappraised?

The valuation date is initially the date when the taxpayer first went into occupation, and 6 April in each subsequent tax year; but the value of the property itself, and its annual rental value, are reassessed not yearly but in five-year cycles. (In consequence the proportion of the value at the valuation date that is attributable to the taxpayer's contribution will also be fixed for five years at a time before it needs to be reappraised; in practice, on any such reappraisal, an adjustment will generally only be made where further money has been spent in the meantime, whether or not contributed to by the taxpayer, which is reflected in the value of the property at the five-year anniversary.)

It therefore follows that Mrs Jones can, on the values stated, be sure of falling within the de minimis exemption if she restricts her occupation to a maximum of 84 days in each tax year until and including 2014/15. The market value and rental value of the property would be reassessed at 6 April 2015, as would the proportion of the value that is attributable to Mrs Jones's contribution(s) – including any further contributions made while since the original purchase of the property.

(See **explanatory note 11**)

(c) Election to mitigate charge

Mrs Jones could elect by 31 January 2012, by completing form IHT500, that the Cornwall property is not subject to an income tax charge, but instead, for so long as she continues to occupy the property, the chargeable proportion of the property value will be treated as part of her estate. The chargeable proportion will be broadly as in **(b) above**, namely such part of the value of the property at the valuation date as can reasonably be attributed to the consideration she provided; but since the valuation date for this purpose is the date of Mrs Jones' death, the proportion will reflect:

(i)   any further capital expenditure on the property by Catherine in the meantime, and

(ii)   any other contributions made by Mrs Jones (after, as well as before, she went into occupation),

in each case so far as reflected in the value of the property at that time.

If Mrs Jones ceases to occupy the Cornwall property then, as for a gift with reservation, the appropriate proportion of the value of the property (on similar principles but calculated at the date she ceases to occupy) will form part of her cumulative lifetime transfers for inheritance tax, as a deemed potentially exempt transfer, if her death occurs within the following seven years.

If Mrs Jones is unlikely to occupy the property for more than two or three years it would be beneficial to elect for inheritance tax to apply as there is a high probability that she would live more than seven years after vacating the property and therefore no tax charge would arise.

If Mrs Jones intends to remain in residence indefinitely it is possible that even 15+ years of charge to income tax would be less than the initial inheritance tax saving of £200,000 (£500,000 @ 40%). The actual inheritance tax payable would, of course, be higher if the value of the property increased over that period. For Example if on the death of Mrs Jones the Cornwall property was worth £1,800,000 (and she had made no further payments reflected in its then value) then the inheritance tax liability on her death in respect of her use of the pre-owned asset might be seen as:

$$1,800,000 \times \frac{420,000}{700,000} = £1,080,000 @ 40\% = £432,000$$

However, the comparison of the potential accumulated income tax charge, weighed against the potential eventual inheritance tax saving, would of course need to take account of the fact that revaluations for the pre-owned assets charge, such as for rental value, fall to be made every five years.

(See **explanatory note 13**)

Explanatory Notes

Associated operations

(1)   Where a transfer of value is made by associated operations carried out at different times, it is treated as made at the time of the last of them (s 268). For the meaning of 'associated operations' see **Example 22**.

(2)   Where any one or more of the earlier operations also constitutes a *transfer of value* made by the same transferor, the value transferred by the earlier operations is treated as reducing the value transferred by all the operations taken together (s 268).

(3)   Thus, the annual waivers in **part a (b)** of the Example, being themselves *transfers of value*, albeit potentially exempt, reduce the value transferred by taking all the operations together. The fact that the waivers are not chargeable does not alter the fact that they were transfers of value (as distinct from chargeable transfers), a chargeable transfer being a transfer of value other than an exempt transfer (s 2(1)).

Ensuring that gifts are properly made

(4)   Care should always be taken to ensure that a gift is properly made. Whilst title to certain assets passes by delivery (eg a watch) there are legally proper ways of transferring title to other assets, such as company shares by a properly constituted and stamped form of transfer and freehold and leasehold properties by

deed (and registration where appropriate). An intended but incomplete gift will not therefore be sufficient for tax purposes, although in fact the donee might enjoy the benefit of the gift. If the donor has done all in his power to perfect a gift, an omission by the donee will not make it imperfect for tax purposes (eg if the donor has delivered a properly constituted and stamped share transfer but the donee has failed to have it registered or the company concerned has refused to register it). A cheque only constitutes a valid gift after it has been cleared by the donor's bank, so that if the donor dies before the cheque has been presented the gift is not complete.

In the 2004 case before the Special Commissioners of *Sellars & Anor* (SpC 401) it was held that where a building society account was changed to the name of a mother and two daughters, but mother was the only person who made transfers into the account and made withdrawals, that the whole of the balance remained in mother's estate even though one-third of the interest had been declared for income tax on the returns of each of the daughters. This was held to be a gift with reservation, not an account held as tenants in common.

As far as loan waivers are concerned, HMRC Inheritance Tax consider that they are not effective for inheritance tax unless the waiver was effected by deed.

Gifts with reservation

(5)   FA 1986 ss 102 and 103 introduced anti-avoidance legislation relating to gifts with reservation and debts, applicable to events occurring on and after 18 March 1986. These rules apply where a donor reserves a benefit from a gift or subsequently enjoys the benefit of the gifted property (eg gift of a house that the donor continues to occupy, or a settlement into a discretionary trust where the settlor is also a beneficiary).

Under these rules a gift with reservation is treated in the same way as any other gift at the time it is made, but special rules apply on the death of the donor. If the reservation ceased more than seven years before death then no charge arises on death. If the reservation ceased within seven years before death then the gift is taxed as if it had been made as a potentially exempt transfer at the time it ceased, on the basis of its value at that time (but without the benefit of any annual exemptions), even though the original gift will also be taxed if it was made within seven years before death. There are regulations to eliminate the double charge to tax. For details see **Example 19**.

Debts are not deductible from the estate of a deceased person unless they were incurred for full consideration for the deceased's own use or benefit and were not created out of property derived from the deceased as a transfer of value or part of an associated operation. Again there are regulations to prevent double charges to tax, which are dealt with in **Example 20**.

(6)   In relation to gifts of land, the gifts with reservation rules are extended by FA 1986 ss 102A, 102B and 102C. The background to the legislation is the 1999 House of Lords' decision in *Ingram v CIR* and the effect of old estate duty law on the inheritance tax provisions.

Some of the estate duty cases drew very fine distinctions. In *Chick v Commissioners of Stamp Duties of New South Wales* (1958), a farmer had made a gift of grazing land to his son in 1934 and in 1935 the land was brought into a partnership in which the farmer was a partner. The farmer was deemed to have reserved a benefit in the land because of his partnership interest. The *Chick* case was followed by legislation under which no reservation was assumed if the later benefits were only available because of full consideration provided by the donor. In *Munro v Commissioners of Stamp Duties of New South Wales* (1934), a farmer gave away land but continued as a partner in the family partnership that farmed the land. He was considered not to have given the land itself, but his interest in the land subject to the rights of the partnership, so that no benefit had been retained. The difference between the two cases is that the *Chick* gift was initially unfettered but the farmer later enjoyed a benefit from the gifted property, whereas the *Munro* gift was subject to the partnership interest at the time it was made. It was stated by Lord Simonds in *St Aubyn v AG* (1952) that a donor does not bring himself within the provisions 'by retaining something which he has never given'.

This principle was considered in the case of *Ingram v CIR*, decided by the House of Lords in 1999. Lady Ingram conveyed the freehold of her property to a bare trustee, who then granted a lease to her and conveyed the freehold reversion to a trust for the family. The High Court held that there was no reservation of benefit, although it was also held that someone could not grant a lease to a nominee, since this would amount to contracting with himself. The Court of Appeal held that the lease was a nullity as the interposing of a mere nominee did not alter the fact that Lady Ingram was effectively both landlord and tenant of the property (*Rye v Rye* (1962)). It was also noted that a nominee cannot effectively contract with his principal (following the Scottish case of *Kildrummy (Jersey) Ltd v CIR* (1990)). This was overruled by the House of Lords, where it was held that 'if the benefits which the donor continues to enjoy are by virtue of property which was never comprised in the gift, he has not reserved any benefit out of the property of which he disposed'. The House of Lords unanimously declined to follow *Kildrummy*, stating that 'a trustee in English law is not an agent for his beneficiary'.

This decision has led to the changes in the law referred to above where a gift is made of an interest in land (for details see **Example 19 explanatory notes 5 to 7**).

Pre-owned assets

(7)   With effect from 6 April 2005 a free-standing income tax charge applies to the benefit of using an asset that was formerly owned by the taxpayer. A similar charge will apply to the use of assets at low cost or to the use of assets purchased with funds provided by the taxpayer. The charge applies to tangible and intangible assets.

(8)   The income tax charge does not apply:

(i)   To property given away before 18 March 1986 (FA 2004 Sch 15 para 3(2); para 6(2) and para 8(2)).

(ii)   If the property was transferred to a spouse/civil partner (or to a former spouse/civil partner under a Court Order) (Sch 15 para 10(1)(c)). This also applies where the property is held in trust and the spouse/civil partner or former spouse/civil partner has an interest in possession (Sch 15 para 10(1)(d)) – there is no requirement that this be an estate interest in possession within IHTA 1984, s 49(1).

(iii)   If the property remains within the estate of the former owner under the 'Gift with Reservation' rules (Sch 15 para 11). Note that FA 2006 s 80 amended FA 2004 Sch 15 para 11 with retrospective effect to provide an exception from the exemption provisions in respect of some interests in possession including those which arose before the exception was introduced.

(iv)   If the property was sold by the taxpayer at an arm's length price (Sch 15 para 10(1)(a)).

(v)   A disposition is ignored for the pre-owned asset rules if it is prevented from being a transfer of value by IHTA 1984, s 17, relating to deeds of variation and certain other post-death rearrangements (Sch 15, para 16). The provision is poorly drafted and would technically not protect, for Example, a variation that gave effect to a negotiated compromise of a dispute over the devolution of the deceased's estate.

(vi)   To property transferred into an interest in possession trust for the benefit of the former owner. This is excluded from the income tax charge because the property remains in the estate of the donor for inheritance tax purposes (Sch 15 para 11(1)) (now only applicable where the interest in possession is a disabled person's interest, since any other retained interest in possession is not an estate interest in possession). However the exemption ceases when the interest in possession comes to an end (Sch 15 para 10(2)) although this would now amount to a gift with reservation under FA 1986 s 102ZA.

(vii)   Where the gift is of property and the former owner has given part of their interest to someone with whom they share occupation or the former owner needs to move back into the gifted property following changes in circumstances (Sch 15 para 11(5)(d)). These rules are the same as gift with reservation rules for inheritance tax.

(viii) The disposal was an outright gift wholly covered by annual small gifts exemptions, or was for the maintenance of the family (Sch 15 para 10(1)(d), (e)).

(ix)   An outright gift of money made more than seven years before the first date of enjoyment of property/chattels acquired with the funds will not be deemed to be consideration (Sch 15 para 10(2)(c)).

(x)   Use of a commercial equity release scheme.

(9)   The pre-owned asset charge does not apply in any fiscal year:

(a)   Where the former owner is not resident in the UK, or

(b)   Where the former owner is resident in the UK but domiciled elsewhere for inheritance tax purposes and the property is not UK property, or

(c)   Where the former owner was previously domiciled outside the UK for inheritance tax purposes the charge does not apply to property disposed of before becoming domiciled in the UK (Sch 15 para 12).

(10)   The income tax charge applies to the use of land or enjoyment of land, chattels and intangible assets (defined as everything other than land or chattels).

For the charge to apply to land the taxpayer must:

- occupy the land (wholly or with others) and

- either the disposal condition or the contribution condition must apply (Sch 15 para 3(1)).

The disposal condition is that at any time after 17 March 1986 the taxpayer owned an interest in the relevant property, or in property the disposal of which has directly or indirectly funded the relevant property, and has disposed of all or part of that interest otherwise than by an excluded transaction (see **note 8** above).

The contribution condition is that the taxpayer has since 17 March 1986 contributed directly or indirectly to the purchase of the relevant property otherwise than by an excluded transaction (see **note 8** above).

(11)   Different rules apply to quantify the deemed income to be charged, depending on whether the charge arises on land, chattels or intangibles.

Land

The charge for land is calculated by taking the appropriate rental value less any amount that the taxpayer is legally obliged to pay the owner of the relevant land in the period in respect of its occupation. The appropriate rental value is:

$$R \times \frac{DV}{V}$$

where:

R is the rent that might reasonably be expected to be obtained on a year to year letting where tenant pays all rates, charges and council taxes and the landlord bears the cost of repairs, maintenance and insurance.

DV depends on the circumstances:

- if the taxpayer previously owned the property or an interest in it, DV is the value of that interest on the valuation date, or the appropriate proportion of that value if he only disposed of a part of that interest;

- if the taxpayer previously owned a property (or an interest in it) which this property replaced, DV is so much of this property's value on the valuation date as is reasonably attributable to the property or interest originally disposed of by him, or to the appropriate proportion of that former property if he only disposed of a part of his interest in it;

- if the contribution condition but not the disposal condition applies, DV is so much of this property's value on the valuation date as is reasonably attributable to the consideration provided by the taxpayer.

V is the value of the relevant land at the valuation date.

For Example, John gave a property worth £100,000 to his son Peter in 1994. Peter sold the property for £350,000 in 1999 buying a further property for £400,000. John moves into the relevant property in 2008 when it had an annual rental value of £36,000. The contribution that could reasonably be attributed to the gifted property would be:

$$\frac{350,000}{400,000}$$

(being the proportion of the cost of the relevant property funded by John's gift)

That proportion is then applied to the annual rental value of the property as at the valuation date of £36,000 in order to ascertain the amount of John's deemed income for a full tax year.

$$\frac{350,000}{400,000} \times 36,000 = £31,500 \ @ \ 40\% = £12,600 \text{ patax payable at the 40\% rate}$$

Valuation date is set out in SI 2005/724 para 2 being 6 April in the relevant tax year, or if later the first day in the tax year on which enjoyment of the asset occurs.

As brought out in the Example at C, the (market) value of the property and its rental value are effectively set for five years at a time, even though there is technically a valuation date in each separate tax year.

The income tax payable is calculated by adding the appropriate rental value to the taxable income of the donor.

Chattels

In the case of chattels the charge is similar to that for land but with a notional amount of interest (on the value of the chattel at the valuation date), with similar rules to land applying to replacement chattels and cash. The rate of notional interest for this purpose is the official rate for beneficial loans to employees – 4.75% for 2009/10 and 4.00% for 2010/11.

Intangibles

For intangibles a charge only arises where they are held within a settlement (within the inheritance tax definition) and the settlor retains an interest (within the income tax definition, but unaffected by any interest of the settlor's spouse or civil partner). Again the liability is based upon notional interest, at the same official rate, on the value of the intangibles concerned at the valuation date.

Available reductions or deductions

Where the asset is only enjoyed (or the settlor is only interested) for part of a year the charge is reduced accordingly. As regards land and chattels (but not intangibles) there is no charge if full consideration is paid for use of the asset, and the charge is reduced by payments made under a legal obligation for the use of the asset. For intangibles, a deduction is allowed for income tax or capital gains tax payable by the taxpayer under specified charging provisions which charge the settlor of settled property, so far as the tax is attributable to the property that attracts the pre-owned assets charge.

(12) If the aggregate notional values before contribution do not exceed £5,000 then this is *de minimis* and there is no charge (Sch 15 para 13).

If a charge arises on the enjoyment of land or chattels, but there the pre-owned assets charge also catches intangible property whose value derives (in whole or in part) from the value of the land or chattels, only the higher of the two chargeable amounts applies (Sch 15 para 18).

There are provisions preventing a double charge to income tax under both the employee benefit in kind rules and the pre-owned asset rules – the employment charge takes priority and the deemed employment income is deducted from the pre-owned assets deemed income (Sch 15 para 19).

(13)   Where a taxpayer is potentially chargeable to income tax by reference to their enjoyment of any land, or chattels, or intangible property for the first time, then they may make an election. The effect of the election, if made, is that the asset is to be treated as caught by the gifts with reservation rules for inheritance tax and therefore no income tax charge arises. This is a deeming provision, the asset does not actually form part of their estate and therefore there is no uplift in value for capital gains tax when death occurs.

If the taxpayer permanently ceases to have occupation or use and enjoyment of the asset then the same consequence applies as under the gifts with reservation rules, namely that a potentially exempt transfer is deemed to have occurred at the cessation of use. If more than seven years then elapse since last enjoyment of the asset then no inheritance tax charge arises on that property on the taxpayer's death.

The election is required by 31 January following the end of the fiscal year of first use. If use first commenced in 2005/06 or earlier the election was required by 31 January 2007 (Sch 15 paras 21–23). Schedule 15 para 23(3)(a) expressly permits HMRC to accept late elections. For HMRC's approach see: Income tax and pre-owned assets guidance section 3 which can be found at http://www.hmrc.gov.uk/poa/poa_guidance3.htm.

Where the whole of the asset would not be attributed to the donor for pre-owned assets purposes then a similar restriction will apply to the proportion treated as caught by the gifts with reservation rules; ie: Chargeable proportion of Asset Value is:

$$\text{Value} \times \frac{\text{DV}}{\text{V}}$$

where DV and V have the meaning set out in **note 11** above, save that in the context of the election provisions:

- the transactions relevant to the calculation of DV include those after the election takes effect as well as those before it, and

- the valuation date is the date of death (if use continues), or of lifetime cessation of use (or of a beneficial interest in possession in settled property).

(14)   The charge is intended to penalise users of inheritance tax avoidance schemes, such as the double trust home loan scheme (the intention of which was to remove the value of the principal private residence from the donors' estate but to enable continued use of the property), or, where the full consideration for the use of the asset is negligible as compared with the open market value of the asset.

(15)   However, the charge will also apply to situations where a taxpayer would not expect a charge to arise. For example where a donor gives away assets (eg cash) and then in the future uses property acquired with those assets without paying a full commercial consideration, and does not fall within any of the exceptions for inheritance tax set out at **note 4 (i)** or pre-owned asset exceptions at **note 8**. Previously if the gift was at least seven years before the death of the donor there were no tax consequences. Since 2005 an income tax charge will arise.

Example

John gave £300,000 in cash to his daughter, Wendy, on the occasion of her marriage in 2005. She used £200,000 of that gift to buy a picture soon afterwards. On 6 June 2010 Wendy moved to Australia on a temporary contract for three years. She left the picture with John who hung it in his hall. The open market value as at May 2010 is £450,000. Wendy returns in 2013 reclaiming possession of the picture on 6 June 2013. John is still alive in July 2020. Assume an Official Rate of 5% throughout, and that John pays tax at 40% in each tax year except 2013/14 when his other income is already sufficient to be liable at 50%.

The cash/picture is not caught by the gifts with reservation rules for inheritance tax because Wendy took full bona fide possession and enjoyment of the cash in 2003 and the tracing provisions do not apply to cash gifts. Because the gifts with reservation rules do not apply, the picture is not excluded from the pre-owned asset charge. An income tax charge arises in principle because John has the use of property purchased with funds provided by him within the last seven years before his use started.

Two thirds of the cost of the picture was paid with John's gift, so (in the absence of other expenditure) that will be the proportion of the picture's value on the valuation date that is reasonably attributable to the consideration provided by John.

The relevant valuation dates are 6 June 2010, 6 April 2011, 6 April 2012 and 6 April 2013, but the value of the picture in all cases is taken at 6 June 2010 since they are all within five years of the first valuation date.

The amount of deemed income for a full tax year can therefore be seen (showing the full statutory fraction) to be:

$$5\% \times £450,000 \times \frac{\frac{2}{3} \times 450,000}{450,000} = 5\% \times \frac{2}{3} \times £450,000 = £15,000$$

John did not have the use of the picture for the whole of 2010/11 or 2013/14, so the amount of deemed income – and his consequent income tax liability – for the four tax years is:

Year	Fraction of year	Deemed income (fraction of £15,000)	Tax liability on deemed income at marginal rate
2010/11	10/12	12,500	£5,000
2011/12	12/12	15,000	£6,000
2012/13	12/12	15,000	£6,000
2013/14	2/12	2,500*	£0*

* Deemed income as calculated is below £5,000 so *de minimis* exemption applies

The income tax charge would be avoided if John elected by 31 January 2011 for gifts with reservation rules for inheritance tax to apply. As he does live to 2019 no inheritance tax charge would in practice arise.

Alternatively John could pay full rental value for the use of the picture. If he is responsible for insurance this could be very low.

(16) See also the companion book, **Tolley's Taxwise I 2010/11**, for calculation of the rate of income tax payable by a donor.

Question

Agnes Brown was a wealthy widow who doted on her nephew Simon. Having not made any gifts previously, she decided in 2002 to begin passing on some of her wealth to Simon and on 17 October 2003 she made a gift to him of a number of investments as follows:

(1)   3,000 shares out of her holding of 16,500 shares in Brown Retailing Ltd, a trading company with an issued share capital of 30,000 shares. The other 13,500 shares are already held by Simon.

(2)   15,000 shares in Landy plc, which were quoted at 180–188p with marked bargains at 180 and 182p.

On 11 November 2005, following the birth of Simon's first child, Agnes settled her remaining shares in Brown Retailing Ltd on discretionary trust, including herself, Simon and his child amongst the class of beneficiaries.

Feeling that perhaps she had favoured Simon to an unfair extent, she gave £100,000 to her niece Pauline on 21 December 2005.

On 10 March 2006 upon the advice of her professional adviser, she excluded herself from all benefit under the discretionary trust dated 11 November 2005.

An offer of £1 million for the whole of the issued share capital of Brown Retailing Ltd was received on 14 November 2008. This was accepted by all shareholders. The trustees reinvested the discretionary trust's proceeds into quoted shares.

Agnes died on 30 September 2010, leaving an estate valued at £700,000 including the following assets:

(i)   a 30% holding valued at £50,000 in Blue Ltd, an unquoted investment company;

(ii)   a 5% holding valued at £60,000 in Pink plc, a trading company on the Alternative Investment Market;

(iii) a 60% holding valued at £100,000 in Green Ltd, an unquoted investment company; and

(iv)   a 40% holding valued at £200,000 in Black Ltd, an unquoted trading company.

Under the terms of her will Agnes added a further £100,000 cash to the discretionary trust. The rest of her estate was divided equally between Simon and Pauline.

On 26 September 2011 the trustees of the discretionary trust appointed £50,000 from the cash received from the executors to Simon on the basis that he was to pay any tax due. At this time the trustees still held the same quoted shares bought in 2008, and no other assets apart from the cash received under Agnes Brown's will.

The value of an ordinary share in Brown Retailing Ltd at the relevant times was as follows:

	17.10.03	11.11.05	10.3.06
	£	£	£
75–100%	25	42	40
50–74%	20	31	30
25–49%	15	24	23
0–24%	10	16	15

There are no other relevant transfers of shares in Brown Retailing Ltd.

Calculate the inheritance tax payable in respect of the above events.

Answer

Agnes Brown — inheritance tax position in lifetime

	£
17 October 2003	
Gifts to Simon:	
3,000 shares in Brown Retailing Ltd	
16,500 shares at £20 (55% holding)	330,000
13,500 shares at £15 (45% holding)	202,500
Loss to estate	127,500
Less: Business property relief 100%	
(see **explanatory note 1**)	127,500
Transfer of value	–
15,000 shares in Landy plc @ ½ (180 + 182) = 181p, giving transfer of value of	27,150
Less: Annual exemptions 2003/04 and 2002/03	6,000
Potentially exempt transfer	21,150
11 November 2005	
Settlement on discretionary trust	
13,500 shares in Brown Retailing Ltd	
at £24 per share (45% holding)	324,000
Less: Business property relief 100%	
(see **explanatory note 2**)	324,000
Transfer of value	–
21 December 2005	
Gift to Pauline	100,000
Less: Annual exemptions 2005/06 and 2004/05	6,000
Potentially exempt transfer	94,000
10 March 2006	
Release of reservation —	
13,500 shares in Brown Retailing Ltd at	
£23 per share (45% holding) – potentially	
exempt transfer (see **explanatory note 5**)	310,500

On death of Agnes Brown — 30 September 2010

	Gross £	Tax on 2010/11 scale £
Transfers within seven years before death:		
Accumulation in seven years before gift on 17 October 2003*	–	–
Gifts to Simon (see **explanatory note 1**):		

		Gross	Tax on 2010/11 scale
Shares in Brown Retailing Ltd	122,553		
Shares in Landy plc	26,097		
		148,650	–

Accumulation in seven years before transfer to trust on 11 November 2005 (to calculate additional tax only, cumulative transfers not affected — see **explanatory note 2**):

			Gross	Tax on 2010/11 scale
17 October 2003				
Gift previously potentially exempt			148,650	–
11 November 2005				
Settlement on discretionary trust as above		–		
Add business property relief no longer available (see **explanatory note 2**)				
		324,000		
Less: Annual exemptions 2005/06 and 2004/05		6,000	318,000	56,660*
			466,650	56,660

(* 466,650 – 325,000 = 141,650 @ 40%)

As death takes place between four and five years after the transfer, the tax payable is reduced by 40% to £56,660 × 60% = £ 33,996.

Accumulation in seven years before gift to Pauline on 21 December 2005:

	Gross	Tax on 2010/11 scale
17 October 2003	148,650	–
11 November 2005 (see above)	–	–
21 December 2005		
Gift to Pauline (annual exemptions reallocated to trust as above — see **explanatory note 2**)	100,000	–*
	248,650	–*

(* 248,650 – 325,000 = Nil)

10 March 2006

Release of reservation — total inheritance tax payable will be the higher of:

(i) Disregarding the original gift and charging the potentially exempt transfer on release, or

(ii) Charging original gift and disregarding subsequent potentially exempt transfer.

	Gross	Tax on 2010/11 scale
	£	£
Accumulation in seven years before gift on 17 October 2003	–	–
17 October 2003		
Gift to Simon — as above	148,650	–
11 November 2005		
Settlement on discretionary trust — ignored	–	–
21 December 2005		

	Gross	Tax on 2010/11 scale
	£	£
Gift to Pauline — as above	100,000	–

10 March 2006
Release of reservation
Potentially exempt transfer now chargeable

	Gross	Tax on 2010/11 scale
(13,500 shares @ £23 per share)	310,500	93,660*
	559,150	93,660

(* 559,150 – 325,000 = 234,150 @ 40%)

As death takes place between four and five years after release of reservation, tax payable is 60% × £93,660 = £56,116

The second calculation is as already calculated above, ie cumulative transfers of £466,650 and tax payable of £33,996

The tax due on death must then be taken into account in both calculations. In the first case, however, the lifetime transfers exceeded the nil threshold at death, so the tax payable on the death estate would be:

		£	£
30 September 2010 — death of Agnes Brown			
Estate on death			700,000
Less: Business property relief			
100% × £60,000 (shares in Pink plc)	60,000		
100% × £200,000 (shares in Black Ltd)	200,000	260,000	
		440,000	
Tax @ 40%			176,000

In the second case the tax would be:

	Gross	Tax on 2010/11 scale
	£	£
30 September 2010 — death of Agnes Brown — accumulation in seven years before death		
17 October 2003	148,650	–
11 November 2005 (see above)	–	–
21 December 2005	100,000	–
	248,650	–
Estate on death (less business property relief)	440,000	145,460*
	688,650	145,460

(* 688,650 – 325,000 = 363,650 @ 40%)

Total tax payable on lifetime gifts and death is:

First calculation	(56,660 + 176,000)	£232,660

Second calculation	(33,996 + 145,460)	£179,456

The first calculation therefore shows the higher total tax liability, and inheritance tax is therefore payable as follows:

	£
By Agnes Brown on creation of discretionary trust	–
By Simon	–
By Pauline	–
By trustees of discretionary trust	56,660
By personal representatives	176,000
On appointment by discretionary trust to Simon on 26 September 2011 (being within two years of death — s 144 — see **explanatory note 6**)	–

Explanatory Notes

Same day transfers

(1) Where two or more transfers of value are made on the same day, the annual exemption is apportioned between them (s 19(3)(b)). Business property relief is deducted in arriving at the amount of a transfer of value. The treatment of the annual exemption in relation to potentially exempt transfers outlined in Example 1 makes the calculation of the potentially exempt transfers by Agnes Brown in this Example particularly difficult. The gift of the shares in Brown Retailing Ltd on 17 October 2003 qualifies for 100% business property relief (see **Example 25 part A(c)** for rates of business property relief) so that the transfer of value is reduced to nil as shown. On the same day as the gift of the Brown Retailing Ltd shares, Agnes made the gift of the shares in Landy plc, the transfer of value being £27,150, which is not eligible for business property relief. Annual exemptions for 2003/04 and 2002/03 are therefore allocated to the gift of shares in Landy plc.

When Agnes Brown died on 30 September 2010, the shares in Brown Retailing Ltd no longer qualified for business property relief. It is understood to be the view of HMRC that the annual exemption should then be reallocated between the gifts as follows:

$$\text{Brown RetailingLtd shares } \frac{127,500}{154,650} \times 6,000 \qquad \text{£4,947}$$

$$\text{Landyplc shares} \frac{27,150}{154,650} \times 6,000 \qquad \text{£1,053}$$

The revised potentially exempt transfers would then be:

Brown Retailing Ltd shares	127,500 –		4,947	122,553
Landy plc shares	27,150 –		1,053	26,097
				£148,650

Alternatively it could be argued that the original allocation of the annual exemption stands despite the withdrawal of business property relief. The gifts to Simon would then be £127,500 in respect of the shares in Brown Retailing Ltd and £21,150 in respect of the shares in Landy plc. In this instance the tax position is the same in any event, as both gifts were made to Simon and there is no inheritance tax liability. However, if a tax liability arose payable by different persons, this point may be taken. The total gifts to Simon would still amount to £148,650 and this amount is included in subsequent calculations.

Business property relief

(2)   For detailed notes on business property relief see **Example 25**. The relief is not available when calculating the tax on a potentially exempt transfer that becomes chargeable as a result of the donor's death within seven years if the relevant conditions are no longer satisfied (s 113A(1)). Similarly, where business property relief has been given against a transfer that was a chargeable transfer in lifetime, the relief is not available when calculating any additional tax payable as a result of the death of the transferor within seven years unless the conditions for the relief are satisfied at that time (s 113A(2)) (see **Example 25 part a(c)**). Note that the withdrawal of business property relief on a transfer that was a chargeable transfer in lifetime only affects the calculation of any additional tax payable on that transfer. The original chargeable transfer is taken into account in the accumulation for the purpose of working out the position on later transfers and on the death estate. In this Example the original chargeable transfer to the discretionary trust on 11 November 2005 qualified for 100% relief so it did not increase the cumulative total at that time. The cumulative total taken into account in calculating the tax on the later gift to Pauline at 24.3 therefore shows the 11 November transfer at nil. For a further illustration see **Example 25**.

The wording of the legislation supports the view that business property relief is effective immediately to the extent that the original transfer is covered by the annual exemption and that only the balance can be affected by the withdrawal of business property relief if the donor dies within seven years. For transfers on or after 28 November 1995, subsection (7A) was introduced into s 113A, which provides that when applying the rules for withdrawing business property relief on transfers within seven years before death, the relief is disregarded in establishing whether there is a potentially exempt or chargeable transfer. The reason for the change is that it had been contended that a transfer that initially qualified for 100% business property relief became a transfer of nil, and was therefore wholly within the £3,000 annual exempt limit, so no chargeable or potentially exempt transfer remained to be reconsidered if the donor died within seven years and no withdrawal of relief could therefore take place. The Revenue did not agree with this view, and the FA 1996 change was made 'for the removal of any doubt'. A similar change was made to s 124A (in subsection 7A) in relation to agricultural property relief.

The change is intended only to establish that a transfer exists, and does not seek to quantify the amount of the transfer. It is considered, therefore, that it does not affect the view stated above that if a slice of the original transfer is covered by the annual exemption, the business property relief on that slice cannot later be withdrawn. This is however not relevant where the original transfer qualified for 100% relief, because the annual exemption would not be used against a nil transfer.

Care needs to be taken in relation to the treatment of the annual exemption when business property relief is withdrawn. Note 1 deals with the situation where the 100% relief is withdrawn from a transfer that was originally potentially exempt, ie the gift to Simon of shares in Brown Retailing Ltd, with the additional complication that another transfer was made on the same day. The Example also illustrates the 100% relief being withdrawn from a transfer that would otherwise have been a chargeable transfer, ie the transfer to the discretionary trust on 11 November 2005. The annual exemptions of 2005/06 and 2004/05 were originally given against the 2005/06 gift to Pauline. When the business property relief is withdrawn at Agnes's death, the annual exemptions will be reallocated to the transfer to the discretionary trust, since the trust transfer occurred earlier in the tax year than the transfer to Pauline.

(3)   No business property relief is available on Agnes Brown's holdings in:

Blue Ltd — an *investment* company

Green Ltd — an *investment* company.

Business property relief of 100% is available on the holding in Pink plc as it is a trading company on the Alternative Investment Market (AIM), and on the investment in Black Ltd, an unquoted trading company.

Consequences of reduction in IHT rates

(4)   In calculating the tax, or additional tax, due on lifetime transfers as a result of Agnes Brown's death within 7 years, the 2010/11 nil rate band is used here in all cases because it is larger (and so the average rate of tax lower) than at the dates of the relevant lifetime transfers: Schedule 2, para 2. It would be different if the

scale at the date of death were harsher: the tax (or additional tax) would then be calculated using the scale (or nil rate band) in force at the dates of the respective original transfers.

[NB – Schedule 2 applies where there is a 'reduction of tax', defined as a reduction of tax by the substitution of a new Table in Schedule 1 (Schedule 2, para 1(a)). It is far from clear how this would apply if the new Table was capable of increasing the tax due at some levels of chargeable transfer but reducing it at others, for Example if the nil rate band were increased to £500,000 but the rate of tax applicable above that figure were 50%.]

Double charges relief

(5)   The situations when a double charge to tax occurs and the reliefs under the Inheritance Tax (Double Charges Relief) Regulations 1987 (SI 1987/1130) are dealt with in **Examples 19 and 20**. The regulations apply to the release of reservation on 10 March 2006 in this Example, when Agnes Brown excludes herself from benefit under the discretionary trust. The release is specifically treated as a potentially exempt transfer by FA 1986 s 102(4), despite the fact that someone else's estate has not been increased, nor has an interest in possession in the trust been created.

In this Example no tax was payable by the trustees of the discretionary settlement in the settlor's lifetime. If any lifetime tax had been payable on such a transfer, then where, as in this Example, the first calculation produced the higher figure, the lifetime tax (up to but not exceeding the part of the death tax payable relating to the transfer) would be deducted from the tax payable by the trustees following Agnes Brown's death (see **Example 20 explanatory note 3**).

Post-death variations of a will

(6)   The assets of the discretionary trust following Agnes Brown's death consist of shares acquired on the takeover of Brown Retailing Ltd in November 2008 and £100,000 added in cash under the terms of Agnes Brown's will. The appointment of £50,000 to Simon on 26 September 2011 is in cash, the shares being retained in full. Accordingly it is a variation of the property settled by will within two years of the date of death and is treated as a disposition at death for inheritance tax and not as a distribution out of the discretionary trust (s 144). (Section 144 applies where a distribution is made out of property settled by will within two years after the death and before any interest in possession has subsisted in the property. The distribution is treated as if it had been made under the terms of the will.) See **Example 60 explanatory note 9** for a problem where such a distribution is made within the first three months after death.

(7)   For detailed notes on post-death variations of a will see **Example 34**.

Question

A.

Relief from inheritance tax is available on 'relevant business property'.

(a)   What is relevant business property?

(b)   What types of business do not qualify for this relief?

(c)   What is the nature of the relief and at what rates is it given?

B.

Relief from inheritance tax is also available for 'agricultural property'.

(a)   Under what circumstances is a transferor entitled to inheritance tax relief when transferring agricultural property and what is the nature of the relief?

(b)   Is the relief available to a transferor of shares or debentures in a farming company?

(c)   Whiteacre is a farm of 200 acres which for the last ten years has been owned and farmed by Arthur personally with assistance from his son.

It has been proposed that Arthur should form a partnership with his son because of his advancing age, failing health and the necessity of providing for his wife when he dies.

Arthur would then grant a lease of the land at full rent to that partnership so that on his death the land will be valued at tenanted value.

The current agricultural value of the land is £2,000 per acre vacant possession; £1,400 per acre tenanted.

Advise Arthur as to the viability of the above proposal, quantifying the value chargeable to inheritance tax on Whiteacre on his subsequent death.

(d)   X owned 800 acres of freehold farmland known as Greenacre let to and farmed by the partnership of X himself, Mrs X and their son Y. The tenancy was granted in 1973 and the partnership has subsisted since before that time.

In July 2010 X died leaving his interest in Greenacre to his son Y (subject to Y paying the inheritance tax thereon). It was valued (tenanted) at £479,000. X left the residue of his estate (including his interest in the partnership) to his wife. He had not made any previous lifetime gifts.

After an accident on the farm Y, who was unmarried, died in September 2010.

Y's estate consisted of:

	£
Greenacre Farm (let to the farming partnership of himself and his mother)	479,000
Interest in the farming partnership	60,000
Other assets	89,000

Compute the inheritance tax payable

(i)   on the death of X

(ii)   on the death of Y assuming he had not made any lifetime transfers and that he left the whole of his estate to his mother.

Answer

A. Business property relief

(a) Relevant business property

Relevant business property means (s 105):

(i)   A sole trader's business, or a partnership share, including professions and vocations.

(ii)   Unquoted *securities* of a company which, together with any unquoted *shares* of the company (including related property in both instances), give the transferor control immediately before the transfer.

(iii)   *Any* unquoted *shares* in a company.

(iv)   Quoted shares and/or securities of a company which, together with any related property, give the transferor control immediately before the transfer.

(v)   Land, buildings, plant or machinery which immediately before the transfer were used wholly or mainly for the purposes of a business carried on by a company of which the transferor then had control, or by a partnership of which he was then a partner.

(vi)   Any land or buildings, machinery or plant which, immediately before the transfer, was used wholly or mainly for the purposes of a business carried on by the transferor and were settled property in which he was then beneficially entitled to an interest in possession.

Quoted shares and securities are defined as shares and securities listed on a recognised stock exchange (ss 105(1ZA), 113A(3B)). Shares or securities on the Alternative Investment Market (AIM) are treated as unlisted and therefore qualify as unquoted under (ii) and (iii) above.

In the case of *CIR v Mallender and others (exors of Drury-Lowe decd)* (2001), it was held that an asset (which in this case was land) used as security for a guarantee was not itself used in the business and was not therefore part of the relevant business property.

The relevant business property concerned must have been owned by the transferor throughout the two years preceding the transfer (s 106) or be property replacing relevant business property where the combined period of ownership of the original and replacement property is at least two years out of the last five years (but relief is then granted only on the lower of the value of the original or replacement property) (s 107). Property acquired as a result of death is deemed to have been owned from the date of death, or for property acquired by a spouse, from the date the deceased spouse acquired it (s 108). The two year rule does not apply where the property was eligible for business property relief on an earlier transfer and either the earlier transfer or the subsequent transfer was made on the death of the transferor (s 109). Where a person starts up a new business, however, (rather than inherits it) and then dies within two years, business property relief is not available.

(b) Non-qualifying businesses

A business, or an interest in a business, or shares in or securities of a company, are not relevant business property if the business, or as the case may be, the business of the company, consists wholly or mainly of:

(i)   Dealing in securities, stocks or shares (except for market makers and discount houses)

(ii)   Dealing in land or buildings

(iii)   Making or holding investments (see **explanatory note 20** re land which is let or subject to a grazing licence).

George & Anor (Exors of Stedman dec'd) v IRC concerned a claim for business property relief by the executors where the deceased owned 85% of the shares in a company carrying on the business of running a caravan park. The Inland Revenue contended the business of the company was making or holding investments. The Court of Appeal allowed the executors' claim on the ground that making or holding investments was only one (and not the main) component of a composite business. (See **explanatory note 20**.)

(c) Nature and amount of relief

The relief applies to transfers of value in lifetime or on death or to the 10 yearly charge on discretionary trusts, the value attributable to relevant business property being reduced by 100% in respect of (a) (i) to (iii) above and 50% in respect of (a) (iv) to (vi) (s 104).

Before 6 April 1996, unquoted shares qualified for relief at only 50% unless, together with related property, they gave the transferor control of *more* than 25% of the votes of the company (and the 25% control had to have been held *throughout* the two years before the transfer, or shorter period under the successions rules in (a) above — s 109A). For chargeable events occurring on or after 6 April 1996 (lifetime transfers, tax uplift on death, etc), 100% relief is available on qualifying unquoted shares regardless of the size of the holding.

The relief is applied automatically without the need for a claim and is given before applying any other relief (eg annual exemptions, as indicated below).

The meaning of 'the value transferred [being] attributable to the value of... relevant business property' was examined in *HMRC v Trustees of Nelson Dance Family Settlement (2009)*. There the transferor settled part of the land used in a farming business that he carried on personally, and business property relief was claimed on the development value of the land so far as it exceeded the agricultural value that attracted agricultural property relief. It was common ground that the subject matter of his transfer of value was not the business that he had carried on, merely part of the assets of that business; but it was held that although in one sense the value transferred was attributable to the value of the land as such, in another sense it was attributable to the value of the business because the value of the business was taken into account in ascertaining the loss to the donor. Section 104 did not require a choice to be made between the two senses, it was sufficient to be able to characterise the transfer in the second sense. But see below if the donor's death occurs within seven years afterwards.

Meaning of control

Control means control of voting on all questions affecting the company as a whole. In considering which shares give control care must be taken with shares that only have votes in special circumstances (eg preference shares entitled to votes when the preference dividends are in arrears). When voting rights relate only to the question of winding-up, or to questions primarily affecting shares of a particular class, then such rights are ignored (s 269(4)). Otherwise the rights are included in determining control. For example, say an unquoted company had a total issued share capital of £100, consisting of 25 ordinary shares of £1 held by A, and 75 preference shares of £1 held by B, the preference shares having votes when the preference dividends were in arrear and on reduction of capital. Neither A nor B *controls* the votes on *all* questions affecting the company as a whole, so neither would qualify for business property relief on any land etc owned personally and used by the company. If the voting rights on the preference shares related only to winding-up, A would then control the company and would be entitled to the 50% relief on land etc owned personally. B's position would be unchanged.

Death of donor within seven years

For lifetime gifts made after 17 March 1986, whether chargeable at the time or potentially exempt, where the death of the donor occurs within seven years, business property relief is available when calculating the tax/additional tax arising as a result of the death providing that:

(1) the original property (or qualifying replacement property — see below) was owned by the transferee throughout the period beginning with the date of the chargeable transfer and ending with the death of the transferor, and

(2) immediately before the death of the donor the original property (or qualifying replacement property) is relevant business property in the hands of the transferee (ignoring the two year period of ownership

rule), except that where property qualified as a transfer out of a controlling holding, it is only necessary for the transferee to retain what he was given (which may not give control). In order for unquoted shares to be relevant business property they must still be unquoted when the donor dies (s 113A(3A)).

If the transferee dies before the donor then the property must qualify at the date of his death rather than the date of the donor's death.

Proportionate relief is available where only part of the property is owned at the date of death (s 113A).

Note that these conditions would seem to be incapable of being satisfied in a case where the relevant business property to whose value the value transferred was attributable was not what was in fact transferred — as in the *Nelson Dance* case above, where land forming part of the assets of the business was transferred but the value transferred was attributable (inter alia) to the value of the transferor's business itself because of the loss to donor principle. The 'original property' is defined as the property which was relevant business property in relation to the lifetime transfer (here the business). The transferee in these circumstances would never own the business itself. So business property relief is likely to be unavailable for the purpose of calculating the additional tax due by reason of the death, even if the donee retains the land that was transferred.

To the extent that the original transfer was covered by annual exemptions, whether the balance was chargeable at the time or potentially exempt, it is considered that the business property relief relating to that part of the transfer is not affected by the death of the donor within seven years. See **Example 24 explanatory note 2**, and the illustration in that Example.

It should be noted that if business property relief is not available in calculating additional tax on a *chargeable* lifetime transfer resulting from the donor's death within seven years, it is only that tax calculation that is affected. The donor's total of cumulative transfers is not altered.

Example

A donor who had made no other transfers settled a building worth £337,000 and used for business purposes into a discretionary trust in July 2009. If it qualified for 50% business property relief, £12,000 of the transfer, reduced to £6,000 after 50% business property relief, would be covered by annual exemptions and the balance of £325,000 would, after 50% business property relief, be a chargeable transfer of £162,500. No tax would be payable because the transfer was below the then nil threshold of £325,000. If the donor died within seven years and the trustees had in the meantime disposed of the property, they would pay tax on £325,000 less the nil threshold at the date of the donor's death, but the donor's lifetime transfers to be aggregated with any subsequent transfers and with his estate would remain at £162,500.

By comparison, if the donor had instead gifted the same building to his son in July 2009 it would be a potentially exempt transfer. On the donor's subsequent death within seven years (son having sold the property), the son would similarly be liable to tax on £325,000 less the nil threshold at the date of the donor's death, but the lifetime transfer to be aggregated with subsequent transfers and with the donor's estate would be £325,000, the business property relief available at the time of the gift not being available to compute the *chargeable transfer* resulting from the donor's death.

Qualifying replacement property

Provision is made for property that replaces all or part of the original property to satisfy the continuing ownership test up to the donor's (or donee's) death providing the replacement property also qualifies as business property, and providing the whole of the proceeds of the original property are used in the purchase of the replacement property within three years after the disposal of the original property, or such longer period as HMRC may allow (s 113B). HMRC interpret 'the whole of the consideration' as meaning the sale proceeds net of any professional costs of the sale and net of any capital gains tax payable on the disposal (IHTM25369).

If unquoted shares in trading companies (for Example on AIM) are sold and replaced with other such shares, then it is understood that the new shares will be treated as replacement property under s 107(1). Replacement shares or property must not be acquired in advance of the disposal of the original property.

Excepted assets

For the purpose of calculating the relief the value of the relevant business property excludes *excepted assets*, ie assets which were neither used wholly or mainly for the purposes of the business throughout the two years preceding the transfer, nor required at the time of the transfer for future use for those purposes.

See the Special Commissioners' case of *Barclays Bank Trust Co Ltd* (SpC 158) for the denial of relief to the extent that there were substantial cash balances held within a company. Note also the Special Commissioners' case of *Farmer & Giles (Farmer's Executors) v CIR* 1999 (SpC 216), which held that in determining whether assets were relevant business property the whole business should be considered 'in the round'. This includes turnover, profits and assets used in the business and investment sides of the business. It could also include time spent by the owners, employees and others on the respective parts of the business. It would appear that if a single set of accounts is prepared for the whole business, there is unified management and the majority of the above tests point to business, then there is a single business for inheritance tax, and let property within the balance sheet is not therefore treated as an excepted asset but as an integral part of the qualifying business.

B. Agricultural property relief

(a) Availability of agricultural property relief

Agricultural property relief is available on the transfer of agricultural property (that is, agricultural land or pasture; also woodland and any building used in the intensive rearing of livestock or fish if the occupation of the woodland or building is ancillary to that of the agricultural land or pasture; and also such cottages, farm buildings and farmhouses occupied with the agricultural land as are of a character appropriate to the property) (s 115).

The cultivation of short rotation coppice (ie the harvesting of trees planted at high density at intervals of less than ten years) is regarded as agriculture, therefore the land used for this purpose is agricultural land and ancillary buildings are farm buildings (FA 1995 s 154).

Agricultural property relief is also available on land taken out of farming and dedicated to wildlife habitats under the Government Habitat Schemes, together with buildings used for the management of the land (s 124C).

The provisions for agricultural property relief are very similar to the rules for business property relief, in that the agricultural value is reduced by (s 116):

(i)	Where the transferor had the right to vacant possession immediately before the transfer or the right to obtain such possession within the next twelve months, extended to 24 months by HMRC Concession F17; or (also by Concession F17) the property is valued at an amount broadly equivalent to the vacant possession value	100%
(ii)	Where the agricultural property transferred is let on a tenancy granted on or after 1 September 1995 (including successions to tenancies following the death of the previous tenant on or after that date – see **explanatory note 14**)	100%
(iii)	Where the transferor has been beneficially entitled to his interest in the property since before 10 March 1981 and satisfies certain conditions (see **explanatory note 10**)	100%
(iv)	Otherwise.	50%

For transfers before 10 March 1992 the rates of relief were 50% for the first and third categories and 30% otherwise.

The percentage deduction only applies to the agricultural value of the property transferred, ie its value on the assumption that the property was subject to a perpetual covenant prohibiting its use otherwise than as agricultural property. In arriving at the agricultural value any loan secured on the agricultural property must be deducted.

Meaning of agricultural land or pasture

The term 'agricultural land or pasture' is given the narrow meaning of bare land. Therefore to obtain relief for any farmhouse etc, it is necessary to show that its occupation is ancillary to that of agricultural land (*Starke*

(Brown's Exors) v CIR (1994)). Furthermore in *Exor of Higginson v IRC* (2002) it was held that the farmhouse must be of a character and size appropriate to the property and the requirements of the farming activities conducted on the agricultural land.

The agricultural value of qualifying for agricultural relief of a farmhouse which is a historic building in an attractive location with a value as a residence independently of its merits as a farmhouse may be much lower than the open market value of the property as in *Lloyds TSB Private Banking Plc v Peter Twiddy (Inland Revenue Capital Taxes)* (10 October 2005, unreported), where the agricultural value was 30% less than its market value. Another decision can be found in *Arnander v HMRC* [2006] STC (SCD) 800 in which the Special Commissioner held that a seven bedroom Grade 2* listed manor house owned together with 110 acres of agricultural land failed to attract relief.

A further recent case on the interaction of farmhouses and agricultural property relief is *Lloyds TSB (personal representatives of Antrobus dec'd) v IRC* (2002) (SpC 336). This case set out five principles which had been established for deciding whether a farmhouse is of a character appropriate to the property. The requirement that the buildings are occupied for agricultural purposes is satisfied if they are tenanted by a person employed solely for agricultural purposes, or by retired farm workers or their widow(er)s, and such occupation is a statutorily protected tenancy or the lease was granted to the employee for life as part of his/her terms of employment.

In the case of *Rosser v IRC* (2003) SpC 368 the Inland Revenue refused a claim to agricultural property relief on a house and barn owned by the deceased on the basis that they were not agricultural land. The case was subsequently referred to the Special Commissioners who allowed the appeal in part — the barn was of a character appropriate to the property and was owned and occupied for the relevant period. Relief was granted on the barn but not the house.

Qualifying conditions

The agricultural property must at the time of the transfer have been either:

(i) occupied by the transferor for the purposes of agriculture throughout the period of two years ending with the date of the transfer or have replaced other agricultural property which, together with the replacement property, was occupied for agricultural purposes for at least two years out of the last five years ending with the date of transfer, or

(ii) owned by the transferor throughout the period of *seven years* ending with the date of transfer and occupied for the purposes of agriculture by him or another throughout that period. In the case of replacement property this condition is satisfied if the other property and the replacement property were owned by him and occupied for the purposes of agriculture by himself or another for at least seven years out of the period of ten years ending with the date of transfer.

The two-year rule in (i) or seven-year rule in (ii) does not apply where: the property was eligible for agricultural property relief on an earlier transfer; either the earlier transfer or the subsequent transfer was made on the death of the transferor; and the property is occupied by the second transferor for agricultural purposes at the date of the subsequent transfer.

Where the transferor had acquired the agricultural property on the death of his spouse/civil partner, their respective periods of occupation and/or ownership are aggregated to determine whether the transferor meets the occupation/ownership requirements (ss 117 to 121).

For lifetime gifts, whether chargeable at the time or potentially exempt, where the death of the donor occurs within seven years, agricultural property relief is only available when calculating the tax/additional tax arising as a result of the death providing that:

(a) the original property (or qualifying replacement property) was owned by the transferee throughout the period beginning with the date of the chargeable transfer and ending with the death of the transferor, and

(b) immediately before the death of the donor the original property (or qualifying replacement property) is relevant agricultural property in the hands of the transferee (ignoring the two-year or seven-year period of ownership rule).

If the transferee dies before the donor then the property must qualify at the date of his death rather than the date of the donor's death.

Proportionate relief is available where only part of the property is owned at the date of death (s 124A).

Annual exemptions and effect of donor's death within seven years

The same provisions apply as for business property relief in relation to annual exemptions, and also for calculating the additional tax payable on a chargeable lifetime transfer as a result of the donor's death within seven years, where the agricultural property is no longer owned by the donee (see **part A(c)**).

Provision is made for property that replaces all or part of the original property to satisfy the continuing ownership test providing the replacement property also qualifies as agricultural property, and providing the whole of the proceeds of the original property are used in the purchase of the replacement property within three years after the disposal of the original property, or such longer period as HMRC may allow (s 124B).

Business property relief on non-agricultural value

Where agricultural property satisfies the conditions for business property relief, business property relief is available in respect of any part of the value transferred that does not qualify for agricultural property relief (s 114). Since agricultural property relief is given only on the agricultural value of the land then business property relief where applicable will be given on any excess over that value.

Where agricultural property is replaced by business property, then providing the agricultural property is qualifying property for business property relief, the period of ownership of the agricultural property (in its character as relevant business property) will be taken into account in deciding whether the conditions for business property relief are satisfied. But in the case of a farming business carried on by a sole trader the farm land as such will not have been relevant business property, and so will not attract this replacement rule.

(b) Transfer of shares or debentures in farming company

Agricultural property relief is available on the transfer of shares or debentures in a farming company, providing the holding gave the transferor control of the company immediately before the transfer and the agricultural property forms part of the company's assets (s 119). Relief is given only on that part of the value of the holding that reflects the agricultural value of the underlying property. The rate of relief is 100% where the company occupies the property or where the property is let on a tenancy granted on or after 1 September 1995, and 50% for property let before that date, and the two year/seven year rules in (i) and (ii) in **part (a)** above apply as if the company were the transferor. (For this purpose the company is treated as having occupied the property at any time when it was occupied by a person who subsequently controls the company.) Furthermore the shares or securities must have been owned by the transferor throughout the two-year or seven-year period.

Business property relief is available on the non-agricultural value of a holding where the relevant conditions are satisfied at 100% on holdings in unquoted farming companies and at 50% on quoted controlling holdings.

Both agricultural property relief and business property relief are given automatically without the need for a claim.

(c) Mitigation of inheritance tax through lease of land

The immediately perceived advantage of the proposal is that the value of the freehold interest in the agricultural land would be reduced from £400,000 (200 × £2,000) to £280,000 (200 × £1,400) on the granting of the tenancy. This act by itself would not have any inheritance tax consequences providing the grant is for full consideration in money or money's worth (s 16).

Furthermore, the rate of agricultural property relief on tenanted property for tenancies granted on or after 1 September 1995 was increased from 50% to 100%, so that unless there are adverse changes in the agricultural property relief provisions, there will be no disadvantage in terms of the rate of relief available. Unless the conditions for agricultural relief were no longer satisfied at the time of Arthur's death, there would therefore be no net value chargeable to inheritance tax at that time. If the conditions were not satisfied, then providing the property remained tenanted, the proposal would achieve the objective of reducing the value of the property in the death estate.

(d)

Inheritance tax payable on the death of X in July 2010

	Gross £	Tax £
Inheritance tax accumulation prior to death	–	–
Estate on death		
Freehold property — Greenacre		
Agricultural value (tenanted)	479,000	
Less: 100% agricultural property relief (**note 13**)	479,000	–	–
Residue of estate to spouse — exempt	–	–
	–	–

Inheritance tax payable on the death of Y in September 2010

	£	£
Greenacre (tenanted since 1973)	479,000	
Less: 50% agricultural property relief (**note 13**)	239,500	239,500
Interest in farming partnership	60,000	
Less: 100% business property relief	60,000	–
Other assets		89,000
		328,500
Tax thereon (no lifetime transfers)		
(328,500 – 325,000 = 3,500 @ 40%)		£1,400

Explanatory Notes

Business property and agricultural property relief legislation

(1) The provisions relating to business property relief are contained in ss 103–114B and those for agricultural property relief in ss 115–124C.

(2) The main provisions are dealt with in the Example, other points of importance being covered in the following notes.

Meaning of control

(3) Control of a company means the control of voting on all questions affecting the company as a whole, subject to what is said in **part A(c)** of the Example (s 269).

Shares or securities which are related property under s 161 are taken into account in determining whether a person controls a company (s 269(2)), except where related property is left out of account under s 176 because of a sale after death (ss 105(2), 122(2)) (see **Example 10** for the related property rules, **explanatory note 4** of that Example dealing with s 176).

The voting powers attaching to shares or securities comprised in a settlement are deemed to be exercisable by the person beneficially entitled in possession to the shares or securities (broadly the person entitled to the income for the time being) (s 269(3)).

Business property relief and agricultural property relief are also available on the occasion of a ten yearly charge on a settlement without an interest in possession. For this purpose the trustees are deemed to be a transferor (ss 66, 103(1)(b), 115(1)(b)).

Agricultural value

(4)   Agricultural value is that which would be the value of the property if it were subject to a perpetual covenant prohibiting its use otherwise than as agricultural property (s 115(3)). The relief does not therefore extend to any value in excess of the agricultural value as defined. For Example, if the value was £100,000 because it was hoped that permission would shortly be forthcoming for a caravan site, but the value on the basis that it must be used perpetually for agriculture was £10,000, the agricultural relief would only be available on the lower £10,000. Depending on the circumstances, business property relief may be available on the excess value (see **part B(a)** of the Example).

Occupation by company

(5)   Occupation of agricultural property by a company controlled by the transferor is treated as occupation by the transferor for the purpose of the minimum two year period of occupation or seven year period of ownership (s 119(1)).

Hence agricultural property owned by a controlling shareholder and occupied by his farming company qualifies for relief.

Parcels of shares acquired over a period of time — matching provisions

(6)   As indicated in the Example, an asset is not relevant business property unless it has been owned by the transferor throughout the two years before the transfer (or it is qualifying replacement property). As far as shares are concerned, they may have been acquired in separate parcels over a period of time and some of the acquisitions may have been within the last two years.

Unlike the capital gains position, there are no matching rules in the inheritance tax legislation, so that there is uncertainty over which shares are contained in a transfer. In practice this may be overcome either by the separate parcels of shares having been originally registered in the names of different nominees or by the share certificates that are cancelled as a result of the gift being those acquired more than two years previously.

Binding contract for sale

(7)   Property that is subject to a binding contract for sale at the time of the transfer is not relevant business or agricultural property unless:

(a)   the sale is to a company that is to carry on the business, the consideration being wholly or mainly shares or securities in the company (which, in the case of agricultural property relief, will give the transferor control of the company), or

(b)   the property is shares or securities of a company and the sale is made for the purpose of reconstruction or amalgamation (ss 113 and 124).

Where partners or company directors have entered into 'buy and sell' agreements whereby on their death the personal representatives are *obliged* to sell and the survivors *obliged* to buy the deceased's interest (funds often being provided by life assurance policies), such an agreement in HMRC's view constitutes a binding contract for sale and business property relief or agricultural relief is not available (Statement of Practice 12/80). If, however, a double option agreement is entered into under which the surviving partners or shareholders have an option to buy and the deceased's personal representatives an option to sell, such options to be exercised within a stated period after the partner's death, this does not cause business or agricultural relief to be lost.

Other reliefs and exemptions

(8)   Business and agricultural property relief are given before any exemptions since they apply to transfers of value (ss 104(1) and 115(1)), such transfers being calculated before reliefs and exemptions (s 3(1)). In relation to potentially exempt transfers that become chargeable transfers, neither relief is available unless the relevant conditions are satisfied at the time of death, as indicated in the Example (ss 113A(1) and 124A(1)).

Gifts subject to a reservation

(9)   Where a gift of business or agricultural property is subject to a reservation, and a transfer of value is treated as made by the donor on his death (or on the donee's death, if earlier), then in considering the availability of business or agricultural relief the donor's transfer is treated as made by the donee (otherwise the donor would not usually be able to satisfy the ownership/occupation requirements) (FA 1986 Sch 20 para 8). Where the requirements for 100% relief are satisfied, the fact that a gift of qualifying property was subject to a reservation will not result in any extra tax charge on death.

As far as the donee's entitlement to relief is concerned, there are provisions to enable him to satisfy the occupation/ownership requirements by reference to the occupation/ownership of the donor (FA 1986 Sch 20 para 8).

For the gifts with reservation provisions see **Example 19**.

Pre 10 March 1981 transfers of agricultural property and transitional relief

(10)   For transfers prior to 10 March 1981, agricultural property relief was 50% of the agricultural value of the agricultural property after reduction for exempt transfers. The relief had to be claimed within two years of the transfer and was limited to relief on £250,000 or on 1,000 acres, whichever was the greater (counting rough grazing land as one-sixth of its actual area).

In order to be eligible to claim relief the transferor had broadly to be a working farmer, although relief could still be claimed after the farmer retired, providing the property had been occupied for agricultural purposes by his family throughout the period between his retirement and the date of the transfer, either under a lease or under some informal arrangements.

Relief was not available on let agricultural land except where it was let to a member of the family (as above) or where it was let to a farming partnership of which the transferor was a member or to a farming company controlled by the transferor.

As a transitional measure, where the transferor has been beneficially entitled to his interest in the property since before 10 March 1981, he is entitled to 100% agricultural property relief providing the following conditions are satisfied:

(a)   He would have been entitled to claim the (then) 50% agricultural property relief had he disposed of his interest before that date, and

(b)   His interest did not at any time between 10 March 1981 and the date of transfer carry a right to vacant possession and did not fail to carry such a right through any act or deliberate omission of his.

Where the former relief would have been limited by reference to value or acreage, the 100% relief is available up to the limit and any excess agricultural value attracts relief at 50%.

Where a transferor has acquired agricultural property on the death of his spouse/civil partner on or after 10 March 1981, the transitional 100% relief is available where the spouse/civil partner satisfied condition (a) above and both spouses/civil partners satisfy condition (b) above.

These transitional provisions thus enable relief to be claimed on the first subsequent transfer at the 100% rather than the 50% rate by retired farmers whose families have continued to work the farm and by partners or controlling directors who let land to the partnership or company.

The transitional relief will not be relevant where a tenancy commences on or after 1 September 1995, because relief is now available on such tenanted property at the 100% rate in any event. Had Arthur in **part B(c)** of the Example not been entitled to the 100% relief under the normal provisions, he would not have been able to claim the transitional relief because he had the right to vacant possession after 9 March 1981 and before the transfer (on his death) on which relief is to be claimed.

Formation of partnership

(11) The formation of a partnership between Arthur and his son would not give rise to any current or potential liability to inheritance tax provided that any reduction in the value of the estate of either resulted from an agreement that was not intended to confer any gratuitous benefit and was such as would have occurred in an agreement made at arm's length between unconnected persons (s 10).

Grant of agricultural tenancy

(12) The grant of the tenancy of Whiteacre by Arthur in **part B(c)** of the Example will not give rise to any liability to inheritance tax because of the exemption provided by s 16 for agricultural tenancies if the grant is made for full consideration. It should be noted, however, that the rent receivable by Arthur will be investment income whereas previously the income was earned income, being embraced in the profits of a farming business carried on by Arthur personally. This will reduce the Class 4 national insurance contributions payable, but will affect the future earnings on which Arthur can claim income tax relief for personal pension premiums (but note that a personal pension premium of up to £3,600 a year may be paid with basic rate tax relief at source by someone who has no earnings). If the tenancy was not granted for full rent, a charge to inheritance tax could arise on the reduction in the value of Arthur's estate and the 'gift' could be 'with reservation' as Arthur would still have a benefit in the land and accordingly could be valued at vacant possession value at the date of Arthur's death.

See **Example 10 part A** regarding the valuation of tenanted agricultural property.

(13) On the death of X in **part B(d)** of the Example Greenacre qualifies for 100% relief because the tenancy was granted before 10 March 1981 and all of the conditions mentioned in **explanatory note 10** are satisfied.

On the death of Y Greenacre qualifies for relief even though Y only owned it for three months because the minimum occupation/ownership rules do not apply on a succession where all of the following conditions are satisfied:

(i)   The value transferred by the earlier transfer qualified for relief

(ii) The property became that of the later transferor as a result of such an earlier transfer and at the time of the subsequent transfer was *occupied* by the later transferor or the personal representative of the earlier transferor for the purposes of agriculture

(iii) The property would have qualified for relief if the normal minimum ownership and occupation conditions had been met

(iv) Either the earlier or later transfer was a transfer on death.

Alternatively Y would still have qualified under the two year occupation test as Y occupied the land as a tenant farmer in the farming partnership for two years even though his ownership did not commence until the death of his father.

The rate of relief on Y's death is only 50%, because the tenancy was granted before 1 September 1995 and Y does not satisfy the conditions for the transitional relief, having not become the owner of Greenacre until his father's death.

Although Y's death is within twelve months of X's death, quick succession relief is not relevant because no tax was payable on X's estate.

(14) The availability of 100% agricultural relief in relation to tenanted property was extended by FA 1996. Where a tenant dies on or after 1 September 1995 and someone else succeeds to the tenancy, the new tenancy is deemed to commence on the date of the first tenant's death. Accordingly, if the landlord dies after the death of the first tenant, but before the succession by the second tenant, 100% agricultural property relief is available on the landlord's death. 100% relief is similarly available where a succession to a tenancy is triggered by a notice of retirement given by the retiring tenant to the landlord, and the succession takes effect after the landlord's death (on or after 1 September 1995) and within 30 months of the notice (s 116(5A), (5B) and (5D)).

Deed of variation

(15) The tax on the death of Y in **part B(d)** of the Example (£1,400) could be avoided by a deed of variation under which the executors of X and of Y (with the agreement of Mrs X as beneficiary of Y's estate) agreed to vary the terms of X's will so that the freehold property devolved to X's widow instead of to Y. This would save the whole of the tax on the death of Y since his estate would then only amount to £89,000 (£239,500 for the farm property no longer being in his estate) which is below the taxable threshold.

The respective executors should have no reservations about this variation, since the estate of Y has in any event been left to his mother, who would simply take the farm property on the death of her husband rather than of her son. See **Example 34** for details of deeds of variation. HMRC accept that the variation rules can still apply where the ultimate destination of the property remains unchanged as here (IHTM 35042).

Furthermore the income tax 'pre-owned' asset rules will not impose an income tax charge on Y as FA 2004 Sch 15 para 16 provides that a party to a deed of variation is not taxed as a former owner simply because of having an interest which they have now signed away (Y's Executor signing on behalf of Y).

Exempt and partially exempt estates

(16) Where business or agricultural property forms part of an estate at death, the benefit of the business or agricultural property relief will be lost if the property is left to an exempt beneficiary. Even if it is not left to an exempt beneficiary, part of the relief will be wasted where there are exempt legacies and the business or agricultural property forms part of the residue of the estate, rather than being left as a specific gift, because the relief is then regarded as applying to the whole estate, including the exempt part of it, so that again relief is wasted to the extent that it is allocated to the exempt legacies. For further notes on this point see **Example 15 explanatory notes 6 to 9.**

Gifts out of and into trusts

(17) Business and agricultural property relief is available on transfers of trust property providing the conditions are satisfied. For life interest trusts, the person with an estate interest in possession is treated as the beneficial owner of the property (s 49) and when the interest comes to an end, he is treated as having made a transfer at that time (s 52). In other cases (including where an interest in possession is not within s 49), the relief is available when relevant property is transferred out of the trust and on the occasion of the ten yearly charge, the trustees being treated as the transferor (ss 103, 113) (see **Example 62 explanatory note 5**).

Detailed notes on the inheritance tax treatment of trusts are contained in **Examples 52 to 65.** See **Examples 60 and 62** in particular for the treatment of business and agricultural property.

Various points need to be borne in mind when placing business or agricultural property into a trust, and the possible effects for the different types of trust need to be carefully considered.

(18) Before 22 March 2006, if property was placed into a life interest trust, the transfer was potentially exempt and will only become chargeable if the donor dies within seven years after the transfer. If the property is business or agricultural property, the relief would be taken into account in arriving at the amount of the potentially exempt transfer. The trustees need to hold the property for two years before any transfer by them would qualify for relief.

If the donor dies within seven years after transferring the property to the trust, so that the potentially exempt transfer becomes a chargeable transfer, the trustees still need to hold the property at that time in order for the relief to be available. (If the donor died within two years this would not prevent the relief being available providing the property was still held in the trust.) If the trust does not satisfy the conditions at the donor's death, the relief is not available against the now chargeable transfer, and the donor's 'clock' of cumulative transfers will include that chargeable transfer.

(19) Since 22 March 2006, the lifetime transfer of property into any trust other than one conferring a disabled person's interest is now an immediately chargeable transfer (at half of the rates of tax payable on death) after being reduced by business or agricultural property relief where available. The trustees need to retain the property for two years before being entitled to relief on any appointments of the property out of the trust. Furthermore, if there are any appointments of the property after that time but within ten years after the trust's creation, then although the relief is available on the transfer the *rate of tax* is based on the full value of the property when settled (see **Example 62 explanatory note 5**). This would not be a problem, however, if the property qualified in full for 100% relief, because the amount chargeable at that rate would be nil. If the donor dies within seven years after the transfer, the tax on the lifetime transfer is recalculated on the death scale, additional tax being payable accordingly. As with life interest trusts, the trustees still need to hold the property when the donor dies in order for the relief to remain available on the donor's transfer (and they would be entitled to the relief even if the donor died within two years providing the property was still held in the trust). If the trust does not satisfy the conditions for relief when the donor dies, the relief is not taken into account in calculating the additional tax on the lifetime transfer, but the amount of the donor's cumulative transfers would not be affected. Relief will not be available against the lifetime transfer to the trust because the trustees have disposed of the property between the time of the gift and the time of death.

Let property, including holiday lettings

(20) Holiday lettings are not agricultural property. HMRC take the view that a property letting business will not usually qualify for business property relief, because it will be regarded as a business of making or holding investments (s 105(3)). This is supported by the Special Commissioners' decisions in *Exors of Moore dec'd* and *Exor of Burkinyoung dec'd (1995)*. In both cases business property relief was denied, even though the taxpayers (or in the *Burkinyoung* case, the managing agents) carried out considerable work as part of the lettings, eg repairs, decoration and maintenance.

Hotels, bed and breakfast and residential homes will usually qualify for relief because of the level of services provided. In the case of *short-term* holiday lettings (eg weekly or fortnightly), where the property owner or his agent is substantially involved with the holidaymakers during the holiday, business property relief will normally be available even if the lettings were for part of the year only (HMRC's Inheritance Tax Manual IHTM25278). Most furnished holiday lettings should satisfy these tests.

In a decision of the *Special Commissioners (Furness v CIR) (1999)*, it was held that a caravan park business qualified for business property relief. Although there were both static and touring caravans, the larger part of the profits came other than from renting out caravan pitches, and the activities of the owner and his staff were greatly in excess of what one would expect in a business concerned wholly or mainly with investments.

The opposite decision was reached in *Weston (exor of Weston dec'd) v CIR (2000)*, where the Court confirmed the Special Commissioner's decision that the greater part of a caravan park's profits came from pitch fees and bank interest rather than caravan sales, so that the business was mainly one of making or holding investments. The same conclusion was reached in *IRC v George & Anor (Exors of Stedman dec'd) (2002)* where the main activities were the letting of sites for 167 residential mobile homes; storage of touring caravans; letting of a shop and warehouse and fields let on grazing licences. This outweighed the ancillary activities of a country club and an insurance agency, so the business was mainly one of making or holding investments. However, that decision was subsequently overturned by the Court of Appeal which reinstated the Special Commissioner's finding that the company was mainly trading.

The comments in the *Farmer & Giles* case mentioned in **part A(c)** of the Example provide a good basis on which to judge whether a business consists mainly of making or holding investments. See however, in the opposite direction, *McCall & anor (PRs of McClean dec'd) v HMRC (2008)*, where land was subject to a grazing agreement. The Court of Appeal in Northern Ireland held that the Special Commissioner had not erred in law when holding that the landowner's business did not consist of growing grass on the land for consumption by the grazier's livestock, but rather of exploiting the land as an investment, so that business property relief was excluded by s 105(3).

Once the hurdle of qualifying for business property relief is crossed then, as the Example indicates, the assets used for the investment side of the business will probably not be regarded as 'excepted assets' and will not therefore be excluded from relief.

Question

On 19 July 2005 Stanley (who has never made a lifetime gift before) gave Elizabeth (his granddaughter) the whole of his shares in Printers Ltd, a trading company, together with the freehold of the land and buildings occupied by the company, but which he owned personally.

On the same day Peter (who has made chargeable transfers within the previous seven years amounting to £180,000 and has fully utilised his exemptions for 2005/06 and 2004/05) gave Elizabeth (his daughter) his shareholding in Printers Ltd.

Prior to the above transfers the shareholdings in Printers Ltd (which had remained unchanged for many years) were:

		Shares
Stanley		4,000
Phyllis	(Stanley's wife)	4,000
Peter	(Stanley's son)	1,000
Barbara	(Peter's sister)	900
Elizabeth	(Peter's daughter)	100
		10,000

and the agreed values for inheritance tax purposes were:

100% holding	£1,600,000	51% holding	£900,000
80% holding	£1,400,000	40% holding	£300,000
60% holding	£1,000,000	10% holding	£40,000

The value of the land and buildings transferred by Stanley was agreed at £800,000.

On 13 November 2010 Stanley died. Elizabeth still owned the property and shares at that date.

(a)   Compute the inheritance tax payable by Elizabeth;

(b)   Assuming that the instalment option will be used, state the date on which the first instalment is due, and the amount payable on that day;

(c)   Explain under what circumstances interest will be payable on the instalments (without calculating the amount of any interest).

Answer

(a)   **Inheritance tax payable by Elizabeth as donee of lifetime transfers:**

On death of Stanley 13 November 2010

Potentially exempt transfers 19 July 2005, now chargeable transfers (see **explanatory notes 2 and 3**):

	Gross £	Tax £
Shares in Printers Ltd	–	–
Land and buildings (see **note 2**)	394,000	27,600*

(* 394,000 – 325,000 = 69,000 @ 40%)

Tax payable (after 60% taper relief) is 40% of £27,600 = £11,040, which is payable over 10 annual instalments.

Peter — inheritance tax accumulation

	Gross £	Tax £
Previous transfers	180,000	–

19 July 2005 — potentially exempt transfer £40,000 less 100% business property relief £40,000 = nil. (No tax payable even if Peter dies within seven years and business property relief is not then available, since cumulative transfers total of £180,000 plus £40,000 is within nil rate band. See **explanatory note 4**.)

(b)   The first instalment of the tax of £11,040 in respect of the land and buildings, amounting to £1,104, is payable on 31 May 2011.

(c)   Interest is payable on the tax in respect of land and buildings from 31 May 2011 to the date of the instalment, calculated on the full amount of tax for the time being unpaid. In addition interest is paid on the instalment from its due date to the actual date of payment of the instalment.

Explanatory Notes

Business property relief

(1)   A transfer of a business or an interest in a business qualifies for business property relief of 100% where the business is carried on for gain (ss 103(3), 104 and 105(1)(a)). Transfers out of a holding of unquoted shares also qualify for business property relief of 100% (ss 104(1)(a) and 105(1)(bb)).

Controlling holdings of quoted shares qualify for business property relief of 50% (ss 104(1)(b) and 105(1)(cc)).

Business property relief of 50% is available on the transfer of land and buildings used for the business of a company of which the transferor has control.

Related property

(2)   Using the related property rules (s 161) (see **Example 10**), Stanley's gift of shares on 19 July 2005 must be valued as a proportion of an 80% holding (ie his own plus his wife's holding), of which one-half relates to him. The related holding determines the size of the holding for the purposes of the rate of business property relief (s 269(2)). The rate of business property relief at 19 July 2005 was 100% on the shares and 50% on the land and buildings, so the original calculation would be:

	£
Value of shares (80%) $1,400,000 \times \dfrac{4,000 \text{ shares}}{8,000 \text{ shares}} =$	700,000
Less: Business property relief (100%)	700,000
Transfer of value	–

The transfer of value on the same day in respect of the land and buildings was:

			£
Value of property			800,000
Less: Business property relief (50%)			400,000
			400,000
Less: Annual exemptions	2005/06	3,000	
	2004/05	3,000	6,000
Chargeable transfer			394,000

For the position where business or agricultural property relief is withdrawn at death because the conditions are no longer satisfied see **Example 24 explanatory note 2**.

Availability of business property relief

(3)   To get the 100% business property relief on the *shares*, Elizabeth merely needs to retain the shares that were transferred to her out of Stanley's holding (s 113A).

To get the 50% relief on the *land and buildings*, as well as retaining them Elizabeth needs to *control* Printers Ltd when Stanley dies (s 113A(3)).

The shares owned by Elizabeth following the gifts on 19 July 2005 and still held by her at 13 November 2010 were:

Original shareholding	100
Gift from Stanley	4,000
Gift from Peter	1,000
Total shares held	5,100

so she has control of Printers Ltd and is therefore entitled to business property relief on the land and buildings.

Because Stanley died more than five but less than six years after the date of gift, taper relief of 60% applies to the tax payable.

(4)   Peter's gift of his Printers Ltd shareholding to Elizabeth on 19 July 2005 qualified for 100% business property relief. The whole of the gift is a potentially exempt transfer. If he should die before 19 July 2012, the potentially exempt transfer will become chargeable, and the business property relief will only then be available if Elizabeth satisfies the qualifying conditions at that time. In fact no tax will be payable on

Peter's gift in any event, since the cumulative transfers (including the unrelieved value of Peter's gift) are within the nil rate band, but if 100% business property relief was not available the gift would be taken into account in the cumulative total for a death within seven years.

(5)   Detailed notes on business property relief are given in **Example 25**.

Instalment option

(6)   Inheritance tax payable on certain assets on death (or on lifetime chargeable transfers where the transferee pays the inheritance tax) may be paid by ten annual instalments (ss 227 and 228). See **Examples 5 and 9**.

The instalment option is available on potentially exempt transfers that become chargeable because of the donor's death within seven years providing the donee still owns the gifted property (or, for transfers of property qualifying for business or agricultural relief, replacement property) at the time of the donor's death.

Unquoted shares and securities (including shares which do not qualify for business property relief, eg shares in property investment companies) that do not represent a controlling holding only qualify as instalment assets if:

(a)   the inheritance tax cannot be paid in one sum without undue hardship, or

(b)   (for shares only) they are valued at more than £20,000 and their nominal value is at least 10% of the nominal value of all the company's shares (or if they are ordinary shares, 10% of the nominal value of the company's ordinary shares), or

(c)   in the case of a transfer on death, the tax payable on the shares or securities, together with the tax on other instalment assets, amounts to 20% or more of the tax payable by the same person on the same transfer.

Furthermore the instalment option on unquoted shares is not available for tax payable in consequence of the donor's death unless the shares are still unquoted when the donor dies (or if earlier, when the donee dies).

The gift of 10% of the shares in Printers Ltd by Peter to Elizabeth would not satisfy any of the conditions listed above so that if tax were to become chargeable the instalment option would not be available.

The instalment option is available as indicated in respect of Stanley's gift to Elizabeth of the land and buildings.

Question

A.

To what extent is domicile relevant for inheritance tax purposes?

Explain the extended meaning given to domicile for the purposes of inheritance tax.

B.

Leonardo, who was born in, and whose home country is, Italy, has lived and worked in the UK since July 1999, but plans to return to Italy following his retirement.

On 31 January 2011 he made a chargeable transfer of £333,000 before deducting exemptions, paying the inheritance tax due himself on the due date, having made no earlier transfers.

His remaining assets, at current values, comprise:

(a)   10,000 £1 shares in Exodus plc (registered in Scotland) quoted on the Stock Exchange at 134p–140p with recorded bargains at 134, 135 and 136.

(b)   10,000 no par value bearer shares in Canadian Timber Limited. The company register is in Ontario, Canada, and the shares are quoted on the Ontario Stock Exchange at the sterling equivalent of 90–92.

(c)   A half share in a painting in the UK which Leonardo and his brother, Vincento, had bought in 1976, each providing one half of the purchase money. Its value is £48,000 but a half share is worth £22,000.

(d)   A house in Pisa, Italy, valued at €200,000.

(e)   Three insurance policies with a UK insurance company on his life:

     (i)   taken out in 2001; the proceeds of £50,000 will be left to his wife, who will receive nothing else,

     (ii)   taken out in 2003 on which he had paid the premiums and under which £15,000 will become payable to his executor,

     (iii)   taken out in 2005 for the benefit of his grand-daughter under which £30,000 becomes payable on his death. Leonardo had paid each annual premium of £600 himself.

(f)   Debts owing to him of:

     (i)   £1,500 by Michael living in the UK, and,

     (ii)   €1,000 by Manolo living in Italy.

(g)   Cash held in bank accounts:

     (i)   in the UK £4,250,

     (ii)   in Italy €3,000.

(h)   His gold watch valued at £800 and gold ring valued at £1,450, both held in the UK.

(i)   His private dwelling-house in London valued at £370,000 plus furniture valued at £20,000.

(j)   His UK trading business which he has run as a sole trader since his arrival in the UK, valued at £160,000.

Assume the current rate of exchange to be €1.12 = £1.

All share certificates and house deeds are held by Leonardo's solicitor at his office in Italy.

Leonardo is considering making further gifts during his lifetime as follows:

(i)   his Canadian Timber Ltd shares to his niece living in Canada,

(ii)   his half share in the painting to his brother, Angelo, living in London,

(iii)   his house in Pisa, Italy, to his daughter living in London,

(iv)   his gold ring to his grandson, living in London, in consideration of his forthcoming marriage,

(v)   his business in the UK to his son, living in London.

(1)   Compute the inheritance tax payable by Leonardo following the January 2011 transfer, stating the date it falls due, and the inheritance tax which would be payable if Leonardo were to die unexpectedly within the week following the transfer, not having made any further gifts, his estate (after the 2001 insurance policy proceeds to his wife) being left to his grandchildren. In the case of tax payable on death, identify the amounts which can be paid in instalments, the period over which instalments are payable, and the extent to which relief from interest is given on tax so payable.

(2)   State whether any amounts would become chargeable to inheritance tax if Leonardo, not having died in February 2011, had made the further gifts in (i) to (v) above in March 2011 and whether any additional tax would arise if Leonardo were then to die at any time in the eight years following the making of those gifts (assuming the inheritance tax legislation remains unaltered).

Answer

A. Relevance of domicile for inheritance tax

Domicile is relevant for inheritance tax purposes because, whilst the tax is charged on gratuitous transfers of UK assets regardless of the domicile of the transferor, it is also charged on gratuitous transfers of assets by persons of UK domicile regardless of where the property is situated.

Therefore it is necessary to know the domicile of the transferor when the transfer involves assets situated outside the UK, or UK authorised unit trusts or open-ended investment companies. The same applies in certain cases to the domicile of the beneficiary of a trust – see **Example 3 Part (a)**.

It is important to remember that since domicile is primarily a concept of private international law – to determine the legal system with which a person is most closely connected – a 'country' for this purpose is a separate legal jurisdiction, not necessarily a separate state. The United States comprises fifty different 'countries'. The point is sometimes of vital importance: residence in one state of the United States when intending to settle permanently in a different state will not give rise to the acquisition of a domicile of choice in either.

For this reason it is technically wrong (though convenient shorthand for tax purposes) to speak of someone being domiciled "in the UK": the United Kingdom comprises three different countries in this sense: England and Wales; Scotland; and Northern Ireland.

Until the Domicile and Matrimonial Proceedings Act 1973 s 1 a married woman acquired the domicile of her husband. However, that ceased to apply with respect to marriages after 31 December 1973. Accordingly in the case of transfers between spouses/civil partners it is necessary to know the domicile of both parties because if the transferor is domiciled in the UK but the transferee is domiciled abroad then the spouse/civil partner exemption is limited to £55,000 (s 18(2)).

A person's country of domicile is usually the country that he regards as his natural home, and a change of domicile requires a high standard of proof. A domicile of origin is acquired at birth. This may be supplanted by the acquisition of a domicile of choice. To do so requires both actual residence in the chosen country and an intention to make that country the person's permanent home; all circumstances of the person's life will be taken into account in deciding his intentions in this context (a conscious statement of intent will of itself usually be of little probative value since it may be self-serving). Positive action will generally be advisable if it is intended to establish a new domicile for tax reasons, eg changing residence, making a new will in the country of choice, obtaining citizenship etc, and severing ties with the previous country. However, retaining electoral voting rights will not be taken into account (FA 1996 s 200). If the domicile of choice is later abandoned without a new domicile of choice being established then the domicile of origin is revived: a person can never be without a domicile in law. (It is considered that Leonardo would have retained his domicile of origin in this Example, as he was born in Italy and intends to return there on retirement. He also retains a house and a bank account in Italy and keeps his documents with his Italian solicitor.)

The domicile of a settlor of settled property, at the time he settled it, is also relevant for inheritance tax since the settled property will then be excluded property to the extent that it comprises assets situated outside the UK, or UK authorised unit trusts or open-ended investment companies.

For inheritance tax purposes domicile has an extended meaning and the following persons are treated as domiciled in the UK (s 267):

(i) Persons who on or after 10 December 1974 were, under the general law, domiciled somewhere in the UK and were so domiciled within the three years preceding the transfer.

(ii) Persons who were resident in the UK on or after 10 December 1974 and in not less than seventeen out of the twenty income tax years ending with the tax year of transfer. For this purpose residence for any part of a tax year will count, so a deemed UK domicile under this rule can arise after not much more than 15 years' continuous residence.

B. Leonardo — inheritance tax payable

1.   *Inheritance tax payable re January 2011 transfer*

Leonardo is domiciled in Italy, therefore property located outside the UK is excluded property. (He is only in his twelfth successive (whole or part) tax year of UK residence so is not affected by the deemed domicile rule at this point.) The inheritance tax position on the transfer on 31 January 2011 is as follows:

			Gross	Tax (2010/11 scale)	Net
			£	£	£
31 January 2011					
Gifts within previous seven years			–	–	–
Chargeable lifetime transfer		333,000			
Less: Annual 2010/11	3,000				
exemptions					
2009/10	3,000	6,000			
Net transfer grossed up*			327,500	500	327,000
			327,500	500	327,000

*Net			Gross
325,000			325,000
2,000	$(\times\dfrac{100}{80})$		2,500
327,000			327,500

Inheritance tax payable by Leonardo on 31 July 2011 = £500.

If Leonardo died in February 2011

	Gross	Tax (2010/11 scale)
	£	£
Gifts within seven years before death:		
31 January 2011		
Chargeable transfer	327,500	1,000*
Cumulative transfers in seven years prior to death	327,500	1,000
(* 327,500 – 325,000 = 2,500 @ 40%)		

Inheritance tax payable by donee on 31 January 2011 transfer:

On death	1,000
Less: due from Leonardo (and so his estate) on lifetime transfer	500
Due from donee 31 August 2011	£500

Estate on death would be

	£	£
Shares in Exodus plc (UK company, listed in UK) 10,000 £1 shares @ 135 (midpoint between 134 and 136, being less than 134 + (¼ × (140 − 134) = 135½))		13,500
Canadian Timber Limited shares — excluded property		–
Painting held in UK — one half share		22,000
House in Italy — excluded property		–
Insurance policies — 2001		50,000
— 2003		15,000
Loans — Michael		1,500
— Manolo — excluded property		–
Cash at bank — UK		4,250
— Italy — excluded property		–
Possessions — gold watch		800
— gold ring		1,450
UK house		370,000
Furniture		20,000
Business	160,000	
Less: 100% business property relief	160,000	–
		498,500
Less: Debts — inheritance tax due on chargeable gift made 31.1.11		500
		498,000
Less: Exempt legacy — widow (2001 insurance policy)		50,000
		448,000

Note

The 2005 life policy for the benefit of Leonardo's grand-daughter does not form part of the estate. The annual premiums do not cumulate, having been exempt as gifts out of income.

As business property is left as part of residue to non-exempt beneficiaries and there is a specific gift to an exempt beneficiary (widow), business property relief will be reduced rateably (s 39A):

		£	£
Estate before reliefs and exemptions (448,000 + 160,000 + 50,000)			658,000
Less: Business property relief			(160,000)
			498,000
Less: Exempt legacy to widow		50,000	
Restricted by reference to business property relief			
$160,000 \times \dfrac{\text{Exempt estate (50,000)}}{\text{Total estate (658,000)}}$		12,158	(37,842)
Estate chargeable to inheritance tax			460,158
Tax thereon @ 40% (lifetime transfers being above nil threshold)			£184,063
Amount payable by instalments			

$$\text{UK house } \frac{370,000}{498,000} \times 184,063 = \pounds136,754$$

Payable by ten equal yearly instalments of £13,675 from 1 September 2011 plus interest on the full outstanding balance.

2.   *Inheritance tax position if gifts in (i) to (v) were made in March 2011 and Leonardo died within following eight years*

(i)   As the Canadian Timber Ltd shares are situated outside the UK, they are excluded property and not chargeable to UK inheritance tax on transfer.

(ii)   The transfer of the half-share of the painting to Angelo would be a potentially exempt transfer of £22,000 (no annual exemptions being available since they are already fully used). No inheritance tax would be due providing Leonardo lived for seven years, otherwise the gift would be added to the transfers of £327,500 made within seven years before the date of the gift and inheritance tax would be due based upon the scale and rate of tax applicable at the date of death.

(iii) The transfer of the house in Pisa to Leonardo's daughter would be excluded as Leonardo is not domiciled in the UK.

(iv) The gift of the ring valued at £1,450 to Leonardo's grandson, whilst not excluded property (unless situated outside the UK at the time the gift was made, for Example handed over when both parties were on holiday in Italy), would be exempt as a gift of not more than £2,500 made by a grandparent in consideration of the grandson's marriage.

(v)   The transfer of the business to Leonardo's son would attract 100% business property relief, so that the potentially exempt transfer would be nil. The transfer would not be liable to inheritance tax unless Leonardo died within seven years after making the transfer. If death occurred within the seven year period, the entitlement to business property relief would have to be reconsidered at that time. The relief would only continue to be available providing the son continued to satisfy the qualifying conditions up to the date of Leonardo's death.

If Leonardo died more than three but less than seven years after giving away the painting or business, any tax payable upon the potentially exempt transfers becoming chargeable would be reduced as follows:

Death more than			
3 years but less than	4 years after gift	— 20%
4 years	5 years	— 40%
5 years	6 years	— 60%
6 years	7 years	— 80%

After seven years no liability would arise on death in respect of these gifts.

Explanatory Notes

Situation of property

(1)   The normal rules of English law apply to determine where property is situated.

(a)   Land is in the country where it is physically situated (but mortgages of land are treated as debts).

(b)   Debts are in the country where the debtor resides.

(c)   Shares are located where the share register is kept. (The place where the shares are quoted, if they are, is not relevant.)

(d)   Life insurance policies are situated where the proceeds are payable (unless under seal, in which case they are situated where the policy is).

(e)   Business property is situated where the business is carried on.

(f)   Tangible property (including currency) is wherever it is physically situated.

(g)   Bank accounts are situated at the branch at which the deposits are payable (subject to what is said in **note 4** re foreign currency accounts).

Excluded property

(2)   Foreign property in foreign ownership is excluded property for inheritance tax purposes. The property must be situated outside the UK and the person beneficially entitled to it must be non-UK domiciled (s 6(1)).

(3)   The following is also excluded property:

(a)   National Savings etc owned by persons domiciled in the Channel Islands or Isle of Man (s 6(3)).

(b)   Certain government securities issued as being exempt from tax where they are owned by persons of a description specified in the conditions of issue of the security concerned (s 6(2)) (see **Example 3 part (a)**). The specified conditions prior to FA 1996 required the holder to be neither domiciled nor ordinarily resident in the UK, but the reference to domicile is excluded in current issues.

In these two cases domicile has its ordinary meaning and not the extended inheritance tax meaning.

For further notes on the meaning and treatment of excluded property see **Example 3 Part (a)**.

Foreign currency bank accounts

(4)   Where a person who is *neither resident, ordinarily resident nor domiciled* in the UK dies, any foreign currency bank accounts with the Bank of England, the Post Office, or an institution authorised under the Banking Act 1987 are left out of account in valuing the estate immediately prior to death. This also applies to such accounts held by trustees of settled property in which the deceased held a beneficial interest in possession unless the settlor was domiciled in the UK at the date of the settlement or the trustees are UK domiciled, resident and ordinarily resident at the time of the beneficiary's death (s 157) (the provision in FA 1989 s 110 deeming trustees of whom one or more is UK resident all to be UK resident regardless of how many foreign resident trustees there are does not apply to this provision). The individual's residence status will be determined using the normal income tax rules.

Works of art

(5)   Where a work of art is normally kept overseas, but becomes liable to inheritance tax on the owner's death solely because it is physically situated in the UK, that liability will be waived by Concession F7. This relief is only available if the work of art was brought into the UK solely for public exhibition, cleaning or restoration. The liability will similarly be waived if a work of art which would otherwise have left the UK to be kept overseas is retained in the UK solely for those purposes.

Business property relief

(6)   For further Examples and notes on the interaction of exempt legacies and business property relief see **Examples 15 and 17**. For details of business property relief, see **Example 25**.

Types of domicile

(7)   For detailed notes on the possible types of domicile an individual might have see **Example 3 Part (c)**.

Question

David, domiciled in England, who had worked a small agricultural holding for many years, died on 1 May 2010 leaving the following estate in England:

'Freehold agricultural land extending to 30 acres and buildings together valued at £123,500 of which the agricultural value was £92,000.

Farming machinery and stores valued at £24,884.

Timber (growing on separate freehold land) valued at £123,000, being operated on a commercial basis. The land itself was valued at £150,000 but was subject to a mortgage of the same amount, for which the lender held no security other than the land.

Leasehold house valued at £157,500.

Household chattels and car valued at £22,850.

A quoted shareholding valued at £80,822 (being a 20% holding that David had owned for many years).

Bank balance £2,303.'

English debts and funeral expenses (all allowable) totalled £7,233.

In addition David owned the following property in Afaria:

'Freehold house valued at 74,500 fars.

Furniture valued at 28,750 fars.

Bank balance 9,580 fars.'

His gardener was owed wages of 830 fars.

He also owned the following property in Nyria:

'Leasehold house valued at 22,450 nyrs.

Furniture valued at 12,250 nyrs.

Bank balance of 3,750 nyrs.'

There were no outstanding liabilities in Nyria.

Death duties abroad, with no interest if paid within six months of death, are calculated on total assets less liabilities at the following flat rates:

Afaria 10%; Nyria 8%.

The UK and Afaria (but not Nyria) have a double taxation agreement.

On 1 May 2010 exchange rates were:

Afaria 1 far = 100/120p; Nyria £1 = 0.48/0.50 nyrs.

On 1 July 2010 the executor obtained probate by presenting a provisional account in which, after appropriate reliefs, realty was included at £75,000, instalment option personalty at £200,000 and non-instalment option personalty at £171,000.

Inheritance tax was not paid on realty or the instalment option personalty.

The timber was sold standing for £127,500, which was received on 1 August 2010, no election having been made for the value at death to be left out of account under ss 125 to 130.

On 20 June 2008 David had made a potentially exempt transfer (after exemptions) of £132,000 to his sister, which was his only lifetime transfer.

By his will he left £30,000 to his brother, with the residue to his sister.

On 30 November 2010 the executor presented a corrective account.

Prepare statements showing:

(a)   Death duty payable in Afaria and Nyria.*

(b)   Any balance of inheritance tax and interest payable in England on 30 November 2010 on the assumption that the minimum amount of inheritance tax was paid at that time, the balance being deferred.

(c)   The amount of tax that can be deferred.

* Assuming the rates of exchange when the duty was paid were unchanged from 1 May 2010.

Answer

(a) Death duty payable overseas

		Fars		£
Afaria	— House	74,500		74,500
	Furniture	28,750		28,750
	Bank balance	9,580		9,580
		112,830		112,830
	Less: Debts	830		830
		112,000	@ 1 far = 100p	112,000
	Death duty in Afaria @ 10%	11,200	@ 1 far = 120p	£13,440
		Nyrs		£
Nyria	— Leasehold house	22,450		44,900
	Furniture	12,250		24,500
	Bank balance	3,750		7,500
		38,450	@ £1 = 0.5 nyrs	76,900
	Death duty in Nyria @ 8%	3,076	@ £1 = 0.48 nyrs	£6,408

(b) Computation of inheritance tax due on 30 November 2010 (Death 1 May 2010)

Inheritance tax paid on account 1 July 2010 on non-instalment option personalty of £171,000:

		Gross £	Tax £
Potentially exempt transfers within seven years before death, now chargeable:			
20 June 2008		132,000	–
Estate on death per provisional account:			
Realty after reliefs	75,000		
Instalment option personalty after reliefs	200,000		
Non-instalment option personalty after reliefs	171,000	446,000	101,200*
		578,000	101,200*

(* 578,000 – 325,000 = 253,000 @ 40%)

Tax paid 1 July 2009 on £171,000 non-instalment option personalty:

$$\frac{171,000}{446,000} \times £101,200 = £38,801$$

				Date of death 1 May 2010	
			£	£	£
Freehold agricultural land and buildings				123,500	
Less:	Agricultural property relief	100% × £92,000	92,000		
	Business property relief	100% × £31,500	31,500	123,500	
				–	

Freehold land less mortgage thereon
(£150,000 – £150,000)

Freehold house in Afaria		74,500	74,500

			brought forward	74,500
Personalty — with instalment option				
Farm machinery and stores		24,884		
Less:	Business property relief — 100%	24,884	–	
Leasehold house in England			157,500	
Leasehold house in Nyria			44,900	202,400
Personalty — without instalment option				
Timber (sold)		123,000		
Less:	Business property relief — 100%	123,000	–	
Quoted shares (20% holding)			80,822	
Chattels			22,850	
Bank balance			2,303	
In Afaria	— chattels	28,750		
	bank balance	9,580	38,330	
In Nyria	— chattels	24,500		
	bank balance	7,500	32,000	
			176,305	
Less:	Debts and funeral expenses — UK	7,233		
	Debts in Afaria	830	8,063	168,242
Chargeable estate				445,142

	Gross £	Tax £
Inheritance tax accumulation in seven years before death	132,000	–
Estate chargeable on death and tax thereon	445,142	100,857*
	577,142	100,857*

(* 577,142 – 325,000 = 252,142 @ 40%)

Estate rate is $\dfrac{100,857}{445,142} \times 100 = 22.657\%$

Since this average rate clearly exceeds the rates paid overseas, the double taxation relief will be the duty paid overseas.

		£	£	£
Liability on estate			100,857	
Less:	Double tax relief —			
	Afaria	13,440		
	Nyria	6,408	19,848	
			81,009	
Less:	Paid on account (see page 28.3)		38,801	42,208
Less:	Tax deferred (at estate rate of 22.657%)			
	Realty			
	House in Afaria £74,500	16,880		

Less:	Double tax relief:				
	$\dfrac{74,500}{112,000} \times £13,440$	8,940	7,940		
	Instalment option personalty £202,400	45,858			
Less:	Double tax relief on house in Nyria:				
	$\dfrac{44,900}{76,900} \times £6,408$	3,741	42,117	50,057	
	Tax repayable to personal representative on non-instalment property				(7,849)
Being:	Tax on non-deferred personalty of £168,242 at estate rate of 22.657%		38,119		
Less:	Double tax relief:				
Afaria	$\dfrac{37,500}{112,000} \times £13,440$	4,500			
Nyria	$\dfrac{32,000}{76,900} \times £6,408$	2,667			
			7,167		
			30,951		
Less:	Paid on account (see page 28.3)		38,801		
			£(7,849)		

Tax payable by personal representative on deferred property

$$\frac{1}{10} \times 50,057$$

	5,006
Total amount repayable 30 November 2010 (no interest due)	(2,843)

(c)

Tax deferred	50,057
Less: First instalment	(5,006)
Amount deferred as at 30 November 2010	£45,051

Explanatory Notes

Converting values of foreign assets and foreign tax

(1) Foreign assets are valued by using the lower value of the exchange rate quoted, ie the more advantageous to the taxpayer. Where foreign tax is paid it is converted to sterling by using the higher value of the exchange rate on the date of payment (restricted to the amount paid if in sterling).

Agricultural and business property relief

(2)

(a)   Agricultural property relief at 100% is available under s 116 on the agricultural value of the farm land and buildings. Business property relief at 100% is available under s 104 on the excess over the agricultural value and on the farming machinery and stores.

(b)   Business property relief is also available at 100% on the growing timber. An election could have been made under s 125 for the timber (but not the land on which it stands) to be left out of account on David's death, but with business property relief at 100% there is no point in doing so. Had it been left out it would have had to be brought in later at its sale value, and only 50% business property relief would have been available on the subsequent sale (s 127(2)) (see **Example 31 explanatory note 10**).

Business property relief is also available on the land on which the timber stands but it is only given on the value of business assets less liabilities so that the land does not attract the relief in this case because its value is wholly eliminated by the mortgage.

Where the only security for the mortgage is the business land, it is not possible to reduce the business property by business property relief and then deduct the mortgage from other assets.

(c)   For detailed notes on agricultural and business property relief and growing timber see **Examples 25 and 31**.

Instalment option

(3)   The option for tax to be paid by ten yearly instalments is available on the following assets in this Example:

Land in the UK and abroad (including leaseholds)

Business and agricultural property

The first instalment is due six months after the end of the month in which the death occurred, ie on 30 November 2010 (s 227(3)).

Payment of tax and interest on underpaid/overpaid tax

(4)   Inheritance tax on death is payable on presentation of the HMRC Account (s 226(2)), ie on 1 July 2010 in this Example, the tax then accounted for being on the provisional amount of £171,000 non-instalment option personalty. The inheritance tax, however, is not due until six months after the end of the month in which the death occurred, ie by 30 November 2010, so the corrective account showing the revised amount payable was submitted in time to stop any interest arising on unpaid tax. In fact the provisional amount paid exceeded the actual liability, so that a refund of £2,843 is due and the question of interest on unpaid tax does not arise.

The amount overpaid on the presentation of the account on 1 July 2010 does not attract an interest supplement. This is not overpaid tax but tax paid in advance of the due date. The amount of £2,843 found to be overpaid at 30 November 2010, on the other hand, will attract interest from that date until it is repaid (the current rate of interest is 0.5% subject to any changes after July 2010).

Interest on unpaid tax on instalment assets is charged only from the date the instalment is payable, except for land which, unless the land is agricultural property or part of an interest in a business, attracts interest on the whole of the tax unpaid.

The first instalment due on 30 November 2010 was paid on time and accordingly no interest was payable thereon.

Interest will therefore arise from 1 December 2010 to the date of payment on the remainder of the tax on the freehold house in Afaria, the English leasehold and the leasehold house in Nyria, whether or not the instalments are paid on time; the present interest rate is 3.0% subject to any changes after July 2010.

In this Example the inheritance tax payable on the estate is less than the amount payable on the provisional account that the personal representatives had submitted. Personal representatives need to be aware that HMRC are taking a harsher attitude to penalties where a provisional account understates the values of the assets — see **Example 33 explanatory note 9**.

Overseas liabilities

(5)   Overseas liabilities are allowable as a deduction from the deceased's estate providing such debts would be allowable if UK debts. Normally the liabilities are deducted primarily from the value of overseas assets with any surplus deductible from UK assets (s 162(5)). If the liability is secured on UK property or is payable in the UK then the debt is deductible from UK property.

Double tax relief

(6)

(a)   Double tax relief is available where the same property is charged to tax both in the UK and overseas. Relief is given under s 158 where the UK has a double tax agreement with the country concerned and otherwise unilaterally under s 159. Where there is a double tax agreement it will usually give greater relief than that available under s 159, but if it does not, the taxpayer is given the benefit of the unilateral relief of s 159.

(b)   Section 159 enables the overseas duty paid to be deducted provided that this does not exceed the UK tax on the same property. In determining whether the UK tax is greater than the overseas tax, the average rate of UK tax is taken. This differs from double taxation relief for income tax where the UK tax applicable to overseas income can be taken as the highest rate of UK tax which applies to that taxpayer in that year of assessment.

The UK tax on the overseas property in this Example is clearly greater than the overseas tax on the same property, the UK average rate being 22.657% compared with 10% in Afaria and 8% in Nyria.

(c)   Section 159 also gives relief where both the UK and another country impose tax on property situated in a third country, or where property is situated in the UK under UK law and in another country under that country's law. Relief is calculated by the formula:

$$\frac{A}{A + B} \times C$$

where A is the inheritance tax, B is the overseas tax and C is whichever of A and B is smaller.

(d)   For a further account of the interaction between Double Taxation and IHT see **Example 3(c)** and **Example 15 note 4**.

Question

A has made cumulative chargeable transfers amounting to £214,000, all in the year ending 5 April 2003.

In May 2003 he gave a fine painting that he had owned for the last ten years to his son S. The picture was worth £95,000 in the open market at the time of the gift.

In November 2003 he gave a similar picture, then worth £100,000 in the open market, to his daughter D.

In both cases any liability for capital gains tax was held over.

On 20 March 2005 S gave his picture, then valued at £117,500, to his wife W, who is an American citizen but domiciled and resident in the UK. She immediately took it to New York to hang in the family gallery.

A died in December 2007 leaving an estate valued at £400,000 equally to his son S and daughter D.

An undertaking was given by the daughter that she would keep the picture in the UK; that she would take reasonable steps for its preservation; and that she would allow reasonable access to the public to view it.

On 3 August 2010 D sold her painting at an international auction room for £150,000, out of which the auctioneers took £15,000 in fees, and capital gains tax on the sale amounted to £8,800.

Both pictures were designated by the Treasury as being of national, scientific, historic or artistic interest. Appropriate claims for relief are made in connection with all transfers.

Calculate the inheritance tax payable as a result of these events.

Answer

Inheritance tax

May 2003	Picture to S	95,000
	Less: Annual exemption 2003/04	3,000
	Potentially exempt transfer	92,000
November 2003	Picture to D — potentially exempt transfer	100,000

On death of A – December 2007

	Gross £	Tax on 2007/08 scale £
Gifts in lifetime:		
Cumulative transfers (year ended 5.4.2003)	214,000	–
May 2003		
Gift of picture to S (potentially exempt transfer now chargeable)	92,000	2,400*
	306,000	2,400*

(* 306,000 – 300,000 = 6,000 @ 40%)

			Gross £	Tax on 2007/08 scale £
November 2003				
Potentially exempt transfer of picture to D, now a chargeable transfer		100,000		
Less: Conditional exemption		100,000		
			–	
Inheritance tax accumulation at death			306,000	2,400
Estate on death			400,000	160,000
			706,000	162,400

Tax payable by S (with interest on unpaid tax from 1 July 2008)
after 40% taper relief

60% × £2,400	£1,440

Tax payable by A's personal representatives (with interest on unpaid tax from 1 July 2008)	£160,000

Chargeable event — sale of picture by D 3 August 2010

	Gross £	Tax at half rate (2010/11 scale) £
A's inheritance tax accumulation	706,000	76,200*

(* 706,000 – 325,000 = 381,000 @ 20%)

Value of picture (sale proceeds)		150,000		
Less: Fees	15,000			
Capital gains tax	8,800	23,800	126,200	25,240
			832,200	101,440
Tax payable by D (with interest on unpaid tax from 1 March 2011)				£25,240

Explanatory Notes

Conditional exemption for works of art and other heritage property

(1)   Conditional exemption from inheritance tax for works of art and other heritage property is provided in ss 30 to 35A. Eligible assets are:

Works of art and other objects or collections or groups of objects that are pre-eminent for their national, scientific, historic or artistic interest

Land of outstanding scenic, historic or scientific interest

Buildings of outstanding historic or architectural interest together with their amenity land and objects historically associated with them.

(2)   Transfers are conditionally exempt if designated by the Treasury *following a claim* made within two years of the event (for Example following death), providing an appropriate undertaking is given by such person as the Treasury consider appropriate (usually the transferee).

(3)   The undertaking depends upon the category, but applies until death or disposal and generally requires reasonable public access, preservation and in the case of objects, retention in the UK, until death or further disposition (s 31). Public access cannot be by prior appointment only, and the owner may be required to publicise information about the conditionally exempt asset.

(4)   The conditional exemption is not available if the transfer would be exempt anyway by reason of transfers to charities or one's spouse/civil partner (s 30). But on a transfer to a spouse/civil partner of property that is the subject of an earlier conditional exemption, the spouse/civil partner would have to renew the undertaking to retain the conditional exemption (s 32).

Availability of conditional exemption

(5)   Conditional exemption is available upon:

(i)   Death.

(ii)   Lifetime transfers where transferor and spouse/civil partner have between them been beneficially entitled to the subject matter throughout the preceding six years.

(iii)   Lifetime gifts not qualifying under (ii) where the transferor acquired the subject matter on an inheritance tax/capital transfer tax conditionally exempt death transfer (s 30(3)).

Potentially exempt transfers

(6)   When a potentially exempt transfer of heritage property is made, no claim for conditional exemption may be made until the transferor dies, and a claim will not then be relevant if the transferor has survived the gift by seven years. If he dies within seven years, s 26A provides that the potentially exempt transfer will nonetheless be exempt if the property has in the meantime been sold by private treaty to an approved body (Sch 3) or surrendered to HMRC in satisfaction of tax (s 230). If the property has been sold other than to

an approved body, no claim for conditional exemption may be made. The circumstances at the transferor's death will determine whether conditional exemption is available, and if an undertaking is already in force for capital gains tax or for maintenance fund purposes it will be treated as an undertaking under s 30 (s 31(4G)).

In this Example both gifts in 2003 are potentially exempt (after deducting the annual exemption from the earlier gift), so claims for conditional exemption for inheritance tax would not be made at the time of the gifts. In order to avoid capital gains tax arising on the gifts, however, it would have been necessary for A to procure the appropriate undertakings as indicated in note 3 from S and D under the provisions of TCGA 1992 s 258, leading to the gifts being treated on a no gain no loss basis (see **explanatory note 13**).

The removal of the picture to America by S's wife W in 2005 does not affect the status of A's gift as a potentially exempt transfer. See **explanatory note 13** for the capital gains tax consequences of S's gift to W.

On the death of A the potentially exempt transfers become chargeable. S cannot claim conditional exemption (because the conditions are not satisfied at the time of A's death) and tax is payable. (The transfer from S to W was an exempt transfer and therefore did not affect the inheritance tax accumulation of S.) D can claim conditional exemption, thus saving inheritance tax of 40% × £100,000 = £40,000 less taper relief of 40% = £24,000 at that time.

Chargeable events

(7)   Inheritance tax is payable following a conditionally exempt transfer when a chargeable event occurs.

A 'chargeable event' is:

(i)   Material breach of undertaking.

(ii)   Death (when a new conditionally exempt transfer might occur).

(iii)   Disposal by sale, gift (when a new conditionally exempt transfer might again occur) or otherwise.

In cases (ii) and (iii), that is death or disposal, a surrender to the Board of HMRC to pay inheritance tax, or a sale by private treaty to an approved body (eg museum) is not a chargeable event (s 32). A private treaty sale to an approved body would be below market value, but above the after tax sum that would arise on an open market sale, thus dividing the benefit of the tax saving between the vendor and the approved body.

(8)   Inheritance tax is chargeable on the value of the subject matter at the time of the chargeable event. The value is the sale proceeds or market value as appropriate. An unconnected sale will usually fix the value at the sale proceeds (s 33(1)(a) and (3)).

(9)   The tax is calculated according to the inheritance tax accumulation of the 'relevant person' at the date of the chargeable event. The relevant person is the person who made the conditionally exempt transfer of the property. If there have been two or more such transfers, but only one within the last 30 years ending with the event then the relevant person is that last person. Otherwise HMRC may select the accumulation of any transferor out of those making appropriate claims in the last 30 years (s 33(5)).

If the relevant person is alive at the time of the chargeable event (which cannot apply in the case of a potentially exempt transfer, because such a transfer only becomes chargeable, and therefore eligible for conditional exemption, on the donor's death), half the scale rate is used, and the rate is not increased to the full rate even if the donor then dies within seven years of the date of the conditionally exempt transfer. If the relevant person is dead at the time of the chargeable event, the full scale rate is charged if the transfer was made on death, and the half scale rate if it was made in lifetime (s 33(1)(b) and (2)).

(10)   When D sold her picture, this was a chargeable event giving rise to a charge under s 32, with inheritance tax payable by her on the net proceeds of sale (s 33(3)). The half rate applies as the conditional exemption was given on a lifetime potentially exempt transfer that became chargeable because of the death of A within seven years after the gift. The tax has therefore been calculated by adding the proceeds to A's lifetime and death transfers, but using half the scale rates in force at the date of A's death. If, however, the rates of tax have reduced between death and the date of the chargeable event, the rates at the time the asset ceases to qualify for exemption apply (Sch 2 para 5). There appears to be an anomaly here in that the half scale rate

can never apply in normal circumstances to a potentially exempt transfer (though the effective charge may be at less than half the scale rate where the potentially exempt transfer was more than five years before death so that taper relief of at least 60% has accrued). It appears therefore that tax could be avoided by claiming conditional exemption on death, if a chargeable event took place soon after the claim had been accepted. It may be that such conduct would be attacked by HMRC as a composite transaction under the Ramsay doctrine, thus treating the chargeable event as occurring on the death and attracting tax at the full rate.

Variation of undertakings

(11)   Once given, an undertaking may be varied by agreement between HMRC and the person bound by the undertaking (s 35A). If that person does not agree with a variation proposed by HMRC within six months, and the First Tier Tribunal (Tax Chamber) considers it to be just and reasonable, the tribunal may direct that it should be made, with effect from a date not less than 60 days after the date of the direction.

Due date of payment of tax

(12)   Where tax becomes payable as a result of the occurrence of a chargeable event, such as the breach of an undertaking as in this Example, the due date is six months after the end of the month in which the event by reason of which it is chargeable occurs (s 226(4)). Interest on overdue tax runs from that due date (s 233(1)(c)).

Capital gains tax

(13)   As far as capital gains tax is concerned, a gift of heritage property in lifetime that is potentially exempt from inheritance tax does not qualify for the gifts holdover relief of TCGA 1992 s 260. The gain may, however, escape tax in the donor's hands under TCGA 1992 s 258 if the appropriate undertaking described in IHTA 1984 s 31 is given as indicated in **note 6**. The effect for capital gains tax purposes is that the person making the disposal by way of gift and the person acquiring it are treated as if the asset was acquired from the one making the disposal for a consideration of such an amount as would secure that on the disposal neither a gain nor a loss would accrue to the one making the disposal (TCGA 1992 s 258(4)).

On sale (other than to an approved body) or material breach the asset is treated as sold for its market value and capital gains tax arises (TCGA 1992 s 258(5)). A gift is treated for this purpose as a sale to an individual (triggering the deemed disposal for market value) unless the undertaking under TCGA 1992 s 258 is renewed by the donee. If inheritance tax is chargeable on the same occasion, any capital gains tax payable reduces the value to be included as a chargeable transfer for inheritance tax (TCGA 1992 s 258(8)).

In the Example, A would have needed to submit undertakings by S and D under s 258, establishing no gain no loss treatment for capital gains tax, to avoid an immediate capital gains tax charge on the 2003 gifts. When S gave his picture to his wife W, the gift would give rise to a deemed disposal at market value be a breach of the undertaking unless the undertaking was renewed by W. (Although TCGA 1992, s 58, providing for no gain, no loss treatment for disposals between spouses or civil partners, generally overrides other provisions of TCGA 1992 fixing the amount of the consideration deemed to be given on a disposal or acquisition, that does not assist S here because the deemed sale under TCGA 1992 s 258(6) is to 'an [unspecified] individual', and so without reference to the identity of the actual donee.) If it was not, S would be deemed to have sold the asset at market value. If W gave the undertaking, it would be breached when she took the asset out of the UK and she would be the one who was deemed to have sold it – and (because it is a breach of undertaking rather than an actual disposal) reacquired it – for market value. Although S also becomes liable to inheritance tax on the 2003 gift of the painting because of his father's death within seven years, he cannot deduct the capital gains tax paid by him (if any) from the inheritance tax value, because the occasion of the inheritance tax charge is the 2003 gift from the father, not the 2005 disposal by S.

As far as D is concerned, she still held the painting at her father's death and the conditional exemption for inheritance tax will therefore apply, the capital gains tax undertaking being treated as an undertaking under s 30 (see **explanatory note 6**). When she sold the painting, both inheritance tax and capital gains tax are charged on that occasion, so the capital gains tax may be deducted from the value to be charged to inheritance tax, as shown in the Example.

Question

Mackenzie Ltd is a property holding and investment company.

The following is a summary of its balance sheet at 31 December 2010:

	£			£
Issued Capital: shares of £1 each	10,000	Freehold Properties		1,720,000
		(Market value £3,000,000)		
Reserves	1,420,000			
		Quoted Investments		1,200,000
Loan Accounts:		(Market value £1,250,000)		
Robert Mackenzie 1,200,000				
James Mackenzie 200,000		Bank Deposit Account	200,000	
Duncan Mackenzie 300,000	1,700,000			
		Bank Current Account	10,000	210,000
	3,130,000			3,130,000

The issued capital had since December 1982 been held by:

Robert Mackenzie		4,000
James Mackenzie	) Robert's sons	3,750
Duncan Mackenzie	)	2,250
		10,000

On 11 January 2011 Mrs Newman, Robert Mackenzie's daughter, and her three children returned to this country from overseas. To provide for them, Robert withdrew £400,000 from his loan account with the company, which enabled him on 15 January 2011 to give £437,500 to Mrs Newman. Some of the company's investments were sold to produce sufficient cash to pay the £400,000 to Robert.

A meeting of the members was held on 18 January 2011 at which it was resolved that one of the freehold properties owned by the company and valued at £900,000 should be conveyed to Miss Diana Crawley, a very close friend of Robert's. The house was conveyed to her on 20 January 2011 without payment.

Assuming that Robert had made previous chargeable transfers totalling £330,000 in 2005/06, that James had made a gift of £81,000 to his son on 31 December 2010 and that Duncan had made no gifts other than £200,000 to his wife in December 2006, calculate the inheritance tax payable in connection with the above.

Answer

Mackenzie Ltd — apportionment of transfer of value on 20 January 2011

Transfer of value by close company on 20 January 2011 apportioned amongst participators:

Robert Mackenzie	0.40	×	900,000	=	360,000
James Mackenzie	0.375	×	900,000	=	337,500
Duncan Mackenzie	0.225	×	900,000	=	202,500
					£900,000

Inheritance tax payable:
Robert Mackenzie

Inheritance tax accumulation

	Gross £	Tax on 2010/11 scale £	Net £
Previous transfers within seven years	330,000	1,000*	329,000

(* 330,000 – 325,000 = 5,000 @ 20%)

15 January 2011					
Gift to daughter			437,500		
Less: Annual exemptions	2010/11	3,000			
	2009/10	3,000	6,000		
Potentially exempt transfer			431,500		
20 January 2011					
Apportioned from Mackenzie Ltd (net amount)					360,000
Grossed up			450,000(*)	90,000	
			780,000	91,000	689,000

(*) £360,000 is wholly within the tax band of 20% for lifetime gifts.

$$\text{The gross transfer is therefore: } 360,000 \times \frac{100}{80} = £450,000.$$

James Mackenzie

Inheritance tax accumulation

			Gross	Tax on 2010/11 scale	Net
			£	£	£
Gift to son on 31 December 2010 is a potentially exempt transfer of:					
Gift			81,000		
Less: Annual exemptions	2010/11	3,000			
	2009/10	3,000	6,000		
			75,000		
20 January 2011					
Apportioned from Mackenzie Ltd (net amount)					337,500
Grossed up			340,625*	3,125	
			340,625	3,125	337,500

* £337,500 – £325,000 = £12,500 is within tax band of 20% for lifetime gifts.

The gross transfer is therefore:	12,500	$\times \dfrac{100}{80}$		15,625
	325,000	@ nil rate		325,000
	337,500			£340,625

Duncan Mackenzie

Inheritance tax accumulation

			Gross	Tax on 2010/11 scale	Net
			£	£	£
Previous transfer to wife — exempt			–	–	–
20 January 2011					
Apportioned from Mackenzie Ltd (net amount)			202,500		
Less: Annual exemptions	2010/11	3,000			
	2009/10	3,000	6,000	196,500*	0	196,500
Net gift grossed up				196,500	0	196,500

* £196,500 – £325,000 = nil within 20% tax band for lifetime gifts. The transfer is wholly within the nil-rate band.

Inheritance tax payable

	£
On conveyance by company	
Robert Mackenzie	90,000
James Mackenzie	3,125
Duncan Mackenzie	0
Payable by Mackenzie Ltd	93,125
By Robert Mackenzie on gift to his daughter	
(£6,000 of transfer covered by annual exemptions, balance of £431,500 potentially exempt transfer)	£nil

Explanatory Notes

Apportionment of close company transfers of value

(1)   Where a close company makes a transfer of value, the transfer is apportioned amongst the participators and each participator is deemed to have made a net transfer of the amount apportioned to him (s 94(1)). HMRC take the view that only actual transfers (as distinct from those apportioned to participators from a close company) can be potentially exempt transfers, so that the apportioned amounts in this Example are immediately reckoned for inheritance tax.

If, however, the estate of a participator increases in consequence of the transfer, that increase is deducted from the amount chargeable on him, because his personal wealth has only decreased by his share of the close company transfer less the consequential increase in his wealth.

(2)   The exempt transfer reliefs for small gifts, normal expenditure out of income and marriage gifts are not available, but the annual exemption is (s 94(5)).

(3)   The surrender of losses under the corporation tax group relief provisions (ICTA 1988 s 402) does not constitute a transfer of value (s 94(3)).

(4)   Where an asset is transferred between group companies on a no loss no gain basis under the provisions of TCGA 1992 s 171, the rights of minority participators are not taken into account for the purpose of apportioning transfers of value under s 94 providing the transfer has only a small effect on the value of the minority participators' rights (s 97). The provisions of s 97 have been extended by FA 2001 s 106 to cover *deemed* intra-group no loss no gain transfers on or after 1 April 2000 under the provisions of TCGA 1992 s 171A. For detailed provisions relating to the tax treatment of groups of companies see the companion book **Tolley's Taxwise I 2010/11**.

Transfers liable to income tax or corporation tax

(5)   The apportionment rules do not apply to any part of the transfer that is liable to income tax or corporation tax in the recipient's hands (s 94(2)(a)). This will eliminate transfers of assets to participators who are employees earning £8,500 or more and to directors, which would be charged to income tax as employment income under the benefits code (ITEPA 2003 s 206) and also transfers to other participators, because they would be charged as distributions (ICTA 1988 s 418). A transfer by a close company to an Employee Benefit Trust may give rise to a transfer of value.

In the circumstances of this Example, HMRC would arguably seek to treat the value of the property as a benefit chargeable to income tax as employment income on the directors, in that an asset has been transferred out of the company at their direction without payment. If this were the case then the inheritance tax apportionment provisions would not apply.

Alterations of capital etc

(6)   Changes in the rights or number of unquoted shares of a close company are treated as if made by a disposal at that time by the participator and are chargeable accordingly (s 98). Such transfers cannot be potentially exempt (s 98(3)).

Effect of apportionment on participators

(7)   The apportioned amounts are included in the inheritance tax accumulations of the participators, unless an individual has not more than 5% of the transfer apportioned to him, in which case although the tax is computed by reference to his inheritance tax accumulation at that time, the transfer is not added to his cumulative total (s 94(4)).

Liability for payment of tax

(8)   The liability to pay the inheritance tax is primarily that of the company, but if the company does not pay by the due date, liability extends to the participators and to the person who received the property transferred, except that a participator to whom not more than 5% of the transfer has been apportioned has no liability (s 202).

Capital gains tax

(9)   Transfers at an undervalue by a close company also have a capital gains tax effect, in that the difference between the price paid (if any) and the market value is apportioned amongst the shareholders and regarded as reducing the capital gains tax base cost of their shares (TCGA 1992 s 125).

(10)   The realisation of investments by the company has nothing to do with the inheritance tax position of any of the shareholders. It is just exchanging one asset for another (but it might trigger a charge to corporation tax on a capital gain).

(11)   The gift of the property to Miss Crawley by the company is a disposal for capital gains purposes. Since the disposal is not at arm's length the company has a chargeable gain of the difference between the market value of the property and its cost plus indexation allowance to date (TCGA 1992 s 17). However, that tax liability is not taken into account in quantifying the loss to the company's estate resulting from the gift (s 5(4)), which equates simply to the market value of the property itself.

Withdrawals from loan account

(12)   The withdrawal by Robert of £400,000 from his loan account with the company does not comprise a transfer of value by him. He has simply put himself in cash funds by exchanging one asset for another.

        The conveyance of the property to Miss Crawley would have been better arranged as a withdrawal of Robert's loan account. The personal capital gains effect at note 9 would have been avoided, and the gift of the property *by him* to Miss Crawley would have been a potentially exempt transfer. An immediate tax cost of £93,125 would have been avoided and the inheritance tax accumulations of all three shareholders not affected. There would however have been a liability to stamp duty land tax on the transfer, the reduction in Robert's loan account being the chargeable consideration (FA 2003 Sch 4 para 8(1)).

Question

In 1986 Mr and Mrs John Webb acquired shares in Pirling Ltd, a small private investment company, of which they have since been directors.

The shares in the company are held as follows:

	Shares held	% of issued share capital
Mr Webb	1,201	26.69
Mrs Webb	1,199	26.64
	2,400	53.33
Others (not related persons)	2,100	46.67
	4,500	100.00

Mr and Mrs Webb are each considering transferring out of their respective holdings 350 shares to their adult son David by way of gift. In the event that they proceed, the transfers will be effected on the same day in January 2011, but Mrs Webb will execute her transfer and complete her gift first.

It is expected that HMRC Shares Valuation Division will agree valuations as follows:

53.33% holding	£500 per share
45.55% holding	£315 per share
37.77% holding	£250 per share

Mr Webb's father died in 2004 when his estate comprised an investment in standing timber valued at £120,000, which he left to John, and other assets of £431,000 (net of the 100% business property relief on the forestry business leaving the timber out of account). An election was made to leave the timber out of account and inheritance tax was paid on the £431,000 at the death scale applicable at that time.

Mr Webb now proposes to sell the timber for £220,000 during 2010/11.

He estimates that felling expenses will amount to £24,000 and that the subsequent cost of restoring roads and fences will be £16,000.

The potentially exempt transfers (after exemptions) made up to 5 April 2010 by Mr and Mrs Webb were £356,000 and £171,000 respectively, all made between 6 April 2007 and 5 April 2008.

Assuming the legislation remains unchanged for future years, calculate:

(i)   The potential liability to inheritance tax of Mr and Mrs Webb resulting from their proposals if one (but not both of them) dies during 2011/12.

(ii)   The inheritance tax liability in respect of the disposal of the timber.

Assume that the nil-rate band in 2011/12 remains £325,000.

Answer

(i) Mr and Mrs Webb — Potential liability to inheritance tax on death in 2011/12 in respect of gifts of shares

Mr Webb

		Gross £	Tax on 2011/12 scale £
Potentially exempt transfers at 5.4.10 now chargeable (* 356,000 – 325,000 = 31,000 @ 40%)		356,000	12,400*
January 2011			
Gift of shares in Pirling Ltd to son			
(working note (b))	165,565		
Less: annual exemptions 2010/11 and 2009/10	6,000		
Potentially exempt transfer now chargeable		159,565	63,826
		515,565	76,226

Inheritance tax payable:

By donees of potentially exempt gifts made in 2007/08 (ie more than three years before Mr Webb's death)

Taper relief of either 20% or 40% would be available depending on the dates of the gifts and the date of Mr Webb's death. If he died less than four years after making the gifts the amount payable would be 80% × £12,400	£9,920
By David on gift of shares (within three years before death therefore no taper relief)	£63,826

Mrs Webb

		Gross £	Tax on 2011/12 scale £
Potentially exempt transfers at 5.4.10 now chargeable		171,000	–
January 2011			
Gift of shares in Pirling Ltd to son			
(working note (a))	332,065		
Less: annual exemptions 2010/11 and 2009/10	6,000		
Potentially exempt transfer now chargeable		326,065	68,826*
		497,065	68,826*

(* 497,065 – 325,000 = 172,065 @ 40%)

Inheritance tax payable:

No tax is due from the donees of the gifts made in 2007/08 because the amount chargeable is below the nil threshold.

By David on gift of shares (within three years before death therefore no taper relief)   £68,826

(ii) Liability to inheritance tax on sale of timber in 2010/11

			Gross £	Tax on 2010/11 scale £
Father's estate net of BPR at death (excluding timber)			431,000	42,400
(431,000 − 325,000 = 106,000 @ 40%)				
Sale of timber		220,000		
Less: Expenses				
Felling	24,000			
Restoration*	16,000	40,000	180,000	72,000**
			611,000	114,400

The person who is entitled to the sale proceeds, ie Mr Webb, is liable to pay the tax, although the tax is calculated by reference to the father's estate.

Inheritance tax payable by Mr Webb is therefore £72,000.

* Allowable expenses are expenses of disposal and of replanting. It is considered that the restoration of the roads and fences would form part of the disposal expenses.

** If the timber constituted 'relevant business property', 50% relief would be available, which would halve the tax payable (see **explanatory note 10**).

Working Notes

Computation of gifts

(a)   *Mrs Webb* (using related property rules)

Value of shares before transfer (53.33% holding)   £

$$\frac{1,199}{2,400} \times (2,400 \ @ \ £500) = \qquad 599,500$$

Value of shares after transfer (45.55% holding)

$$\frac{849}{2,050} \times (2,050 \ @ \ £315) = \qquad 267,435$$

Reduction in estate   332,065

(b)   *Mr Webb* (using related property rules)

Value of shares before transfer (45.55% holding)

$$\frac{1,201}{2,050} \times (2,050 \text{ @ } £315) = \qquad 378,315$$

Value of shares after transfer (37.77% holding)

$$\frac{851}{1,700} \times (1,700 \text{ @ } £250) = \qquad 212,750$$

Reduction in estate $\qquad \underline{165,565}$

Explanatory Notes

Business property relief on shares

(1)   Business property relief is not available in respect of the transfer of shares by Mr and Mrs Webb because they are shares in an investment company. See **Example 25** for detailed notes on business property relief.

Consecutive transfers

(2)   Care must be taken to calculate the transfers in the correct order. The Example states that Mrs Webb makes her transfer first, thus her accumulation must be used to record the loss in value attributable to the loss of control. Note that although the shares held by Mr Webb also lose value that loss is not due to a transfer of value made by Mr Webb and is therefore not chargeable. HMRC could use the associated operations provisions to counter the loss to the Exchequer but do not normally do so unless the transactions are actually linked or form part of an avoidance package.

For notes on associated operations, see **Examples 22 and 23**.

Even though the associated operations provisions may not apply, the related property provisions will apply. See notes to **Example 10** for further details.

(3)   If Mr Webb were to make his transfer of shares first then the potential liabilities (using related property rules) would become:

Mr Webb

£

Value of shares before transfer (53.33% holding)

$$\frac{1,201}{2,400} \times (2,400 \text{ @ } £500) = \qquad 600,500$$

Value of shares after transfer (45.55% holding)

$$\frac{851}{2,050} \times (2,050 \text{ @ } £315) = \qquad 268,065$$

Reduction in estate $\qquad \underline{332,435}$

Inheritance tax payable on death in 2011/12

		Gross £	Tax on 2011/12 scale £
Cumulative chargeable transfers (as before)		356,000	12,400
January 2011			
Gift of shares in Pirling Ltd to son	332,435		
Less: annual exemptions 2010/11 and 2009/10	6,000		
Potentially exempt transfer now chargeable		326,435	130,574
		682,435	142,974

Mrs Webb

	£
Value of shares before transfer (45.55% holding)	
$\dfrac{1,199}{2,050} \times (2,050 \ @ \ £315)$	377,685
Value of shares after transfer (37.77% holding)	
$\dfrac{849}{1,700} \times (1,700 \ @ \ £250)$	212,250
Reduction in estate	165,435

Inheritance tax payable on death in 2011/12

		Gross £	Tax on 2011/12 scale £
Cumulative chargeable transfers (as before)		171,000	–
January 2011			
Gift of shares in Pirling Ltd to son	165,435		
Less annual exemptions 2010/11 and 2009/10	6,000		
Potentially exempt transfer now chargeable		159,435	2,174
		330,435	2,174

(* 330,435 – 325,000 = 5,435 @ 40%)

A comparison of the potential inheritance tax liabilities in respect of the gifts of shares is:

	Mrs Webb makes first transfer		Mr Webb makes first transfer	
	Accumulation	Tax	Accumulation	Tax
		£		£
On death in 2011/12 of				
Mr Webb	515,565	63,826	682,435	130,574
Mrs Webb	497,065	58,826	330,435	2,174
		122,652		132,748

This illustrates that the order in which transfers are made may alter not only the potential total liabilities, but also where the burden of the tax falls and the future accumulation for inheritance tax. This will be particularly important not only where there are different beneficiaries but also in the context of future gifts.

Growing timber

(4)   Where an estate *on death* includes growing timber, an election may be made under s 125 to leave the timber (but not the land on which it stands) out of account in valuing the estate at death. The election must be made within two years of the date of death and is only available if the deceased either had been beneficially entitled to the land throughout the previous five years, or had become entitled to it without consideration (for Example, by gift or inheritance).

(5)   The election may not be made if the woodland is occupied with agricultural land and the occupation is ancillary to that of the agricultural land. In those circumstances, however, agricultural relief would be given if the necessary conditions were fulfilled.

For details of agricultural relief, see **Example 25**.

(6)   Following an election, the subsequent disposal by sale or gift of the timber gives rise to a charge to inheritance tax under s 126 on the sale price less allowable expenses, or if the disposal is for less than full consideration, the market value (s 127(1)). Allowable expenses are the costs of sale and expenses of replanting within three years of disposal, or such longer time as the Board allows (s 130(2)).

(7)   The disposal proceeds are treated as value transferred at the date of *death*, forming the top slice of the property passing on death and thus attracting the highest rates of tax (s 128). But where there have been reductions in the rates of tax, the death scale current at the time of *disposal* is used (Sch 2.4). The tax is due six months after the end of the month in which the disposal takes place, with interest payable from that date. Section 208 provides that the person entitled to the proceeds of sale (or the person who would be entitled if the disposal were a sale) is liable for the tax.

Instalment option

(8)   If the disposal of the timber is itself a chargeable transfer, or a potentially exempt transfer that becomes chargeable because of the donor's death within seven years, (for Example if Mr Webb had given the standing timber to his son instead of felling and selling it), the value transferred thereby is reduced by the tax charged under **explanatory note 7** in arriving at the chargeable transfer (s 129). See **Example 32**. Section 229 provides that a claim may be made for the tax chargeable on such a transfer to be paid by ten equal annual instalments, commencing six months after the end of the month in which the transfer is made. Although this would be possible for a chargeable lifetime transfer, such as to a relevant property trust, it could not apply to a potentially exempt transfer, nor to any additional tax on a chargeable lifetime transfer, because the liability would not exist until after the donor's death. It appears, therefore, that this provision should have been amended to take account of the current treatment of potentially exempt transfers and additional liabilities on chargeable lifetime transfers. It is considered that the instalment option would in practice be available, with the first instalment being due six months after the end of the month in which the donor died. If any instalment is paid late, interest is payable only on the late instalment and not on the full amount outstanding (s 234).

Death before disposal

(9)   If the person who inherits woodlands on which an election has been made dies before the timber is disposed of, no inheritance tax charge can arise in respect of the earlier death (s 126(1)).

Furthermore, a new election may then be made on the second death.

Business property relief for growing timber

(10)   Where woodlands constitute 'relevant business property', ie where they are operated on a commercial basis, they qualify for 100% business property relief. But if an election is made to leave such timber out of account on a death, the net sale proceeds on subsequent sale are reduced by only 50% (s 127(2)). Elections should not therefore be made where the 100% relief is available (although part of the 100% relief may not be effective because of the way the estate devolves — see **Examples 15 and 17**). Where an election has already been made, as it was (unwisely) in this Example, and the timber is subsequently sold, the relief can only be given at the 50% rate, which was not revised when the rates of business property relief were increased in 1992. The availability of the 50% relief depends on the forestry business having been eligible for business property relief (at whatever rate) on the death of Mr Webb's father.

For notes on business property relief see **Example 25**.

Transitional estate duty provisions

(11)   Under the transitional provisions that were introduced when estate duty was replaced by capital transfer tax (now inheritance tax), a liability to estate duty will arise on the sale of timber that was left out of account on a pre 13 March 1975 death. But if an inheritance tax transfer of value (other than to a spouse) intervenes (for Example, the death of the person beneficially entitled) estate duty will not be chargeable at all and the transfer will be dealt with under the inheritance tax provisions (Sch 7.2). Such a transfer is expressly precluded from being a potentially exempt transfer and will therefore be a chargeable transfer unless covered by exemptions (FA 1986 Sch 19 para 46). This provision strictly applies to the whole of any property of which any part, however small, is subject to the deferred estate duty charge. By HMRC Concession F15, any part of the property that is not subject to the deferred charge will not be prevented from being a potentially exempt transfer.

Question

Mr Rosewell, a UK domiciled individual, owned a set of four Rennie Mackintosh chairs which he wanted to give to his son. Rather than gift them as a set, he gifted them individually to his son in August 2005, 2006, 2007 and 2008 so as to lower the gifted value.

The relevant values were:

	2005	2006	2007	2008
Number of chairs	£	£	£	£
Four	40,000	44,000	48,000	52,500
Three	30,000	33,000	36,500	40,000
Two	17,500	19,250	21,000	23,500
One	6,250	6,875	7,500	8,250

In September 2008 Mr Rosewell gifted £322,500 cash into a discretionary trust of which he is a beneficiary. The trustees agreed to pay any tax due, and retained the whole trust fund in cash.

Mr Rosewell's father (a widower) had died in May 2001. In his will he left woodlands including standing timber with a then value of £125,000 to Mr Rosewell. The father's estate was worth £575,000 excluding the timber and the executors elected to exclude the timber from the chargeable estate. In February 2008 Mr Rosewell gifted the woodland to his son, who agreed to pay any tax due. The land was then worth £375,000 and the timber £150,000. The woodland was not run as a business by either Mr Rosewell or his father.

After the transactions detailed above Mr Rosewell's estate was worth £200,000 net of liabilities. Under his will he left half of the estate to his wife and the balance equally between his son and daughter.

Mr Rosewell is concerned about the inheritance tax exposures were he to die, for Example, in December 2010. His health has significantly deteriorated in the last few months. He has made no other gifts or transfers apart from those stated above.

Explain the inheritance tax implications of the above transactions if Mr Rosewell were to die on 30 December 2010 (assuming all assets retain their current values and that the legislation remains unchanged).

Answer

Inheritance tax implications of transactions by Mr Rosewell in the event of his death on 30 December 2010

Position on gifts in lifetime

Gifts of Rennie Mackintosh chairs to son (using associated operations rules for second and subsequent gifts)

			£	£
August 2005	Value of set of four chairs		40,000	
	Value of three chairs		30,000	
	Transfer of value		10,000	
	2005/06 annual exemption	3,000		
	2004/05 annual exemption	3,000	6,000	
	Potentially exempt transfer			4,000
August 2006	Value of four chairs		44,000	
	Value of two chairs		19,250	
	Loss to donor		24,750	
	Less: earlier transfer		10,000	
	Transfer of value		14,750	
	2006/07 annual exemption		3,000	
	Potentially exempt transfer			11,750
August 2007	Value of four chairs		48,000	
	Value of one chair		7,500	
	Loss to donor		40,500	
	Less: earlier transfers (10,000 + 14,750)		24,750	
	Transfer of value		15,750	
	2007/08 annual exemption		3,000	
	Potentially exempt transfer			12,750
August 2008	Value of four chairs		52,500	
	Less: earlier transfers (10,000 + 14,750 + 15,750)		40,500	
	Transfer of value		12,000	
	2008/09 annual exemption		3,000	
	Potentially exempt transfer			9,000

Gift with reservation to discretionary trust

		Gross	Tax (2008/09 scale)
		£	£
Sept 2008	Settlement on trust	322,500	2,100

(* 322,500 – 312,000 = 10,500 @ 20%)

Tax payable by trustees £2,100

Gift of woodlands to son

The gift of the woodlands to Mr Rosewell's son would trigger a charge to inheritance tax in respect of the timber in Mr Rosewell's father's estate, based on the value at the date of disposal. Since the estate was well in excess of the current inheritance tax threshold the tax charge would be £150,000 @ 40% = £60,000, payable by Mr Rosewell six months after the end of the month of disposal, ie by 31 August 2009. The tax would reduce the value of the transfer to the son, as follows:

		£	£
February 2009	Market value of woodlands (375,000 + timber 150,000)	525,000	
	Less: Tax payable re father's estate	60,000	
	Potentially exempt transfer		465,000

On Mr Rosewell's death – 30 December 2010

Since Mr Rosewell made a gift with reservation to the discretionary trust, the double charges regulations must be used when computing the tax following his death. The first calculation is to charge the gift in the death estate and ignore the transfer to the trust, and the second to charge the gift to the trust and exclude it from the death estate.

First calculation (ignoring gift to trust)

		Gross	Tax (on 2010/11 scale)
		£	£
Gifts within seven years before death:			
August 2005	PET re gift of chairs	4,000	–
August 2006	PET re gift of chairs	11,750	–
August 2007	PET re gift of chairs	12,750	–
August 2008	PET re gift of chairs	9,000	–
Sept 2008	Gift to trust — ignored	–	–
Feb 2009	Gift of woodlands	465,000	71,000*
		502,500	71,000*

(* 502,500 – 325,000 = 177,500 @ 40%)

Value of estate on death:		
Free estate	200,000	

Less:	Spouse exemption	100,000	100,000		
Settled property			320,400**	420,400	168,160
				929,900	
Total tax payable					239,160

** Initial value of trust £322,500 less tax of £2,100 paid by trustees out of the amount settled.

Second calculation (excluding value of trust from death estate)

			Gross	Tax (on 2010/11 scale)
			£	£
Gifts within seven years before death:				
August 2005	PET re gift of chairs		4,000	–
August 2006	PET re gift of chairs		11,750	–
August 2007	PET re gift of chairs		12,750	–
August 2008	PET re gift of chairs		9,000	–
Sept 2008	Chargeable transfer to discretionary trust		322,500	14,000*
(* 360,000 – 325,000 = 35,000 @ 40%)			360,000	14,000*
Feb 2009	Gift of woodlands		465,000	186,000
Value of estate on death		200,000		
Less:	Spouse exemption	100,000	100,000	40,000
			925,000	
				240,000
Less:	tax paid in lifetime			2,100
Total tax payable				237,900

Since the first calculation shows the higher tax figure, that calculation applies. The tax of £2,100 paid by the trustees in lifetime is, however, allowed as a credit against the tax payable in respect of the trust property at death, reducing the total payable to £237,060 (see **explanatory note 5**). Inheritance tax is therefore payable as follows:

By son re woodlands		71,000
By trustees of discretionary trust 320,400 @ 40%	128,360	
Less: paid in lifetime	2,100	126,060
By personal representatives		40,000
		237,060

Explanatory Notes

Associated operations

(1) The attempt by Mr Rosewell to reduce the value of the gift of the chairs by giving them in different tax years is blocked by the associated operations provisions of s 268 (for details see **Examples 22 and 23**). Spreading the gifts does, however, enable the annual exemptions to be used.

Growing timber

(2)   The provisions enabling growing timber to be left out of a deceased's estate are dealt with in **Example 31**. Where the disposal of the timber is a chargeable transfer or, as in this Example, a potentially exempt transfer that becomes a chargeable transfer, the tax charged in respect of the original estate as a result of the disposal of the timber reduces the value transferred, as illustrated for Mr Rosewell (s 129). See **Example 31 explanatory note 8** regarding paying tax by instalments.

Gifts with reservation and double charges regulations

(3)   By including himself as a beneficiary of the discretionary trust, Mr Rosewell has made a gift with reservation. The effect is that the gift to the trust is chargeable when made, but the value of the trust property will still be included in his estate on his death for inheritance tax purposes so long as he is included as a beneficiary. See **Example 24** for an illustration of the deemed potentially exempt transfer if such a reservation in lifetime is released.

(4)   The effect of the gifts with reservation rules is to charge tax twice, and the double charges regulations (SI 1987/1130) give relief for the double charge by providing for tax to be charged at the higher of two calculations, the first being to charge the gift in the death estate and ignore it in lifetime and the second to charge the gift in lifetime and exclude it from the death estate. For the detailed provisions and further illustrations see **Examples 19, 20 and 24**.

(5)   When making the first calculation, in which the gift to the trust in lifetime is ignored and is included in the death estate at its then value, the tax paid on the gift in lifetime is not taken into account. If, however, the first calculation proves to give the higher figure of tax payable, the tax paid in lifetime is credited against the tax attributable to the property that is subject to the reservation. Note, however, that this credit is taken into account *after* deciding which of the two calculations shows the higher figure (SI 1987/1130 reg 5(4)). In this Example, had the lifetime tax been deducted before making the comparison, the second calculation would have shown the higher tax figure (£237,900 compared with £237,060).

When giving credit for the tax paid in lifetime in the second calculation, that figure will be restricted to the tax payable on death shown in the earlier part of the calculation. That restriction does not apply in this Example.

Capital gains tax implications of gift of chairs

(6)   Mr Rosewell's gifts of the chairs to his son also have implications for capital gains tax. There are two separate provisions affecting the capital gains calculations. The first is the connected persons provisions of TCGA 1992 ss 19 and 20. Where assets are disposed of within a period of six years to one or more connected persons (such as Mr Rosewell's son in this Example) and their value taken together is higher than their separate values, the disposal value is taken to be a proportionate part of the aggregate value, and the legislation provides that earlier tax charges should be adjusted appropriately. The second is the chattels exemption of TCGA 1992 s 262, which provides that chattels such as antiques are exempt if sold for £6,000 or less, with marginal relief for proceeds above £6,000. If articles that constitute a set are sold on different occasions to the same person (or connected persons) the transactions are treated as a single transaction for the purpose of the exemption, earlier tax charges similarly being required to be adjusted appropriately. See the companion to this book, **Tolley's Taxwise I 2010/11**, for full details of the capital gains tax provisions.

Question

(a)   In relation to inheritance tax there is a statutory duty laid on solicitors, accountants and others (except barristers) to make a return to the Board of HMRC when they have been acting in a professional capacity on behalf of a settlor in certain given circumstances.

When does that statutory duty arise and what are its limitations?

(b)   A client who has undertaken to discharge any inheritance tax payable informs you that he has received a Notice of Determination from HMRC in which it is specified that the value of a holding of 2,500 shares in T Ltd (25% of the equity) which he had transferred to a discretionary settlement, has been determined at £20 per share.

If your client considers that the value of the shares is not more than £5 each, what advice would you offer?

(c)   As in (b) above, a client who has undertaken to discharge any inheritance tax payable informs you that he has received a Notice of Determination from HMRC in which it is specified that the value of a plot of land (Blackacre), transferred to the trustees of a discretionary settlement, should be £250,000.

If your client considers that the value of Blackacre is overstated in the Notice of Determination, what further advice would you offer?

(d)   When and in what circumstances is it possible to obtain a grant of representation to a deceased person without first delivering an HMRC Account?

How is the legal personal representative protected against any subsequent claim from the Revenue for inheritance tax in connection with the death when a grant has been issued in this way, and in what circumstances is such protection lost?

Can he still be called on to complete an HMRC Account?

(e)   When and in what circumstances is it necessary to render an account of transfers of value made during the lifetime of the transferor or charges relating to a relevant property trust?

Answer

(a) Duty to make return to HMRC re settlements

Section 218 provides that where any person, other than a barrister, has in the course of his trade or profession been concerned with the making of a settlement where the settlor is domiciled in the UK and the trustees are not or will not be resident in the UK, he must within three months of the making of the settlement make a return to the Board of HMRC. The return must state the names and addresses of the settlor and of the trustees.

For this purpose the trustees are regarded as non-resident unless the general administration of the settlement is carried on in the UK and the trustees or a majority of them are also resident in the UK (s 218(3)).

A return is not required where the settlement was created by a will (which would include a settlement created by deed of variation by a beneficiary otherwise absolutely entitled under the will, because of the deeming effect of s 142(1)), or where such a return has already been made by another person, for example the trustees (s 218(2)).

(b) Notice of Determination relating to value of shares

The client should be advised to appeal in writing against the determination of the value of the shares specified in the notice. The appeal must be made within 30 days of service of the notice and must state the client's grounds of appeal, ie that the true value of the shares is not more than £5 each (s 222(1)).

The appeal is made in the first instance by notice in writing given to the Board of HMRC. The client may then choose to notify the appeal direct to the tribunal under ss 223A, 223D, or to require HMRC to review the matter in question (ss 223A, 223B).

There is no set time limit for taking either of those steps provided the notice of appeal has been given to HMRC within the 30-day period mentioned; but HMRC can themselves offer to review the matter in which case the client would have 30 days in which to accept the offer of a review (or to notify the appeal to the tribunal), failing which he will be bound by HMRC's view of the matter as stated in their offer unless the tribunal gives permission for late notification of the appeal (ss 223C, 223H).

If a review is carried out by HMRC (after being required to do so by the client, or after he has accepted their offer of a review) and the client is dissatisfied with its conclusion as notified to him by HMRC, the client has 30 days (or longer if he can get permission from the tribunal) in which then to notify the appeal to the tribunal.

See generally **explanatory note 6** for more detail in relation to the procedure for appeals and reviews.

(c) Notice of Determination relating to value of land

The client should be advised to appeal in writing against the determination of the value of Blackacre as at **(b) above**. However, because the question in dispute is a question as to the value of land in the United Kingdom, it may be notified at the appropriate stage to the 'appropriate tribunal' in the first instance (the Upper Tribunal (Lands Chamber) for land in England and Wales, or the Lands Tribunal for Scotland or the Lands Tribunal for Northern Ireland for land in those respective jurisdictions). Even if it is notified to the First-tier Tribunal, any question in dispute as to the value of land in the UK must anyway be determined on a reference to the 'appropriate tribunal' (s 222(4A)–(4B)).

(d) Grant of representation to deceased's estate, exempt and excepted estates

Personal representatives are not required to produce an account to the probate registry to obtain a grant of representation; instead they complete a Probate Summary in the form of supplementary page IHT421 to the form IHT400 (previously form P26A). The HMRC account (with the probate summary) must be sent to HMRC Capital Taxes and the inheritance tax on the non-instalment property (together with any instalments that have already fallen due in respect of instalment-option property) must be paid before the grant is issued; the probate registry will not issue the grant until they have received the probate summary stamped by HMRC to confirm this.

Excepted estates

To apply for a grant of representation for an excepted estate the personal representative completes form IHT205 (C5 in Scotland) or IHT 207 for those domiciled abroad. The form is given to the Probate Registry.

There is an excepted estate where the conditions set out below are satisfied.

There are three types of excepted estate set out in SI 2004/2543 applicable from 1 November 2004 with respect to deaths on or after 6 April 2004 and this is further amended with respect to deaths on or after 1 September 2006 by SI 2006/2141. The three types of excepted estate are: low value excepted estates; exempt excepted estates and excepted estates of foreign domiciliaries.

(A)   Low value excepted estates: Under paragraph 4(2) the conditions are:

    (i)   the deceased was domiciled in the UK at the date of death;

    (ii)   the estate consists only of property passing under the deceased's will or intestacy or under a trust, nominated property, or joint property passing by survivorship;

    (iii)   where any trust assets were held in a single trust in which the deceased had an interest in possession and had a value not exceeding £150,000;

    (iv)   not more than £100,000 represents the value of property situated outside the UK;

    (v)   the deceased is not a person by reason of whose death one of the alternatively secured pension fund provisions applies;

    (vi)   the deceased died without having made any chargeable transfer in the seven years before his death except cash, quoted shares or quoted securities, or land and buildings (and contents), with a total gross value not exceeding £150,000. Paragraph 4(7) indicates that business property relief and agricultural property relief are disregarded for this purpose;

    (vii)   the gross value of the estate plus transfers within seven years of death plus exempt transfers to spouse/civil partner, charities etc within seven years of death do not exceed the nil-rate band at death.

(B)   Exempt excepted estates: Under paragraph 4(3) the conditions are:

    (i)   the deceased was domiciled in the UK at the date of death;

    (ii)   the conditions set out in A above at (ii) to (vi) apply;

    (iii)   the gross value of chargeable assets of the estate (before deducting liabilities, reliefs or exemptions), when added to the cumulative chargeable gifts made in the seven years before death, does not exceed £1,000,000 and the net chargeable estate after deduction of spouse/civil partner and charity exemptions only does not exceed the nil-rate band.

(C)   Under paragraph 4(5) the estate is exempt if the deceased was never domiciled (or deemed domiciled) in the UK, the estate consists only of cash or quoted shares which pass by will, intestacy or survivorship and whose gross value does not exceed £150,000, and the alternatively secured pension fund provisions do not apply.

The requirement for an HMRC account to be submitted is relaxed by regulations issued under the provisions of s 256. The regulations enable a grant of representation to be issued without the completion of an HMRC account in the case of excepted estates. The procedures are explained in HMRC's Customer Guide to Inheritance Tax.

An estate is not an excepted estate if the deceased had made a gift with reservation of benefit which either continued until death or ceased within seven years before death.

Protection from liability to inheritance tax:

After 35 days (the 'prescribed period') from the issue of the grant all persons potentially liable for inheritance tax in respect of the excepted estate are automatically discharged from liability and any charge for such tax on any property comprised in the estate is removed.

The protection is lost:

(1)   in the case of fraud or failure to disclose material facts or

(2)   if it subsequently comes to light that there is further property which causes the excepted estate conditions not to be satisfied (eg the gross value exceeds £1,000,000, or other property exceeds the stipulated limits) or

(3)   if within the 'prescribed period' a notice in writing is issued by HMRC to the personal representatives requiring delivery of an HMRC account.

If it is discovered at any time that the estate is not an excepted estate then the personal representative must deliver a Corrective Account (C4) to the Revenue within six months of the discovery.

If an estate ceases to be an excepted estate because of a deed of variation then again a C4 is required within six months of the date of variation. HMRC say it will help them process accounts more quickly if copies of the signed IHT205/C5 or if appropriate the instrument of variation are attached to the C4.

The Revenue have agreed to adopt this procedure instead of insisting on a full form IHT400 being delivered (see HMRC IHT Newsletter Aug 2004).

(e) Rendering an account of lifetime transfers of value or charges under a relevant property trust

Under section 216 persons liable to inheritance tax are required to submit an account in respect of *chargeable transfers* made in lifetime, or occasions of charge under the regime for relevant property trusts, before the end of twelve months from the end of the month in which the transfer is made or occasion occurs, unless:

(i)   another liable person has already done so (s 216(5)) or

(ii)   one of the exceptions in 1 to 3 below applies and HMRC have not served notice requiring the delivery of the account.

An account is also required in the case of alternatively secured pension funds following the death of a member of the scheme or a relevant dependant of the member. The account is required from the scheme administrator of a registered pension scheme within twelve months of the end of the month in which the individual died.

Whilst a potentially exempt transfer is a transfer of value, it is not a chargeable transfer unless the transferor dies within seven years. Accordingly there is no requirement to notify HMRC Inheritance Tax on the making of such a transfer – still less of the making of an exempt transfer. On the death of the transferor the transferee is primarily liable for any inheritance tax on the potentially exempt transfer and is obliged to submit an account within twelve months from the end of the month in which the transferor died (s 216(6)). The personal representatives of the transferor have a secondary liability for any inheritance tax arising, and they are required under s 216 to give details of all chargeable transfers made by the deceased with the seven years before his death. If they cannot establish the exact value of any property, the account may contain a provisional figure, but they must undertake to deliver a further account as soon as the exact amount is ascertained.

Where a person holds property subject to a reservation (or within seven years after the release of a reservation) then on the death of the donor that person must deliver to the Board an account of such property within twelve months from the end of the month in which the donor died (s 216(6)(ab)).

If someone who has submitted an account discovers that it is materially incorrect, he must submit an amended account within six months after the discovery of the defect (s 217).

Under s 219A HMRC may require anyone liable to deliver an account under s 216 or 217 to produce relevant documents and accounts. The person receiving the notice may appeal against it within 30 days from the date on which the notice was given and the appeal is governed by the same rules as if it were against a Notice of Determination (s 219B).

In the same way as for excepted estates (see **(d) above**), several exceptions have been prescribed to the obligation to deliver accounts other than on death, by regulations made by HMRC under s 256:

(1)   **Excepted transfers**

A chargeable transfer made on or after 6 April 2007 is an excepted transfer under SI 2008/605, regulation 3, if the value transferred (when added to that transferred by previous chargeable transfers by the transferor within the preceding seven years):

(i)   does not exceed the nil rate band for the time being, and the value transferred is attributable only to cash and/or quoted shares or securities; or

(ii)   does not exceed 80% of the nil rate band for the time being, and the value transferred (before available exemptions and disregarding business and agricultural property reliefs) does not exceed the hitherto unused part of the nil rate band.

(2)   **Excepted terminations**

The termination of an estate interest in possession in settled property is an excepted termination under SI 2008/605, regulation 4, if the value transferred in consequence of the termination (disregarding business and agricultural property reliefs):

(i)   (when added to that transferred by previous chargeable transfers by the transferor within the preceding seven years) does not exceed the nil rate band for the time being, and the value of the property in which the interest subsisted is attributable only to cash and/or quoted shares or securities; or

(ii)   (when added to that transferred by previous chargeable transfers by the transferor within the preceding seven years) does not exceed 80% of the nil rate band for the time being, and the value of the property in which the interest subsisted does not exceed the hitherto unused part of the transferor's nil rate band; or

(iii)   does not exceed the amount of the transferor's available annual or marriage/civil partnership exemptions made available by him to the trustees by notice given to them within six months after the termination under s 57.

These provisions also apply to the termination of an interest in possession of a bereaved minor under a bereaved minor's trust within s 71A; but in practice a deemed transfer of value in such a case would be limited to the extremely rare case where the minor's interest in possession had subsisted since before 22 March 2006 and the beneficiary is still under age 18: the settled property does not form part of the minor's estate (s 49(1B)) but it appears to be envisaged that a deemed transfer of value under s 52 is still possible (even where a flat-rate exit charge under s 71B does not arise) if the interest comes to an end without the minor becoming absolutely entitled.

(3)   **Excepted settlements**

A settlement is an excepted settlement for the purpose of any occasion of charge to inheritance tax arising under Part 3, Chapter 3 on or after 6th April 2007, under SI 2008/606 regulation 4, if:

(i)   no qualifying interest in possession subsists in the settlement immediately before the occasion of charge,

(ii)   there are no related settlements (ie settlements created by the same settlor on the same day),

(iii)   throughout the trust's existence the trustees have been UK resident (tested in terms of the general administration being ordinarily carried on in the UK and the trustees or a majority of them (and of each class of trustees if more than one) being UK resident), and

(iv)   either:

(A)   the assets have always comprised only cash of a value not exceeding £1,000 and the settlor has not added any capital to the trust after its creation (essentially covering pilot trusts) (regulation 4(2)), or

(B)   the settlor has at all times since making the settlement (until his death if he is no longer living) been domiciled in the UK, the charge arises under s 64 (ten-yearly charges for relevant property), s 65 (exit charges for relevant property) or s 71E ('good' exit charges for age 18-to-25 trusts), and the value transferred by the notional chargeable transfer used for ascertaining the rate of tax (disregarding all liabilities and reliefs) does not exceed 80% of the nil rate band for the time being (regulation 4(3)–(8)).

In the case of an excepted termination or an excepted settlement (properly treated as such), and in the absence of fraud or a failure to disclose material facts, the trustees of the settlement (but not other liable parties) are discharged from liability for any tax on the event in question six months after its occurrence (and in the case of an excepted settlement any Inland Revenue charge for the tax is extinguished) unless in the meantime HMRC have issued a notice requiring an account of the property concerned.

Explanatory Notes

Accounts, returns and provision of other information

(1)   An *Account* is a document completed by a transferor (or other person liable for inheritance tax) providing details of a disposition or event to which a liability to inheritance tax may apply.

A *Return* is a document submitted by a person about transactions affecting others.

(2)   In addition to the returns dealt with in **part (a)** of the Example, the Board has power to require a person to provide information as specified in a notice under s 219. This does not extend to information in respect of which a lawyer could maintain a claim of professional privilege, except that solicitors may be obliged to disclose the names and addresses of clients. There is no right of appeal against a s 219 notice.

A notice under this paragraph may be combined with one relating to income tax.

The s 219 requirement to provide information is extended by FA 1990 s 125 to require someone to provide information in respect of tax liabilities outside the UK that are of a similar nature to inheritance tax if this is provided for in a double tax agreement, and the s 219 requirements also apply from 28 July 2000 where a tax information exchange agreement has been made by the UK with the country concerned (s 220A).

Both double taxation and information exchange agreements may provide that information may not only be exchanged with, but also obtained for, the relevant overseas country.

(3)   The Board also has power (under s 219A) to require a person to produce documents or provide accounts for the purposes of enquiring into an account; determining whether an account is correct; and making determinations. An appeal against such requirements lies to the Special Commissioners under s 219B, but no further appeal is permitted.

Notice of Determination

(4)   The notice of determination by the Board under s 221 dealt with in **part (b)** of the Example may be issued to the transferor, or to any person liable for any of the tax chargeable on the value transferred, or to anyone making a claim in respect of the value transferred.

The notice may specify all or any of the following:

(a)   Date of transfer

(b)   Value transferred and value of any property to which the value transferred is wholly or partly attributable

(c)   Transferor

(d)   Tax chargeable and persons liable

(e)   Tax overpaid and date from which interest will be added on overpayment (and rate of interest)

(f)   Any other relevant matter (s 221(1) and (2)).

(5)   The determination of any fact relating to a transfer is to be in accordance with the account or return submitted if the Board is satisfied that it is correct but otherwise is to be made by the Board to the best of their judgment (s 221(3)).

Appeals against Notices of Determination and Reviews by HMRC

(6)   Once notice of appeal has been given to HMRC within 30 days after service of a Notice of Determination, three possibilities arise (s 223A):

(a)   the appellant requires a review by HMRC,

(b)   HMRC offer a review, or

(c)   the appellant notifies the appeal to the tribunal or (where the issue is the value of land in the UK) to the appropriate tribunal as referred to in **part (e)** of the Example.

Those possibilities are essentially mutually exclusive for the time being, but as will be seen the appellant regains the right to notify the appeal to the tribunal after a review by HMRC. Once a review by HMRC has been offered or required, no further HMRC review can be required or offered.

The tribunal to be notified will in principle be the First-tier Tribunal (Tax Chamber), but that tribunal may transfer to the Upper Tribunal a case that has been categorised as Complex (SI 2009/273 rule 28). However, appeals where the matters to be decided are substantially confined to questions of law may be notified to the High Court instead (provided it can at the relevant time still be notified to the tribunal) if either:

(i)   it is agreed between the appellant and HMRC that the appeal will be to the High Court, or

(ii)   the High Court gives leave on an application by the appellant (s 222(2) and (3)).

If the question to be determined by the tribunal turns on a question as to the value of land (for Example, in **part (b)** of the Example, if the value of the shares turned on the value of land owned by the company) the tribunal may refer any question as to the value of land to the 'appropriate tribunal' (see **part (c)** of the Example), rather than the taxpayer being required to make a fresh appeal (s 222(4A)).

1. Review required by appellant

If the appellant requires HMRC to review the case they must within 30 days (or such longer period as is reasonable) notify the appellant of their view of the matter in question, and then have 45 days (or longer as agreed) in which to notify the appellant of the conclusions of the review and their reasoning; if they fail to do so within that period, the review is treated as having upheld HMRC's view of the matter as initially notified in response to the appellant's requirement for review, but HMRC must still notify the appellant of the conclusion that the review is treated as having reached (ss 223B, 223E).

The appellant can then notify the appeal to the tribunal within the 'post-review period' (or later if the tribunal gives permission); the post-review period is 30 days starting with the date of the document in which HMRC give notice of the conclusion of their review, or (if they failed to do so within the time allowed) the period between expiry of HMRC's time limit for the review and 30 days after they notified the appellant of the deemed conclusion (s 223G).

2. Review offered by HMRC

If HMRC offer a review they must also notify the appellant of their view of the matter in question; the appellant then has 30 days in which to accept the offer of review, or to notify the appeal to the tribunal.

If the appellant does accept the offer of review then the review proceeds in the same way as if it had originally been required by the appellant (see **1 above**); the 45 day time limit for HMRC to notify their conclusions starts with the day when they received notification of the appellant's acceptance of the offer of review (s 223G).

If on the other hand the appellant fails to accept the offer within the time allowed then HMRC's view as notified is conclusive and the consequences are as if, on the date that they gave notice of that view, the tribunal had determined the appeal in accordance with the terms of HMRC's view (s 223C). The appellant is still able to notify the appeal to the tribunal, but only if the tribunal gives permission, which would be unlikely unless he could show good reason for having failed to accept the offer of review s 223H).

3. Notification of appeal to the tribunal

As indicated in **part (b)** of the Example, there is no set time limit for notifying the appeal to the tribunal after giving notice of appeal to HMRC within the 30 day period from the Notice of Determination. The right to notify the tribunal is disapplied (temporarily) once HMRC have notified their view of the matter in response to a requirement for review under s 223B, or have offered a review (with their view) under s 223C; notification is then allowed only if permitted by ss 223G, 223H as referred to in **1 and 2 above** (s 223D(5)). The procedure is laid down in SI 2009/273 as amended.

Once the appeal has been notified to the tribunal, the tribunal is to decide the matter in question. It must confirm the determination (if relevant, as varied under s 223E on HMRC's review) unless the tribunal is satisfied that it ought to be varied (or further varied) or quashed (s 224).

(7)   An appeal against a decision of the First-tier Tribunal (other than certain excluded decisions of a mainly procedural kind) may be made by either party to the Upper Tribunal, but only on a point of law that arises from that decision, and only with permission (from either such tribunal): Tribunals, Courts and Enforcement Act 2007 s 11. The procedure is laid down in SI 2008/2698 as amended.

A similar right of appeal – again only on a point of law and again only with permission – is available from the Upper Tribunal to the Court of Appeal (in Northern Ireland or England and Wales as the case may be, or in Scotland the Court of Session) under s 13 of the same Act.

Excepted estates

(8)   Where an estate is an excepted estate the personal representatives will swear a revised form of oath stating that the gross value of the estate does not exceed the appropriate amount.

Persons required to deliver an account

(9)   The provisions requiring those liable to inheritance tax in lifetime to render an account are dealt with in **part (d)** of the Example.

The personal representatives of a deceased person must deliver an account of all property which formed part of the estate at death unless the estate is an excepted estate. Where there are no personal representatives then:

(a)   every person in whom property of the estate vests, or who is beneficially entitled to an interest in possession on or after the deceased's death, and

(b)   where property passes to a settlement without an interest in possession, every person for whose benefit any of that property, or income from it, is applied

must deliver an account to the Board specifying the property in which he has an interest.

The account is submitted on HMRC account form IHT400. This is accompanied by a worksheet (IHT(WS)). HMRC produce additional materials in the form of IHT400 Notes – Guide to completing your

Inheritance Tax account, IHT400 Helpsheet – Working out the interest on Inheritance Tax payments and IHT400 Rates and Tables. More information can be found at http://www.hmrc.gov.uk/inheritancetax/more-iht400.pdf.

Penalties

(10) The penalty regime is discussed in question 5.

In addition to that commentary it should be noted that for deeds of variation made on or after 1 August 2002 that give rise to an increase in the inheritance tax liability, s 245A has been amended by FA 2002 s 120 to include a penalty where personal representatives fail to send the Revenue a copy of the variation and notify the amount of additional tax payable (see **Example 34 explanatory note 5**).

(11) Personal representatives should be aware that HMRC are taking a harsher attitude to the question of penalties where they consider that an HMRC Account containing estimated valuations has been submitted without the personal representatives having made 'the fullest enquiries that are reasonably practicable in the circumstances' as required by s 216(3A). In a case before the Special Commissioners (*Robertson v CIR, SpC 309*, (2002)), they sought to impose a penalty of £10,000 on an executor who had submitted an account within six weeks after the testator's death containing estimated figures which were later found to be substantially understated, even though corrective accounts had been submitted less than six months after the death. The Special Commissioners found in favour of the executor, commenting that the Revenue had wholly failed to show that the executor was guilty of negligence. He had acted in accordance with accepted practice in submitting estimated figures and making prompt arrangements for professional valuations. The Revenue were held to have acted wholly unreasonably and the executors were entitled to costs in connection with the hearing. Despite the executor's success in this case, it would be advisable for personal representatives to ensure that they have made all enquiries that are *reasonably practicable* before including estimated figures in HMRC Accounts.

Estates

Question

Dr and Mrs Slowe made their wills without professional advice, each leaving the whole of his/her estate to the surviving spouse with the proviso that should the spouse predecease him/her the estate should be divided between their children.

On 31 December 2010 they were involved in a road accident in which Dr Slowe (aged 50) died instantly. Mrs Slowe (aged 51) was seriously injured and died seven days later. They had two children, John (aged 25) and Jill (aged 18).

At death Dr Slowe's interest in the group practice in which he was a partner was valued at £250,000. He also owned assets valued at £50,000, and the family home, valued at £500,000, was in his sole ownership. He had no interest in any settlements nor had he made any lifetime gifts.

Mrs Slowe had assets of her own valued at £75,000 and was the life tenant of the estate of her late father, who died on 20 February 1988, the reversionary interest passing to her children equally. The settlement was valued at £325,000 on 7 January 2011. During her lifetime Mrs Slowe had made chargeable transfers amounting to £85,000 (all less than three years before death).

(a)   Compute the inheritance tax payable by reason of the deaths of Dr and Mrs Slowe taking into account any possible transfer of their nil-rate bands.

(b)   Consider whether it would be possible to mitigate that liability.

(c)   Comment on what the tax position would have been if they had died simultaneously.

(d)   Assuming professional advice had been obtained before death so that the wills had included an appropriately worded survivorship clause, recompute the inheritance tax payable consequent upon their deaths.

(e)   Prepare a table comparing the tax payable at (a) and (d), and comment on the difference in tax payable at (d) with what would have been payable under (b) and (c).

Answer

(a) Inheritance tax payable on death of Dr Slowe — 31 December 2010

Nil, since all property passes to Mrs Slowe which is an exempt transfer.

Inheritance tax payable on death of Mrs Slowe — 7 January 2011

		£	£
Free estate			
Family home			500,000
Other assets —	Own	75,000	
	Husband's estate:		
	Assets from partnership	250,000	
	Other assets	50,000	375,000
			875,000
Settled property			
Life interest in estate of late father			325,000
Amount subject to inheritance tax			1,200,000

Inheritance tax accumulation

	Gross £	Tax £
Cumulative transfers prior to death	85,000	–
Amount liable on death	1,200,000	254,000*
	1,285,000	254,000*

(* 1,285,000 – 650,000 (see **note 10**) = 635,000 @ 40%)

Estate rate $\dfrac{254,000}{1,200,000} \times 100 = 21.1667\%$

Inheritance tax payable:		
By personal representatives	875,000 @ 21.1667%	185,209
By trustees of settled property	325,000 @ 21.1667%	68,791
		£254,000

(b) Mitigating Mrs Slowe's inheritance tax liability

The personal representatives of Mrs Slowe could, within two years after Dr Slowe's death, make a written disclaimer of the gift to her under his will (s 142). This would result in an intestacy, and under the intestacy rules a 28-day survivorship period applies to the spouse entitlement, so the effect of such a disclaimer would be that Dr Slowe's estate would pass to the children. The same effect would be obtained if, again within two years of Dr Slowe's death, Mrs Slowe's personal representatives entered into a written variation under s 142 to redirect the assets to the children.

If a deed of variation or disclaimer is executed, it will not be a transfer of value and inheritance tax will be calculated as though the deed displaced the provisions of the will (ie computed as in **part (d)** of the Example) *providing* in the case of a variation (not a disclaimer) that the instrument of variation contains a statement that the variation is intended to have that effect.

Since additional tax would be payable on Dr Slowe's estate, then within six months after the date of such a variation Dr Slowe's personal representatives, together with Mrs Slowe's personal representatives, would have to notify HMRC Capital Taxes of the amount of extra tax and send a copy of the variation. See **explanatory note 5** for further details.

(c) Simultaneous deaths (commorientes)

Where two or more persons die at the same time or in circumstances where it cannot be known which survived the other(s), it is assumed under the rule of commorientes that the elder died first and accordingly that the younger is deemed to have survived the elder (Law of Property Act 1925 s 184). However, for inheritance tax purposes s 4(2) provides that they shall be assumed to have died at the same instant.

Any bequest from one to the other will accordingly be ignored for inheritance tax purposes since neither survived the other. Therefore if Dr and Mrs Slowe had both died at the same time (or if it could not be determined who died first) then for the purposes of general law (ie the actual devolution of the assets) Mrs Slowe (being the elder) would be deemed to have died first, and her estate would pass under her will to her husband. On the death of Dr Slowe his estate (now including his wife's estate) would pass under his will to the children.

For inheritance tax purposes, however, Dr Slowe would be deemed to have died at the same time as Mrs Slowe and his estate for inheritance tax would not include his wife's assets.

Even so, when computing the inheritance tax liability on the estate of Mrs Slowe the assets other than the settled property would in fact pass to Dr Slowe's estate and therefore would be exempt (s 18), whereas the settled property would revert under the terms of the settlement to the children and a liability would arise as follows:

Inheritance tax payable on simultaneous deaths

Mrs Slowe (elder)	£	£
Free estate	75,000	
Less: Exempt transfer to Dr Slowe	75,000	nil
Settled property		
Life interest in estate of late father		325,000
Amount subject to inheritance tax		325,000

Inheritance tax accumulation

	Gross	Tax
	£	£
Cumulative transfers prior to death	85,000	–
Amount liable on death	325,000	34,000*
	410,000	34,000*

(* 410,000 – 325,000 = 85,000 @ 40%)

Inheritance tax payable:	£
By personal representatives	nil
By trustees of settled property	34,000

	£	£
Dr Slowe (younger)		
Family home		500,000
Interest in practice	250,000	
Less: 100% business property relief	250,000	–
Other assets (excluding Mrs Slowe's assets of £75,000)		50,000
Amount subject to inheritance tax		550,000

Inheritance tax accumulation

	Gross £	Tax £
Cumulative transfers prior to death	–	–
Amount liable on death	550,000	90,000*
Inheritance tax payable by personal representatives		90,000*

(* 550,000 – 325,000 (see **note 10**) = 225,000 @ 40%)

(d) Survivorship clauses

To prevent devolution and taxation problems relating to deaths at or near the same time, it is common to include a survivorship clause in a will. For Example, the bequest to the spouse is made conditional upon that person surviving for a specified period such as thirty days after the first death. Such clauses are effective for inheritance tax purposes providing the specified period does not exceed six months (s 92) and tax is computed as if the dispositions which take effect at the end of the period (or on the earlier death of the contingent legatee) had taken place at the first death. If survivorship clauses had been included in the wills of Dr and Mrs Slowe (or if Mrs Slowe's personal representatives had disclaimed the inheritance or entered into a variation as indicated in **part (b)** above) the tax position on their deaths would have been as follows:

Inheritance tax payable on death of Dr Slowe — 31 December 2010

	£
Family home	500,000
Interest in practice 250,000	
Less: 100% business property relief 250,000	–
Other assets	50,000
Estate on death for inheritance tax	550,000

Inheritance tax accumulation

	Gross £	Tax £
Cumulative transfers prior to death	–	–
Estate on death	550,000	90,000
Inheritance tax payable by personal representatives (as in (c))		90,000

Inheritance tax payable on death of Mrs Slowe — 7 January 2011

	£
Free estate	
Assets	75,000
Settled property	
Life interest in estate of late father	325,000
Estate on death	400,000

Inheritance tax accumulation

	Gross £	Tax £
Cumulative transfers prior to death	85,000	–
Estate on death	400,000	64,000*
	485,000	64,000*

(* 485,000 – 325,000 (see **note 10**) = 160,000 @ 40%)

Estate rate

$$\frac{64,000}{400,000} \times 100 = 16.0\%$$

Inheritance tax payable:

		£
By personal representatives	£75,000 @ 16%	12,000
By trustees of settled property	£325,000 @ 16%	52,000
		64,000

(e) Comparison of tax payable

	Under (a) above (without variation) £	With survi- vorship clause £
By personal representatives of Dr Slowe	–	90,000
By personal representatives of Mrs Slowe	185,209	12,000
	185,209	102,000
By trustees of settled property	68,791	52,000
	254,000	154,000

Tax of £154,000 would also be payable if a disclaimer or variation as at (b) were executed.

The tax payable in the event of simultaneous deaths (c) is £124,000 (£34,000 + £90,000). The difference of £30,000 compared with the tax payable had the survivorship clause or a variation or disclaimer operated is because Mrs Slowe's own assets of £75,000 are in the event of simultaneous deaths exempt from inheritance tax since they none the less pass under her will to her husband (but are not reckoned in his estate for inheritance tax purposes); whereas they are chargeable in her estate if they pass directly to her children as they would under the survivorship clause or variation/disclaimer, and attract tax at 40% = £30,000.

Explanatory Notes

Inheritance tax on estates of Dr and Mrs Slowe

(1)   Because Dr Slowe predeceased his wife the whole of his estate passed to her under the will. This is an exempt transfer and no inheritance tax is payable (s 18). Accordingly when Mrs Slowe died there was no quick succession relief because her estate had not been increased by a chargeable transfer (s 141).

Conversely, Mrs Slowe will benefit from 100% of Dr Slowe's unused nil-rate band. This means that if the increase is claimed, her nil-rate band will be increased by £325,000 for 2010/11 – the year of her death (see **explanatory note 10**).

(2)   Mrs Slowe's estate includes the value of her husband's share in the professional partnership. As she is not a partner this does not qualify for business property relief. For notes on business property relief see **Example 25**.

(3)   The wording of the wills resulted in the second estate being increased in value and attracting a large amount of tax, whilst the first estate lost the benefit of its business property relief because the relievable asset passed to an exempt beneficiary in whose hands it could not attract the relief: neither Mrs Slowe nor Dr Slowe's executors carried on the business. The failure to use Dr Slowe's nil-rate band, which would have been serious before 9 October 2007, is now not a problem provided a claim is made within the time allowed to transfer the benefit of his nil-rate band to his widow's estate. The benefit from the deed of variation would be very substantial because the total inheritance tax payable would be reduced from £254,000 to £154,000, giving an overall saving of £100,000. Such a deed would not have been necessary in the particular circumstances if the wills had contained a survivorship clause. However, if Mrs Slowe had survived by longer than the time specified in such a survivorship clause there would still have been a loss of business property relief, and the better approach in Dr Slowe's will would have been to ensure that his interest in his professional practice should pass to a chargeable beneficiary (which could be a discretionary trust) even if his wife survived him, and not get aggregated with his widow's estate.

Deeds of variation

(4)   In this Example the use of the provisions in s 142 (alteration of dispositions taking effect on death) would be fairly straightforward and could be used to rewrite the provisions of Dr Slowe's will to advantage. In practice complications can occur if the family cannot agree on a revised disposition of the estate, or if one or more of the original beneficiaries is an infant and therefore does not have the legal capacity to agree to a variation. Court consent would be needed to reduce an infant beneficiary's entitlement.

(5)   As indicated in **part (b)** of the Example, a variation of the way in which a deceased's estate is distributed, either under a will or under an intestacy, is effective for inheritance tax providing the instrument of variation includes a statement that it is intended to have that effect, made by those making the variation, and by the personal representatives of the deceased whose estate is subject to the variation if additional tax is payable (s 142(2), (2A)). The personal representatives can only refuse to make the statement if they hold insufficient assets to discharge the additional tax liability (s 142(2A)). If a beneficiary has died before the date of the variation, his personal representatives can act in his stead, but the authority of the beneficiaries of that estate will be needed where the variation reduces the interest of the survivor's estate, and should in practice join in the variation to avoid queries from HMRC over that authority.

Where the effect of a variation is that additional tax is payable, the beneficiaries and the personal representatives of the deceased whose estate is subject to the variation must notify IR Capital Taxes of the amount of extra tax and send a copy of the variation within six months after the date it is made (s 218A). Penalties apply for failure to comply (s 245A(1A)).

Instruments of variation are also effective for capital gains purposes providing the instrument contains a statement by those making it that it is intended to have that effect (TCGA 1992 s 62(7)).

(6)   The property which may be subject to variation or disclaimer under s 142 includes 'excluded property' (as to which see **Example 3**) but not property in which the deceased had retained a benefit (see **Example 19**) or

settled property in which the deceased at the time of his death had an estate interest in possession (s 142(5), and see **Example 52**). (Someone who *becomes entitled* to an interest in settled property may disclaim, but not vary, his entitlement under s 93.) Where an asset is held jointly as joint tenants, and one of the joint tenants dies, then even though the survivor acquires the deceased's share automatically, he may use a deed of variation to redirect his entitlement to someone else. Section 142 can also be used in cases of intestacy. The provisions do not, however, apply to any disclaimer or variation which is made for consideration in money or money's worth, other than consideration which takes the form of another interest in the same estate which also qualifies for relief under the same provision (s 142(3)) (the same applies to a disclaimer under s 93). Where a variation results in property being held in trust for not more than two years from the date of death, the disposition at the end of the short-term interest in possession is treated as made by the deceased at the date of death (s 142(4)). This provision prevents a variation being used to obtain the benefit of the surviving spouse exemption by redirecting property left as part of the chargeable estate to the spouse for a period of up to two years after the death and claiming potentially exempt transfer treatment when that interest comes to an end and the property passes to others. Section 142(4) only deals with interests which are provided by the variation (read with the will) to come to an end within that period – if they terminate by death or by some act separate from the variation then the usual consequences would follow and s 142(4) would not apply. Similarly, a fixed-term interest ending more than two years after the death will not be caught by s 142(4), though HMRC will take a careful look at the matter (IHTM35095).

(7)   The survivorship clause and a deed of variation affect the devolution of the property itself. The treatment for inheritance tax purposes where there are deaths at the same instant does not, however, affect the provisions of the will, commorientes applying where relevant and thus making a survivorship clause valuable from the devolution point of view, quite apart from for tax purposes.

Commorientes

(8)   The deeming provisions of s 4(2) apply when it is not known which of two or more persons have died first (see **part (c)** of the Example). They do not, however, apply where there is evidence that one died before the other(s) when, in the absence of a survivorship clause or a family deed, the best one can hope for in terms of tax relief is quick succession relief. The insertion of a survivorship clause in a will is therefore most important since as indicated earlier a deed of variation is not always practicable; in the will of the older spouse or civil partner it is good practice to disapply the survivorship provision in circumstances such that the commorientes rule would apply, so as to capture the additional saving of inheritance tax highlighted in **parts (C)** and **(E)** of the example. It should however be borne in mind that, if one spouse has insufficient assets to absorb a single nil-rate band and the other has more than is covered by a single nil rate band, a survivorship clause does risk losing the benefit of the transferable nil-rate band (see explanatory **note 10** and **Example 1 part (III)**) if the poorer spouse happens to be the second to die, but without having fulfilled the survivorship condition. This situation can only be rectified by means of a variation in relation to the estate of the (wealthier) spouse who died first.

For notes on quick succession relief see **Example 21**.

Deeds of variation — effect on other taxes etc

(9)   It should be noted that a deed of variation is effective both for inheritance tax and for the 'death' rules (TCGA 1992 s 62) of capital gains tax (providing the variation includes a statement to that effect) and does not give rise to a charge to stamp duty or stamp duty land tax. The inheritance tax effect is valid for all purposes of inheritance tax (s 142). In the case of *Marshall v Kerr* (1994) HL, it was confirmed that the capital gains tax effect was restricted to eliminating a capital gains charge by not treating the redirection of the assets as a disposal by the original beneficiaries, and that it did not affect other capital gains tax provisions (so that if, for example, the variation consisted of creating a trust in which the original beneficiary had an interest, the beneficiary would be regarded as a settlor for TCGA 1992 s 77 and would be charged on the trust's gains — see **Example 50 part c**).

It is possible to make a deed of variation effective for capital gains tax and not inheritance tax, or vice versa. If the variation was not effective for inheritance tax, the redirected assets would be treated as being transferred under the normal inheritance tax rules, so that the transfers would be potentially exempt unless they were to a discretionary trust. Where a discretionary trust is created through a deed of variation, which is effective for inheritance tax the settlement is regarded as commencing at the date of death, so that the ten-year anniversaries date from that time.

The deed of variation does not affect the income tax position. Any income arising before variation is charged to tax on the original beneficiary. Furthermore, if a parent varies in favour of his/her infant child, this constitutes a settlement within the terms of ITTOIA 2005 ss 620, 648 and any subsequent income arising before the child becomes 18 or marries under that age is chargeable as income of the parent under ITTOIA 2005 ss 629, 631, 632.

TCGA 1992 s 68C (and ITA 2007 ss 472, 473) affects variations of wills or intestacies etc occurring on or after 6 April 2006, irrespective of the date of death of the deceased person in question.

Section 68C applies where a transfer of property following a death is varied in circumstances where TCGA 1992 s 62(6) applies. The main conditions for section 62(6) to apply in respect of a variation are that the variation is made within two years after the deceased person's death, and the instrument of variation contains a statement that the provision is to apply.

The section also applies in any case where property becomes settled property in consequence of the variation but would not otherwise have become settled property. In such circumstances, a person listed below will be treated for TCGA purposes (except where the context otherwise requires) as having made the settlement and as having provided the property for the purposes of the settlement.

Four categories of person (in all cases referring effectively to the original beneficiary) are identified in this context:

- The first category comprises anyone who, immediately before the variation, was entitled to the property (or to property from which it derives) absolutely as legatee.

- The second category relates to a person who would have become entitled to the property (or to property from which it derives) absolutely as legatee but for the variation.

- The other two categories relate to individuals who would have fallen into either of the first two categories had they not been infants or other persons under a disability.

Section 68C provides for a different result where property which is not settled property immediately before the variation (in practice, because it is still vested in the deceased's personal representatives, in that capacity not as trustees) would have become comprised in a settlement (whether it is a settlement which arose on the deceased person's death or a pre-existing settlement), but the effect of the variation is that the property, or property derived from it, becomes comprised in a different settlement. In such circumstances, the deceased person (not the original beneficiary making the variation) will be treated for TCGA purposes (except where the context otherwise requires) as having made that other settlement.

Similarly, where, immediately before the variation, property is comprised in a settlement and is property of which the deceased person is a settlor, and the effect of the variation is that the property, or property derived from it, becomes comprised in another settlement the deceased person is to be treated for TCGA purposes as having made that other settlement.

Where the deceased person is treated as having made a settlement, he or she is treated for TCGA purposes as having made the settlement in question immediately before their death. This will not apply in any case where the settlement in question arose on the death of the deceased person.

Transfer of the nil-rate band

(10)   Sections 8A to 8C, introduced by FA 2008, allow a claim to be made to transfer any unused IHT nil-rate band on a person's death to the estate of their surviving spouse or civil partner who dies on or after 9 October 2007. This applies where the IHT nil-rate band of the first deceased spouse or civil partner was not fully used in calculating the IHT liability of their estate. When the surviving spouse or civil partner dies, the unused amount may be added to their own nil-rate band. A full explanation of the transferable nil-rate band provisions can be found in **Example 1**.

Where a valid claim to transfer unused nil-rate band is made, the nil-rate band that is available when the surviving spouse or civil partner dies will be increased by the proportion of the nil-rate band unused on the first death. For example, if on the first death the chargeable estate is £162,500 and the nil-rate band is

£325,000, 50% of the nil-rate band would be unused. If the nil-rate band when the survivor dies is £350,000, then that would be increased by 50% to £525,500.

The amount of the nil-rate band that can be transferred does not depend on the value of the first spouse or civil partner's estate. Whatever proportion of the nil-rate band is unused on the first death is available for transfer to the survivor.

It is important to remember that even if all the assets passing under the will are left to the surviving spouse or civil partner, there may be other components of the aggregate 'estate' on death for IHT purposes (such as assets in trust with an estate interest in possession, or gifts to other people made within seven years of death) which involve chargeable transfers. If present, these may use up some or all of the nil-rate band in the normal way, and so reduce the amount of unused nil-rate band that may be available for transfer.

In this case in (a) none of his nil-rate band was utilised on the death of Dr Slowe so 100% of the rate in force at the date of Mrs Slowe's death is available ie £325,000. The amount to be taken off her estate before the application of IHT is therefore £650,000 (£325,000 × 2).

In (c) Mrs Slowe dies first but she has used all of her nil-rate band against the life interest trust (even before taking account of her lifetime transfers – her estate is £410,000 and therefore none is available on the subsequent death of Dr Slowe. However, if most of the value of the life interest trust had not given rise to a chargeable transfer (eg if all but £12,500 of the trust property had been excluded property by reference to foreign situs and a non-UK domiciled settlor) it appears that a transfer of the unused portion of Mrs Slowe's nil-rate band to Dr Slowe's estate would have been possible even though her free estate does not form part of his taxable estate as a result of the commorientes rules. The effect simply exaggerates the benefits of the latter rules in the rare situation where they apply. The revised calculations would be as follows:

Inheritance tax payable on simultaneous deaths

Mrs Slowe (elder)	£	£
Free estate	75,000	
Less: Exempt transfer to Dr Slowe	75,000	nil
Settled property		
Life interest in estate of late father (non-excluded property)		12,500
Amount subject to inheritance tax		12,500

Inheritance tax accumulation

	Gross	Tax
	£	£
Cumulative transfers prior to death	85,000	–
Amount liable on death	12,500	–
	97,500*	–

*utilising only 30% of Mrs Stowe's nil-rate band – no tax

Dr Slowe (younger)	£	£
Family home		500,000
Interest in practice	250,000	–
Less: 100% business property relief	250,000	–
Other assets (excluding Mrs Slowe's assets of £75,000)		50,000
Amount subject to inheritance tax		550,000

Inheritance tax accumulation

	Gross £	Tax £
Cumulative transfers prior to death	–	–
Amount liable on death	550,000	–*
Inheritance tax payable by personal representatives		–*

*subject to claim, nil-rate band increased by 70% unused on Mrs Slowe's death:

£325,000 × 170% = £552,500, which exceeds chargeable estate

In (d) again Dr Slowe dies first but as his estate on death amounts to £550,000 the nil-rate band will have been fully utilised on his death with no surplus available to Mrs Slowe.

Question

Edward (aged 65 and just retired) is considering settling his entire assets worth £728,000 on his wife Mary for life with the remainder to their only son, Brian (to be held on trust to pay the income to him with power to release capital and with remainders over on Brian's death), completely excluding himself from any interest in the settlement.

The settlement may either be made now or included in Edward's will to take effect after his death.

Edward had made lifetime gifts of £306,000 to his brother Jon on 5 September 2009 utilising his unused annual exemptions and part of the nil-rate band. He had made no gifts in the year to 5 April 2009, but had used his annual exemptions for years prior to that. Edward died on 12 December 2011.

The value of the trust at the date of Mary's death on 3 February 2016 is £900,000. Assume that the nil-rate band for 2015/16 is £350,000 and that Mary left her entire free estate to charity.

Indicate the taxation implications of Edward's proposals, and explain the general principles governing the taxation of such settlements.

Answer

The taxation implications of Edward's proposals are as follows:

Inheritance tax

Settlement on spouse during lifetime

The settlement of his assets by Edward on Mary will be a chargeable transfer and subject immediately to IHT unless Mary is a disabled person within s 89(4)–(6), because the life interest falls outside the provisions of s 49(1A).

		Gross	Tax on 2010/11 scale
2009/10			
Gift to Jon – potentially exempt transfer £306,000			
2010/11			
Transfer of assets to settlement		728,000	
Less: Annual exemption 2010/11		(3,000)	
		725,000	80,000

*£725,000 – 325,000 @ 20%

Settlements made on or after 22 March 2006 are now generally subject to the rules which previously applied only to discretionary trusts. Therefore, the assets held by the trustees of an interest in possession settlement will not usually form part of the estate of the life tenant where the settlement was made after 21 March 2006. So on Mary's death her life interest will not form part of her estate.

This, however, has its drawbacks. In particular, as seen above the creation of the settlement will represent a chargeable event (previously, lifetime transfers into interest in possession settlements constituted PETs). Furthermore, the settlement will be subject to the ten-year charge and exit charge rules for relevant property trusts.

The following trusts will remain outside the rules previously limited to discretionary trusts:

(a) Bare trusts (where the beneficiary continues to be treated as entitled to the assets held under the bare trust; the trust property of a bare trust is not settled property).

(b) Interest in possession trusts where the interest in possession is what may be referred to as an estate interest in possession (see **Example 52**), namely:

    (i) an immediate post-death interest (IPDI) (see below);

    (ii) a disabled person's interest (broadly an interest in possession for a person incapable of looking after their affairs because of mental disorder, or a person in receipt of an attendance allowance or a disability living allowance);

    (iii) a transitional serial interest (TSI) (see below) (s 49(1A)); or

    (iv) owned by the beneficiary who has owned it continuously since before 22 March 2006.

To be a transitional serial interest in a settlement (s 49B–E):

    (i) the settlement must have been set up before 22 March 2006; and

> (ii) immediately before 22 March 2006, there must have been an individual with a beneficial interest in possession in the settlement;
>
> (iii) that person's interest must have come to an end after 21 March 2006 but before 5 October 2008; and
>
> (iv) the person with the current interest in the settlement became beneficially entitled to that interest at that time; and
>
> (v) the interest is not a disabled person's interest or an interest of a bereaved minor (IHTA 1984 s 49B).

The rules for bereaved minors are found in s 71A. They apply only for settlements which:

(a) are set up under the English intestacy rules or by:

> (i) a parent of the beneficiary in their will, or
>
> (ii) the Criminal Injuries Compensation Scheme,

(b) give the minor the capital and income of the trust absolutely when the minor reaches the age of 18.

Settlement on spouse on death of settlor

An immediate post-death interest (IPDI) under s 49A occurs where an individual becomes beneficially entitled on or after 22 March 2006 to an interest in possession in settled property provided certain conditions are met:

(a) the interest in settled property arises immediately on the death of the settlor by reason of will or intestacy; and

(b) the person becomes beneficially entitled to an interest in possession on the death of the settlor whether or not he or she dies intestate;

(c) the trust is not a bereaved minor's or disabled person's trust.

If the conditions are met the new trust will not be subject to the rules applying to relevant property trusts.

Edward has already made gifts of £306,000. His estate is valued at £728,000.

On Edward's death

5 Sept 2009	Gift to Jon		306,000
Less:			
Annual exemptions	2008/09	3,000	
	2009/10	3,000	6,000
			300,000

The chargeable gift of £300,000 after exemptions is charged within the nil-rate band of £325,000. The balance of the estate held on trust for Edward's wife is exempt under s 18.

On Mary's death

Mary is treated as beneficially entitled to the underlying settled property by virtue of her IPDI (s 49), and it therefore forms part of her estate for the purpose of the deemed transfer of value on her death under s 4. Mary's free estate passes to charity and is therefore exempt, so the settled property comprises Mary's only chargeable estate. Edward had used £300,000 of his £325,000 nil-rate band through the gift to Jon, so 7.7% of it is available for transfer to Mary's estate, subject to a claim by her personal representatives or (if they do not claim) by the trustees of Edward's will trust. Mary's nil-rate band of £350,000 is thus increased by that percentage to (£350,000 × 107.7% =) £376,950

Value of Mary's chargeable estate at 3 February 2016	900,000
Tax due (£900,000 – 376,950) @ 40% =	£209,220

Prior to FA 2006 Sch 20 para 4 Brian's interest in possession would also have led to the settled property being comprised in his estate. However, since it is created out of an existing settlement after 6 October 2008 it is neither a TSI nor an IPDI. Whilst the assets remain in trust the relevant property rules will apply (see **Example 60**).

Release of life interest

If, prior to her death, Mary relinquished or assigned her life interest in the settlement in favour of Brian, this would be a deemed transfer of value, against which her annual (and if relevant marriage) exemptions for the year of release and previous year would be available unless otherwise used used if Mary gave the requisite notice to the trustees within six months (s 57 and see **Example 55 explanatory note 3**). The treatment of the balance would depend on:

(a)   whether Mary's life interest was an estate interest in possession (an IPDI or a disabled person's interest (DPI)) or not (lifetime settlement where Mary is not a disabled person), and

(b)   whether or not Brian became absolutely entitled immediately on the release or assignment (which on the facts stated would depend on the trustees exercising their power to release capital before or simultaneously with Mary's release or assignment); if he did not, his interest in possession (unless he was himself a disabled person at the date the property was originally settled so that his interest would be a DPI) would be a non-estate interest in possession in any event, and the trust fund would become relevant property if it was not so before.

Brian's interest	*Absolute entitlement or DPI*	*Continuing IIP other than a DPI*
Mary – estate IIP	potentially exempt transfer	immediately chargeable transfer
Mary – non-estate IIP	relevant property exit charge	no IHT event – trust property remains relevant property

Additionally, if Mary's life interest was an estate interest in possession, she would be regarded as making a gift of the underlying trust property for the purpose of the gift with reservation rules (FA 1986 s 102ZA), so that any benefit subsequently enjoyed by her (or any interest retained by her under the terms of the trust) would result in those rules catching the property and taxing it as part of her estate on her death (or as a failed potentially exempt transfer if the benefit had ended during her lifetime but within seven years before her death).

Assignment to settlor

Edward, if he settled the trust in his lifetime, would be excluded from benefit by the terms of the settlement, but that would not prevent his becoming a beneficiary if Mary chose to assign her life interest to him. If she did this, the consequences would again depend in part on whether her life interest was a DPI by virtue of her status as a disabled person when the trust was settled. Edward would not become absolutely entitled — he would merely take over Mary's right to income for the rest of her life, after which Brian's interest would take affect as previously. The position (assuming that Edward was not himself a disabled person at that time, so that the life interest in his hands would not be a DPI) can be summarised as follows:

(a)   With a non-estate interest in possession the trust property would already be within the relevant property regime, and it would continue so without an IHT charge by reference to the assignment. However, although the gift with reservation rules would not have applied in Edward's case prior to Mary's assignment because he was excluded from benefit, they would apply once he became entitled to Mary's life interest; accordingly, on his death while Mary was still alive the trust property would be taxed as part of his estate on his death (without prejudice to any charge under the relevant property rules (FA 1986 s 102(3)). Alternatively, on the reservation ceasing during his lifetime (eg if he in turn assigned or relinquished the life interest, or if it came to an end through Mary's death while Edward was still living), Edward would be deemed to have made a potentially exempt transfer of the trust property concerned (FA 1986 s 102(4)), which would become chargeable if he were to die within seven years afterwards.

(b)   If on the other hand Mary's interest was a DPI then (as with a relinquishment in favour of Brian on a continuing trust, see above) the assignment would give rise to a deemed transfer of value which (apart from annual exemptions so far as made available by her to the trustees by notice as above) would be an immediately chargeable transfer. The property concerned would become relevant property as Edward's interest in possession is taken not be a DPI as above. As a result of amendments to the 'gift with reservation' rules introduced in 2003 to counteract the decision in IRC v Eversden [2003] EWCA Civ 668 and [2003] STC 822, Edward is not protected from those rules by the fact that the original gift to the trust attracted spouse exemption as a result of Mary's DPI (FA 1986 s 102(5)(a)).

The application of the gift with reservation rules in relation to Mary by virtue of FA 1986 s 102ZA, if her life interest was a DPI and so an estate IIP, would be the same as above.

Capital Gains Tax

Settlement by will

If Edward waits until his death to make the transfer into the settlement for Mary, there will be no capital gains tax payable because death is not a chargeable occasion for capital gains tax, although the deceased's assets are regarded as acquired at probate value by those on whom they devolve (ie legatees, trustees, or personal representatives as the case may be) (TCGA 1992 s 62). The trustees would therefore be deemed to acquire the trust property at probate value.

Lifetime settlement

If Edward makes the transfer into the settlement for Mary during his lifetime, then the capital gains tax exemption for absolute transfers between spouses does not apply. Gift relief under TCGA 1992 s 165 or s 260 is not available in respect of disposals of assets to the trustees of a trust in which the settlor has an interest where the disposal is made on or after 10 December 2003. Section 169F provides that any interest of the spouse is to be treated as the interest of the settlor.

These provisions also claw back or prevent any gifts relief in relation to disposals to trusts which become settlor-interested settlements within a certain time period. This period begins immediately after the disposal and ends immediately before the sixth anniversary of the start of the tax year next following that in which the disposal is made.

As Mary will have a life interest in the new settlement, Edward will be deemed to have an interest in the settlement and holdover relief will not be available.

Death of life tenant

When a life tenant dies then, provided the life interest was an estate interest in possession, the trust property is treated as having been disposed of and immediately reacquired at probate value, but as with the death of someone owning assets absolutely, there is no capital gains tax charge on the trust assets. (If the settlement had been made in lifetime and any gains had been deferred under the holdover provisions of s 165 or s 260 prior to 10 December 2003 – which however is not possible here because of the trust being treated as settlor-interested as referred to above – the deferred gains would become chargeable on the life tenant's death. If any of the property in the trust at that time is qualifying property for holdover relief under s 165, the deferred gains on that property could be the subject of a further claim for holdover relief.)

If therefore Mary's life interest is an IPDI or a DPI, on her death neither the trustees nor Brian will be liable to capital gains tax in respect of the assets in the settlement. Those assets which devolve upon Brian (some may have to be sold in order to pay inheritance tax unless Brian wishes to retain all the assets and fund the tax by other means — perhaps by instalments if the property is instalment option property) will do so for capital gains purposes at their market value at the date of his mother's death, and those retained by the trustees in order to sell them to raise cash for the payment of inheritance tax will also have a base value equivalent to their market value at that time (TCGA 1992 s 73).

If on the other hand Mary's life interest is not an estate interest in possession – as would be the case if Edward made the settlement in his lifetime and Mary was not a disabled person at the time – then her death would not give rise to any deemed disposal by the trustees unless and until Brian became absolutely entitled.

Release of life interest

If Mary relinquishes her entitlement during her lifetime, the position will be the same as on her death with a non-estate interest in possession: unless and until Brian becomes absolutely entitled there will be no deemed disposal by the trustees, but when he does, the trustees will be deemed to make a disposal at that time at the then market value, any gains held over if the settlement was created in lifetime becoming chargeable, and capital gains tax will be payable accordingly (less any annual exemption available to the trustees and subject to any available holdover relief) (TCGA 1992 s 71).

Trustees' own gains

If, during the continuation of the trust, the trustees themselves realise capital gains on the disposal of trust assets, for Example on the switching of investments, then the trustees will be liable to tax on the gains at 28%, subject to availability of the annual exemption (TCGA 1992 Sch 1.2(1)). The annual exemption for a trust (other than one which fulfils the conditions for a disabled person's trust in TCGA 1992 Sch 1.1 – which are different from those for a DPI for inheritance tax purposes) is half that available to individuals (£5,050 for 2010/11), providing it is the only settlement created by the settlor since 6 June 1978 (see **Example 50 part c**).

Enterprise investment scheme relief

Providing the beneficiaries of the trust are confined to individuals and charities, then gains realised by the trustees may be deferred to the extent that they are reinvested in cash by subscribing for ordinary shares in a qualifying unquoted trading company under the enterprise investment scheme, the money raised being used within twelve months for a qualifying business activity (TCGA 1992 Sch 5B).

For further notes on the capital gains tax position of trusts see **Example 50**.

Income Tax

Lifetime settlement

If the settlement is made by Edward in his lifetime, then since Mary is entitled to the income it will be treated as a settlement in which he retains an interest, and all income arising, whether distributed by the trustees or retained by them, will be liable to income tax as part of Edward's statutory total income during his lifetime (ITTOIA 2005 s 624). The settlement is not sufficient to transfer income from Edward to Mary for income tax purposes because he is giving her only a right to income and not outright ownership of the assets. Following Edward's death, the income whether distributed or not will be treated as Mary's income. This will also apply if the settlement is made on Edward's death.

Tax liability of trustees

The trustees in each case will have a basic rate liability (or lower rate or dividend ordinary rate liability if the income is savings income) unless the income is mandated direct to Mary in order to save administrative cost and inconvenience, any liability at the higher rate (or dividend upper rate) being assessed on Edward, or Mary his widow, as the case may be. Edward would be entitled to recover any tax paid by him from the trustees or from Mary (ITTOIA 2005 s 646).

Charge on Edward and Mary after his death

Where income is treated as Edward's income, the amount on which he is charged to tax cannot be reduced by any trust expenses, since he is only permitted to deduct amounts that would have been deductible if he had received the income directly (ITTOIA 2005 ss 619, 621, 623). Furthermore, for income other than dividends, the income is taxed as miscellaneous income, so it cannot be taxed at the savings rate of 20% whether or not Edward is liable at higher rates. Dividend income is, however, charged at the dividend ordinary rate of 10% or upper rate of 32½% (ITTOIA 2005 ss 619, 621, 623.

From 2010/11 there are three rates of tax for dividends. Dividends otherwise taxable at the 20% basic rate will continue to be taxable at the 10% dividend ordinary rate and dividends otherwise taxable at the 40% higher rate continue to be taxable at the 32.50% dividend upper rate. Dividends otherwise taxable at the 50% additional rate are taxable at a new 42.50% dividend additional rate (FA 2009 s 6(3) and Sch 2 para 3 (amends ITA 2007 s 8).

After Edward's death, Mary is taxed as the beneficiary of an interest in possession trust. Unless the income has been mandated direct to her, the trust expenses will be paid out of the taxed income of the trust, and the balance remaining will be paid to her, the trustees giving her a certificate indicating the amounts of tax deducted at the basic, lower or dividend ordinary rate of tax as the case may be. The tax deducted will count towards the tax payable by her or will be repayable if it exceeds her liability. This does not apply to dividend tax credits, which are not repayable.

Question

Your client, Charles, a wealthy widower, is a director and majority shareholder in an unquoted trading company that was established many years ago.

His wife died suddenly six months ago, leaving her estate comprising shares in quoted companies, life insurance policies, cash, jewellery and personal possessions, valued in total at £335,000, to Charles.

Charles is aged 62 and is considering retiring within the next year or so. He is also considering disposing of some of his assets, either by sale or possibly by gift, but is undecided whether to dispose of them during his lifetime or by will on his death.

Taxation will be a major factor influencing his decision regarding the disposition of his assets, and he has stated that he wishes to minimise any tax liability arising.

He has estimated his total estate to have a value of approximately £1,140,000, including the £335,000 left to him by his deceased wife, broadly comprised as follows:

His 70% shareholding in the unquoted family trading company, valued at £140,000

His 18% shareholding in an unquoted company which supplies the family company, valued at £60,000, (the other shares being held by his brothers and sister)

Quoted shares valued at £108,000

His private residence valued at £495,000

A plot of land on which he and his wife had planned to build a bungalow for their retirement valued at £40,000

A life insurance policy on his life with a market value of £40,000 and a surrender value of £36,000

Furniture, jewellery and other chattels with a total value of £25,000, the highest value item being valued at £2,500

Cash at bank, building society and at home — total value £232,000

Private motor car valued at £9,000

He has one daughter and two grandsons, one of whom joined him last year in the family company. He has also developed a considerable interest in Heartbeat (UK) — a registered charity.

(a)   In relation to both capital gains tax and inheritance tax, summarise:

    (i)   the events giving rise to a charge

    (ii)   the amount chargeable

    (iii)   the rates of tax

    (iv)   some common exemptions and reliefs

    (v)   whether phasing of disposals is advantageous

    (vi)   the advantages/disadvantages of lifetime disposals as compared to a transfer on death

    (vii)   the benefits, if any, of Charles emigrating.

(b)   Suggest action that Charles might take and disposals he might make which would result in a nil or small tax liability, and which would reduce the tax payable on his eventual death.

Answer

(a) Capital gains tax summary

(i) *Chargeable disposals*

The capital gains tax provisions apply to the disposal of chargeable assets during lifetime. No charge is made on death. 'Disposal' includes sales, gifts and loss or destruction of assets; chargeable assets are all assets other than those that are specifically exempt. Options, debts, currency other than sterling, and rights are included, but not bettings winnings or damages for personal or professional injuries.

(ii) *Calculation of gain or loss*

The chargeable gain (or allowable loss) is calculated by comparing the value on disposal with the sum of the cost price, costs of acquisition and costs of sale. All assets owned on 31 March 1982 will be deemed to have had a cost equivalent to their market value at that date.

Treatment of losses

Chargeable gains are reduced by losses of the same year. In addition, they are reduced by losses brought forward (or carried back from the year of death), but not so as to waste the annual exemption of the year of disposal.

(iii) *FA 2010 changes to CGT (F (No 2) A 2010 s 2 & Sch 1)*

The annual exemption for 2010/11 is set at £10,100 for individuals and £5,050 for trustees.

From 23 June 2010, there will be two main rates of Capital Gains Tax (CGT), 18% and 28%, replacing the single rate of 18% for all gains. The rate paid by individuals will depend upon the amount of their total taxable income (F (No 2) A 2010 Sch 1 ss 2 amends TCGA 1992 s 4)

Individuals who are taxed at the basic 20% rate on their total taxable income will be taxed at 18% on their capital gains falling within the basic rate band and those taxable at the higher rates of 40% and 50% will be liable at the 28% rate.

For individuals, where total taxable income and gains after all allowable deductions (including losses, personal allowances and the CGT annual exemption) are less than the upper limit of the basic rate income tax band (£37,400 for 2010/11), the rate of CGT is 18%. For gains (and any parts of gains) above that limit the rate will be 28%.

So for the tax year 2010/11, most people will start paying higher rate income tax only on income over £43,875 although this will depend on whether they have any other allowances or allowable expenses etc.

To summarise:

(1)   If total taxable income is below that amount, gains up to the unused amount of the band are chargeable at 18%.

(2)   Any amounts that exceed any unused amount of the basic rate band are chargeable at 28%.

(3)   If total taxable income uses up the whole of the basic rate band all capital gains are charged at 28%.

Gains arising in 2010/11, but before 23 June 2010, will continue to be liable to CGT at 18% and will not be taken into account in determining the rate (or rates) at which gains of individuals arising on or after 23 June 2010 should be charged.

Certain CGT reliefs allow gains on disposal of an asset to be deferred until sometime after the disposal. For instance, a gain can be reinvested in shares under the Enterprise Investment Scheme (EIS) and, subject to conditions, can be deferred until the EIS shares are disposed of. The CGT rate(s) on a gain deferred in this way will be the rate(s) at the time the deferral ends and the gain becomes liable to tax. Gains on disposals before 23 June 2010 which are deferred until 23 June 2010 or later will therefore be liable to CGT at the 18 or 28% rates, in the same way as gains arising on disposals on or after that date.

Gains qualifying for entrepreneurs' relief will be taxed at a rate of 10%, and the lifetime limit of gains qualifying for entrepreneurs' relief will be raised to £5 million (from the previous figure of £2 million which applied from 6 April 2010 – the figure for 2009/10 being £1 million). (FA 10 no2 Sch 1 ss4 & 5 amends TCGA 1992 S169H & N)

F (No 2) A 2010 changes for trustees & personal representatives

For **trustees**, the CGT rate will be 28% for gains arising on or after 23 June 2010, except in certain cases where entrepreneurs' relief applies when the rate will be 10%. (F (No 2) A 2010 Sch 1 ss 2 amends TCGA 1992 s 4).

For **personal representatives**, the CGT rate will be 28% for gains arising on or after 23 June 2010 and 18% prior to that date (F (No 2) A 2010 Sch 1 ss 2 amends TCGA 1992 s 4).

Example

In 2010/11 Jan's taxable income, after all allowable deductions and the personal allowance, is £30,400. The upper limit of the income tax basic rate band is £37,400.

Jan sells an asset in May 2010 and realises a chargeable gain of £20,000.

In January 2011, Jan sells another asset, realising a chargeable gain £20,100. Jan has no allowable losses to set against these gains, and the annual exemption for 2010/11 is £10,100. Neither of the gains qualifies for entrepreneurs' relief.

Jan's taxable income is £7,000 less than the upper limit of the basic rate band (£37,400 – £30,400). Jan sets the annual exemption against the later gain (because part of that gain is liable to tax at the higher CGT rate), leaving £10,000 taxable (£20,100 – £10,100). The first £7,000 of the £10,000 is taxed at 18% and the remaining £3,000 is taxed at 28%.

The £20,000 chargeable gain Jan realised in May 2010 before the change of rates on 23 June 2010 is taxable at the old 18% rate. (see below and **Example 40 note 10**).

(iv) FA 2008 changes to CGT under FA 2008 s 8 and Sch 2, the taxation of capital gains was reformed. A number of other changes to simplify the capital gains tax regime were made, including:

- the withdrawal of taper relief;

- the withdrawal of indexation allowance;

- the abolition of the 'kink test' for assets held at 31 March 1982;

- abolition of halving relief; and

- simplification of the share identification rules.

Other CGT reliefs will continue to have effect. For Example:

- private residence relief will continue to be available for principal private residences;

- business asset roll-over relief continues to be available;

- business asset gift hold-over relief also continues to apply;

- any unused allowable losses from past years will continue to be allowed to be brought forward in order to reduce any gains.

Where gains are to be deferred until the occurrence of a later event, the effect of the changes is that, where a gain arose in a tax year earlier than 2008/09 was deferred; the computation of the deferred amount should take account, if appropriate, of the kink test, halving relief and indexation allowance. This figure of deferred gain will not be affected by these changes.

However, taper relief will not be due if these gains come into charge in 2008/09 or a later tax year. This is because taper relief was due only when a gain is brought into charge, and the deferred amount does not include taper relief.

In the case of an unconditional contract to sell made before 5 April 2008 to take effect after this date – the existing pre-5 April 2008 rules will apply and taper relief and/or indexation may be available. This is because the contract is deemed to be made at the date it was entered into.

In the case of a conditional contract to sell made before 5 April 2008 – the disposal date will be treated as the date that the conditions were satisfied. If this is post-5 April 2008 then the revised rules will apply.

UK resident settlor-interested settlements

Sch 2 para 5 repeals TCGA 1992 ss 77 to 79. These provisions had the effect that gains in respect of which the trustees of a UK resident settlor-interested settlement would otherwise have been chargeable to CGT are in certain circumstances charged on the settlor. The introduction of a single rate of CGT for trustees and individuals means that the application of ss 77 to 79 would have no effect on the rate at which the gains were charged to CGT.

Settlements for vulnerable persons

For details of the FA 2008 changes to capital gains see **Example 47 note 4**.

Entrepreneurs' relief

Individuals

Under FA 2008 s 9 and Sch 3 entrepreneurs' relief applies to individuals and trustees who dispose of the whole or part of a trading business, or of shares in a trading company in which they have a qualifying interest.

Entrepreneurs' relief may be available in respect of gains made by individuals on the disposal of:

- all or part of a trading business the individual carries on alone or in partnership;

- assets of the individual's or partnership's trading business following the cessation of the business;

- shares in (and securities of) the individual's 'personal' trading company (or holding company of a trading group);

- assets owned by the individual and used by his/her 'personal' trading company (or group) or trading partnership.

An individual is able to make claims for relief on qualifying disposals made on or after 6 April 2008. Claims may be made on more than one occasion up to a 'lifetime' limit of £2 million (and £5 million after 23 June 2010). Disposals on or before 5 April 2008 do not affect the lifetime limit. The limit will only begin to diminish when the relief is claimed.

Transitional provisions also allow relief to be claimed in certain circumstances where gains that have been deferred from disposals made on or before 5 April 2008 become chargeable after that date. The first £2 million (F (No 1) A 2010 s 4) (£1 million before 5 April 2010) of gains qualify for the relief which effectively taxes qualifying gains at 10%. Gains in excess of £2 million are charged to CGT at the rate of 18% for gains incurred before 22 June 2010 (see below for the rules after that date.)

For gains incurred up to 22 June 2010 the relief works as follows:

(1)   Schedule 3 introduced section 169N into TCGA 1992. Where a claim is made in respect of a qualifying business disposal the relevant gains (see s 5) are to be aggregated, with any relevant losses (see s 6) being deducted.

(2) The resulting amount is reduced by 4/9ths.

(3) But if the total of current gains less losses and the amounts resulting in relation to earlier relevant qualifying business disposals (if any), exceeds £2 million (£1 million limit before 6 April 2010), the reduction is to be made in respect of only so much (if any) of the amount resulting as (when added to that total) does not exceed £2 million (£1 million limit before 6 April 2010).

The amount arrived at is to be treated as a chargeable gain accruing at the time of the disposal to the individual or trustees by whom the claim is made.

The changes to CGT rates from 23 June 2010 mean the 4/9 reduction no longer achieved an effective rate of 10%. Finance (No 2) Act 2010 Sch 1 ss 5 includes provision to charge gains on disposals that qualify for entrepreneurs' relief on or after 23 June 2010 at a 10% rate. The previous 4/9ths reduction will cease to apply from that date.

The amount of an individual's gains that can qualify for entrepreneurs' relief is subject to a lifetime limit of £2 million (£1 million for disposals before 6 April 2010).

For trustees, the £2 million limit is that of the beneficiary of the settlement who meets the conditions for the trustees to claim the relief.

Finance (No 2) 2010 Sch 1 ss 5 sets out the provision to increase the limit to £5 million with effect from 23 June 2010.

Where individuals or trustees make qualifying gains above the previous £2 million limit before 23 June 2010 (£1 million limit before 6 April 2010), no additional relief will be allowed for the excess above the old limit. But if they make further qualifying gains on or after 23 June 2010, they will be able to claim relief on up to a further £3 million of those additional gains (or up to £4 million where the earlier £1 million limit applied), giving relief on accumulated qualifying gains up to the new limit of £5 million.

In determining at what rate(s) an individual should be charged to CGT on any other gains, those gains qualifying for entrepreneurs' relief are set against any unused basic rate band before non-qualifying gains.

To summarise:

For gains arising before 23 June 2010 (FA 2008 Sch 3, F (No 1) A 2010 s 4)

The first £2 million of gains (limit was £1 million for 2009/10) will qualify for the relief which effectively taxes qualifying gains at 10%. Gains in excess of £2 million will be charged to CGT at the normal rate of 18%.

The relief works as follows:

(1) Where a claim is made in respect of a qualifying business disposal the relevant business gains are to be added together, with any relevant business capital losses being deducted.

(2) The resulting amount is to be reduced by 4/9ths.

(3) But if the total of current gains less losses and the amounts means that the tally of business capital gains exceeds £2 million (£1 million before 6 April 2010), the reduction is to be made in respect of only so much (if any) of the amount resulting as (when added to that total) does not exceed £2 million (£1 million before 6 April 2010).

(4) The resulting gain is then taxed at 18%. This gives an effective tax rate of 10% once the gain is reduced by 4/9ths ($18\% \times 5/9 = 10\%$)

For gains arising after 23 June 2010 (FA (No 2) 2010 Sch 1 ss 4 & 5 amends TCGA 1992 s 169H & N)

The amount of gains that can qualify for entrepreneurs' relief is subject to a lifetime limit of £2 million (£1 million for disposals before 6 April 2010). This is taxable at 10%.

This limit is to increase to £5 million from 23 June 2010.

For gains above the previous £2 million limit arising before 23 June 2010 (£1 million limit before 6 April 2010), no additional relief will be allowed for the excess above the old limit.

If there are further qualifying gains on or after 23 June 2010, relief can be claimed up to a further £3 million of those additional gains (or up to £4 million where the earlier £1 million limit applied), giving relief on accumulated qualifying gains up to the new limit of £5 million.

In working out what rate of CGT applies on any other gains, those gains qualifying for entrepreneurs' relief are set against any unused basic rate band before non-qualifying gains.

Trustees

Trustees can claim relief on certain disposals of business assets and company shares and securities where a 'qualifying beneficiary' has a qualifying interest in the business in question. Trustees must make claims jointly with the 'qualifying beneficiary'. Any relief given on the trustees' gains will reduce a beneficiary's lifetime limit on relief (TCGA 1992 s 169O).

If, on the same day, there is both a disposal of trust business assets in respect of which an individual is the qualifying beneficiary and a qualifying business disposal by the individual, TCGA 1992 s 169N(8) applies as if the disposal of trust business assets were later.

Example – the effect of the change of the lifetime limits on multiple gains

Matthew has previously used £1 million of his lifetime entrepreneurs' relief limit. In 2010/11 his taxable income, after all allowable deductions and the personal allowance, is £27,400. The upper limit of the income tax basic rate band is £37,400.

In May 2010, Matthew realises a chargeable gain of £2.5 million on the disposal of a business. In March 2011 Matthew sells another business, realising further chargeable gains of £5 million. Both disposals qualify for entrepreneurs' relief (subject to the lifetime limits). Matthew has no allowable losses to set against these gains, and the annual exemption for 2010/11 is £10,100. He has no other gains for 2010/11.

The £2.5 million gain realised in May 2010 is subject to the £2 million lifetime limit for entrepreneurs' relief (for qualifying disposals from 6 April 2010), of which Matthew has previously used £1 million. The gain is reduced by 4/9 of £1 million and the remainder charged to CGT at the single rate of 18%.

The increase in the lifetime limit from 23 June 2010 means that £3 million of the £5 million gain from March 2011 is chargeable at the 10% rate of CGT. Matthew's taxable income is £10,000 below the basic rate band (£37,400 – £27,400).

But the £3 million of the gain charged at 10% is taken into account in priority to other gains in determining whether total income and gains exceed the basic rate band. So the remaining £2 million gains, less the annual exemption, are charged at the higher rate of 28%. There is more on the relief in **Example 40**.

See pages (ix to xi) for the rates applying to personal representatives and trustees.

(iv) Exemptions and reliefs

Exempt assets include:

Principal private residence (subject to certain conditions)

Private motor cars

Tangible movable assets (chattels) that are wasting assets, including racehorses, but excluding chattels used in a business on which capital allowances have been or could have been claimed

Other chattels (including business chattels) if sold for less than £6,000

Gifts of assets to charities.

Reliefs include:

Rollover relief or holdover relief enabling gains to be deferred when qualifying business assets are sold and replaced. Where gains are rolled over to reduce the cost of the replacement asset, taper relief (see (ii) above) is available when the replacement asset is disposed of, based upon the period of ownership of the *new* asset. Where gains are held over against the acquisition of depreciating assets, the taper relief when the replacement asset is disposed of is based on the period of ownership of the *original* asset.

Deferral relief when a gain is reinvested by a cash subscription either for unquoted shares in a qualifying trading company under the enterprise investment scheme or for shares in a venture capital trust. The gain is deferred until the qualifying shares are sold or replaced, taper relief being based on the period of ownership of the *original* asset.

Gifts holdover relief enabling gains to be regarded as reducing the donee's acquisition cost for capital gains tax, in respect of gifts of business assets, agricultural land, shares giving 5% voting control in an unquoted trading company, or gifts subject to an immediate charge to inheritance tax.

(v)   *Advantages of phasing disposals*

By disposing of assets over a period of years a number of annual exemptions may be used. Note that unused annual exemption cannot be carried forward, and unused losses cannot be carried back (except losses of the year of death, which may be carried back against gains in excess of the annual exemption in the three previous years, latest first). But this does not apply to disposals of items to the same person if they form part of a set.

(vi)   *Disposals in lifetime or on death*

On death there is no charge to capital gains tax and there is an automatic uplift to market value at that time for those entitled to the assets, whereas a disposal in lifetime may give rise to a charge. If a gain has been rolled over or held over against the cost of qualifying replacement business assets, the death of the taxpayer means that the gain never gets charged to tax. By contrast, where holdover relief has been claimed on a gift of an asset, the donee's capital gains tax cost is reduced as indicated in (iv), thus resulting in a higher gain when the donee disposes of the asset. The donee's acquisition cost is not affected by the subsequent death of the donor.

(vii)   *Effect of emigration*

Capital gains tax is chargeable on worldwide assets of taxpayers who are resident or ordinarily resident in the UK.

If a taxpayer ceases to be both resident and ordinarily resident then he will not be liable to UK capital gains tax unless the assets are situated in the UK and are used in a trade carried on in the UK. A charge can also occur on accrued gains on the export of a UK company or trust.

Charles can therefore avoid UK capital gains tax by emigration if gains are realised after he has become neither resident nor ordinarily resident, except in relation to any assets used in the UK for the purposes of a trade. If, however, he returned to the UK and became resident or ordinarily resident within five complete tax years of the date of departure, gains on assets held on emigration that were realised while he was non-resident would be chargeable in the tax year of return. Any such gains realised in the tax year of departure would be taxed as gains of that tax year. Finance (No 2) Act 2005 provisions prevent the exploitation of double tax agreements during the period of absence. If a gain has been charged to tax in another country, and is also charged in the UK on the taxpayer's return within five years then the tax paid overseas is deductible from the UK liability. If a taxpayer is resident or ordinarily resident in the UK, but under a double tax treaty would be treated as non-resident (such that a gain would be taxed at a low or nil rate) then UK capital gains tax will be payable overriding the DTA provisions (F (No 2) A 2005 s 32 amending TCGA 1992 s 10A). Similar provisions were introduced for trustees (F (No 2) A 2005 s 33 introducing TCGA 1992 s 83A).

Inheritance tax summary

(i)   Chargeable transfers

Inheritance tax is chargeable on certain lifetime gifts, on wealth at death and on certain transfers into and out of trust. If a taxpayer makes a lifetime gift to an individual, or to certain trusts such as a trust for the disabled, then provided the donor survives the gift by seven years or more, it is not liable to inheritance tax. This is known as a potentially exempt transfer, and it covers virtually all lifetime gifts that an individual might make, except to a discretionary trust, which are chargeable at the time they are made. Certain gifts are totally exempt from tax (see (iv) below).

(ii)   Chargeable amount

Where a lifetime gift is immediately chargeable, the chargeable amount is the difference between the value of the donor's estate before the transfer and its value after the transfer. If the donor bears the inheritance tax then that tax will reduce the value of the estate after the transfer, increasing the chargeable transfer. This is known as grossing up the gift.

(iii)   Rates of tax

Any *chargeable* transfers of the last seven years are added together. To that total is added the value of the current chargeable transfer, which is charged to tax as the highest part of the total. For 2010/11 there is no inheritance tax on the first £325,000 of cumulative transfers. Lifetime chargeable transfers in excess of £325,000 are taxed at 20%, which is half of the full rate.

The nil-rate band for 2010/11–2014/15 remains at £325,000.

Potentially exempt gifts made within seven years before death become chargeable transfers on death, any chargeable transfers within the seven years before the gift being taken into account in calculating the tax payable. The value taken into account is that at the time of the gift, but the rate of tax used is the full rate (not the half rate) applicable at the date of death (currently 40%). If the gift was made more than three years before death then any tax payable on the gift is reduced by a taper relief.

Where a transfer was chargeable in lifetime, and the donor dies within seven years, tax is recalculated at the full rate on the scale in force at the date of death, taper relief being available as for potentially exempt transfers, and the tax payable, if any, being reduced by the tax paid in lifetime, but no repayment being available if the lifetime tax exceeds the tax due at death.

Tax on the death estate is calculated by adding the estate to chargeable transfers within the seven years before the death.

(iv)   Exemptions and reliefs

Exemptions include:

Transfers between spouses and civil partners (unless transferee is not UK domiciled, when exempt limit is £55,000 – for more information see **Example 3 (c)**)

Annual exemption for lifetime gifts	— £3,000 pa
Small lifetime gifts to same person	— not exceeding £250 pa
Normal expenditure out of income	
Gifts in consideration of marriage or registration of a civil partnership	— £5,000 by a parent
	— £2,500 by a grandparent or a party to the marriage/civil partnership
	— £1,000 by any other person

Gifts to charities, political parties, housing associations, or for national purposes

Conditional exemption for heritage property

Gifts made more than seven years before death (see (i) above).

Reliefs include:

Business property relief (relief being at 100% on an interest in a business or unquoted shareholdings; controlling holdings in quoted companies qualify for 50% relief)

Agricultural property relief (at 100% for owner-occupied property and property let on leases granted on or after 1 September 1995 and 50% for other let property)

Quick succession relief, reducing the tax payable where a donee dies within five years after receiving a chargeable transfer.

It is also possible to use a deed of variation within two years after death to alter the way a deceased person's estate is distributed (see **Example 34**).

(v)   Advantages of phasing disposals

Regular gifts could be covered by the exemption for normal expenditure out of income providing they are habitual (eg by payments of regular premiums under an insurance policy), and leave the taxpayer with sufficient income to live in his normal style.

Other lifetime gifts would be potentially exempt in so far as they are not covered by the annual exemption of £3,000. If the previous year's annual exemption was not used, that would also be available to reduce the transfer. The earlier year's annual exemption is only available after the later year has been used in full. Any of the previous year's exemption not then utilised will be lost. Potentially exempt transfers only become chargeable transfers if the donor dies within seven years. Transfers that are not potentially exempt are taxed at one-half of the full rate once the nil threshold is exceeded.

Even though a gift is not covered by a specific exemption, no tax is payable in lifetime or on death to the extent that the gift is covered by the nil threshold (taking into account gifts made within the previous seven years).

(vi)   Disposals in lifetime or on death

Although gifts made more than three but less than seven years before death attract taper relief, that is irrelevant unless the cumulative total at the time of the lifetime gift exceeds the nil threshold applicable at the date of death, since no tax will be payable to which any taper relief can apply.

Because lifetime gifts are accumulated with earlier chargeable transfers (made within seven years before the date of the gift) it is possible for gifts made within seven years before death to increase the overall burden of inheritance tax.

Subject to the above, potentially exempt lifetime gifts are normally advantageous as they are completely exempt after seven years, are not chargeable in any event if covered by the nil threshold, and if chargeable, possibly attract taper relief. Any part of the nil threshold used to cover such transfers would, however, reduce the amount available on the death estate.

In the case of assets attracting 100% business property relief it may not be advantageous to make a lifetime transfer. This is because a liability to capital gains tax can arise on the gift. The gain may be held over for capital gains purposes (see point (iv) under capital gains tax summary above), but it will reduce the base value to the donee (point (vi) of the capital gains tax summary above), whereas on death there is an automatic uplift to market value for capital gains tax purposes without any capital gains tax being payable. There would, however, be no liability to inheritance tax at the time of a lifetime gift because of the 100% relief, nor if the donor died within seven years, providing the gifted business assets were still held and still qualified.

(vii)   Effect of emigration

Inheritance tax is chargeable on worldwide assets of a person domiciled in the UK. To emigrate without changing domicile has no effect.

Even if Charles changes his domicile he will still be deemed UK domiciled for three years, and thereafter will be liable to inheritance tax on UK based property no matter where his domicile is.

See **Example 3 (c)** for more information on deemed domicile.

(b) Suggested course of action for Charles

Although the transfer to Charles on his wife's death was exempt because of the spouse exemption, her nil-rate band has been wasted (unless she had made chargeable or potentially exempt gifts in the seven years before her death). The following points should be considered in order to improve the present and potential future tax position.

(i)   Charles should consider a deed of variation to redirect some of the assets left to him by his wife. This could go directly to his daughter, or to the grandchildren, thus utilising the nil-rate threshold of his wife at her death and avoiding the value of the appropriate assets becoming part of his estate. Alternatively he could direct his wife's estate to a discretionary trust, for which he is a trustee, so that he can still exercise some control over the assets.

The deed would also be effective for capital gains tax (providing the deed contains a statement that it is intended to have that effect), avoiding any tax if the assets have increased in value since the wife's death (although if the variation included a trust in which Charles had an interest, he would be regarded as the settlor and would be charged on the trust's gains).

(ii)   Charles could make transfers of his shareholding in the family trading company in 2010/11, covering any capital gains tax liability with gifts holdover relief. The gifts would initially be potentially exempt transfers covered by 100% business property relief for inheritance tax. If Charles died within seven years, then providing the donees had retained the shares given to them, business property relief of 100% would still be available so long as the company's activities still qualified. If Charles does not wish to give all of the shares directly to his family, trusts could be used.

(iii)   Further gifts could be made in so far as no liability to capital gains tax is crystallised (eg cash gifts; chattels worth less than £6,000; possibly the land owned if it has a high base value); or on which gifts holdover relief would be available (eg shares in supplier company or gifts to a discretionary trust; although the latter would be chargeable transfers for inheritance tax, the gifts could be restricted so that they were covered by available reliefs and the nil threshold).

(iv)   Thereafter annual gifts could be made utilising the capital gains tax annual exemption, currently £10,100. For inheritance tax, such gifts would be reduced by the £3,000 annual exemption. Gifts could include quoted shares and/or the unquoted shares in the supplier company. The latter would attract 100% business property relief for inheritance tax.

(v)   Care must be taken not to allow the taxation advantages of a gift to outweigh the personal requirements of the taxpayer.

(vi)   Either in lifetime or on death Charles could make gifts to charity. These would reduce the estate without giving rise to a liability either to capital gains tax or inheritance tax, and he can make gift aid payments of any amount to charity and save higher rate tax on the gross equivalent, providing he makes an appropriate gift aid declaration. He can also obtain higher rate relief for gifts to charities of quoted stocks and shares, and also shares on the Alternative Investment Market (AIM), and this also applies to gifts of UK land and buildings. All such gifts are valued at their open market value plus any incidental costs of making them.

Explanatory Note

For further notes on liability to inheritance tax see **Examples 1 to 4**; business property relief see **Example 25**; deeds of variation see **Example 34**; and domicile see **Example 27**. Capital gains tax is dealt with in detail in the companion book **Tolley's Taxwise I 2010/11**.

Question

Mr Gregory is a 68-year old widower for whom you act as tax adviser. He came to see you on 31 May 2010 and told you that he had just been informed by his doctor that he had only a few months left to live. He intends that all his wealth should pass to his only son Neil (who will be his sole executor). He has heard that in some circumstances it might be advantageous either to transfer some of his assets immediately to Neil as a gift or alternatively to sell some of his assets and then to transfer the sale proceeds to Neil as a gift.

Mr Gregory is not currently in a position to make cash gifts as he has just drawn out the last of his savings from his bank account. He provides you with the following information concerning his assets:

(i) He owns 2,000 shares in Bingo plc, a quoted company, currently valued at £480. He had acquired the shares for £14,350 in December 1990.

(ii) He had acquired 20,000 £1 shares at par out of an issued share capital of 200,000 shares in Peck Limited, a retail company, in February 2007. His shares have been valued recently at £1.20 each. The investment qualified for income tax relief at 20% under the enterprise investment scheme.

(iii) He had acquired 10,000 £1 shares out of an issued share capital of 10,000,000 shares in Zingo plc, a quoted land dealing company, for £7 each in November 1993. The shares are currently worth £30 per share.

(iv) All tax liabilities have been agreed and paid on the due date up to 5 April 2010. Mr Gregory does not expect to have any income tax liabilities outstanding on his death, as his income should be just enough to cover his outgoings up to that time. It is estimated that the income tax computation up to the date of his death will show a repayment due of £1,250.

Other relevant information is as follows:

(v) He had taxable capital gains in the previous four years of assessment as follows:

	2006/07 £	2007/08 £	2008/09 £	2009/10 £
Net gains	13,000	12,200	–	12,825
Less: Annual exemption	(8,800)	(9,200)	–	(10,100)
Taxable gains	4,200	3,000	nil	2,725

(Mr Gregory is a higher rate taxpayer.)

(vi) In January 2009 he had made an outright gift of his principal private residence to his son Neil who now resides there. Mr Gregory went to live with his brother. The value of the residence at that time was £250,000 but it has since risen to £400,000. Neil has now suggested that Mr Gregory should come to live with him rent-free. Mr Gregory has refused to go to live with Neil partly on personal grounds, but also because he believes that if he does, problems might arise in connection with inheritance tax. The gift of his residence is the only gift which Mr Gregory has made so far.

(vii) His son Neil, who is due to get married shortly, has recently started up in business and has indicated that he will need to convert any assets which he receives from his father into cash by 31 December 2010 at the latest, in order to invest in the business.

(a) Indicate the optimum tax strategy for Mr Gregory regarding lifetime gifts.

(b) Assuming that Mr Gregory had in fact gone to live with Neil in his former private residence, state the inheritance tax consequences which would have arisen.

(c) Assuming that Mr Gregory adopts the strategy suggested under (a) above, calculate the inheritance tax liability arising on the basis that he died on 30 September 2010.

The rate of interest on repayments for the purpose of the Example is 4% (the actual current rate with effect from 29 September 2009 is 3%).

Answer

(a) Tax strategy re lifetime gifts

Disposals of assets in lifetime may attract capital gains tax on their growth in value. Furthermore, if the disposal is a gift, it may be reckonable for inheritance tax.

Mr Gregory is almost certain to die within seven years, and therefore even if a gift was initially a potentially exempt transfer for inheritance tax, it would become chargeable on his death. The taper relief for inheritance tax applicable after three years will almost certainly not be available.

By comparison, assets retained until death obtain a capital gains tax free uplift to probate value, thus avoiding a liability to capital gains tax. A gift in lifetime may therefore attract a liability to both capital gains tax and inheritance tax, whereas the same asset given on death would only be liable to inheritance tax.

Against that double charge, a gift in lifetime attracts any unused inheritance tax annual exemptions or marriage exemption and the value subsequently chargeable on death because the seven-year period has not been survived is the value at the date of the gift. Mr Gregory gave his house to his son in January 2009. The value at that date of £250,000 will be reduced by the annual exemptions for 2008/09 and 2007/08 and will be included in calculating the inheritance tax on Mr Gregory's death at £250,000 – £6,000 = £244,000, not at its current value of £400,000.

As Mr Gregory does not have long to live, the increase in value up to the date of death of any asset given away now is likely to be minimal, but the inheritance tax annual exemptions of 2009/10 and 2010/11 are available. In ordinary circumstances an exemption is available for gifts that are normal expenditure out of income. Although there is no fixed minimum period during which regular gifts have to have been made to constitute 'normal expenditure', it is necessary that a pattern of actual or intended payments has been established (*Bennett & Others v CIR* (1994)). Thus a 'death bed' resolution to make periodic payments for life does not create an exemption for such payments under the normal expenditure out of income provisions.

To create a liability to capital gains tax would not be advisable. If, however, the disposals realised net capital losses, any losses in the tax year of death may be carried back against the capital gains liabilities of the three preceding years, latest first, tax being repayable accordingly. The loss carryback relief is not wasted against gains already covered by the annual exemption. As Mr Gregory is likely to die before 5 April 2011, immediate crystallisation of losses would be useful. Care must be taken not to give loss-producing assets to connected persons such as Neil, as a loss on a disposal to such a person can only be utilised against future gains on disposals to the same person, which are very unlikely if death is imminent.

The recommended stategy would be to:

(i) Sell the shares in Bingo plc, realising a capital loss as follows:

	£
Cost of shares December 1990	14,350
Sale proceeds in say July 2010	480
Loss on Bingo plc shares	13,870

(ii) Relieve the loss on the Bingo plc shares against gains of the three years preceding death (assuming death in 2010/11):

	2009/10	2008/09	2007/08	
	£	£	£	£
Gains	12,825*	–	12,200*	
Loss re Bingo plc shares	(2,725)		(3,000)	(5,725)

	2009/10	2008/09	2007/08	
	£	£	£	£
	10,100		9,200	
Less: Annual exemption	(10,100)		(9,200)	
	–		–	
Available loss (as above)				13,870
Unused losses				8,145

*Before taper relief

The tax saving from carrying back the loss to 2009/10 is £2,725 @ 18% = £490. The due date of payment for the 2009/10 tax is 31 January 2011, so if Mr Gregory died before that date the capital gains tax originally due would not be paid. Otherwise it would be repaid. The repayment due as a result of carrying back the loss to 2007/08 is £3,000 @ 40% = £1,200.

As far as repayment supplement is concerned, although the *tax saving* is calculated by reference to the tax position of the earlier year, the claim relates to the later year, and repayment supplement is payable only if the repayment is made after 31 January following that later year. Where losses are carried back from the year of death, the deduction is made automatically without the need for a claim (TCGA 1992 s 62(2)). TMA 1970 Sch 1B.2(7) provides, however, that for supplement purposes the carryback is treated in the same way as if a claim was required. In this Example, supplement would only be payable if the tax was repaid after 31 January 2012. The tax will almost certainly have been repaid by that date, but if it has not been, repayment supplement will be payable from that date at 4% per annum (the actual current rate with effect from 29 September 2009 is 3%).

(iii)   Make a gift during 2010/11 to Neil of the appropriate number of shares in Zingo plc.

	£	£
The gain on each Zingo plc share would be:		
Market value		30.00
Less: Cost	7.00	
		7.00
Gain per share		23.00

The available capital loss in 2010/11 after carry back against 2009/10 and 2007/08 is £8,145 as indicated in (ii) above, which covers a gift of 354 shares (@ £23.00 gain per share). The available exemptions for inheritance tax are:

		£
Annual	2010/11	3,000
	2009/10	3,000
Marriage (on gift to Neil)		5,000
		11,000

This covers a gift of 366 shares (@ £30 each). Mr Gregory should therefore give Neil 366 shares in Zingo plc.

(Note that the sale or gift of shares in Peck Limited would give rise to a clawback of enterprise investment scheme relief at 20%, since they will not have been held for three years until February 2011.)

By gifting 366 shares instead of 354 (see above re maximum gift for CGT purposes) the loss to be set back is restricted by £276 (12 × £23.00). This however is better than paying inheritance tax on £360 (12 shares @ £30).

If larger gains than £8,145 were made, the losses available to carry back would be reduced to below £5,725 and the capital gains tax repayment for earlier years would be reduced accordingly. As a result Mr

Gregory's annual capital gains tax exemption cannot be used in 2010/11, because to use the annual exemption, gains would need to exceed the losses of £13,870, and no losses would be left to carry back. The executors are unlikely to make losses when they convert assets to cash for Neil because they take the assets at probate value, and even if they did, those losses are not available to carry back against Mr Gregory's gains.

(b) Inheritance tax consequences of Mr Gregory going to live with Neil

It is reasonable to assume that Mr Gregory's illness is such that he is unable to maintain himself. Provided such an eventuality was not foreseeable in January 2009 (at the time of the original gift of the property), then Mr Gregory could return to his former residence without breaching the gifts with reservation rules or the use of pre-owned asset provisions.

FA 1986 Sch 20 para 6(1)(b) provides such an exemption in relation to gifts of an interest in land when the donor's circumstances change in a way that was unforeseen at the time of the original gift and the benefit provided by the donee to the donor represents reasonable provision for the care and maintenance of an elderly or infirm relative. This provision also applies to prevent a pre-owned asset charge (FA 2004 Sch 15 para 11(5)(d)).

Without such exemption Mr Gregory's return to his former residence would nullify the original gift and would return the value of the house to his estate. In addition the original gift, which was a potentially exempt transfer, would still be included in the lifetime chargeable gifts if death occurred within seven years after the original gift. However, relief is given to prevent double charging (FA 1986 s 104 and SI 1987/1130).

(c) Inheritance tax as a result of Mr Gregory's death on 30 September 2010

		£	Gross £	Tax (2010/11 scale) £
Gifts in lifetime:				
January 2009				
Gift to Neil — house		250,000		
Less: Annual exemptions 2008/09	3,000			
2007/08	3,000	6,000		
Potentially exempt transfer now chargeable			244,000	–
July 2010				
Gift to Neil				
366 shares in Zingo plc @ £30 per share		10,980		
Less: Marriage exemption	5,000			
Annual exemptions 2010/11	2,980			
2009/10	3,000	10,980	–	–
			244,000	–
Mr Gregory's estate at death —				
30 September 2010				
Proceeds of sale of Bingo plc shares		480		
Income tax repayment		1,250		
Capital gains tax repayment**	490			
Shares in Zingo plc				
10,000 – 366 = 9,634 @ £30		289,020		
Shares in Peck Limited				

20,000 @ £1.20	24,000			
Less: Business property relief 100%	24,000	–	291,240	84,096*
			535,240	84,096*

Inheritance tax liability on death
of Mr Gregory —   £84,336

(* 535,240 – 325,000 = £210,240 @ 40%)

** Assuming that the 2009/10 tax of £490 was discharged, the repayment will consist of 2007/08 gains of £3,000 less loss used in 2010/11 of £276 = £2,725 @ 18% = £490

Supplementary note

The general principles of inheritance tax are dealt with in earlier Examples. In particular normal expenditure out of income is dealt with in **Example 1**, gifts with reservation in **Example 19** and pre-owned assets in **Example 23**. The capital gains tax provisions are outlined in **Example 36**. Capital gains tax is dealt with in detail in the companion to this book, **Tolley's Taxwise I 2010/11**.

Question

Thomas and Maria have been married for many years. Their daughter, Julia, was born in February 1968 and their son, Edmund, in October 1969. Thomas started in business on his own account in 1965 as a manufacturer of domestic hardware. Their relevant financial history is as follows:

March 1965	—	The family home is bought by Maria for £6,000.
May 1979	—	Thomas buys 100,000 ordinary shares in Huntingdon Ltd, a trading company that has since become listed on the Stock Exchange. The value at 31 March 1982 was 25p per share.
September 1988	—	Thomas buys 25,000 ordinary shares in Portsmouth plc for £45,000.
31 March 1989	—	Thomas transfers all his business assets (except plant of £30,000 which he retains personally) to a new company, Thomas Ltd, in consideration for ordinary shares valued at £300,000 (Maria holding one share as nominee). Business assets immediately before the transfers were:

	£
Goodwill	110,000
Plant, at cost less depreciation	55,000
Vehicles, at cost less depreciation	30,000
Stock, at cost or lower market value	65,000
Debtors	90,000
Cash	40,000
Creditors	(60,000)
	330,000

Thomas Ltd continues the trade without a break.

November 2003	—	Maria gives the family home (then valued at £80,000) in equal shares to Julia and her husband Henry. Maria and Thomas then move to their second home (which cost £62,000 in 1988, at which time an election had been made for capital gains tax that the original home remained the principal private residence).
June 2006	—	Maria places £32,500 cash into trust for Edmund for life, with remainder to Julia or her children (Julia has a son and a daughter). The trustees invest the money in a building society account which pays interest monthly.

Thomas gives 70% of the shares in Thomas Ltd to Edmund.

Company assets, at historical cost, are:

	£
Goodwill on acquisition from Thomas	110,000
Freehold factory bought July 1989	225,000
Shares in 100% subsidiary, allotted May 1992	100,000
Other non-chargeable assets	368,000
	803,000

In June 2006 goodwill is valued at £400,000. The factory is used for the trade (which is to continue) and is worth £600,000. The subsidiary's only assets are a portfolio of investment properties worth £230,000. (Ignore deferred tax.)

October 2006	—	Thomas places his holding of shares in Huntingdon plc (then valued at £130,000) into a discretionary trust. The beneficiaries are Julia, Edmund and all their descendants. Thomas's holding was less than 5% and he did not work for the company. The trustees decide to accumulate all the income arising. The gain arising on the transfer was £60,402 after available reliefs.
May 2010	—	Edmund dies intestate. He is unmarried and without children. In addition to his shares in Thomas Ltd (which have not changed in value since June 2006) he leaves a house worth £165,000 and other investments of £70,000. Under the rules of intestacy his estate will pass to Thomas and Maria.

No person elects to rebase all their chargeable assets to 31 March 1982 values.

Shares in Thomas Ltd at June 2006 are to be valued:

(i)   as to a 100% holding, on an assets basis;

(ii)   as to a 70% holding, on an assets basis discounted by 20%;

(iii)   as to a 30% holding, £225,000 for the holding.

Any inheritance tax on lifetime transfers is paid by the donor.

(a)   Work out the gain on the gift by Thomas of 70% of his shares in Thomas Ltd taking into account any available CGT reliefs.

(b)   Identify and quantify all chargeable and potentially exempt transfers, advising how much inheritance tax is payable on chargeable transfers, when it is payable, and any other factors that may be relevant.

(c)   Advise the beneficiaries under Edmund's intestacy of the main planning points that arise on his death.

Answer

(a) Capital gains tax liabilities 6 April 2003 onwards

			£
November 2003	—	Gift of family home by Maria — covered by principal private residence exemption — no chargeable gain.	
June 2006	—	Cash into trust by Maria — no chargeable disposal.	
		Gift by Thomas to Edmund of 70% of shares in Thomas Ltd:	
		Valuation of Thomas Ltd — assets basis	
		Factory	600,000
		Subsidiary	230,000
		Non-chargeable assets	368,000
		Goodwill	400,000
			1,598,000
		Valuation of gift: 70% × (1,598,000 × 80%)	894,880
		Cost — March 1989 (70% × 300,000)	210,000
		Gain	684,580

Holdover relief will be available, for any gain relating to the chargeable business assets – restricted to the fraction:

$$\frac{\text{Chargeable business assets}}{\text{Total chargeable assets}} \text{ ie } \frac{600,000 + 400,000}{600,000 + 400,000 + 230,000}$$

Available for relief:

$$\frac{1,000,000}{1,230,000} \times 684,580$$

	£
Heldover gain	556,569
Gain chargeable on Thomas for 2006/07 (684,580 – 556,569)	£128,011

October 2006	—	Gift by Thomas of shares in Huntingdon plc to discretionary trust
		The gain of £60,402 can be held over under TCGA 1992 s 260, as disposition is immediately liable to inheritance tax.
		Note The base cost of shares in Huntingdon plc to the trustees is 130,000 – 60,402 = £69,598.
May 2010	—	No liability to capital gains tax on death of Edmund.

(b) Inheritance tax

Inheritance tax position of Maria

November 2003				£	£
—	Gift of house				80,000
	Less:	Annual exemptions	2003/04	3,000	
			2002/03	3,000	6,000
	Potentially exempt transfer				74,000

The transfer will only become chargeable if Maria dies before November 2010, but no tax will be payable in any event, since the transfer is below the nil threshold (although the nil threshold available against Maria's estate at death would be correspondingly reduced).

June 2006				£	£
—	Gift of cash into interest in possession trust				32,500
	Less:	Annual exemptions	2006/07	3,000	
			2005/06	3,000	6,000
	Potentially exempt transfer				26,500

Again the transfer will only become chargeable on the death of Maria, this time before June 2013, but again the cumulative transfers are in any event covered by the nil threshold.

Inheritance tax position of Thomas

June 2006			£
—	Gift of 70% of shares in Thomas Ltd to Edmund.		
	Valuation of gift:		
	Holding before gift — 100% of 1,598,000		1,598,000
	Holding after gift — 30% minority		225,000
	Loss to estate		1,373,000
	Less: business property relief		
	100% × 1,373,000	1,368,000*	
		1,598,000	1,175,384
			197,616

(* The investment holding subsidiary is an excepted asset for business property relief)

Less:	Annual exemptions	2006/07	3,000	
		2005/06	3,000	6,000
Potentially exempt transfer				191,616

Note   The shares that were returned to Thomas following the death of Edmund would also form part of Thomas's estate. However should he die within seven years, ie before June 2013, relief will be given to prevent double charging. No liability will arise on the potentially exempt transfer itself, since it is below the nil threshold.

October 2006		
—	Gift of shares in Huntingdon plc to discretionary trust	
	Value of gift	£130,000

No inheritance tax is payable at the time of the gift as the cumulative total of gifts immediately liable to inheritance tax is below the 2006/07 threshold of £285,000. If Thomas should die before June 2013, the gift would be aggregated with the June 2006 potentially exempt transfer that then became chargeable and inheritance tax would be payable to the extent that the aggregate amount exceeded the nil threshold at the time of death. If he should die after June 2013 but before October 2013 no tax would be payable on the gift to the discretionary trust, but it would be aggregated with later gifts and the death estate, thus increasing the inheritance tax payable.

Inheritance tax position re death of Edmund in May 2010

	£	£
Value of free estate:		
Shares in Thomas Ltd (70% holding) (1,598,000 × 70%, less 20%)	894,880	
Less: Business property relief (100% available as second transfer was on death even though not owned for two years)		
$100\% \times 894{,}880 \times \dfrac{1{,}368{,}000^{*}}{1{,}598{,}000}$	766,080	128,800

(* The investment holding subsidiary is an excepted asset)

	£
House	165,000
Other investments	70,000
	363,800
Settled property — trust of Maria	32,500
	396,300

Inheritance tax payable (396,300 − 325,000) @ 40% = £28,520

		£
Payable by:		
Personal representatives:	$\dfrac{363{,}800}{396{,}300} \times 28{,}520 =$	26,181
Trustees:	$\dfrac{32{,}500}{396{,}300} \times 28{,}520 =$	2,339
		28,520

Of the total liability, the tax relating to the Thomas Ltd shares can be paid by instalments without interest to the due date and that relating to the house by instalments with interest from 1 December 2010; therefore the amount actually due from the personal representatives on application for probate will be:

Shares

$$\frac{128{,}800}{363{,}800} \times 26{,}181 \times \frac{1}{10} = 927 \quad \text{(with interest on balance only if paid late)}$$

$$\text{House } \frac{165,000}{363,800} \times 26,181 \times \frac{1}{10} \quad = \quad 1,187 \qquad \text{(with interest on balance from 1 December 2010)}$$

$$\text{Other investments } \frac{70,000}{363,800} \times 26,181 \quad = \quad 5,038$$

$$\underline{\underline{£7,152}}$$

(c) Advice to Thomas and Maria as beneficiaries of the estate of Edmund

The value in Edmund's estate is reverting to yourselves. As the oldest generation, you are likely to die before other members of the family. It may be preferable for Edmund's estate to go to your daughter Julia or to your grandchildren. If this course of action is decided on then it could be achieved by use of a deed of variation. Such a deed would not save inheritance tax on Edmund's death but might significantly reduce the potential liability on your own deaths. The deed must be executed within two years of Edmund's death.

It should be noted that if an instalment option asset (ie either the Thomas Ltd shares or Edmund's house) is sold, the outstanding instalments of inheritance tax become payable immediately.

The funding of the inheritance tax could be achieved by Thomas Ltd purchasing its own shares from the estate. This would qualify for special treatment and HMRC clearance should be obtained for the purchase not to be treated as a distribution by Thomas Ltd.

If no deed of variation occurs then should either of you die within five years after Edmund's death (ie before May 2015) quick succession relief would be available in your estates in respect of the assets inherited from him. In the same way, should the devolution of Edmund's estate be varied in favour of Julia and she were to die or make a chargeable transfer of her interest in the settled property devolving on her following Edmund's death, before May 2015, quick succession relief would be available by reference to the tax payable on Edmund's death.

Explanatory Notes

Valuation of assets for capital gains tax and inheritance tax

(1)   This Example shows the way in which both capital gains tax and inheritance tax may be relevant when gifts are made, and the different rules that apply when dealing with each tax. Note particularly that in valuing a shareholding, the open market value of the holding is taken for capital gains tax (TCGA 1992 s 272), hence the gift of 70% of Thomas's 100% holding in Thomas Ltd to Edmund in June 2006 is discounted by the 20% reduction for a 70% holding, whereas for inheritance tax the 'loss to the donor' principle applies, the shares therefore being taken into account for inheritance tax as a 100% holding, reduced to a minority holding. (See Revenue's Tax Bulletin August 1996 concerning when two or more separate assets may be treated as a single unit of property for valuation purposes.) The value of the gift is therefore different for capital gains tax and inheritance tax, ie:

Capital gains tax   £894,880
Inheritance tax   £1,373,000

When considering the capital gains tax acquisition value for those who inherit a deceased's assets, on the other hand, TCGA 1992 s 274 provides that where the value of an asset has been *ascertained* (whether in any proceedings or otherwise) for the purposes of inheritance tax, that value is taken to be the market value of the asset at the date of death for capital gains tax (overriding the normal 'open market value' provisions in TCGA 1992 s 62). This enables the higher 'loss to the donor' amount to be used in those circumstances, including any value attributable to related property.

Where, however, no tax is due because of reliefs or exemptions, the value of assets will not be *ascertained* for inheritance tax, so their capital gains acquisition value would be the open market value. This would apply, for Example, where 100% business property relief is available on family company shares, or where a transfer of such shares is covered by the nil threshold. It has been suggested that where this would give lower acquisition values, the problem could be overcome by having a minimal amount of 'excepted assets', not qualifying for business property relief, within the company (see **note 2**), so that a valuation would then be necessary. The Revenue have, however, stated that if very little or no tax was at stake, it was unlikely that an ascertained value would be negotiated by Shares Valuation Division (Tax Bulletin April 1995).

In the case of *Stonor & Mills (Dickinson's Executors) v CIR* (2001) (SpC 288), no inheritance tax was payable on the estate because of the nil-rate band and the charities exemption. The executors sold freehold properties from the estate for significantly more than the probate value, resulting in large capital gains. They tried to get the Revenue to accept the sale values as amended probate values, but the Revenue refused on the grounds that an investigation into values was not necessary since charity relief had been claimed. The executors then made a claim under s 191 (land sold within three years after death – see **Example 10 part b**) to substitute the sale proceeds for the probate value, thus increasing the capital gains tax base cost and eliminating the gains. It was held that since no one was liable to pay any tax on the estate no one was entitled to make a s 191 claim.

(2) Capital gains tax holdover relief on gifts under TCGA 1992 s 165 is also available only on business assets and not on assets held as investments (other than farming land owned by an agricultural landlord, which can qualify for s 165 relief). Gifts relief under TCGA 1992 s 260 is available on any asset, providing the gift is immediately liable to inheritance tax, hence the relief on the October 2006 gift by Thomas to the discretionary trust.

Transfer of business to company

(3) Thomas will not have been able to hold over the chargeable gains on the transfer of his personal business to Thomas Ltd in 1989, since not all of the assets were transferred in consideration for shares. Hence the value of the shares received, £300,000, is not reduced by holdover relief.

Cross references

(4) See **Example 4 explanatory note 7** for the position when both capital gains tax and inheritance tax are payable on the same transfer. For detailed notes on business property relief see **Example 25**, on quick succession relief see **Example 21**, on the instalment option see **Example 5** and on deeds of variation in relation to a deceased's estate see **Example 34**. Note in this Example that a variation would not result in additional tax payable on Edmund's estate, since there are no exempt beneficiaries. Had additional tax been payable, the amount would have had to be notified to HMRC Capital Taxes and a copy of the variation sent, within six months after the deed was effected. Capital gains tax is dealt with comprehensively in the companion to this book **Tolley's Taxwise I 2010/11**.

Question

Y died on 5 April 2009 leaving small bequests to each of three friends and the residue to his son X, for life.

The administration of the estate was completed by the personal representatives on 5 April 2011.

Details of the estate income (which is wholly interest) are as follows:

	Expenses borne £	*Leaving residuary income* Net £	Gross equivalent £	Payments to X £	*made on*
2009/10	1,130	1,760	2,200	1,600	3 March 2010
2010/11	1,150	2,880	3,600	3,040	20 June 2011

(a)   Indicate the tax liability of the personal representatives in relation to the estate income and state what their responsibilities for reporting the income are under self-assessment.

(b)   Calculate for 2009/10 and 2010/11 the amounts of estate income to be included in X's taxable income.

(c)   State whether the estate income that would have been included in X's taxable income would have been different had he been absolutely entitled to the residue (as compared with his limited (life) interest).

Answer

(a) Personal representatives — income tax liability and self-assessment

Tax rates (FA 2008 s 4, s 5 and Sch 1)

Personal representatives are liable to tax either at the basic rate of 20% or the dividend rate of 10% on any chargeable income. Changes to the Trust and Estate return (SA900) rules

Different filing dates for paper and online returns

Paper returns will now have to be filed by 31 October. Consequently for the 2009/10 return it means filing the form by 31 October 2010. An automatic penalty will be charged if a paper return is received after this date.

Online returns must be filed by 31 January. If it is intended to file a return after 31 October it will need to be filed online. So the deadline for filing the 2009/10 return online is 31 January 2011. Once again, an automatic penalty will be charged if it is received after this date.

The filing obligation is satisfied by the first return received by HMRC and this also triggers any late filing penalty. So if, for Example, a paper 2009/10 return is filed after 31 October 2010, it is not then possible to avoid a late filing penalty by filing the return online.

Online filing has the obvious advantage of an immediate acknowledgement of receipt. However, as far as the Trust & Estate return is concerned, it does not provide an automatic tax calculation. HMRC still has to process online Trust & Estate returns in the same way as paper returns.

It is necessary to register first to use the online facility at online.hmrc.gov.uk. However, HMRC does not provide an online version of the Trust & Estate Tax Return series (SA900+) and so proprietary software will be necessary. It is possible to amend returns online.

For HMRC to calculate the liability – the return must be filed by 31 October, whether it is a paper or online return. This is later than the existing deadline.

If HMRC receive the return after 31 October they will apparently still calculate the liability, if asked but they cannot guarantee to do so before the 31 January payment date.

The deadlines for paying tax are unchanged.

Withdrawal of substitute returns

HMRC no longer accept or approve computer generated substitute versions of the Trust & Estate Tax Return series (SA900+). This means that either a paper return must be filed or the return filed online.

Change to the enquiry window

The closure of the enquiry window, the statutory period in which HMRC may open an enquiry into a return, will be linked to the date on which that return is delivered.

Where a return is filed on time, the enquiry window will close twelve months after the return is delivered. So where a return is received before the filing deadline, the enquiry window will close earlier than under the existing legislation.

(b) Estate income to be included in taxable income of life tenant, X

Where a person has a life interest in a will settlement, the amounts to be included in his statutory income during the period of administration are the grossed up equivalents of the net income payments actually made to him in the tax year (ITTOIA 2005 ss 649–662). The amount of the grossing addition depends on the rate of tax on the underlying income, – see (a) above.

Thus the amount to be included in the statutory income of X in 2009/10 is £1,600 × 100/80 = £2,000.

Upon the completion of the administration, any amounts due to the life tenant which remain unpaid are deemed to be paid as income of the tax year in which the administration is *completed* (ITTOIA 2005 ss 649–662).

Since the administration is completed in 2010/11, X will be deemed to have received the balance due to him in that tax year, ie £3,040 × 100/80 = £3,800.

(c) Effect on X's estate income if he had had an absolute interest in residue

Where a person has an absolute interest in the residue of an estate, the amounts to be included in his statutory income during the period of administration are the same as for a life tenant, ie the net income payments actually made to him, grossed up at the appropriate rate. However, the maximum amount that can be included is the 'aggregated income entitlement' to date, that is the total amount taxable in any year cannot exceed the aggregate amount of the residuary income to which the person is entitled, less amounts paid in previous tax years (ITTOIA 2005 s 668).

Upon the completion of the administration, any amounts not paid, up to the aggregated income entitlement, are deemed to be paid to the beneficiary immediately before completion.

The amounts taxable on X would therefore be the same as in (b) above, ie a gross amount of £2,000 in 2009/10 and a gross amount of £3,800 in 2010/11.

Explanatory Notes

Self-assessment position of personal representatives

(1)   If all the estate income is taxed income and there are no capital gains, then in most cases no amounts have to be entered on the return and only the information section needs to be completed (see **Example 41** re Mrs Daley).

The personal representatives supply beneficiaries with form R185 (estate income) showing income payments split according to whether the underlying income was taxed at the basic, lower or dividend ordinary rate of tax and whether the tax is repayable or non-repayable (see **explanatory note 7**).

Income of beneficiaries

(2)   All payments made to a beneficiary with a limited interest (usually a life interest) will be income. For a beneficiary with an absolute interest, payments must be treated as being liable to income tax in the hands of the beneficiary, up to the gross equivalent of the amount of income received by the estate. In the legislation references to amounts paid include assets transferred to beneficiaries, or debts set off or released, the amount for such items being their value at the relevant date (ITTOIA 2005 s 681).

Where assets have been transferred to absolute beneficiaries during the administration period, therefore, the gross equivalent of their value must be taken into account as a distribution of estate income even though the distribution was of capital, so particular care must be taken in calculating the amount to be shown on forms R185 (estate income). See **Example 40** for the capital gains implications of transferring assets to a beneficiary during the administration period.

Beneficiaries with an absolute interest

(3)   For someone with an absolute interest in the estate, if the amounts to be deducted from the income of the estate exceed the income in any year, the excess is carried forward and deducted from future income in computing the aggregated income entitlement (ITTOIA 2005 s 666(2), (6)).

(4)   If, when the administration is completed, it is found that the total residuary income of the estate is less than the amounts paid to someone with an absolute interest (for Example, because large bills are paid in the later

stages of the administration), then the amount included in the statutory income of the person concerned is reduced to the actual net income. This is done by reducing the income of the tax year in which the administration is completed, then, if necessary, the previous year, and so on (ITTOIA 2005 s 668).

Identification of income received by beneficiaries

(5)   The rate of tax for the different categories of income is known as the 'applicable rate' (ITTOIA 2005 ss 663, 670, 679).

'Just and reasonable' apportionments of income bearing tax at different rates are to be made between beneficiaries with interests in residue. After making any such apportionments, payments to beneficiaries are regarded as being out of brought forward and current income charged at the basic rate in priority to other income, and as being out of brought forward and current savings income charged at the 20% rate (which will include pre 6 April 1999 dividends) in priority to dividends charged at the ordinary rate of 10% (ITTOIA 2005 ss 670, 679).

Changes in the applicable rate

(6)   As indicated in the Example, amounts payable on completion of the administration are deemed to be income of the tax year in which the administration is completed, and they are therefore regarded as having been taxed at the applicable rate in force for that year, even if the rate of tax actually deducted from the income was different. This treatment applies only where the *applicable rate* changes. Where income was previously treated as being subject to a *different* applicable rate, any brought forward amounts are still regarded as having been taxed at the applicable rate that was relevant when they were received. For dividends received before 6 April 1999, the applicable rate was 20%, and that rate has remained unchanged. If any pre 6 April 1999 dividends were undistributed and were therefore brought forward to 1999/00 or a later year, they would be regarded as distributed (along with any other savings income) in priority to post 5 April 1999 dividends and the applicable rate would be 20%.

Forms R185

(7)   Personal representatives supply beneficiaries with an income certificate form R185 (estate income) showing the amounts paid as income and tax deducted (or treated as deducted), split between savings income (with tax at the lower or dividend ordinary rate) and other income (with tax at the basic rate). The beneficiaries include the information from the R185 in the trusts etc pages in their personal returns.

The tax on some of the income may be shown as non-repayable (ITTOIA 2005 s 680). Non-repayable tax at the 20% rate arises on life policy gains. From 6 April 1999 (ITTOIA 2005 s 680) provides that non-repayable tax also includes tax credits on dividends, and the applicable rate for all non-repayable tax except that on life policy gains is the dividend ordinary rate of 10%.

This also applies to beneficiaries with only a limited interest in residue.

Completion of administration

(8)   When the administration of the estate is complete, the personal representatives will have assigned the interest in the assets to the trustees of the life interest settlement, who take those assets for capital gains tax purposes at their value at the date of death. This will normally be the probate value, but where a probate value was not *ascertained* for inheritance tax (because no inheritance tax was payable) the capital gains 'open market value' rule applies (see **Example 38 explanatory note 1**). Once the interest in the assets has been assigned to the trustees, the trustees are responsible for making the relevant income tax self-assessment returns, using forms R185 (trust income) and paying any tax due. The beneficiary is then liable to tax on the amount shown on the R185. See the Examples in the book relating to trusts and **Example 43** in respect of the income tax position of a life interest will trust.

Enterprise investment scheme and venture capital trusts

(9)   Where someone has invested under the enterprise investment scheme or venture capital trust scheme, their death does not trigger the withdrawal of the income tax relief on the shares nor will it cause deferred gains

to become chargeable. The personal representatives would be liable to capital gains tax on sale of the shares, the acquisition cost being the market value at the date of death.

Question

John Bird died on 30 September 2010. By his will he left one half of his estate to his wife (aged 65) and one half to his son (aged 42). His executors, Mrs Bird and her son Rupert, obtained probate on 1 February 2011. There was no inheritance tax payable. The estate, which was valued at £500,000 (gross), included the following assets:

Asset	Probate value £
950 shares of £1 each in Bird Enterprises Ltd, a trading company (the other 50 shares being owned by Mrs Bird, who was a director working part-time and had subscribed for the shares at par in February 1990). Rupert was an employee in the company.	235,000
10,000 shares in Computer Games plc, a quoted company	17,500
3,600 shares in Midwest Bank plc held in an ISA following the flotation of the former building society	10,200

Mrs Bird and her son decided to sell Bird Enterprises Ltd because without its founder, Mr Bird, they were too dependent on the skills of individual employees. Although a number of outside offers were made, on 31 March 2011 they accepted a bid of £332,500 from the management for the whole of the company.

The Midwest Bank received a takeover offer of £2.50 per share from a High Street bank on 3 April 2011 which Mrs Bird and her son accepted.

On 10 February 2011 Micro plc made a cash offer of £3.30 per share or 4% Redeemable Loan Stock to the same value in any proportions for each share in Computer Games plc (the loan stock is within the definition of qualifying corporate bonds (QCB)).

The administration of the estate was completed late January 2011.

Neither Mrs Bird nor her son will have any further capital disposals in 2010/11

(a)   State the capital gains tax payable for 2010/11 if all of the above transactions are undertaken by Mrs Bird and her son as executors (and they accept cash for the Computer Games shares).

(b)   Set out alternative suggestions which would have mitigated the tax payable.

Answer

(a) Capital gains tax payable for 2010/11

Estate of John Bird deceased

	£	£	£
Bird Enterprises Ltd — sale proceeds 950 shares March 2011		332,500	
Probate value September 2010	235,000		
Costs of title 0.75%	1,763	236,763	95,737
Midwest Bank plc —			
Sale proceeds April 2011 3,600 shares @ £2.50		9,000	
Probate value	10,200		
Costs of title 0.75%	77	10,277	(1,277)
Computer Games plc —			
Sale proceeds February 2011 10,000 shares @ £3.30		33,000	
Probate value	17,500		
Costs of title 0.75%	132	17,632	15,368
			109,828
Annual exemption			(10,100)
Chargeable gains for the year			99,728
Capital gains tax payable by executors @ 28% (see **Example 36 a (iii)**)			£27,924

Mrs Bird

	£	£
Bird Enterprises Ltd —		
Sale proceeds 50 shares March 2011	17,500	
Cost	50	
	17,450	
Annual exemption		(10,100)
Qualifying chargeable gains for the year		7,350
Capital gains tax payable by Mrs Bird @ 10% on £7,350 (see **note 10** re: entrepreneurs' relief)		735
Total capital gains tax payable by executors and Mrs Bird		£28,659

(b) Ways of mitigating tax payable

The overall tax payable could be mitigated as follows:

Transferring shares in Bird Enterprises Ltd to beneficiaries before sale

If Mrs Bird and her son as executors had transferred the shares to themselves as individuals prior to the sale, the transfer would be deemed to occur at the date of death (TCGA 1992 s 62(4)). Their revised personal capital gains tax position for 2010/11 (subject to any losses arising to them as individuals) would be:

Mrs Bird

	£	£	£
Bird Enterprises Ltd —			
Sale proceeds 525 shares March 2011 (166,250 + 17,500)		183,750	
Cost of 50 shares in February 1990	50		
Probate value of 475 shares September 2010	117,500	117,550	
			66,200
Annual exemption			(10,100)
Qualifying chargeable gains for the year			56,100
Capital gains tax payable by Mrs Bird @ 10% on £56,100 (see **note 10** re entrepreneurs' relief)			£5,610

Rupert Bird

	£	£
Bird Enterprises Ltd —		
Sale proceeds 475 shares March 2011	166,250	
Probate value September 2010	117,500	48,750
Annual exemption		(10,100)
Qualifying chargeable gains for the year		38,650
Capital gains tax payable by Rupert @ 10% on £38,650(see **note 10** re entrepreneurs' relief)		£3,865

Such a transfer would, however, be taken to be a distribution of income, giving rise to taxable income in the hands of the beneficiaries to the extent that undistributed income had arisen in the estate, and would therefore trigger a charge to higher rate tax. Since the administration was completed within the same tax year as the transfer, however, this is irrelevant, since the income would already have been distributed.

Shares in Computer Games plc

The executors could transfer the whole of the shares to themselves as beneficiaries, enabling the beneficiaries to take loan stock, or they could take loan stock themselves as executors and pass it on to themselves as beneficiaries, thus deferring the capital gain. On 3 April 2011, however, they had incurred a loss on the disposal of the Midwest Bank plc shares. To use that loss and also their annual exemption, the executors could take the cash offer on 7,403 Computer Games plc shares and loan stock in respect of 3,183 shares, giving the estate a capital gains liability of:

	£	£
Sale proceeds 7,403 shares @ £3.30	24,430	
Proportion of probate value:		

	£	£
$\dfrac{7{,}403}{10{,}000} \times 17{,}632$	13,053	11,377
Loss on Midwest Bank plc shares as in (a) above		(1,277)
		10,100
Annual exemption		(10,100)
Chargeable gains		

See **explanatory note 4**.

This enables both the executor's annual exemption and the loss on the Midwest Bank shares to be fully utilised. (Losses incurred by executors can only be offset against a gain accruing to them as executors in the same or a future year and cannot be transferred to beneficiaries. A similar tax saving could have been achieved if the Midwest Bank shares had been transferred to the beneficiaries before the Bank was taken over, so that the loss would arise to Mrs Bird and Rupert. The Computer Games plc shares on which the cash offer was taken could then be reduced so as to realise gains of approximately £10,100 as before.)

Effect of above suggestions

As a result of the above, the capital gains tax payable for 2010/11 would be reduced from £28,659 to (5,610 + 3,865) £9,475, ie by £19,184. Mrs Bird and Rupert would, however, each have redeemable loan stock in Micro plc with accrued gains of:

	£
1,721 shares @ £3.30	5,679
Proportion of probate value $\dfrac{1{,}721}{10{,}000} \times 17{,}500^{*}$	(3,012)
Accrued gain	2,667

* See **explanatory note 4**.

Even so, if the loan stock was redeemed in a year in which the beneficiary had no other gains, the accrued gain would be covered by the annual exemption of the year of disposal.

Explanatory Notes

Treatment of personal representatives

(1)   On death the deceased's assets are acquired by the personal representatives at market value, but there is no deemed disposal by the deceased and no capital gains tax is payable as a result of the death.

(2)   The personal representatives — the executors in this Example — are treated as a separate single and continuing body of persons. All their dealings as personal representatives are completely separate from their dealings as individuals. Capital gains and losses are accordingly computed and assessed on them as personal representatives. Under self-assessment any tax due on capital gains is payable on 31 January following the end of the tax year. The rate of tax on personal representatives' gains is 28% for gains on and after 23 June 2010. (TCGA 1992 s 4). See **Example 36 a (iii)**.

(3)   The personal representatives are entitled to an annual exemption of the same amount as an individual for the tax year of death and the following two tax years. If the administration of the estate has not been completed in that time there is no annual exemption for later years and any gains arising are chargeable at the 28% rate for gains on and after 23 June 2010..

Probate valuation costs

(4)   When computing the gain or loss on sales of assets by the personal representatives, the cost of acquiring the assets can be increased by the costs incurred in valuing them for probate (*CIR v Richards' Executors* 1971).

SP2/04 sets out the scale of expenses allowable under TCGA 1992 s 38(1)(b) for the costs of establishing title in computing the gains or losses of personal representatives on the sale of assets comprised in a deceased person's estate.

Gross value of estate		*Allowable expenditure*
A	Not exceeding £50,000	1.8% of the probate value of the assets sold by the personal representatives.
B	Over £50,000 but not exceeding £90,000	A fixed amount of £900, to be divided between all of the assets of the estate in proportion to the probate values and allowed in those proportions on assets sold by the personal representatives.
C	Over £90,000 but not exceeding £400,000	1% of the probate value of the assets sold.
D	Over £400,000 but not exceeding £500,000	A fixed amount of £4,000, to be divided as at B above.
E	Over £500,000 but not exceeding £1,000,000	0.8% of the probate value of the assets sold.
F	Over £1,000,000 but not exceeding £5,000,000	A fixed amount of £8,000, to be divided as at B above.
G	Over £5,000,000	0.16% of the probate value of the assets sold, subject to a maximum of £10,000.

The scale has effect where the death in question occurred on or after 6 April 2004.

A deduction for probate valuation costs only applies where the sale is by the personal representatives and not where the sale is by the beneficiaries themselves. It should be noted that the actual costs, if any, of the *beneficiary* relating to the acquisition of the asset are deductible (TCGA 1992 s 64(1)(a)), and also any costs of the personal representatives *in transferring* assets to them (s 64(1)(b)). As Mrs Bird and Rupert have undertaken the transactions themselves it is unlikely there are any such costs.

HMRC have agreed the following scale of allowable expenditure under TCGA 1992 ss 38 and 64(1) for expenses incurred after 6 April 2004 by corporate trustees in the administration of estates and trusts. The Commissioners for Revenue and Customs will accept computations based either on this scale or on the actual allowable expenditure incurred.

The scale is as follows:

Transfers of assets to beneficiaries etc

(i)   *Publicly-marketed shares and securities*

(A)   One beneficiary – £25 per holding transferred.

(B)   Two or more beneficiaries between whom a holding must be divided – as (A) above to be divided in equal shares between the beneficiaries.

(ii)   Other shares and securities – as (i) above with the addition of any exceptional expenditure.

(iii)   Other assets – as (i) above with the addition of any exceptional expenditure.

For the purpose of this statement of practice, shares and securities are regarded as marketed to the general public if buying and selling prices for them are regularly published in the financial pages of a national or regional newspaper, magazine, or other journal.

Actual disposals and acquisitions

(i)   Publicly-marketed shares and securities – the investment fee as charged by the trustees.

(ii)   Other shares and securities – as (i) above, plus actual valuation costs.

(iii)   Other assets – the investment fee as charged by the trustees, subject to a maximum of £75, plus actual valuation costs.

Where a comprehensive annual management fee is charged, covering both the cost of administering the trust and the expenses of actual disposals and acquisitions, the investment fee for the purposes of (i), (ii) and (iii) above will be taken to be £0.25 per £100 on the sale or purchase moneys.

Deemed disposals by trustees

(i)   Publicly-marketed shares and securities – £8 per holding disposed of.

(ii)   Other shares and securities – actual valuation costs.

(iii)   Other assets – actual valuation costs.

Valuation for capital gains tax where no inheritance tax payable

(5)   Where no inheritance tax is payable on death, the values included in the application for probate will not be binding on HMRC for capital gains tax unless specifically agreed with them (see **Example 38 explanatory note 1**). The personal representatives may therefore wish to file form CG34 after the sale of shares in Bird Enterprises Ltd to agree the acquisition cost and gain prior to the submission of the self-assessment return.

Shares held in a PEP

(6)   Although the shares in Midwest Bank plc were held in a single company PEP and were not therefore liable to capital gains tax, that treatment ceases on death. The shares are held by personal representatives as a normal chargeable asset. Therefore the loss between death and disposal is available for relief (a gain would have similarly been a chargeable gain).

Considerations to be taken into account on deciding appropriate course of action

(7)   The executors must carefully consider the taxation implications of selling assets themselves or transferring them to the beneficiaries. These include:

Sale by executors

Capital gains tax rate is 28% for gains on or after 23 June 2010 (TCGA 1992 s 4(3) as substituted by F(No 2)A10 Sch 1 para 2) – 18% for gains before that date.

Annual exemption is available in year of death and two following years only

Base costs of assets include costs of the estate (SP 2/04)

Losses are only available against gains of the estate

Sale by beneficiaries

Capital gains tax rate is 18% (for basic rate taxpayers) or 28% (for higher rate taxpayers) for gains arising after 23 June 2010. For gains before this date the rate was 18%. The appropriate rate will be 10% if entrepreneurs' relief applies.

Each beneficiary has own annual exemption

Acquisition value is probate value (subject to what is said in **Example 38 explanatory note 1**)

Acquisition date is date of death

Personal losses may be offset against gains on assets acquired; losses on assets acquired may be offset against personal gains

The distribution of a capital asset triggers an income tax charge in the hands of the beneficiary to the value of any undistributed income arising in the estate (see **Example 39 explanatory note 2**).

Furthermore, the tax may be borne by different beneficiaries. In this Example the cash to be distributed following a sale by the executors in respect of the three shareholdings held in the estate would be:

		£
Sale proceeds:	Bird Enterprises Ltd	332,500
	Computer Games plc	33,000
	Midwest Bank plc	9,000
		374,500
Less: Capital gains tax		28,659
Divided equally		345,841

Thus Mrs Bird has suffered capital gains tax of half of £28,659 = £14,329. Rupert's share of the tax is £14,330.

If the proposals in (b) had taken place the tax would have been:

	Mrs Bird £	Rupert £
Re Bird Enterprises Ltd	5,610	3,865
Re estate	–	–
	5,610	3,865
Tax saved	8,719	10,465

Thus Rupert would have had a larger saving compared with Mrs Bird.

Because Rupert has not used his annual exemption for 2010/11 it would be better for the beneficiaries to make the disposals than the executors.

Private residence exemption

(8) Where following a death, the private residence is to be sold by the personal representatives, a chargeable gain may arise between death and sale. Under TCGA 1992 s 225A, the private residence exemption is available if the property has both before and after the death been used as the main residence of individuals who are entitled to 75% or more of the sale proceeds either absolutely or for life.

Gifts holdover relief

(9) Personal representatives do not qualify for gifts holdover relief under TCGA 1992 s 165 or s 260, but trustees do. Where the residue of the estate is left on trust, the personal representatives should ensure that assets on which gifts holdover relief is to be claimed have been formally appropriated to the trustees before being gifted. The trustees are then treated as acquiring the assets at the date of death.

The Finance Act 2006 changes to IHT for trust also impinge on the CGT holdover provisions in so far that:

• transfers into and out of trusts that now come within the 'relevant property' rules will automatically be eligible for hold-over relief under TCGA 1992 s 260(2)(a);

- hold-over relief under TCGA 1992 s 260(2)(d) is restricted to trusts that meet the IHT rules for trusts for minor children;

- the special rules in TCGA 1992 ss 72, 73 relating to the death of a person entitled to an IIP are restricted to assets that are subject to an IIP which meets the revised IHT rules.

Entrepreneurs' relief (FA 2008 Sch 3, F (No 1) A 2010 s 4 and F (No 2) A 2010 Sch 1 ss 4 & 5 amends TCGA 1992 s 169)

(10) **Individuals**

Under FA 2008 s 9 and Sch 3 entrepreneurs' relief applies to individuals and trustees who dispose of the whole or part of a trading business, or of shares in a trading company in which they have a qualifying interest.

Entrepreneurs' relief may be available in respect of gains made by individuals on the disposal of:

- all or part of a trading business the individual carries on alone or in partnership;

- assets of the individual's or partnership's trading business following the cessation of the business;

- shares in (and securities of) the individual's 'personal' trading company (or holding company of a trading group);

- assets owned by the individual and used by his/her 'personal' trading company (or group) or trading partnership.

An individual is able to make claims for relief on qualifying disposals made on or after 6 April 2008. Claims may be made on more than one occasion up to a 'lifetime' limit of £2 million (and £5 million after 23 June 2010). Disposals on or before 5 April 2008 do not affect the lifetime limit. The limit will only begin to diminish when the relief is claimed.

Transitional provisions also allow relief to be claimed in certain circumstances where gains that have been deferred from disposals made on or before 5 April 2008 become chargeable after that date.

From 06 April 2010 until 22 June 2010, the first £2 million (FA 2010 no 1 s 4) (£1 million before 5 April 2010) of gains qualify for the relief which effectively taxes qualifying gains at 10%. Gains in excess of £2 million are charged to CGT at an effective rate of 18% for gains incurred before 22 June 2010 (see below for the rules after that date.)

For gains incurred up to 22 June 2010 the relief works as follows:

(1)   Schedule 3 introduced section 169N into TCGA 1992. Where a claim is made in respect of a qualifying business disposal the relevant gains (see s 5) are to be aggregated, with any relevant losses (see s 6) being deducted.

(2)   The resulting amount is reduced by 4/9ths.

(3)   But if the total of current gains less losses and the amounts resulting in relation to earlier relevant qualifying business disposals (if any), exceeds £2 million (£1 million before 5 April 2010), the reduction is to be made in respect of only so much (if any) of the amount resulting as (when added to that total) does not exceed £2 million (£1 million before 5 April 2010).

The amount arrived at is to be treated as a chargeable gain accruing at the time of the disposal to the individual or trustees by whom the claim is made.

The changes to CGT rates from 23 June 2010 mean the 4/9 reduction no longer achieved an effective rate of 10%. Finance (No 2) Act 2010 Sch 1 s 5 includes provision to charge gains on disposals that qualify for entrepreneurs' relief on or after 23 June 2010 at a 10% rate. The previous 4/9 reduction will cease to apply from that date.

From 06 April 2010 until 22 June 2010, the amount of an individual's gains that can qualify for entrepreneurs' relief is subject to a lifetime limit of £2 million (£1 million for disposals before 6 April 2010).

For trustees, the £2 million limit is that of the beneficiary of the settlement who meets the conditions for the trustees to claim the relief.

F (No 2) A 2010 Sch 1 ss 4 & 5 amends TCGA 1992 s 169H & N setting out the provision to increase that limit to £5 million from 23 June 2010.

Where individuals or trustees make qualifying gains above the previous £2 million limit before 23 June 2010 (£1 million limit before 6 April 2010), no additional relief will be allowed for the excess above the old limit. But if they make further qualifying gains on or after 23 June 2010, they will be able to claim relief on up to a further £3 million of those additional gains (or up to £4 million where the earlier £1 million limit applied), giving relief on accumulated qualifying gains up to the new limit of £5 million.

In determining at what rate(s) an individual should be charged to CGT on any other gains, those gains qualifying for entrepreneurs' relief are set against any unused basic rate band before non-qualifying gains.

To summarise:

For gains arising before 23 June 2010 (FA 2008 Sch 3, F (No 1) A 2010 s 4)

The first £2 million of gains (limit was £1 million for 2009/10) will qualify for the relief which effectively taxes qualifying gains at 10%. Gains in excess of £2 million will be charged to CGT at the normal rate of 18%.

The relief works as follows:

(a)   Where a claim is made in respect of a qualifying business disposal the relevant business gains are to be added together, with any relevant business capital losses being deducted.

(b)   The resulting amount is to be reduced by 4/9ths.

(c)   But if the total of current gains less losses and the amounts means that the tally of business capital gains exceeds £2 million (£1 million before 6 April 2010), the reduction is to be made in respect of only so much (if any) of the amount resulting as (when added to that total) does not exceed £2 million (£1 million before 6 April 2010).

(d)   The resulting gain is then taxed at 18%. This gives an effective tax rate of 10% once the gain is reduced by 4/9 (18% × 5/9 = 10%)

For gains arising after 23 June 2010 (F (No 2) A 2010 Sch 1 ss 4 & 5 amends TCGA 1992 s 169H & N)

The amount of gains that can qualify for entrepreneurs' relief is subject to a lifetime limit of £2 million (£1 million for disposals before 6 April 2010). This is taxable at 10%.

This limit is to increase to £5 million from 23 June 2010.

For gains above the previous £2 million limit arising before 23 June 2010 (£1 million limit before 6 April 2010), no additional relief will be allowed for the excess above the old limit.

If there are further qualifying gains on or after 23 June 2010, relief can be claimed up to a further £3 million of those additional gains (or up to £4 million where the earlier £1 million limit applied), giving relief on accumulated qualifying gains up to the new limit of £5 million.

In working out what rate of CGT applies on any other gains, those gains qualifying for entrepreneurs' relief are set against any unused basic rate band before non-qualifying gains.

Trustees

Trustees can claim relief on certain disposals of business assets and company shares and securities where a 'qualifying beneficiary' has a qualifying interest in the business in question. Trustees must make claims jointly with the 'qualifying beneficiary'. Any relief given on the trustees' gains will reduce a beneficiary's lifetime limit on relief. TCGA 1992 s 169O.

If, on the same day, there is both a disposal of trust business assets in respect of which an individual is the qualifying beneficiary and a qualifying business disposal by the individual, TCGA 1992 s 169N(8) applies as if the disposal of trust business assets were later.

Example – the effect of the change of the lifetime limits on multiple gains

Matthew has previously used £1 million of his lifetime entrepreneurs' relief limit. In 2010/11 his taxable income, after all allowable deductions and the personal allowance, is £27,400. The upper limit of the income tax basic rate band is £37,400.

In May 2010, Matthew realises a chargeable gain of £2.5 million on the disposal of a business. In March 2011 Matthew sells another business, realising further chargeable gains of £5 million. Both disposals qualify for entrepreneurs' relief (subject to the lifetime limits). Matthew has no allowable losses to set against these gains, and the annual exemption for 2010/11 is £10,100. He has no other gains for 2010/11.

The £2.5 million gain realised in May 2010 is subject to the £2 million lifetime limit for entrepreneurs' relief (for qualifying disposals from 6 April 2010), of which Matthew has previously used £1 million. The gain is reduced by 4/9ths of £1 million and the remainder charged to CGT at the single rate of 18%.

The increase in the lifetime limit from 23 June 2010 means that £3 million of the £5 million gain from March 2011 is chargeable at the 10% rate of CGT. Matthew's taxable income is £10,000 below the basic rate band (£37,400 – £27,400).

But the £3 million of the gain charged at 10% is taken into account in priority to other gains in determining whether total income and gains exceed the basic rate band. So the remaining £2 million gains, less the annual exemption, are charged at the higher rate of 28%.

Shares and securities

The relief will have effect for gains on disposals of shares in (and securities of) a trading company (or the holding company of a trading group) provided that throughout a one-year qualifying period the individual making the disposal:

• is an officer or employee of the company, or of a company in the same group of companies;

• owns at least 5% of the ordinary share capital of the company and that holding enables the individual to exercise at least 5% of the voting rights in that company.

Where the company (or group) does not cease to trade, the one-year qualifying period is the year ending on the date the shares or securities are disposed of. Where the company (or group) ceases to trade before the disposal of the shares or securities, the one-year qualifying period ends on the date trading ceased, and the disposal must be made within three years of the date of cessation.

In this case Mrs Bird and Rupert are director and employee respectively and have shareholdings in excess of 5% which they have owned for over one year. Entrepreneur's relief therefore applies to the gains on their disposal of Bird Enterprises Ltd shares.

Question

Mr and Mrs Daley were killed in a road accident on 18 August 2010. Under their wills each appointed their son Arthur as executor. They had each left their entire estate to the other, subject to a 30-day survivorship clause. As default beneficiaries, Mr Daley left his used car business to his son together with one half of residue, the other half being divided between various charities. Mrs Daley, who only had building society investments worth £50,000, named her son as the only beneficiary in default of her husband.

Mr Daley's estate is expected to be valued for probate at:

		£	£
Used car business			900,000
Private residence			440,000
Quoted securities			8,900
National Savings Certificates			41,600
ISA at Midnorth Building Society			10,100
Government securities (interest paid gross)			26,800
Life policies			82,500
Pension policies			104,200
Bank accounts			1,400
Premium bonds			20,000
			1,635,500
Less:	Mortgage	125,000	
	Other debts, funeral expenses	10,500	135,500
			1,500,000

Because of business property relief and exemption for charities, no inheritance tax will be payable. Arthur, as executor, will convert all his father's assets (including the business) to cash, and pay the liabilities and legacies. He will use a current account with his bank, and will invest surplus funds on the money market. A premium bond prize of £100,000 was received after his father's death. Arthur anticipates completing the administration of the estate by the end of 2011.

Arthur will also obtain probate on his mother's estate, and will cash the investments and pay all debts and legacies by March 2011.

Arthur has contacted your firm for advice as to his obligations as executor under self-assessment. Set out the taxation points to be considered from death to the completion of the administration of the estate for both Mr and Mrs Daley.

Answer

Tax liabilities of Mr Daley deceased — executor's obligations

Arthur should notify HMRC as soon as possible after his father's death. They will send form R27 asking if probate is to be applied for. Arthur will return the form marked accordingly and in due course he will forward probate, together with a copy of the will, to HMRC.

Cessation of used car business

The death of Mr Daley will denote a cessation of the business for income tax purposes. Ideally accounts should be drawn up to the date of death and submitted with the final self-assessment return, otherwise the accounts covering the date of death must be apportioned.

2009/10 tax return

If the 2009/10 tax return of Mr Daley had not been filed before his death, Arthur as executor is responsible for filing it by 31 October 2010 if filing a paper return or 31 January 2010 for a return filed online. See **note 4**. He is also responsible for paying the outstanding tax for 2009/10 by that date. Interest will be charged on tax paid late, although by Concession A17, interest on tax falling due after death will not start to run until 30 days after the grant of probate.

If the tax is not paid by 28 February 2011 (ie 28 days after the due date), a surcharge of 5% is payable. This increases to 10% if the tax is still unpaid by 31 July. Interest is also payable on any surcharge not paid within 30 days. If there was a reasonable excuse for non-payment throughout the period of default, HMRC (or Commissioners) may set aside the surcharge. Inability to pay is not in itself a reasonable excuse.

FA 2007 s 96 amended the enquiry window for income tax self-assessment tax returns. The enquiry window will close one year after delivery of the return. Therefore, where a return is received before the filing deadline the enquiry window will close earlier than under current legislation. For example, if the 2010/11 return was received by HMRC on 31 August 2011, HMRC will have until 31 August 2012 to enquire into the form.

If deliberate errors both concealed and not concealed are discovered, HMRC can issue an assessment for years ending not earlier than six years before death (ie for 2004/05 onwards) and such assessments must be issued not later than three years after 31 January following the end of the tax year in which the death occurred, ie three years after 31 January 2012 (TMA 1970 s 40). Normally penalties may be charged where there are deliberate errors. Under the Human Rights legislation, however, it is probably not possible to impose tax geared penalties on personal representatives in respect of tax evasion by the deceased. See **Example 5 (c)** for more detail on the FA 2008 legislation on penalties.

However, it appears that consequent to guidance given to HMRC, penalties will still be sought from personal representatives in these situations by way of addition to the settlement offer. Upon request HMRC will issue a letter stating that if in the future there is an adverse decision on the matter in the courts, the penalty will be repaid with interest.

2010/11 tax return

Following Mr Daley's death in August 2010, HMRC will, on request, issue a tax return for 2010/11 before the end of that tax year (and also before the end of the tax year in which the administration of the estate will be completed). When returns have been submitted HMRC will give early confirmation if they do not intend to enquire into the return.

Because of Mr Daley's death it will be appropriate for Arthur to apply to HMRC to reduce the payment on account due on 31 January 2011 in respect of 2010/11. The application should be made on the return, or on form SA 303.

Any tax due for the year of death (or earlier years) will be a liability of the estate.

Tax position on investments

The ISA investment retains its tax exemption until death. Thereafter the normal income and capital gains tax rules apply. An ISA insurance policy will pay out on death and consequently the personal representatives will need to claim the death benefit. Before the claim is accepted by the insurer there are no income tax or capital gains tax implications but any interest paid as a result of late settlement of the claim will be taxable and paid net of tax.

The premium bond continues to be tax-exempt, including the prize received. The amount received will add to the residue of the estate and be distributed accordingly as capital.

Under ITA 2007 s 636 (2) (based on ICTA s 721), if Arthur as personal representative transfers securities to a beneficiary in the interest period in which Mr Daley died, neither Arthur nor the legatee are treated as making or receiving payments. Therefore, in these circumstances no accrued income profit or accrued income loss can arise. However, because the transfer itself is not excluded, ITA 2007 s 681 (exemption for unrealised interest received after a transfer) may still be an issue.

Interest on investments and dividends on shares are taxable when received. They are *not* apportioned for income tax over the period to which they relate. For probate and inheritance tax purposes, however, dividends receivable after death on ex dividend shares (exclusive of the tax credits) and amounts of interest accrued to the date of death on securities (less lower rate tax) are included in the value of the estate. ITA 2007 s 640 introduces rules for small holding of securities and excludes interest on securities that form part of a deceased person's estate, unless the nominal value of securities held by the personal representatives as such exceeds £5,000 on any day:

(a)   in the tax year in which the interest period ends; or

(b)   in the previous tax year.

In relation to a transfer with unrealised interest of securities that form part of a deceased person's estate, the deceased's personal representatives are an excluded transferor or excluded transferee unless the nominal value of securities held by the deceased's personal representatives as such exceeds £5,000 on any day:

(a)   in the tax year in which the settlement day falls; or

(b)   in the previous tax year.

Where there is a transfer of variable rate securities that form part of a deceased person's estate, the deceased's personal representatives are an excluded transferor unless the nominal value of securities held by the deceased's personal representatives as such exceeds £5,000 on any day in the relevant tax year or the previous tax year (see **Example 43**).

Relief is given where an absolute beneficiary is liable to higher rate tax and the estate paid inheritance tax on net accrued income (see **Example 43 explanatory note 4**).

Tax liabilities of Arthur as executor of Mr Daley's estate

Arthur will receive a trust and estate self-assessment return (form SA 900) for the period 19 August 2010 to 5 April 2011, and in due course for the period 6 April 2011 to the date of completion of the administration of the estate. The returns must be filed by 31 October for a paper return or 31 January 2011 for a return filed online (see **note 4**) following the end of the relevant tax year, or by 30 September following the tax year if HMRC are to compute the tax liabilities.

Personal representatives are not entitled to personal allowances and are charged tax on the estate income at the basic rate if it is non-savings income, the lower rate if it is savings income other than dividends, and the dividend ordinary rate on dividends. Any capital gains arising on the disposal of assets in excess of probate values are liable to tax at 18%, after deducting an annual exemption (£10,100 for 2010/11) in the tax year of death and the next two tax years.

Used car business

Because the period of trading by the estate will be less than two years the actual basis of assessment will apply, ie:

2010/11	19 August 2010 to 5 April 2011
2011/12	6 April 2011 to date of sale

Supplementary pages will be required to be completed. If only one set of accounts is prepared details will be shown on the first return, with the profits for the period after 5 April 2011 deducted. On the second return the box indicating that all details have been shown on the previous return will be ticked. The profits (after capital allowances) will be shown with the exclusion of the amount assessed in the earlier year. There is no liability for Class 4 national insurance contributions.

Investment income

Investment income received gross must be declared and tax paid at the savings rate. This will include interest on government securities, on investments for a fixed term over £50,000, and on overseas investments. Interest is also paid gross on all quoted eurobonds, now defined as interest-bearing securities issued by a company (or building society) and listed on a recognised stock exchange (ITA 2007 s 882). Other interest will have had tax deducted at source. This is also shown on the self-assessment return.

Any charge arising under the accrued income scheme on a sale by the executor will be taxed at 20%. Where there is any accrued income relief, the relief is given by deducting it from the gross income received, thus reducing the amount chargeable at 20%.

Changes to self-assessment payments on account limits

Statutory Instrument 1996/1654 – Income Tax (Payments on Account) Regulations was amended to increase the figure at regulation 3 from £500 to £1,000. The regulation has effect on and after 6 April 2009 for income tax due for 2009/10.

It applies to self-assessment payments on account (POA) for 2009/10 and later years. Consequently the first payments on account affected were those due in January 2010 and July 2010.

Payment of tax

If the net income tax payable for 2010/11 exceeds £1,000 (£500 for years up to and including 2008/09), or 20% of the total income tax liability for the year (including tax deducted at source), then payments on account will be required for 2011/12.

Capital gains tax is not included in calculating payments on account. The 2010/11 income tax and capital gains tax will be due on 31 January 2012. As the administration of the estate is likely to be almost complete at that time it should be possible accurately to determine the actual liability for 2011/12. Unless covered by the de minimis limits, one half of that liability (excluding capital gains tax), or one half of the 2010/11 net tax liability if less, will be due on 31 January 2012. The second instalment will be due on 31 July 2012 and the balance, together with any capital gains tax, on 31 January 2013.

Arthur as executor may prefer to pay the whole amount at an early date in order to complete the administration of the estate.

The same provisions as to interest on overdue tax and surcharges apply as stated above in relation to the tax position of Mr Daley deceased.

Tax liabilities in relation to Mrs Daley

Tax position of Mrs Daley deceased

Arthur has similar obligations as stated above in respect of his mother's estate. Since her only assets are building society accounts, however, it may be that it will only be necessary to submit a tax repayment return to the date of her death. Even that will not be necessary if Mrs Daley had elected to receive interest gross.

Tax position in relation to Mrs Daley's estate

Following a taxpayer's death, any election to receive interest gross ceases to have effect and all subsequent payments are made net of tax at the savings rate. Since Mrs Daley's only asset is building society interest, Arthur will be able to tick the second box in Step 1 on the trust and estate tax return confirming that he is the personal representative of a deceased person and that all the following points apply:

All the income arose in the UK

He does not wish to claim reliefs

No annual payments have been made out of capital

All income has had tax deducted before it was received (or is UK dividends with tax credit)

There are no chargeable disposals

There are no accrued income charges or reliefs, no income from relevant discounted securities, offshore income gains or gains on life insurance policies etc.

Arthur can then go straight to **Example 19** in the return to give his, or his agent's, telephone number and sign the declaration at **Example 22**. When the administration of the estate is complete the date of completion is shown at **Example 21**. It is likely that this will occur in 2010/11, so that only one return will be required in relation to Mrs Daley's estate.

Explanatory Notes

(1)   Where HMRC enquire into a return, they will issue a closure notice stating their conclusions and showing the revisions to the self-assessment and the additional tax due (TMA 1970 s 28A). The personal representatives then have 30 days in which to appeal in writing against conclusions stated or amendments made by the closure notice, giving the grounds of appeal (TMA 1970 ss 31, 31A).

(2)   The personal representatives may give HMRC notice of an amendment to the self-assessment return (within the permitted twelve months after the filing date for the return) whilst an enquiry is in progress. The amendment will not restrict the scope of the enquiry but may be taken into account in the enquiry. If it affects the tax payable, it will not take effect unless and until it is incorporated into the s 28A closure notice (see **note 2** above) (TMA 1970 s 9B).

(3)   Questions relating to the subject matter of an enquiry may be referred to the Special Commissioners for their determination while the enquiry is in progress on a joint written application by the personal representatives and HMRC. Either party may withdraw from the referral process providing they give notice before the first hearing of the matter by the Special Commissioners. The determination will be binding on both parties as if it were a decision on a preliminary issue under appeal (TMA 1970 ss 28ZA–28ZE (and ss 31A–31D for companies)).

Revised filing dates for paper and online self-assessment returns

Paper substitutes for SA returns

(4)   Computer generated substitute versions of the SA Return will no longer be approved or accepted for:

- SA Individual Returns – (SA100 series)

- SA Trust Returns – (SA900 series)

For the time being, HMRC will continue to accept approved substitutes for the remaining SA returns (including those for trustees of registered pension schemes) and for all other forms they currently approve substitutes for.

Changes to SA filing dates

Anyone who required to file a self-assessment tax return has:

- until 31 October to do so, if they choose to send a paper return; or

- until the following 31 January if they file online.

This allows an additional three months for online filing compared with paper.

The filing obligation is satisfied by the first return received by HMRC and this also triggers any late filing penalty. So if, for Example, a paper 2009/10 return is filed after 31 October 2010, it is not then possible to avoid a late filing penalty by filing the return online.

In addition, in certain other cases, HMRC will allow extra time beyond the statutory deadline of 31 October – until 31 January – for paper filing without incurring a penalty. These include:

- trustees of registered pension schemes; and

- SA taxpayers (see below), for whom facilities to file online are not yet available.

In the event that there are problems with HMRC systems close to the filing deadline, taxpayers will not be penalised for late submission of a return due to such problems provided that they, or their agent, file within a reasonable period once the service is restored.

FA 2007 s 88(1F) – if a notice is given after 31 July the return must be submitted during the period of three months beginning with the date of the notice (for paper returns) or on or before 31 January (for online returns).

FA 2007 s 88(1G) – if a notice is given after 31 October the return (whether paper return or electronic) must be submitted within three months from the date of the notice.

SA taxpayers who are unable to file online

Those SA taxpayers who do not have the choice of online filing, will be allowed to file on paper up to 31 January, without incurring any penalty that might otherwise be due for paper filing after 31 October.

If such paper output is used for returns which could be filed online, it will be accepted provided it is identical to the official HMRC return but must be submitted to HMRC by the paper filing date of 31 October.

(5)   For detailed notes on the self-assessment provisions see the companion to this book, **Tolley's Taxwise I 2010/11.**

Trusts

Question

Outline the provisions determining the rates of tax applicable to trust income and the way in which the tax payable is accounted for.

Answer

Rates of tax on trust income

Certain trust income is taxed as income of the settlor. Certain other trust income is charged at the 'trust rate', or in the case of dividend income, the dividend trust rate.

Under FA 2009 s 6(4) (amending ITA 2007 s 9) – the dividend trust rate increased from 32.50% to 42.50% and the trust rate has increased from 40% to 50% with effect from 2010/11.

Under ITA 2007 s 491, the first £1,000 of relevant income is not charged at the special trust tax rates, but is instead charged at the income tax rate appropriate to the type of income, known as standard rate band. Therefore, if payments are received net of tax (for Example, building society interest) up to the limit of the standard rate band, then the trustees have no further tax to pay.

For more detailed information see **Example 47**.

Otherwise trustees are liable to tax at the dividend ordinary rate of 10% on tax credit inclusive dividend income, the basic rate of 20% on other savings income and non-savings income. The trust income is determined using the principles applicable to each type of income.

Trustees in their capacity as such are not entitled to personal allowances, nor are they liable to pay income tax at the higher rate.

Treatment of expenses

Any expenses applicable to the particular income are deducted in arriving at the assessable income, but there is no relief for the general trust expenses. Such expenses are regarded as paid first out of dividend income, then out of other savings income, then out of non-savings income (ITA 2007 s 486 — see **Example 43 at note 10** for details of relief for expenses when the rate applicable to trusts or the dividend trust rate applies).

HMRC have confirmed that the standard rate band set out in FA 2005 s 14 will apply to trust income *net* of trust management expenses so potentially it will apply to other charges as well.

Although the management expenses are deducted from the trust income taxed at the lowest rate first, the standard rate band will apply in the order — basic rate income at 20% first, followed by dividends at 10%.

Income certificates to beneficiaries (forms R185)

At the end of each tax year the trustees give income beneficiaries a certificate of their entitlement to trust income (form R185), and of income tax paid thereon by the trustees, and that income will be included in the statutory income of the beneficiary, whose unused personal allowances and starting rate band, if any, will be available to give an income tax repayment, and upon whom any higher rate or dividend upper rate tax will be charged. The trustee's certificate will show the rates at which tax has been paid. For trusts liable to the trust rate, the tax rate shown will be 40%. For other trusts the rates will be 20% on non-savings income and non-dividend savings income. A 10% tax rate is charged on dividends, distributions on which tax is treated as paid (ie dividends on which a non-resident is not entitled to a tax credit (ITTOIA 2005 s 399), bonus issues of redeemable securities (ITTOIA 2005 s 400(4), (5)), scrip dividends (ITTOIA 2005 s 411), close company loans written off or released (ITTOIA 2005 s 416), and dividends from abroad. The 10% tax credits will be shown as non-repayable.

Trust rate and dividend trust rate

ITA 2007 ss 9, 479–483 provide that distribution income received by trusts is chargeable at the 'dividend trust rate' of 32.5% and at the 'rate applicable to trusts' of 40% otherwise.

As mentioned above, under FA 2009 s 6(4) (amending ITA s 9) — the dividend trust rate has increased from 32.50% to 42.50% and the trust rate increased from 40% to 50% from 2010/11.

Trustees are liable at the s 9 rates where they have a power to accumulate income or where they have a discretion as to whether or not the income is made available to income beneficiaries.

With effect from 6 April 2006

Trustees of settlor-interested trusts are taxed at the special trust rates instead of at only up to basic rate.

The dividend trust rate applies to distribution type income, ie UK dividends, dividends from abroad taxed as miscellaneous income, qualifying distributions arising to non-UK resident trustees, non-qualifying distributions (ie bonus issues of redeemable securities – ITTOIA 2005 s 400(4), (5)), scrip dividends (ITTOIA 2005 s 411 – but see **Example 49 part b(a)**), close company loans written off or released (ITTOIA 2005 s 416), and amounts taxable under ITA 2007 ss 481 and 482 (purchase by company of own shares etc – see below). In each case there is an actual or notional tax credit to reduce the tax payable by the trustees (except for dividends from abroad).

The additional tax of 32.50% is payable by trustees on distributions in respect of the balance of the dividend trust rate of 42.50%.

If the trustees make discretionary payments to beneficiaries, however, they must make the payments net of 50% tax and they cannot treat the dividend credit as tax already paid in calculating how much of the tax at 50% has already been paid by them. This significantly increases the tax burden on such payments. For the detailed provisions see **Example 48**.

Income Tax adjustments between settlors and trustees

On enactment, the Finance (No 2) Bill currently (October 2010) before Parliament will amend the Income Tax adjustment mechanism for those individuals who are taxed on the income arising to a trust they have set up (settlor-interested trusts), in relation to repayments of tax for 2010/11 and subsequent years.

Where the person who sets up a trust (the settlor) may benefit from its property or income, the income is treated as the settlor's and taxed accordingly. However, tax is first collected from the trustees. The adjustment mechanism ensures that the same income is not taxed twice and that the settlor neither gains nor suffers a loss.

In relation to the trust income, the settlor is entitled to recover from the trustees the amount of any extra tax he need pay and must pay over to them any repayment received in respect of an 'allowance or relief' above that which he could otherwise have obtained (ITTOIA 2005 s 646).

Clause 7 of the Bill proposes to extend this repayment obligation to all repayments of tax obtained by a settlor in relation to trust income; for example, where he is liable to income tax at a lower rate (say 40%) than the trustees (50%).

Purchase by company of own shares etc

Where a company redeems, repays or purchases its own shares from trustees of a settlement, ITA 2007 ss 481 and 482 (purchase by unquoted trading company of own shares to be treated as a capital payment rather than a distribution) does not apply and the payment is treated as income of the trustees liable at the dividend trust rate of 42.50% on the grossed up equivalent, as indicated above. This treatment applies to life interest trusts as well as accumulation/discretionary trusts, but not to unit trusts, charitable trusts, pension funds or where the income is treated as belonging to the settlor (ITA 2007 ss 481 and 482).

Income not liable to ITA 2007 ss 479–483 rates

Where someone has a life interest in a trust fund, or part thereof, or is entitled to an annuity from the fund, that person cannot avoid liability at the higher rate of tax simply because the trustees do not pay out all of the trust income to which that person is entitled, since the income is in any event included in his statutory income, by reference to the statement of trust income and form R185 (trust income), and he will be a creditor of the trust for any balance of income due to him. Liability at the ss 479–483 rates does not therefore apply to income to which someone is absolutely entitled as against the trustees.

Nor do the ss 479–483 rates apply to income treated for tax purposes as that of the settlor *before* it is distributed (eg where the settlor has settled funds and he and/or his wife are discretionary income beneficiaries — in that event all income is assessable on the settlor under ITTOIA 2005 ss 625–629). The rates *do* apply to income paid to infant, unmarried children of the settlor, even though such income is treated as the settlor's under ITTOIA 2005 ss 629–632 (see below).

The rate applicable to trusts does not apply to capital receipts such as lease premiums, even though they are partly charged to income tax (see **Example 48** for an illustration).

Income of charitable trusts ITA 2007 s 524 and income from property held for certain occupational and personal pension funds is also excluded from ss 479–483 (see **Example 48 explanatory note 6**).

Income taxed as income of settlor

Income taxed as the settlor's income under ITTOIA 2005 ss 629–632 or ITTOIA 2005 ss 625–629 (see above under *Income not liable to ITA 2007 ss 479–483 rates*) is treated as the highest part of the settlor's income (other than employment income lump sum compensation payments under ITEPA 2003 s 403 and life policy gains under ITTOIA 2005 s 465). The settlor can recover any tax paid by him from the trustees or from the person who received the income (ITTOIA 2005 s 646).

Where the settlor has retained an interest in the trust, and income is therefore taxed as his income before distribution, the charge under ITTOIA 2005 ss 619, 621, 623 on dividend income is at the dividend ordinary rate of 10% or upper rates of 42.50% as the case may be. Any other income is charged as miscellaneous income at 20% or 50%.

By comparison, if income is treated as the settlor's income under ITTOIA 2005 ss 629–632, ie because it is paid to his infant, unmarried child, it will have been liable to tax in the hands of the trustees when it arose at either 50% for non-dividend income or 42.5% for dividend income. When any distribution is made, however, it will come out of the general pool of trust income and it will not be dividend income. The distribution will be made net of 40% tax, but the trustees will not be able to include the 10% dividend tax credit in accounting for that tax. This will therefore result in a higher tax charge where a dividend is paid to an infant child via a discretionary trust compared with a direct settlement by the parent on the child. Using the Example above of a net dividend of £90 paid to a discretionary trust with a tax credit of £10, the net distribution to the child would be 50% of £90 = £45 (tax £45). If the settlor had made a direct settlement on the child the additional tax payable would be only £32.50, ie:

Gross income (90 dividend + tax credit 10)	100.00
Tax @ 42.50% (£32.50 payable after tax credit)	42.50
Net receipt	£57.50

This principle applies even where the first £1,000 of income is taxed at the standard rates as only the tax paid is included within the tax pool to frank distributions to beneficiaries.

Filing dates for self-assessment returns

Paper substitutes for SA returns

Computer generated substitute versions of the SA return will no longer be approved or accepted for:

• SA individual returns – (SA100 series)

• SA trust returns – (SA900 series).

For the time being, HMRC will continue to accept approved substitutes for the remaining SA returns (including those for trustees of registered pension schemes) and for all other forms they currently approve substitutes for.

Changes to SA filing dates

Anyone who is required to file a self-assessment tax return has:

- until 31 October to do so, if they choose to send a paper return; or

- until the following 31 January if they file online.

This allows an additional three months for online filing compared with paper.

The filing obligation is satisfied by the first return received by HMRC and this also triggers any late filing penalty. So if, for Example, a paper 2009/10 return is filed after 31 October 2010, it is not then possible to avoid a late filing penalty by filing the return online.

In addition, in certain other cases, HMRC will allow extra time beyond the statutory deadline of 31 October – until 31 January – for paper filing without incurring a penalty. These include:

- trustees of registered pension schemes; and

- SA taxpayers (see below), for whom facilities to file online are not yet available.

In the event that there are problems with HMRC systems close to the filing deadline, taxpayers will not be penalised for late submission of a return due to such problems provided that they, or their agent, file within a reasonable period once the service is restored.

FA 2007 s 88(1F) – if a notice is given after 31 July the return must be submitted during the period of three months beginning with the date of the notice (for paper returns) or on or before 31 January (for online returns).

FA 2007 s 88(1G) – if a notice is given after 31 October the return (whether paper return or electronic) must be submitted within three months from the date of the notice.

SA taxpayers who are unable to file online

Those SA taxpayers who do not have the choice of online filing, will be allowed to file on paper up to 31 January, without incurring any penalty that might otherwise be due for paper filing after 31 October.

If such paper output is used for returns which could be filed online, it will be accepted provided it is identical to the official HMRC return but must be submitted to HMRC by the paper filing date of 31 October.

Payment dates

All sources of income, and also any capital gains, are dealt with in the self-assessment, and trustees make payments on account of income tax (not capital gains tax) in the same way as individuals.

The tax payment dates are:

31 January in the tax year	1st payment on account, being one half of the total tax payable for the previous tax year (including the tax at the rate applicable to trusts or dividend trust rate where appropriate but excluding capital gains tax), as reduced by any tax deducted at source
31 July after end of tax year	2nd payment on account (same amount as 1st payment)
31 January after end of tax year	Full liability for year (including capital gains tax) less payments on account and tax deducted at source

For a detailed illustration see **Example 47**.

Question

T, a widower, who had been in business as a sole trader for many years, died on 6 April 2009.

By his will S, his accountant, was appointed executor and trustee and the whole estate was left in trust to his son, U, absolutely, with a charity being the longstop beneficiary.

The will did not bar the application of the Apportionment Act 1870, and empowered S to continue T's business so that it could be sold as a going concern.

By the will, S is allowed a fixed annual sum of £1,500 for his services as executor and trustee.

T's income-producing assets apart from the business consisted of:

£20,000 listed 10% loan stock in X plc — interest receivable 31 July and 31 January. Interest was received on the due dates and S apportioned it between capital and income under the Apportionment Act 1870.

Building society deposit — net interest receivable 30 June and 31 December. Interest of £160 was received in June and £64 in December 2010. S apportioned the June interest between capital and income under the Apportionment Act 1870.

Property let unfurnished producing rental income during 2010/11 of £1,130 with allowable expenses of £430. At 5 April 2010, there were unutilised losses arising from this property of £100.

The business accounts were made up to 5 April each year. Accounts were produced for the two years to 5 April 2010 and 2011 showing tax adjusted profits of £17,200 and £16,420 respectively.

The deceased had a mortgage of £16,000 on his home, provided by a relative. The interest paid by S for the period from 6 April 2010 until December 2010, when the property was sold, was £900.

T, until his death, had been the life tenant of a settled fund, the sole asset of which was an investment of £40,000 listed 8% debenture stock in Z plc. The due dates for receipt of the interest were 6 April and 6 October. The trustees normally paid the income to T shortly after it was received, and paid to S the income due until T's death, on 31 July 2010.

A loan was taken out by S to enable inheritance tax to be paid on the estate personally. The loan interest charged for 2010/11 was £500.

Certain administration expenses were paid on 31 March 2011. These were allocated as to £500 for capital and £1,195 for income. On that date S was paid the annual sum of £1,500 due to him.

(a)   Prepare a statement showing the trust income for 2010/11 together with supporting notes explaining your treatment of each of the items mentioned above.

(b)   Show the entries on the R185 (trust income) to be given to U for 2010/11.

(c)   Explain the manner in which double taxation has occurred in respect of the income reported for U. Outline any tax relief U may be entitled to under ITTOIA 2005 s 669. The taxable estate was £500,000 and IHT paid was £75,000.

Answer

(a) Statement of trust income 2010/11

Refer to note		£	£	*Tax* £
1	Trading profit	16,420		
2	Unfurnished lettings	700	17,120	
	Savings income			
3	£20,000 10% loan stock, X plc	2,000		
4	Life tenancy (debenture interest)	1,600		
5	Building society interest ((160 + 64) × 100/80)	280	3,880	56
			21,000	56
	Less: charges on income:			
6	Executor's remuneration (annuity)	1,500		
7	Loan interest re payment of IHT	500	2,000	
	Total income of trust		19,000	56
	Tax thereon:			
	Non-savings income 15,120 @ 20%	3,024		
	Savings income (non-dividend) 3,880 @ 20%	776		
	19,000	3,800	3,800	
6	*Add:* Tax deducted from executor's remuneration (1,500 @ 20%)	300		
	Total tax due	4,100		4,100
	of which tax payable by self-assessment is (see **explanatory note 7**)			4,156
			15,200	
	Less: trust expenses:			
8	Mortgage interest	900		
9	Administration expenses	1,195	2,095	
	Net income of trust		13,105	
	Less: apportioned to capital per (b)		1,652	
	Net income available for beneficiary		11,453	
	Comprising:			
	Non-dividend savings income (3,880 − 776)	3,104		
	Less: apportioned to capital	1,652		
		1,452		
10	Used to pay trust expenses (part)	1,452	–	
	Non-savings income (15,120 − 3,024)	12,096		
10	Used to pay trust expenses (balance)	643	11,453	
	Gross equivalent is 11,453 × 100/80 =		14,316	

(b) Computation of income treated as capital

Refer to

note		£
3	£20,000 10% loan stock X plc	
	1 February 2010 to 6 April 2010 66/182 × £1,000	359
4	Life tenancy	
	7 October 2010 to 6 April 2010	1,600
5	Building society interest received	
	[Change dates to 1 January 2010 and 6 April 2010]	106
		2,065
	Income tax @ 20%	413
	Net income apportioned to capital	1,652

Form R185 (trust income) to be given to U for 2010/11

11		Gross	Tax	Net
	Savings income	–	–	–
	Non-savings income	£14,316	£2,863	£11,453

(c)

Where, owing to the apportionment rules, income is included in the estate and charged to inheritance tax, and is also charged as income after death, an absolute beneficiary may claim to reduce his income for higher rate or upper rate purposes (not for savings, basic or dividend ordinary rate tax) by the inheritance tax charged on the grossed-up amount of the accrued income (ITTOIA 2005 s 669).

As a beneficiary with an absolute interest in a share of his late father's estate, U has been assessed on income that arose in the period prior to death but which was received after death.

This has resulted in an element of double taxation as this income was also taken into account when establishing the value of his father's estate on death and therefore was also subject to inheritance tax.

However, if U is a higher rate taxpayer, an element of tax relief is available. The relief is computed by multiplying the income taxed twice by the average rate of inheritance tax on T's estate.

This amount is deducted from U's share of the estate income in determining the amount of income to be taxed at higher rates.

For a more detailed explanation see **explanatory note 9**.

Estate taxable	£500,000
Inheritance tax paid	£75,000
Average rate	15%
Income treated as capital from (b)	£1,652
IHT attributed @15%	£248
Gross up at 20%	£62
	£310
Tax credit	£62

To deduct from R185 figures to give

	Gross	Tax	Net
Non-savings income	14,296	2,863	11,453
Less: s 669 relief	(310)	(62)	(248)
	£14,006	£2,801	£11,205

This will need to be shown on the trust tax return – stating that s 699 relief of £248 (net) has been claimed.

Notes relating to statement of trust income

(1)   The death of T constitutes a cessation of the sole trade for tax purposes. The trustees are regarded as commencing the business from that date The first year of charge is 2010/11. Tax will be charged on the profit from 7 April 2010 to 5 April 2011. (Trustees are not liable to Class 4 national insurance contributions – Social Security Contributions and Benefits Act 1992 Sch 2.5.)

(2)   The income from lettings is:

Rent income in 2010/11	1,130
Allowable expenses	430
	£700

The unutilised losses of T personally are not available for carry forward against the income of the will trust.

(3)   Despite the income from the 10% loan stock having to be allocated to the capital of the estate in so far as the proportion up to the date of death of T is concerned (Apportionment Act 1870), the entire income *received* after death has to be included for *income tax purposes* as that of the will trust (See **explanatory note 7**).

(4)   The settlement income is *received* after death, and despite the allocation to estate capital under the Apportionment Act, is for *income tax purposes* regarded as income of the will trust (See **explanatory note 7**).

(5)   Building society interest will partly have to be allocated to capital of the estate under the Apportionment Act, but since it is *received* after death it is for *income tax purposes* regarded wholly as income of the will trust.

The interest is paid after deduction of lower rate tax, except where the recipient is unlikely to be a taxpayer and has provided an appropriate certificate to the building society. As a trust is not entitled to personal allowances it cannot give such a certificate.

(6)   The £1,500 pa payable to S as executor is regarded as an annuity, from which income tax at the basic rate must be deducted when making the payment (ITA 2007 s 449). See **explanatory note 6** for the way in which the tax is accounted for.

Had the will contained a professional executor's charging clause, the amount paid to S would be an administration expense, payable out of the net income.

(7)   The interest paid on the loan to pay inheritance tax is allowable in calculating the trust income (ITA 2007 s 383).

(8)   The mortgage interest paid is a trust expense payable out of taxed income.

(9)   Administration expenses have to be paid out of taxed income.

(10)   Trust expenses are the expenses of administration and as such are regarded as paid out of income which has already suffered tax. They must be distinguished from expenses relating to a particular source, like those

of the trade and of the lettings in this case which are allowable in computing the income from that particular source.

Trust expenses are treated as being set against income in the following order (ITA 2007 s 486):

(i)   Income carrying non-repayable credits (ie dividends, dividends on which a non-resident is not entitled to a tax credit (ITTOIA 2005 s 399), bonus issues of redeemable securities (ITTOIA 2005 s 400(4), (5)), scrip dividends (ITTOIA 2005 s 411), and close company loans written off or released (ITTOIA 2005 s 416).

(ii)   Taxed dividends from abroad.

(iii) Non-savings and savings income other than that in (i) and (ii).

The set-off order is in fact the most beneficial, in that it maximises the amount of tax paid by the trust that may be passed on to beneficiaries.

(11) Although for income tax purposes, any income received after death is treated as income of the estate and charged on the trustees, as stated in notes 3, 4 and 5, any part of that income that has been apportioned to trust capital is not available to the life tenant and is excluded from his income. The form R185 therefore excludes the net amount of £1,652 apportioned to capital.

Explanatory Notes

Apportionment of income

(1)   The Apportionment Act 1870 requires income accrued up to the date of death to be taken into the estate. This is compulsory for inheritance tax, but for succession purposes the Act may be excluded, so that, for Example, all income received after death goes to the life tenant, rather than some being treated as part of estate capital. For income tax purposes, any income received after the date of death is regarded as income of the estate. Note that the date of death is counted as one of the days prior to the date of death.

This may lead to double taxation, ie for inheritance tax in the estate and for income tax.

Most modern and competently drafted wills or trust deeds will specifically exclude the application of all apportionments.

Where the deceased was life tenant of a trust fund, any income accrued to the date of death (net of tax) is part of his estate for inheritance tax, the settled fund being reduced accordingly. Again this may result in double taxation.

Where double taxation occurs, some relief is available to an *absolute* beneficiary (not a beneficiary with a life interest) in respect of higher rate tax — see **Example 43 (c) and explanatory note 9.**

(2)   Where income is received prior to death it is not apportioned even if all or part of it relates to a period after death. Where income received after death is to be accrued up to the date of death as indicated in note 1 above, the amount to be included in the estate for inheritance tax is as follows:

Shares

Where the shares are cum dividend, no apportionment is necessary. Where they are ex dividend, the forthcoming dividend (exclusive of the tax credit) is taken into the estate.

Other securities

The price must include the accrued interest (less tax at the lower rate) as at the date of death.

Rents

Where the amount received after death relates wholly or partly to a period before death it must be apportioned on the basis that the income accrues evenly from day to day.

Salaries, pensions, annuities

These are again accrued on a day-to-day basis and the amount receivable (net of tax) must be apportioned to the periods before and after death.

Income of life tenant during administration of estate

(3)   Where a person has a life interest in the residue of an estate, the amounts to be included in his statutory income during the period of administration are the grossed up equivalents of the actual income payments made to him (see **Example 39** for further details). Where part of the income has been apportioned to trust capital under the provisions of the Apportionment Act 1870, the amounts actually paid to the life tenant will be less than the net income of the trust, as shown in **part (b)** of the Example.

Income of beneficiary with absolute interest during administration of estate

(4)   Where a person has an absolute interest in the residue of an estate (ie a right to capital as well as to income) again the amounts included in total income during the administration period will be the grossed up equivalent of the actual income payments made to him (see **Example 39**).

If interest is paid on overdue inheritance tax, it is not an allowable deduction for someone with an absolute interest (IHTA 1984 s 233(3)). (For someone with a life interest, his income is the gross equivalent of the amounts actually paid to him, so that interest on overdue tax is effectively allowed for higher rate purposes.)

Nature of payments from estate to beneficiaries

(5)   Payments from the estate to beneficiaries are treated as made first from income taxed at the 20% basic rate, then savings income (excluding dividends) taxed at the 20% basic rate, then dividend income taxed at 10% (ITTOIA 2005 s 679).

The different types of income (net of expenses) and the tax deducted therefrom are shown separately on forms R185, with tax relating to the income in **note 10(i)** of the Example shown as being non-repayable.

Executor's remuneration

(6)   The executor's remuneration of £1,500 represents an annuity, which is a charge on income and reduces the trust's income for tax purposes. Tax relief has, however, already been retained out of the payment at 20%. In order to ensure that the tax retained is balanced by an equivalent amount of tax payable (so that the trust suffers no tax on that slice of its income), the trust's income is first reduced by the annuity, and tax is calculated on the resulting trust income at the appropriate rates. The tax payable is then increased by basic rate tax on the amount of the annuity. For an illustration of the treatment where charges exceed the trust income see **Example 44 part b.**

Changes to Self-assessment payments on account limits

(7)   Statutory Instrument 1996/1654 – Income Tax (Payments on Account) Regulations was amended to increase the figure at regulation 3 from £500 to £1,000. The regulation has effect on and after 6 April 2009 for income tax due for 2009/10.

It applies to self-assessment payments on account (POA) for 2009/10 and later years. Consequently the first payments on account affected were those due in January 2010 and July 2010.

Self-assessment

(8)   The self-assessment provisions apply to trustees and personal representatives in the same way as for individuals. Payments on account are due on 31 January in the tax year and 31 July following, each equal to half of the total income tax payable (net of tax deducted at source) for the previous tax year (unless it

was below the de minimis thresholds). A balancing payment is then due on the following 31 January (which will include any capital gains tax payable). At the same time the first payment on account for the next year is due.

Payments on account will not be made for the tax year in which a trust commences, since no tax was payable for the previous year. In this Example therefore all the tax payable by self-assessment, amounting to £4,100, will be due for payment on 31 January 2011. Note that this tax figure is made up of the tax of £3,024 on the non-savings income plus the tax of £776 on the savings income of £3,600 not taxed at source plus the tax of £300 deducted at source from the executor's remuneration.

The first payment on account for 2011/12 is also due on 31 January 2012. Since there is no capital gains tax in the tax figure of £4,100, the first payment on account for 2011/12 will be half of that figure, ie £2,050. The total amount payable by the trustees on 31 January 2012 is therefore £6,150.

ITA 2007 s 882 now provides that tax is not deducted from payments of interest on quoted eurobonds, which are defined as interest-bearing securities issued by a company and listed on a recognised stock exchange.

For further notes on self-assessment see **Examples 41, 46, 47 and 48**.

Will trusts

(9)   Often it will be necessary for the executors to administer the estate of a deceased person and then to transfer their responsibilities to the trustees of the life interest settlement in respect of the residue of the estate. In this Example the trustees and personal representatives are the same. Furthermore the whole of the estate is left in trust to the son. In practice in these circumstances, it is usual to treat all of the income as belonging to the trustees from the date of death and to allow the expenses of administration etc against that income. More correctly the executor should issue a form R185 (estate income) and complete a self-assessment return for the period of administration of the estate and then do the same as trustee, ie issue form R185 (trust income) and complete a further self-assessment return for the remaining part of the same tax year.

Relief for inheritance tax attributable to income accrued at death (ITTOIA 2005 s 669)

(10) Income that accrued during the lifetime of the deceased but was paid after death is treated under inheritance tax rules as part of the estate of the deceased person. The same income is treated as part of the net statutory income of the estate and therefore enters into the computation of residuary income.

Where this happens, a residuary beneficiary D who is liable to tax at the higher rate may claim a deduction from the residuary income of an amount equal to the inheritance tax applicable to the accrued income (ITTOIA 2005 s 669).

Instructions for working out the deduction are set out in the legislation as follows:

A reduction is made in the residuary income of D's estate for that tax year in ascertaining the extra liability, if any, of a person with an absolute interest in the whole or part of the residue of D's estate or any other estate to which that residuary income is relevant.

A person's extra liability is the amount by which the person's liability to income tax exceeds the amount it would be if:

(a)   income charged at the higher rate were charged:

(i)   in the case of income chargeable at the lower rate instead of the basic rate, at the lower rate, and

(ii)   in any other case, at the basic rate, and

(b)   income charged at the dividend upper rate were charged at the dividend ordinary rate.

The amount of the reduction under subsection (2) is calculated as follows:

Step 1

Calculate the net pre-death income by subtracting from the pre-death income any liabilities which have been taken account both:

(a)   in determining the value of D's estate for the purposes of inheritance tax, and

(b)   in calculating the residuary income of D's estate for the tax year.

Step 2

Calculate the inheritance tax attributable to net pre-death income by multiplying the inheritance tax to be charged by:

where:

NPDI is the net pre-death income, and

VE is the value of D's estate.

Step 3

Gross up the inheritance tax attributable to net pre-death income by reference to the basic rate for the tax year.

The amount of pre-death income taken into account in determining the value of D's estate is taken to be the actual amount of income accruing before D's death, less income tax at the basic rate for the tax year in which D died.

Finance Act 2009 Sch 2 para 21 amends ITTOIA s 669(3) to ensure that the reduction in residuary income can be calculated by reference to the additional rate or the dividend additional rate.

Question

A.

Herbie Fritter is the life tenant of a trust fund set up by his grandfather.

The trust income in 2010/11 consisted of taxed interest on £80,000 3% Treasury Stock which had been held for many years.

Trust expenses amounted to £320.

Herbie is a widower aged 70, whose only other income in 2010/11 is a state retirement pension of £7,710.

(a) Prepare a statement showing the trust income and show the details to be stated on the income certificate given to Herbie.

(b) Compute Herbie's income tax repayment for 2010/11.

B.

Assume the same facts as above except that Herbie is an annuitant entitled to an annuity from the trust amounting to £3,200 per annum gross.

The trustees paid the full annuity in 2010/11, being authorised to use capital to make up the deficiency.

(a) Show the position of the trustees and the figures on the certificate to be given to Herbie.

(b) Compute Herbie's income tax repayment for 2010/11.

Answer

A. Herbie Fritter — Trust Income

(a) *Statement of trust income 2010/11*

	Net £	Tax £	Gross £
3% Treasury Stock interest	1,920	480	2,400
Trust expenses paid therefrom	320		
Regarded as net amount with tax deduction of		80	
and a gross equivalent of			400
Net amount, tax thereon and gross equivalent remaining	1,600	400	2,000

Certificate by trustees to Herbie (R185 (non-discretionary trusts))

Gross	Tax	Net
£2,000	£400	£1,600

A.

(b) *Herbie's income tax repayment claim 2010/11*

	£	Tax £
Retirement pension	7,710	
Savings income from trust	2,000	400
	9,710	
Age allowance	9,490	
Taxable income	220	
Tax payable @ 10% starting rate for savings income (see **note 7**)		22
Repayment due		378

B. Tax payable by trustees under ITA 2007 s 963

(a) *Statement of trust income 2010/11*

	Net £	Tax £	Gross £
Trust income after expenses as before	1,600	400	2,000
Annuity to Herbie	2,560	640	3,200
Further tax to be paid by trustees		240	

The annuity is income in Herbie's hands, even though part of it was paid out of capital. Having accounted for tax at 20% on the full amount of the payment, the trustees will give Herbie the appropriate certificate on form R185 as follows:

Gross	Tax	Net
£3,200	£640	£2,560

B.

(b) *Herbie's income tax repayment claim 2010/11*

	£	Tax £
Retirement pension	7,710	
Annuity	3,200	704
	10,910	
Age allowance	9,490	
Taxable income	1,420	
Tax payable @ 20% on £1,420 (see **note 7**)		284
Repayment due		420

Explanatory Notes

Paying expenses out of capital

(1)   Had the trustees been empowered to pay the expenses from capital, their income of £2,400 would have been intact. In **part A** of the Example, Herbie would have received £1,920 net, the gross equivalent of which would have been the full £2,400 received by the trustees.

If Herbie had been liable to tax at 40% or 50%, his higher or additional rate liability would be increased if the trust expenses were paid out of the trust capital.

Payment of annuities

(2)   Annuities reduce the payer's income for tax purposes (the payer being the trust in **part B** of the Example). It is, however, provided by ITA 2007 s 901 that tax must be deducted from annuities at the basic rate. The tax relief is therefore normally given by allowing the payer to retain the tax deducted, but an equivalent amount of the payer's income must be taxed at the *basic rate*. The net result is that no tax is suffered on that part of the payer's income. If there is insufficient income to cover the annuity, tax must be accounted for at the basic rate on the excess under ITA 2007 s 963, and no tax relief is available on the payment, since it is made out of trust capital.

Assessments under ITA 2007 s 963

(3)   Where tax is payable under ITA 2007 s 963 as indicated in **note 2** above, HMRC issue assessments outside the self-assessment system for the amount due. Interest on such assessments runs from 31 January after the tax year to which the assessment relates, regardless of when the assessment is issued.

Interest on government stocks

(4)   From 6 April 1998, interest on all government stocks is paid gross where the stocks are acquired on or after that date, unless the holders apply to receive the interest net (ITA 2007 s 892). Those like Herbie's trustees who already hold such stocks are treated as having *opted* for net payment, but they may apply for the gross payment rules to apply. If such an application has been made, the interest received would normally be taken into account in calculating the half-yearly payments on account, but in this Example it would be covered by the de minimis limit of £1,000 (see **note 5**) so that half-yearly payments would not be required.

Payments on Account – change of limit

(5)   It is worth noting that SI 1996/1654 – Income Tax (Payments on Account) Regulations 1996 was amended by SI 2008/838 to raise the de minimis figure at regulation 3 from £500 to £1,000 with effect for 2009/10 and later years.

The first payments on account affected were those for 2009/10 due in January 2010 and July 2010.

Self-assessment

(6)   See **Example 47** for detailed notes on the treatment of trusts under self-assessment.

Tax on savings income

(7)   Tax is chargeable on an individual's taxable income in excess of his personal allowance (and any other deductions such as blind person's allowance or allowable expenses), up to the basic rate limit of £37,400 at the basic rate of 20%, except so far as his income other than dividend and savings income is less than the starting rate limit for savings income of £2,440 (ITA 2007 ss 10, 12, 16 as amended). If taxable non-savings income (eg earnings and pensions etc) is more than this limit, then the 10% savings rate will not be applicable and savings income will be taxed in full at 20%.

Savings income is defined in ITA 2007 s 18. The commonest category is interest, but it also includes profits from deeply discounted securities, accrued income profits, taxable life assurance chargeable gains of individuals and personal representatives, and certain purchased life annuity payments. The definition does not include other annuities, such as Herbie's in **part B** of the Example, which is taxable under ITTOIA 2005 ss 683–686.

What this means is that if an individual has total income, including some savings income, of between £6,475 and £8,915 the 10% rate will apply to at least part of their savings income. For people over 65 who are receiving the higher personal allowance these figures will be increased.

However, if the personal allowance has been utilised against non-savings income (as explained above), but the remaining non-savings income is less than £2,440, the balance of the £2,440 against can be used to tax savings income at the 10% rate. Only the balance of savings income remaining is then chargeable at 20%.

For Example – Keith aged 60, has taxable employment and pension income of £7,040 and savings interest (before any tax is taken off) of £1,000. Keith's tax free personal allowance for 2010/11 is £6,475 so he only has tax to pay on £565 (£7,040 – £6,475) on his non-savings income. This means that he has used up £565 of the £2,440 starting rate band of 10% for savings income, leaving £1,875 available. His savings income of £1,000 will be taxed in full at 10% only.

However, if Keith's non-savings income amounted to £25,000 (before tax), he will be taxed in full at 20% on his savings income, as taxable non-savings income is more than his personal allowance of £6,475 plus the savings rate starting limit of £2,440.

Taxable income (apart from dividends, dealt with below) over £37,400, up to the higher rate limit of £150,000, is taxed at the 40% higher rate whether or not it is savings income. Beyond the higher rate limit, introduced by FA 2009 Sch 2 with effect for 2010/11 and subsequent years, the applicable rate is 50%.

Dividends or distributions from unit trusts (but not interest) form the highest tranche of income and so are taxed at the dividend rate that corresponds to the highest appropriate band of income:

(a)   Dividends below the basic rate limit of £37,400 are taxed at the dividend ordinary rate of 10%, which is fully covered by the related tax credit (non-repayable).

(b)   Dividends between the basic rate limit and the higher rate limit are taxed at the dividend higher rate of 32.5%.

(c)   Dividends in excess of the higher rate limit are taxed at the dividend additional rate of 42.5%.

Loss of personal allowances for higher earners

(8)   In addition to the introduction of a 50% tax rate from 2010/11, the basic personal allowance for income tax will be gradually reduced to nil for individuals with adjusted net incomes above £100,000, on a basis of £1 reduction for each additional £2 of income. (The effect of this is a marginal tax rate of 60% for income between £100,000 and £112,950.) The calculation of adjusted net income is the same as that already in place for reducing the higher age allowances for those over age 65 whose incomes are in excess of £22,900 (FA 2009 s 4).

Question

A and his wife B died in a car crash on 6 April 2009, being survived by their four children C, D, E and F.

The children's dates of birth are:

C	20 January 1988
D	6 October 1992
E	11 November 1993
F	23 May 1995

By their wills, in addition to bequests to more distant relatives and friends and gifts of their residuary estates to charities, A and B created the following separate trusts for their children. Neither of them had made any other trusts in their lifetimes.

Under A's will

For C, an annuity of £1,500 to be paid out of the income from 20,000 £1 shares in X plc. It is stipulated that if the income of any year is insufficient to meet the annuity in full, capital is to be used to make good the deficiency. Because of falling profits, X plc was only able to pay a 4% dividend during 2010/11.

For D, 10,000 shares in Y plc if he attains 25 years of age. By Trustee Act 1925 s 31, the income may, at the discretion of the trustees, be applied for D's maintenance while he is under 18; once D attains 18 years of age the income has to be paid to him. The dividends received from Y plc shares in 2010/11 (exclusive of tax credits) totalled £1,600, of which £1,150 was in the period to 6 October 2010 and £450 after that date. Maintenance paid to D between 6 April and 5 October 2010 was £290. £300 was paid to D in February 2011.

Under B's will

For E, an absolutely vested interest in 10,000 8% preference shares of £1 each in Z plc. The capital cannot be paid to E until the child's 18th birthday, but power is given for payments to be made for E's maintenance out of income. Any income not distributed will be accumulated until E becomes 18. £700 was paid to E during 2010/11.

For F, Rannoch House if he attains 18 years of age. The house is currently let at an annual rent of £7,500 from 6 April 2010 but was empty in the period from B's death on 6 April 2009 until 5 April 2010 for major renovation work so no rents were received in this period. Consequently no election for the special income tax treatment for trust with vulnerable beneficiary was made for 2009/10 but the trustees wish to consider making such an election for 2010/11.

No maintenance was paid to F during 2010/11 as he has a part time job from which he earns £2,500 a year with no tax deducted. He has no other income.

By 5 April 2010 the estate had been administered and the funds to satisfy the bequests to C, D and E had been set aside.

(a)   Calculate the income tax payable by the trustees of each of the above funds for 2010/11 and state the deadline for any vulnerable person's election in relation to the F Trust.

(b)   State the amounts which will be treated as taxable income of each beneficiary for 2010/11.

Ignore the Apportionment Act 1832, which was excluded by both A's and B's wills.

Answer

(a) Income tax payable by trustees for 2010/11

C Trust:

			Gross £	Tax £
Dividends (20,000 × 4% = 800 + 89 (tax credit of 1/9))			889	89
Less charges: Annuity (part) (cf ITTOIA 2005 s 397(3))			889	89
			–	–
Tax on trust income			–	–
Tax on charges	889	@ 20%	178	178
Total tax payable by trustees under self-assessment (see ITA 2007 s 964) (due 31 January 2012)				178
Tax payable by trustees under ITA 2007 s 963 assessment re annual payment made out of capital (see **explanatory note 1**):				
Balance of annuity of (1,500 – 889)	611	@ 20%		122

Form R185 to the annuitant will show:

	Gross £	Tax £	Net £
Annuity	1,500	300	1,200

D Trust:

The trustees are liable to tax in respect of dividend income at the dividend trust rate of 42.5% on the tax credit inclusive amount until the beneficiary has an absolute interest in income (6 October 2010). From that date the trust becomes an interest in possession trust (for income tax purposes – see **explanatory note 6** for the inheritance tax position) until D becomes entitled to the capital at age 25. From then on the tax payable on the dividends at trust level is covered by the tax credits, so the trustees are not liable to pay any tax thereon. The position is therefore as follows.

Dividend income (6 April 2010 to 5 October 2010)	1,150			
Tax credits £1,150 × 1/9	128			
	£1,278			
Tax payable at dividend ordinary rate	500 *	@ 10% =		50
dividend trust rate	778	@ 42.5% =		331
* see **explanatory note 2**				381
Less: Tax credits				128
Tax payable by trustees on trust income (to tax pool)				£253

	Net	Tax	Gross
Tax on distribution pre 6.10.10	290	290	580

Less tax in tax pool as above	253	
Further tax due under ITA 2007 ss 497/498	37	37
Total tax payable by trustees under self-assessment (due 31 January 2012)		290

E Trust:

Income received

10,000 × £1 × 8% = £800 + tax credit £89 = £889.

Tax at the dividend trust rate does not apply as E has an absolute right to the income.

The tax liability on the dividend income is at 10%, covered by the tax credit. Although the trustees will have to send in a tax return form SA 900, they will not need to make any income entries since the tax on the income was covered by tax credits. The due date for submitting the return is 31 January 2012.

F Trust:

Because, under the will of a deceased parent of his, F will become absolutely entitled to all of the trust assets on reaching 18 and only he can benefit from the income in the meantime, the F Trust is a qualifying trust for a bereaved minor and a vulnerable person election can be made in relation to it, which will entitle the trustees to claim special treatment for income tax (and for capital gains tax were that applicable to the trust) (FA 2005 Chapter 4). The income tax liability would then be calculated by reducing the normal trust tax payable (referred to in FA 2005 s 27 as TQTI) by the excess of that figure over the extra amount of tax the vulnerable beneficiary would pay (FA 2005 s 28 Vulnerable Person's Liability (VQTI)) on the assumption that the trust income is the highest part of his or her income and disregarding any relief given by way of a reduction of income tax (eg married couple's allowance).

The vulnerable person election must be made jointly by the trustees and F (no doubt acting by his legal guardian) (FA 2005 s 37), and if it is to have effect from 6 April 2010 the deadline for making it is 31 January 2012.

The calculation of the trustees' income tax liability, as set out in FA 2005 ss 26–28 is:

Steps	
TLV2	Compute F's liability to income on the basis that any income distributed to him by the trustees is disregarded and that any reliefs given by way of an income tax deduction (for Example – married couple's allowance) are also ignored for this purpose.
TLV1	This is the tax due computed on the same assumptions as for TLV1 but assuming further that the trust income relating to the vulnerable beneficiary was in fact charged on F as the highest part of his income.
VQTI	VQTI = TLV1 – TLV2
TQTI	This is the tax due on the trustees without reference to the vulnerable person rules.
The relief	The trustees' income tax liability is reduced by TQTI – VQTI. The trustees' reduced liability is thus VQTI.

F Trust: calculation of vulnerable person relief – 2010/11

This calculation assumes enactment of the increased personal allowance of £7,475 (see Stop Press note at the beginning of the book and **explanatory note 7** to **Example 44**).

TLV2	F's income ignoring the trust income is his wages of £2,500 which is within his personal allowance – no tax is payable on this.

				£
	Earnings			2,500
	Personal allowance (restricted)			2,500
				0

				£
TLV1	Earnings			2,500
	Trust income (rental business profit (assumes no expenses)			7,500
				10,000

				£
	Income including trust (TLV1)			10,000
	Personal allowance			6,475
	Taxable income			£3,525

Tax payable thereon

		£		£
		3,525	@ 20%	705

VQTI   TLV1 minus TLV2 equals VQTI (705 − 0 = 705)
So VQTI is £705

TQTI   Tax on trustees (assumes no management expenses for purpose of this Example)

		£		£
	basic rate	1,000 *	@ 20%	200
	trust rate	6,500	@ 50%	3,250
		7,500		3,450

* the full trust basic rate band of £1,000 is available as the other trust made by B, the E Trust, does not comprise settled property (ITA 2007 s 466(3)(c)), and B has therefore only created one settlement for the purpose of ITA 2007 s 492

The relief   Trustees' income tax liability reduced by TQTI − VQTI

		£
	TQTI	3,450
	The relief (3,450 − 705)	2,745
	Revised liability	705

(b) Amounts treated as taxable income of the beneficiaries for 2010/11

C	Annuity	£1,500	Tax deducted	£300
D	Discretionary trust income to 5 October 2010			
	£290 × 100/50	580	Tax deducted	£290
	Income of trust from 6. October 2010			
	— Dividends			
	£450 × 100/90	500	Tax credit (non-repayable)	£50
		£980		
E	Dividend income vested (that is, an absolute entitlement to it whether or not distributed)	£889	Tax credit (non-repayable	£89
F	— Nil			

In all cases the beneficiary's income is below the level of the single personal allowance. Dividend tax credits are, however, not repayable. Unless their personal allowances are covered by other income, C will be able to reclaim the whole of the tax deducted of £300 and D will be able to reclaim the tax of £290 deducted from his maintenance. Neither D nor E will be able to reclaim the tax credits of £50 or £89 respectively in relation to the dividend income that they are treated as receiving.

F neither received nor was entitled to any income from the F Trust so has no liability on it. The calculations in relation to the vulnerable persons election determine the (reduced) liability of the trustees and do not give rise to a liability for the vulnerable person himself.

Explanatory Notes

Payment of annuities

(1)   Where an annuity is payable, tax must be deducted at the basic rate, and tax must be accounted for at that rate on an equivalent amount of income. The effect is to cause tax to be charged on the dividend income of the C trust at 20% rather than the dividend rate of 10%. ITA 2007 s 963 provides that tax also has to be paid at the basic rate on the part of the annuity paid out of the capital of the trust. HMRC issue assessments outside the self-assessment system in respect of such tax. Although the tax on such an assessment is payable 30 days after it is issued (unless an appeal and postponement application is made) (TMA 1970 s 59B(6)), interest on unpaid tax runs from 31 January after the tax year to which the assessment relates (see **Example 44 explanatory note 3**).

Now that dividend credits are not repayable, the fact that the trust's dividend income is effectively taxed at 20% will not disadvantage C.

For a further illustration of the treatment of an annuity see **Example 44 part B**.

Contingent interest

(2)   At present D only becomes entitled to the trust capital (the shares in Y plc) if he attains the age of 25; but see 45.2(a) as to the income arising. Until age 18 the trustees have the power to accumulate income and therefore the dividend income received by the trust before D's 18th birthday on 6 October 2010 is chargeable to tax at the dividend trust rate (now 42.5%). As and when payments are made to D during that time, since 6 April 2010 they are net of tax at 50%, and the tax may be reclaimed by D if appropriate, as indicated in the Example. The trustees must, however, account for the 50% tax deducted from the payments and they cannot treat the dividend credit relating to the amount distributed as tax paid by them when calculating how much tax they must pay. They could not, therefore, have paid an actual distribution of more than £575 (equating to £1,150 gross), to D before 6 October 2010, ie:

	£	Available income £
Trust income		
Dividend 1,150 × (100/90)	1,278	1,150
Tax due (per 45.2 at D)	381	
Less tax credit	128	
Tax payable	253	(253)
If distribution restricted to £1,175 gross		
Tax at 50% on £1,175	575	
Already paid	253	
Further tax payable	322	(322)
Net income available for distribution		575

For a more detailed illustration of these provisions see **Example 48**.

The trustees have the benefit of only half the usual basic rate band for trustees of discretionary and accumulation trusts, because there are two separate current trusts under A's will: ITA 2007 s 492.

From his 18th birthday D is entitled to the income arising after that time whether it is actually distributed or not. The amount of £300 paid to him after his 18th birthday in the tax year is irrelevant, since he is entitled to the full dividend received in that period (subject only to trust management expenses) and will eventually receive the rest. In particular the payment cannot be a discretionary distribution of pre-18th birthday income because any balance of undistributed income fell to be capitalised on his attaining age 18 under Trustee Act 1925 s 31(2).

Absolute interest – bare trust

(3)   Although E is under 18, he has a vested interest in the preference shares in Z plc.

Contrast the interest of E (vested) with that of D (contingent). Although E cannot personally have the shares in Z plc until he is 18, or even the income for his personal unrestricted use, the shares belong to him. If he dies the asset (and any accumulated income) will form part of his estate. The income from the shares forms part of his statutory income. By comparison D's interest in the shares of Y plc is conditional upon his living to age 25. If he dies then the asset will fall into residue and pass to charity. D has no right to the income until he is 18 (other than at the discretion of the trustees). Thereafter he has an absolute right to income which is taxed in his name. Only after the contingency has been eliminated (ie on attaining age 25) will the shares vest in D. There is a considerable body of case law on the question of whether an interest under a will is vested or contingent, and it involves a detailed knowledge of the general law of trusts, which is outside the scope of this book.

Trust with vulnerable beneficiary

(4)   The rate applicable to trusts and the dividend trust rate were originally raised in FA 2004, with effect for the tax year 2004/05, as a tax avoidance deterrent. To prevent tax changes having an adverse effect on trusts with vulnerable beneficiaries, particularly trusts for disabled people and for children with a deceased parent, FA 2005 Chapter 4 (ss 23–45) brought in provisions to protect such individuals. These provisions are all the more helpful now that the rates have been further increased: from 2010/11, the dividend trust rate has been increased from 32.5% to 42.5% and the trust rate from 40% to 50% (see Answer at **Example 42**).

Vulnerable person election

(5)   Trustees holding settled property on qualifying trusts for the benefit of a vulnerable person may make an election, jointly with the vulnerable beneficiary which will allow the trustees then to make a claim year by year for the special tax treatment provided by FA 2005 Chapter 4 to apply for that year. Such an election is irrevocable, and will apply from its effective date until any of the following occurs:

(a)   the beneficiary ceases to be a vulnerable person,

(b)   the trusts cease to be qualifying trusts, or

(c)   the trusts are terminated.

The election must state the date from which it is to be valid and must be made no later than 12 months after 31 January following the tax year in which that date falls.

If one of those events occurs, the trustees have 90 days from the time they become aware of its occurrence to notify HMRC (s 37).

Although the election itself is irrevocable, a claim to the special tax treatment can be made, or not made, by the trustees on a year by year basis while the election remains in force (s 24). The claim, if made, covers both income tax and capital gains tax – it cannot be made for one without the other.

Vulnerable persons

(6)   There are two categories of vulnerable person (s 23(7)):

(a)   A disabled person, defined as a person with a mental disability who is incapable of administering his property or managing his affairs, or, a person in receipt of attendance allowance or disability living allowance at the middle or highest rates (or who would be so entitled to such an allowance if they were UK resident) (s 38).

(b)   A relevant minor, being a child aged under 18 at least one of whose parents has died (s 39)

If these categories (and the requirements for trusts for them to count as qualifying trusts, see below) seem familiar, it may be because they were taken as models for more restrictive categories of privileged treatment for inheritance tax purposes (see further **explanatory note 6** below) when the treatment of settled property was overhauled in FA 2006 (though the extended meaning of 'parent' in IHTA 1984 s 71H does not apply for the purpose of the vulnerable persons rules in FA 2005).

Qualifying trust — disabled persons

(7)   To be a qualifying trust for a vulnerable disabled person, the terms of the trust must secure that, during his lifetime or until the trust terminates,

(a)   no capital distribution can be made other than for the benefit of the disabled person, and

(b)   that person must be entitled to all of the income arising from the trust fund, or no income of the trust may be applied for the benefit of any other person (s 34).

Qualifying trust — relevant minors

(8)   A trust is a qualifying trust for a relevant minor if it is:

(a)   a statutory trust for a minor under the intestacy rules of England and Wales (Administration of Estates Act 1925 ss 46, 47(1)), or

(b)   a trust which:

(i)   secures that the relevant minor will become absolutely entitled to both capital and income (including accumulations) not later than age 18, and that no income or capital can be distributed or applied before that time other than for the benefit of the relevant minor, and

(ii)   was established either under the will of a deceased parent of the relevant minor, or under the Criminal Injuries Compensation Scheme (s 35).

It must therefore be noted that any trusts established by parents, by will or intestacy, for their minor children, where the children do not become entitled to the settled property until an age over 18 (eg accumulation and maintenance trusts in the extended form they often took before FA 2006) will not qualify. Hence the D Trust in the **Example** does not qualify but the F Trust does.

Part qualification

(9)   References to qualifying trusts include trusts where only part of an asset is held on qualifying trusts provided that part, and any income arising from it, can be identified (s 36).

In such cases, or generally where the trustees' total income includes income which is not qualifying trusts income, only the relevant proportion of management expenses will be allowed against the qualifying trusts income when calculating TQTI. The management expenses are to be apportioned for this purpose by reference to the amount of qualifying trust income as a proportion of the total income of the trustees (s 27(2)).

Part years

(10)   Where the trust only qualifies for part of a tax year then income and expenses are related to the qualifying and non-qualifying periods based upon when income arises (s 29).

Special tax treatment – Income tax

(11)   FA 2005 ss 25–29 as amended sets out the special tax treatment rules so far as income tax is concerned. The mechanics of working out the reduction in the trustees' tax liability, with a UK resident beneficiary, are set out in detail for the F Trust in **part (a)** of the Example, but basically the trustees will be able to take account of the vulnerable beneficiary's personal allowance and income tax bands to reduce the amount of income tax payable.

For income tax purposes, the trustees therefore include in their return the tax that would normally be due by them, and then calculate what the tax would be if the income had arisen directly to F, taking into account his other income, gains and allowances. The difference is claimed as a deduction.

Special tax treatment – Capital gains tax

(12)   The special tax treatment for capital gains tax is restricted to cases where the trustees are ordinarily resident in the UK the relevant tax year, or are resident in the UK during any part of the tax year (s 30(1)(c). It also does not apply in the tax year of the death of the vulnerable beneficiary (s 30).

Subject to that, relief in respect of capital gains accruing to the trustees is, since FA 2008, computed in a very similar way to the income tax relief illustrated in part (a) of the Example for the F Trust, the effect of which is to reduce the trustees' liability to that which would have been the vulnerable person's liability if the trustees' gains had accrued to him direct. In more detail, the steps for a UK resident vulnerable beneficiary are:

TLVB	The vulnerable person's capital gains tax liability for the year apart from this relief.
TLVA	What TVLB would be if the qualifying trusts gains accrued direct to the vulnerable person instead of to the trustees, without any deduction for allowable losses. (It appears that this applies to allowable losses whether of the trustees or of the vulnerable person; this may influence whether the trustees wish to make a claim for a year in which significant losses have been realised, bearing in mind that the claim cannot be made for income tax without also operating for capital gains tax.)
VQTG	TLVA minus TLVB.
TQTG	The trustees' liability on the qualifying trusts gains apart from this relief.
The relief	The trustees' capital gains tax liability is reduced by TQTG – VQTG, so that the effective reduced liability equals VQTG.

For 2010/11 these amounts will each be calculated at the 18% or 28% rates according to whether the qualifying trusts gains accrued before, or on or after, 23 June 2010, and in the latter case (in the case of TVLA and TVLB) whether the vulnerable person's income and gains (including qualifying trusts gains for TVLA) exceed his basic rate band or the otherwise unused part of it. As for general capital gains tax purposes, allowable losses (where taken into account, see TVLA above) and annual exempt amounts can be allocated in the most beneficial way. (TCGA 1992 ss 4, 4A as amended/inserted by Finance (No 2) Bill 2010.)

Non-UK resident vulnerable persons

(13)   Where the beneficiary is not ordinarily resident in the UK during the tax year, and not resident in the UK during any part of it, the calculations for TVL1, TVL2, TVLA and TVLB are to be carried out on the assumption that he is resident and domiciled in the UK throughout the relevant tax year. Certain additional assumptions are made in calculating TVLA and TVLB for the capital gains tax relief, essentially to secure that overseas losses of the vulnerable person which would be disallowed on grounds of his actual non-UK residence are nevertheless allowed in calculating his liability excluding the qualifying trust gains. (FA 2005 ss 28(4), 32, 41(2) and Sch 1.)

Self-assessment

(14)   See **Example 47** for further details on the way in which income is shown in the self-assessment tax return of the individual.

Inheritance tax status of testamentary trusts for children

(15)   Until Finance Act 2006, there were favourable inheritance tax rules for accumulation and maintenance (A & M) trusts under which beneficiaries were to become entitled to at least in interest in possession by age 25. Such trusts were not subject to the periodic or exit charges applicable to relevant property trusts (and lifetime transfers into these trusts were exempt from IHT so long as the settlor survived seven years).

Following the amendments made by FA 2006 Sch 20, any trust under a will for a child of the deceased will be subject to the relevant property regime unless:

(a)   the child has an immediate interest in possession from the deceased's death (which will be an immediate post-death interest unless the child is a disabled person in which case it will be a disabled person's interest); if the child is under age 18 at the deceased's death and the will is governed by English law this would require special drafting to negate the effect of Trustee Act 1925 s 31 which postpones an interest in possession to age 18 (IHTA 1984 s 49A); or

(b)   the child is a disabled person, no interest in possession subsists, and the terms of the trust are such that, if any capital is applied during his lifetime, not less than half of the amounts so applied are applied for the child's benefit – in which case the child will have a deemed interest in possession which is a disabled person's interest (IHTA 1984 s 89(2)); or

(c)   the child (bereaved minor) is under age 18 and the terms of the trust are such that he will become absolutely entitled to both capital and income (including accumulations) not later than age 18, and that no income or capital can be distributed or applied before that time other than for the benefit of the bereaved minor (IHTA 1984 s 71A – a "bereaved minor's trust"); or

(d)   the child is under age 25 and the terms of the trust are as in **paragraph** (c) above but reading age 25 for age 18 IHTA 1984 s 71D – an "age 18-to-25 trust"). In this case the trust will remain within s 71D whether or not an interest in possession arises in the child's favour before he reaches age 25; but if it arises immediately on the deceased's death, or within two years after it (IHTA 1984 s 144) then the interest in possession will be within **paragraph** (a) above and s 71D will not apply; or

(e)   the child is absolutely entitled so that any trust involved (if the child is still under age 18) is a bare trust and the property concerned is not settled property.

Immediate post-death interests and disabled person's interests lead to the trust property being treated as part of the beneficiary's own estate for inheritance tax purposes (IHTA 1984 s 49). The same obviously applies in relation to a bare trust. This is the position for the E Trust in the Example, and also for the C Trust; IHTA 1984 s 50 contains rules for ascertaining how much of the trust property (here the shares in X plc) is to be treated as underlying an annuity, which is an interest in possession and in this case an immediate post-death interest.

A bereaved minor's trust carries no inheritance tax consequences other than the charge on the deceased's estate itself – even on the death of the beneficiary under age 18 – unless some event is brought about as a result of which the terms of the trust no longer qualify as a bereaved minor's trust (without the bereaved minor having become absolutely entitled). In such an event inheritance tax would be charged under IHTA 1984 s 71B on the value affected at a rate determined by the time elapsed since (in effect) the deceased's death, using the table in IHTA 1984 s 70(6) (0.25% per quarter for the first ten years, 0.20% per quarter for the next ten years and so on). The F Trust is a bereaved minor's trust.

An age 18-to-25 trust, such as the D Trust in the Example, benefits from an equivalent exemption to the extent that capital is distributed (typically in exercise of a power or advancement) in the period up to the beneficiary's 18th birthday (or in fact, for technical reasons, before he reaches 18 and 3 months). Distributions from then on, including the absolute entitlement on his 25th birthday, or if the property leaves the age 18-to-25 regime on the beneficiary's death, will attract an inheritance tax charge under the special regime in IHTA 1984 s 71F. The rate is determined under a formula not dissimilar to that for relevant property trusts, involving establishing the effective rate on an assumed chargeable lifetime transfer and discounting this to 30% of Q fortieths of itself where Q is the number of fully elapsed quarters since the beneficiary's 18th birthday. Two particular features of this formula can be noted:

(i)   By definition only a maximum of seven quarters can have elapsed between the beneficiary's 18th and 25th birthdays; so, with the maximum lifetime rate of inheritance tax at 20%, and 30% of this therefore 6%, the maximum possible rate of tax under this formula is 4.2%;

(ii)   The factors that go to make up the assumed chargeable transfer are all determinable as at the death of the deceased — primarily the value of the trust property immediately after the death, and the deceased's chargeable transfers in the seven years before his death). None of them depends on the value of the trust property from time to time thereafter. In many cases where the deceased had not made inroads into his nil rate band in the seven years before his death, the rate of tax under s 71F at a beneficiary's 25th birthday can be foreseen to be 0% (or not significantly more) even when the beneficiary is still a baby at his parent's death, subject only to changes to the structure of the legislation in the meantime.

If the property leaves the age 18-to-25 trust regime for any other reason than its being distributed to or for the benefit of the beneficiary (including an absolute entitlement arising for him) by his 25th birthday, or his death under that age, then s 71G imposes the same 'flat rate per quarter' charge at that time as was noted above under s 71B for bereaved minors' trusts.

Question

Garth, a bachelor aged 45, was injured in a road accident some years ago and the Court awarded the sum of £50,000 compensation to be paid to him.

Garth created a settlement of this sum under which he was himself to receive the income for life, the capital upon his death being divisible amongst certain relatives.

The trust income for the year ended 5 April 2011 comprised:

		£
Building society interest (amounts received)		1,280
Taxed interest from government stocks (gross amounts)		660
National Savings Bank interest (investment account)		76
Rents receivable		4,739
Repairs and maintenance of rented property	329	
Insurance	205	(534)
Dividends from UK companies (amount received)		1,800

Trust expenses amounted to £450. There was a loss brought forward of £205 on the rented property.

In 2010/11 Garth's only personal income, other than non-taxable social security allowances, consisted of interest on National Savings Bank income bonds of £4,000 (paid gross).

(a)   Prepare a statement showing the trust income for 2010/11.

(b)   Compute Garth's personal tax position for 2010/11.

Answer

Garth — Trust Income

(a) *Garth's Trustees — Statement of Trust Income 2010/11*

	£	Gross £	Tax £
Rent receivable	4,739		
Less: Expenses	(534)		
Loss brought forward	(205)	4,000	
Savings income			
Building society interest			
(1,280 × 100/80)	1,600		320
Government stocks interest	660		132
NSB interest	76	2,336	
Dividends (1,800 + 200)		2,000	200
Total income of trust		8,336	652
Tax thereon:			
Non-savings income	4,000 @ 20%	800	
Non-dividend savings income	2,336 @ 20%	467	
Dividend income	2,000 @ 10%	200	1,467	1,467
	8,336		
of which tax payable by self-assessment is			815
Net income of trust treated as Garth's income		6,869	

(b) *Garth — Income tax liability 2010/11*

	£	Tax £
NSB interest	4,000	–
Trust dividend income	2,000	200
Other trust income (both savings and non-savings)	6,336	1,267
	12,336	1,467
Personal allowance	6,475	
	5,861	
Tax thereon:		
Dividend income	2,000 @ 10%	200	
Balance	3,861 @ 20%	772	972
		495
Non-repayable dividend tax credits		200
Repayment due		295

Explanatory Notes

Settlement in which settlor retains an interest

(1)   For income tax purposes, income from a settlement is treated as the settlor's income if he or his wife has retained an interest in the settlement (ITTOIA 2005 s 625).

Garth is therefore assessable on the trust income whether he receives it or not, since he was the settlor, and no relief is available for the trust expenses of £450. For further notes on settlements in which the settlor retains an interest, see **Example 35**.

ITTOIA 2005 ss 622–627 is part of the anti-avoidance legislation in ITTOIA 2005 Part 5 Chapter 5, which also provides, in ITTOIA 2005 ss 629, 631, that payments to unmarried minor children of the settlor are treated as the settlor's income (see **Example 42**).

(2)   Where a settlor retains an interest in a discretionary settlement, until 2005-06 the income was not liable to the trust rate or the dividend trust rate, but that exclusion was reversed when the results of HMRC's 'trust modernisation' project were enacted in FA 2006. Since then those rates apply, if the income must or may be accumulated or distributed at discretion, whether or not the trust is settlor-interested; but in the Example those rates do not apply because Garth has a life interest.

(3)   Special provisions apply for capital gains tax where a settlor retains an interest in a non-resident settlement — see **Example 51** for details.

(4)   ITTOIA 2005 s 685A gives statutory effect to a pre-existing practice of not taxing beneficiaries of settlor-interested settlements on discretionary income payments they receive from the trustees where the underlying income has already been taxed in the hands of the settlor. To the extent that it applies, the usual rules as to discretionary income payments by trustees (ITA 2007 ss 494–495 – the tax pool system) will not apply; instead the beneficiary (not being the settlor himself, but including the settlor's spouse or civil partner) who receives the discretionary annual payment is to be treated as receiving the sum with an additional rate (50%) tax credit, to the extent that the section applies to the income he receives. It applies only to a proportion of the discretionary annual payment corresponding to the proportion of the trustees' income (of current and previous years of assessment) that has been charged to income tax under ITTOIA 2005 s 619 in the hands of the settlor.

The tax which the beneficiary is treated as having paid is not repayable, and cannot be used to reduce a tax bill on other income. To prevent unintended changes in the beneficiary's liability on his other income (since trust income is generally charged before savings and/or dividend income) this notional income is treated as the highest part of his income.

Where the recipient of the annual payment is the settlor then the annual payment is not a taxable receipt in the settlor's hands, nor does it carry the additional rate credit that applies for other beneficiaries of a settlor-interested discretionary trust.

Gifts to charity

(5)   Where a UK resident trust that is caught by the anti-avoidance legislation of ITTOIA 2005 Part 5 Chapter 5 (see **note 1**) gives money to a charity, the amount taxable on the settlor is reduced by the amount (plus tax) given to the charity (ITTOIA 2005 ss 628, 630).

This means that the income given to the charity will be net of tax at the relevant rate applicable to the trustees, ie 50% for discretionary trusts and the basic, lower or dividend ordinary rate for interest in possession trusts. Where the trust's income exceeds the amount given to the charity, the amount given to the charity is treated as made rateably out of the trust's different sources of income (unless the trust stipulates that the charity should receive certain sources of income). Trust management expenses are similarly allocated between income that goes to the charity and the remainder of the trust income.

The rate of tax recoverable by the charity depends on the tax payable by the trust. Say a trust gives a charity £500 out of the trustees' bank interest. If the trust is a discretionary trust with income (after management expenses) of £10,000, the interest would be net of 50% tax, so that the tax thereon would be (500 × 50/50 =) £500. The charity would receive £500 from the trustees plus a tax refund of £333, making £1,000 in all. If the trust is an interest in possession trust, the tax on the gift of £500 would be (500 × 20/80 =) £125. The charity would receive £500 from the trustees plus a tax refund of £125, making a total of £625.

(6)   For the purpose of the anti-avoidance provisions mentioned in note 1, an interest free or low interest rate loan is an 'arrangement' that, if made with any element of bounty, is within the definition of settlement, so that income from the investment of such a loan is capable of being treated as the settlor's income. The protection of ITTOIA 2005 ss 628, 630 (see **explanatory note 5** above) applies where the loan is made to a charity.

Self-assessment

(7)   See **Example 47 explanatory note 7** for the entries on self-assessment returns in relation to trusts in which the settlor retains an interest. HMRC Helpsheet 270 contains detailed information on how to decide whether an interest has been retained and also relating to parental settlements on minor children (as to which see **Example 64**). Where gifts or loans are made to charity as outlined in **notes 5 and 6** above, the income does not have to be included in the settlor's self-assessment return.

Settlor-interested trusts

(8)   A settlement may be made by a settlor on himself for a number of reasons. In this Example Garth may well have made the settlement so that trustees can administer his assets on his behalf whilst he is suffering from a mental or physical disability. Other reasons for such settlements would include:

(a)   A couple with no children, but each having relatives, wishing to ensure that each set of relatives obtained the appropriate share of their respective estates (rather than the whole devolving upon the relatives of the spouse/civil partner who died last as could occur in intestacy).

(b)   To provide certainty for the next generation(s) by creating a settlement under which each of husband and wife would receive the income during their lifetime, their children having the knowledge that the destination of the capital could not be altered by such events as the remarriage of a widow/widower.

(c)   A couple with children from different relationships who wish to ensure that their own offspring obtain the appropriate share of their respective estates (removing the possibility that the destination of the capital could be altered after their own deaths, whilst providing income for their co-habitant in the meantime).

Practical consequences

(9)   Until FA 2006, tax on the income of a settlor-interested trust was collected primarily from the settlor, except so far as it was deducted at source from income payable to the trustees or charged on them at basic rate as persons in receipt of the income. In particular the trustees were not liable to pay tax on it at rates higher than the basic rate, even in the case of a discretionary or accumulation trust. If the settlor was a higher rate taxpayer he would pay the additional tax, and having done so he was (and still remains) entitled to recover the tax so paid from the trustees (ITTOIA 2005 s 646).

This system was changed by FA 2006 s 89, which also provided for the income taxed on the settlor to retain its original character (allowing him the benefit of the different rates applicable to different types of underlying income). If the trust is of a discretionary or accumulation type, the trustees must pay the trust rate (now 50%), or the dividend trust rate (now 42.5%); the settlor receives a corresponding tax credit, and since the 50% rate is only applicable to individuals whose income exceeds £150,000 it will often now be the case that the settlor is entitled to a refund of part of the tax suffered by the trustees. If the trust confers an interest in possession then the trustees remain liable only at the basic rate, so the chance of the settlor having additional tax to pay as a result of the income being deemed to be his is greater.

The pre- and post-election Budgets in 2010 proposed that the settlor's right to repayment from the trustees of additional tax for which he found himself liable under these provisions should be matched by an obligation on him to refund to the trustees any tax refund that he obtains through being liable at a lower rate than that paid by the trustees (hitherto such an obligation only arose where his refund was due to some allowance or relief); it is likely that the legislation to implement this will be included in the promised autumn 2010 Finance Bill.

Trustees

Trustees must now include all of the trust income on the trust and estate return (SA900). As well as ticking box 8.12 to report that the trust is settlor-interested, they also need in the case of a discretionary or accumulation trust to tick box 8.16.

Where discretionary income payments are made to the settlor, they do not form part of his income (ITTOIA 2005 s 685A(5)) and do not need to be disclosed on the SA900. Where they are made to some beneficiary other than the settlor, s 685A takes them outside the usual tax pool arrangements (see **explanatory note 4** above), and the tax credit they carry is not repayable; so trustees do not need to gross up the payments or account for additional tax to cover the credit. Such payments should therefore not be shown under Q14 in the SA900 – they should be reported instead in the 'Additional information' box 21.11.

Where the settlement is partly settlor-interested and partly not, it is necessary to allocate discretionary payments between the settlor-interested part and the non-settlor-interested part. Rather than try to match them to the underlying income from which they were paid, ITTOIA 2005 s 685A(2) provides for a statutory apportionment. The amount of the discretionary payments from the settlor-interested part is the same proportion of the total discretionary payments as the proportion of total income that is chargeable on the settlor.

So, for Example, if the settlor's interest extends only to 30% of the trust fund and the trustees' total income is £5,000, £1,500 is chargeable on the settlor; if the trustees make discretionary payments to other beneficiaries of £2,000, then the entry in box 21.11 of form SA900 (additional information) is:

2,000 × (1,500/5000) = 600

The difference (2,000 – 600 = 1,400) goes in Q14 as normal.

Settlor

The SA107 has a separate section for settlor income (boxes 7 to 15). Only the net amount of taxed payments is to be included; there are separate boxes for savings, dividend and other income, in each case where taxed in the trustees' hands at the basic or trust rates or their dividend equivalents, as well as for income where no tax has been suffered/deducted.

Beneficiaries other than the settlor

As seen in **explanatory note 4**, in the hands of a beneficiary other than the settlor the 50% tax credit attaching to discretionary payments from a settlor-interested settlement is not repayable and is dealt with outside the trustees' tax pool. Instead, tax treated as having been deducted is notional tax, which is ring-fenced – it cannot be set sideways against any other income of the beneficiary, and cannot be repaid. Whereas discretionary receipts dealt with through the tax pool system are to be shown on a net basis in box 1 on the SA107 (supplementary pages for trusts etc), those from a settlor-interested trust are shown on a gross basis in box 2; beneficiary returns the actual amount they receive – there is no grossing up. So whatever the beneficiary's marginal rate, the notional tax covers their liability on that income – if they are anything other than a top rate taxpayer, part of the notional tax will appear to be lost. This reflects the policy that the changed system brought in by FA 2006 was as to mechanics not liability; when it was realised that the new system was capable of pushing other income into a higher tax bracket. Retrospective changes were introduced by FA 2008 to make clear that the payment is treated as the highest part of the beneficiary's income (as to which see ITA 2007 s 1012 for the priority between different provisions which specify the same thing). Unless the legislation is further amended, however, the fact of including such payments in the beneficiary's income at all (which, by Inland Revenue practice, it was not before 2006) is capable of leading to the restriction or loss of his personal allowance if it takes his total income over £100,000, or to the restriction of relief for pension contributions if it takes it over the planned thresholds of £130,000 or £150,000.

Interest on government stocks

(10)   Garth's trustees could make an election to receive interest on the government stocks gross (see **Example 44 explanatory note 4** for details). If this was done in relation to interest receivable from 2010/11, tax would not be payable on the 2010/11 interest until 31 January 2012, but the tax would be included in payments on account for later years, unless covered by the de minimis limits (now £1,000, see **Example 44, explanatory note 5**).

Question

The Colenso Trust was created by Charles in 1985. Under the terms of the trust deed the trustees have discretionary power to pay income to any of the named beneficiaries and to accumulate any income that is not so applied.

Charles has created seven other settlements (Trusts T to Z) at different times before and after the Colenso Trust; except as stated below, all of them were made since 6 June 1978, and continued in existence throughout 2010/11:

- Trust T, under which Charles has a vested remainder interest, has had UK resident trustees at all material times;

- Trust U was wound up in 2007 after the FA 2006 changes to inheritance tax;

- Trust V was made offshore in 1970 but the trustees have been UK resident continuously since 1992 and the trust fund is now held and administered for exclusively charitable purposes;

- Trust W (with UK trustees) came to an end when the life tenant died on 30 September 2010;

- Trust X (with non-UK trustees) holds nothing but a continuing life assurance policy on Charles's life, and thus produces no income or chargeable gains;

- Trust Y (with UK trustees) was formed on 10 March 2011 when Charles took out a new life assurance policy on his life written in trust on a contingent basis; and

- Trust Z has UK trustees and the primary beneficiary is disabled, with a vulnerable person election in force (see **Example 45 explanatory note 4**).

The income and expenses of the trustees of the Colenso Trust for the year ended 5 April 2011 were as follows:

Income

	£
Dividends from UK companies (amount received)	2,520
Rent of property let unfurnished	2,850
Interest on National Savings investment account	465

Expenses

		£
Property expenses	— ground rent	34
	— repairs	646
Accountancy fees		588

The income tax liability of the trust for 2009/10 amounted to £1,696, of which tax credits covered £546. In addition the trustees had made payments on account of £486 on each of 31 January 2010 and 31 July 2010.

The trustees had a tax pool brought forward at 6 April 2010 of £326, and no brought forward allowable losses. During the year the trustees made sales of quoted shares showing the following results after deducting base values and expenses of sale:

- 4 May 2010 – gain £700

- 18 May 2010 – loss £1,500

- 25 August 2010 – gain £2,000

- 19 November 2010 – gain £2,310

- 10 January 2011 – loss £200.

One of the beneficiaries of the trust is Clery, a widower who was born in 1926.

The trustees paid £4,200 to Clery out of the trust income in 2010/11.

His other income for that year was a state pension of £4,415 and income from purchased life annuities totalling £20,000 gross, of which the capital content was £16,000.

(a)   Prepare a statement of income and gains for the Colenso Trust for 2010/11.

(b)   Compute the tax pool to carry forward to 2011/12 or s 496 tax payable.

(c)   Show the tax payable by the trustees under self-assessment.

(d)   Calculate Clery's repayment of income tax for 2010/11.

Answer

The Colenso Trust

(a) *Statement of trust income and gains 2010/11*

			£	Gross £	Tax £
Rent receivable			2,850		
Less: expenses			680	2,170	
Savings income					
NSB interest				465	
Dividends (2,520 + 280)				2,800	280
Total income of trust				5,435	280
Tax thereon:					
On amount equal to grossed up trust expenses (paid out of dividend income and not chargeable at dividend trust rate)					
(588 × 100/90) =	653	@ 10%	65		
On balance of dividends at dividend trust rate					
(2,800 – 653)	2,147	@ 42.5%	912		
On standard rate band (see **explanatory note 1**)	200	@ 20%	40		
On remaining income at trust rate	2,435	@ 50%	1,218		
	5,435		2,235		2,235
Of which tax payable by self-assessment is					1,955
Used to pay trust expenses			588	2,823	
Net income of trust				2,612	

Capital gains:

	6.4.2010 – 22.7.2010 £	23.7.2010 – 5.4.2011 £	Tax £
Chargeable gains	700	4,310	
Allowable losses	(1,500)	(200)	
Use pre-23.7.2010 losses most beneficially	1,500	(1,500)	
	700	2,610	
Use annual exemption most beneficially	–	(1,263)	
Liable @ 18%	700		126
Liable @ 28%		1,347	377
			503

(b)   *Tax pool and position under ITA 2007 ss 496–498*

		£
Unutilised tax brought forward at 6 April 2010		326
Tax already accounted for by trustees at:		
Standard rate	200	
Trust rate	654	
Dividend trust rate, net of tax credits (2,147 @ 32.5%)	698	
		1,552
		1,878

Tax on payments made out of income to Clery:

$$4,200 \times \frac{50}{50}$$

	£
	4,200
Tax payable under ss 496–498	2,322
Tax pool exhausted so amount to carry forward to 2011/12	£0

(c)   *Tax payable by trustees under self-assessment (POA — payment on account)*

		£	£	Tax payable £	Re 2010/11 £
31.1.10	1st POA 2009/10			486	
31.7.10	2nd POA 2009/10			486	
31.1.11	Balancing payment 20098/10:				
	Tax due (1,696 – tax credits 546)	1,150			
	Less POAs	972	178		
	1st POA 2010/11 (½ × 1,150)		575	753	575
31.7.11	2nd POA 2010/11			575	575
31.1.12	Balancing payment 2010/11:				
	Income tax as in (a)	2,235			
	ss 496–498 liability as in (b)	2,322			
	Capital gains tax as in (a)	503			
	Total liability	5,060			
	Less tax credits	280			
	Tax due	4,780			
	Less POAs	1,150	3,630		3,630
	1st POA 2011/12 ½ × (4,780 – CGT 503)		2,138	5,768	
	Total tax paid directly for 2010/11				4,780
31.7.12	2nd POA 2011/12			2,138	

(d) *Clery's income tax repayment claim 2010/11*

			£	Tax £
Trust income $£4,200 \times \dfrac{100}{50}$			8,400	4,200
State pension			4,415	
Savings income:				
Purchased life annuities (income element)			4,000	800
			16,815	5,000
Age allowance (over 75)			9,640	
			7,175	
Tax payable thereon:				
On non-savings income	3,175	@ 20%	635	
On savings income	4,000	@ 20%	800	1,435
Repayment due				3,565

Explanatory Notes

Income tax rates applicable to trusts

(1) For 2010/11 the income of accumulation and discretionary trusts is liable to tax at the newly-increased dividend trust rate of 42.5% if it is dividend income (see **Example 42** for details) and otherwise at the trust rate of 50% (ITA 2007 s 9).

Under ITA 2007 s 491, the first £1,000 of relevant income will generally not be charged at the trust rate, but will instead be charged at the income tax rate appropriate to the type of income. Therefore, if payments are received net of tax (for Example, building society interest) up to the limit of the standard rate band, then the trustees will have no further tax to pay.

However, that £1,000 standard rate band is restricted by ITA 2007 s 492 where a settlor has made more than one settlement that is in existence at any time during the tax year in question. The reference to £1,000 is replaced by an amount obtained by dividing £1,000 by the number of settlements made by the same settlor, or by £200 if there are more than five other current settlements such that the quotient would be less than £200. For this purpose a settlement will be counted even if:

- its period of existence during the tax year in question does not overlap with that of the subject settlement or of another settlement made by the same settlor (where one or more settlements are made or terminated during the tax year);

- its trustees are not UK resident;

- it is not a discretionary or accumulation trust;

- it does not have any income in the tax year;

- a vulnerable person election is in force for it;

- it is a settlor-interested trust; or even

- (anomalously since the trust rate itself does not apply to charitable trusts) it subsists for charitable purposes only. HMRC have at least stated that "Ordinary donations to third party charities would not be counted as separate settlements when considering the amount of standard rate band due" (see TSEM3016a).

On this basis all of Charles's other settlements in the Example, except for Trust U which had come to an end before 2010/11, are taken into account for restricting the standard rate band of the Colenso Trust; division of the basic £1,000 by 7 (six other trusts plus the Colenso Trust) produces a figure below £200 so the Colenso Trust's standard rate band is £200.

The section sets out the position where there is more than one settlor of a settlement, and in such circumstances the amount is the amount obtained in relation to the settlor who had made the largest number of current settlements.

HMRC have confirmed that the new standard rate band (restricted as relevant) will apply to trust income *net* of trust management expenses.

Although the management expenses are deducted from the trust income taxed at the lowest rate first, the standard rate band will apply in the order – basic rate income at 20% first, followed by dividends at 10%.

Apart from the standard rate band explained above, trustees are liable to tax at the trust rate or dividend trust rate on income as the case may be if:

(a)   the income is to be accumulated or payable at the discretion of the trustees, and

(b)   it exceeds the trust expenses paid out of income, grossed up at the appropriate rate of tax. The expenses are treated as coming first out of dividends and other income carrying a non-repayable tax credit, then out of dividends from abroad, then out of non-dividend savings income, then out of non-savings income (see ITA 2007 ss 486-486 and **Example 43 note 10**). The grossing up rate for the expenses is 10% for dividend income, 20% basic rate for non-dividend savings income and for non-savings income. The expenses are not allowable deductions for basic or for dividend ordinary rate tax, so tax is charged on an equivalent amount of income at the appropriate rate (10% in this Example).

(2)   See **Example 48** for an illustration of a trust liable at the trust rate where there is a non-UK resident beneficiary.

(3)   In this Example, it may be possible to agree that some of the accountancy fees relate to the property income, rather than treating them as general trust expenses, thereby reducing the assessable income and the overall tax liability of the trust.

Self-assessment returns

(4)   The HMRC Trusts, Settlements and Estates Manual states in Section TSEM1405 that a new trust that does not have any income or gains does not have to notify them of the existence of the trust (though this does not affect the trust from being taken into account for the restriction of the standard rate band for other settlements as in **explanatory note 1** above). Existing trusts which do not have any income or gains may ask HMRC to close the trust's record. The trustees are, of course, obliged to notify HMRC by 5 October following the relevant tax year, in the same way as individuals, if they do have income and/or gains chargeable to tax (TMA 1970 s 7).

(5)   Where a self-assessment return is required, all types of trusts and estates complete the same return (SA 900).

Revised filing dates for paper and online self-assessment returns

(6)   **Paper substitutes for SA returns**

Computer generated substitute versions of the SA return are no longer to be approved or accepted for:

SA Individual Returns – (SA100 series) (but see below as to limited cases where online filing is not yet possible);

SA Trust Returns – (SA900 series).

For the time being, HMRC will continue to accept approved substitutes for the remaining SA Returns (including those for trustees of registered pension schemes) and for all other forms they currently approve substitutes for.

Changes to SA filing dates

Anyone who is required to file a self-assessment tax return will have:

- until 31 October to do so, if they choose to send a paper return; or

- until the following 31 January if they file online.

This allows an additional three months for online filing compared with paper.

The filing obligation is satisfied by the first return received by HMRC and this also triggers any late filing penalty. So if, for Example, a paper 2008/09 return is filed after 31 October 2009, it is not then possible to avoid a late filing penalty by filing the return online.

In addition, in certain other cases, HMRC will allow extra time beyond the statutory deadline of 31 October – until 31 January – for paper filing without incurring a penalty. These include:

- Trustees of Registered Pension Schemes; and

- Certain categories of SA taxpayers (see below) for whom facilities to file online are not yet available.

In the event that there are problems with HMRC systems close to the filing deadline, taxpayers will not be penalised for late submission of a return due to such problems provided that they, or their agent, file within a reasonable period once the service is restored.

FA 2007 s 88(1F) – if a notice is given after 31 July the return must be submitted during the period of three months beginning with the date of the notice (for paper returns) or on or before 31 January (for online returns).

FA 2007 s 88(1G) – if a notice is given after 31 October the return (whether paper return or electronic) must be submitted within three months from the date of the notice.

SA taxpayers who are unable to file online

Those SA taxpayers who do not have the choice of online filing because of current limitations of HMRC systems (see http://www.hmrc.gov.uk/carter/sa-exclusions.htm), will be allowed to file on paper (including computer generated paper output provided it is identical to the official HMRC return) up to 31 January, without incurring any penalty that might otherwise be due for paper filing after 31 October.

Interest in possession trusts are not required to show any *taxed* income in the return, except where accrued income relief is due on the income. (Accrued income *charges* are untaxed income and must be shown.) The trustees will still, however, need to know the overall tax position in order to be able to ascertain the income payable to the life tenant to be shown on form R185 (trust income) (see **note 8**). The returns for discretionary trusts show both taxed and untaxed income and the amount of the unused tax pool (if any) brought forward from the previous year. For both types of trust, supplementary pages have to be completed where income arises from a trade, partnership, land and property or from abroad, or where there are capital gains, or where the trust is non-resident or dual resident.

(7) To minimise administration burdens, HMRC have a scheme under which trustees responsible for at least 50 trusts dealt with in a single tax office may receive a single notice calling for trust returns and may make a single declaration when submitting a batch of returns. Trustees wishing to operate the scheme must make a written application. More information can be found in the HMRC Trusts, Settlements and Estates Manual at TSEM 3052.

Changes to self-assessment payments on account limits

(8)   SI 1996/1654 – Income Tax (Payments on Account) Regulations 1996 was amended by SI 2008/838 to raise the figure at regulation 3 from £500 to £1,000 with effect for2009/10 and later years.

The first payments on account affected were those for 2009/10 due in January 2010 and July 2010.

Trusts in which settlor retains an interest

(9)   Where the settlor retains an interest in the trust, all income (other than certain income derived from charitable gifts and loans — see **Example 46 explanatory notes 5 and 6**), *before* deducting expenses, is taxable on the settlor. The amount included on the trust pages of the settlor's personal tax return depends on whether the settlor also has an absolute entitlement to income.

Where the settlor does have an absolute entitlement, the amounts of income will be entered on the trust pages of the settlor's return net of management expenses. The management expenses must, however, also be treated as his income, so they have to be entered as 'other income' under Question 13 in the main part of the return, grossed up by the appropriate tax rate (dividend rate or basic rate according to the income used to meet the expenses). Exceptionally, tax may not have been deducted from the income at all, for Example if the trustees are non-resident. Even if the expenses are grossed up at the dividend rate, the rate of tax payable on them by the settlor will be the basic rate.

If the settlor is not absolutely entitled to income, then the amounts entered in the trust pages of the return will be the whole of the trust income *before* management expenses.

See HMRC Help Sheet 270 for further details.

Forms R185 and beneficiaries' own tax returns

(10)   It is advisable for trustees to compute the overall tax position of the trust as quickly as possible after 5 April each year to comply with their responsibilities under self-assessment.

Where the beneficiary is absolutely entitled to the income it will be essential to do so, in order that the R185 may be completed and forwarded to the beneficiary in plenty of time for him to complete his own self-assessment return or to claim a repayment as the case may be (especially as the beneficiary may plan to submit his tax return on paper, with therefore three months shorter time limit than the trustees face if filing online – see **explanatory note 6** above). For such beneficiaries, if all the income is taxed at source and there are no expenses, it is usual to mandate the income directly to the beneficiary and to include the income in the beneficiary's return as if it was his own income. In the case of a bare trust, ie where the beneficiary has an absolute right to both income and capital, all of the trust income is deemed to be that of the beneficiary and entered as such on the beneficiary's tax return. Trustees of bare trusts are not required to send trust returns but may, if they wish, send a trust return of the trust income, but not capital gains. This does not affect the beneficiary's liability to make his own returns.

Income paid out to discretionary beneficiaries

(11)   Under ITA 2007 ss 496–498, trustees are required to account for tax at the 50% trust rate on income paid out in exercise of their discretion to beneficiaries, and the beneficiaries will be given form R185 showing the income as non-savings income with tax deducted at 50%. The tax suffered is available for repayment, as illustrated in the Example. (Different rules apply if the trust is settlor-interested, see **Example 46 explanatory note 9**.)

Tax does not have to be accounted for under ss 496–498 on capital payments, nor on payments of accumulated income that have become part of capital. If, however, the payment is advanced in such a way that it becomes income in the hands of the beneficiary, ss 496–498 applies. For Example where trustees are empowered to make payments to bring a beneficiary's income up to a certain level, such payments will be income whether paid out of current or accumulated income or capital (but see **Example 44 explanatory note 2** as to annuities paid wholly or partly out of trust capital)..

The trustees can reduce the tax to be accounted for under ss 496–498 by the following (excluding any tax on income that has been used to cover trust expenses (see **note 1(b)**):

(i) Tax paid on income liable to the trust rate, including tax deducted at source.

(ii) The excess of the tax paid at the dividend trust rate on distributions and dividend type income over the dividend ordinary rate.

(iii) The whole of the tax paid at the dividend trust rate on dividends from abroad.

(iv) Any pool of unused tax brought forward at 5 April 1999 (see **note 11**).

(v) Tax at the basic or lower rate on the first £1,000 (or lower limit as in **explanatory note 1**) of trust income.

(12) If a beneficiary of a discretionary trust has not received a form R185, he should gross up the income received for tax deducted at 50%. If there is any doubt that part of the payment received is not income, or as to whether it was paid from a settlor-interested trust (see **Example 46 explanatory note 4**), the amount should be shown on his personal return as a provisional figure with a tick in box 23.2 and the reason for the figure being provisional should be shown in the additional information box at 23.5. The beneficiary should not delay submitting his return because of the failure of the trustees to provide a form R185.

Sections 496–498 tax pool

(13) In many instances, the pool of tax under ss 496–498 will exceed the amount that is due, so no amount will be payable. Furthermore tax could be paid on income that is used to cover non-deductible expenses (see **Example 48**). From 6 April 1999, however, none of the tax credits on dividends are included in the tax pool, whereas the payments out of income will still have repayable tax of 50% (34% prior to 5 April 2004, or 40% between then and 5 April 2010) deducted. Except to the extent that there is an unused pool of tax brought forward, this will restrict the maximum payment out of dividend income to 50% of the net dividend, giving a ss 496–498 liability of 50% of the net dividend (see **Example 45 explanatory note 2** and **Example 48 explanatory note 9** for illustrations).

Note that the unused pool brought forward at 6 April 1999 will include tax credits on any pre 6 April 1999 dividends that have not been paid out to beneficiaries, and those credits remain available to cover ss 496–498 tax on discretionary payments after 5 April 1999.

(14) The ss 496–498 tax payable is added to the tax due under self-assessment and is accounted for in the balancing payment. It also counts, however, in the calculation of the payments on account for the following year. Thus it can increase the tax payable on 31 January following the end of the tax year by 150% of the ss 496–498 liability.

The trustees may not intend to make distributions to beneficiaries in the following tax year and may be tempted to apply to reduce the payments on account by the amount of the ss 496–498 tax. Payments on account are, however, compared with the actual tax due for the subsequent year, and if the reduced payment is below the actual liability for that year, interest is payable on the difference (restricted to the amount of the reduction). It does not matter that the claim to reduce the payments on account was in respect of ss 496–498 tax and the additional liability arises because of an increase in tax because of increased income, tax rate increases, reduced expenses or for any other reason.

Capital gains tax

(15) A trust with UK resident trustees is liable to capital gains tax on the trustees' chargeable gains less allowable losses (including those brought forward from earlier years) so far as required to reduce the total gains to the level of the available annual exempt amount, and the annual exemption itself (as to which see **explanatory note 16** below).

The rate at which that net amount is charged depends, in 2010/11, on the dates on which the gains were realised during the tax year: for the first time (and still subject to enactment at the time of writing – provisions are included in clause 2 and Sch 1 of the July 2010 Finance Bill) a change to the rate of capital gains tax has been made to take effect other than for the tax year as a whole. Part of the amount may therefore, in this transitional year, be charged at one rate and part at another.

The rate applicable to gains realised before 23 June 2010 is 18%; that applicable to all gains realised by trustees or personal representatives on or after that date is 28%. (For individuals the 28% rate will apply only to the extent that the gains, taken as the top slice of the individual's taxable income after personal allowance, exceed the basic rate limit.) It is provided that allowable losses, and the annual exempt amount, may be set against gains in the way that is most beneficial to the taxpayer, as illustrated in **part (a)** of the Example.

In this context a reminder is apposite that where a transaction involves a contractual commitment to sell being undertaken other than at the same time as the sale is completed, it is the date of the contract (or, in the case of a conditional contract including one granting an option, the date on which the sale become unconditional or the option is exercised) which is the date of the disposal (TCGA 1992 s 28).

A number of former reliefs — taper relief, indexation allowance (other than for companies), the "kink test" alternative to 31 March 1982 valuation for assets held at that date, and the halving of deferred gains relating to certain acquisitions from someone who held the asset at that date — were abolished with effect for 2008/09 onwards and remain unavailable despite the upward adjustment of capital gains tax rates. Other reliefs such as main residence relief, hold-over relief (for business assets or where there is an interaction with inheritance tax), and business asset roll-over relief, remain available subject to the rules applicable to them respectively.

The amount due is payable on 31 January following the tax year, but is not included in the calculation of payments on account for the following year, nor is it available for inclusion in the tax pool for ss 496–498 liability.

(16)   The basic annual exempt amount for a trust is one half of that applicable to individuals (half of £10,100 for 2010/11 = £5,050). However, in the same way as the £1,000 standard rate band for income of a discretionary or accumulation trust (see **explanatory note 1** above), this basic trust exemption is diluted where the settlor has created other trusts which still continue; but the rules for this dilution are different in the capital gains tax context.

If the subject settlement has UK resident trustees, any other trust made by the same settlor must be counted in any tax year (whether or not it is settlor-interested) if:

*   both it and the subject settlement were made after 6 June 1978 (in whatever order);

*   it is not a disabled person's trust;

*   its trustees were UK resident at some point during the tax year;

*   it existed at some point during the tax year (this is not stated explicitly, but if a trust has come to an end through absolute entitlement its property is not settled property (TCGA 1992 s 60), and the trust is therefore not a "settlement" in the tax year at all); and

*   some at least of its settled property is held other than for charitable purposes or for the purposes of a registered pension scheme or certain other related types of pension scheme.

If there are any other trusts meeting those criteria as well as the subject settlement, the basic annual exempt amount (half that of an individual) is divided between them equally (irrespective of whether they have any chargeable gains in that tax year), subject to a minimum exemption equal to one-tenth of the amount available to individuals, ie £1,010 for 2010/11.

In this Example Trusts T, W and X, as well as the Colenso Trust, meet those criteria, so each has an annual exemption for 2010/11 of one quarter of the basic £5,050 trust exemption, or £1,262.50. As to the others:

*   Trust U is not counted because it had been wound up before 2010/11.

*   Trust V is not counted both because it was made before 1978 and because its property is held for exclusively charitable purposes.

*   Trust Y is not counted because its trustees were not UK resident at any time during 2010/11.

- Trust Z is less immediately clear since the tests for a qualifying trust for a vulnerable beneficiary (FA 2005 s 34(2)) are slightly different from those for a disabled person's trust for the purposes of the annual exemption (TCGA 1992 Sch 1 para 1(1), as to which see **Example 50 part B**); but on analysis if a trust is eligible for a vulnerable beneficiary election then it will usually be a disabled person's trust for the purpose of the annual exemption. (The only ways in which the annual exemption test is narrower concerns trustees' powers that may be disregarded in applying the basic tests, cf s 34(3), (4) and para 1(2); or seemingly if the trust can come to an end during the disabled beneficiary's lifetime.) It is assumed here that Trust Z is not affected by those distinctions, and it is therefore also not counted for the purpose of diluting the annual exemption of the Colenso Trust.

If there is more than one settlor of the subject trust, dilution will occur by reference to whichever of those settlors made the largest number of other trusts meeting the criteria described, subject again to the minimum exemption (for 2010/11) of £1,010.

Question

A trust was established on 6 April 1991. The trust deed stipulates that after paying an annuity of £6,500 per annum to the settlor's sister, the remaining income of each year is to be distributed or accumulated as the trustees deem fit.

The assets placed into the trust consisted of certain properties let unfurnished on landlord's repairing short leases, and cash. The latter was placed on bank deposit and used to fund investments in government securities and quoted shares.

At 6 April 2009 the pool of unutilised tax brought forward under ITA 2007 ss 496–498 was £3,750.

The receipts and payments of the trust for 2009/10 and 2010/11 were as follows:

	2009/10 £	2010/11 £
Receipts		
Rents receivable	11,300	11,300
Premium received on granting of 21 year lease	–	10,000
Interest on £10,000 9% Government Stock (gross amount)	900	900
Bank interest received (see below)	1,400	1,500
Dividends from quoted UK companies (including tax credits)	3,200	2,762
Payments		
Trustees' expenses properly chargeable to income	405	450
Trustees' expenses re investment advice	–	100
Loan interest (see below)	200	550
Repairs to the let properties	100	400
Annuity to settlor's sister (gross amount)	6,500	6,500
Discretionary payments of cash from the trust income:		
to A, who is resident in the UK	3,366	–
to B, who is neither resident nor ordinarily resident in the UK	–	3,700

The amounts stated in respect of bank interest received are the gross amounts. The interest was received net of tax. The loan was obtained to finance an extension to one of the let properties. Interest on the 9% Government Stock, which is received net of 20% tax, is exempt from tax in the hands of a non-resident. The trustees' expenses for investment advice have been charged to income by authority of the trust deed.

For 2008/09, the amount of income tax paid on account equalled the liability for the year of £4,208.

Calculate:

(1) The income of the trust for 2009/10 and 2010/11, showing any liability in respect of income chargeable at special trust rates under ITA 2007 s 479, and the due dates of payment of tax.

(2) The income available for distribution to discretionary beneficiaries for 2009/10 and 2010/11 (individually).

(3) The trust's position under ITA 2007 ss 496–498 at the end of 2010/11.

(4) Any income tax that may be reclaimable by the non-UK resident beneficiary in respect of the discretionary payment made to him.

Note:

Ignore capital gains tax, and interest on tax or tax refunds.

Answer

(1) Statement of trust income

2009/10

			Gross £	Tax deducted or credited £
Property income (see **explanatory note 6**)			11,000	
Savings income				
Interest on Government Stock			900	180
Bank interest			1,400	280
Dividends			3,200	320
			16,500	780
Less: Charges (annuity)			6,500	
Net total income of trust			10,000	
Tax thereon:				
On amount equal to grossed up trust expenses, excluding those for investment advice (405 × 100/90) =	450	@ 10%	45	
On £1,000 of income at standard rate under ITA 2007 s 491 (20% on property income)	1,000	@ 20%	200	
On dividend income not used for expenses, at dividend trust rate				
(3,200 – 450)	2,750	@ 32.5%	894	
On balance at trust rate	5,800	@ 40%	2,320	
	10,000			
Tax deducted from annuity	6,500	@ 20%	1,300	
Total income tax due			4,759	4,759
Of which tax payable by self-assessment is				3,979

Amounts of income tax payable by trustees direct to HMRC under self-assessment for 2009/10 and payments on account for 2010/11 are as follows:

		£	£
31 January 2010:			
½ × 4,208			2,104
31 July 2010:			
½ × 4,208			2,104
31 January 2011:			
Total income tax payable for 2009/10		4,759	
Less: Payments on account	4,208		
Tax/tax credits at source	780	4,988	
		(229)	(229)
			3,979
First payment on account for 2010/11 (½ × 3,979)		1,990	

Total amount payable		1,761
31 July 2011:		
Second payment on account for 2010/11 (see **explanatory note 6**)		1,989

2010/11

		Gross	Tax deducted or credited
		£	£
Property income (see **explanatory note 6**)		16,350	
Savings income			
Interest on Government Stock		900	180
Bank interest		1,500	300
Dividends		2,762	276
		21,512	756
Less: Charges (annuity)		6,500	
Net total income of trust		15,012	
Tax thereon:			
On amount equal to grossed up trust expenses, excluding those for investment advice (450 × 100/90) =	500 @ 10%	50	
On lease premium (see **explanatory note 6**)	6,000 @ 20%	1,200	
On £1,000 of income at standard rate under ITA 2007 s 491 (20% on property income)	1,000 @ 20%	200	
On dividend income at dividend trust rate (2,762 – 500)	2,262 @ 42.5%	961	
On balance at trust rate	5,250 @ 50%	2,625	
	15,012		
Tax deducted from annuity	6,500 @ 20%	1,300	
Total income tax due		6,336	6,336
Of which tax payable by self-assessment is			5,580

Amounts of income tax payable by trustees direct to HMRC under self-assessment for 2010/11 and payments on account for 2011/12 are as follows:

		£	£
31 January 2011:			
As above ½ × 3,979			1,990
31 July 2011:			
½ × 3,979			1,989
31 January 2012:			
Total income tax payable for 2010/11		6,336	
Less: Payments on account	3,979		
Tax/tax credits at source	756	4,735	
		1,601	1,601
			5,580
First payment on account for 2011/12 (½ × 5,580) (see **explanatory note 13**)		2,790	
Total amount payable		4,391	
31 July 2012:			

Second payment on account for 2011/12 (see **explanatory notes 6 and 13**)	2,790	

(2) Income available for distribution to discretionary beneficiaries

		2009/10 £		2010/11 £
Trust income (excluding lease premium) after annuity and expenses		9,550*		8,512**
Less: Tax at Standard Rate (20%) under ITA 2007 s 491	200		200	
Tax at trust rate per part (1)	2,320		2,625	
Tax at dividend trust rate per part (1)	894		961	
Trustees' expenses for investment advice (see **explanatory note 7**)	–	3,414	100	3,886
Available for beneficiaries		6,136		4,626
Amount actually distributed was		£3,366		£3,700
Leaving undistributed income of		£2,770		£926

*£10,000 total income net of annuity as at part (1), less expenses £450 (grossed up with dividend tax credit for consistency).

£15,012 total income net of annuity as at part (1), less lease premium (capital) £6,000 and expenses £500 (gross equivalent as before). Note that in so far as the amount shown as available to the beneficiaries includes dividend income, it cannot all be distributed without the trustees incurring a further tax liability, except to the extent that there is unutilised tax brought forward (see **explanatory note 9).

(3) Trust's position under ITA 2007 ss 496–498 at end of 2010/11

		2009/10 £		2010/11 £
Tax at 40% on amounts paid at trustees' discretion to beneficiaries:				
$£3,366 \times \dfrac{40}{60}$		2,244		
Tax at 50% on amounts paid at trustees' discretion to beneficiaries:				
$£3,700 \times \dfrac{40}{60}$				3,700
Less: Tax already accounted for by trustees:				
On trust income charged at standard rate under FA 2005 s 14		200		200
on trust income chargeable under ITA 2007 s 479 –				
at trust rate 40%		2,320		
at trust rate 50%				2,625
at dividend trust rate excluding non-repayable tax credits				
(2,750 @ 22.5%)		619		
(2,262 @ 32.5%)				735
Unutilised tax b/f		3,750		4,645
		6,889		8,205

		2009/10		2010/11
Utilised	2,244	2,244	3,700	3,700
Unutilised tax c/f	4,645		4,505*	–
Amount due from trustees under ITA 2007 ss 496–498		–		–

* The amount of £4,505 carried forward represents tax paid at the trust rate plus the excess of the dividend trust rate over the dividend ordinary rate, and it can be used to cover tax at 50% on the gross equivalent of future income distributions.

(4) Tax reclaimable by non-resident beneficiary (see explanatory note 10)

2009/10	No distribution to B – no repayment.
2010/11	Distribution of £3,700 to B (who is neither resident nor ordinarily resident in UK) comes from trust income that includes £900 from Government Stock that is exempt from tax in B's hands.

The part of the total tax (£3,700) paid on the discretionary payment of trust income in 2010/11 that represents the interest on the Government Stock is therefore repayable, thus:

$$£3,700 \times \frac{900}{15,512} = £215$$

* Being taxable income of £21,512 before charges, less lease premium of £6,000 which is a capital receipt.

Explanatory Notes

Trusts liable to the trust rate and dividend trust rate (special trust rates)

(1)   A trust that can accumulate income, or pay income to the beneficiaries at the discretion of the trustees, is liable to tax on non-dividend income at the rate applicable to trusts (40% in 2009/10, 50% in 2010/11), and at the dividend trust rate (32.5% and 42.5% ion those respective years) on 'distribution income', ie UK dividend income and certain other income carrying non-repayable tax credits, and foreign dividends (ITA 2007 s 479). In the case of UK dividends and other income carrying a non-repayable tax credit of 10%, the trustees have to pay the balance (22.5% for 2009/10 and 32.5% for 2009/10) of the tax credit inclusive amount. In the case of dividends from abroad, the trustees have to pay the full dividend trust rate for the particular year (subject to a claim for double tax relief where foreign tax has been paid). See **Example 42** for details of income carrying non-repayable tax credits and for details of amounts that are not chargeable at the trust rate.

In this Example, the amounts excluded from the charge under s 479 are the lease premium (see **note 6**) and the annuity to the settlor's sister. The trustees have to account for tax on such amounts at the basic rate. (See Example 44 explanatory note 2 for annuities.) Under self-assessment, tax is not charged separately for each source of income, and the tax under s 479 is accounted for as part of the overall figure.

Amount on which special trust rates are charged

(2)   The liability under s 479 applies to the *income* of the trust after deducting any excluded amounts per note 1 and allowing for the trustees' expenses of managing the trust. Trust expenses are regarded as being met first from income taxed at the dividend trust rate, then other savings income, then non-savings income, grossed up appropriately. See **Example 43 note 10** for further details.

In the case of *CRC v Trustees of the Peter Clay Discretionary Trust (2008) CA* – the trustees of a discretionary trust claimed that their expenses in managing the trust should be apportioned between income and capital. HMRC rejected this on the basis that only expenses that related wholly to income could be attributed to income; expenses which related partly to income and partly to capital should be charged wholly to capital. The Special Commissioners had concurred with the trustees, but the High Court allowed HMRC's subsequent appeal. The trustees appealed.

The court ruled that under general law, only expenses which had been incurred exclusively for the benefit of the income beneficiaries could be charged against income. Those relating both to income and capital had to be charged against capital.

However, if professional fees incurred by trustees for accountancy services could be apportioned between fees attributable to dealing with the trust income and those attributable to dealing with capital, the fees charged by the executive trustee for dealing with those services should also be apportioned.

Non-resident discretionary trusts and non-resident life tenants

(3)   Where a discretionary trust has income not chargeable to UK income tax, because it is not resident in the UK, or deemed to be not resident under a double tax treaty, the management expenses must be apportioned between the taxable and non-taxable income of that year, and only the proportion applicable to taxable income is allowable in computing the tax under ITA 2007 s 487(1)–(4).

Similar provisions disallow a proportion of trust expenses in computing the income of a non-resident beneficiary with a life interest (ITA 2007 s 501).

Income of certain types listed in ITA 2007 s 813, including savings and investment income and annual payments (which is how income distributions from discretionary trusts are classified), although strictly taxable income, may not be charged to tax on non-residents because of ITA 2007 s 811, which broadly limits the charge to the tax, if any, deducted at source. Any such income from which tax is *not* deducted is treated by s 487(5)(6) as non-taxable income for the purposes of s 487(1)–(4).

Interest on government stocks

(4)   If the trustees had so elected, the interest on the Government Stock in the Example would have been paid gross. There is a cash flow advantage of receiving gross interest, because payments on account are made half-yearly on 31 January in the tax year and 31 July following, with a later balancing payment (or repayment), on the next following 31 January. See **Example 44 explanatory note 4** for the rules for paying gross interest on *all* government stocks.

Bank and building society interest

(5)   Tax is deducted from both building society interest and bank interest paid to trustees of discretionary trusts, providing in the case of bank interest on deposits made before 6 April 1995 that the trustees or HMRC have notified the bank since that date that the income is income of a discretionary trust (ITA 2007 Sch 2 para 154(1)(2)(3)).

Lease premiums

(6)   In relation to the let property, although the lease premium is a capital amount, it is chargeable in part to income tax under ITTOIA 2005 s 277 thus reducing the amount of the credit to capital.

Therefore the taxable property income is:

	2009/10		2010/11
	£		£
Rents receivable	11,300		11,300
Premium		10,000	
Property business receipt:			

					2009/10		2010/11
$10,000 \times \dfrac{(50-(21-1))}{50} = 10,000 \times \dfrac{30}{50}$						6,000	6,000
	Balance – consideration for part disposal for capital gains tax					4,000	
					11,300		17,300
Less:	Expenses	– Repairs	100			400	
		– Loan interest	200		300	550	950
					11,000		16,350

As a capital receipt, however, the lease premium (not being listed in ITA 2007 s 482) is not subject to the rate applicable to trusts, and is therefore deducted in calculating the tax payable under ITA 2007 s 479 (see **note 1**).

Since the lease premium is a non-recurring item, the trustees might think it appropriate to apply to reduce the payments on account for 2011/12. If, however, the final liability proves to be higher than the payments on account actually made (up to the total of the payments due without a claim, ie £5,580), interest would be charged on the shortfall from the half-yearly payment dates, the rate of interest at the time of writing being 3.0% per annum (from 29 September 2009).

If the payments on account had exceeded the liability for 2010/11, interest at the appropriate rate (0.5% per annum from 29 September 2009) would be paid on the overpayment from the respective dates that the half-yearly instalments were paid to the date the repayment order was issued. There should therefore be a non-taxable credit to income in the trust accounts, equal to the interest that would have been received, the credit to capital for the lease premium being reduced accordingly (in addition to being reduced by the income tax on the premium plus capital gains tax, if any).

Investment advice

(7)   The cost of investment advice is of a capital nature and is not allowable for additional rate tax notwithstanding the authority of the trust deed to charge it to income (*Carver v Duncan and Bosanquet v Allen (1985)*). Nonetheless, the trust deed authorises the expenses to be charged to income, so that the amount available for distribution to income beneficiaries is reduced accordingly.

Income payments to discretionary beneficiaries

(8)   Any income payments made to beneficiaries of discretionary trusts, other than to the settlor of a settlor-interested trust (ITTOIA 2005 s 685A(5)) are treated for income tax as being amounts paid net of tax, at 40% in 2009/10 or 50% in 2010/11.

Whether the resultant tax credit is repayable in the beneficiary's hands, and whether the actual payment by the trustees has to be grossed up by them for the purpose of applying ITA 2007 ss 496-498, requiring the deduction and payment of tax by the trustees, depends on whether the income falls to be charged on the settlor by virtue of the rule for settlor-interested trusts in ITTOIA 2005 s 619. See **Example 46 explanatory note 4** for settlor-interested trusts and **Example 47 explanatory note 11** for others.

Note that the amount of tax that can be set against the trustees' liability on discretionary distributions, under ITA 2007 ss 496-498, will not always cover the full amount of tax paid by the trustees, because the trustees' expenses have to come out of the taxed income of the trust. This makes no difference, however, where, as in the Example, the expenses have come out of dividend income, so that the dividend credits are used to cover the tax on expenses, because the dividend credits, being non-repayable, are not taken into account under ss 496–498 in any event.

In many instances the 'pool' of tax under ss 496–498 will exceed the amount that is due, so that no amount will be payable, as shown in **part (3)** of the Example. In this Example there is the further point that the cost of investment advice was not allowable in calculating the tax due at the rate applicable to trusts, but nevertheless reduced the income available for distribution.

(9)   The fact that dividend credits have since 6 April 1999 not been repayable means that unless there is an unused pool of tax brought forward, the maximum distribution that can be made out of dividend income, without creating an income tax liability that exceeds available income, was 60% until 5 April 2010 and 50% thereafter.

The effect on the amount available for beneficiaries in **part (2)** of the Example is as follows:

	2009/10	*2010/11*
	£	*£*
Tax credit inclusive dividend income (net of trust expenses)		
(3,200 — 450)	2,750	
(2,762 – 500)		2,262
Less: Tax credits 10%	275	226
Tax credit exclusive amounts	2,475	2,036
60% thereof	1,485	
50% thereof		1,018
Amount shown as available for beneficiaries per **part (2)**	6,136	4,626
Dividend income included therein as above	2,750	2,262
Less: Tax at dividend trust rate of 32.5%	894	
Tax at dividend trust rate of 42.5%		961
	1,856	1,301
Actual amount available as above	1,485	1,018
Further reduction required	371	283
Reducing amount available for distribution to	5,765	4,343

As stated above, higher distributions could be made to the extent that the tax was covered by the pool of unutilised tax brought forward from year to year.

Tax credits on pre 6 April 1999 dividends *were* repayable and were thus included in the ss 496–498 pool. If those dividends had not been distributed before 6 April 1999, therefore, the credits will be available to cover tax on a post 5 April 1999 distribution. The rate at which a pre-1999 tax pool based on dividend income is used up, against distributions made out of actual post-1999 dividend income, will however have increased as the trust rate was raised from 34% to 40% in 2004/05 and again from 40% to 50% in 2010/11.

FOTRA securities

(10)   Government securities held by someone who is neither resident nor ordinarily resident in the UK are free of UK tax, such securities being referred to as FOTRA securities (ITTOIA 2005 ss 713–716 and ITTOIA 2005 ss 153, 713). If a discretionary trust holds such securities and makes distributions to beneficiaries who are both not resident and not ordinarily resident in the UK, then under Concession B18, a repayment claim may be made based upon the proportion of exempt income over total income (before charges) of tax credits attributed to distributions. Under the concession, the distribution is treated as made rateably out of income on a last in first out basis. Relief is available for payments out of income arising not earlier than 6 years before the end of the tax year of payment, providing the trustees have filed tax returns and paid all tax, interest, surcharges and penalties due. Claims must be made within five years from 31 January following the relevant tax year.

The claim by B re the distribution of £3,700 to him in 2010/11 will be regarded as relating wholly to the 2010/11 trust income, since that income exceeds the amount of the distribution.

The tax accounted for by the trustees for 2010/11 on the distribution of £3,700 is £3,700 per **part (3)** of the Example. The repayment available to B is the proportion of that amount that the £900 interest on the Government Stock bears to the 2010/11 total income before charges of (21,512 – 6,000 =) £15,512 (the lease premium not being taken into account since it is a capital receipt). This amounts to £215 as shown in **part (4)** of the Example.

Income paid to settlor's children

(11) Where income is paid to an unmarried minor child of the settlor, it is treated as income of the settlor in the year of distribution (ITTOIA 2005 ss 629, 631) and taxed as the highest part of that income (ITTOIA 2005 ss 619, 621, 623 – see **Example 42** for details). Provided the trust is UK resident, full credit is given to the settlor for the tax paid by the trustees at the trust rate (ITA 2007 ss 493–494).

By Revenue concession A93 this treatment is extended to tax paid by non-resident trusts to the extent that the distribution to the child is made out of income that arose not earlier than 6 years before the end of the year of distribution (on a last in first out basis). Credit will be given to the extent that the distribution is made from income chargeable to UK tax and the trustees have complied with their UK obligations, ie filed tax returns and paid all tax, interest, surcharges and penalties due. No credit will be given for non-repayable tax, eg on dividends. Such tax will not, however, be taken into account in calculating the gross income taxable on the settlor under the concession. Claims under the concession must be made within five years from 31 January following the tax year in which the beneficiary received the payment from the trust.

Anti-avoidance provisions re payments made by discretionary trusts to companies

(12) To prevent companies circumventing the rules by routing dividends through discretionary trusts, thus receiving the income not in the form of dividends but as annual payments from which income tax had been deducted, CTA 2010 s 610 (formerly ICTA 1970 s 687A) provides that payments made to a *company* by a discretionary trust are not liable to corporation tax in the receiving company's hands, but the income tax deducted from the payments by the trustees is not repayable. This does not apply if the recipient company is a charity, heritage body etc, and it only applies to a non-resident company if the payments would otherwise be chargeable to corporation tax as income of a UK branch or agency. It is not common for companies to receive payments from discretionary trusts, but these provisions are aimed at preventing possible abuse.

Changes to self assessment payments on account limits

(13) SI 1996/1654 – Income Tax (Payments on Account) Regulations 1996 was amended by SI 2008/838 to raise the de minimis figure at regulation 3 from £500 to £1,000 with effect for 2009/10 and later years. The first payments on account affected were those for 2009/10 due in January 2010 and July 2010.

Question

A.

Mrs Spencer, who was born on 3 April 1937, has a life interest in income under a will trust established by her late husband who died on 30 May 2008.

The trust fund consists of loan stocks and similar securities having a nominal value of £50,000, the interest on which is received gross. In addition a small building society deposit account is held on which interest is received net of income tax.

During the year to 5 April 2011 the trustees had the following transactions:

(i)   On 16 December 2010 contracted to purchase £69,780 nominal of 7% Treasury Stock for settlement on 17 December 2010. The interest payment dates of this stock are 22 May and 22 November.

(ii)   On 5 May 2010 contracted to sell £2,059 nominal National Midland 9% Unsecured Loan Stock for settlement on 6 May 2010. The interest payment dates of this stock are 30 June and 31 December.

During the year to 5 April 2011 the trustees received the following income (no expenses being incurred):

	£
Building society interest received (net)	400
Gross income from securities	5,000

Mrs Spencer's only other income comes from state and occupational pensions totalling £20,000 gross less tax deducted of £2,000 for 2010/11.

(a)   Compute the accrued income relief or charge on the will trust and state how this will be dealt with.

(b)   Compute the income tax payable by or repayable to Mrs Spencer for 2010/11.

B.

Outline the tax problems for trusts in relation to:

(a)   Scrip dividends.

(b)   Demergers.

Answer

A. Mrs Spencer – accrued income scheme

(a)   *Accrued income relief or charge on will trust*

Purchase of Treasury Stock:

Interest accrued to date of settlement	23.11.10 to 17.12.10	=	25 days

$$\text{Accrued } 7\% \times £69,780 = £4,885 \times \frac{25}{365} \qquad = \qquad £334$$

Trustees are entitled to accrued income relief on this amount.

Sale of National Midland Stock:

Interest accrued to date of settlement	1.1.10 to 6.5.10	=	126 days

$$\text{Accrued } 9\% \times £2,059 = £185 \times \frac{126}{365} \qquad = \qquad £64$$

Trustees are liable to an accrued income charge on this amount.

Taxation treatment:

Accrued income charges and reliefs are taken into account in the tax year in which the next interest payment date falls after the settlement date. Accrued income charges are taxed, on the trustees, at (in principle) the rate applicable to trusts (see **note 1**), not on Mrs Spencer as life tenant, because although it is taxed as income it actually represents an accretion to capital. Accrued income relief is given by reducing the assessable interest. Charges and reliefs are not netted off unless they relate to the same kind of stock with the same interest payment dates.

The first receipt of interest on the 7% Treasury Stock will be in May 2011. From that income accrued income relief of £334 will be deducted, the balance being taxable as trust income of 2011/12. If the stock is sold before May 2011 then the accrued income relief will be deducted from the accrued income charge on sale.

The next interest payment date on the National Midland Stock was June 2010, so the £64 is taxed in 2010/11 and in principle is liable to tax at the rate applicable to trusts of 50%. But since the trustees have no other trust rate income it falls within the trustees' standard rate band and will in fact be charged at the basic rate by virtue of ITA 2007 s 491. Accordingly the liability will be £64 @ 20%.

As both stocks are exempt from capital gains tax no related adjustments for that tax are required.

(b)   *Income tax payable by or repayable to Mrs Spencer for 2010/11*

	£	Tax paid £
Pension income	20,000	2,000
Will trust (savings income):		

Securities	5,000		
Building society interest	500	5,500	100
Total income		25,500	2,100
Age allowance 9,490 less half of (25,500 – 22,900)		8,190	
		17,310	
Tax thereon: 11,810 @ 20% basic rate	2,362		
Savings income 5,500 @ 20%	1,100		3,462
Tax payable			1,362

B.

(a) *Scrip dividends*

Where a UK resident company offers scrip shares as an alternative to a cash dividend, certain shareholders taking the scrip option are treated as having income equal to the 'appropriate amount in cash' (ITTOIA 2005 s 411). This means the amount of the cash option, unless it differs by more than 15% from the market value of the shares (ITTOIA 2005 ss 410–413), in which case the deemed income is the market value of the shares on the first day of dealing. The notional income is deemed to be net of the dividend ordinary rate of tax of 10% and is grossed up accordingly. The grossing addition represents a notional tax credit, which is not repayable to non-taxpayers.

This treatment applies where an *individual* is beneficially entitled to the *shares*, or where the shares are received by personal representatives or by trustees for whom a cash dividend would be liable at the 'dividend trust rate' under ITA 2007 s 479.

Where the shares give rise to deemed income in this way, the 'appropriate amount in cash', before grossing up, is treated as the capital gains cost of the scrip shares. Such scrip dividend shares are treated as a separate free-standing acquisition and not as part of the existing under the reorganisation rules (TCGA 1992 s 142); but this does not prevent them from being added to the pool of such shares under TCGA 1992 s 104 if forming part of the trust capital (see further below).

(i) Life interest trusts

As far as life interest trusts are concerned, the trustees must decide whether, in the light of trust and general law and the terms of the particular trust, the shares are received as capital or income.

HMRC's Statement of Practice (SP 4/94) gives their view of the position. They will not seek to challenge the view taken by the trustees (providing the facts support that view) if they have treated the scrip shares either as belonging to the life tenant, or as belonging to trust capital, or as being part of trust capital, but with the life tenant being compensated for the loss of the cash dividend he would have had.

If life tenant is treated as beneficially entitled to the shares

If the life tenant is treated as beneficially entitled to the shares, the trustees would be regarded as holding the shares as bare trustees (except in Scotland, where different rules apply). Any transfer to the beneficiary would therefore be disregarded. For income tax purposes the life tenant would have notional income equal to the appropriate amount in cash. For capital gains tax, the shares would not form part of the trust holding and the life tenant would be regarded as having purchased the shares separately for the 'appropriate amount in cash'. Any sale of the scrip shares by the trustees would be regarded as a sale by the life tenant, so if the shares were sold at the time of issue under the terms of a cash offer from a broker, the last in first out identification rule would apply (see below), and there would in fact be an allowable loss because the amount paid by the broker would be less than the issue price of the shares.

If shares are treated as belonging to trust capital

If the trustees treat the shares as belonging to trust capital, there are no income tax implications and the shares are treated as normal scrip shares for capital gains tax and added to the trust's existing holding at a *nil cost*. The trust's position when the shares are disposed of will depend on whether they have exemptions etc available to cover the potential gain. The tax liability (at present tax rates) could be nil or 50%.

If shares are treated as belonging to trust capital with cash payment to life tenant

If the trustees treat the shares as capital, but make a cash payment to the life tenant to compensate him for not getting the dividend, the treatment of the shares in the trustees' hands is the same as in the previous paragraph. The cash payment to the life tenant is not, however, an income dividend but a payment out of trust capital, so that income tax must be deducted at 20%. There may still be a problem with how much cash to pay, because if the life tenant is a basic rate taxpayer, the effective tax rate on actual dividends is only 10%. The trustees must account for the tax on the payment under ITA 2007 s 963 (see **Example 44 part B**), and will show the payment separately on the form R185 issued to the life tenant.

If shares are treated as belonging to capital and immediately sold

FA 2008 s 8 and Sch 2 simplified the rules for pooling of shares.

The changes mean that in identifying securities disposed of after 5 April 2008, all identical securities owned are treated as part of a single pool (a *section 104 holding*), and the allowable expenditure in respect of that holding will be the sum of:

- the market value at 31 March 1982 of all securities in the section 104 holding that were held at that date; and

- the actual cost or CGT acquisition value of all securities in the section 104 holding acquired from April 1982 onwards. (In the case of scrip shares they are acquired at nil cost as above, so no addition will be made to the base cost of the section 104 holding.)

Where there is an existing section 104 holding at 5 April 2008, the record of the holding should distinguish between the original cost and indexed cost. It is the original cost (not the indexed cost) of an existing section 104 holding that is taken into account in computing the allowable expenditure in a revised section 104 holding from 6 April 2008 onwards; any previously accrued but unused indexation allowance will have been lost at that date.

Where there were any additions to a section 104 holding between 30 November 1993 and 5 April 2008 under transactions (such as transfers between husband and wife or, post-December 2005, civil partners) that are treated for capital gains tax purposes as giving rise to neither a gain nor a loss to the person making the disposal, the amount of the original cost will not include any element of indexation allowance. (In such cases the indexation element was added to the indexed cost of the holding separately from the original cost.)

The abolition of the kink test, indexation allowance, and taper relief simplified the previous pooling rules. The single *section 104 holding* includes all shares acquired before the date of disposal, and the order of matching is now:

- assets acquired on the date of disposal;

- assets acquired in the 30 days following the date of disposal; and

- assets in the enlarged section 104 holding.

The primary effect of s 104 as amended is to provide that a holding of 'securities' (s 104 uses 'securities' to refer to assets such as shares) is treated as a single asset, growing or diminishing as securities are acquired and disposed of. Before the 2008 changes, for CGT purposes a section 104 holding could not contain securities acquired before 6 April 1982, nor after 5 April 1998.

As a result of the FA 2008 amendments, securities acquired that are identified under s 106A(5) with securities disposed of in the 30 days preceding that acquisition, cannot form part of a section 104 holding.

(ii) Discretionary and accumulation trusts

The treatment of scrip dividends received by discretionary and accumulation trusts is not clear. As indicated in the second paragraph of this section, such trusts are treated as having notional income under ITTOIA 2005 ss 409–414) if a cash dividend would have been income to which ITA 2007 s 479 applies, the notional income being regarded as accompanied by a notional tax credit at 10% of the tax credit inclusive amount. If, however, the scrip dividend is required under the terms of the trust to be treated as trust capital, there is an argument that it cannot be charged to the dividend trust rate under ITA 2007 s 479 (but that even so, since the scrip shares are within ITTOA 2005 ss 409–414, they would be treated as a free-standing acquisition for capital gains tax with a base cost equal to the 'appropriate amount in cash'). HMRC do not share this view, and consider that the trustees are liable to tax at the excess of the dividend trust rate of 42.5% over the grossed up amount of the scrip dividend, so that a further 32.5% tax is payable. Only the tax actually paid is taken into account when calculating how much tax is payable by the trustees under ITA 2007 ss 496–498 on distributions to beneficiaries (see **Example 42** for further details). The shares have a base cost for capital gains tax equal to the appropriate amount in cash (on which income tax will have been paid), and are added to the section 104 holding in which the source shares are contained unless a disposal is matched with some other shares according to the rules of TCGA 1992 s 106A outlined above.

In the case of *Howell v Trippier (2004)* (reported as *Red Discretionary Trustees v HMIT* at Special Commissioners level), the discretionary trust received a stock dividend. The settlement trustees elected to receive dividends consisting of further shares in the relevant company. The market value of the stock dividends represented taxable income — the trust return was submitted on the basis that the stock dividend was taxable at the dividend ordinary rate but the Inland Revenue amended the return to increase income tax payable to the dividend trust rate. The Court of Appeal dismissed the trustees' appeal and confirmed that the dividends were taxable at the dividend trust rate.

(b) *Demergers*

Demergers treated as exempt distributions

There is specific legislation in relation to demergers in CTA 2010 Part 23 Ch 5 (ss 1073–1099). The legislation prevents some of the tax problems that a demerger would otherwise cause. Providing the relevant conditions are satisfied, a demerger may be classed as an 'exempt distribution', and in that event the distribution is not treated as income in the hands of the shareholders. For capital gains tax it is treated either as a reorganisation under TCGA 1992 ss 126–131 (by s 192) or a reconstruction under TCGA 1992 ss 136 and 139, depending on the type of demerger, and there is therefore neither chargeable gain nor allowable loss.

Direct demergers and indirect demergers

Demergers may either be direct demergers, where a company distributes shares in one or more 75% subsidiaries direct to its shareholders, or indirect demergers, where a company transfers either a trade or shares in its 75% subsidiaries to another company and that other company makes an issue of shares to the transferor company's shareholders.

Where there is a direct distribution in the form of shares, the shares are regarded as income in the hands of trustees (although exempt from tax as indicated above). It was, however, held in the case of *Sinclair v Lee (1993)* that this did not apply to an indirect demerger. (See further **explanatory note 5** below.) The case related to ICI/Zeneca, where ICI transferred shares in its wholly owned subsidiary Zeneca Ltd to Zeneca Group plc (which was not ICI's subsidiary), and Zeneca Group plc issued shares to ICI shareholders. On the facts, this was held to be a capital distribution, the ICI holding being split for capital gains purposes into separate ICI/Zeneca holdings according to the market value of the shares on the first day after the demerger (for unquoted shares the relevant date would be the date of disposal).

This does not, however, determine the treatment of trust holdings for all demergers and it is necessary to look at the particular circumstances, and also the provisions of the particular trust. HMRC made a detailed statement of their views in the October 1994 issue of the Tax Bulletin, a summary of which follows.

Where there is a direct demerger, the shares are regarded as *income* of the trust, because under company law they are a dividend paid out of accumulated profits. If, exceptionally, they were treated as capital, the capital gains tax treatment for the trustees would be as for individuals.

In an indirect demerger, the HMRC view is that the shares would normally be an addition to capital (following *Sinclair v Lee*), the capital gains treatment of the trustees being the same as for individuals, but this is not necessarily true of all indirect demergers.

Discretionary trusts

The trustees are treated in the same way as individuals, ie they are not liable to income tax or capital gains tax. If shares are then distributed to beneficiaries, they are treated for capital gains tax as a disposal of a proportionate part of the holding at market value, the cost plus the available indexation allowance for that part of the holding being allowed against the deemed proceeds.

If the trustees exercise a power to accumulate the 'income' as part of the trust fund, and later distribute the shares as capital, no income tax arises. If the shares are distributed as income rather than accumulated, the distribution is treated as being net of (now) 50% tax (the value of the distribution being the lower of the value at the date of the demerger and the value when distributed). Since income tax will not have been paid on the demerged shares under ITA 2007 s 479, the trustees may have to pay tax under ITA 2007 s 496/498 (unless there is a sufficient pool of tax already accounted for). (See **Example 48** for details of ITA 2007 s 479 and ss 496–498.)

Life interest trusts

The following relates to the treatment of English life interest trusts. (Different rules apply in Scotland.)

In a direct demerger, the shares would belong to the life tenant directly, so they would not form part of the trust's holding, the capital gains tax cost of which is unaffected. The life tenant would be treated for capital gains as acquiring the shares at market value at the date of the demerger (the distribution being other than at arm's length – TCGA 1992 s 17(1)), even though there would have been no reduction of the trustees' allowable cost. (If the trustees retained the shares, there would be a disposal of them by the life tenant to the trustees, and unless he was paid their cash value, he would be the settlor of shares into the trust.)

In an indirect demerger, the shares would usually be treated as capital as indicated above, so that they would not affect the life tenant. If *exceptionally* they were treated as income, the capital gains tax position would be the same as for a direct demerger, except that s 17(1) would not apply (because there would be no disposal by the transferor company *directly* to the shareholder), and the beneficiary's capital gains tax cost would be nil.

For direct demergers, there would be no income tax on the life tenants nor on the trustees under ITA 2007 ss 9, 497, 498, since the shares are treated as belonging to the life tenant. The same would apply where, exceptionally, shares are treated as income in an indirect demerger. If the shares are treated as capital, the trustees would have no income tax liability. If, however, they then distributed the shares under provisions in the trust deed, such that the shares were income in the hands of the life tenant, the trustees would have to deduct tax and pay it over to HMRC under s 963.

Explanatory Notes

Accrued income scheme

(1)   The accrued income scheme provisions are in ITA 2007 ss 616–681.

The accrued income scheme causes particular difficulties in relation to trusts. The scheme treats amounts that are capital sums under the general (and trust) law as being income for tax purposes and tax is charged (or refunded) accordingly.

The fact that the sums are to be accumulated as part of capital, rather than being income of a beneficiary, is, however, recognised by ITA 2007 s 482, which provides that the trustees are taxed in respect of accrued income charges at the rate applicable to trusts, ie 50%. However ITA 2007 s 491 provides that, within the standard rate band, such deemed income is chargeable at, in effect, the basic rate. Mrs Spencer's trust is only liable to tax at special trust rates on accrued income of £64; as this is less than £200 it is certain that the whole will be chargeable at the basic rate (ie 20%). (Even if Mr Spencer had made many other trusts that were still current, so that the full standard rate band of £1,000 fell to be shared between them, it cannot be reduced below £200 for each trust, see ITA 2007 s 492 and **Example 47 explanatory note 1.**)

These rules can lead to an anomaly. The trustees could receive a reduction for accrued income relief at the basic rate but be liable at the dividend trust rate on an amount in excess of their standard rate band and have to pay tax at 50% on the excess.

Because the accrued income charges represent capital sums, they do not form part of a beneficiary's income and are not shown on form R185.

The trustees then have the problem of how to deal with accrued income charges and accrued income reliefs in the trust accounts. The Accounting Recommendations of the Institute of Chartered Accountants state that where a life tenant may be interested in such accruals, consideration should be given to accounting for the interest and the associated tax on an accruals basis when the securities are purchased and sold. The alternative view, which the authors prefer, is that the accruals treatment should not apply to accrued income charges, and that the tax on accrued income charges should be debited to the capital account of the trust in the year of the liability, as it would have been if it had been capital gains tax. This is also the view of the author of the Society of Trust and Estate Practitioners' (STEP's) Accounting Guidelines (2005), see Appendix 4 to that publication.

There is also doubt as to the treatment of accrued income relief. The relief reduces the trustees' income for tax purposes as shown in **part A (a)** above, and the beneficiary's income for tax purposes is similarly reduced, so that in 2011/12 Mrs Spencer's interest from the 7% Treasury Stock shown on form R185 will be the gross interest of (7% × £69,780 =) £4,885, reduced by £334, giving taxable income of £4,551. Tax thereon amounts to £910 compared with tax on £4,885 of £977. The reduction of £334 at 20% = £67 in the tax payable will have been reflected in the amount payable by the trustees under self-assessment. If tax had been deducted at source from the interest, the trustees would have a tax refund of £67. The question then is how much should the trustees actually pay to Mrs Spencer. HMRC have stated that this is a matter for the trustees in accordance with the general law, and whatever is paid will not affect the tax treatment. There are several possibilities:

(a)   Taxable income £4,551 less tax £910 = £3,641.

(b)   Actual gross income £4,885 less tax thereon £977 = £3,908.

(c)   As (b) plus tax reduction of £67 = £3,975.

The trustees have actually received net income of £3,908 and have had a tax reduction of £67, and some people therefore favour paying the beneficiary £3,975 as in (c). Before the introduction of the accrued income scheme, however, the part of the purchase price representing accrued interest, ie £334, would have been part of the capital cost of the security. The authors take the view that the logical approach is to regard that treatment as unchanged for trust accounting purposes, and to treat the £67 as a reduction in the cost and to pay to the beneficiary what would previously have been paid, ie £3,908. Thus both accrued income charges and accrued income reliefs would be dealt with through the trust capital account. This again appears to be the approach followed in the STEP accounting Guidelines.

Scope of accrued income provisions

(2)   The accrued income provisions apply to 'transfers'. This means 'transfer by way of sale, exchange, gift or otherwise' (ITA 2007 s 620(1)(2)), and would include a settlement of securities by an individual, and a transfer of securities to beneficiaries on termination of a trust, as well as the trustees buying and selling the trust securities. The provisions do not apply where securities become vested in an individual's personal representatives on his death (ITA 2007 s 620(1)(2)). Nor do they apply if the personal representatives transfer the securities to legatees or to those entitled on an intestacy in the interest period in which the individual died (ITA 2007 s 636). There is no exemption for a transfer in a later interest period.

Scrip dividends and demergers

(3)   The problems of trustees who receive scrip dividends or shares on a demerger are outlined in **part B** of the Example. HMRC have given detailed comments on their views, but there are many grey areas which it would be difficult to resolve, even with amended legislation, because of the mismatch between trust law and tax law.

As far as scrip dividends are concerned, where the shares are worth the same as the cash dividend, the simple way to avoid problems is to take the cash. The enhanced scrip dividends which were offered by listed companies a few years ago were worth half as much again as the cash dividend, and there was the option of obtaining the extra cash by selling immediately, thus giving rise to the particular problems mentioned in the Example. Such offers have not been made recently, although enhanced scrip offers may arise in other circumstances.

Purchase by company of own shares etc

(4)   Where a company redeems, repays or purchases its own shares from the trustees of a settlement, the excess of the amount paid over the original issue price is treated as if it were an income distribution with a notional tax credit attached, and the trustees are liable to tax at the excess of the dividend trust rate of 42.5% over the tax credit rate of 10%, so that a further 32.5% is payable (ITA 2007 ss 481–482). This does not apply where the trust income is treated as belonging to the settlor, or where the trust is a unit trust, charitable trust, or pension trust (or presumably where the trust is a bare trust — see **Example 64 explanatory note 8**), but it applies to all other trusts, including interest in possession trusts.

If the purchase is by an unquoted trading company in order to benefit its trade, and specified conditions are satisfied, the purchase is treated as a chargeable disposal for capital gains tax rather than as an income distribution (CTA 2010 ss 1033–1048).

Proposed reform of trust law affecting demergers

(5)   Following a Law Commission report on the subject in 2009 (LC315), the Ministry of Justice conducted a consultation exercise between March and June 2010 in relation to a draft Trusts (Capital and Income) Bill. Its provisions in draft would *inter alia* treat tax-exempt corporate distributions as capital of a trust, but would give the trustees an express power to compensate an income beneficiary out of capital if satisfied that, but for the distribution, there would have been a receipt from the corporate body that would have been a receipt of income for the purposes of the trust.

Cross references

(6)   See **Example 44 explanatory note 4** for the provisions that apply for receiving interest gross on government stocks, **Example 43 explanatory note 7** for the provisions that apply for receiving interest gross on listed company securities and **Example 47** for the self-assessment provisions in relation to trusts.

Question

A.

The termination of a life interest in settled property can occur in various circumstances, including:

(a)   where, on the death of the life tenant, the settlement (or a part) comes to an end,

(b)   as in (a) but the property passes to the original settlor,

(c)   where, on the life tenant's death, there is a successive life tenancy, and

(d)   where the interest ceases otherwise than on the death of the life tenant.

State the capital gains tax situation in each of the events (a) to (d) above, giving appropriate statutory references.

B.

Where capital gains tax is payable by trustees, state the position regarding the capital gains tax rate and the annual exemption, and indicate the position if the settlor has retained an interest in the settlement.

Answer

For the non-statutory terminology 'estate IIP' and 'privileged minor's IIP' see **Example 52**. In this Example the term 'privileged IIP' will be used to include both.

A. Termination of life interests in settled property – capital gains tax treatment

(a) *Where the settlement or part thereof comes to an end on the death of the life tenant*

The settled property to which someone becomes entitled is deemed to be disposed of at market value and immediately reacquired by the trustees; but where that occurs on the death of a beneficiary who had a privileged IIP no chargeable gain (or allowable loss) arises on the disposal except as indicated below (TCGA 1992 ss 71–73). In other words there is an adjustment to the base cost of the settled property and the trustees then hold that property as bare trustees for the person entitled thereto.

Where the asset disposed of, or part thereof, was the subject of a claim for gifts holdover relief under TCGA 1992 s 165 or s 260 when the trustees acquired it, then a chargeable gain will arise, restricted to the amount of the heldover gain.

Where the life interest did not extend to the whole of the settled property to which someone became entitled on the life tenant's death, then there is no exemption from the capital gains charge on the deemed disposal, but any gain arising is reduced by a proportion representing the life tenant's interest (TCGA 1992 s 73).

A further instance where a chargeable gain arises is where deferral relief has been claimed in respect of a subscription for enterprise investment scheme shares (see **explanatory note 7**).

If the interest in possession of the life tenant was not a privileged IIP, then any gain or loss on a s 71 deemed disposal will be a chargeable gain or allowable loss, treated in the same way as in **part (d)** below.

(b) *As in (a) but the property passes to the original settlor*

If the original settlor becomes absolutely entitled on the death of the life tenant, and the life tenant's interest was a privileged IIP, then there is a deemed disposal and reacquisition of the settled property as in **(a)** above, but the consideration is deemed to be such that no gain or loss accrues to the trustees, rather than being at market value. Where the deemed disposal is of an asset held by the trustees at 31 March 1982, then the original settlor is also deemed to have held the assets on that date. Therefore on a subsequent disposal by the original settlor his base cost will be the asset's market value as at 31 March 1982 even though the asset was actually owned by the trustees, not by the settlor, on that date.

As in **(a)**, if the interest in possession was not a privileged IIP this rule does not apply, and any gain or loss will be treated in the usual way as per **(d)** below.

(c) *Where, on the life tenant's death, there is a successive life tenancy*

If the life tenant's interest was a privileged IIP, then the consequences are similar to those in **(a)** above. The settled property is deemed to be disposed of at market value and immediately reacquired by the trustees, but no chargeable gain arises on the disposal (TCGA 1992 s 72), other than any gain held over under the gifts holdover provisions (TCGA 1992 s 74) or enterprise investment scheme deferral relief provisions (see **explanatory note 7**).

If the life tenant's interest was not a privileged IIP, there is no deemed disposal on the life tenant's death unless the trust comes to an end as in **(a)** above. The base value of the trust assets in the trustees' hands remains unchanged.

(d) *Where the life interest ceases otherwise than on the death of the life tenant*

Whether the life interest is an estate IIP or not, such a termination has no capital gains tax effect if the property remains in trust, and the capital gains tax base value of the property remains the same. If, however, a beneficiary (whether the life tenant or someone else, which would include the trustees of a separate settlement where relevant), become absolutely entitled to any property against the trustees at that time, there is a deemed disposal at market value, and deemed reacquisition as bare trustees for the beneficiary, and the trustees are chargeable to capital gains tax accordingly (TCGA 1992 s 71).

If the beneficiary is UK resident, however, a claim may be made by the trustees and beneficiary jointly for any gain to be held over under one of two provisions of TCGA 1992:

(i)   under s 260 if the deemed disposal entails a chargeable transfer for inheritance tax or would entail an inheritance tax charge but for one of a specified range of reliefs (notably in connection with accumulation and maintenance trusts, bereaved minor's trusts and age 18-to-25 trusts); or

(ii)   under s 165 and Sch 7 if the property consists of any of the following:

   •   Assets used in a business by the trustees or the life tenant

   •   Unquoted shares in a trading company

   •   Shares in a trading company in which the trustees hold 25% or more of the voting rights

   •   Property that would qualify for agricultural property relief (Sch 7 paras 1–3).

Since 16 June 1999, where a beneficiary becomes absolutely entitled:

(i)   Losses on actual disposals by the trustees before the beneficiary becomes absolutely entitled cannot be transferred to the beneficiary. Such losses will remain losses of the trustees, for which relief may be obtained within the trust according to the normal rules.

(ii)   Losses arising on the deemed market value transfer to the beneficiary that the trustees cannot use against gains arising at the time of the transfer of the property or earlier in the same tax year will be treated as made by the beneficiary who has become absolutely entitled to the asset, but the loss will be ring-fenced in the beneficiary's hands: he will be able to use the loss only to reduce a gain on the disposal of the particular asset, or in the case of land, an asset derived from the land.

These rules, in TCGA 1992, s 71(2)–(2D), were introduced by FA 1999 s 75 to prevent abuse of the rules by artificial schemes enabling people unconnected with a trust to purchase the trust losses, including schemes set up specifically to manufacture losses within trusts to be used in this way.

See **explanatory note 4** re the connected persons rules.

If someone with an interest in a settlement (either a life interest or a reversionary interest) disposes of his interest, the disposal is not subject to capital gains tax unless the interest had been acquired for money or money's worth by him or by a predecessor in title of his (TCGA 1992 s 76(1)). This exemption does not, however, apply (even if the interest disposed of was not acquired for money or money's worth) to:

(1)   disposals which take place at a time when the trustees are neither resident nor ordinarily resident in the UK (TCGA 1992 s 85). In such a case some relief is available where the trust became non-resident after 18 March 1991 (triggering a deemed disposal of the assets by the trustees at that time) and the beneficiary's interest was acquired before the change of residence; the beneficiary's base value for his interest under the trust is in effect updated to the date of the change in residence (s 85(2)–(9)).

(2)   disposals of an interest in a trust whose trustees have at any time been not resident or not ordinarily resident in the UK (s 76(1A), (1B)).

On a person becoming absolutely entitled to the assets of the settlement, he is deemed to have disposed of his interest for the then market value of the assets (TCGA 1992 s 76(2)) – alongside the deemed disposal by the trustees of the assets to which he becomes entitled, and reacquisition as bare trustees for that beneficiary. The beneficiary's deemed disposal will not result in a chargeable gain – even if it would otherwise be caught by one of the exclusions at **1** and **2** above – unless the interest had previously changed hands for money or money's worth; in such a case s 76(2) in effect ensures a charge on the beneficiary in respect of the gain in the value of his (or his predecessor in title's) investment in the interest.

Special rules apply where there is a disposal for actual consideration (other than in the form of another interest under the same settlement, unless that other interest had previously changed hands for actual consideration) of an interest under a trust that is settlor-interested at the date of the disposal, or has been so at any time in the [receding two tax years. If the trust is UK resident or ordinarily resident in the tax year of disposal, and the settlor is or has been resident or ordinarily resident in the UK in the current year or in any of the previous five tax years, then the beneficiary's disposal of his interest will trigger a deemed disposal and reacquisition of the trust assets by the trustees at market value (or of a relevant part or fund of them if the interest does not extend to the whole). It is irrelevant whether the person disposing of the interest in the trust is not UK resident; any tax is payable by the trustees, but they are given a statutory right to recover it from the beneficiary who made the disposal. (TCGA 1992 s 76A and Schedule 4A.) However, provision is made by para 10 of that Schedule to prevent double-counting as between the beneficiary's disposal of his interest and the trustees' deemed disposal, the general effect of which is to preserve the charge on the higher of the two net gains or to allow the smaller of the two allowable losses.

B. Capital gains tax rate etc

Charging gains to tax

Subject to what follows, UK resident trustees are chargeable to tax on their chargeable gains less allowable losses as for individuals. In the main, reliefs available to individuals such as private residence relief and business assets roll-over relief are also available to trustees; but as regards private residence relief it is important to remember that it will be unavailable to trustees (except in a heritage property maintenance fund trust) if the base value of the property in question is to any extent reduced (directly or indirectly) as a result of a claim for gift relief under TCGA 1992 s 260, whether that claim was made before or after the disposal on which private residence relief would otherwise be available (TCGA 1992 s 226A).

There are anti-avoidance provisions in TCGA 1992 s 79A that prevent losses arising on trustees' disposals being set against gains they make on assets that had been transferred to the trust if the transferor or someone connected with him had bought an interest in the trust and had claimed gifts holdover relief on the transferred assets.

The capital gains tax rate for trusts with effect from 23 June 2010 is 28%, which also applies to personal representatives of a deceased's estate (TCGA 1992 s 4). The change of rate from 18% in mid-tax year gives rise to a need for transitional provisions; for the main principles of these see **Example 47 explanatory note 15**.

Trusts in which settlor retains an interest

The former capital gains tax equivalent to the income tax provisions for taxing the settlor on income of a settlor-interested trust, in TCGA 1992, ss 77–79, was abolished for UK trusts by FA 2008, though in the case of non-UK resident (or dual resident) trusts a similar (and more wide-ranging) regime applies under TCGA 1992 s 86 and Schedule 5.

To complement the rule in TCGA 1992 s 169B that denies gift relief under the provisions of TCGA 1992 s 165 or s 260 in respect of disposals of assets by a settlor to the trustees of a trust in which he has an interest, the trustees holding assets that were the subject of a gift relief claim on the transfer to the trustees will face a clawback charge under s 169C if the trust becomes settlor-interested within a certain time period. This does not apply if the terms of the trust meet 'disabled beneficiary' conditions, in favour of a disabled settlor, or in the case of a heritage property maintenance fund trust. The conditions are similar to, but not identical to, those described in the next section relating to the annual exemption available to a disabled person's trust.

This period begins immediately after the disposal to the trustees that benefited from gift relief and ends at the end of the sixth tax year thereafter.

Capital gains tax annual exemption

Where tax is chargeable in the name of the trustees on a held-over gain, or under the provisions in **part A (d)** above, or on disposals of trust assets by the trustees, the trustees can claim an annual exemption equal to half the amount exempt for an individual, ie £5,050 for 2010/11.

If, however, the same person is the settlor in relation to more than one trust created after 6 June 1978 (with certain exceptions including trusts for the disabled and charitable trusts), the exemption of £5,050 is divided between those trusts, with a minimum exempt slice for each trust of £1,010 (TCGA 1992 Sch 1 para 2(3)). This rule applies to settlements arising under a will or intestacy as well as those created in lifetime. (For more details see **Example 47 explanatory note 16.**)

If the trust is a trust for the disabled, the full annual exemption of £10,100 is available, reduced pro rata if there is more than one disabled trust established by the same settlor after 9 March 1981, with again a minimum slice for each trust of £1,010 (TCGA 1992 Sch 1 para 1). Where there was more than one settlor of the subject disabled person's trust, but again only taking account of other disabled person's trusts made by each of them.

The requirements in this context for a trust for the disabled differ from those for inheritance tax in IHTA 1984 s 89(1), and also from those which apply in relation to eligibility to make a vulnerable person's election in FA 2005 s 34. In relation to the annual exemption, the terms of the trust must secure that, during the lifetime of the disabled person (or until forfeiture of a protected life interest of his), not less than half of any capital that is applied must be applied for his benefit, and (unless he is entitled to at least half the trust income) no income may be applied for the benefit of anyone other than the disabled beneficiary. The possibility of breach of those conditions by means of an exercise of the statutory power of advancement can be disregarded so long as the power is not actually exercised in an offending way.

Explanatory Notes

Types of trust and IHT and CGT treatment following Finance Act 2006

(1) The main types of trust are bare trusts, trusts with an interest in possession (IIP), discretionary trusts and accumulation and maintenance (A&M) trusts (though the latter expression now has very little taxation significance).

Where someone is a bare trustee this means that the beneficiary is absolutely entitled to the trust property as against the trustee. The capital gains tax (CGT) treatment is therefore to look through the trust and to deem the trustee's acts as being those of the beneficiary (TCGA 1992 s 60); and equally for inheritance tax (IHT) the trust property is not settled property but property to which the beneficiary is beneficially entitled in his own right (and thus part of his estate). For further details see **Example 64**.

As seen in **part A** of the Example, the CGT treatment of life interest trusts is dependent on the IHT categorisation of the IIP, as to which see further **Example 52** (TCGA 1992 ss 72, 73).

Most interest in possession trusts are life interest trusts, but sometimes an interest may cease earlier, for Example if a widow remarries. (An annuity is another form of interest in possession, and there detailed rules for both IHT and CGT purposes to identify the extent of the settled property that is to be treated as underlying the annuity: see IHTA 1984 s 50(2)–(4), TCGA 1992 s 72(3)–(5).)

A protected life interest (where the life interest is automatically replaced by a discretionary trust of income in the event of the life tenant's bankruptcy, attempted assignment of his interest or related events – see Trustee Act 1925 s 33) is an interest in possession while the life interest has not been "forfeited" in that way, and its tax treatment is no different from other interests in possession. If and when a forfeiture occurs, the trust switches to the income tax and CGT rules for discretionary trusts, following the trust law treatment; but for IHT, if the IIP was a privileged IIP in the first place, the forfeiture will be disregarded and it will remain a privileged IIP (IHTA 1984 s 88).

Inheritance Tax Act 1984 sets out the rules for 'relevant property' trusts, which now include not just discretionary trusts but also many trusts which before FA 2006 would have ranked as [privileged] IIP trusts or A&M trusts. These include (but see further **Examples 59 to 62**):

- an immediate 'entry' tax charge of 20% on lifetime transfers that exceed the IHT threshold into 'relevant property' trusts;

- a 'periodic' tax charge on the value of trust assets once every ten years, at a rate established by reference to a variety of factors but so that (ever since a single rate above the nil rate band was introduced in 1988) the formula cannot produce a rate higher than 6% every ten years; and

- an 'exit' charge proportionate to the periodic charge when funds are taken out of a trust between ten-year anniversaries (or, if no ten-year anniversary has yet occurred, at a proportion of a rate established at the outset of the life of the settlement.

(2)　Until 22 March 2006 any IIP (with very limited exceptions) led to the life tenant being treated for IHT as beneficially entitled to the underlying settled property, so that it counted as part of his estate (hence the non-statutory term "estate IIP" used in this book, see **Example 52**): IHTA 1984 s 49. As a result, a lifetime transfer into an IIP trust, or from one life tenant to another, attracted potentially exempt transfer treatment, escaping IHT if the transferor lived for seven years thereafter. The trust was not affected by the relevant property regime.

IIPs that were already within that regime on that date retain the same treatment while the same beneficiary remains entitled to the same IIP; and the first replacement IIP within the same settlement, if the switch took place before 6 October 2008 (or in favour of the life tenant's spouse on his death, or under certain trusts of life assurance policies), would also attract the same treatment as "transitional serial interests" (IHTA 1984 ss 49B-49E).

However, in all other cases an IIP will only be an estate IIP in one of two ways:

(a)　if it is an actual or deemed IIP in favour of a disabled person within IHTA 1984 ss 89-89B – this is the only category where estate interest in possession treatment can apply in the case of a trust made in the settlor's lifetime since 22 March 2006; or

(b)　if it arises under a will or intestacy and takes effect immediately on the deceased's death – an 'immediate post-death interest' within IHTA 1984 s 49A. (The administration period, and any survivorship clause where the survivorship requirement is no longer than six months from the death, are disregarded for this purpose (IHTA 1984 ss 91–92), and post-death rearrangements which result in an IIP in settled property and attract statutory backdating treatment for IHT purposes under IHTA 1984 ss 142–147 will also fulfil the requirements of taking effect immediately on the death.

(3)　Trustees are treated for CGT purposes as a single deemed person distinct from those who may from time to time occupy the position of trustee, and, if that deemed person is UK resident, gains arising on the disposal of trust assets are assessable on the trustees (other than bare trustees, as indicated in **explanatory note 1** above) (TCGA 1992 s 69, which also sets out the rules for determining the residence status of the deemed person).

Creation of settlement

(4)　When a settlement is created the settlor is deemed to have disposed of the entire property transferred to the settlement at its market value, even if he retains an interest as beneficiary or is a trustee under the settlement, and he is therefore chargeable to capital gains tax accordingly (subject to any available reliefs and exemptions).

If the assets transferred are business assets (as defined by TCGA 1992 s 165) or the transfer is *immediately* chargeable to inheritance tax (whether or not there is any actual inheritance tax payable (TCGA 1992 s 260)) then provided the trustees are UK resident the settlor can avoid incurring a personal CGT liability on the gain by making an election to hold it over so that it reduces the trustees' base acquisition cost, and unlike other gifts relief elections the donees do not have to join in the election. For gifts into settlement on or after 10 December 2003 this facility is not available if the settlor retains an interest or the trust becomes settlor-interested within six years. For nearly all lifetime transfers into family trusts since 2006, gifts holdover relief will be available under s 260: apart from special cases such as heritage maintenance fund trusts and employee trusts, and even where the trust is primarily for the settlor's own benefit, the only case where the transfer will not be immediately chargeable to IHT, but only *potentially exempt*, will be where the trust confers a disabled person's interest at the outset.

In a life interest trust, the heldover gains crystallise when the life tenant dies, as indicated in **part A** of the Example. In a discretionary trust, the heldover gains are similarly triggered when assets are transferred to beneficiaries (see **note 6**). In both cases this will be subject to any further holdover relief claim that the circumstances may allow.

If the settlor's disposal gives rise to losses rather than gains, then under the 'connected persons' rules, the losses can only be set against gains on other disposals to the trustees. These rules will also apply as between the trustees and any beneficiaries with whom they are connected; but note that (except in relation to companies of which they collectively exercise control) trustees are no longer connected with the settlor's spouse and relatives after the settlor's death. Even if the trustees and beneficiaries *are* connected, this does not prevent the trustees' losses arising from the disposal to the beneficiaries being transferred to the beneficiaries to the limited extent allowed by TCGA 1992 s 71(2)–(2D), as indicated in **part A (d)** of the Example.

Emigration of trustees

(5)   Emigrating trustees are charged not only on gains held over at the time the funds were settled but on the whole of any increase in value of the trust assets up to the time of emigration (TCGA 1992 s 80). If the emigration occurs solely as a result of the death of a UK resident trustee and the trustees become UK resident again within six months thereafter, the deemed disposal on emigration is disapplied, except in relation to assets that were disposed of by the trustees between the death and the re-immigration of the trust, or where a gain on their disposal would be protected from UK CGT by a double tax agreement. There is a similar rule for trusts which become UK resident solely by reason of the death of a non-UK resident trustee and which re-emigrate within six months: the emigration charge in such a case is limited to assets that were acquired in the UK-resident period with the benefit of hold-over relief (TCGA 1992, s 81). For detailed notes on non-resident trusts see **Example 51**.

Persons becoming absolutely entitled to trust property

(6)   TCGA 1992 s 71 applies not only when a beneficiary under an interest in possession trust becomes absolutely entitled as against the trustees, as outlined in **part A (d)** of the Example, but also where a beneficiary of a discretionary trust becomes so entitled. The trustees are deemed to have disposed of the assets to the beneficiary at market value at that time and are chargeable to capital gains tax accordingly.

The gifts holdover relief provisions of ss 165 and 260 outlined in **explanatory note 3** are, however, available if the conditions are satisfied and the beneficiary is UK resident. A distribution from a relevant property trust will be a chargeable event for inheritance tax, triggering an exit charge under IHTA 1984 s 65 and thus satisfying the s 260 requirement, unless (s 65(4)) it takes place within three months after the creation of the settlement or within three months after a ten-year anniversary.

Where a discretionary trust is created by will, distributions to beneficiaries within the two years after the death (but not within the first three months) are treated as if made under the will for inheritance tax purposes (IHTA 1984 s 144 – see **Example 60 explanatory notes 10 and 12**). For capital gains tax purposes, however, if such a distribution was of chargeable assets that had grown in value since the date of death, the trustees would be liable to tax on the gain arising under TCGA 1992 s 71 (subject to any available annual exemption), unless the business gifts holdover relief of s 165 was available. Relief under s 260 would not be available because the distribution would not be a chargeable event for inheritance tax. One way of avoiding a capital gains tax charge in these circumstances would be for the trustees to appoint assets to a beneficiary *before* the assets were appropriated to the trustees by the personal representatives. The trustees would then be bare trustees (as to which see **explanatory note 1**), and as and when the assets were appropriated to them by the personal representatives, their acquisition would be deemed to be that of the beneficiary, who would thus take over the personal representatives' acquisition cost.

Creation of life interest out of discretionary trust

(7)   On any restructuring of the terms of a trust – for Example if property is held under a discretionary trust and a life interest is created in the property – it has to be established whether a separate settlement has been created or whether the original settlement continues (*Roome v Edwards (1981)* and *Bond v Pickford (1983)*). If the original settlement is treated as continuing, the restructuring will have no immediate capital gains consequences.

If the restructuring was held to involve the relevant assets passing into a separate settlement, this would be an occasion of charge under TCGA 1992 s 71, since another 'person', ie the trustees of the new settlement, would become entitled to the trust property as against the trustees of the original settlement. In most cases nowadays the restructuring would not result in an exit charge for inheritance tax under IHTA 1984 s 65 (see **note 6** above), such as to permit a claim to holdover relief under TCGA 1992 s 260; a trust that is once within the relevant property rules will only cease to be so if a disabled person's interest is created. If on the other hand an estate IIP existed before the restructuring, the restructuring may well give rise to a deemed transfer of value by the beneficiary with that IIP, which would now with very few exceptions be a chargeable transfer on entry into the relevant property regime such as to attract holdover relief subject to the trustees being UK resident.

Enterprise investment scheme deferral relief

(8)   If trustees reinvest gains by making a cash subscription for enterprise investment scheme (EIS) shares, they may claim deferral relief under the provisions of TCGA 1992 Sch 5B (but not EIS income tax relief or capital gains exemption) (Sch 5B para 17). This applies to interest in possession trusts (except where the IIP is for a fixed term) in which any of the beneficiaries is an individual or a charity, and to discretionary trusts in which all beneficiaries are individuals or charities. Where, however, a life tenant with an estate IIP dies and EIS shares pass to a succeeding life tenant or remainderman, the deemed disposal under TCGA 1992 s 71(1) or s 72(1) (see **part A(a)** of the Example) triggers the deferred gain, even if no gain arises on the shares themselves.

Anti-avoidance provisions — apportionment of gains of non-resident companies

(9)   There are provisions in TCGA 1992 s 13 to attribute gains in a non-resident company to UK resident participators if the company would have been a close company if UK resident. For gains realised after 20 March 2000, where the UK participators are trustees, the gains cannot be prevented from being so attributed by reason of the provisions of a double tax agreement (TCGA 1992 s 79B). For further details of the provisions of TCGA 1992 s 13 see **Example 51 explanatory note 17**.

Question

A.

In May 1988 Stephen Jones set up a discretionary trust for the benefit of his four cousins. The trust paid inheritance tax of £44,000 on a chargeable transfer of £330,000. Stephen acted as trustee, together with his solicitor and a close friend. All capital gains arising, totalling £110,000 were held over. Stephen has never set up any other trusts.

In February 1989 Stephen emigrated (permanently) and the administration of the trust was transferred to new trustees all of whom were and are resident outside the UK. Had the trust's assets been disposed of at that time capital gains of £155,000 would have arisen (including the gain held over).

The beneficiaries, Matthew, Mark, Mary and Matilda were all minors at the date of the settlement, and have been resident and ordinarily resident in the UK at all times. However, although all the children were born in the UK, Matthew's domicile at birth was in Massachusetts, USA, and this remains unchanged to date.

The trustees subsequently undertook the following transactions:

June 1997	Disposal of a freehold office property for £360,980 (net of costs). The property was part of the original trust fund. It had cost Stephen Jones £50,000 in early March 1982 and was worth £100,000 in May 1988.
September 1997	Disposal of quoted shares in Jonah plc for £25,000. These shares had been acquired by the trustees in March 1990 for £9,650.
May 1998	Purchase of warehouse property in England for £150,000.
June 1998	Sale of UK residential investment property for £200,000. This property had been bought by the trustees in December 1988 for £62,034 including costs.
June 2009	Sale of chargeable non-business assets for £244,652 which had originally been settled by Stephen. The gain was £111,400. There was no heldover gain in respect of these assets.

In addition to distributing all income year by year, the trustees made capital distributions out of the settlement as follows:

	Matthew £	Mark £	Mary £	Matilda £
May 1996	–	–	60,000	20,000
December 1997	90,000	60,000	–	70,000
May 1999	6,000	6,000	6,000	–
August 2010	40,000	40,000	40,000	45,000

The re-referenced retail prices index for the dates given was:

March 1982	79.44
May 1988	106.20
December 1988	110.30
February 1989	111.82
March 1990	121.40
June 1997	157.50
September 1997	159.30
April 1998	162.60

Calculate the capital gains chargeable on the trustees and the beneficiaries in respect of the above transactions, stating if any supplementary charge will apply.

The capital gains tax annual exemption for individuals was as follows:

1997/98	£6,500
1998/99	£6,800
1999/2000	£7,100
2000/01	£7,200
2001/02	£7,500
2002/03	£7,700
2003/04	£7,900
2004/05	£8,200
2005/06	£8,500
2006/07	£8,800
2007/08	£9,200
2008/09	£9,600
2009/10	£10,100
2010/11	£10,100

The annual exemption for discretionary trusts is half the above amounts (except where several trusts have been made by the same settlor). The rate of capital gains tax payable by such trusts was 34% for 1997/98 to 2003/04; 40% from 2004/05 to 2007/08; 18% from 2008/09 to 2009/10, and for gains in 2010/11 arising before 23 June 2010; and 28% for gains arising later in 2010/11 than that.

B.

Set out the capital gains that would have been chargeable on the trustees and beneficiaries in respect of the settlement in A if, although Stephen Jones had emigrated in 1989, the trustees had remained UK resident.

C.

Set out the capital gains that would have been chargeable on the trustees and settlor on the assumption that the settlement was on Stephen Jones for life and then to his four cousins at age 60 (with a right to income in the meantime after cessation of Stephen Jones's life interest).. Assume also that he did not emigrate in 1989, but the administration of the trust was transferred to non-resident trustees in February 1989 that the capital payments up to May 1998 were all made to Stephen Jones, that on 1 December 1998 Stephen Jones excluded himself from any further benefit from the trust by releasing his life interest in favour of his cousins and that the capital payments in May 1999 and July 2010 were made to the cousins.

D.

Explain briefly how the capital gains tax rules relating to the residence status of trustees changed under Finance Act 2006.

E.

How did the capital gains tax rules on non-resident trusts changed as a result of FA 2008 Schedule 7?

Answer

A. Overseas trusts – capital gains tax treatment – pre-1991 trust

Capital gains on creation of settlement

When a settlement is created, the settlor is deemed to have disposed of the entire property in the settlement at its market value, even if he retains an interest as beneficiary or is a trustee of the settlement, and he is therefore chargeable to capital gains tax accordingly (subject to available reliefs and exemptions).

When the assets transferred are business assets (TCGA 1992 s 165) or the transfer is immediately chargeable to inheritance tax (TCGA 1992 s 260), then providing the settlement is a UK resident settlement (see TCGA 1992 s 166) and (from 10 December 2003 onwards) it is not a settlor-interested settlement (within the broad definition of that term employed by TCGA s 169B), the settlor can avoid being liable for tax on the gains at that time by making an election to hold them over so that they reduce the trustees' base acquisition costs. For disposals prior to 19 March 1989 the holdover relief was under FA 1980 s 79 and covered all assets, although no relief was then available on a subsequent disposal for inheritance tax paid.

Since Stephen Jones had created a UK resident discretionary trust, the transfer of assets to the trust would be chargeable to inheritance tax. (If he had retained an interest in the trust, the trust income would be chargeable on him; this would also have applied to any capital gains realised by the trustees while Stephen Jones was UK resident – even while the trust was also UK resident – for tax years up to and including 2007/08. For capital gains following the emigration of the trusts see **part c**.)

The gain arising on the creation of the settlement were held over under FA 1980 s 79.

Capital gain on emigration of Stephen Jones

The emigration of Stephen Jones in February 1989 did not create a liability for capital gains tax on any gains held over, or on any increase in value to the date of emigration.

Export of trust prior to 19 March 1991

When the trust was taken over by non-resident trustees in February 1989, the gains of £110,000 held over on the creation of the trust became chargeable but the accrued gains of £45,000 on the trust's assets were not chargeable as they were not realised (TCGA 1992 s 168) (see **explanatory note 9** for emigration of a trust on or after 19 March 1991). The liability for the capital gains tax on the heldover gains was that of the trustees, although if the amount was not paid within twelve months from the due date (31 January 1990) then the Revenue could recover the tax from Stephen Jones.

Subsequent disposals

Although the trustees, as non-residents, are not chargeable to UK capital gains tax, the capital gains on disposals by the trustees must still be calculated as though they were still resident in the UK. (It sometimes happens that such calculations are only commissioned after many years when a distribution to a UK resident beneficiary has been made or is in prospect.) The gains are then apportioned to beneficiaries in proportion to any capital sums they have received from the trust in that or any earlier year, except to the extent that those capital sums have already been allocated to earlier capital gains. The apportioned amounts cannot exceed the actual capital sums received, and are chargeable on the beneficiaries in the year of apportionment. Only beneficiaries who are resident or ordinarily resident in the UK *and* domiciled in the UK are assessed to capital gains tax on gains apportioned to them (TCGA 1992 s 87). The normal annual exemption for capital gains tax is available to the UK domiciled beneficiaries on the apportioned amounts, and is applied against the gains attributed to them in priority to their own gains. The apportioned gains did not, however, attract taper relief in the beneficiaries' hands while that relief applied, since the gains will have been reduced by any available taper relief when they arose in the trust. It is not possible to offset a beneficiary's own capital losses against apportioned gains. (While taper relief was in force (1998/99 to 2007/08 inclusive) a settlor's own capital losses could be set against gains attributed to him under s 86, but only after they had so far as possible been set against his own gains; that restriction was removed with the abolition of taper relief with effect from 6 April 2008. See **explanatory notes 5, 10** and **11** in respect of the attribution of gains to resident settlors and also **explanatory note 17** re anti-avoidance provisions applicable from 21 March 2000.

The position in respect of the non-resident trust is as follows:

Gains

	£	£
1997/98		
Sale proceeds freehold office property June 1997		360,980
Market value May 1988	100,000	
Indexation allowance $(\dfrac{157.5 - 106.2}{106.5}) = .484$	48,400	
	148,400	
Gain		212,580
Sale proceeds Jonah plc shares September 1997		25,000
Cost March 1990	9,650	
Indexation allowance $(\dfrac{159.3 - 121.4}{121.4}) = .313$	3,020	
	12,670	
Gain		12,330
Total gains for 1997/98 (212,580 + 12,330) =		£224,910
1998/99	£	£
Sale proceeds UK property June 1998		200,000
Cost December 1988	62,034	
Indexation allowance to April 1998		
$(\dfrac{162.6 - 110.3}{110.3}) = .475$	29,466	
	91,500	
Total gains for 1998/99		108,500
2010/11		
		£
Gain on disposal of non-business assets July 2010		111,401
Total gains for 2010/11		111,401

Apportionment of gains

	Matthew £	Mark £	Mary £	Matilda £	Total £
1997/98					
Capital payments to date	–	–	60,000	20,000	80,000
Capital payments in year	90,000	60,000	–	70,000	220,000
	90,000	60,000	60,000	90,000	300,000
Apportioned gain (90:60:60:90)	67,473	44,982	44,982	67,473	224,910
Excess capital payments to date cf	22,527	15,018	15,018	22,527	75,090
1998/99					
Apportioned gain (restricted to actual payments to date)	22,527	15,018	15,018	22,527	75,090
Actual gain					108,500
Apportioned above					75,090
Unallocated gain of 1998/99 cf					33,410
1999/2000					
Capital payments in year	6,000	6,000	6,000	–	18,000
Apportioned gain (restricted to actual payments)	6,000	6,000	6,000	–	18,000
Unallocated gain bf					33,410
Apportioned in 1999/2000					18,000
Unallocated gain of 1998/99 cf					15,410
2010/11					
Capital payments in year	40,000	40,000	40,000	45,000	165,000
Apportionment of unallocated gain (40:40:40:45)	27,006	27,006	27,006	30,382	111,400
Apportionment of gain of year (restricted to actual payments)	3,736	3,736	3,736	4,202	15,410
Excess capital payments cf	9,258	9,258	9,258	10,416	38,190*

The apportioned gains will be chargeable on the beneficiaries (except Matthew prior to 2010/11, who is not UK domiciled) in the year of apportionment, eg Mark will be chargeable on £44,982 in 1997/98, £15,018 in 1998/99, £6,000 in 1999/2000, and £30,742 (27,006 + 3,736) in 2010/11, less his annual exemption in each case unless otherwise used.

In Matthew's case the £27,006 matched against current year's gains in 2010/11 is chargeable except so far as Matthew is a remittance basis user (so that he would not have any annual exemption) and does not remit the capital payment into the UK. He is not charged on his share of the unallocated gain brought forward from before 2008/09.

In 2010/11 the capital gains tax payable by the beneficiaries other than Matthew on their shares of the unallocated gain of £15,410 brought forward is increased by a supplementary charge, as the gain arose in 1998/99, and was not distributed in that year, or the following year (1999/2000). The charge runs from 1 December in the tax year following that in which the gain was made to 30 November in the tax year following that in which the capital payment was made (although the period cannot start earlier than six years before that 30 November date). The charge therefore runs from 1 December 2000 to 30 November 2010 = 9 years but limited to six years (maximum period) @ 10% per annum, so the capital gains tax payable by each beneficiary other than Matthew is increased by 60% (see **explanatory note 14**). The apportioned gain may, however, be treated as the lowest part of the chargeable gains of the year. For example:

Assume Matilda has no gains in her own right in the year 2010/11, and that her income for that year (net of her personal allowance) falls £5,000 short of the higher rate threshold. Her liability will be:

Total apportioned gains	34,584			
Less Annual exemption	10,100			
Capital gains tax chargeable on	24,484			
Tax payable @ 18% on	5,000	=	900	
Tax payable @ 28% on balance	19,484	=	5,455	6,355
Of which proportion relating to 1998/99 is 4,202/34,584		=		£772
Supplementary charge re 1998/99	£772 @ 60%	=		£463

(to be shown in box 9 on the capital gains summary sheet SA108 of the self-assessment tax return).

By comparison, if in 2010/11 Mary had capital gains of £7,100 in her own right from a disposal in May 2010, and had income (net of her personal allowance) that already exceeded the basic rate band, her liability would be:

Total apportioned gains	30,742			
Less annual exemption	10,100			
(see**explanatory note 8**)				
	20,642			
Own gains	7,100			
Capital gains tax chargeable on	27,742			
Tax relating to personal pre-23 June 2010 gains @ 18%	7,100	=	1,278	
Tax relating to apportioned gains from capital payment post 22-June 2010 @ 28%	20,642	=	5,780	7,058
Of which proportion relating to 1998/99 is 3,736/40,000 × £5,780		=		£540
Supplementary charge re 1998/99	£540	@ 60%	=	£324

B. Position if trust had remained UK resident after Stephen Jones emigrated

If the trustees had remained UK resident, the gain held over when the trust was created would not be chargeable until the underlying assets were disposed of. The revised capital gains on the trustees' disposals would be chargeable on them in the tax year in which the disposal took place. The trust would have an annual exemption of one half of the exemption for individuals and tax would be payable on the remaining gains at the rate applicable to trusts (later 'trust rate') from time to time prior to 6 April 2008 and at the rate of 28% for the 2010/11 gain realised after 22 June 2010. There would be no relief by reference to the non-domiciled beneficiary, Matthew. The position would therefore be:

	£	£
1997/98		
Sale proceeds freehold office property June 1997		360,980
Market value May 1988	100,000	
Less heldover gain:		
Cost March 1982	50,000	
Indexation allowance $(\dfrac{106.2 - 79.44}{79.44}) = .337$	16,850	
	66,850	
Market value on transfer to trust	100,000	
Gain held over	33,150	
Less halving relief (settlor acquired before 31 March 1982)	16,575	16,575
		83,425
Indexation allowance on £83,425 .484 as in A		40,378	123,803
Gain		237,177
Gain		237,177
Gain on Jonah plc shares acquired by trustees in March 1990 (as in A)		12,330
Total gains		249,507
Less annual exemption (½ × 6,500)		3,250
Gains chargeable at 34%		246,257
1998/99		
Gain on sale of UK property bought by trustees in December 1998 (as in A)		108,500
Less annual exemption (½ × 6,800)		3,400
Gains chargeable at 34%		105,100
2010/11		
Gain on sale of non-business chargeable assets July 2010 as in A		111,400
Less annual exemption (½ × 10,100)		5,050
Gains chargeable at 28%		106,350

C. Position if Stephen Jones had been life tenant and had remained UK resident but the trust had emigrated

The creation of a life interest settlement on Stephen Jones in May 1988 would give rise to chargeable gains which could be held over under FA 1980 s 79 as before. The heldover gain would then be chargeable on Stephen Jones on the export of the trust in February 1989 as in A above.

The subsequent disposals by the trust would be treated as in A, ie there would be a capital gains tax computation as though the trustees were still resident in the UK. Since the trust emigrated before 19 March 1991, the provisions of TCGA 1992 s 86 charging a settlor who retains an interest in a trust on gains as they arise would not apply before 1999/2000, in respect of gains arising on or after 17 March 1998 (see below). Gains arising before 17 March 1998 would be chargeable on Stephen Jones when distributions were made to him, with a supplementary charge if not distributed in the tax year in which the gain arose or the following tax year (as in A above).

By virtue of FA 1998 s 132 any gain arising on or after 17 March 1998 on a pre-19 March 1991 settlement whose trustees are not UK resident became chargeable on the settlor if he or his immediate family (or companies they control) can benefit from the settlement. Gains arising between 17 March 1998 and 5 April 1999 were deferred until 6 April 1999 to allow settlors to reorganise their affairs. Stephen Jones did this in December 1998 by releasing his life interest in favour of his cousins (though the release would not have achieved exemption from the s 86 charge if any persons referred to in **explanatory note 10** had been eligible beneficiaries). The release would be a potentially exempt transfer for inheritance tax since the cousins became entitled to interests in possession on the release of the prior life interest before 22 March 2006 (see **Examples 52** and**55**).

The gains attributable to Stephen Jones would be as follows (before his personal annual exemption or any personal losses prior to 6 April 1998):

	£
1997/98	
Capital payments to date	80,000
Capital payments in year	220,000
	300,000
Gains chargeable on Stephen Jones (actual)	224,910
Excess capital payments to date	75,090
1998/99	
Actual gains	108,500
Gains chargeable on Stephen Jones — excess capital payments to date	75,090
Unattributed gain of 1998/99 cf	33,410

As Stephen Jones excluded himself from benefit on 1 December 1998, the unattributed 1998/99 gain of £33,410 carried forward would not be chargeable on him, but would be apportioned among the four cousins along with subsequent gains and taxed as and when capital payments were made to them. The first capital payment was made in 1999/2000 and would be treated as in **part A** of the Example.

D.

Until the introduction of FA 2006, there were different rules determining the residence status of trustees for income and capital gains tax. These were harmonised by that Act so that trustees are treated as resident and ordinarily resident in the UK if either:

(a)   all the trustees are resident in the UK; or

(b)

   (i)   at least one trustee is resident in the UK, and

   (ii)   a settlor in relation to the settlement was resident, ordinarily resident or domiciled in the UK when the settlement is made (ITA 2007 s 475, TCGA 1992 s 69).

An additional rule introduced in the process is that, for the purpose of the above test, a trustee who is not resident in the UK is to be treated as so resident at any time when he acts as trustee in the course of a business which he carries on in the UK through a branch, agency or permanent establishment here. This rule is far from easy to apply in practice because of the uncertainties surrounding the concept (for corporate trustees) of a permanent establishment; HMRC's guidance on the matter can be found at http://www.hmrc.gov.uk/cnr/trustee-res-guidance.pdf, and further guidance, published by three professional bodies and agreed with HMRC, can be found at http://www.step.org/pdf/TAXGUIDE%203-10%20trustee%20residence%20%282%29.pdf.

The new rules came into effect on 6 April 2007.

E.

Prior to FA 2008 non-UK domiciled, but UK resident, individuals were exempt from both the settlor charge under TCGA 1992 s 86 and the beneficiary charge in TCGA 1992 s 87.

Following the amendments contained in FA 2008 the exemption from the settlor charge for non-UK domiciled settlors of non-UK resident trusts remained but, as from 6 April 2008, the beneficiary charge in TCGA 1992 s 87 applies to non-UK domiciled beneficiaries. The charge to tax under TCGA 1992 s 87 is subject to the remittance basis where the non-UK domiciled beneficiary has claimed the remittance basis under ITA 2007 s 809B or is entitled to it under ITA 2007 s 809D; and there are complex transitional rules where gains or capital payments occurred before 6 April 2008.

In addition, non-resident trustees were given an option to rebase trust assets to the market value as at 6 April 2008 so that trust gains accruing, but not realised, prior to 6 April 2008 would not be chargeable if matched to capital payments made on or after 6 April 2008 to non-UK domiciled beneficiaries. This option is open only to the trustees, and neither settlor nor beneficiaries have the right to make the election.

As a result of the changes:

Capital payments made from 6 April 2008 to non-UK domiciled beneficiaries are generally chargeable to tax.

The remittance basis applies if the non-UK domiciled beneficiary is a remittance basis user in the year when trust gains are treated as accruing to him. This is so whether the trust gains accrue on UK or non-UK assets. A capital distribution is treated as remitted if the distributed property is received in or brought to the UK. Benefits in kind will be treated as remitted if enjoyed or used in the UK.

Surplus capital payments brought forward from 2007/08 are not taxed unless (as previously) the non-UK domiciled beneficiary is both resident and domiciled in the UK when trust gains are treated as accruing to him. Surplus capital payments to non-UK domiciled beneficiaries made prior to 12 March 2008 can be franked against future post 5 April trust gains, but only to the extent that

- there are no capital payments made after 5 April 2008 to which the post 5 April 2008 gains can be attributed first, and

- there are no pre-April 2008 gains accruing by virtue of the rebasing election.

Capital payments to non-UK domiciled beneficiaries between 12 March and 5 April 2008 which are not matched to pre-6 April 2008 gains are left out of account in 2008/09 and subsequent years for the purposes of TCGA 1992 s 87.

If the trustees have made a rebasing election, the pre-6 April 2008 element of any gain treated as accruing to the beneficiary is matched with any surplus capital payments made between 12 March and 5 April 2008.

Trust gains brought forward from 2007/08 and treated under section TCGA 1992 s 87(4) as accruing to non-UK domiciled beneficiaries by virtue of capital payments made on or after 6 April 2008 are not taxed unless the non-UK domiciled beneficiary has become both resident and domiciled in the UK. Although the capital payment is received after 5 April 2008, if it is matched to trust gains realised prior to 6 April 2008 or to the pre-6 April 2008 element of any gain on a rebasing election, it is not necessary in this case for the non-UK domiciled beneficiary to be a remittance basis user.

Trusts which are non-UK resident on 6 April 2008 were given the option to elect for rebasing to the market value as at 6 April 2008 in relation to all assets held by the trust both directly and by its underlying companies. The effect, if the election is made, is that the pre-6 April 2008 element of any trust gains treated as accruing to non-UK domiciled beneficiaries after that date will not be taxed. The election must be made no later than 31 January following the first tax year (starting with 2008/09) in which either a UK resident beneficiary receives a capital payment or the trustees transfer any property to another settlement such that TCGA 1992 s 90 applies.

Any supplemental charge under TCGA 1992 s 91 for remittance basis users will be calculated based on the year in which the capital payment is made by the trustees, not the year in which it is remitted to the UK by the non-UK domiciled beneficiary.

A general matching rule was introduced, in s 87A, to the effect that a last in, first out rule is used to match any trust gains with capital payments made on or after 6 April 2008. This applies to all beneficiaries, not just non-UK domiciled beneficiaries, and applies in place of the original first in, first out rule in computing supplemental tax.

Explanatory Notes

Legislation relating to offshore trusts

(1)   The capital gains tax charges relating to offshore trusts contain many points of difficulty. On 21 May 1992 the Revenue issued a lengthy Statement of Practice (5/92) and also concession D40 dealing with the approach they will take in applying certain areas of the rules. The Revenue gave additional guidance in their Tax Bulletin of April 1995. The changes made by FA 1998 and, more recently, FA 2008 have, however, introduced many more areas of complexity and anomaly. Significant further changes were introduced by FA 2000, which are dealt with briefly below.

Effect of emigration of trust on trustees

(2)   If an election to hold over a settlor's gains had been made under TCGA 1992 s 165 or s 260 (or previously under FA 1980 s 79), the heldover gain crystallised if donee trustees emigrated before 19 March 1991. The amount chargeable was the gain originally held over (TCGA 1992 s 168).

For trusts emigrating on or after 19 March 1991, the emigrating trustees are charged not only on gains held over at the time the funds were settled but on the whole of any increase in value of the trust assets up to the time of emigration (see **note 9**). Since 19 March 1991 TCGA 1992 s 168 has accordingly no longer applied where a trust becomes non-resident and now relates only to the emigration of donees who are individuals.

(3)   Where a heldover gain has been charged under TCGA 1992 s 168 as a result of the emigration of the donee, the base cost at which the donee is deemed to have acquired the asset is its full value at the time of the gift, so that the trustees are treated as having acquired the assets at their value on the creation of the settlement. Where that was before 31 March 1982, HMRC apparently took the view that a general 31 March 1982 rebasing election could only be made by the trustees, even though any charge to capital gains tax would be made on the beneficiaries, but the point is no longer relevant after 5 April 2008 since 31 March 1982 value will be taken as the acquisition cost in all such cases after that.

(4)   Where a heldover gain was triggered on or after 6 April 1988 but before 6 April 2008 and was wholly or partly attributable to a disposal before 6 April 1988 of an asset acquired before 31 March 1982, only half of the heldover gain was charged to tax (TCGA 1992 Sch 4.4). This halving relief is illustrated in **part B** of the Example.

Attribution of gains of offshore trusts to beneficiaries or settlor

(5)   TCGA 1992 s 87 charges beneficiaries to tax on gains made by a non-resident trust to the extent that they receive capital payments from the trust. (There are equivalent charging provisions in s 89 for trusts which are UK resident but had been offshore at some time since 10 March 1981, and in Sch 4C where property has been transferred between settlements in circumstances that attract a deemed disposal under Sch 4B which was targeted at schemes known as flip-flop schemes.) Before FA 1998 this applied where the trustees were neither resident nor ordinarily resident at any time in the tax year, if at any time in that year or at the time when he made the settlement the settlor was domiciled and either resident or ordinarily resident in the UK. In respect of gains realised and capital payments made on or after 17 March 1998, the conditions relating to the settlor's residence and domicile no longer apply (FA 1998 s 130). Both before and after 17 March 1998, however, a beneficiary is not charged unless he is resident or ordinarily resident in the UK; and, until the FA 2008 amendments summarised in **part E** of the Example, he was also not charged unless he was domiciled in the UK at some time in the year in which the gains were apportioned to him (TCGA 1992 ss 2(1), 87(7)). Note that where the income tax provisions of ITA 2007 ss 727, 731 apply (transfer of assets abroad – liability of non-transferors on benefits received), any distributions or benefits are treated as being made first from accumulated income before being treated as capital payments under TCGA 1992 s 87. In this example all income has been remitted in addition to the capital payments made.

If the settlor retains an interest in the trust, gains are charged on him as and when they arise under the provisions of TCGA 1992 s 86 if the settlement becomes non-resident on or after 19 March 1991, or if funds are added or the beneficiaries are varied on or after that date, and in any event from 6 April 1999 in respect of gains arising on or after 17 March 1998 (see **explanatory notes 10 and 11**). Gains taxed on the settlor are not charged on the beneficiaries (s 87(3)).

As and when chargeable gains are made that are not taxed on the settlor under s 86, they are apportioned to the beneficiaries and charged to tax, but only to the extent that capital payments of an equivalent amount have been paid to the beneficiaries, either in the year in which the gains are made or in an earlier year (for this purpose 'the beneficiaries' could include the settlor if not chargeable under s 86). (See **explanatory note 17** for anti-avoidance provisions to counter schemes to avoid the charge on the beneficiaries.) Any gains that have not been distributed in this way are carried forward and apportioned as and when capital payments are made, as in 1999/2000 and 2010/11 in **part A** of the Example. The capital payments carried forward at the end of 1997/98 represented amounts that the beneficiaries had already received in respect of which no chargeable gains had arisen. When chargeable gains next arose in 1998/99 they were apportioned to the beneficiaries because of the excess capital payments at 5 April 1998.

(6)   It should be noted that the chargeable gains can exceed the capital payments received in a year because of amounts received in prior years (but not before 10 March 1981) (TCGA 1992 s 87(4), (5), (10)). Therefore Mary, who does not receive any capital payments in 1997/98, has a liability in that year on gains of £44,982, since she had received capital payments in excess of that amount in earlier years. On the other hand, a charge to tax may occur in a year in which no gains are made, because capital payments are made when there are unallocated gains brought forward. In 1999/2000 there are no gains but Mark and Mary are charged on brought forward gains because of the capital amounts received. Furthermore, if those unallocated gains brought forward were realised in an earlier year than the immediately previous year, a supplementary charge is payable, as shown (see **note 14**).

(7)   Prior to 2008/09 Matthew was not chargeable on the gains apportioned to him as, although he is resident and ordinarily resident in the UK, he is not UK domiciled. The apportionment nevertheless removed the gains from the record so far as the other beneficiaries were concerned. From 2008/09 onwards Matthew will in principle be charged to capital gains tax to the extent that post 6 April 2008 gains are matched with a post 6 April 2008 capital payment to him; but if he has the benefit of the remittance basis (with a claim where required) under ITA 2007 ss 809B–809E (with the loss of his annual exemption if the remittance basis is available only by virtue of a claim under s 809B) then he is charged only when he remits the capital payment into the UK.

(8)   Transitional rules in respect of the mid-year change of capital gains tax rate in 2010/11 (see **Example 47 explanatory note 15**), so far as relating to the offshore trust rules discussed in **explanatory notes 5** to **7** , are contained in F (No 2) A 2010 Sch 1 paras 21 and 22. Gains attributed to a settlor under s 86 will – surprisingly beneficially – be treated as arising before 23 June 2010 so as to attract the 18% rate, even where the gains are realised by the trustees after 22 June 2010. So far as concerns gains attributed to beneficiaries under s 87 (or s 80 or Sch 4C), gains resulting from matching capital payments received before 23 June 2010 are treated as arising before 23 June 2010 (even if they are matched with gains realised by the trustees later in 2010/11); correspondingly gains resulting from matching capital payments received on or after 23 June 2010 are treated as arising after 22 June 2010 (even if they are matched with gains realised by the trustees before 23 June 2010, whether in 2010/11 or earlier). This rule does not deal explicitly with capital payments treated as received by virtue of continuing benefits (see **explanatory note 16**) but it is thought that the benefit can if necessary be time-apportioned between the two parts of the tax year.

By virtue of TCGA 1992 s 4B (inserted by F (No 2) A 2010 Sch 1 para 3), where a person's chargeable gains are taxable at different rates, his annual exemption (and any allowable losses) may be deducted from those gains in whatever way is most beneficial. This will usually mean, as here, deducting them from the gains that are liable at 28%; the benefit is that much greater in this example to the extent that part of the attributed gain liable at 28% is also exposed to the supplementary charge.

Emigration of trust on or after 19 March 1991

(9)   In **part A** of the Example the trust became non-resident in February 1989 and the gains held over on creation of the settlement became chargeable at that time, but not accrued gains on the trust's assets, as they had not been realised. If trustees of a settlement become non-resident on or after 19 March 1991, then they are deemed to have disposed of and immediately reacquired the settled property at market value on the day they become non-resident, so that not only any heldover gains but also accrued gains become chargeable

at that time (TCGA 1992 s 80). TCGA 1992 s 168 imposing a separate charge on heldover gains, as illustrated in **part A**, therefore no longer applies where trustees become non-resident on or after 19 March 1991.

The deemed disposal under TCGA 1992 s 80(2) does not apply to trading assets of a branch or agency which remain chargeable to UK capital gains tax under TCGA 1992 s 10. Rollover relief on replacement of business assets under TCGA 1992 ss 152–156 cannot be claimed if the new assets are acquired after the trust becomes non-resident and are outside the UK tax charge. These provisions also apply to dual resident trusts that are exempt from UK tax on gains because of a double tax treaty.

The deemed disposal under TCGA 1992 s 80(2) is also disapplied (subject to revenue protection exceptions in the case of assets disposed of during the period of non-residence, and assets protected by double taxation arrangements) if the trust becomes non-resident solely by reason of the death of a trustee and the trust is repatriated within 6 months thereafter; but since 6 April 2007 this would only be relevant in the case of settlements whose settlor had no UK residence or domicile connections at the time he made the settlement (see **part D** of the Example).

On the emigration of a trust, beneficiaries would normally be treated as having acquired their interest in the trust at the market value at the date of the trust's emigration. Where a trust becomes non-resident on or after 21 March 2000, this uplift to market value does not apply where the trust has a stockpile of gains at the date of emigration that have not been attributed to beneficiaries (TCGA 1992 s 85).

Trusts in which the settlor retains an interest

(10) Where a settlement with non-resident trustees is made on or after 19 March 1991, or becomes non-resident on or after that date, and the settlor is resident or ordinarily resident and domiciled in the UK, and the settlor or his spouse/civil partner, children, children's spouses/civil partners, a company controlled by one or more of those persons, or an associated company, can benefit from the settlement, then the gains of the settlement are attributed to the settlor (TCGA 1992 s 86). For settlements with non-resident trustees made on or after 17 March 1998, grandchildren and their spouses (and, since 5 December 2005, their civil partners) are added to the list of defined persons for s 86 (FA 1998 s 131). This also applies to pre-17 March 1998 trusts if they become non-resident or if funds are added or grandchildren become beneficiaries on or after that date (or a grandchild who was already a beneficiary enjoys a benefit for the first time on or after that date that he would not have been able to enjoy under the terms of the settlement as it stood at that date) (FA 1998 Sch 22).

Before FA 2002 a trust's gains were reduced by taper relief before being attributed to a settlor and the settlor could not use his personal losses to reduce the gains. The abolition of taper relief with effect from 6 April 2008 simplifies this calculation.

The settlor can recover the tax he has paid from the trustees without that amount being treated as a capital payment by the settlement. For this purpose he may require the Revenue to issue him with a certificate of the tax paid (TCGA 1992 Sch 5.6). There is no provision for the settlor to obtain payment from the trustees before he has paid the tax, even though the disposal proceeds relating to the gains will be in the trust; HMRC take the strict view on this point, but (at least where large amounts are at stake) will co-operate to provide a certificate rapidly so as to enable a quick reimbursement. If the settlor fails to take all reasonable steps to recover the tax, then that amount will be considered to be an addition to the settlement unless the trust is unable to remit the amount because of local restrictions. (It may also constitute an addition to the settlement, and a chargeable transfer, for inheritance tax purposes.)

The provisions of s 86 do not apply in a tax year in which the settlor dies, nor in which the last of those individuals who cause him to have an interest dies, or, where the interest is that of a spouse/civil partner, they cease to be married/the civil partnership is dissolved.

(11) Before FA 1998 a non-resident trust made before 19 March 1991 was only subject to the provisions of TCGA 1992 s 86 outlined in **explanatory note 10** if funds were added or the beneficiaries were varied to include any of the defined persons.

With effect from 6 April 1999, gains of pre-19 March 1991 non-resident trusts are no longer excluded from the provisions of TCGA 1992 s 86 (TCGA 1992 Sch 5). Unremitted gains of the period 17 March 1998 to

5 April 1999 were deemed to arise on 6 April 1999, thus bringing them within the provisions. The charge was delayed to enable trusts to reorganise their affairs, for example by excluding the range of defined persons as beneficiaries, or by becoming resident or by winding up the trust. There are, however, anti-avoidance provisions in FA 1989 Sch 23 to prevent exploitation of the transitional period.

The revised provisions do not apply to 'protected settlements', ie where the beneficiaries are confined to:

(i)   children of the settlor or his spouse/civil partner who are under 18;

(ii)   unborn children of the settlor or his spouse/civil partner;

(iii)   future spouses/civil partners of the settlor or his children;

(iv)   persons outside the defined categories (eg cousins, as in **part A**of the Example).

> This protection ceases, however, when the child reaches age 18. Furthermore, distributions to grandchildren are caught as a result of FA 1998 s 131 (see **explanatory note 10**). The Revenue have, however, stated that the existence of grandchildren (of whatever age) as beneficiaries of a pre-19 March 1991 settlement at 6 April 1999 will not cause the settlement to fall outside the 'protected' category (Tax Bulletin December 1998).

(12)   Where capital payments are made on or after 6 April 1999 to beneficiaries of pre-19 March 1991 trusts in which the settlor has an interest, they will be matched with any unallocated gains that arose before 17 March 1998, and only when all such unallocated gains have been matched with capital payments will capital payments to beneficiaries be regarded as having been already charged on the settlor. Before 6 April 2008 this matching was on a first in, first out basis (attracting the supplementary charge if appropriate – see **explanatory note 14**); since that date, as indicated in **part E** of the Example, matching is on a last in, first out basis so that the incidence of the supplementary charge may be deferred (but potentially at the cost of more years' worth of supplementary charge when it does bite).

Settlor who is temporarily non-resident

(13)   To be liable to UK capital gains tax the settlor must be UK resident or ordinarily resident in the tax year that gains arise. Under TCGA 1992 ss 10A and 86A, however, a UK domiciled settlor can also be liable if after becoming non-resident he returns to the UK having been away for fewer than five complete tax years. The charge, on gains arising or attributed to him in the period of absence, is made in the tax year of return to the UK, but it is reduced by any gains that have been charged on UK resident beneficiaries during his period of non-residence.

From 2003/04 (or earlier by election) until 2007/08 inclusive (after which taper relief was abolished), gains will not normally be reduced by a trust's taper relief before being attributed to a settlor (FA 2002 s 51 and Sch 11) (see **explanatory note 10**). This does not, however, apply where the gains on which a returning settlor is charged have been reduced by gains already attributed to UK resident beneficiaries during the settlor's absence. The gains in such circumstances will continue to be reduced by the trust's taper relief before they are attributed to the settlor and will not be able to be reduced by the settlor's losses (TCGA 1992 s 86A as amended by FA 2002 Sch 11 para 5).

Supplementary charge

(14)

Before FA 1991 there was no financial cost to deferring payment of capital gains tax on gains realised by offshore trusts through not remitting the gains. Where such gains are assessable on beneficiaries for 1992/93 onwards, the tax payable is increased by a supplementary charge (TCGA 1992 ss 91–97). The charge runs from 1 December in the tax year following that in which the trustees' gains arose to 30 November in the tax year after that in which the gain is apportioned to the beneficiary as a result of a capital payment (any capital payments being regarded as applying to the earliest unallocated gains first). If the period would otherwise exceed six years, however, it starts on 1 December six years before the 30 November charging date (TCGA 1992 s 92(4)(5)). The supplementary charge does not apply where gains are matched by capital payments in the same or following tax year. Gains made before 6 April 1990 were treated as made in 1990/91. Trustees could distribute such gains before 6 April 1992 without any supplementary charge on the beneficiary. Later gains may be distributed in the same or the following tax year without the supplementary charge becoming payable, subject to the 6 April 1990 fund of undistributed gains being matched with payments first. The charge is at an annual rate of 10% of the tax on the capital payment, giving an overall maximum possible rate (for gains attributed by reference to capital payments received after 22 June 2010) of 60% of 28% = 16.8%, in addition to the capital gains tax of 28% already payable ie a total charge of 44.8%.

In **part A** of the example, the 1997/98 capital gain is more than matched by capital payments made in or before that year, so that the whole gain is apportioned to beneficiaries in that year. The 1998/99 gain of £108,500 is distributed as to £75,090 in that year and £18,000 in 1999/2000, but £15,410 remains unallocated until 2010/11, so that the supplementary charge arises on that part of the 2010/11 assessable gains which derives from that brought-forward balance.

(15) Prior to 6 April 2008 careful planning of capital payments could, in some cases, reduce the overall amount of supplementary charge payable. Say, for example, an overseas trust has two beneficiaries, one liable to capital gains tax at 20% and the other at 40%, and the trustees were to make a capital payment which would partly relate to gains of a year to which the supplementary charge would apply and partly to a later year for which the supplementary charge was not relevant. If a capital payment was made to the lower taxed beneficiary first, this would relate to earlier gains before later gains, so that any part of the payment that attracted the supplementary charge would suffer the additional charge on a 20% tax bill. A payment in a subsequent year could then be made to the higher taxed beneficiary out of gains not liable to the supplementary charge. This ceased to be the case when the 18% flat rate of capital gains tax was introduced in 2008/09, but may again be the case (to a lesser degree) since an individual's liability to the higher 28% rate depends on his total income and gains being above the basic rate limit for income tax. Similar planning points could apply where there is a non-UK domiciled beneficiary like Matthew in this example who is subject to the remittance basis and does not remit his capital payment, or where, although UK domiciled, a beneficiary is not resident or ordinarily resident in the UK.

Treatment of interest-free loans

(16) Many non-resident trustees have regarded payments to beneficiaries to be by way of loan (often interest-free), rather than capital payments to which gains would be apportioned. Such a loan was considered in a criminal case in relation to a confiscation of property order (R v Harvey (1998)). The loan was secured by way of a charge on the offender's property. The loan was disregarded, because it was stated to be in reality a gift and that the charge was unlikely to be enforced. The Revenue took a similar view for tax purposes in relation to offshore trusts, and succeeded in the cases of Billingham v Cooper and Edwards v Fisher, heard by the Court of Appeal in 2001. In both cases overseas trustees had made interest-free loans, repayable on demand, to UK resident (settlor) beneficiaries of pre-March 1991 trusts. Although the Revenue conceded that such loans had little initial benefit, they contended that the continuation of the loans, through the failure of the trustees to call them in when repayable on demand, meant that benefit was provided on a continuing basis. The Court of Appeal agreed, stating that in giving effect to the purpose of TCGA 1992 ss 87 and 97, it needed to be considered what benefit a beneficiary actually received, so that the 'loan' payments to beneficiaries were within the capital payments and supplementary charges rules. Similar principles are applied to occupation or use of trust assets in kind for less than commercial consideration (eg rent-free occupation of property).

Apportionment of gains of non-resident companies

(17) A chargeable gain that arises in a non-resident company which would be a close company if resident in the UK is apportioned between its participators. In so far as a participator (alone or with his associates) has at least 10% (5% prior to 7 March 2001) of the gain apportioned to him, and is UK resident or ordinarily resident (and, if an individual, domiciled) in the UK, he is chargeable to capital gains tax on the apportioned amount. These provisions apply to UK resident trustees as well as to individuals (see **Example 50 explanatory note 8** for special anti-avoidance provisions for trustees). Although chargeable to capital gains tax, the gain is computed using corporation tax rules, with indexation allowance (but not taper relief, prior to its abolition) applying (see **Tolley's Taxwise I 2010/11 Example 70** for details) (TCGA 1992 s 13).

Such gains may also be apportioned to non-resident trustees (s 13(10)), and may in turn be chargeable on the settlor or beneficiaries under the provisions considered in **explanatory notes 5** and **6** above. The computation of the gain may be affected by a rebasing election made by the trustees under FA 2008 Sch 7 para 126 (see **part E** of the Example).

Where the applicable rate of capital gains tax in 2010/11 depends on the date a gain was realised (see **Example 47 explanatory note 15** and **explanatory note 8** above), a gain apportioned under s 13 will be dealt with by reference to the date of the company's disposal.

These provisions do not apply to gains on the disposal of an asset used for the purposes of a trade carried on by the non-resident company wholly outside the UK, or to trading currency.

If the gain is distributed within four years of the date the gain is realised or, if earlier, three years after the end of the accounting period in which the gain is realised (within two years after the gain was realised for gains realised before 7 March 2001), then the capital gains tax on the apportioned amount can be offset against the income tax on the distribution (or capital gains tax if a capital distribution) that is payable by the participator to whom it was apportioned. (This rule does not protect gains that are apportioned to non-UK resident trustees but the attributed to the settlor or beneficiaries under the provisions discussed in **explanatory notes 5** and **6** above.) If not so relieved, the tax is treated as an expense for capital gains tax in computing any subsequent gain on the disposal of the participator's interest in the company (TCGA 1992 s 13).

Question

Explain, with appropriate reference to both statute and case law, what is meant by an 'interest in possession' in settled property, commenting specifically on the impact that powers granted to the trustees may have on the position.

Summarise the ways in which settlements with an 'interest in possession' are treated for inheritance tax purposes and explain the position both before and after the changes made by Finance Act 2006.

Answer

Meaning of 'interest in possession'

The Inheritance Tax Act 1984 uses the term 'interest in possession' but it is not defined clearly in the legislation. The meaning of the expression is essentially one of the general law: it must be an interest in the trust property (ie an entitlement, as distinct from a mere right to be considered as an object of a discretionary power); and the interest be in possession (as distinct, primarily, from being in reversion such as to come into possession only at some time in the future).

The definition put forward by the Revenue, and accepted by the House of Lords in *Pearson and Others v CIR (1980)*, is that 'an interest in possession in settled property exists where the person having the interest has an immediate entitlement to any income produced by that property as the income arises; but that a discretion or power, in whatever form, which can be exercised after income arises so as to withhold it from that person negatives the existence of an interest in possession. For this purpose a power to accumulate income is regarded as a power to withhold it, unless any accumulations must be held solely for the person having the interest or his personal representatives.' Thus an interest in possession can be summarised as being a present right of present enjoyment, without any further decision of the trustees being required.

Having the present right of present enjoyment means that the beneficiary must have a right to enjoy the income (if any) of the settlement as it arises. A beneficiary may have an interest in possession in property which produces no income. It is not necessary for the beneficiary to be entitled to the gross income from the settled property: the fact that the trustees may deduct their administrative expenses from the gross income does not defeat a beneficiary's interest in possession. Because of this a beneficiary will still have an interest in possession even if he has to wait until expenses have been deducted before receiving the income.

There have been a number of cases in which the issue has been whether or not an interest in possession was created by reason of provisions allowing a beneficiary to reside in property owned by the trustees. This issue is essentially just one manifestation of the same test, namely a present right of present enjoyment. See for Example *IRC v Lloyds Private Banking (1998)*, *Woodhall's Executor v IRC (2000)*, *Faulkner v IRC (2001)*, *Cook and Daw v IRC (2002)*, *Oakley and Hutson v IRC (2005)*, *Judge v HMRC (2005)* and *Fairbairn's Trustees v HMRC (2007)*.

An interest in possession will not subsist in settled property if the trustees have powers that affecting the net income remaining after payment of administration expenses. Purely administrative powers such as power to pay taxes, to charge fees or pay insurance do not defeat an interest in possession. On the other hand the existence of dispositive powers such power to accumulate income, or a power to pay or apply income to or for the benefit of another beneficiary, will prevent an interest in possession from subsisting in the settled property.

However, it is immaterial whether or not powers exist which could bring an interest in possession to an end; if an interest meets the foregoing characteristics then, while it continues, it is an interest in possession, and the exercise of the powers in question would merely bring the interest to an end, not prevent its existence for the time being.

Inheritance tax treatment of settlements

Where property is held in trust, the inheritance tax treatment of that property depends on the type of trust. The Inheritance Tax Act 1984 divides trusts into three categories:

- those where there is an interest in possession that results in the beneficiary being treated as beneficially entitled to the underlying settled property under IHTA 1984 s 49; as a result the property is within the beneficiary's estate for IHT purposes, and since 2006 these IIPs can be referred to as '**estate IIPs**';

- those where there is no estate interest in possession (and generally no interest in possession at all), but which are given a degree of privileged status (see **Example 59 explanatory note 8**); and

- all other trusts. The property in these (unless excluded property, typically within IHTA 1984 s 48(3),(3A)) will be in the 'relevant property' regime, which since 2006 can be regarded as the mainstream IHT rules for trusts; prior to 2006 the relevant property rules were largely confined to discretionary trusts. Since then many interest in possession trusts will be within the relevant property regime.

Estate interests in possession since FA 2006

As a preliminary point, in certain circumstances an interest in possession may be treated as existing for inheritance tax purposes even though none exists within the definition explored above. (The treatment of such trusts for income tax and capital gains tax will follow the nature of the trust itself: there is no actual interest in possession and the deeming is solely for inheritance tax purposes; but it will of course be the inheritance tax treatment which affects the availability of capital gains tax holdover relief under TCGA 1992, s 260 if an asset leaves the settlement.) Examples include the tenant's interest under a lease for life granted otherwise than for full consideration (IHTA 1984 s 43(3)); a discretionary trust of income that arises on forfeiture of a protected life interest under Trustee Act 1925 s 33; or a disabled person's trust under IHTA 1984 s 89(2) or 89A. However these deemed interests in possession will only be estate IIPs if they fall into one or other of the four categories listed below.

Since 22 March 2006 the four cases where an interest in possession will be within IHTA 1984 s 49, such as to be an estate IIP, are as follows, provided in all cases the interest in possession is not in favour of a bereaved minor in circumstances where the trust falls within the rules for bereaved minors' trusts in s 71A (see below):

(a)   *Pre-2006 interests* (a non-statutory term): Where the beneficiary has been entitled to the IIP since before 22 March 2006.

(b)   *Transitional serial interests*: Where the beneficiary became beneficially entitled to the IIP in succession to:

   (i)   the estate IIP of a beneficiary who had been beneficially entitled to that IIP since before 22 March 2006, and where the succession (in lifetime or on death) took place before 6 October 2008 (s 49C);

   (ii)   the estate IIP of the beneficiary's spouse or civil partner who had been beneficially entitled to that IIP since before 22 March 2006, and where the succession took place on the death of the spouse/civil partner (s 49D); or

   (iii)   one of a succession of estate IIPs, going back to before 22 March 2006, in a contract of life insurance held in the trust immediately before that date, so long as each succession (other than the first within (i) above) took place on the death of the beneficiary with the previous estate IIP (s 49E).

(c)   *Immediate post-death interests*: Where the settlement was effected by will or under the law relating to intestacy and the beneficiary became beneficially entitled to the IIP on the death in question (s 49A).

(d)   *Disabled person's interests*: These are of four related types:

   (i)   Where the beneficiary was a disabled person (within the definition in IHTA 1984 s 89(4)–(6) – broadly, incapable of looking after his affairs because of mental disorder, or in receipt of disability living allowance at the middle or higher rate or of attendance allowance) at the date the property in question was originally settled, and either

   • has a deemed interest in possession within s 89(2) (which requires that, during his lifetime, there is no actual interest in possession and that, if any of the trust property is applied during his lifetime, at least half of the amounts so applied must be applied for his benefit) (s 89B(1)(a)), or

   • became beneficially entitled to his (actual) interest in possession on or after 22 March 2006 (s 89B(1)(c)); or

   (ii)   Where (on or after 22 March 2006) the beneficiary makes the settlement for his own benefit and he satisfies HMRC that, at that time, he has a condition which makes it reasonable to expect that he will as a result become a disabled person within the definition just mentioned, and either

   • the beneficiary-settlor has a deemed interest in possession within s 89A (the conditions of which are similar to s 89(2) but so that *any* application of trust property during his lifetime must be for his benefit (not merely one half of any property applied), and with the additional requirement that, if the settlement is capable of being brought to an end during his lifetime, then as a result either he will be absolutely entitled or another disabled person's interest within (i) above will subsist) (s 89B(1)(b)), or

- the beneficiary-settlor has an (actual) interest in possession and *any* application of trust property during his lifetime must be for his benefit (s 89B(1)(d)).

With effect from 9 December 2009 a fifth category was added, namely:

(e) *Purchased IIPs*: Where the beneficiary became entitled to the IIP on or after 9 December 2009, at a time when he was domiciled in the UK, and did so under an arm's length transaction within s 10 (s 5(1B)).

If an interest in possession is a disabled person's interest then it cannot also be an immediate post-death interest or a transitional serial interest, even if it would otherwise meet the requirements for those respective categories.

The rules for bereaved minors' trusts are found in IHTA 1984 s 71A and, if applicable, take priority over those for estate IIPs (though an IIP in favour of a minor will be unusual). They apply only where the settlement in question:

(1) was set up for the benefit of a beneficiary under age 18 at least one of whose parents has died (note the extended meaning of 'parent' in s 71H which includes step-parents and those with parental responsibilities):

- by a parent of the beneficiary in their will,

- by the English intestacy rules on the death of the beneficiary's parent or remoter ancestor (this could only arise in the case of remoter ancestors if the intervening generation(s) have already died, though this would change if the disclaimer provisions of the Civil Law Reform Bill, consulted on in draft by the Ministry of Justice in early 2010, were enacted and brought into force), or

- under the Criminal Injuries Compensation Scheme,

(2) ring-fences the income for the benefit of the beneficiary during his minority, and

(3) gives the beneficiary the capital and income of the trust absolutely when he reaches the age of 18.

Inheritance tax treatment of trusts with an estate interest in possession

Where s 49 does apply, the value of the settled property in which the estate IIP subsists forms part of the estate of that person for IHT purposes.

There are two consequences:

(a) Distributions of capital to the beneficiary with the estate IIP do not attract an inheritance tax charge, unlike the position with relevant property trusts. The supporting capital was previously part of the taxpayer's estate in the form of trust property and is now part of his estate in the form of free estate.

(b) On the beneficiary's death the settled property is aggregated with his free estate and tax is charged on the entirety. If the estate IIP comes to an end in any other way, or is disposed of by the beneficiary in his lifetime, this involves a deemed transfer of value by the beneficiary, with effects on his inheritance tax accumulation as if he had made the gift out of his free capital.

Since 22 March 2006, such a transfer in the beneficiary's lifetime is a PET (or exempt, if in favour of his spouse/civil partner) only if

- another individual becomes absolutely entitled,

- a disabled person's interest arises,

- (during the transitional period to 5 October 2008 only) a transitional serial interest arises, or

- the estate IIP was an immediate post-death interest (not a disabled person's interest) and the property becomes held for a minor child of the deceased settlor under a bereaved minor's trust (IHTA 1984 s 3A(1A)).

In other cases where the trust continues (other than for wholly charitable purposes) the termination of the estate IIP will involve an immediately chargeable transfer and the property will no longer form part of the beneficiary's estate; but if the beneficiary remains interested it will be caught by the gifts with reservation rules at his death or when the reservation ceases.

Although the tax liability in respect of the settled property will usually be imposed on the trustees rather than on the beneficiary with the estate IIP, the effect of this treatment is to increase the rate of tax on any subsequent chargeable transfer by the beneficiary or, in the case of a liability on death, to increase the estate rate and therefore the tax payable on the beneficiary's free estate at death by reason of the aggregation of the free estate and the settled property.

Inheritance tax treatment of relevant property trusts (with or without an interest in possession)

The relevant property rules can be briefly summarised as follows (see further **Examples 59 to 62**):

(a)   On the tenth anniversary of the creation of the settlement it is subject to a ten-year charge (s 64).

The charge, on the value of the relevant property after deducting any business property relief or agricultural property relief, is 30% of the tax that would be payable on a notional chargeable transfer (see (c)(i) below); for many years it has been impossible for the resultant rate to exceed 6%, but this would be affected if, for Example, the scale of rates on death were to change to include a rate higher than 40%.

A further such charge will occur every ten years thereafter.

(b)   There is also an exit charge when property in such a settlement ceases to be relevant property (either because the property leaves the settlement or for any other reason, for Example the property becoming subject to an estate interest in possession – now in practice confined to a disabled person's interest) (s 65).

The charge in this event is at a proportion of the rate used on the last ten-year anniversary (X fortieths where X is the number of complete quarter-years that have elapsed since that ten-year anniversary). This will be suitably adjusted if further property has been settled since the ten-year anniversary, or if property which was not relevant property at that time has become relevant property since then (s 69).

If there has not yet been a ten-year anniversary, the rate to which the X fortieths fraction is applied is again worked out by reference to a notional chargeable transfer, different to that used for the ten-yearly charge (see (c)(ii) below) (s 68).

(c)   The rate scale used when to work out the tax on these notional chargeable transfers is what could be called the scale for lifetime chargeable transfers, ie one half of the normal (death) scale applicable at the date of charge. The trust has its own inheritance tax accumulation, based primarily on that of the settlor when he put property into the trust.

  (i)   The notional chargeable transfer used to work out the tax on a ten-yearly charge (which is then used in relation to subsequent exit charges) is generally a transfer of the relevant property itself, plus other property in the trust that has never yet been relevant property, and any property in related settlements (made on the same date). In the latter two cases the valuation date is immediately after the property in question was settled, whereas the relevant property is valued at the date of the ten-yearly charge. The IHT accumulation to be used will be that of the settlor in the seven years before he made the trust, but will include also the amount on which exit charges ((**b**) **above**) have been imposed in the ten years leading up to the ten-yearly charge (s 66).

  If the settlement was made before the introduction of capital transfer tax on 27 March 1974, the only components of the notional transfer are the value of the relevant property at the date of the ten-yearly charge, and the amount subjected to exit charges in the preceding ten years.

(ii)   The notional chargeable transfer used to work out the tax on an exit charge occurring before any ten-year anniversary has occurred is based on the value of the trust property (and of that in any related settlement) immediately after it was settled (without the benefit, for this purpose, of any reliefs), using the settlor's IHT accumulation in the preceding seven years (s 68).

Explanatory Notes

Privileged trusts with a non-estate interest in possession

(1)   It is technically possible for an interest in possession to subsist in favour of the beneficiary of either of the two new (relatively limited) forms of privileged trusts for younger beneficiaries introduced by FA 2006:

(a)   a bereaved minor's trust, subsisting under the will or intestacy of the beneficiary's deceased parent where the child is still under age 18 and will become absolutely entitled to capital by age 18 (IHTA 1984 s 71A).

(b)   an age 18-to-25 trust where the beneficiary is still under age 25 and will become absolutely entitled to capital by age 25 (IHTA 1984 s 71D). Such a trust may subsist either under the will of the beneficiary's deceased parent, or in favour of a beneficiary under a pre-2006 trust which until 5 April 2008 was within the former regime for accumulation and maintenance trusts in IHTA 1984 s 71.

It will be rare for an interest in possession to subsist while the beneficiary is under age 18, because Trustee Act 1925 s 31 has the effect of precluding an interest in possession pending attainment of that age (*Stanley v IRC (1944)*). Deliberate drafting to exclude the effects of that section would be needed. But if the beneficiary does have an interest in possession during his minority then it shares some limited characteristics with an estate IIP (but specifically without bringing the trust property within the beneficiary's estate) and could on that account be termed a 'privileged minor's IIP':

• distributions of capital for the beneficiary's benefit, or such that he becomes absolutely entitled not later than age 18, will not attract an inheritance tax charge (IHTA 1984 ss 71B(2)(a), (c), 71E(2)(a), (d)) – though this is of course the case whether or not he has an interest in possession;

• a capital gains tax uplift in base value applies on the beneficiary's death under age 18 (TCGA 1992 s 72(1A), (1B), 73(2A).

Once the beneficiary has passed age 18 without having become absolutely entitled (under an age 18-to-25 trust) – whether or not he attains an interest in possession at that point – both these advantages evaporate, though the trust remains outside the relevant property regime and the rate of tax on his absolute entitlement or death may well be more favourable.

A pre-2006 accumulation and maintenance trust may still, for the time being, remain within IHTA 1984 s 71 (and so outside the relevant property regime) if, since 5 April 2008 or before, the terms of the trust secure that absolute entitlements will arise not later than age 18 (irrespective of the relationship of the beneficiaries to the settlor, or whether the trust was formed in lifetime or on death). However, unlike a bereaved minor's trust it is by definition impossible for an accumulation and maintenance trust to confer an interest in possession since the absence of an interest in possession is one of the criteria for the application of IHTA 1984 s 71 (see s 71(1)(b)).

Creation of interest in possession settlement

(2)   Until 2006 the lifetime formation of an interest in possession trust for an individual – though triggering a chargeable disposal of the assets in question for capital gains tax purposes (see **Example 50 explanatory note 4**) – would not involve an immediate chargeable transfer:

• either it was neutral if in favour of the settlor himself,

- or it was an exempt transfer if in favour of the settlor's spouse or civil partner, or to the extent that it was covered by annual or marriage gift exemptions or the normal income expenditure exemption,

- or it was a potentially exempt transfer if in favour of any other individual – so that (apart from the gift with reservation rules) an actual charge to inheritance tax would be escaped if the settlor survived for seven years, and even if he failed to do so the value transferred would be fixed at the date of the transfer even if the trust property had increased in value by the time the settlor died.

Similarly the formation of an accumulation and maintenance trust involved merely a potentially exempt transfer (and a capital gains tax disposal).

Since 22 March 2006, the transfer of assets to either sort of trust (even if for the benefit of the settlor or his spouse or civil partner) will constitute an immediately chargeable transfer for inheritance tax (save where covered by the annual or normal income expenditure exemptions), and the trust will be within the relevant property regime, with the sole exception of a transfer to a trust conferring a disabled person's interest. Care is needed in cases where the trust is for the settlor's benefit: see the Example in **note 4** below.

The transfer will still involve a disposal for capital gains tax purposes; but because it is immediately chargeable – provided the trustees are UK resident, and subject to the important exception of settlor-interested trusts (TCGA 1992 s 169B–169C) – holdover relief will be available under TCGA 1992 s 260 so that an immediate capital gains tax charge need not be incurred.

Furthermore, if a UK resident beneficiary later becomes absolutely entitled to the same asset under the relevant property trust, holdover relief should again be available to allow him to take over the trustees' base value which in turn they would have taken over from the settlor. (See however the warning about entitlements within three months after commencement of the settlement, or after a ten-year anniversary, in **Example 50 explanatory note 6.**)

Discretionary or relevant property trusts

(3)   Detailed notes on the tax treatment of discretionary trusts are given in **Examples 59 to 63.**

Example

(4)   Hardy settles £500,000 for himself for life, with remainder to his wife. The transfer is a chargeable lifetime settlement and so inheritance tax will be payable at the 20% lifetime rate on the excess over his available nil rate band. The settlement will be subject to ten-year and exit charges as appropriate.

If Hardy has nothing more than the right to income, there will be no gift with reservation: the "gift" (as opposed to transfer of value) is merely of the reversionary interest, see *Commissioner of Stamp Duties (NSW) v Perpetual Trustee Co (1943)* and cf IHTM14392. (Care would therefore be needed in relation to the pre-owned assets charge, the application of which would depend on the nature of the trust assets; let land would be safest.)

However, if there is a power to release capital to Hardy, or he is the object of some other power of appointment, the transfer will be treated as a gift of the whole property and caught by the reservation of benefit rules. Consequently, the trust fund (of whatever value at that time) will be subject to inheritance tax as part of Hardy's estate when he dies. Some relief from the double charge (on creation of the settlement and on death) would be available under the double charges regulations SI 1987/1130: see further **Examples 19, 20 and 24.**

The problem would have been worse had Hardy settled assets which gave rise to a chargeable gain. The transfer would have given rise to a capital gains tax liability with no scope for any holdover relief (because the donee trust was settlor-interested).

Question

A.

Robin died on 31 July 2005 and the inheritance tax on his estate was payable out of residue, at an estate rate of 25%.

His will provided for the following:

(1)   A bequest to his married daughter Merle of 25,000 shares of £1 each in Fieldfare plc, quoted on the Stock Exchange at 398–406p.

(2)   The creation of a settlement, the assets of which amounted to £30,000, under which the income was payable to Merle for life, then to Merle's daughter Jenny for life, with remainder to Merle's son Martin.

On 1 August 2008 Merle gave Jenny 12,500 of the shares in Fieldfare plc that she had inherited from her father. The shares were quoted on that day at 272–276p. She had made previous potentially exempt transfers amounting to £286,000 (after exemptions), all on 30 September 2002.

Merle and Jenny were involved in an accident and as a result Merle died on 30 September 2008, leaving her free estate to her son Martin. Jenny survived, in a coma, for eleven months but eventually died on 31 August 2009, having made no lifetime transfers, and leaving her estate to her brother Martin.

Their respective estates were valued for probate as follows:

	Merle 30.9.08 £	Jenny 31.8.09 £
12,500 shares each in Fieldfare plc	36,750	38,000
Other assets (net of liabilities)	24,025	276,250
Settled fund (net of liabilities)	32,000	22,750

Compute the inheritance tax payable:

(a)   on the death of Merle

(b)   on the death of Jenny.

Jenny's date of birth is 15 January 1981.

B.

How would the principles of your answer differ (without computations) if all the events mentioned had taken place a year later?

•   Robin's death on 31 July 2006

•   Merle's gift of Fieldfare shares on 1 August 2008 (with previous transfers on 30 September 2003)

•   Merle's death on 30 September 2009

•   Jenny's death on 31 August 2010.

Answer

A. Deaths and gift between 2005 and 2009

(a) Inheritance tax payable on death of Merle (30 September 2008)

		Gross £	Tax on 2008/09 scale £
Gifts within seven years before death:			
During 2002/03		286,000	–
1 August 2008			
Gift to Jenny 12,500 shares @ 273	34,125		
Less: Annual exemptions 2008/09	3,000		
2007/08	3,000	6,000	
Potentially exempt transfer now chargeable		28,125	850*
Cumulative transfers in seven years prior to death		314,125	850*
(* 314,125 – 312,000 = 2,125 @ 40%)			

Estate of Merle deceased

	Date of death 30 September 2008 £
Free estate:	
12,500 shares in Fieldfare plc	36,750
Other assets (net of liabilities)	24,025
	60,775
Settled property (Robin's will trust) (net of liabilities)	32,000
Chargeable to inheritance tax on death	92,775

		Tax on 2008/09 scale £
Cumulative transfers in seven years prior to death	314,125	850
Chargeable estate on death	92,775	37,110*
	406,900	37,960

(* £92,775 @ 40% = £37,110)

Inheritance tax payable:

On gifts within seven years
before death

Payable by transferees of gifts in 2002/03 (previously potentially exempt transfers)		nil
Payable by Jenny (or her executors) re gift of shares on 1 August 2008, previously potentially exempt		£850
On estate at death as computed		37,110

Less: Quick succession relief re gift of shares from Robin (see **explanatory notes 5 and 6**)

$$40\% \text{ of } \left(\frac{100,000}{133,333} \times 33,333 \right) \qquad 10,000$$

Quick succession relief re settled property (see **explanatory notes 5 and 7**)

$$40\% \text{ of } \left(\frac{30,000}{40,000} \times 10,000 \right) \qquad 3,000 \qquad 13,000$$

Inheritance tax payable on Merle's estate   £24,110

Payable by executors:

$$\frac{60,775}{92,775} \times 24,110 \qquad\qquad £15,794$$

Payable by trustees of settled property:

$$\frac{32,000}{92,775} \times 24,110 \qquad\qquad £8,316$$

(b) Inheritance tax payable on death of Jenny (31 August 2009)

Estate of Jenny deceased

	Date of death 31 August 2009
Free estate:	
12,500 shares in Fieldfare plc	38,000
Other assets (net of liabilities)	276,250
	314,250
Settled property (Robin's will trust) (net of liabilities)	22,750
	£337,000

Inheritance tax payable:

	£
On £337,000 (337,000 − 325,000 = 12,000 @ 40%)	4,800

£

Less:	Quick succession relief re gift of shares from Merle (see **explanatory note 9**)		
	80% of $\left(\dfrac{27,275}{28,125} \times £\,850\right)$	659	
	Quick succession relief re settled property (see **explanatory note 10**)		
	100% of $\left(\dfrac{23,684}{32,000} \times £\,8,316\right)$	6,155	
	Total quick succession relief available	£6,814	
	But relief restricted to total tax chargeable		4,800
			–

Accordingly no inheritance tax is payable on Jenny's death.

B. Deaths and gift a year later, between 2006 and 2010

Robin's death is now after 22 March 2006. Merle's life interest in the fund of £30,000 is an immediate post-death interest, but Jenny's successor life interest in it cannot now be a transitional serial interest – not because she did not succeed to it until after 5 October 2008, but because that status can only apply where Merle had become beneficially entitled to her interest in possession before 22 March 2006.

Jenny's interest in possession is also not a disabled person's interest, even though she was in a coma, and so mentally disabled, for the whole time she was entitled to it between Merle's death and her own. She can only be a "disabled person" within the definition in s 89(4)–(6) if her disability existed at the time the property was transferred into the settlement, ie in this case on Robin's death.

The settled property will therefore not form part of Jenny's estate on her death on 31 August 2010; without it, her estate is below the 2009/10 nil rate band of £325,000, and thus no inheritance tax is due on it even before invoking quick succession relief in respect of Merle's gift.

Instead, despite Jenny's interest in possession, the settled fund will have been within the relevant property regime in the period between Merle's and Jenny's deaths. An exit charge arises under s 65 on Martin becoming absolutely entitled when Jenny dies, and this is within the first ten years after the settlement commenced. Assuming that Robin's will did not create any other settlements, the rate of tax under s 68 will be established by reference to:

- the effective rate on a notional transfer, at the 20% lifetime rate, of the £30,000 initial value of the trust fund by a transferor with Robin's inheritance tax accumulation immediately before his death,

- multiplied by three tenths,

- multiplied by four fortieths (sixteen completed quarters expired between 31 July 2006 and 31 August 2010, less twelve completed quarters expired between 31 July 2006 and 30 September 2009).

However, Robin's inheritance tax accumulation immediately before his death must have been less than £295,000, since the estate rate at his death was well below 40% even with the 2006/07 nil rate band of £285,000; the calculation has the benefit of the 2010–11 nil rate band of £325,000. Accordingly the effective rate in the first stage of the s 68 calculation would be 0%, and on any view the rate after the full s 68 calculation will therefore come out at 0%.

Because Jenny's life interest was not an estate IIP, there is no exemption from capital gains tax on any unrealised gains within the trust fund on Martin's becoming absolutely entitled on her death. However, the fact that (with a 0% rate) no inheritance tax is actually charged on the relevant property exit charge does not stop it from being a chargeable transfer for inheritance tax, so if Martin is UK resident it is open to him and the trustees to claim holdover relief under TCGA 1992 s 260.

Otherwise the position is as in part A, but with the 2006/07 nil rate band of £285,000 on Robin's death and the 2009/10 nil rate band of £325,000 on Merle's death.

Explanatory Notes

Quick succession relief

(1)   Under the provisions of s 141, quick succession relief applies where the value of a person's chargeable estate for inheritance tax purposes was increased by a chargeable transfer made not more than five years before

    (a)   his death

        or

    (b)   a lifetime charge on settled property in which the deemed transferor had an interest in possession (where the earlier transfer was or included the making of the settlement or was made after the making of the settlement) The terms of this limb of s 141 are such that it can only refer to an estate IIP, even though no express restriction was introduced by FA 2006.

The rates of quick succession relief are as follows:

Period between earlier and later transfers	Percentage relief
1 year or less	100%
1+ to 2 years	80%
2+ to 3 years	60%
3+ to 4 years	40%
4+ to 5 years	20%

The percentage relief is calculated on the part of the tax paid on the previous transfer that the net value then transferred bears to the gross chargeable transfer at that time, or, in the terms of s 141 itself, "a percentage of the tax charged on so much of the value transferred by the first transfer as is attributable to the increase [in the recipient's estate]": some of the tax charged on that gross value transferred is attributable to the tax itself.

Where the later transfer is made on death, whether it relates to free estate or settled property, the quick succession relief reduces the total tax chargeable because of the death, as shown in the Example, so that the apportionment of the tax payable between free estate and settled property is of the tax as reduced by quick succession relief.

Successive transfers

(2)   Where an individual who has a life interest in possession in settled property transfers parts of his interest therein at different times and more than one later transfer occurs within five years of his acquisition of the life interest, then quick succession relief is available on the second and subsequent transfers within the five years, but only to the extent of any tax not used up on the earlier transfers. In this connection a transfer uses up the full amount of tax paid on the earlier transfer of which the tax relievable on the later transfer is a percentage (s 141(4)(5)).

For Example:

A grants a life interest to B by will trust. Within two years B releases part of his interest to a discretionary trust (C), then in the fifth year after A's death B releases the remainder of his interest to a second discretionary trust (D).

Proportion of tax on A's transfer relevant to the increase in B's estate is say £25,000. Transfer of part interest within two years to C trust attracts tax of say £8,000 and transfer of remainder to D trust within five years tax of say £7,000.

The quick succession relief available on the transfer to C trust is 80% × £25,000 so the amount of £8,000 is fully covered by quick succession relief, representing £10,000 of the original £25,000 (£8,000 = 80% × £10,000) leaving £15,000 still available. The transfer to D trust attracts quick succession relief of 20% of £15,000 = £3,000 to set against the tax payable of £7,000.

Valuation of quoted securities

(3)   Quoted securities are valued one quarter up from the lower of the two quoted prices. Thus on Robin's death a quotation of 398–406p per share becomes 400p.

Gift by Merle to Jenny of inherited shares

(4)   Quick succession relief was not available on Merle's gift of the Fieldfare plc shares to Jenny despite Merle having acquired the shares by a chargeable transfer on death less than five years earlier, because it only applies where the *later transfer* is on death or termination of an estate interest in possession in settled property.

Position on death of Merle

(5)   As Merle's death occurred more than three years but within four years after Robin's death, quick succession relief is available at 40%. The quick succession relief applies both on the shares transferred to her and on the life interest in the settled fund that passes to Jenny on Merle's death.

(6)   The value of the shares transferred to Merle on Robin's death was:

25,000 shares in Fieldfare plc @ 400p (see **explanatory note 3**)	100,000
Tax thereon (25% of gross = 25/75 of net)	33,333
Gross transfer	£133,333

(7)   The value of the assets transferred to the settled fund on Robin's death was:

Assets	30,000
Tax thereon (25% of gross = 25/75 of net)	10,000
Gross transfer	£40,000

Position on death of Jenny

(8)   The liabilities in Jenny's estate will have included the inheritance tax on the gift from Merle and the value of the settled property will have been reduced by the inheritance tax payable by the trustees because of the death of Merle.

(9)   Jenny's death occurred within two years after the gift of shares from Merle, so in **part A** of the Example 80% quick succession relief is available thereon.

The value of the shares transferred was:

Chargeable transfer – gross	28,125
Less: Inheritance tax on death of Merle	850
Net chargeable transfer	£27,275

(10)   Jenny's death occurred within one year of Merle's death, so the rate of quick succession relief on the assets in the settlement is 100%.

The net value transferred on Merle's death was:

Settled fund	32,000
Inheritance tax payable thereon	8,316
	£23,684

The value of £22,750 at Jenny's death reflects the movement in the value of the fund for reasons other than the liability for tax.

Jenny's death also occurred within five years after that of Robin. However, although the same fund is charged on both deaths, Jenny's estate was not increased by Robin's chargeable transfer and so quick succession relief is not applicable on Jenny's death by reference to Robin's chargeable transfer.

(11)   In **part A** of the Example Jenny's interest in Robin's will trust is a transitional serial interest, and therefore an estate IIP, (see further **Example 52**) because:

   (i)   the settlement was set up before 22 March 2006 (on Robin's death); and

   (ii)   immediately before 22 March 2006, there was an individual (Merle) with a beneficial interest in possession in the settlement; and

   (iii) that person's interest must have come to an end after 21 March 2006 but before 6 October 2008 (on 30 September 2008 on Merle's death); and

   (iv)   Jenny became beneficially entitled to that interest at that time;

   (v)   the interest is not a disabled person's interest (see **part B** of the Example); and

   (vi)   Jenny is not a minor and therefore the trust for her cannot be subject to the rules for bereaved minors' trusts in s 71A.

Consequently, Jenny is treated as beneficially entitled to the assets in the fund at her death.

(12)   For more details regarding the inheritance tax regime for relevant property trusts touched on in **part B** of the Example see **Examples 59 to 62**.

Question

Mr Maxford died on 7 January 2011. He was UK domiciled. The following information is held:

(1)   He had previously owned a 14% shareholding (70,000 shares) in Maxford plc, an unquoted trading company, for many years.

(2)   In February 2001 he gifted 30,000 of the Maxford plc shares to trustees of a discretionary trust for his children.

(3)   In May 2005 he gifted 20,000 of the Maxford plc shares to a trust in which his daughter has a life interest. (He was excluded from benefit under both trusts and the trustees retained the shares.)

(4)   The agreed share values at the time of both gifts were:

Shareholding	Per share value
	£
11% to 15%	10.00
5% to 10%	5.00
Below 5%	3.00

In February 2007 Maxford plc was listed on the Alternative Investment Market. All donees had retained their shares.

(5)   In 1992 he had inherited a 51% shareholding in Minota plc, a company whose shares are listed on the London Stock Exchange. In July 2007 he gifted a 10% shareholding then worth £680,000 to his daughter and she held them at his death when they were worth £200,000.

(6)   No other transfers had been made. Donees agreed to pay any tax due in respect of transfers to them.

His estate at death comprised:

(i)   His house worth £800,000.

(ii)   A life interest in his uncle's estate. The uncle had died in June 2006 with an estate worth £235,000 on which inheritance tax of £27,500 was suffered. On Mr Maxford's death his daughter became entitled to the capital, which was then worth £300,000.

(iii)   20,000 shares in Maxford plc valued at £10 per share.

(iv)   Holdings of quoted shares as follows:

Number / %	Company	Value at death
		£
7,000	Green plc	107,000
3,500	Blue plc	42,000
6,000	Red plc	8,000
41%	Minota plc	850,000

In the six months following death the following share sales occurred:

Shares sold	Company	Gross proceeds
		£
6,000	Green plc	84,000
2,000	Blue plc	35,000
600	Red plc	950

In his will, Mr Maxford left his Maxford plc shares to his daughter. His house was left equally to his widow and daughter, subject to his widow having full use and enjoyment of the house for her lifetime or for so long as she wished. The balance of his estate went to his son.

(a)   Calculate the inheritance tax payable as a result of the death of Mr Maxford.

(b)   Calculate the allocation of any tax due between the free estate and settled property.

Answer

(a) Inheritance tax payable as a result of death of Mr Maxford

Position on gifts in lifetime

		Gross £
February 2001	Gift of 30,000 Maxford plc shares to discretionary trust –	
	Value of 70,000 shares @ £10	700,000
	Value of 40,000 shares @ £5	200,000
	Loss to estate	500,000
	Less: business property relief	500,000
	Chargeable transfer	–
May 2005	Gift of 20,000 Maxford plc shares to life interest trust –	
	Value of 40,000 shares @ £5	200,000
	Value of 20,000 shares @ £3	60,000
	Loss to estate	140,000
	Less: 100% business property relief	140,000
	Potentially exempt transfer	–
July 2007	Gift of 10% holding of Minota plc shares to daughter	680,000
	Less: 50% business property relief	340,000
		340,000
	Less: Annual exemptions 2007/08 and 2006/07	6,000
	Potentially exempt transfer	334,000

On Mr Maxford's death 7 January 2011

Lifetime transfers in seven years before death

No additional tax is payable on the February 2001 gift, since this was more than seven years before Mr Maxford's death. (It is, however, included in the inheritance tax accumulation until February 2008, with the capacity to affect the July 2007 gift accordingly if there had been some restriction on the business property relief through the presence of excepted assets within the company.)

Business property relief remains available on the other gifts providing the transferees have retained what they were given and the property still qualifies as relevant business property. A listing on the Alternative Investment Market does not affect the status of unquoted shares, so that the May 2005 gift to the life interest trust will still retain entitlement to the 100% relief. The position on the July 2007 gift of Minota plc shares to the daughter is as follows:

	Gross £	Tax on 2010/11 scale £
Cumulative transfers in previous seven years	–	–

	Gross £	Tax on 2010/11 scale £
July 2007 PET now chargeable	334,000	3,600*
	334,000	3,600*

(* 334,000 – 325,000 = 9,000 @ 40%)

As the Minota plc shares have fallen in value at the date of death, the daughter may claim under s 131 to have the tax on her gift recomputed as follows:

Value of gift as above		334,000
Value on death	200,000	
Less: 50% business property relief	(100,000)	
Annual exemptions	(6,000)	94,000
Reduce transfer by		240,000

This reduces the tax figure to nil. The amount included in the inheritance tax accumulation, however, remains at £334,000.

Estate at death

		£	£
House		800,000	
Less: Spouse exemption (see **explanatory note 4**)		800,000	–
20,000 shares in Maxford plc @ £10		200,000	
Less: 100% business property relief		200,000	–
Quoted shares**:			
Green plc	7,000 shares	107,000	
Blue plc	3,500 shares	42,000	
Red plc	6,000 shares	8,000	
Minota plc	41% (see **explanatory note 2**)	850,000	1,007,000
Free estate			1,007,000
Settled property – immediate post-death interest in uncle's estate			300,000
			1,307,000

** See **explanatory note 5**.

Inheritance tax thereon:

Cumulative transfers in previous seven years	334,000	–
Estate at death	1,307,000	526,400*
	1,641,000	526,400

(* 1,641,000 – 325,000 = 1,316,000 @ 40%)

Tax on estate	526,400
Less: Quick succession relief re uncle's estate (4 to 5 years)	

$$20\% \times \frac{207,500}{235,000} \times 27,500$$

	4,856
	521,544

(b) Allocation of tax between free estate and settled property

	£
Tax on estate as above	521,544

$$\text{Estate rate} = \frac{521,544}{1,307,000} \times 100 = 39.904\%$$

	£
Tax on free estate 1,007,000 @ 39.904%	401,832
(payable by personal representatives, reducing son's residue accordingly)	
Tax on settled property 300,000 @ 39.904%	119,712
(payable by trustees, reducing daughter's entitlement accordingly)	
	521,544

Explanatory Notes

Business property relief

(1)   Business property relief for unquoted shares in a trading company has been at 100% since 6 April 1996.

Thus the Maxford plc shares retained by Mr Maxford until his death qualify for 100% business property relief in the death estate. Since they were left as a specific gift to his daughter, there is no restriction of the exempt legacy of the house to the spouse by reference to the business property relief (see **Example 15** for further details).

(2)   Since 10 March 1992 quoted shares in a trading company have qualified for business property relief of 50% if they give the transferor control immediately before the transfer, hence the relief in respect of the gift of the Minota plc shares to the daughter. There is no relief in the death estate on the Minota plc shares retained by Mr Maxford, since he no longer had a controlling holding; but the fact that the daughter's holding is not a controlling holding in its own right does not cause a loss of relief when computing the tax on death (s 113A(3)(b), (4)(a)).

Fall in value of gift

(3)   The claim for tax to be computed on the value of a gift at death where that is lower than the value at the time of the gift does not affect the cumulative transfers figure for the purpose of later transfers, so the amount included in lifetime transfers remains at £334,000. For detailed notes on such claims see **Example 12**.

Legacy of house to spouse and daughter

(4)   The stipulation in Mr Maxford's will that his spouse was entitled to full use of the property created a life interest in the daughter's share of the property (*IRC v Lloyds Private Banking (1998)*). Mrs Maxford therefore owns half the property outright and has a life interest in the other half. In both cases the spouse exemption applies. For detailed notes on interests in possession and property see **Example 52**.

Sale of quoted shares at a loss within twelve months after death (ss 178–189)

(5)   Although 6,000 of the Green plc shares were sold at a loss within twelve months after death, no relief may be claimed, since the overall result of the sales was a profit as follows:

			Death Value £	Realised Value
Green plc	6,000 shares	6,000/7,000 × 107,000	91,714	84,000

			Death Value	Realised Value
			£	
Blue plc	2,000 shares	2,000/3,500 × 42,000	24,000	35,000
Red plc	600 shares	600/6,000 × 8,000	800	950
			116,514	119,950

For detailed notes on claims for a loss on quoted shares see **Example 8.**

Question

A.

(a) Brian is the life tenant of a settlement created before 22 March 2006, comprising quoted securities. On 31 December 2007, when the fund was valued at £169,000, he released his life tenancy for the benefit of the succeeding life tenant, Carol.

Brian had made a previous transfer in the form of a gift to his brother on 26 March 2006 of £186,000.

After relinquishing his interest in the settlement he made a gift of £60,000 to a friend on 8 June 2008.

On 2 April 2011 Brian died leaving free estate of £120,000 to his brother.

Calculate the inheritance tax payable.

(b) Carol, who succeeded to the life tenancy from Brian in (a) above, was killed in a road accident on 1 May 2008, having made no previous transfers.

The settlement was then valued at £175,000. On the death of Carol the property passed to her son David, the remainderman, absolutely.

Carol left free estate of £159,000, which passed to David under the intestacy rules.

(i) Calculate the inheritance tax position on her death;

(ii) Calculate the effect of the subsequent death of Brian, and

(iii) State what advice you would expect to have been given to Carol's personal representatives in relation to the trust fund when investigating the position immediately after her death.

B.

Antony and Benjamin each have a life interest in half of a trust fund, with remainder to Denis, the assets of the whole fund consisting entirely of a loan of £120,000 to a close company, repayable at seven days' notice.

On 30 June 2006 Antony sold his interest to Clive for its full market value of £20,000.

Before Antony sold his interest to Clive he had made a chargeable transfer of £294,000 to a discretionary trust in August 2000, but had not made any later transfers of value.

Antony died on 30 September 2010 leaving an estate of £448,000.

Clive, before his acquisition of Antony's interest, had made a potentially exempt transfer (after exemptions) of £200,000 in February 2005 and made no further gifts.

Benjamin died on 30 December 2010. Before his death he had made potentially exempt transfers (after exemptions) in the previous seven years amounting to £226,000 and his estate was valued at £100,000, excluding his interest in the trust.

Sufficient of the loan was repaid for the trustees of each fund to meet their inheritance tax liabilities on each occasion, and from the first such occasion the trustees therefore maintained separate accounts for each fund.

Compute the inheritance tax payable by the trustees of each fund by reference to the above events.

Where relevant, proper notice was given to the trustees of availability of exemptions within the appropriate time limit for both **part A** and **part B** of the Example.

Answer

A.

(a) Brian

Inheritance tax accumulation

26 March 2006			
Gift to brother			186,000
Less: Annual exemptions	20054/06	3,000	
	2004/05	3,000	6,000
Potentially exempt transfer			£ 180,000
31 December 2007			
Release of life tenancy			169,000
Less: Annual exemptions	2007/08	3,000	
	2006/07	3,000	6,000
Potentially exempt transfer			£163,000
8 June 2008			
Gift to friend			60,000
Less: Annual exemption 2008/09			3,000
Potentially exempt transfer			£57,000

Death of Brian — 2 April 2011

Inheritance tax payable on gifts within seven years before death

	Gross	Tax (on 2010/11 scale)
	£	£
26 March 2006		
Gift to brother	180,000	–
31 December 2007		
Release of life tenancy	163,000	7,200*
	343,000	7,200*
(* 343,000 – 325,000 = 18,000 @ 40%)		
8 June 2008		
Gift to friend	57,000	22,800
Cumulative chargeable transfers at death	400,000	30,000
Free estate on death	120,000	48,000
	520,000	78,000

Inheritance tax payable

		£	By
Re 26 March 2006 gift		nil	
Re 31 December 2007 release of life interest			
(3–4 years before death)	7,200		
Less: Taper relief 20%	1,440	5,760	trustees of settlement
Re 8 June 2008 gift		22,800	friend
(less than 3 years before death)			
On free estate		48,000	personal representatives

A.

(b)

(i)   Estate of Carol — Inheritance tax position as at date of death 1 May 2008

		£
Free estate		159,000
Settled property		175,000
		334,000
Inheritance tax on 2008/09 death scale (no previous transfers)		8,800*
(* 334,000 – 312,000 = 22,000 @ 40%)		
Payable by:		
Personal representatives	$\dfrac{159,000}{334,000} \times 8,800 =$	4,189
Trustees of settlement	$\dfrac{175,000}{334,000} \times £8,800 =$	4,611
		8,800

(ii)   Estate of Carol — Revision of inheritance tax position following death of Brian

	£	£
Free estate		159,000
Settled property	175,000	
Less: Inheritance tax payable by reference		
to now chargeable transfer dated 31.12.07	5,760	169,240
		328,240
Inheritance tax payable (* 328,240 – 312,000 = 16,240 @ 40%)		6,496*

Less: Quick succession relief by reference to earlier chargeable transfer on 31.12.07:

		£	£
100% ×	$\dfrac{157,240}{163,000} \times £5,760$		5,556
Tax payable			940
Payable by:			
Personal representatives	$\dfrac{159,000}{328,240} \times 940 =$		455
Trustees of settlement	$\dfrac{169,240}{328,240} \times 940 =$		485
Repayable to: Personal representatives (4,189 − 455)			3,734
Trustees of settlement (4,611 − 485)			4,126**
			£7,860

See also **explanatory note 11.

(iii) Advice to Carol's personal representatives following her death

Carol has not made any previous transfers and her free estate of £159,000 is, on its own, below the threshold for inheritance tax on her death. But her estate for inheritance tax purposes includes in addition the settled property by reason of her estate IIP. Unless steps can be taken to avoid this, therefore, the possession of the life interest causes tax to be payable on the free estate at that time, in the sum of £4,189, as well as giving rise to a liability in the settlement itself.

This is a substantial price to pay for the free estate's entitlement to income on the trust fund for a matter of just four months (on a fund of around £170,000 an annualised income yield of some 7.4% after income tax would be required to make it worth accepting the liability in the free estate, even before taking account of the tax on the settled property which would also be borne beneficially by David as remainderman.

Carol's personal representatives should therefore have been advised to ensure that they did nothing to accept any right to benefit from the trust fund before they had established whether Carol herself had done so; and, if she had not, then to disclaim the life interest that came into possession by virtue of Brian's surrender. David as beneficiary of Carol's free estate would also need to join in the disclaimer by way of authority to the personal representatives to abandon an asset of the estate in this way; on the facts given, this is doubly in his interest since the income for the four-month period would then pass to him as the next beneficiary under the trust, but even if the trust fund had passed to someone else in the light of Carol's death the arithmetic is likely to support a disclaimer if this course is still open. (An additional factor to take into account in the latter scenario, if Brian were known to have a poor life expectancy, would be the adjustments to the inheritance tax position that would flow from his death before 31 December 2014, cf (ii) above.)

Acts on Carol's part which might have amounted to acceptance of the life interest would include the receipt of an income payment since the surrender of Brian's interest, or pressing the trustees for such a payment, or even joining (in her own right rather than as a trustee) in executing Brian's deed of surrender. The computations in (i) and (ii) above assume that a disclaimer did not prove feasible.

B. Antony

Inheritance Tax Accumulation

Cumulative transfers to date			294,000
30 June 2006			
Sale of life interest in trust			
Value transferred		60,000	
Less: Proceeds of sale		20,000	
		40,000	
Less: Annual exemptions	2006/07	3,000	
	2005/06	3,000	6,000
Potentially exempt transfer			£34,000

30 September 2010 — Death of Antony

	Gross	Tax (on 2010/11 scale)
	£	£
Tax payable by trustees on potentially exempt transfer 30 June 2006:		
Cumulative transfers within seven years before 30 June 2006 –		
Chargeable transfers in August 2000	294,000	–
Potentially exempt transfer 30 June 2006	34,000	1,200*
	328,000	1,200*

(* 328,000 – 325,000 = 3,000 @ 40%)

Tax payable by personal representatives on estate at death:

Cumulative transfers within seven years before

	Gross	Tax (on 2010/11 scale)
30 September 2010	34,000	–
Estate on death	448,000	62,800*
	482,000	62,800*

(* 482,000 – 325,000 = 157,000 @ 40%)

Inheritance tax payable:

By trustees (4–5 years before death)	
1,200 subject to taper relief at 40%	£720
By personal representatives	£62,800

Clive

Inheritance Tax Accumulation

Potentially exempt transfer February 2005	£200,000
30 September 2010	

Transfer of life interest because of death of Antony			60,000
Less: Annual exemptions	2010/11	3,000	
	2009/10	3,000	6,000
Potentially exempt transfer			£54,000

Benjamin — Date of death 30 December 2010

Inheritance Tax Accumulation

		Gross	Tax (on 2010/11 scale)
		£	£
Potentially exempt transfers within seven years before death, now chargeable		226,000	–
Value chargeable on death:			
Free estate	100,000		
Settled property	60,000	160,000	24,400*
		386,000	24,400*

(* 386,000 – 325,000 = 61,000 @ 40%)

Tax payable:
By personal representatives

$$\frac{100,000}{160,000} \times £24,400 = \qquad\qquad 15,250$$

By trustees

$$\frac{60,000}{160,000} \times £24,400 = \qquad\qquad 9,150$$

£24,400

Summary of Inheritance Tax payable by Trustees

		£
By trustees of Antony's trust fund		
On sale of Antony's life interest to Clive 30 June 2006	potentially exempt transfer	nil
On Antony's death 30 September 2010:		
Re potentially exempt transfer 30 June 2006		720
Re termination of life interest (by reference to inheritance tax accumulation of Clive who held the interest in possession, providing Clive lives until after 30 September 2017)	potentially exempt transfer by Clive (see **explanatory note 12**)	nil
By trustees of Benjamin's trust fund		
On Benjamin's death 30 December 2010		9,150

Explanatory Notes

Termination of estate interest in possession

(1)   Where a person, before 22 March 2006, had an interest in possession in the whole or any part of a settlement, the appropriate part of the capital of the trust fund continues to be treated for inheritance tax purposes as belonging to that person absolutely (s 49(1)). (An interest in possession broadly means an entitlement as of right to *income* from a settlement. For further notes on this point, and the other cases ("estate IIPs") where the same treatment applies after 21 March 2006, see **Example 52**.)

Clive acquired his interest after 21 March 2006; but he took it, before 6 October 2008, in succession to Antony who had been entitled to it since before 22 March 2006 and Clive's interest is therefore a transitional serial interest. This is not affected by the fact that the succession took place by purchase rather than without consideration. Clive's interest is accordingly an estate IIP and he is treated as beneficially entitled to the assets in the fund until the life interest he bought comes to an end on Antony's death.

If the person with an estate IIP dies (s 4(1)) or his interest terminates under the terms of the trust, or he disposes of the interest by releasing or assigning it (s 52), there will be a potential charge to inheritance tax. It would be unfair for the person in possession of the interest to have to pay any inheritance tax arising as that person has no control over the assets of the settlement. Any tax is therefore payable by the trustees (s 201(1)). If the transfer is, or becomes, a chargeable transfer, however, the value transferred it is added to the inheritance tax accumulation of the person with the interest in possession (s 52), and the tax is calculated as though the transfer had been made by that person.

After the transfer/termination the trust assets are no longer included in the estate of the transferor, but instead in that of the transferee (provided he became absolutely entitled or has an estate IIP). If, however, the transferor dies within seven years after the date of transfer, the potentially exempt transfer rules apply in the normal way and tax on the potentially exempt transfer is chargeable on the normal scale, any tax arising being payable by the trustees.

(2)   The termination of an estate interest in possession during the lifetime of the person beneficially entitled to that interest is treated under s 52(1) as a transfer of value equal to the value of the property in which the interest in possession subsisted. The estate of the transferor immediately before the transfer is deemed to include the whole of the property in which he had an interest in possession and therefore the reduction in value of the estate as a result of the assignment is the full value of the property in which he had an interest in possession less any amount received as consideration for the assignment (s 52(2)). Where consideration is received, exemption cannot be claimed as a commercial transaction because s 52(1) and (2) expressly provide for tax to be payable. The easiest way to look at it is that whilst the life tenant's IHT estate has been depleted by the underlying value of the trust fund which it is deemed to contain, it has at the same time increased by the proceeds received, so that the transfer of value is the difference between the two.

Availability of exemptions

(3)   For events after 21 March 2006, if the termination of an estate IIP occurs during the person's lifetime and

   (i)   another individual becomes absolutely entitled,

   (ii)   a disabled person's interest arises,

   (iii)   (not later than 5 October 2008) a transitional serial interest arises, or

   (iv)   the estate IIP was an immediate post-death interest (not a disabled person's interest) and the property becomes held for a minor child of the deceased settlor under a bereaved minor's trust

(and the individual becoming entitled in (i)–(iii) is not the spouse or civil partner or the person whose interest terminates, such as to attract spouse exemption) then the transfer is a potentially exempt transfer and will only become a chargeable transfer should the former life tenant die within seven years. The transfer is, however, a *deemed* transfer of value and accordingly the small gifts exemption and exemption for normal expenditure out of income do not apply (ss 20(3), 21(5)).

On the other hand the annual and marriage gifts exemptions are expressly made available providing the transferor gives the trustees of the settlement a notice informing them of the availability of the exemptions, within six months after the date of *termination*, in a form prescribed by HMRC (s 57). Both the annual and marriage exemptions would be taken into account in arriving at the potentially exempt transfer (ss 51(2), 57). Other exemptions are also available (see **explanatory note 5**).

Notice is required within that six months period even though the transfer is a potentially exempt transfer and the exemption may never have to be used against the trust fund if the former life tenant survives (and would thus be wasted if the life tenant made subsequent transfers of value from his free estate in the same tax year). It is therefore not always obvious that it would be in the life tenant's best interests to make his exemptions available to the trustees, unless the six month period lasts beyond the end of the current tax year and he can judge the position with full knowledge of how matters have evolved.

As to the form of any notice, the Form 222 formerly published by HMRC has not been available from them for some years, and is not known to have been formally prescribed in any case. Their Inheritance Tax Manual states merely that the notice should be given 'in writing' (which is probably implicit in the term "notice" in any case). The position is less than satisfactory for trustees presented with the relevant information which, in the absence of a prescribed form, does not meet the express terms of the legislation; it must remain open to the person giving it (or some other donee of his) to argue subsequently, if it suited him, that the exemption in question was not transferred to the trustees and remained available for later use.

(4)   Even though any tax that may arise on the termination of the life interest is payable by the trustees and not by the transferor, his accumulation is increased by the amount of the transfer if it becomes a chargeable transfer, thus increasing his and his estate's tax liability on any later transfers. Brian in **part A**, and Antony and Clive in **part B**, of the Example would therefore at least want to consider surrendering their annual exemptions to the trustees for use against the transfers if they had made no other transfers against which the exemptions could be utilised.

(5)   If the termination of an estate IIP occurs on the death of the person entitled to it, the value of the assets in the settlement is added to the free estate and tax calculated on the aggregate. The trustees are then liable to pay a proportionate part of the total inheritance tax payable.

For both lifetime and death terminations the exemptions for transfers to spouse/civil partner (if entitled absolutely or to another estate IIP), charities or political parties are available.

If on the other hand the interest in possession that comes to an end, or is disposed of, is not an estate IIP, the death of the life tenant will not give rise to any inheritance tax consequence as the trust fund would not be deemed to form part of the life tenant's estate.

Release of Brian's life interest

(6)   On the release of Brian's pre-2006 life interest in **part A** of the Example there is a transfer of value based on the underlying assets in the settlement. Since Brian is entitled to the whole of the income of the trust, the whole capital value of the fund is deemed to be transferred. Because another interest in possession for an individual (Carol) follows on from Brian's pre-2006 interest, and the release took place before 6 October 2008 when the transitional period came to an end, Carol's interest in possession qualifies as a transitional serial interest (TSI) and is therefore an estate IIP. For this reason the transfer is at that point potentially exempt (after deducting annual exemptions, following due notice by Brian to the trustees of their availability).

On the death of Brian his accumulation is recomputed for the seven years prior to death, with the potentially exempt transfers now being treated as chargeable transfers. The rates used for the recomputation are those applicable at his death on 2 April 2011. In the case of transfers occurring more than three years before death, taper relief reduces the tax on those particular transfers without affecting the overall computation.

Death of Carol and subsequent death of Brian

(7)   In the absence of a disclaimer removing the settled property from Carol's estate at her death, tax of £4,189 is payable by her personal representatives on her free estate by 1 December 2008, six months after the month of her death, or earlier application for letters of administration,

When the position is recomputed on the subsequent death of Brian, however (see **explanatory note 10**), this liability is reduced to £455 through a combination of a lower value transferred (because of the tax debt which has to be deducted from the settled property) and quick succession relief on the settled property which benefits the two portions of the estate rateably. The personal representatives will be entitled to a refund of the difference, which will carry interest from 1 December 2008 (or later date of original payment) to the date of repayment.

The liability of the trustees on Carol's death (£4,611) is also reduced (to £485) for the same reasons when recomputed in the light of Brian's death. However in this case the resulting rebate of £4,126 will be offset against the liability of £5,760 that crystallised on Brian's death when the potentially exempt transfer (in favour of Carol's life interest) became chargeable. The trustees will therefore have to pay the additional £1,634 (5,760 – 4,126) – which, like the rest of the tax payable by reason of Brian's death, will fall due on 1 November 2011 – but this will not prevent their being entitled to interest on the rebate of £4,126 up to that date, again from 1 December 2008 (or later date of original payment).

Disclaiming interest in a settlement

(8)   A person who becomes entitled to an interest under a settlement (any type of interest, not just a life interest) may as a matter of the general law disclaim (refuse to accept) his entitlement so long as he has done nothing to accept it. A disclaimer must be of the whole interest and not just part of it. Merely obtaining information about it does not amount to acceptance. The ability to disclaim passes to that person's personal representatives in the event of its still subsisting (through non-acceptance) at his death.

Providing such a disclaimer is not made for money or money's worth, the person is treated for inheritance tax purposes as never having become entitled to the interest (s 93). Once benefits have been accepted, any purported disclaimer would not operate as a disclaimer under the general law, and could therefore not benefit from the rule in s 93. The normal tax consequences would therefore follow in relation to the succession to the interest; furthermore it would be necessary to establish whether the purported disclaimer had no legal effect at all (in which case the person who made it would remain entitled to the benefit of the interest), or whether as a matter of interpretation it operated as a lifetime gift to the next beneficiary in line, with tax consequences accordingly.

There is no parallel to IHTA 1984 s 93 in the capital gains tax legislation, and the provision for disclaimers in TCGA 1992 s 62(6) is inapplicable because the trust fund did not comprise assets of which Carol was competent to dispose (within the definition in s 62(10)). In reality, on the facts of **part A**, David was not in a position to direct the trustees (subject to liens etc) how to deal with the trust assets until Carol's death or an earlier disclaimer by her, so a deemed disposal of trust assets under TCGA 1992 s 71 would have occurred at that time and not on the surrender of Brian's interest.

If a disclaimer were not made, a CGT-free re-basing of the trust assets in David's hands would occur on Carol's death as she had an estate IIP (see **Example 50 part A(a)**); but with a valid disclaimer (even if made by her personal representatives after her death) that is no longer the analysis because the deeming effect of IHTA 1984 s 93 applies for all inheritance tax purposes. The chances are therefore that HMRC would treat the termination of the settlement on her death as involving a chargeable disposal for capital gains tax (albeit subject to the possibility of a claim to holdover relief under TCGA 1992 s 260 – in just the same way as if it had come to an end in her lifetime by reason of a disclaimer (or surrender) made by Carol herself (see **Example 50 Part A(d)**).

Quick succession relief etc

(9)   If, on death, a person's estate has been increased by a chargeable transfer within the previous five years then quick succession relief is available. The total tax chargeable on death is reduced by a percentage of that part of the tax charged on the previous transfer that the net value then transferred bore to the gross chargeable transfer at that time. The percentage is as follows:

Time between transfer and death	*Percentage relief*
1 year or less	100%
1+ to 2 years	80%
2+ to 3 years	60%

3+ to 4 years	40%
4+ to 5 years	20%

For further notes on quick succession relief see **Example 53**.

(10) The release of the life interest by Brian in **part A** of the Example on 31 December 2007 was potentially exempt, not chargeable at that time, so that no quick succession relief was due on Carol's death on 1 May 2008. However, when Brian dies on 2 April 2011 his release of his life interest which was previously potentially exempt becomes chargeable (s 3A(4)) with tax payable of £5,760.

Whilst this liability does not arise until nearly three years after Carol's death, it nonetheless affects the value of the trust property on Carol's death on 1 May 2008 since it derives from the now chargeable transfer by Brian on 31 December 2007. (It could be understood as a contingent liability that was not allowable until it crystallised, though this is not how the legislation treats it.)

The recharacterisation of Brian's potentially exempt transfer as a chargeable transfer also makes quick succession relief available by reference to the death of Carol on 1 May 2008, giving a repayment of inheritance tax to the trustees and her personal representatives (see **explanatory note 7** above). The time between the two chargeable transfers is less than one year, and the percentage is therefore 100% (s 141). The tax of £5,760 charged on the earlier transfer reduces the gross chargeable transfer of £163,000 so that, for the purpose of working out the quick succession relief, the increase in the estate of Carol resulting from Brian's chargeable transfer is only £157,240.

Retaining funds to meet potential liabilities

(11) This Example illustrates that trustees of settlements will have a potential tax liability for seven years after a release of an estate IIP. Accordingly funds must be retained for that period to meet those liabilities. The point may become even easier to overlook as estate IIPs become gradually less common following the FA 2006 changes. Thus on the death of Carol the trustees should not distribute to the remainderman, David, all of the assets remaining after the tax of £4,611 on her death, since by doing so they would find themselves with a personal liability for tax on the subsequent death of Brian should they be unable to recover from David the additional net tax due of £1,634 (5,760 – 4,126, see **explanatory note 7** above) by reference to Brian's death.

(12) In **part B** of the Example, there are two inheritance tax consequences when Antony dies:

(a) the 2006 potentially exempt transfer (by Antony in favour of Clive) becomes chargeable. Although it was the only chargeable transfer within the seven years before Antony's death, so that it is within his nil rate band for the purpose of calculating the tax on his estate, it nevertheless incurs a liability on the trust fund because it was itself made within seven years after the earlier transfer to the discretionary trust in 2000. (This demonstrates that lifetime gifts which constitute immediately chargeable, as distinct from potentially exempt, transfers may remain relevant to the calculation of inheritance tax due by reason of the death for up to practically 14 years after they were made.)

(b) Clive's TSI (whose duration was only ever for the balance of Antony's lifetime – if Antony had outlived Clive then the IIP would have continued in favour of Clive's estate, though no longer as a TSI but rather under the relevant property regime) terminates as the trust fund passes to the remainderman, Denis. This is a potentially exempt transfer by Clive after deduction of annual exemptions for 2009/10 and 2008/09, and provided Clive lives for at least a further seven years it will not give rise to a charge. If, however, Clive were to die within that time the transfer would become chargeable by reference to his accumulation. The tax would be payable out of the trust funds; in transferring the trust assets to the remainderman Denis, therefore, the trustees should provide for this contingent liability.

On the death of Benjamin his interest in possession, dating from before 22 March 2006 and therefore an estate IIP, is chargeable in the normal way, that is by aggregation with his free estate, and the tax on the total is apportioned rateably to the various parts of his estate.

Reversion to settlor or spouse/civil partner

(13)   If an estate interest in possession comes to an end during the settlor's lifetime, and the settled property reverts to the settlor, tax is not chargeable (s 53(3)). Furthermore tax is not chargeable if the settlor's spouse/civil partner (or widow/widower or surviving civil partner if settlor had died less than two years earlier) becomes beneficially entitled to the property and is domiciled in the UK (s 53(4)).

   In either case the entitlement must be absolute if it is to benefit from this exemption; this may involve less favourable capital gains tax implications if the assets have grown in value, see **Example 50 part A(b)**. The exemption does not however apply if the settlor or spouse/civil partner acquired the reversionary interest for a consideration in money or money's worth (s 53(5)); but the inapplicability of the inheritance tax exemption will not affect the operation of the capital gains tax rules.

Question

(a)   Fred, who had been entitled to an annuity under a fund settled by his aunt's will on her death in 1985, died on 31 August 2010. The amount of the annuity was £5,000. The value of the fund as a whole on that date was £500,000 and it produces an average annual income yield of 10%. Assume the current yield shown in the FTSE Actuaries Index for British Government Stocks (Irredeemables) was 4.17%.

Calculate the value of the annuity fund for inheritance tax purposes on the death of Fred.

(b)   Jim, the life tenant of a settled fund, also died on 31 August 2010. His life tenancy, to which he had become entitled in 2002, was subject to an annuity of £5,000 in favour of Gordon. The value of the fund as a whole was £500,000 on that date and the annual income yield was 6%. Assume the current actual dividend yield of the FTSE Actuaries All Share Index was 3%.

Calculate the value of the fund underlying the life tenancy for inheritance tax purposes on the death of Jim.

Answer

(a) Fred deceased — 31 August 2010

Value of Annuity Fund

	£
Without s 50(3)	
Annuity £5,000	
Income of fund (£500,000 × 10%) £50,000	
Share of capital attributable to Fred	
$\dfrac{5,000}{50,000} \times 500,000$	50,000
	———
With s 50(3)	
Annuity £5,000	
Notional income of fund (£500,000 × 4.17%) £20,850	
Minimum share of capital attributable to Fred	
$\dfrac{5,000}{20,850} \times 500,000$	119,904
	———
Value for inheritance tax of Fred's annuity fund	£119,904

(b) Jim deceased — 31 August 2010

Value of part remaining after an annuity

	£
Without s 50(3)	
Annuity £5,000	
Income of fund (£500,000 × 6%) £30,000	
Share of capital attributable to Jim	
(ie after annuity of £5,000)	
$\left(\dfrac{30,000 - 5,000}{30,000}\right) \times 500,000$	416,667
	———
With s 50(3)	
Annuity £5,000	
Notional income of fund (£500,000 × 3%) £15,000	
Value of fund	500,000
Less: Maximum value of annuity fund	
$\dfrac{5,000}{15,000} \times 500,000$	166,667
	———
Minimum value of part remaining	333,333

Value for inheritance tax of fund underlying Jim's life tenancy	£416,667

Explanatory Notes

(1) A person who has an interest in possession (including an annuity) in settled property is treated for the purposes of inheritance tax as owning the underlying settled property absolutely provided the interest was acquired before 22 March 2006 or is one of the following (s 49(1), (1A)):

  •   an immediate post-death interest (s 49A)

  •   a disabled person's interest (ss 89–89B) or

  •   a transitional serial interest (ss 49B–49E).

  For full details of those three categories – which with pre-2006 interests in possession can be referred to as 'estate IIPs' – see **Example 52**.

(2) Where one beneficiary of a settlement is entitled to a fixed amount of income and another to the remainder of the income, then to arrive at their respective shares of the trust fund the fund is divided in proportion to their shares of income (s 50(1)). The income arising over the previous twelve months is usually used for this purpose.

(3) However, if only one of the interests in the settlement is to be valued for the purpose of calculating a chargeable transfer, s 50(3) contains anti-avoidance provisions to prevent loss of tax to HMRC where the yield of the fund may have been arranged to reduce the taxable amount.

  The anti-avoidance provisions *do not apply* where chargeable transfers of *both* of the interests are made *at the same time*, since the whole of the supporting capital will in those circumstances be caught in any event.

(4) The value of the annuity fund becomes:

  (a)   In the case of a transfer of the annuity — not *less* than its capital value using the current yield on the FTSE Actuaries Index for British Government Stocks (Irredeemables).

  (b)   In the case of a transfer of the remainder — not *more* than its capital value using the current actual dividend yield on the FTSE Actuaries All Share Index.

  The use of these particular indices is prescribed by SI 2000/174, effective from 18 February 2000. The figures are obtainable from the Financial Times.

(5) The value of Fred's annuity fund included in his estate is therefore the higher of £50,000 (arrived at using the actual income yield of the fund) and £119,904 (arrived at using the notional income yield of 4.17% being the yield on British Government Irredeemable Stocks).

  In arriving at the value of the property supporting Jim's life tenancy, the value of the annuity fund using the actual income yield is 1/6th of £500,000 = £83,333. Since this is less than the maximum permitted value of £166,667 using the All-Share Index, the anti-avoidance provision in s 50(3) does not apply in valuing Jim's interest for inheritance tax purposes on his death.

Question

Amelia Dobbin, a widow, died on 15 July 2010.

Her first husband, George Sedley, who died in 1971, had by his will left the residue of his estate to her absolutely. In 1973 she made a settlement of this absolute interest under which she took a life interest with remainder to her son Paul.

At her death the settled fund consisted of investments valued at £249,000.

Her second husband, William Dobbin, who died in July 1974, settled the residue of his estate on her for life with the remainder to Rebecca, his daughter by a previous marriage.

This settled fund on Amelia Dobbin's death was valued at £300,000.

Amelia had made two transfers of value prior to her death.

On 1 January 1999 she transferred assets to Rebecca's husband, the value of the transfer being £70,900. On 10 June 2008 she gave £172,000 to Paul.

For many years up to the date of her death Amelia had owned, and farmed as sole trader, 200 acres of agricultural land (which is included in the balance sheet of the farming business), the open market value of which at her death is £400,000 and the agricultural value £300,000. The other assets of the farming business are valued at £96,000.

Amelia's free estate at death, apart from the farm land and other business assets, consisted of £40,000 Crawley Corporation 6% Stock 2012, quoted at 92–94 ex div (interest paid 15 February and 15 August), furniture and effects valued at £13,500, income due to her from the settlements £4,320 and a bank balance of £8,590.

Her liabilities and funeral expenses amounted to £4,370.

By her will she left £50,000 to a registered charity, £2,000 to a major British political party, and the residue to a close friend.

(a)   Prepare a statement of the amount on which inheritance tax is chargeable on Amelia's death.

(b)   Compute the inheritance tax payable, stating by whom it will be borne.

Assume that George Sedley's estate was not of such value that it is possible to claim a transfer of nil-rate band from him on Amelia's death in 2010. Assume also that William Dobbin left in excess of £30,000.

Answer

Amelia Dobbin deceased

(a)   *Calculation of amount on which inheritance tax is chargeable on death — 15 July 2010*

Free estate

			£
Agricultural property:			
Agricultural value	300,000		
Less: Agricultural property relief 100%	300,000		–
Business property:			
Non-agricultural value (£400,000 – £300,000)		100,000	
Farm business assets		96,000	
		196,000	
Less: Business property relief 100%		196,000	–
£40,000 Crawley Corporation 6% stock @ 92½% ex div			37,000
Interest due (half year)	1,200		
Less: Income tax @ 20%	240	960	37,960
Furniture and effects			13,500
Income due from settlements			4,320
Bank balance			8,590
			64,370
Less: Funeral expenses and liabilities		4,370	60,000

Less:	Exempt legacies		
	Charity	50,000	
	Political party	2,000	
		£52,000	

Giving a deduction after agricultural and business
property relief attributable thereto of

$$£52,000 \times \frac{60,000 \text{(free estate after APR / BPR)}}{556,000 \text{(free estate before APR / BPR)}} \qquad 5,612$$

	£
Net value of free estate chargeable to inheritance tax on Amelia's death	54,388

Settled property

		£
1973	Settlement by Amelia on herself for life	
	Investments	249,000
1974	Surviving spouse settlement	
	Transitional exemption (see **explanatory note 4**)	–
Total estate chargeable to inheritance tax on Amelia's death		303,388

(b) *Inheritance tax payable at death — 15 July 2010*

On potentially exempt transfers within seven years before death (ie 16 July 2003 to 15 July 2010):

				Gross £	Tax £
10 June 2008					
Gift to son			172,000		
Less: Annual exemptions	2008/09	3,000			
	2007/08	3,000	6,000		
Potentially exempt transfer now chargeable				166,000	–
				166,000	–

On estate at death:

	Gross £	Tax £
Inheritance tax accumulation within seven years before death as above	166,000	–
Chargeable assets at death and tax thereon	303,388	57,755*
	469,388	57,755*

(* 469,388 – 325,000 = 144,388 @ 40%)

The inheritance tax of £57,755 is borne as follows:

By personal representatives

		£
Value of free estate (as reduced by APR and BPR)	60,000	
Less: Exempt transfers (as reduced by APR and BPR)	5,612	
	£54,388	
$£57,755 \times \dfrac{54,388}{303,388} =$		10,354

By trustees of 1973 settlement

		£
Value of settled property	£249,000	
$£57,755 \times \dfrac{249,000}{303,388} =$		47,401
		£57,755

Explanatory Notes

Valuation of quoted securities

(1)   Quoted securities are valued at a quarter up from the lower of the quoted prices (or halfway between the highest and lowest bargains marked if less), any accrued income therefore being included in the quotation. If quoted ex interest, the whole of the forthcoming income (net of lower rate income tax) must be added

to the resultant valuation, since the whole of that income would have been forthcoming had a sale been made at the point of death, not just the part accrued on a day to day basis up to the death.

Agricultural and business property relief

(2)   For detailed notes on agricultural property relief and business property relief see **Example 25**.

(3)   The free estate is reduced by the exempt legacies to the charity and political party. Such legacies are completely exempt (ss 23, 24). However unless agricultural and business property is left as a specific legacy rather than as part of the residue of the estate, the benefit of agricultural property and business property relief is allocated over the exempt and chargeable free estate, thus effectively diluting the value of those reliefs where there are exempt legacies (s 39A, and see **Examples 15 and 17**).

For detailed notes on the charity and political party exemptions see **Example 1**.

Estate duty — surviving spouse exemption

(4)   Where one party to a marriage died before 13 November 1974 and the other dies after 12 March 1975 (the date on which estate duty was abolished and capital transfer tax/inheritance tax commenced to be chargeable on death) any property which would have been exempt from estate duty under the 'surviving spouse' exemption of FA 1894 s 5(2) is left out of account for inheritance tax (Sch 6.2).

The estate duty exemption applied only to property in which the spouse had a limited interest (eg for life or widowhood) and of which she/he was at no time competent to dispose, and not to property that passed absolutely. The property comprised in the settlement established by Amelia's second husband on his death in July 1974 is therefore left out of account for inheritance tax under this transitional provision.

(5)   Although Amelia at her death only had a life interest in the 1973 settlement comprising the assets from her first husband's estate, she did at one time (between 1971 and 1973) have an absolute interest in those assets, having herself created the settlement in her own favour. The transitional relief at note 4 does not therefore apply.

Until the major changes in FA 2006, a settlement upon oneself with remainder to specified persons was a useful way of determining in one's lifetime the destination of specified property upon death. For further notes on this point see **Example 46 explanatory note 8**. The assets comprised in the settlement itself remained in the settlor's estate for inheritance tax purposes through the interest in possession rules, so there would not be even a potentially exempt transfer when such a settlement was made, no transfer of value having taken place. The settled fund remained chargeable to inheritance tax on the death of the settlor, so no tax was avoided, but the lifetime settlement determined the devolution on death, thus safeguarding against any possible family problems arising, say, from remarriage or other doubts within a family.

Since 22 March 2006 the making of any settlement in the settlor's lifetime, even in the settlor's own favour, entails an immediately chargeable transfer (with a lifetime charge to inheritance tax to the extent that the settlor's nil rate band is exceeded, and with potential effects on the settlor's death up to 14 years later, see **Example 55 explanatory note 12(a)**), unless the settlement confers a disabled person's interest (on the settlor or some other person; for what is meant by a disabled person's interest see **Example 52**).

Inheritance tax – transfer of nil-rate band

(6)   For an account of the new provisions relating to the transfer of the nil-rate band from one spouse to another see **Example 1 (iii)**. In summary, anyone who dies after 8 October 2007 who has previously been in a marriage or civil partnership, where the marriage or civil partnership came to an end on the death of the other spouse or civil partner, may make use of any nil-rate band which was not used on the death of the predeceasing spouse or civil partner, irrespective of when the predeceasing spouse or civil partner died. Where the first spouse dies before 25 July 1986, ie the date when IHT replaced capital transfer tax, it is still possible to claim transfer of nil-rate band which was not used on their death. However, the unlimited exemption for gifts to a surviving spouse, taking effect on death only came into force from 13 November 1974. Between 22 March 1972 and 12 November 1974 estate duty exemption for a gift to a spouse was limited to £15,000. The nil-rate band was also £15,000. William Dobbin died between those dates but left an estate in excess of £30,000. There can be no transfer of nil-rate band to Amelia. Before 22 March 1972

there was no spouse exemption from estate duty. George Sedley died before that date and the question assumes that there is no transferable nil-rate band as a result of his death.

Potentially exempt transfers

(7)   Amelia made potentially exempt transfers on 1 January 1999 and 10 June 2008. The earlier transfer became completely exempt on 1 January 2006. The second transfer became a chargeable transfer by reason of her death on 15 July 2010, but since it is below the nil threshold no tax is payable (and taper relief is not therefore relevant). It does, however, reduce the nil band available against the death estate.

Question

Richard died in 1994 and left his estate consisting of marketable securities in trust for his brother Alan for life and thereafter absolutely to Alan's son, Lawrie.

Lawrie died on 1 June 2010. His estate, including his interest in expectancy on the death of Alan, was left to his only daughter Gladys for life and thereafter to his nephew John absolutely.

Lawrie's estate comprised:

Personal assets £335,000

Interest expectant on the death of Alan valued at £32,000.

His funeral expenses amounted to £1,700 and his debts, including £100 owed to his turf accountant, amounted to £3,400. He had made no lifetime transfers.

Alan died on 31 December 2010, the value of the settled property on that date amounting to £55,000. Alan's personal estate was valued at £233,000. He had made one previous transfer on 6 October 2007, being a gift of quoted shares then valued at £143,000.

Calculate the inheritance tax payable on the above events.

Answer

Inheritance tax computation on death of Lawrie (1 June 2010)

Value of estate for inheritance tax

			£
Free estate			335,000
Reversionary interest:			
Interest in expectancy on death of Alan – excluded property, therefore			Nil
			335,000
Less: Funeral expenses		1,700	
Debts	3,400		
Less: Turf accountant	100	3,300	5,000
Chargeable to inheritance tax			330,000
Inheritance tax on 2010/11 scale (330,000 – 325,000 = 5,000 @ 40%)			2,000

Inheritance tax computation on death of Alan (31 December 2010)

Inheritance tax accumulation

				Gross £	Tax £
6 October 2007					
Shares transferred			143,000		
Less: Annual exemptions	2007/08	3,000			
	2006/07	3,000	6,000	137,000*	–
Estate at death:					
Free estate			233,000		
Settled property – Richard's settlement			55,000	288,000	40,000**
				425,000	40,000**

(** 425,000 – 325,000 = 100,000 @ 40%)

*This will have been a potentially exempt transfer when it was made, but becomes a chargeable transfer since death occurred within seven years. No tax is payable, however, because it is below the nil threshold.

Tax of £40,000 on estate is payable as follows:

By trustees of settled property

$$\frac{55,000}{288,000} \times £40,000$$ 7,639

By personal representatives

$$\frac{233,000}{288,000} \times £40,000$$

$$\frac{32,361}{£40,000}$$

Explanatory Notes

Reversionary interests

(1) A reversionary interest in a settlement is excluded property whether it is transferred in lifetime or on death unless it was acquired for a consideration, or unless it is one to which the settlor or his spouse/civil partner is beneficially entitled (or for interests acquired on or after 10 March 1981, has been at any time beneficially entitled (s 48)). Accordingly the value of the reversion in this Example is excluded from Lawrie's estate for inheritance tax purposes.

For detailed notes on excluded property see **Example 3**.

(2) The reason for excluding reversionary interests from a person's estate for inheritance tax purposes was that the capital value of the settlement (as distinct from the value of the right to receive the income for the time being) is included in the estate of the person presently entitled to receive the income for interests in possession created before 22 March 2006 and for some interests in possession created after that date.

For other interests in possession created on or after 22 March 2006, the settlement is subject to a separate charging regime based upon the value of the trust property and, therefore, it is still appropriate to exclude reversionary interests from tax on a general basis.

Quick succession relief

(3) The settled property does not give rise to quick succession relief on the death of Alan since it was *not* chargeable on the death of Lawrie (see **Examples 53 and 55**).

The settlement made by Richard granted a life interest to Alan and a reversion to Lawrie.

That made by Lawrie granted a life interest to Gladys with reversion to John.

The fund left by Richard therefore devolves as follows:

Lawrie therefore never had an interest in the income of the settlement made by Richard and was therefore not chargeable to inheritance tax on the transfer of the reversion on his death. This passed as part of his estate from which Gladys is to enjoy the income for her life and will not be chargeable to inheritance tax until Gladys's interest in the fund ceases (ordinarily upon her death). On Alan's death on 31 December 2009, however, the trust fund created by Richard is reduced by inheritance tax of £7,639, reducing the value in the estate of Lawrie from which Gladys is to enjoy the income. It does not reduce the inheritance tax payable on Lawrie's death, because the trust fund was excluded property.

Treatment of debts in deceased's estate

(4)   Debts may be deducted from the chargeable estate if they are:

(i)   Reasonable funeral expenses, including the cost of a tombstone (s 172).

(ii)   Liabilities imposed by law or incurred for a consideration in money or money's worth (including income and other taxes) (s 5(3), (5)).

(iii)   Liabilities for inheritance tax providing they are paid from the estate (ss 5(4) and 174(2)).

A debt may not be deducted, however, to the extent that the creditor has received gifts from the deceased (FA 1986 s 103). For details see **Example 20**.

The amount due to the turf accountant is not incurred for consideration in money or money's worth and cannot therefore be deducted in arriving at the chargeable estate of Lawrie.

Question

The trustees of a discretionary settlement made by Harold on 1 November 1968 make the following appointments under powers given to them in the settlement, the cumulative transfers in the ten years prior to 1 November 1998 being £189,000.

(i)	1 July 2001	£40,000	cash to Andrew absolutely
(ii)	1 April 2008	£60,000	cash to Harold's wife Mary
(iii)	1 August 2010	£92,800	quoted securities to Brian absolutely

Harold, the trustees and the beneficiaries are all domiciled and resident in the United Kingdom. One other trust made by Harold (also with UK resident trustees) is still in existence throughout 2010.

The appointments all provide that any tax payable is to be borne by the recipient beneficiaries.

(a)   Calculate the inheritance tax payable (if any) as a result of each of the above appointments and also the amount payable on the 1998 and 2008 ten-year anniversaries.

The value of relevant property on 31 October 1998 was £162,000 and on 31 October 2008 £302,000.

The chargeable gain accruing to the trustees as a result of Brian's absolute entitlement on 1 August 2010 was £12,525, and they made no other disposals for capital gains tax during 2010/11.

(b)   If Harold added £25,000 to the original settlement on 1 November 2004 (at which time his gross chargeable transfers for the seven years to that date amounted to £240,000 including the £25,000 then transferred) calculate the revised tax liabilities assuming that the value of relevant property at 31 October 2008 was £338,000, including the addition to the settlement which was valued at £36,000 on that date.

The payment of £60,000 to Mary on 1 April 2008, and the appointment of quoted securities to Brian on 1 August 2010, can both be shown to be wholly derived from the funds in Harold's original settlement.

(c)   How would your answer to (b) differ if the addition of £25,000 on 1 November 2004 had been made not by the Harold but by Mary (with the same record of previous transfers)?

Answer

(a) Inheritance tax position of settlement made 1 November 1968

	Gross £	Tax £

1 November 1998
Ten-yearly charge (see **explanatory notes 3 and 4**):
Distributions in previous ten years (ie amounts subject to

	Gross £	Tax £
exit charges)	189,000	–
Value of relevant property on 31 October 1998	162,000	25,600*
	351,000	25,600*

Actual rate is 30% of effective rate

$$\frac{25,600}{162,000} \times 30\% = 4.741\%$$

Tax payable by trustees is £162,000 × 4.741% =£7,680
* Tax is calculated on 1998/99 scale
   (351,000 – 223,000 = 128,000 @ 20%)

1 July 2001
Exit charge – on distribution to Andrew
Amount chargeable = £40,000
Actual rate at previous ten-year anniversary recomputed for change of rates
2001/02 scale 351,000 – 242,000 = 109,000 @ 20% = £21,800
Actual rate is 30% of effective rate

$$\frac{21,800}{162,000} \times 30\% = 4.03\%$$

Number of complete quarters between 1 November 1998
and 30 June 2001 = 10
Tax payable by trustees and deducted from distribution to Andrew

$$£40,000 \times 4.03\% \times \frac{10}{40} = £403$$

1 April 2008
Exit charge – on distribution to Mary
Amount chargeable = £60,000
Actual rate at previous ten-year anniversary recomputed
for change of rates
2007/08 scale 351,000 – 300,000 = 51,000 @ 20% = £10,200
Actual rate is 30% of effective rate

$$\frac{10,200}{162,000} \times 30\% = 1.89\%$$

Number of complete quarters between 1 November 1998 and
31 March 2008 = 37

Tax payable by trustees and deducted from distribution to Mary

$$£60,000 \times 1.89\% \times \frac{37}{40} = £1,049$$

1 November 2008
  Ten-yearly charge
  Distributions in previous ten years (ie between

1 November 1997 and 31 October 2008)	100,000	–
Value of relevant property on 31 October 2008	302,000	18,000**
	402,000	18,000**

  (** 402,000 – 312,000 = 90,000 @ 20%)
  Actual rate is 30% of effective rate

$$\frac{18,000}{302,000} \times 30\% = 1.788\%$$

Tax payable by trustees is £302,000 × 1.788% =	£5,400

1 August 2010
(i) Capital gains tax deemed disposal on appointment to Brian
  Trust annual exemption of £5,050 shared with one other trust

Chargeable gain accruing to trustees	12,525
Annual exemption for this settlement: half of £5,050	2,525
Gain chargeable to tax	£10,000
Capital gains tax payable by trustees (to be borne by Brian) @ 28%	£2,800

(ii) Inheritance tax exit charge – on distribution to Brian

Total value	92,800
Less: Capital gains tax borne by Brian	2,800
Amount chargeable	£90,000

  Actual rate at previous ten-year anniversary recomputed for change of rates

2010/11 scale 402,000 – 325,000 = 77,000 @ 20%	£15,400

  Actual rate is 30% of effective rate

$$\frac{15,400}{302,000} \times 30\% = 1.529\%$$

Number of complete quarters between 1 November 2008 and
1 August 2010 = 7
Inheritance tax payable by trustees (to be borne by Brian)

$$£90,000 \times 1.529\% \times \frac{7}{40} = £241$$

Summary:

Capital gains tax	2,800
Inheritance tax	241
Total tax to be paid by Brian, or raised from securities before distribution	3,041

(b) Additions to existing settlement by Harold

1 November 2004
  Recalculation of amount charged at previous

(1998) ten-year anniversary because of addition to property
in the settlement:

Distributions in ten years to 31 October 1998		189,000
Value of relevant property at 31 October 1998	162,000	
Value of property added 1 November 2004	25,000	187,000
		376,000

1 April 2008

Exit charge – on distribution to Mary

Amount chargeable = £60,000

Revised rate at previous ten-year anniversary following addition to
settlement, using 2007/08 scale:

376,000 – 300,000 = 76,000 @ 20% = £15,200

Actual rate is 30% of effective rate

$$\frac{15,200}{187,000} \times 30\% = 2.439\%$$

Number of complete quarters between 1 November 1998 and 31 March
2008 = 37

Tax payable by trustees and deducted from distribution to Mary

$$£60,000 \times 2.439\% \times \frac{37}{40} = £1,354$$

	Gross £	Tax £

1 November 2008

	Gross £	Tax £
Ten-yearly charge (see **explanatory note 7**)		
Distributions in previous ten years subject to an exit charge	100,000	–
Chargeable transfers made by Harold in seven years preceding addition to settlement (240,000 – 25,000)	215,000	
Deemed accumulation for notional transfer	315,000	600*
Value of relevant property on 31 October 2008:		
Derived from original fund	302,000	
Derived from addition	36,000	
	338,000	67,600
	653,000	68,200†

(* 315,000 – 312,000 = 3,000 @ 20% = £600)

(† 653,000 – 312,000 = 341,000 @ 20% = £67,200)

Actual rate is 30% of effective rate

$$\frac{67,600}{338,000} \times 30\% = 6\%$$

proportionately reduced where relevant property added in previous ten
years.

Tax payable by trustees:

On relevant property held for preceding ten years

£302,000 @ 6%   18,120

On relevant property added 1 November 2004

$$£36,000 @ 6\% \times \frac{16}{40}$$

		864
		£18,984

1 August 2010

		Gross	Tax
(i)	Capital gains tax on appointment to Brian as before		£2,800
(ii)	Inheritance tax exit charge – on distribution to Brian		
	Amount chargeable after CGT deduction as before	£90,000	
	Actual rate at previous ten-year anniversary recomputed for change of rates using 2010/11 scale		
	Distributions in previous ten years subject to an exit charge	100,000	
	Chargeable transfers made by Harold in seven years preceding addition to settlement (240,000 – 25,000)	215,000	
		_____	
	Deemed accumulation for notional transfer	315,000	–*
	Value of relevant property on 31 October 2008	338,000	65,600†
	(no distinction between original and added property)	653,000	65,600†

* within 2010/11 nil rate band £325.000

† 653,000 – 325,000 = 328,000 @ 20%

Actual rate is 30% of effective rate

$$\frac{65{,}600}{338{,}000} \times 30\% = 5.825\%$$

Number of complete quarters between 1 November 2008 and 1 August 2010 = 7

Inheritance tax payable by trustees (to be borne by Brian)

$$£90{,}000 \times 5.825\% \times \frac{7}{40} = £917.44$$

Summary:

Capital gains tax	2,800
Inheritance tax	917
Total tax to be paid by Brian, or raised from securities before distribution	3,717

(c) Addition to existing settlement by Mary

The result of the addition being made by someone other than the original settlor is that there are now two people who are settlors in relation to the settlement. Section 44(2) provides that in such a case 'and if the circumstances so require [Part 3 of the IHTA 1984 (except for s 48(4)–(6) dealing with FOTRA securities as excluded property)] shall have effect in relation to [the settlement] as if the settled property were comprised in separate settlements'. HMRC equate 'the circumstances so require' to 'in a straightforward case' (IHTM42553).

So the addition (and the property derived from it) would be treated as the making of a separate settlement by Mary. That separate settlement would first have property comprised in it on 1 November 2004, which is therefore its commencement date; and so its first ten-year anniversary will fall on 1 November 2014. The inheritance tax accumulation attributed to the notional chargeable transfer used to work out the rate then applicable will include Mary's chargeable transfers in the seven years prior to (but not including) the date of the addition (£215,000 in the Example, ie £240,000 less the £25,000 addition itself); distributions from the property derived from Harold's 1968 settlement will not be counted for that purpose as they will only affect the deemed separate settlement made by him.

Therefore on the basis that the appointments on 1 April 2008 and 1 August 2010 can both be shown to have been wholly derived from the original settlement, the inheritance tax exit charges on each of them will be as in **part (a)** above. Correspondingly the ten-year charge on 1 November 2008 would be worked out, only on the original property, in the same way as in **part (a)**.

The other point to note in relation to the addition by Mary is that she is evidently a beneficiary of the settlement since she received a distribution on 1 April 2008. Therefore the settled property from time to time representing her addition will be within the gifts with reservation rules so far as she is concerned. This does not preclude the levying of inheritance tax charges under the relevant property regime in the usual way; but it will mean that on Mary's death the property in question will be subject to inheritance tax by aggregation with her estate. (Alternatively if she ceases to be a beneficiary, or to the extent that distributions are made from this fund to other beneficiaries, the reservation will cease and Mary will be treated as having made a potentially exempt transfer at that time.)

Explanatory Notes

Charging relevant property trusts to inheritance tax

(1)   Until 2006 the relevant property regime (and its equivalent in the early days of capital transfer tax) was essentially for trusts (other than those for which specially privileged treatment was though appropriate) whose charging regime could not rationally be linked to the lifetime of a beneficiary. Primarily this meant discretionary and accumulation trusts. For all interest in possession trusts the underlying capital was treated as part of the beneficiary's estate and taxed on his death, in the same way as had been the case in the days of estate duty before capital transfer tax was introduced.

The Finance Act 2006 changed that focus, and the relevant property regime became the primary inheritance tax regime for settled property. The cases where a new interest in possession would be within the old regime were severely limited – to immediate post-death interests and disabled person's interests; but transitional provisions for beneficiaries whose interests in possession date from before 22 March 2006, and for those who succeeded to those interests before 6 October 2008 (or, in a limited number of cases, later than that) will ensure that there are plenty of 'estate IIPs' in existence for many years to come.

See **Example 52** for an explanation of what interests in possession can be classified as estate IIPs, and of how the settled property is taxed when an estate IIP subsists or comes to an end.

The relevant property regime is centred on the imposition of a tax charge every ten years at 30% of the lifetime rate (approximating broadly to a charge at the full lifetime rate once in a generation) based on certain assumptions. These assumptions (in the form of a 'notional chargeable transfer' used to compute the rate) take account of other (non-relevant) property in the same trust and property in any trusts made on the same date; and crucially (for settlements made, or property added, on or after 27 March 1974 when capital transfer tax was announced) the settlor's inheritance tax accumulation in the seven years prior to his putting property into the trust (or the highest such accumulation if he contributes property on different dates) is permanently attached to the settlement for this purpose. (See **notes 3 and 7**, and **Example 60** for trusts made after 26 March 1974.)

The ten-yearly charge is supplemented by a proportional, or 'exit', charge when property leaves the relevant property regime (**notes 5 and 6**), subject to some exceptions (see **note 10**).

Unlike the regime for estate IIPs, the relevant property regime does not involve the settled property being deemed to be comprised in anyone's estate (though where something turns on ownership, for Example business property relief or agricultural property relief, the owners are the trustees). Therefore the trustees cannot make transfers of value or chargeable transfers. Any occasion on which tax is charged under the relevant property regime (or the subsidiary regimes for certain 'privileged' types of trust, also in Chapter 3 of Part 3) nevertheless is treated as a chargeable transfer for the purpose of any other references to chargeable transfers in the IHTA 1984 (s 2(3)).

Pre-27 March 1974 settlements under the relevant property regime

(2)   The basic rules of the relevant property regime are somewhat modified in relation to a settlement that was created before 27 March 1974. Except where property is added to the trust on or after that date, the trust's inheritance tax accumulation will not include any element by reference to the settlor's position; furthermore the only property which counts towards the notional transfer which determines the rate is relevant property within the same trust.

Ten-yearly charge

(3)   On the tenth anniversary of the creation of the settlement and every subsequent tenth anniversary (but not before 1 April 1983) a charge to inheritance tax arises. This is known as the principal or 'ten-yearly' charge (s 64).

The charge is made on any *relevant property* (see **note 8**) held in the trust immediately before the ten-year anniversary. See **note 9** re reducing the tax on relevant property that has not been relevant property throughout the ten-year period.

The rate of tax is determined by reference to a notional transfer of the relevant property made immediately before the ten-year anniversary, where the notional transferor had previously made chargeable transfers of a specified amount see **note 4**), and *one half* the normal death scale rate in force at the date of the charge is used to arrive at the tax on the notional transfer. There is no grossing up (s 64). The rate of tax charged on the relevant property in the trust is 30% of the effective rate of tax on the notional transfer. With the current half scale rate of 20% this gives a maximum charging rate of 6% (see **note 11** re business or agricultural property relief and the instalment option).

The rules for arriving at both the notional transfer itself and the previous transfers are different for pre-27 March 1974 trusts and trusts made on or after that date. For the detailed rules relating to post-26 March 1974 trusts see **Example 60**.

Cumulative transfers at ten-year anniversary

(4)   For pre-27 March 1974 trusts, the inheritance tax accumulation at the anniversary date will normally only show transfers occurring during the preceding ten years. Those transfers will comprise:

(a)   the amounts on which exit charges have been made under s 65 (see **notes 5 and 6**), and

(b)   at the first ten-year anniversary only, distribution payments (as defined under the old rules) up to 8 March 1982 (the equivalent during that time of the relevant property exit charge). This cannot be relevant for a ten-year anniversary charge occurring on or after 1 April 1993.

Thus, in the Example, the charge in 2008 uses the exit charges of the preceding ten years:

	£
1 July 2001	40,000
1 April 2008	60,000
	100,000

These previous transfers are cumulated with the relevant property in the trust at the ten-year anniversary to compute the tax at one half normal rates on the notional transfer and arrive at the effective rate. The tax charge on the relevant property is then at 30% of the effective rate (s 66). In each case the tax is calculated at the rates in force at the date of the charge.

Special rules apply when property has been added to the settlement, or has become relevant property (for Example on the termination of a prior estate IIP as in **Example 53 part B**), during the ten-year period. These are detailed in **note 7**.

Exit charges

(5)   In addition to the ten-yearly charge (**explanatory notes 3 and 4**) a charge to inheritance tax arises when property in a settlement ceases to be relevant property (s 65). This charge is known as the exit charge. If the tax is payable out of the relevant property remaining in the trust, the distribution is grossed up using the rate of tax payable on the distribution (ie after reducing it under note 6 below, if appropriate, according to the complete quarters since the last ten-year anniversary) (s 65(2)). (For an illustration of grossing up see **Example 60**.) The method of computing exit charges occurring after the first post-31 March 1983 ten-year anniversary of the settlement is the same for both pre-27 March 1974 settlements and settlements made on or after that date. (Different rules apply to exit charges before the first ten-year anniversary, but that is not now relevant to settlements made before 27 March 1974. See **Example 60 explanatory note 5**.)

(6)   The charge on distributions after the first ten-year anniversary is found by using the rate of tax computed at the previous ten-year anniversary (but where the scale of rates has been reduced the rate deemed to have applied at that anniversary is recalculated using the revised scales (Sch 2.3), as shown in **part (a)** of the Example). The exit charge rate is arrived at by applying to that previous rate the fraction x/40 where x is the number of complete quarters in the period since the previous ten-year anniversary (s 69). If, therefore, the distribution occurs at the anniversary, or within three months thereafter, no exit charge is payable. The charge is levied on the difference between the value of relevant property before the distribution and its value thereafter. Thus the 'loss to the donor' principle applies to discretionary settlements. The maximum rate for an exit charge is 5.85%, ie 6% (maximum rate at previous ten-year anniversary) × 39/40.

        Special rules apply where property has been added to a settlement since the date of the last ten-year charge (see **note 7**).

Added property

(7)   Where property has been added to a pre-27 March 1974 settlement after 8 March 1982 as a result of a chargeable transfer by the settlor, then on the occasion of the following ten-year anniversary the inheritance tax accumulation is deemed to commence with the distributions subject to an exit charge in the previous ten years, plus the aggregate of the values transferred by the settlor in the seven years preceding the date of the addition to the settlement disregarding transfers made on that day. Where two or more additions have been made then the higher of the two (or more) possible figures will be used (s 67(4)). Thus a modest addition to an existing settlement can give rise to a substantial increase in the tax payable. In the Example the ten-yearly charge on 1 November 2008 would increase from £5,400 to £17,784 if £25,000 was added to the settlement on 1 November 2004.

        This rule is not triggered if the transfer of value resulting from the addition is wholly an exempt transfer – ie covered in full by the annual exemption (s 19) or, perhaps more significantly, by the exemption for normal expenditure out of income (s 21).

        Although the total value of relevant property added in the previous ten years is chargeable to tax and is added to the accumulation to arrive at the rate of tax, the rate of tax chargeable on that added property is reduced by one-fortieth for each complete quarter before the date that the property became relevant property. In the Example the property was added after six years (24 quarters) and therefore tax was payable on the added property of £16,000 @ 6% × 16/40 = £384; being a charge for the last four of the ten years (16 quarters) (s 66(2)).

        In addition to affecting the subsequent ten-year charge the addition will also increase the exit charge on any distribution occurring after its settlement. This is because it is necessary both for pre- and post-27 March 1974 settlements to recompute the tax rate on the previous ten-year anniversary by including in the calculation the value of property added subsequently as though it were relevant property at that time (s 69(2), (3)). This is illustrated by the difference in rates in **part (b)** of the Example in relation to the distribution on 1 April 2008 to Mary where the tax increased from £1,049 to £1,354.

        If the £60,000 paid in **part (b)** to Mary on 1 April 2008 had come partly from the original settlement and partly from the added property then two separate computations would be required. The fraction applicable to the added property will not take into account the complete quarters (since the date of the previous anniversary) occurring before the day that the property was added (ss 68(3), 69(4)).

Thus, assuming that £54,000 came from the original settlement and £6,000 from the added property, the computation would be:

1 April 2008   £
  Exit charge – on distribution to Mary
  Original property = £54,000
  Revised rate at previous ten-year anniversary 2.439%
  Number of complete quarters = 37
  Tax payable:

$$\pounds 54,000 \times 2.439\% \times \frac{37}{40} = \qquad\qquad 1,218$$

Property added on 1 November 2004 – £6,000
Complete quarters 1 November 1998 to 1 November 2004 = 24

$$\text{Appropriate fraction is } \frac{37-24}{40} = \frac{13}{40}$$

Tax payable:

$$\pounds 6,000 \times 2.439\% \times \frac{13}{40} = \qquad\qquad 48$$

$$\underline{\qquad 1,266}$$

Where there is no indication as to whether a distribution is paid out of the original property or added property, it is treated as coming out of each proportionately.

Property will be deemed to have been added if the settlor makes any chargeable transfer which results in the value of the property in the settlement increasing, unless

• the addition was merely of value, without adding to the settled property as such, and

• it can be shown that the transfer was not primarily intended to increase the value of the settlement, and

• the actual increase was not more than 5% of the pre-addition value (s 67(2)).

Meaning of 'relevant property'

(8)   If an interest in possession subsists in settled property, the property will not be relevant property if the interest in possession is an estate IIP (see **Example 52**), or in certain circumstances if it is owned by a company whose business consists wholly or mainly of acquiring interests in settled property. The company must have bought the interest for full value from a beneficiary in whose hands it was an estate IIP (s 59).

In all other cases the settled property will be subject to the relevant property regime unless it falls within one of the following special exceptions:

(i)   Charitable trusts (whether temporary or permanent)

(ii)   Property held on the terms of one of the restrictive types of trust for children and young people applicable since FA 2006, namely:

        • bereaved minor's trusts

        • age 18-to-25 trusts or

- accumulation and maintenance trusts (see **Example 64**) set up before 22 March 2006 (and still remaining within the more circumscribed conditions that have applied for such trusts since 6 April 2008)

(iii)   Maintenance funds for historic buildings etc

(iv)   Pension funds

(v)   Employee and newspaper trusts (unless there is an interest possession that is not an estate IIP and which, if owned by a company whose business consists wholly or mainly of acquiring interests in settled property, was not an estate IIP in the hands of the beneficiary from whom the company bought it for full value)

(vi)   Trade or professional compensation funds

(vii)   Protective trusts where the discretionary trust was triggered by a forfeiture before 12 April 1978

(viii)   Privileged trusts for disabled persons where funds were settled before 10 March 1981

(ix)   Excluded property.

(9)   If property in a settlement has not been relevant property throughout the whole of a given ten-year period then the charge on that property will not take into account the complete quarters (since the date of the previous ten-year anniversary) occurring before the day that the property became relevant property (s 69(4), applying s 68(3)). See **Example 53 part B** and **Example 61** for an illustration of this point.

Capital gains tax and relevant property exit charges

(10)   Under IHTA 1984 s 165(2), if a beneficiary becomes absolutely entitled to settled property by virtue of the event which gives rise to an inheritance tax charge under Part 3 Chapter 3 (which includes relevant property exit charges), then the amount of the capital gains tax is deductible from the amount otherwise chargeable to inheritance tax, provided the capital gains tax is borne by the beneficiary – as is the case in the Example for the appointment to Brian.

A similar rule applies in relation to an individual's chargeable transfer if the capital gains tax is borne by the donee. If on the other hand the tax in such a case is borne by the transferor, it is not taken into account as an additional loss to his estate (s 5(4)).

For the rates of capital gains tax for disposals during 2010/11 see **Example 47 note 15**, and for the division of the trust annual exemption between different trusts made by the same settlor see **Example 47 note 16**.

Conversion of relevant property into non-relevant property

(11)   An exit charge can (and in certain cases does) arise if trustees convert relevant property into property that is not relevant property. Such a charge is prevented in most instances, however, by specific provisions. Thus there is no exit charge when property ceases to be relevant property because it is transferred to an employee trust (subject to detailed conditions – see s 75), or becomes held for charitable purposes without limit of time, or becomes the property of a national body such as a museum or the National Trust, or a political party or a non-profit making body (s 76). This is subject to the proviso that the property does not cease to be used for the purposes of the body concerned.

An important exemption from the exit charge is available in the case of a settlement made by a settlor who was not domiciled, or deemed domiciled, in the UK at the time. In such a case property situated outside the UK is excluded property, as is property comprising holdings in a UK authorised unit trust (AUT) or open-ended investment company (OEIC). Since excluded property is not relevant property (see **note 8(ix)**), an exit charge would otherwise arise if trustees of such a trust moved trust property out of the UK (physically as with chattels, or by exchanging a UK asset for a non-UK one). Section 65(7) provides exemption in such a case.

Unfortunately, possibly by oversight, a corresponding exemption was not added in relation to the acquisition of a holding in an AUT or OEIC when they were added to the categories of excluded property where non-UK domiciled persons are concerned (s 48(3A) added by FA 2003), so if the settlor was not UK domiciled trustees should exercise considerable care if investing in such holdings.

Although an exit charge does not arise when a distribution for charitable purposes is made from a temporary charitable trust (ie where the income, and perhaps the capital, is for the time being applicable solely for charitable purposes but the trust will convert, or is capable of being converted, for other purposes at some time in the future), a special charge is made under s 70 on the cessation of the trust or on a non-privileged distribution. This is calculated by reference to the time that the property has been so held (but not before 13 March 1975) and is the sum of

- 0.25% for each of the first forty quarters

- 0.20% for each of the next forty quarters

- 0.15% for each of the next forty quarters

- 0.10% for each of the next forty quarters

- 0.05% for each of the next forty quarters

Thus the maximum rate of 30% cannot apply until 2025.

If the trust pays the tax then the amount must be grossed up.

Instalment option

(12)   It should be noted that where inheritance tax is payable on property eligible for the instalment option, that option is available to trustees of a settlement, provided that the property remains in the settlement (s 227(1)(c)). For details of property eligible see **Example 5 at explanatory note 7**. If the property is business or agricultural property qualifying for 50% relief, the 6% maximum rate of charge for discretionary trusts is effectively 3% on that property, and when paid by instalments over ten years this becomes 0.3% a year.

Question

Nicholas Carraway, whose gross chargeable transfers in the preceding seven years totalled £132,000 and who had no available annual exemptions, settled a sum of £100,000 on 6 April 1990 in a discretionary trust, personally paying the inheritance tax chargeable on the scale at that time.

On 21 September 1992 the trustees made a distribution of £4,000 to A, subject to payment of tax out of that amount.

On 1 April 1994 the trustees made a distribution of £6,000 to B, subject to payment of tax out of that amount.

The market value of the trust fund on 5 April 2000 was £150,000.

On 27 May 2004 the trustees made a distribution of £20,000 to C, paying the tax out of the remainder of the settled fund.

The market value of the trust fund on 5 April 2010 was £300,000.

On 10 October 2013 the trustees made a final distribution of £330,000 to D, subject to payment of tax out of that amount.

Compute the inheritance tax payable on each chargeable occasion.

Assume for this purpose that the inheritance tax legislation remains unchanged for later years.

Also assume that the 2010/11 rates will continue into 2013/14.

Answer

Tax position of settlement (settlor having paid the tax on the settlement)

Initial value of settlement = £100,000

Inheritance tax – effective rate (originally calculated using 1990/91 scale but revised using 1992/93 scale to calculate tax on distribution 21 September 1992):

	Gross £	Tax £
Settlor's previous transfers within seven years before commencement of settlement	132,000	–
Initial value of settlement	100,000	16,400*
	232,000	16,400*

(* 232,000 – 150,000 = 82,000 @ 20%)
Actual rate is 30% of effective rate

$$\frac{16,400}{100,000} \times 30\% = 4.92\%$$

21 September 1992
    Exit charge on distribution to A
    Amount chargeable = £4,000
    Actual rate applicable at formation of settlement
      (revised using 1992/93 lifetime scale) – 4.92%
    Number of complete quarters between 6 April 1990
      and 21 September 1992 = 9
    Tax payable by trustees and deducted from distribution to A

$$£4,000 \times 4.92\% \times \frac{9}{40} = £44$$

1 April 1994
    Exit charge on distribution to B
    Amount chargeable – £6,000
    Actual rate applicable at formation of settlement
      (revised using 1993/94 lifetime scale):
    232,000 – 150,000 = 82,000 @ 20% = £16,400
    Actual rate is 30% of effective rate

$$\frac{16,400}{100,000} \times 30\% = 4.92\%$$

    Number of complete quarters between 6 April 1990
      and 31 March 1994 = 15
    Tax payable by trustees and deducted from distribution to B

$$£6,000 \times 4.92\% \times \frac{15}{40} = £111$$

	Gross £	Tax using 2000/01 scale £
6 April 2000		
Ten-yearly charge (using one half of death rate at 6.4.00)		
Settlor's previous transfers within seven years before commencement of settlement	132,000	
Distributions subject to exit charges in previous ten years (£4,000 + £6,000)	10,000	
	142,000	–
Value of relevant property – 5 April 2000	150,000	11,600**
	292,000	11,600**

(** 292,000 – 234,000 = 58,000 @ 20%)

Actual rate is 30% of effective rate

$$\frac{11,600}{150,000} \times 30\% = 2.32\%$$

Tax payable by trustees is £150,000 × 2.32% = <u>£3,480</u>

27 May 2004

Exit charge on distribution to C

Actual rate at previous ten-year anniversary
   (revised using 2004/05 lifetime scale):
292,000 – 263,000 = 29,000 @ 20% = £5,800

Actual rate is 30% of effective rate

$$\frac{5,800}{150,000} \times 30\% = 1.16\%$$

Number of complete quarters between 6 April 2000 and
   26 May 2004 = 16

Rate of exit charge applicable

$$1.16\% \times \frac{16}{40} = 0.464\%$$

Distribution (net) – £20,000

$$\text{Gross equivalent thereof } £20,000 \times \frac{100}{99.536} = £20,093$$

Exit charge payable by trustees £20,093 × 0.464% = £93
(not deducted from £20,000 distribution to C)

6 April 2010		
Ten-yearly charge (using one half of death rate at 6.4.10)		
Settlor's previous transfers within seven years before commencement of settlement	132,000	
Distributions in preceding ten years subject to an exit charge	20,093	
	152,093	–
Value of relevant property – 5 April 2010	300,000	25,419†
	452,093	25,419†

(† 452,093 – 325,000 = 127,093 @ 20%)

Actual rate is 30% of effective rate

$$\frac{25,419}{300,000} \times 30\% = 2.542\%$$

Tax payable by trustees is £300,000 × 2.542% = £7,626

10 October 2013

Exit charge on distribution to D

Amount chargeable – £330,000

Actual rate at previous ten-year anniversary

revised using 2013/14 lifetime scale:

452,093 – 325,000 = 127,093 @ 20% = £25,419

Actual rate is 30% of effective rate

$$\frac{25,419}{300,000} \times 30\% = 2.542\%$$

Number of complete quarters between 6 April 2010 and
    9 October 2013 = 14

Tax payable by trustees and deducted from final distribution

$$£330,000 \times 2.542\% \times \frac{14}{40} = £2,936.01$$

Explanatory Notes

Ten-yearly charge on post 26 March 1974 relevant property settlements

(1)   The rules relating to settlements containing *relevant property* took effect from 9 March 1982, replacing an earlier regime under FA 1975 which (as to ten-yearly charges) never actually took effect because (after postponements) the first ten-year anniversary of an existing settlement could not fall before 1 April 1983. (The pre-1982 rules were capable of giving rise to charges on what were known as *distribution payments*, the then equivalent of the exit charges described in **note 4**, and also, if the trustees were not UK resident, to annual charges in effect on account of the next ten-yearly charge – as to which see **note 3**.) There is essentially a single regime covering relevant property in general, but there are some variants in the case of pre-27 March 1974 settlements and these are dealt with in **Example 59**.

Until 22 March 2006 when the classification of trusts was substantially altered by FA 2006, relevant property was broadly confined to discretionary trusts. Since that date it will include many trusts with an interest in possession, and most trusts which, apart from the rule change, would have enjoyed privileged treatment as accumulation and maintenance trusts. Relevant property is defined in detail in **Example 59 explanatory note 8**.

(2)   A charge arises under the 1982 legislation on each tenth anniversary of the settlement. This charge is applied to the *relevant property* held in the trust at the anniversary date, without grossing up (s 64).

For post 26 March 1974 settlements the ten-yearly charge is arrived at as follows (s 66):

(a)   The settlement is deemed to make a notional transfer immediately before the ten-year anniversary comprising:

(i) the value of the relevant property in this settlement immediately before the ten-year anniversary, ie its value on the day before the anniversary

(ii) the value immediately after it became comprised in the settlement of any property which was not then relevant property and has not subsequently become relevant property whilst remaining comprised in the settlement (eg where part of the settled property has always been subject to an estate interest in possession)

(iii) the value of the property in any related settlement at the time the related settlement commenced (s 66). A related settlement is a settlement made by the same settlor and commencing on the same day (excluding settlements in which all the property is held without time limit for charitable purposes) (s 62). It is immaterial whether the making of that settlement involved a chargeable transfer or an exempt transfer or even (if it created an estate IIP for the settlor) no transfer of value at all.

(b) The notional transfer in **(a)** is added to the notional previous transfers to arrive at the effective rate of tax on the notional transfer in **(a)(i)**.

The notional previous transfers are:

(i) Any chargeable transfers made by the settlor in the seven years prior to the creation of the settlement (excluding transfers made on the day the settlement commenced), except where **(e)** below applies. (It should be noted that if any potentially exempt transfers made before the transfer into settlement become chargeable because of the donor's death within seven years, this will affect the cumulative total of chargeable transfers. This could happen before or after the date of the ten-year charge, and if it was after, the ten-year charge would have to be recomputed accordingly.)

(ii) Any amounts on which exit charges have been levied under s 65 within the previous ten years (see **note 4**).

(iii) In the case of the first ten-year anniversary if it occurred before 9 March 1992, any distribution payments (see **note 1** above) made under the old rules before 9 March 1982 but within the ten years before the anniversary.

To compute the tax charge on the notional transfer the lifetime rate – ie one half of the death rate — of tax is used.

(c) Having arrived at the effective rate of tax on the notional transfer, take 30% of that effective rate to arrive at the actual rate applicable to the ten-yearly charge. (However, if or to the extent that the chargeable relevant property had not been relevant property throughout the ten-year period, the rate on such property is further reduced by $\frac{1}{40}$th for each complete quarter that had elapsed in the ten-year period before the property became relevant property.) At current rates this gives a maximum charging rate of 6% (or 3% on property that qualifies for 50% business or agricultural property relief, payment of which can be spread over ten years free of interest if the instalment option is available – see **Example 5 explanatory note 7**).

(d) Apply the *rate* arrived at in **(c)** above to the *relevant property* in the trust at the ten-year anniversary, ie to the property at **(a)(i)** above. Note that the effect of including **(a)(ii) and (iii)** in the notional transfer is to give a higher total for the *notional* transfer, and thus possibly a higher tax rate, but the charge is levied on the relevant property **(a)(i)** only.

(e) In the same way as for pre-27 March 1974 settlements, where property has been added to the settlement within the previous ten years and at least part of the addition comprised a chargeable transfer (as to which see further **Example 59 explanatory note 7**), then although the charge on that property is proportionately reduced as indicated in **(c)** above, the settlor's previous cumulative transfers at **(b)(i)** become the chargeable transfers made by him in the seven years preceding the addition to the settlement, if that gives a higher total. Where more than one addition has taken place then either the commencement date or any one of the addition dates is used, whichever gives the highest cumulative total for the previous seven years (s 67).

Where the total used is at one of the addition dates then it is possible that this total will include earlier transfers to the settlement. This would result in a transfer being included twice, eg if the addition was made less than seven years after the commencement of the settlement, the settlor's seven year cumulative total at the date of the addition will include the original chargeable transfer on the creation of the settlement, and (unless it has been the subject of an exit charge) that property will also form part of the relevant property in the settlement (ie included at **(a)(i)** above). In such circumstances the seven year cumulative total is reduced by the net amount put into the settlement.

Similarly that seven year cumulative total may include the value of property which has ceased to be relevant property at the date of the ten-year charge and has been the subject of an exit charge under s 65 (ie included at **(b)(iii)** above). Then the seven year cumulative total is reduced by the value attributable to the property subject to that exit charge (s 67(3)(b), (5)).

A double counting relief also applies where property has been the subject of an exit charge but has since become relevant property again. (This will be very uncommon since the changes made by FA 2006, but before 22 March 2006 a typical Example would have been on the creation of an interest in possession within the last ten years which had subsequently ended.) The value of such property would thus appear both as relevant property (under **(a)(i)** above) and also as property on which an exit charge had been levied in the last ten years (under **(b)(iii)** above). In such circumstances the latter amount is reduced by the smaller of:

- the value at the time of the exit charge; or

- the value on the day before the ten-year anniversary (s 67(b)).

(3)   Under the pre-9 March 1982 rules, a proportional periodic charge was payable annually where trustees were not resident in the UK but this charge was abolished when the rules were changed. Any unused tax credit arising from the payment of such annual charges is available against *any* payments under the revised rules, ie both ten-yearly charges and exit charges (s 85).

Exit charges

(4)   A further charge to inheritance tax arises when property in a settlement ceases to be relevant property (or if the trustees make a disposition which devalues the relevant property in the settlement). This is known as the 'exit charge' (s 65). No exit charge arises, however, if such an event occurs within the first three months after a ten-year anniversary, or within the first three months after the settlement is made (s 65(4)).

Where an exit charge occurs after there has been a ten-year anniversary of the settlement, its rate is linked to that which applied on the ten-year anniversary (or would have applied but for any later changes in the amount (rather than value) of property that is relevant property, and but for any fractional reduction that applied at the ten-year anniversary because the property had not been relevant property throughout the preceding ten years): see **note 5**.

If there has not yet been a ten-year anniversary, that approach cannot be used and a different formula has to be employed to produce the 'linked' rate: see **note 6**.

In either case, the full rate so ascertained is then reduced by applying the fraction of x/40 where x is the number of *complete* quarters in the period since the preceding ten-year anniversary (or since the settlement was formed) (ss 69(4), 68(2)).

If the property was not relevant property throughout the period since the preceding ten-year anniversary, or since the settlement commenced, the rate of tax on that property is reduced by deducting, from what would otherwise be x in the x/40 fraction, the number of complete quarters that had expired before it became relevant property. In such a case x in the x/40 fraction can never be less than 1 (ss 69(4), 68(3)).

The value transferred on an exit charge is the difference between the value of relevant property before the distribution and its value after the distribution. Thus the 'loss to the donor' principle applies and grossing up is necessary if the tax is not to be borne out of the fund that ceases to be relevant property (see **note 6**). The rate used for grossing up is the actual rate found under the relevant formula, taking account therefore of the appropriate reduction using the x/40 fraction.

Exit charge after a ten-year anniversary has occurred

(5) For both pre- and post-27 March 1974 settlements where a ten-year anniversary has already occurred (even if there was no relevant property at that date), the exit charge is calculated (using the time-fraction referred to in note 4) by reference to the rate of tax computed at the previous ten-year anniversary, recalculated using one half of the death scale in force at the date of the distribution (if lower) (s 69). When property has been added to a settlement, or has become relevant property, since the date of the last ten-year charge, it is necessary (for this purpose alone) to recompute the ten-yearly charge as if that property had been relevant property at the date of the ten-yearly charge, but taken at its value when it in fact became relevant property (s 69(2)). For details see **Example 59 at explanatory note 7.**

Exit charge before first ten-year anniversary

(6) Where an exit charge arises before the first ten-year anniversary then for post 26 March 1974 settlements the rate to which the time-fraction in **note 4** is applied is 30% of the effective rate (s 68(2)).

This effective rate is found by applying the lifetime rates (ie one half of the death rates) of inheritance tax then applicable to a notional chargeable transfer which is the sum of:

(a) the value of all the property in the settlement immediately after the settlement commenced, whether it is relevant property or not, plus

(b) the value of the property in any related settlement immediately after it commenced, plus

(c) the value of any added property at the time of its addition to the settlement (this includes accumulated income that has been treated as an accretion to capital, the date of addition being the date that the accumulation was so treated),

based on assumed previous chargeable transfers equal to any chargeable transfers made by the settlor in the seven years prior to the day on which the settlement was created. Note that the value of property immediately after the settlement in question commenced, in each of cases **(a) to (c)** above, is not necessarily the same as the value transferred by the settlor in contributing it to the settlement: in particular no deduction can be made in this context for business property relief or agricultural property relief.

Various problems arise in respect of a settlor's premature death within seven years of making a settlement. These include

(i) additional tax being due through recomputation at death rates of the tax due on the original transfer to settlement, and

(ii) a failed PET made by the settlor prior to the formation of the settlement, which would both

- add to the settlor's inheritance tax accumulation which affects the settlement for as long as it comprises relevant property and

- increase the tax on the transfer which created the settlement.

The problems can be illustrated in this brief Example:

A always used up his annual exemption by a gift of £3,000 to his nephew on 20 April each year. A died on 1 May 2010.

On 1 May 2004 A gave his daughter £65,000

On 12 June 2005 he gave his son £100,000

On 1 September 2006, he set up a discretionary settlement with funds of £321,000, paying the tax due himself.

Original IHT position:

Gifts to son and daughter – PETs – Set up of discretionary trust

This is a chargeable transfer of £321,000. A has a nil cumulative total and the nil-rate band for 2006/07 was £285,000. The excess of £36,000 is grossed up as tax is paid by the settlor (36,000 × 100/80 = 45,000).

Chargeable transfer (gross)	£330,000
Tax paid by settlor (330,000 – 285,000 = 45,000 @ 20%)	£9,000

On subsequent death of Mr A (1 May 2010)

Failed PETs to son and daughter

Transfers of £100,000 to his son and £65,000 to his daughter are within Mr A's nil-rate band for 2010/11 so no further tax payable. The cumulative total of transfers is however now increased to £165,000.

Transfer to discretionary trust

	£
Chargeable transfer to trust	330,000
Cumulative transfers	165,000
	495,000
Tax at death rate (495,000 – 325,000 = 170,000 @ 40%)	68,000
Less: paid in 2006/07	9,000
Additional tax payable by trustees	59,000

If the settlor's death occurs before a distribution out of the trust, the charge on the distribution is calculated accordingly. If the settlor dies after the distribution is made the exit charge may be increased and additional tax will then be payable. This is because, as above, any failed PETs on death will increase the amount of the settlor's previous transfers in the seven years before the commencement of the settlement. If aware of earlier PETs, therefore, well-advised trustees will make a suitable retention from any property distributed within the first seven years; but often they may be unaware of the settlor's earlier PETs and therefore – although in reality the trustees may need to consider relying on indemnities – the counsel of perfection would be to assume provisionally that no nil rate band is available until the settlor has survived a full seven years from the making of the settlement.

The effect of the settlor's death on occasions of charge is considered in more detail in **Example 62**.

If a gift into settlement was free from IHT because of the availability of BPR or APR, and the property involved is subsequently disposed of by the trustees within seven years after it was settled, the trustees should prudently consider replacing it with other agricultural or business property so as to shelter any charge within IHTA 1984 ss 113B and 124B in the event of the settlor failing to survive the seven year period.

Grossing up

(7)   If the exit charge is to be borne out of the fund that incurs the exit charge then no grossing up is necessary (s 65(2)(a)). The trustees, not the beneficiary in the case of a distribution, are liable for the tax, and so will deduct it from the distribution.

However, if the tax is to be paid out of the relevant property retained in the settlement then the chargeable amount must be grossed up (s 65(2)(b)). In the Example the distributions to A, B and D did not require any grossing up as the tax was to be borne by, and so deducted from, the distribution. C, however, was to receive £20,000 on a net basis, after payment of tax. The fund of relevant property has therefore been reduced by £20,000 plus the tax thereon £87, a total transfer of £20,087.

This is calculated by using the formula of:

$$\text{Net transfer} \times \frac{100}{(100 - \text{rate of tax})} = \text{gross transfer}$$

In this Example the rate of tax is 0.464% and therefore the calculation is:

$$\pounds 20,000 \times \frac{100}{(100 - 0.464)} = \pounds 20,093$$

Tax planning

(8)   Although the treatment of discretionary trusts is complex, they have a useful role to play in tax planning.

If a settlor has not made any chargeable transfers, he can presently transfer assets to the value of £325,000 into a discretionary trust every seven years without either incurring inheritance tax or (provided the trust is not settlor-interested) incurring any immediate charge to capital gains tax (since the holdover relief in TCGA 1992 s 260 is available on *chargeable* transfers, whether any inheritance tax is payable on those transfers or not). Any transfers out of the trust in the first ten years will then not attract inheritance tax because the initial value of the trust property (**note 6(a)** above) is within the nil rate band (subject to what is said below about business and agricultural property).

Care needs to be taken, however, if the settlor has already made potentially exempt transfers, because a liability on the transfer to the trust could then arise if he died within seven years, and also on distributions out of the trust. The rule of thumb must be to make chargeable transfers into a relevant property trust *before*, rather than after, any potentially exempt transfers.

Furthermore, now that all lifetime transfers into trust are subject to the relevant property regime (except where a disabled person's interest arises, see **Example 52**) it will be possible in many cases for trusts to maintain the flexibility of discretionary trusts rather than be constrained by the use of interest in possession settlements or accumulation and maintenance trusts. (On the other hand where the trust will have significant dividend income that is planned to be distributed rather than accumulated and capitalised it may still be preferred to create an interest in possession, even though for inheritance tax purposes this will not be an estate IIP, because of the income tax considerations discussed in **Example 48 explanatory note 9.**)

If the property transferred into trust qualifies for 100% or 50% business or agricultural relief, this increases the amount that can be transferred without tax being payable, subject to what is said above about potentially exempt transfers. Distributions of the business or agricultural property out of the trust will also qualify for the appropriate rate of relief provided the trustees have by then fulfilled the required period of ownership or occupation. However, if a distribution is of unrelieved property (or the rate of relief is less than 100%) then the rate of tax on an exit charge within the first ten years will not be guaranteed (subject to changed legislation) to be nil even where the transfer into the trust was within the nil rate band, because the whole of the value of the business or agricultural property is taken into account in calculating the initial value of the settlement (see **note 5(a)** above). Any exit charges on distributions within the first *ten* years are based on the full unrelieved value of the property when settled. (The same point applies where the transfer into the trust was partly covered by annual exemptions in addition to the maximum available nil rate band.) For further details see **Example 62 at explanatory note 5**.

Spouse as discretionary beneficiary under a trust created by will

(9)   It is possible to include a spouse/civil partner as one of the discretionary beneficiaries, thus ensuring that property is not left directly to the surviving spouse/civil partner to swell that spouse's/civil partner's own estate. Prior to the introduction of a transferable nil-rate band between spouses and civil partners (announced in the 2007 Pre-Budget Report and incorporated into FA 2008 Sch 4, see **Example 1(iii)**), this was a common ploy, in the will of the first of a couple to die, in order to reduce inheritance tax on the second death.

In many cases it is no longer considered necessary to make use of a discretionary trust in the will of the first spouse to die because this will not result in any tax saving on the death of the survivor. The following Examples illustrate the point.

Example A – Use of discretionary will trusts prior to transferable nil-rate band

Mr and Mrs Forster have estates in their sole names of £301,000 and £282,000 respectively. In addition they own a freehold house as joint tenants valued at £400,000. Their wills each leave all of their estate to the other (or to their only child in the case of the second spouse to die). They have not made any lifetime gifts. If both had died before 9 October 2007 their potential liability to inheritance tax would have been:

		£
On first death:		
Inter-spouse transfer – exempt		nil
On second death:		
Estate of Mr Forster		301,000
Estate of Mrs Forster		282,000
House		400,000
		983,000

Tax thereon (983,000 – 300,000 = 683,000 @ 40%) = £273,200

If, however, their wills had provided for an amount equal to the nil band for inheritance tax to devolve upon a discretionary settlement, from which spouse, child and, say, grandchildren could benefit, with the residue of the estate devolving on the spouse, then the nil-rate band of the spouse dying first would be utilised, viz:

On first death (say Mr Forster)	£
Free assets	301,000
Pecuniary legacy to discretionary trust	300,000
Residue to spouse	1,000
½ share of house (passes to spouse by survivorship)	200,000
Exempt transfer	201,000
Value of Estate	
Own assets	301,000
½ share of house	200,000
	501,000
Less: exempt transfer	201,000
Chargeable estate	300,000
Covered by nil threshold.	
On Mrs Forster's death	
Own assets	282,000
Residue from husband's estate	1,000
House	400,000
	683,000

Tax thereon (683,000 – 300,000 = 383,000 @ 40%) = £153,200

Thus taking both deaths together the discretionary trust would at the time of the second death (before 9 October 2007) save inheritance tax equal to the value of the nil-rate band on the first death (£300,000 @ 40% = £120,000). Provided the value in the discretionary trust does not increase faster than the rate of increase of the nil-rate band, no further tax will be payable on capital distributions from the trust. The surviving spouse would be able to have use of the income (and capital) of the trust with the agreement of the trustees (but distributions must not be made with in first three months – see **note 9** below). The income of the trust would be subject to income tax at 50% (apart from the trustees' modest standard rate band not exceeding £1,000), but this will be recoverable to the extent that it exceeds the beneficiary's personal tax liability if the income is distributed (see **Example 47** for further details).

Example B – Use of discretionary will trusts after transferable nil-rate band

Assume the same facts as in **Example A** but the survivor (Mrs Forster) dies between 9 October 2007 and 5 April 2008. The potential inheritance tax liability without the use of a discretionary trust is:

	£
On first death:	
Inter-spouse transfer – exempt	nil
On second death:	
Estate of Mr Forster	301,000
Estate of Mrs Forster	282,000
House	400,000
	983,000

Tax thereon (983,000 – 600,000* = 383,000 @ 40%) =   £153,200

* Mr Forster has not used his nil-rate band at all so Mrs Forster's nil-rate band is augmented by 100% and she has £600,000 rather than £300,000 available.

If Mr and Mrs Forster's wills had provided for an amount equal to the nil-rate band to devolve upon a discretionary settlement, from which spouse, child and, say, grandchildren could benefit, with the residue of the estate devolving on the spouse, then the nil-rate band of the spouse dying first would be utilised, so the survivor's nil-rate band is not increased at all. Thus, the second calculation produces the same result (inheritance tax of £153,200 is payable on Mrs Forster's death) and there is no advantage in making use of the discretionary trust.

If Mrs Forster had died *after* 5 April 2008, the statutory nil rate band at her death would have increased from £300,000 and so the potential nil rate band on her death, with the benefit of a 100% transfer, would therefore be more than this £600,000. If the value of the property in the discretionary trust under Mr Forster's will had not increased, therefore, the trust would have resulted in a smaller overall value falling within the combined nil rate bands, and therefore a higher overall inheritance tax charge, than if Mrs Forster had inherited outright or the trust had conferred an estate IIP on her instead. Where such trusts are used it is possible to unravel them within two years of the first death (see **note 10** below).

However, there are still circumstances where a discretionary will trust may have a role to play, for instance:

- to hold property whose value is thought likely to escalate after the first death at a greater rate than (double) the expected growth in the statutory nil rate band; or

- to hold property which will attract APR or BPR on the first death, but is unlikely to do so on the survivor's death (whether because the property will have been sold by then or because the business was dependent on a professional qualification of the first to die and cannot be carried on by the survivor); or

- to receive agricultural or business property, with the benefit of APR or BPR, which the trustees might consider selling to the surviving spouse in the hope that she may fulfil the relevant period of ownership or occupation thereafter and thus obtain double relief for the family at the end of the day.

In some cases it is therefore felt better to draft wills to include a discretionary trust of the nil rate band, and/or of relievable property, leaving open the option of unravelling the trust (or converting it to interest in possession form for the survivor) within two years after the first death if the circumstances at that time are not such that a continuing discretionary trust is felt to be beneficial.

Distribution, or restructuring, within two years after death

(10)   If a relevant property trust is created by will, distributions out of it within two years after the death are treated as having been made under the will (IHTA 1984 s 144) rather than being treated as amounts on which an exit charge is payable. This is a very useful provision enabling maximum flexibility to be built into a will so that the estate may be distributed taking into account the situation at the time of the death, rather than having to review the will regularly to ensure that its provisions are still appropriate.

To be within the provisions of s 144 as it stood before FA 2006, a distribution must in principle be one on which tax would otherwise be chargeable (though the rule also extends to distributions to employee trusts, charities or political parties, or maintenance funds for historic buildings, so long as these would incur a charge apart from the exemptions in s 75, s 76 or Sch 4 para 16(1) respectively. It must not therefore occur within the first three months after death (or, in a case where the will leaves property to the trustees of an existing pilot discretionary trust, within three months after a ten-year anniversary of that trust that happens to fall within two years after the settlor's death – the commencement of the settlement in that case will be when property was first put into the pilot trust), because exit charges do not apply to such distributions (see **note 4**). In the case of *Frankland v CIR (CA 1997)*, within three months after the creation of a discretionary trust by will, the trust property was transferred to a trust in which the surviving spouse had a life interest. The intention was to avoid the inheritance tax on the death estate through the substitution of an exempt spouse transfer for the taxable transfer to the discretionary trust. It was held that s 144 did not apply because there would have been no exit charge on the transfer to the life interest trust (s 65(4), **note 4** above). This trap affects distributions to charities as well as outright distributions to a surviving spouse; the position for appointments of a life interest has changed in part since the reforms in FA 2006, see **note 12**.

(11)   Where distributions of assets from a discretionary trust within two years after death are treated as made at death as indicated in **note 10** above, the capital gains tax position must be considered if the assets are liable to that tax and have increased in value since death. The capital gains tax gifts holdover relief of TCGA 1992 s 260 only applies if the distribution is chargeable to inheritance tax (see **Example 50 explanatory note 3**), which it is not where IHTA 1984 s 144 applies. Capital gains tax cannot therefore be held over unless the assets qualify for business gifts holdover relief under TCGA 1992 s 165 (as to which see **Example 50 part A(d)**). See **Example 50 explanatory note 5** for a way in which, with forethought on the part of the executors, a capital gains tax charge on the distribution may be avoided.

(12)   Section 144 was amended by FA 2006 to ensure that backdating effect of the provision extends to the appointment of an interest in possession out of a relevant property trust established by the will. Except where the beneficiary was a disabled person at the death, so that the IIP would be a disabled person's interest, such an appointment within the two-year period will give rise to an immediate post-death interest notwithstanding the requirement of s 49A that the interest should have taken effect immediately on the death (so that, apart from the new s 144(4)–(6), the property affected would not have ceased to be relevant property and would therefore no have triggered the backdating provision). The same provisions deal with appointments on terms that meet the requirements for a bereaved minor's trust (s 71A) or an age 18-to-25 trust (s 71D), though it is arguable that the requirement of those sections (that the trusts should have been 'established by the will') would anyway have been fulfilled as a matter of interpretation, reading the appointment with the original terms of the will. Because the mechanism of the new provision does not depend on an event that would otherwise give rise to an exit charge, the three-month trap evident in the *Frankland* case (**note 10** above) does not apply in these cases, though it is unfortunately left to catch the unwary where property does leave the relevant property regime within the three-month period. Thus, if backdating under s 144 is to apply:

(a)   three months must elapse from the death (or ten-year anniversary) in the case of appointments or distributions to the deceased's surviving spouse or civil partner absolutely, or to a charity, or the creation of a disabled person's interest; but

(b)   there is no need to wait for the three month period to expire if the appointment or distribution creates an interest in possession for someone who definitely was not a disabled person at the deceased's death within the definition in s 89(4)–(6), or trusts that meet the requirement for a bereaved minor's trust or an 18-to-25 trust.

Question

On 6 June 2001 H, who had made no previous transfers of value, settled £80,000 on himself for life, with remainder to his wife, W, for life, with remainder on her death on discretionary trusts for the benefit of their children and grandchildren.

H died on 5 May 2002 when his own assets were valued at £90,000.

His cumulative chargeable transfers at that date were £95,000.

By his will he left all his property to his children equally.

His wife, W, died on 4 April 2005 leaving assets valued at £184,000.

By her will she settled £50,000 cash on discretionary charitable trusts without limit of time, and the residue to her brother for life with remainder to his children.

She had made chargeable transfers of value totalling £114,750, all less than seven years before her death.

The settled fund from her husband's death was valued at £110,000 upon her death.

On 8 August 2005 the trustees of H's settlement appointed £30,000 gross to the eldest child, William, for life with remainder to his children who attained 18 or being daughters sooner married, whom failing to revert to the main trust fund.

On 10 April 2010 William and his wife (who had no children) were killed in a car accident.

After payment of inheritance tax and other expenses in connection with his death, the fund appointed to William, which then fell back into the settlement created on 6 June 2001, was valued at only £24,000.

The rest of the property in that settlement was valued at that date at £96,000.

The recombined settlement may be taken to have the following values:

As at 5 June 2011	£113,640
As at 4 May 2012	£125,410
As at 3 April 2015	£157,624

Calculate the inheritance tax payable in connection with the appointment on 8 August 2005 and on the first ten-year anniversary.

(So far as future events are concerned assume that the law set out in IHTA 1984 as amended does not change.)

Answer

6 June 2001	–	H settles £80,000 on himself for life
	–	No IHT payable as no loss to his estate
5 May 2002	–	H dies, settlement passes to spouse for life – exempt transfer
4 April 2005	–	W dies, and is deemed settlor of discretionary trust dated 6 June 2001

Tax position of deemed settlor W at date of her death, 4 April 2005

		Gross £	Tax on 2004/2005 scale £
Cumulative transfers in seven years to date of death		114,750	–
Free estate on death	184,000		
Less: Charitable settlement (exempt)	50,000		
	134,000		
Interest in possession in husband's 2001 settlement	110,000	244,000	38,300*
		358,750	38,300*

(* 358,750 – 263,000 = 95,750 @ 40%)

IHT payable:

£

By personal representatives

$$\frac{134,000}{244,000} \times £38,300 =$$ 21,034

By trustees of settlement

$$\frac{110,000}{244,000} \times £38,300 =$$ 17,266

38,300

Initial value of related settlement (W's will trust)

Free estate		184,000
Less: to charitable trusts		50,000
		134,000
Less: IHT payable by personal representatives		21,034
		£112,966

Initial value of discretionary settlement (ie value at time it was deemed to commence)

Value of fund in which W had an interest in possession at her death		110,000
Less: IHT payable by trustees		17,266
		£92,734

8 August 2005 – Exit charge on creation of life interest for William

		Gross £	Tax on 2005/06 scale £
Settlor's 7-year cumulative total at time settlement deemed to commence		114,750	–
Notional transfer			
Initial value of settlement	92,734		
Initial value of related settlement	112,966		
Initial value of added property	nil	205,700	9,090*
		320,450	9,090*

(* 320,450 – 275,000 = 45,450 @ 20%)

Actual rate is 30% of effective rate

$$\frac{9,090}{205,700} \times 30\% = 1.326\%$$

Quarters since settlement deemed to commence
4 April 2005 to 8 August 2005 = 1 quarter
Tax payable:

$$1.326\% \times \frac{1}{40} \times 30,000 = £10$$

6 June 2011 ten-year charge

	Original settlement	Property reverting to settlement	
Values (net of IHT on his death) on William's fund reverting to settlement	96,000	24,000	120,000
	80%	20%	100%
Same proportions of value immediately before ten-year anniversary	90,912	22,728	113,640
Date property last became relevant property	4 April 2005	10 April 2010	
Complete quarters since 6 June 2001 until property last became relevant property	15	35	
			£

Assumed cumulative total:

Settlor's 7-year cumulative total at time settlement deemed to commence			114,750
Exit charges in last 10 years			30,000
			144,750
Less:	Amount included in that cumulative total (exit charge) and also reflected in value of relevant property at ten-year anniversary		22,728
			122,022
Assumed transfer at 10-year anniversary:			
Relevant property at 5 June 2011			113,640
Initial value of related settlement			112,966
			226,606

	Gross	Tax on 2010/11 scale
	£	£
Assumed cumulative total	122,022	Nil
Assumed transfer at 10-year anniversary	226,606	4,726*
	348,628	4,726*

(* 348,628 – 325,000 = 23,628 @ 20%)

Actual rate is 30% of effective rate

$$\frac{4,726}{226,606} \times 30\% = 0.626\%$$

		Original settlement	Property reverting to original settlement
Quarters excluded from appropriate fraction (above)		15	35
Quarters counted for appropriate fraction (balance of 40)		25	5
Tax payable:		£	
Original settlement	0.626% × 25/40 ×	90,912	356
Returned property	0.626% × 5/40 ×	22,728	18
Value of settlement, and total tax, at 10-year anniversary		£113,640	374

Explanatory Notes

Settlement on self

(1)   A transfer of value normally occurs when a person transfers property to a settlement.

However, until 22 March 2006, if the settlor retained an interest in possession in the property in the settlement then there was no loss to his estate and therefore no transfer of value. Since that date, that treatment can only apply if the settlor's interest is a disabled person's interest (as to which see **Example 52**)

In all other cases there will be a transfer of value even where the settlor has an immediate interest in possession; moreover, the settled property will always be relevant property, and the transfer of value (beyond the annual exemption or normal income expenditure exemption) will always be a chargeable transfer, unless a disabled person's interest is conferred on some other party. (In that case, if the other party is the settlor's spouse or civil partner the spouse exemption will apply, otherwise it will be a potentially exempt transfer.)

Where the settlor or his spouse did have an estate interest in possession at the outset (much less common from 22 March 2006 for the reason stated), if the property subsequently became held on discretionary trusts, or (subject to the possibility of a transitional serial interest up to 5 October 2008) an interest in possession arises in favour of anyone other than the settlor or his spouse, then for the purpose of the relevant property rules the settlor or spouse (whoever last had the interest in possession) is deemed to have created a separate settlement at that time (unless the original settlement was made before 27 March 1974) (s 80).

Accordingly the discretionary settlement in the Example is not deemed to be made until W dies, since until then H, and then W, had successive interests in possession before 22 March 2006, being entitled as of right to the income.

Related settlements

(2)   Any other settlements created at the time of W's death would normally be related settlements (s 62(1)).

However the charitable trust is not regarded as related as the assets are held for charitable purposes without limit of time (s 62(2)) – see **Example 60 explanatory note 2 (a) (iii)**.

Furthermore the transfer to the charitable trust is an exempt transfer (s 23) thus reducing the estate chargeable on W's death.

The inheritance tax payable on W's death in respect of the settlement is met by the trustees, thus reducing the initial value of the discretionary settlement from £110,000 to £92,734.

Exit charges

(3)   The interest in possession appointed to William was an estate interest in possession because William became beneficially entitled to it before 22 March 2006 (see **Example 52**). The appointment therefore resulted in the appointed fund ceasing to be relevant property, which is the primary event giving rise to an exit charge under the relevant property regime (see **Example 60 explanatory note 4**). If the interest in possession had been appointed on or after 22 March 2006 it would not have been an estate IIP (unless William had been a disabled person at the date the property was originally settled in 2001, so that the interest in possession would have been a disabled person's interest, see **Example 52**); and the appointed fund would therefore have remained within the relevant property regime despite the interest in possession, with no inheritance tax exit charge accordingly.

(4)   The effective rate of tax on an exit charge depends upon whether the distribution occurs before the first ten-year anniversary (s 68) or after that date (s 69).

Although the settlement was deemed to be created by the death of W, the anniversary date is fixed by s 61 as being the tenth anniversary of the date when the original settlement commenced (s 61(2)).

(5)   For the purpose of computing the assumed cumulative total and notional transfer, the date of the deemed creation of the settlement applies and accordingly the settlement commences with W's seven-year cumulative total immediately prior to her death, the settlement created by her will becoming a related settlement.

(6)   Although the cycle of ten-year anniversaries runs from the date of the actual original settlement (**note 4** above), the quarters that are counted towards the appropriate fraction, to determine the rate on the exit charge, start from the commencement of the settlement, which here is W's death (4 April 2005) as explained in **note 1** (s 68(2)).

Ten-yearly charge

(7)   On the tenth anniversary of the original settlement (6 June 2011) a ten-yearly charge arises under s 64 even though only slightly more than six years have elapsed since the settlement was deemed to commence on W's death.

As the property subject to the exit charge (appointment of life interest to William) is also included in the value of relevant property (because of the death of William and his wife and the consequent reversion of the property to the discretionary settlement), the assumed cumulative total is reduced by the lower of:

(a)   the exit charge £30,000; or

(b)   the proportionate value at the ten-year anniversary of the property which has reverted (s 66(5)).

At the time the property reverted to the settlement it was valued at £24,000 and the other property in the settlement at £96,000. Accordingly 20% (£24,000 out of £120,000) of the value at 6 June 2011 (£113,640), or £22,728, derives from the fund that had been appointed to William and subsequently reverted.

(8)   The charge at the ten-year anniversary is reduced by the number of complete quarters prior to the appropriate date. Again the appropriate fractions reflect the fact that part of the property only became relevant property on 4 April 2005, and part last reverted to the settlement on 10 April 2010 (s 66(2)).

(9)   See **Examples 59, 60 and 62** for further details of discretionary trusts.

Question

On 6 June 2000 Smith retired from the family farming partnership which had commenced 20 years earlier when he had taken his brother and their sons into partnership.

His cumulative chargeable transfers at that date were £189,352 arising out of transfers of value made in December 1993, and he had not yet made any potentially exempt transfers.

At the time of his retirement he transferred the freehold interest in one of his farms, valued at £100,000, which had been leased for the last twelve years to a non-family tenant farmer, to the trustees of a discretionary settlement (the *B Trust*) which he created at the same time in favour of the children of his brother, who had recently been killed in a farming accident for which Smith felt some moral responsibility. He agreed to pay any inheritance tax due.

On the same date he settled £100,000 of the cash due to him from the partnership on a second discretionary settlement in favour of his own children (the C *Trust*).

The trustees of this settlement paid any inheritance tax due.

On 5 May 2001 Smith added £24,000 in cash to the B Trust (on which the trustees are to pay the inheritance tax due).

On 6 May 2001 Smith gave his own children £195,000 in cash.

On 1 January 2002 the trustees of the B Trust appointed £18,000 to the late brother's eldest son.

On 9 September 2003 when the B Trust consisted of the farm and 12,000 £1 shares in ABC plc, Smith added a further 120,000 £1 shares in ABC plc to that trust and paid the inheritance tax himself.

On 2 February 2006 the trustees of the B Trust appointed 66,000 shares in ABC plc to the eldest daughter absolutely.

The assets in the B Trust were:

	Market value of farm	Shares in ABC plc at value for inheritance tax
9 September 2003	£200,000	140p each
2 February 2006	£210,000	150p each
5 June 2010	£300,000	200p each
6 June 2010	£300,000	201¾p each

Calculate the inheritance tax payable by the trustees in connection with the two appointments from the B Trust and on the first ten-year anniversary of that trust.

Ignore capital gains tax and assume that Smith the settlor is still living.

Answer

Tax position of settlor — Smith

				Gross	Tax (on 2000/01 scale)	Net
Inheritance tax accumulation						
6 June 2000				£	£	£
Cumulative transfers to date (December 1993)				189,352	–	189,352
B Trust – Farm			100,000			
Less:	Agricultural property relief 50%					
	(see **explanatory note 5**)		50,000			
			50,000			
Less:	Annual	1999/00	3,000			
	exemptions					
		1998/99	3,000			
			6,000			
				2,000**		
Net transfer, grossed up (see **explanatory note 4**)				48,000	48,838	838	48,000
				238,190	838	237,352
C Trust – Cash			100,000			
Less:	Annual exemption					
				4,000**	96,000	19,200	76,800
				334,190	20,038*	314,152

(* 334,940 – 234,000 = 100,940 @ 20%)

(** Apportionment of annual exemptions — see **explanatory note 1**)	B Trust	C Trust	Total
Total value transferred by transfers of value	50,000	100,000	150,000
Percentage of total value transferred	33.33%	66.67%	100%
Exemptions as above, apportioned	2,000	4,000	6,000

Tax position of settlements:

Initial value of B Trust	£100,000
Initial value of C Trust	
(a related settlement) – £100,000 less tax £19,200	£80,800

5 May 2001 — Property added to B Trust

Tax position of settlor — Smith

				Gross	Tax (2001/02 scale)
				£	£
Inheritance tax accumulation					
Cumulative transfers in last 7 years (see **explanatory note 9(i)**)				145,588	–
Added property			24,000		
Less: Annual exemptions	2001/02	3,000			
	2000/01	3,000	6,000	18,000	–
				163,588	–

(* 163,588 – 242,000 = Nil)

Initial value of added property =   £24,000

Tax position of B Trust

1 January 2002

Exit charge on distribution to late brother's eldest son (Note – as farm is not sold the distribution must come from property added on 5 May 2001 and the tax calculation is affected accordingly)

		Gross	Tax (2001/02 scale)
		£	£
Settlor's 7-year cumulative total at time settlement commenced (s 68(4)(b)) – see **explanatory note 9**		189,352	–
Notional transfer (s 68(4)(a) and (5))			
Initial value of settlement (B Trust)	100,000		
Initial value of related settlement (C Trust)	80,800		
Initial value of added property (to B Trust)	24,000	204,800	30,430
		394,152	30,430*

(* 394,152 – 242,000 = 152,152 @ 20%)

Effective rate:

$$\frac{30,430}{204,800} \times 100\% = 14.859\%$$

Appropriate fraction (s 68(3)):

Complete quarters since settlement commenced
    6 June 2000 to 1 January 2002   6 quarters

Less: Complete quarters before property added
    6 June 2000 to 5 May 2001   3 quarters
                              3 fortieths

Tax payable on cash distribution to son:

Value distributed   18,000

Tax   60

$$14.859\% \times 30\% \times \frac{3}{40} \times 18,000 =$$

9 September 2003 — further added property

Tax position of settlor — Smith

			Gross	Tax (2003/04 scale)	Net
			£	£	£
Cumulative transfers in last 7 years — see **explanatory note 9(ii)**		–	163,588	–	163,588
Added property 120,000 shares @ 140p		168,000			
Less: Annual 2003/04 exemptions	3,000				
2002/2003	3,000	6,000			
Net transfer					162,000
Grossed up*			179,647	17,647	
			343,235	17,647	325,588
* Cumulative net transfers	325,588				
Nil rate band	255,000				
Excess grossed up at 20%	70,588	$\times \dfrac{100}{80} =$	88,325	17,647	

Initial value of added property - £168,000 (tax paid by settlor)

Tax position of B Trust

2 February 2006
Exit charge on distribution to eldest daughter (Shares deemed to have been appropriated pro-rata out of property added on 5 May 2001 and 9 September 2003, since the farm is still owned)

		Gross	Tax (2005/06 scale)
		£	£
Assumed Transfer:			
Settlor's 7-year cumulative total at time settlement commenced (see **explanatory note 9**)		189,352	–
Notional transfer			
At 1 January 2002 (above)	204,800		
Initial value of further added property	168,000	372,800	57,430
		562,152	57,430*

(* 562,152 – 275,000 = 287,152 @ 20%)

Effective rate: $\dfrac{57,430}{372,800} \times 100\,\% = 15.405\,\%$

Actual rate before appropriate fraction is 30% of effective rate, ie 30% × 15.405% = 4.622%

Appropriate fraction:

Quarters since settlement commenced

6 June 2000 to 2 February 2006	22
Less: Complete quarters before first addition (as above)	3
	19
6 June 2000 to 2 February 2006	22
Less: Complete quarters before second addition	
6 June 2000 to 9 September 2003	13
	9

Tax payable on distribution of 66,000 ABC plc shares at £1.50 to daughter

Value distributed £99,000:

re 2000 addition (12,000 shares)

$$4.622\,\% \times \frac{19}{40} \times £\,99{,}000 \times \frac{12{,}000}{132{,}000} = \qquad\qquad 198$$

re 2001 addition (120,000 shares)

$$4.622\,\% \times \frac{9}{40} \times £\,99{,}000 \times \frac{120{,}000}{132{,}000} = \qquad\qquad 936$$

£1,134

6 June 2010 – ten-year charge (see **explanatory notes 8, 9 and 10**)

	£	Gross (2010/11 scale) £	Tax £
Assumed cumulative total:			
Settlor's 7-year cumulative total at time settlement commenced (see **explanatory notes 9 and 10**)		189,352	
Exit charges in previous 10 years			
1 January 2002	18,000		
2 February 2006	99,000	117,000	
		306,352	–
Assumed transfer:			
Relevant property – value as at 5 June 2010			
Farm	300,000		
Less: Agricultural property relief 50%	150,000		
	150,000		
66,000 shares in ABC plc @ 200p	132,000		
	287,000		
Initial value of related settlement	80,800	362,800	68,830*
		669,152	68,830*

(* 669,152 − 325,000 = 344,152 @ 20%)

Effective rate:

$$\frac{68,830}{362,800} \times 100\% = 18.97\%$$

(Note that with the present single rate structure the effective rate will always be 20% if the assumed cumulative total exceeds the nil threshold, and in that event the subsequent calculations are not necessary. It is still, however, necessary to value the respective parts of the settled fund if it has not all been settled for the full ten years.)

Appropriate fraction

	Complete quarters before fund became relevant property	Resulting numerator	Shares	Value for IHT
Farm – settled for full ten years	0	40		150,000
Shares – 6/66 added 5 May 2001	3	37	6,000	12,000
Shares – 60/66 added 9 September 2003	13	27	60,000	120,000

Farm – no reduction (settled for full ten years)

Shares – 6/66 added 5 May 2001 = three quarters reduction giving 37/40

Shares – 60/66 added 9 September 2003 = 13 quarters reduction giving 27/40

IHT payable:

Farm – original fund	$18.97\% \times 30\% \times \dfrac{40}{40} \times £150,000$	8,537
6,000 shares – first addition	$18.97\% \times 30\% \times \dfrac{37}{40} \times £12,000$	632
60,000 shares – second addition	$18.97\% \times 30\% \times \dfrac{27}{40} \times £120,000$	4,610
		£13,779

Explanatory Notes

Same day transfers

(1)   Where two transfers are made on the same day, the annual exemptions are divided between the transfers proportionally to the value transferred, even if one of the transfers was a potentially exempt transfer. In this Example both transfers are immediately chargeable.

The transfer to the B Trust is added to the inheritance tax accumulation before the gift to the trustees of the C Trust because the tax on the former gift is to be met by Smith, whereas the trustees of the C Trust are to meet the tax due on that later transfer and the total tax on both gifts would be higher if they were included the other way round (s 266(1)).

Related settlement

(2)   Because the C Trust is made on the same day as the B Trust they are related settlements to each other (s 62).

Although the amount settled by Smith in the C Trust was £100,000, inheritance tax of £19,200 was payable by the trustees, giving an initial value of £80,800 applicable to that related settlement.

(3)   The tax on the B Trust is paid by Smith (the settlor) and therefore its initial value remains at £100,000.

(4)   The chargeable transfer of £48,000 so far as his own inheritance tax accumulation is concerned has to be grossed up (at lifetime rates) since he bears the tax. Thus, on the scale applicable in 2000/01:

		Net		*Gross*
Cumulative transfers to date		189,352		189,352
Balance of nil-band	44,648	44,648		44,648
		234,000		234,000
	3,352	3,352	$\times \dfrac{100}{80} =$	4,190
	£48,000	£237,352		£238,190

giving tax of (4,190 – 3,352 =) £838 (= 4,190 × 20%).

Exit charge

(5)   The rate of tax payable on the exit charges depends on whether the property leaving the settlement came from the original settlement (or property held at the previous ten-year anniversary) or property added, because of the differing periods for which the respective funds have been relevant property.

In this Example the original settlement of the B Trust was a farm which is still owned throughout the period under consideration, so therefore the distributions must always be from the added property.

Note however that where property has qualified for annual exemptions and/or business or agricultural relief in calculating the tax due on its transfer into the settlement, this is not taken into account in calculating the initial value of the settlement, so any exit charges on distributions within the first ten years are based on the full value of the property when settled, as shown in the Example in relation to the exit charge on 1 January 2001 (s 68). If the distribution itself consists of qualifying business or agricultural property, the relief is available in arriving at the value of the distribution (providing the trustees satisfy the conditions for relief). When calculating the ten-yearly charge, business or agricultural property relief is taken into account in arriving at the value of the trust property, as shown in the Example in the calculation on 6 June 2010 (s 66).

The rate of agricultural property relief on the transfer of the farm to the settlement in 2000 was 50% for tenanted agricultural property rather than 100% for owner occupied property etc, because the tenancy had been granted before September 1995 (see **Example 25**). Where rates of relief increase after a settlement, the increased rate may be taken into account in computing any *additional* liability to inheritance tax resulting from a death within seven years where the date of death is *after* the date of increase. However the increased rate is *not* applied to calculations of the accumulated transfers brought forward where the original chargeable transfer was before the date of increase even if that amount is used to calculate liabilities after that date.

Agricultural property relief will be available to the trustees in respect of the ten-year charge on 6 June 2010, but again only at 50% as the lease was granted prior to 1 September 1995 and vacant possession is not available within twelve months.

Exit charge – rate of tax when property has been added

(6)   The effective rate of tax on an exit depends upon whether the distribution occurs before the first ten-year anniversary (in which case s 68 applies) or after the first ten years (then s 69 applies) (see **Example 60 explanatory notes 4 to 6**).

In this Example both exit charges are before the first ten-year anniversary, so the effective rate is calculated by adding a notional transfer to the settlor's seven-year cumulative total at the time the settlement commenced.

The notional transfer is the sum of the initial values of the original settlement, related settlements and added property (including accumulated income treated as an accretion to capital).

The effective rate is reduced to an appropriate fraction comprising the number of complete quarters from the date the settlement commenced to the date of the charge, divided by 40.

However when the property leaving the settlement is not part of the original settlement then the numerator is reduced by the number of complete quarters from the date of settlement to the date the property is added.

The tax payable on the distribution is then 30% of the appropriate fraction of the effective rate.

(7)   On the occasion of the second distribution it should be noted that the rate must be recomputed using the inheritance tax rates then applicable (if lower) and, because further property has been added, the notional transfer has been increased.

Provisions to avoid double counting on a ten-year charge

(8)   Where property has been added to the settlement after 8 March 1982 when the law relating to discretionary trusts altered (strictly because 'the settlor has made a chargeable transfer as a result of which the value of the property comprised in the settlement was increased') the rules in s 67 apply when calculating the tax charge on the ten-year anniversary.

The 'assumed cumulative total' to be used includes the highest of the settlor's seven-year cumulative total as at the date the settlement commenced and his seven-year cumulative totals at the time of additions, reduced when appropriate as explained below.

If no reductions were made this procedure might result in double counting, eg if the addition is made less than 7 years after the commencement of the settlement, the settlor's seven-year cumulative total at the date of the addition will include the sum originally settled as well as earlier additions which (unless the property has been the subject of an exit charge) form part or all of the relevant property in the settlement now subject to the ten-year charge. It will also reflect the initial value of any related settlement.

In such circumstances the seven-year cumulation is reduced by so much as is attributable to property whose value is taken into account in the 'assumed transfer' (s 67(5)(a)).

Similarly the seven-year cumulative total at the time of an addition may reflect the value of property which has ceased to be relevant property at the date of the ten-year charge and has been the subject of an exit charge in the previous ten years. Once again the seven-year cumulation is reduced by the amount attributable to the property in respect of which the exit charge was made (s 67(5)(b)).

Double counting relief also applies where property has been the subject of an exit charge on the creation of an interest in possession within the last ten years, but has since become relevant property again. Its value would appear both as relevant property and as property on which an exit charge had been levied in the last ten years. In such circumstances, the latter amount is reduced by the smaller of the value at the time of the exit charge and the value at the time of the ten-year charge, as illustrated in **Example 61** (s 67(6)).

(9)

(i)   In the Example Smith's seven-year cumulative total at the time of the first addition (5 May 2001), and the available reduction in calculating the effective rate on the ten-year charge on the B Trust, is:

		Cumulative Total £	Available Reduction £
(a)	his 7-year cumulation prior to the creation of the B Trust — December 1993 – now spent because more than seven years before addition	–	–
(b)	relating to the creation of the B Trust of which £1,588 is attributable to the tax paid and £48,000 is attributable to relevant property in the settlement at the time of the 10-year charge (the farm)	49,588	48,000
(c)	by reference to the creation of the related settlement (C Trust). Of this sum £19,200 was used by the trustees to pay the tax so that only £76,800 is attributable to the initial value of the related settlement in the 'assumed transfer'	96,000	76,800
		145,588	124,800

(ii)   Smith's seven-year cumulative total at the time of the second addition (9 September 2003), and the available reduction in calculating the effective rate on the ten-year charge on the B Trust, is:

		Cumulative Total £	Available Reduction £
(a)	his 7-year cumulation prior to the creation of the B Trust (spent, see (i) (a) above)	–	–
(b)	relating to the creation of the B Trust, as in (i) (b) above	49,588	48,000
(c)	by reference to the creation of the related settlement (C Trust), as in (i) (c) above	96,000	76,800
(d)	by reference to the first addition of £24,000. The chargeable £18,000 (after annual exemptions) is therefore attributable to relevant property in the settlement at the time of the 10-year charge or to property that is the subject of the exit charge on 1 January 2002	18,000	18,000
(e)	Gift to children – potentially exempt	–	–
		163,588	142,800

In both cases transfers on the same date as the addition (ie including the addition itself) are excluded from the cumulative total, though the net addition may feature in the notional transfer itself.

(iii)   The assumed cumulative total is therefore the highest of:

		£	£
(a)	Settlor's 7-year cumulative total prior to the creation of the settlement		189,352
(b)	Settlor's 7-year cumulative total on first addition (see (i) above)	145,588	
	Less: Available reduction	124,800	20,788
(c)	Settlor's 7-year cumulative total on second addition (see (ii) above)	163,588	
	Less: Available reduction	142,800	20,788

Accordingly the cumulative total on creation of the settlement ((iii) (a) above) is used.

Effect of settlor's death

(10)   Note that if Smith had died before 6 May 2008 then the potentially exempt gift of £195,000 to his children would have become chargeable. This would alter the calculation of liability at the time of the second

addition (even though death occurred after the tax had been agreed). The seven-year cumulative total at the date of the second addition would then be:

	Cumula- tive Total £	Available Reduc- tion £
As 9(ii) (a) to (d) above	163,588	142,800
(e) Gift to children – now chargeable	195,000	–
	358,588	142,800

The assumed cumulative total would therefore now be the highest of:

		£	£
(a)	Settlor's 7-year cumulative total prior to the creation of the B Trust (2000)		189,352
(b)	Settlor's 7-year cumulative total on first addition to the B Trust (2001)	145,588	
	Less: Available reduction	124,800	20,788
(c)	Settlor's 7-year cumulative total on second addition to the B Trust (2003)	358,588	
	Less: Available reduction	142,800	215,788

This would revise the inheritance tax liability on 2 February 2006 and also on subsequent occasions of charge, such as the ten-year anniversary on 6 June 2010, as follows:

Exit charge 2 February 2006

	Gross £	Tax (2005/06 scale) £
Assumed transfer:		
Settlor's cumulative total as above	215,788	–
Notional transfer (see above under 'Tax position of brother's children's settlement')	372,800	62,718
	588,588	62,718*

(* 588,588 – 275,000 = 313,588 @ 20%)
Actual rate is 30% of the effective rate

$$\frac{62,718}{372,800} \times 100 \times 30\% = 5.047\%$$

Tax payable:
  re 2000 addition (12,000 shares)

$$5.047\% \times \frac{19}{40} \times £99,000 \times \frac{12,000}{132,000} = \qquad 216$$

  re 2002 addition (120,000 shares)

$$5.047\,\%\ \times \frac{9}{40}\times £\,99{,}000\times \frac{120{,}000}{132{,}000}=$$

1,022

£1,238 (previously
£1,134)

6 June 2010 – ten-year charge

	Gross £	Tax (on 2010/11 scale) £
Settlor's cumulative total as above	215,788	–
Exit charges in previous 10 years (see above at 62.5)	117,000	
	332,788	1,558*
Assumed transfer (see above at 62.5)	362,800	72,560
	695,588	74,118**

(* 332,788 – 325,000 = 7,788 @ 20%)
(** 695,588 – 325,000 = 370,588 @ 20%)

$$\frac{72{,}560}{362{,}800}\times 100\,\%\ =20\,\%$$

IHT payable:

Original fund	20% × 30% × £150,000	9,000
1st addition	$20\,\%\times30\,\%\times\dfrac{37}{40}\times £\,132{,}000\times\dfrac{6{,}000}{66{,}000}$	666
2nd addition	$20\,\%\times30\,\%\times\dfrac{27}{40}\times £\,132{,}000\times\dfrac{60{,}000}{66{,}000}$	4,860

(previously
£14,526   £13,779)

(11)   The relevant value of the property comprised in the settlement is its value on the day preceding the tenth anniversary – in this case 5 June 2010 (s 64).

Associated operations

(12)   If two or more settlements of an identical or substantially similar nature were set up over a short term, HMRC Capital Taxes took the view that the associated operations provisions of s 268 (as to which see **Example 22**) would apply. This would have resulted in the settlements being treated as a single settlement set up at the time of the last settlement, with only one nil rate band. In the case of *Rysaffe Trustee Co (CI) Ltd v IRC* (2002), however, the High Court held that as a matter of general law the creation of five identical settlements must be treated as five separate settlements, not one. It was up to the settlor to determine if he wished to create more than one settlement and the associated operations provisions of s 268 could not apply.

(13)   For further notes on discretionary trusts see **Examples 59, 60 and 61**.

Question

A has a protected life interest within Trustee Act 1925 s 33(1) in a trust fund valued at £250,000 created by his uncle; after A's death the trust fund is to pass to A's nephew (the uncle's son) absolutely. On 1 July 2005 A purported to assign that life interest to his brother. The trustees pointed out that the attempted alienation was ineffective and brought the protected life interest to an end, substituting for it a statutory discretionary trust of income under which the beneficiaries were A, his wife and their children.

A also has a life interest under the will of his father who died on 1 April 2006; on A's death this fund is to pass to A's son absolutely.

On 1 May 2009 A sold this life interest to a Reversionary Interest Society for £200,000 – the full market value of the interest. The assets of the trust fund were worth £564,000 at that time.

He did not advise the trustees of the fund of the availability of annual inheritance tax exemptions.

On 21 April 2010 A, who was fit and well, sold his house, then valued at £200,000 on a vacant possession basis, to his daughter D for £170,000 but reserving to himself a lease of the property for 99 years determinable by one month's notice given by the landlord at any time after his death. The value of the lease at that time was £80,000.

On 1 May 2010, before his daughter had paid the £170,000 (although all documentation had been completed), A was killed in a car accident. His other assets totalled £30,000 net – he had spent the money received from the Reversionary Interest Society.

His uncle's discretionary, formerly protective, trust fund was then valued at £305,000.

By his will, A created a discretionary trust of the whole of his free estate in favour of his children. On 12 March 2012 the trustees appointed a sum of £10,000, free of tax, to a son, S, absolutely.

The only previous transfer which either A or his daughter had made before the events described was a gift of £108,000 (after annual exemptions) that A made in July 1997.

(a) Calculate the inheritance tax payable as a result of these transactions and consequent upon A's death.

(b) Calculate the rate at which inheritance tax will be payable on future appointments out of the discretionary trust created by A's will.

(c) Calculate the inheritance tax consequences if A's daughter gives the necessary notice in the light of A's death so that the lease of the house terminates on 1 January 2011 when the vacant possession value of the house is £215,000.

(d) State (without calculation) the inheritance tax consequences if she decides not to give such notice but then dies unexpectedly on 31 March 2011.

Answer

(a) Inheritance tax on transactions and death

Inheritance tax accumulation — A

1 July 2005
    Forfeiture of protected life interest – No transfer of value –
    A deemed to retain an interest in possession (s 88(2))

		Gross	Tax on 2009/10 scale
		£	£
1 May 2009			
Cumulative chargeable transfers within previous 7 years (ie since 2 May 2002)		–	–
Sale of life interest under father's will trust			
Value of trust fund	564,000		
Less: Amount received	200,000	364,000	7,800*
		364,000	7,800*

(* 364,000 – 325,000 = 39,000 @ 20%)

21 April 2010
Sale of house to daughter			
Market value with vacant possession	200,000		
Less: Amount receivable	170,000		
	30,000		
Less: Value retained through lease for life	80,000		
	No loss to A	–	
Accumulation at death on 1 May 2010		364,000	

Inheritance tax accumulation — daughter

21 April 2010

Amount payable for house			170,000
Less:	Value of reversion on lease for life (see **explanatory note 3**):		75,000
	$\dfrac{200,000 - 170,000}{80,000} \times 200,000 = {}$ *		
Loss to daughter's estate			95,000
Less: Annual exemptions	2010/11	3,000	
	2009/10	3,000	6,000
Chargeable transfer – see **explanatory note 3**			89,000
No previous transfers so nil tax			

*

$$\frac{\text{Consideration x received for grant of lease}}{\text{Arm'slength consideration for grant of lease}} \times \text{Vacant possession value of house}$$

Death of A — 1 May 2010

	£	£
Free estate		
Net assets	30,000	
Lease 'for life' – not part of A's estate for inheritance tax purposes, see **explanatory note 3**	–	
Amount due from daughter re house sale	170,000	200,000
Settled property		
Deemed life interest in protective trust		305,000
		505,000

Inheritance tax due on death estate

	Date of death 1 May 2010	
		Tax on 2010/11
	Gross	scale
	£	£
On gifts within 7 years before death		
Transfers within 7 years before 1 May 2010		
(ie on and after 2 May 2003)		–
1 May 2009 – sale of life interest	364,000	15,600*
	364,000	15,600*

(* 364,000 – 325,000 = 39,000 @ 40%)

On estate at death		
(Nil threshold already exceeded by lifetime transfers)		
£505,000 @ 40%		202,000
Tax payable		£
By trustees of father's will trust	15,600	
Less: paid on original transfer	7,800	7,800
By personal representatives:		

$$\frac{200,000}{505,000} \times 202,000$$

		80,000

By trustees of protective trust

$$\frac{305,000}{505,000} \times 202,000$$

		122,000

Termination of life interest owned by Reversionary Interest Society

1 May 2010 – A's death brings the interest to an end and his son becomes absolutely entitled. Apart from the additional tax arising from A's death within seven years after selling the interest (above), no further inheritance tax charge arises. The trust property was not in an individual's estate immediately before A's death, nor was it relevant property.

Appointment of £10,000 by the trustees of A's will to S

12 March 2012 – Appointment is within two years after the death and is deemed to have been made by A under his will (s 144). No further tax is payable.

(b) Discretionary trust created by A's will

		£
A's estate		190,000
Less:	appointment to son	10,000
		180,000
Less:	tax payable by executors	76,000
Net amount received by discretionary settlement created by the will		104,000

Rate of tax on distributions before the first ten-year anniversary on 1 May 2020

Distributions made before 1 May 2012 will (like the appointment on 12 March 2012) be treated for inheritance tax purposes as having been made on A's death without having entered the settlement (s 144).

A's seven-year cumulative total at *commencement of settlement* (ignoring transfers of value made on that day, that is the transfer of value deemed to have been made on A's death), was £364,000. The position of the settlement subject to s 144 is therefore as follows:

	£
Cumulative total of settlor	364,000
Net amount received as above	104,000
	468,000

As the cumulative total in respect of the notional transfer in s 68 is above the threshold, the 'effective' rate of tax on the notional transfer is 20%, so that the rate of tax on distributions made after the second anniversary of A's death but before the first ten-year anniversary is N/40ths of 6% (30% × 20%), 'N' being the number of complete quarters since 1 May 2010.

If the tax rates have been reduced when the distribution occurs, the 'effective rate' is recalculated using the new reduced rates.

Rate of tax at ten-year anniversaries

This is 30% of the 'effective rate' found by assuming a transfer of value equal to the value of the trust fund immediately before the ten-year anniversary (ie on 30 April 2020, 30 April 2030 and so on), made by a transferor whose cumulative total is deemed to be £364,000 (the settlor's cumulative total as above) *plus* the amounts taxed on exit from the discretionary trust in the preceding ten years, using one half the death scale current at the date of the ten-year anniversary.

If any property subject to the ten-year charge was not 'relevant property' throughout the whole of the preceding ten years or was not comprised in the settlement throughout the whole of that period, then (in relation to that property alone) the 'effective rate' above is reduced by 1/40th for each complete successive quarter which expired before the property became relevant property.

The value charged to tax is the value of the 'relevant property' in the settlement immediately before the anniversary on the appropriate 30 April.

Rate of tax between ten-year anniversaries

This is the 'appropriate fraction' (ie $(X–Y)/40$ – where 'X' is the number of completed quarters since the last ten-year anniversary and 'Y' is the number of those quarters completed before the property became relevant property, or 0 if it was relevant property throughout) of the rate charged on the last ten-year anniversary.

If the tax rates have been reduced since the last ten-year anniversary, the current lower rates are substituted.

(c) Inheritance tax on termination of lease for life

The lease for 99 years determinable after A's death continues after A's death until brought to an end, by expiry of the daughter's notice, on 1 January 2011. In the meantime A's personal representatives (and the discretionary trust under A's will) have a continuing interest in possession in the deemed settlement constituted by the lease 'for life' (s 43(3)). This is still a non-estate interest in possession and the house as a whole remains relevant property.

On expiry of the daughter's notice the lease (deemed settlement) comes to an end and the daughter becomes absolutely entitled to the house free from the lease, giving rise to an exit charge under the relevant property rules since the house has ceased to be relevant property (s 65).

The settlor of the deemed settlement was the daughter as it was she who paid more than the value of the house subject to the reserved lease. The settlement had commenced on 21 April 2010 so the exit charge occurs before any ten-year anniversary; two complete quarters had elapsed between then and the exit charge on 1 January 2011. The position of the settlement is:

	£
7-year cumulative total of settlor immediately before settlement commenced	nil
Initial value of settled property under deemed settlement:	
Value of house free of lease	200,000
Notional transfer – within 2010/11 threshold so effective rate 0%	200,000

Thus there is no inheritance tax to pay on the exit charge. If the daughter had given the notice soon after A's death so that it expired before 21 July 2010, no exit charge would have occurred in the first place (s 65(4)), but this makes no practical difference in the circumstances.

(d) If the daughter had died without terminating the lease

The value of the daughter's reversionary interest is a fixed proportion of the unencumbered value of the house from time to time, for as long as the deemed settlement under s 43(3) continues; on the facts that proportion here is 37.5% (see **explanatory note 3**). Its value is included in the daughter's estate because it is not excluded property (s 48(1)(c)), and will be taxed as part of her free estate on her death accordingly subject to any spouse exemption etc.

Insofar as the daughter paid too much for the house subject to the lease for life, she can be seen to have made a gift of the excess of £50,000 (£170,000 cash plus £80,000 lease less £200,000 vacant possession value). The gift was not in fact into a settlement (the deemed settlement is of the house as a whole, not of the lease, and the excess in reality took the form of cash rather than the lease; the cash is not represented by the house even if unsettled cash gifts were subject to the tracing rules for the gifts with reservation provisions); so the house is not caught by the gifts with reservation rules so as to be charged on the daughter's death.

For the ten months since A's death and before her own the daughter could have brought the lease to an end by one month's notice given at any time, but she decided not to do so. Had she done so at least a month before her death, the settlement would have come to an end on expiry of the notice (see **(c)** above) and the whole unencumbered value of the house would then have been in her estate at her death. HMRC may therefore seek to pursue a claim that the daughter's estate should be taxed as though she had made a transfer of value equal to the difference between vacant possession value and the statutory value of her reversionary interest, by virtue of s 3(3); after all, the daughter's decision not to give notice, after considering the matter, shows that the failure to exercise that right to give notice was deliberate and not inadvertent.

However, it is thought that such a claim could be resisted for a combination of two reasons:

(a)   A deemed disposition under s 3(3) occurs, if at all, at the latest time the person could have exercised a right in question. The daughter's mere decision not to exercise it did not amount to abandonment of the right, and so should could have changed her mind at any time and given notice right up to the moment she died. Any such notice would not have expired, and brought to an end the lease for life and so the deemed settlement, until a month after her death; so the settlement would have still been in existence at her death.

(b)   Section 3(3) applies if the failure to exercise the right in question results in the person's estate being diminished, and that of another person (or of settled property not subject to an estate IIP) being increased. The fixed proportions of value attributed to the reversionary interest and the interest in possession (see **explanatory note 3**) mean that, while the settlement continued as above, the failure to give notice did not result in any diminution as such in the daughter's estate before or at her death; merely in its not *increasing* when the notice expired a month after the death.

Explanatory Notes

(1)   *1 July 2005 – purported assignment to brother*

When A's life interest comes to an end there is no transfer of value because A is deemed to retain his interest in possession (s 88(2)).

(2)   *1 May 2009 – sale of life interest*

A's life interest under his father's will is an immediately post-death interest, and therefore an estate interest in possession even after the FA 2006 changes (see **Example 52**).

Although the sale by A of his life interest to the Reversionary Interest Society is a commercial transaction for full value, s 10 does not prevent its giving rise to a transfer of value because s 52(2) expressly provides that a transfer of value arises with an allowance for the sale price received, ie a lifetime transfer of £564,000 (the value of the assets comprising the trust fund) less the £200,000 received = £364,000.

The transfer is not a potentially exempt transfer because the interest does not become comprised in the estate of another individual, nor is another individual's estate increased as a result of the transfer, and it therefore falls outside s 3A.

Section 57 allows the annual and marriage exemptions to be applied to events on the happening of which tax is chargeable under s 52 (ie the coming to an end during lifetime of estate interests in possession in settled property) provided the transferor (the person with the estate interest in possession which came to an end) gives the trustees a formal notice within six months, telling them of the availability of the exemption and the extent to which he is making it available.

As no such notice has been given the exemptions are not available to the trustees.

The assigned life interest in the hands of the Reversionary Interest Society is not an estate interest in possession because it is not beneficially owned by an individual. However it is a qualifying interest in possession within s 59 because it was an estate IIP in the hands of the person from whom the Society acquired it, and it was acquired for full value by a company whose business consisted wholly or mainly of acquiring interests in settled property. The qualifying interest in possession prevents the property in A's father's will trust from being relevant property, and so there is no inheritance tax charge when the settlement comes to an end on A's death.

(3)   *21 April 2010 – lease for life*

For the purposes of inheritance tax a lease for life (which includes a lease that is determinable on or at a date ascertainable only be reference to a death) is deemed to be a settlement of the property leased, unless it was granted for full consideration in money or money's worth – s 43(3). The leasehold interest in such a case is thus an interest in possession in that settled property, and the superior interest (typically the freehold) is a reversionary interest in it.

In a case where a property is transferred for no cash consideration but reserving a lease for life to the transferor, this does not in terms fit the terms of the statutory exclusion from s 43(3) namely that the lease was 'granted' for full consideration. However HMRC will treat the lease for this purpose as though it had been granted by the transferee in return for (and, logically, immediately after) the transfer of the unencumbered freehold interest; that consideration will thus be more than full consideration paid to the transferee, and there would be no deemed settlement. Instead, on those facts, the transferor would have made a transfer of value equal to the full value of the property less the value of the lease (on normal valuation principles) that he retained.

In the Example, A's daughter undertakes to pay him cash for the transfer of the house as well. It is assumed that the principle outlined in the previous paragraph will still be applied; on that basis, it appears that the daughter could be treated as having granted the lease for life (worth £80,000 on a full consideration basis) in return for £30,000 (being the difference between the £200,000 vacant possession value of the house and the £170,000 cash sum that she has undertaken to pay). Therefore the lease for life can be seen to have been "granted" by her for less than full consideration, and s 43(3) will give rise to a deemed settlement accordingly.

The settled property under this deemed settlement is the whole (unencumbered) house. In place of normal valuation principles applying to the two parties' interests in it, the proportions of the property's value from time to time ('V') that are to be attributed to them are fixed, for as long as the deemed settlement subsists, by reference to the relationship between the consideration given for the lease when it was granted ('X') and the consideration which would have been given for it at that time between unconnected parties ('Y'). Of these figures, only V varies with time; the fractions of V attributed to:

(a)   the landlord's (reversionary) interest (which is not excluded property – s 48(1)(c)) is X/Y (s 170), which in the Example is 30,000/80,000 or 37.5%, and

(b)   the lessee's interest is the entire balance, or (Y – X)/Y (s 50(6)), which in the Example is (80,000 – 30,000)/80,000 or 62.5%.

This latter rule, in s 50(6), is predicated on the lessee's interest being an estate IIP, as all interests in possession owned by individuals were before 2006. However, in the Example A became beneficially entitled to his interest in possession after 22 March 2006; since he was not a disabled person at the time, his interest in possession is not an estate IIP, and so s 50(6) seems to be irrelevant in such a case. Some aspects of the treatment of deemed settlements arising from s 43(3) were less than clear even before the FA 2006 changes; leases for life were not addressed in those changes and the position since then is if anything more confusing, but it would appear that:

(i)   the house as a whole comprises the settled property which is therefore relevant property;

(ii)   because A's interest is an interest in possession but not an estate IIP, no property or value enters A's estate on the lease being created; the interest in possession (lease) itself is not part of his estate (s 5(1),(1A)); and

(iii)   the daughter's transfer of value resulting from the transaction cannot therefore be a potentially exempt transfer, and is therefore an immediately chargeable transfer except so far as covered by annual exemptions.

A has disposed of the house but is still in occupation of it, so the pre-owned assets income tax rules are potentially in point for him. However, his disposal (taking account of the reserved lease, which is "a right expressly reserved by him over the property") was for more, not less, consideration than he would have been paid in a transaction between unconnected parties, and the sale is thus an excluded transaction for the purpose of those rules.

(4)   *1 May 2010 – position on A's death*

On A's death the tax on transfers of value made within the last seven years is recalculated using the full-scale rates in force at the date of death and by accumulation with transfers within the seven years preceding each gift.

The difference between the tax calculated on this basis and the tax originally calculated using the lifetime rates in force at the time of the transfer is due from the trustee of A's father's will trust (s 201).

A's own assets on death include the sum of £170,000 due to him from his daughter.

His chargeable estate also includes the value of the property in the protective trust in which his life interest is deemed to continue (see **explanatory note 1**), but not the interest in possession under the deemed settlement arising from the lease for life (see **explanatory note 3**).

(5)   *Capital gains tax position on A's death*

When A's nephew becomes absolutely entitled to the assets in A's uncle's trust on A's death, the deemed disposal of the trust assets under TCGA 1992 s 71 will give rise to chargeable gains in the trustees' hands in the usual way, subject to the possibility of hold-over relief under TCGA 1992 s 260 if the nephew is UK resident. Although A's interest in possession (before the purported assignment) is deemed to continue until his death for inheritance tax, despite the forfeiture of the protected life interest, that treatment does not apply for capital gains tax purposes and the trust is discretionary at A's death.

The same applies in relation to the assets to which A's son becomes absolutely entitled on A's death under A's father's will trust – even though that occurs on the termination of an actual life interest – because the life interest was not then owned by the person whose death brought it to an end but rather by the Reversionary Interest Society.

There are no capital gains tax implications of the deemed settlement in relation to the lease for life. That deeming is solely for inheritance tax purposes, and the capital gains tax treatment of the house and the interests in it follows the factual position. There is therefore no disposal by the daughter (whether personally or in her capacity as a trustee of the deemed settlement) on A's death, or on the giving or expiry of the notice to terminate the lease: she acquired the freehold interest at the outset, and the terminability, or actual termination, of the lease following A's death does not alter what she owns. The daughter's base cost will not be the whole £170,000 she paid, but will be restricted by TCGA 1992 s 18 to the market value of what she acquired from her father namely the property subject to the lease. As seen in **explanatory note 3**, she overpaid by £50,000 and her base cost will therefore be £120,000.

In A's hands the lease loses most of its value on his death because it becomes terminable by the landlord on one month's notice; but this loss on one of the assets of which he was competent to dispose is not an allowable loss, any more than a gain arising on his death would have been a chargeable gain.

(6)   *12 March 2012 – distribution within two years after death*

Example 34 illustrates how s 142 allows beneficiaries within two years after a death to vary the dispositions without that variation being itself a transfer of value, and for the tax payable in connection with the death to be calculated as though the variation had been made by the deceased himself.

Similarly, s 144 provides that distributions made within two years after death out of property settled by the deceased's will in which there has been no estate IIP are similarly treated as having been made at the time of the death and are not therefore subject to an exit charge. (See **Example 60 explanatory notes 10 and 12** for the position on transfers within the first three months, which may not benefit from that basic rule, and **explanatory note 11** for the interaction of s 144 with capital gains tax.)

The £10,000 appointed by the trustees of A's will to A's son is therefore deemed for the purposes of inheritance tax to have been given to him by his father A under his will with effect from A's death, and does not give rise to any exit charge under the relevant property rules.

(7)   See **Example 60** for the rules for calculating the rate at which inheritance tax will be payable on appointments after the first ten-year anniversary out of the discretionary trust created by A's will.

Question

A.

You receive a letter from a wealthy client:

10 August 2010

Dear William

As you will recall, I had previously intended to transfer £375,000 into a settlement for my young children. We had discussed creating an accumulation and maintenance settlement in early 2006 but I had a short stay in hospital and when I came out you advised me that the rules had changed and that accumulation and maintenance settlements were no longer be available.

Due to the uncertainties of the Government's proposals you suggested that I write to you again later in the year when things had settled down. I had another bout of illness and with one thing and another it has taken me rather longer to write to you.

I am still interested in making a settlement for my children all of whom are, as you know, still under 18. I recall reading that it is now possible to put assets into trust for children which can be kept until they are 25 (rather than the age of 18 as originally proposed). Is this something that you would recommend? As you know I think it highly irresponsible for any parent to let an 18-year old receive substantial capital; whilst not entirely happy about it, I would be less concerned about my children receiving their entitlement at 25.

If not, what other strategies would you suggest I consider.

Please let me know what reporting requirements and other ongoing tax-related responsibilities this will entail.

Yours sincerely

Bernard

PS As you may recall when my wife Celia died in December 2005 she left £250,000 on trust for the children in her will, and the rest of her estate to me. The terms of the trust mean that the children do not get the money until they are 25. I remember that you advised me at the time that this was an accumulation and maintenance trust so I wonder if this trust is affected by the changes?

B.

Another of your clients of more modest means than Bernard wants to know whether there would be any tax advantages if he and his wife transferred funds to their children. The children are aged 15, 12 and 10. Prepare notes on the points to be made to the client.

Answer

A. Accumulation and maintenance settlement

31 August 2010

Dear Bernard,

Thank you for your letter of 10 August.

You are quite right in recalling that it is no longer possible to create an accumulation and maintenance settlement of the kind which we had discussed before your hospitalisation in early 2006. Some amendments were made to the Government's proposals as outlined in the 2006 Budget but the benign tax treatment given to accumulation and maintenance settlements has ended.

If it is any consolation, even accumulation and maintenance settlements made before the 2006 Budget were affected by the changes although the previous tax treatment was left in place until 5 April 2008. If you had been able to settle the funds on an accumulation and maintenance settlement before 22 March 2006, the trust would have still been affected by the new rules unless steps had been taken to rearrange with effect from 6 April 2008 so it would have been necessary to consider rearranging these trusts before 6 April 2008 if at all possible.

You correctly refer to the changes which allow some trusts to retain funds until a child reaches the age of 25 (rather than 18). For trusts made after 21 March 2006, this can only apply if the trust was set up under the will of the child's parent (or under the Criminal Injuries Compensation Scheme). However, there were transitional arrangements for trusts that were already in existence at that date, and the trust set up by Celia for your children will qualify. Trusts that take advantage of this slight relaxation will, strictly, face an inheritance tax charge when capital is taken from the trust from the share of a beneficiary who is over the age of 18. However, this should not be relevant in practice in the case of Celia's trust because of the way the charge is calculated. My records for Celia's estate show that she had not made any significant chargeable transfers in the seven years before she died, and in those circumstances the rules focus purely on the initial value of the trust which as you say was £250,000. That is well within the present nil-rate band of £325,000; it would have to drop below £250,000 before distributions would attract a positive rate of inheritance tax, though if it fell much from its present level it would be necessary to submit a return even though no tax might be due.

One important consequence of Celia leaving £250,000 to the children in her Will is that she used much of her nil-rate band, which was £275,000 when she died. If she had left everything to you there would have been no inheritance tax to pay because gifts between spouses are exempt for inheritance tax purposes, but there would have been the prospect of that £250,000 all being taxed at 40% on your own eventual death since your estate already exceeds the nil-rate band. The recommended approach at the time Celia died was to leave as much of the nil-rate band as possible to persons other than the spouse because her nil-rate band would otherwise be 'wasted' – the legacy she left can be seen, under the rules then applicable, to have saved an eventual £100,000 of tax.

You might recall that in 2008 the Chancellor announced that nil-rate bands of spouses were to be transferable, so that if Celia had left everything to you, your nil-rate band would effectively double on your death. Since Celia in fact used just over 90% of her nil-rate band to make a gift to the children your nil-rate band will not be enhanced by 100% on your death, but only by the balance of 9% (though calculated by reference to the statutory figure at your death, not the lower level in force when she died). It therefore makes sense for you to consider making lifetime gifts into trusts for your children in the expectation that you survive by a further seven years so that these will no longer be taken into account in assessing the lifetime chargeable transfer on your death.

If you wish to make a lifetime gift to your children, therefore, you have broadly two options. First, you can make an outright gift (to a bare trust on behalf of your children). This means that they can insist on receiving the capital as soon as they are 18. Such a gift would constitute a potentially exempt transfer and will escape inheritance tax altogether provided you live for seven years after the gift. In view of your understandable objections to giving 18-year olds substantial sums of money, I would not recommend that you followed this option. However, you should note that it is the most inheritance tax-friendly solution (though any income generated while they were still under 18 and unmarried would still be taxed as if it were yours).

Alternatively, you can settle the funds into a trust. Since 22 March 2006, the inheritance tax treatment has been the same for both interest in possession trusts (essentially those where the beneficiaries have a right to receive the income from a fixed interest in the trust) and discretionary trusts (those where the trustees have a lot more freedom about paying income and capital to the beneficiaries). In the circumstances I would suggest that you consider using a discretionary trust as that gives you the greatest flexibility in the future – there is no requirement to distribute income or capital by any given age.

If you proceed, inheritance tax will be payable at 20% on the funds entering the trust, except so far as covered by your annual exemption. However, on the basis that you have made no chargeable transfers to date, the first £6,000 will be covered by your annual exemption for this year and for last year, and the next £325,000 by the nil-rate band. (Please note that the enhancement mentioned above in respect of the transferable nil-rate band does not apply to lifetime gifts.)

Therefore, assuming for the sake of illustration that you were to gift £375,000 and to specify that any tax was to be borne by the trust, the trustees would be required to pay inheritance tax of £8,800 (£369,000 – £325,000 @ 20%). If instead you chose to pay the tax yourself, the tax charge would be calculated on a 'grossing-up' basis and would work out at £11,000 ((£369,000 + £11,000) – £325,000 @ 20%).

This tax will be payable (assuming you make the gift before the end of next month) by 30 April 2011. Otherwise, it will be payable six months after the end of the month in which you make the gift.

Further tax will be payable out of the trust fund should you die within seven years of making the gift. This will be payable six months after the end of the month in which you die.

If the tax is not paid on the due date, interest is charged at the rate in force at that time (currently 3%).

In both cases (the immediate lifetime charge, and the further tax on death), there is technically a 12 month period allowed for filing a return (plus the remainder of the month current at the date of the event in question); but because interest starts to run well before the end of that time limit it is unwise to leave submitting the return over until the end of the 12 months, at least without having reviewed the figures carefully and put money down with HMRC against the tax liability that is expected.

Initial and ongoing reporting requirements:

In relation to yourself

(i)   In principle you must file an inheritance tax return within 12 months after making the gift to the trustees, as above. However, if after all you limit the size of the gift to what is covered by your annual exemptions and statutory nil-rate band (or to 80% of the nil-rate band if the gift is made in the form of anything other than cash or quoted shares or securities), you are only required to file such a return in your lifetime if HMRC notify you to that effect. Your personal representatives would need, in the return for your estate, to disclose the gift in any case if you died within seven years afterwards, and the trustees as donees would in that case need to file a return of the gift as well.

(ii)   In addition to that, you will need to include in your tax return for the year ended 5 April 2011 full details of any chargeable assets disposed of in order to raise the funds for (or transferred in kind to) the settlement, so that any chargeable gains arising may be calculated. If there are any such gains beyond your annual exemption of £10,100, and any available losses in the present or earlier tax years, the capital gains tax rate applicable will be 28% to the extent that the gains plus your income exceed the basic rate limit for income tax – this went up from 18% on 23 June 2010.

(iii)   Income arising under the settlement will not affect you in so far as it is accumulated for the benefit of your children; but if, while the children are under eighteen years of age and unmarried, the trustees make any payment for their maintenance, education or benefit the amount so paid will be regarded as your income for tax purposes, and will consequently need to be included in your personal income tax return; this applies as much to capital payments as to income, except that in the case of capital the amount is limited to the income that arose (or later arises) while they are still unmarried minors. You would be entitled to recover any tax paid by you under these provisions from the trustees or from the children who receive the income. However, the majority of the trust's income (beyond the first £1,000) will be taxed in the trustees' hands at the highest rates that could apply to your own personal income, and conceivably your own liability on the amount in question may be less than what the trustees had paid; in that event, if you obtained a tax repayment, you would be bound to pay it over to the trustees rather than retaining it for yourself. I should also mention that, to the extent that the trust's income consisted of dividend income, there is an increased income tax cost of making income payments compared with dividend income received directly. (See generally points **(ii) and (iii)** below under the heading *In relation to the trustees*).

(iv) Equivalent reporting responsibilities will apply if you make any additions to the settlement in future years.

In relation to the trustees

(i) The trustees should inform HMRC that the settlement has been created and ask for a reference for the settlement.

(ii) Tax return forms must be prepared and submitted by the trustees for each year ended 5 April. The forms give details of the income of the trust, the trustees' expenses and outgoings, disposals and deemed disposals for capital gains tax purposes, details of any distributions made to the children and may include the calculation of the self-assessed tax liability. The income of a discretionary settlement is chargeable at the trust rate — currently 42½% for dividends and 50% for other income, except that the first £1,000 of income, plus the amount used for expenses, is charged at 10% for dividends and 20% for other income. If a time came when the children were given a right to the income arising for the time being, the charge on the trustees would be restricted to 10% on dividend income and 20% on other income, though the children (so long as they were no longer minors, or were married though under 18) would have credit for tax borne by the trustees and would either have additional tax to pay, or would obtain a tax refund (except for the underlying tax credits on dividends) according to their personal circumstances.

(iii) If the trustees distribute any income for the maintenance or education of one or more of the children when they are still under eighteen and unmarried, then as stated above, such income will be treated as your income for tax purposes. Even so, the amount of any such income will be declared in the trust tax return and will be included in calculating the income liable at the 42½% and 50% rates. The trustees will deduct tax at 50% from the payments and if the underlying income includes dividends, the dividend credits cannot be taken into account as refundable tax paid by the trustees, thus reducing the amount that can be distributed without giving rise to an additional tax liability. Once the children have married or reached age 18, distributions (or income entitlements, if conferred by the trustees) will no longer give rise to liability (or a right to refund) on your part as described in point **(iii)** above under *In relation to yourself*; instead the children would include income distributions (or entitlements as the case may be) on their own tax returns, with credit for the tax paid by the trustees; this would effectively be the same as in **(ii)** above, but using the higher amounts of tax at the trust level while the trust remains discretionary.

(iv) The capital gains of the discretionary settlement will be chargeable at 28% after the deduction of allowable losses and of the annual exemption (£5,050 for 2010/11, reduced if you have created more than one settlement that is current during the relevant tax year). If assets are distributed in kind, the trustees will be treated as disposing of them at that time for capital gains tax purposes; but if the recipient beneficiary is UK resident then the trustees and the beneficiary can instead secure that the beneficiary takes over their base cost through a claim for hold-over relief – with an unfortunate technical exception in a case where the distribution occurs within three months after the trust is made or after one of the ten-yearly inheritance tax charges mentioned in **(v)** below.

(v) Inheritance tax will be payable on the tenth anniversary (and every subsequent ten years) on the value of the trust assets. The top charging rate is currently 6% but the trustees have the benefit of the nil-rate band (currently £325,000) before any tax is payable.

(vi) Charges will also be payable by the trustees whenever capital distributions are made by the trust, other than during the first three months of any ten-year period. This basic rate of this charge is 6% although in practice the actual rate will be a lot lower. This is partly because the calculation takes into account the nil-rate band at the time of the distribution, and partly because, in addition, the basic rate of the charge is reduced to a fraction of itself, n/40, where n is the number of complete quarters since the last ten-year anniversary (or the creation of the trust). Thus the maximum proportion of the basic charge that will be payable under this heading is 39/40ths, in the final quarter of each ten-year period.

In relation to your children

(i)   The children have no reporting responsibility until they reach age eighteen (or, theoretically, marry under that age).

(ii)   When income is distributed to your children, this will be shown on their tax returns (which you will complete whilst they are minors). This reporting obligation arises even where the income is taxed as though it were yours (point **(iii)** above under *In relation to yourself*), but in that case they will have no liability.

I shall be happy to discuss any of the above points with you in more detail if you wish, and to assist in the completion of relevant forms.

Yours sincerely,

William

B. Transferring funds to infant children

(1)   Where funds are transferred to children under 18, there is little opportunity to obtain any income tax advantages. The funds transfer would be treated for income tax as a settlement. Unless it is covered by one of the exceptions listed below, settlement income that is paid to or would otherwise be treated as the income of a child of the settlor who is under 18 and unmarried is treated as the parent's income and not the child's (ITTOIA 2005 s 629). A settlement includes 'any disposition, trust, covenant, agreement, arrangement or transfer of assets' (s 620).

(2)   Each parent may, however, give each such child a capital sum from which not more than £100 gross income arises each year. If income exceeds the limit the whole amount is taxable (s 629(3)).

(3)   Before 9 March 1999, there were income tax advantages if the parents arranged for funds for each child to be held under a 'bare trust', under which the child had an absolute right to the property and income, but the trustees (who could be the parents) were the legal owners, effectively holding as the child's nominee. The disadvantage of such trusts was that the child could not be prevented from obtaining legal ownership of the funds at age 18.

The income tax advantages of bare trusts by parents in favour of their minor children are no longer available for trusts created on or after 9 March 1999. Subject to the de minimis amount of £100 referred to in note 2 above, the income arising will be taxed as that of the parent under s 629.

(4)   The changed rules for bare trusts do not alter the capital gains treatment, which treats gains arising as the child's gains against which the annual exemption (currently £10,100) is available, the rates of tax on any gains beyond his exemption being, since 23 June 2010, 18% to the extent that the child's income has not used up his basic rate band for income tax, and 28% above that level. Funds could therefore be invested for the child purely for capital growth, with no income arising. This does not, however, give the former benefits of being able to use the child's personal allowance and lower tax rates against income.

(5)   Other possibilities, which also do not make use of the children's allowances and lower tax rates are as follows:

(a)   National Savings and Investments Children's Bonus Bonds for children under 16.

(b)   Friendly society policies (with premiums up to £270 per annum).

(c)   Contributions of up to £2,880 net per child into a personal pension plan. The basic rate tax relief of 20% is added to the amount invested in the plan, so that for a contribution of £2,880 the plan investment would be £3,600.

(6)   Where a child aged 16 or 17 opens a cash individual savings account (ISA) with funds provided by the parents then this will be treated as a settlement and the income arising will be taxable on the parent until each child's 18th birthday or earlier marriage (subject to the de minimis amount of £100) even though income within an ISA is normally tax free.

Explanatory Notes

Payments re settlor's infant, unmarried children

(1)   The income of discretionary and accumulation settlements is charged at the dividend trust rate (currently 42½%) if it is dividend or similar income (see **Example 42** for details) and at the rate applicable to trusts (currently 50%) if it is non-dividend income.

Under ITA 2007 s 491 the first £1,000 of relevant income will not be charged at the special trust tax rates, but will instead be charged at the income tax rate appropriate to the type of income, known as standard rate band. Therefore, if payments are received net of tax (for Example, building society interest) up to the limit of the standard rate band, then the trustees will have no further tax to pay.

The standard rate band will apply to trust income *net* of trust management expenses, so potentially it will apply to other charges on income as well.

Although the management expenses are deducted from the trust income taxed at the lowest rate first, (the basic rate at 20% first, followed by dividends at 10%).

See **Examples 42, 47 and 48** for further details on the standard rate band, its interaction with trust expenses and additional liabilities where amounts are distributed, and its restriction where more than one trust made by the same settlor is in existence for the time being.

Although any payment made by the trustees for the maintenance or education of a child of the settlor who is under 18 and unmarried is deemed to be the settlor's income, it is not so treated *before* the payment is made. The trustees are therefore liable to tax at the 50% rate, and any payments for the children are grossed up at that rate (ITA 2007 ss 493–498). See **Example 42** under heading *Income taxed as income of settlor* for the effect of the treatment of dividend income on the overall tax charge where dividend income is paid to minor children via a discretionary trust.

Notification of liability to tax

(2)   Since the trustees are chargeable to income tax on the trust income that arises, they must notify HMRC that they are so liable within six months after the end of the first relevant tax year. This is the same requirement as that of an individual taxpayer and carries a penalty of up to 100% of the tax due in the event of failure to notify (TMA 1970 s 7).

Person becoming absolutely entitled as against the trustees; gifts holdover relief

(3)   When a person becomes absolutely entitled to trust assets as against the trustees, other than on the death of a life tenant, the assets are deemed to have been disposed of by the trustees at market value for capital gains tax purposes. Any capital gain arising may be held over (subject to the recipient's UK residence) under the provisions of TCGA 1992 s 260, because s 260(2)(a) specifically allows a gain to be held over on a disposal which is a chargeable transfer for inheritance tax purposes. (This includes exit charges under the relevant property regime – hence the technical exception referred to in **part A** of the Example, **point (iv)** under In relation to the trustees, because an exit charge in those circumstances is disapplied by IHTA 1984

s 65(4), though there would still be the possibility of holding over the gain if the assets in question qualified as business assets, or were such as to attract agricultural property relief for inheritance tax, by virtue of TCGA 1992 s 165 and Schedule 7.)

Requirements for and advantages of accumulation and maintenance type settlements

(4)   Accumulation and maintenance settlements cannot be established after 21 March 2006. Those already in existence continued within the same regime until 5 April 2008, after which time that particular regime would only continue if the capital was (or had become) payable to the beneficiaries when they reach the age of 18, and (if the beneficiaries were not grandchildren of a common grandparent) the trust had not been in that regime for more than 25 years.

If an accumulation and maintenance settlement ceases to qualify within those narrower rules, because of the 25-year rule, the trustees are liable to an inheritance tax charge at (in practice) a fixed rate of 21%. Thereafter it would be within the relevant property regime and the normal ten-yearly and exit charges would apply.

(5)   Settlements which ceased to be A & M settlements on 6 April 2008 simply because of the requirement to pay capital by the age of 18 did not incur an inheritance tax charge on that event; and they moved at that time into the age 18-to-25 trust regime, which is in some respects similar to the relevant property regime during the first ten years of a trust's existence but in other respects more beneficial (no periodic charge, and no charge while the beneficiary is under age 18; the quarters for the n/40 fraction are only counted from a beneficiary's 18th birthday.

Reporting potentially exempt transfers that become chargeable

(6)   Potentially exempt transfers that become chargeable because of the death of the donor within seven years must be included in the account delivered by the personal representatives, along with details of the deceased's estate (IHTA 1984 s 216). Section 216 also requires potentially exempt transfers to be reported by the donee, the donee being primarily liable for payment of the tax.

Bare trusts

(7)   Bare trusts used to provide a simple way of enabling children's personal allowances and lower tax rates to be used against funds from the parent, so long as the income merely accumulated for the children's benefit without actually being paid to them. The parents could act as trustees and there thus need be no administration costs.

The earlier income tax advantages of bare trusts by parents in favour of their children under 18 were negated with effect from 9 March 1999 (with a saving for bare trusts made before that date and not added to since) – see now ITTOIA 2005 s 629.

The advantages continue for bare trusts created by parents before that date providing no funds are added. Except for dividend credits, the tax deducted at source from the accumulated income may be reclaimed to the extent that it exceeds the child's liability.

The revised rules do not prevent bare trusts being created by a parent's will, or by other relatives. It is not, however, possible for a parent to circumvent the rules by creating a bare trust for a relative's or friend's children and for the relative/friend to do the same for his children by way of a reciprocal arrangement (ITTOIA 2005 s 620).

(8)   Property held on a bare trust is in the legal ownership of the trustees and must remain in their ownership if and so long as the beneficiary is a minor (since a minor cannot give a valid receipt). As and when the beneficiary is over 18 he may call for the legal ownership to be transferred to him at any time.

Under self-assessment, trustees are not required to complete tax returns in respect of bare trusts (although they may send a return of *income*, but not capital gains, if they wish – see **Example 47 explanatory note 10**), and the child must show the income and gains in his own return.

(9)   Because the property is held for the beneficiary absolutely, it is not settled property for capital gains tax (TCGA 1992 s 60), and any gains are taxable on the beneficiary, so that the full annual exemption (£10,100 for 2009/10) is available unless used against other gains.

(10)   There is now an equivalent to TCGA 1992 s 60 in the income tax legislation in the shape of ITA 2007 s 466. The trustee is effectively only a nominee, so the provisions of ITA 2007 s 479 charging tax at the excess of the dividend trust rate of 42½% over the tax credit rate of 10% where a company purchases the trustees' shares (see **Example 49 explanatory note 4**) do not apply.

(11)   For inheritance tax, too, the property is not settled property since it is held for the beneficiary absolutely; any accumulations of income while he is under 18 belong to him nevertheless (and to his estate, at whatever age he dies). So a transfer to a bare trust is a potentially exempt transfer, so that tax will not be payable providing the donor survives the transfer by seven years.

Other tax-efficient ways of benefiting children

(12)   In addition to creating bare trusts that do not produce income but offer capital growth, parents may use funds for the benefit of their children without being caught by the income tax parental settlement rules as follows, as indicated in the Example at **part b note 5**:

    (a)   National Savings and Investments Children's Bonus Bonds may be purchased for children under 16 (maximum holding per child £3,000 in latest issue plus holdings in earlier issues). Interest on the bonds is tax-free. They run for 5 years at a time, so a bond bought just before the child's 16th birthday will mature just before the child's 21st birthday.

    (b)   Premiums of up to £270 per annum for each child may be paid on a qualifying friendly society policy. The proceeds of the policy are tax-free and the society does not pay tax on its income and gains in respect of such policies.

    (c)   Personal pension contributions of up to £2,880 net, £3,600 gross, per child may be paid each year. The child may not, however, draw any benefits from a pension plan until pension age is reached (age 55 from 2010).

These tax-efficient payments do not, however, give any opportunity for using the child's personal allowance and lower rates of tax.

Question

You were contacted in May 2010 by the trustees of the Green grandchildren's trust, a trust with UK based trustees and so resident in the UK.

The following details are known:

(1)   The trust's main asset is a 27% holding of ordinary shares in Green plc, an unquoted UK trading company. The shareholding was acquired by gift in January 1988 from the settlor. The shares were worth £850,000 at that time and a gain of £650,000 was held over. The settlor had acquired the shares in 1968. This shareholding is now worth about £2 million. It is anticipated that the company may be floated on the London Stock Exchange in the next year or so, in which case the shares could increase in value to over £5 million.

(2)   The trust's main source of income is dividends from its shareholding in Green plc. Normally about half the dividend is distributed to the beneficiaries.

(3)   The trust was created as an accumulation and maintenance trust which provides for a grandchild of the settlor to receive a life interest at age 25 with capital distributions subject to trustees' discretion. No alteration was made to the trust before 6 April 2008.

(4)   There are currently eight grandchildren with age ranges 21 to 30 – so that all of them were 18 or over on 6 April 2008. It is unlikely that any further beneficiaries will come into existence, and the trustees have established eight accounts (with equal numbers of shares) within the trust for administration purposes. Only two of the beneficiaries work for Green plc. The trustees are under pressure to completely wind up the trust and distribute to the beneficiaries. The trustees have already resolved in principle to distribute fully all retained income within the trust.

(5)   The trust had a brought forward tax credit pool for ICTA 1988 s 687 purposes of £650,000 at 6 April 1999, being mainly tax at the trust rate on dividends.

One of the trustees died recently, and the proposed replacement trustee, who has seen a taxation memorandum placed with the trust deeds by the settlor at the outset, has requested a meeting with the trustees' advisers to review the position generally and to understand how the various changes in income tax, capital gains tax and inheritance tax have affected the trust, and in particular the question whether to retain income and/or capital in the fund or distribute.

Draft technical notes for the meeting with the trustees.

Answer

Technical notes for meeting with trustees of Green grandchildren's trust

When income is relevant to a grandchild's tax position

(1)   Once a grandchild has reached 25 he has a life interest in his share of the trust fund, which means that he is entitled to the relevant share of income whether it is distributed or not. Before reaching age 25, he is taxable only on income distributed to him or for his maintenance; the trustees are given power to accumulate income while he is under 18 (and beyond that so long as 21 years had not expired since formation of the trust), and after that 21-year accumulation period the income is distributable in the trustees' discretion among all the grandchildren still under age 25 for the time being. In either case the grandchild is entitled to the usual personal allowance – now £6,475 – and is subject to the usual tax treatment of an individual.

This treatment of distributions applies whether the grandchild is still a minor or not, because the trust was made by the beneficiaries' grandparent; had the trust been made by a parent of the beneficiaries, distributions for the benefit of a beneficiary under age 18 (and unmarried) would have been treated as income of the parent-settlor, not of the beneficiary, up to the amount of income received by the trustees.

When tracing the tax changes over the past 11 years, the starting point is to consider the income – here dividends – in the hands of the trustees to whom it arises, and only then see the effect of this on the beneficiary's position so far as he is liable to tax.

Tax treatment of dividends before 6 April 1999

(2)   Before 6 April 1999 dividends carried a repayable tax credit of 25% of the cash dividend (20% of the tax credit inclusive amount), so that a cash dividend of £80 represented a dividend of £100 with a credit of £20, which was repayable to a non-taxpayer. Trust expenses were deducted from net trust income to give the amount available for distribution to beneficiaries.

Beyond that the trustees had no liability on dividends arising from the share of a grandchild with a life interest (ie a grandchild over 25) because the income is his whether distributed or not (see **point 1** above). If the grandchild's personal allowance covered his income, he could therefore claim repayment of the dividend credit. If the grandchild was a basic rate taxpayer no further tax was payable. A higher rate taxpayer had to pay a further 20% of the tax credit inclusive amount (25% of the cash dividend).

Where the dividend income was subject to accumulation, or was payable only at the trustees' discretion, it was taxable at the 34% rate applicable to trusts. Any amounts of income distributed to or for the benefit of a grandchild were treated as net amounts from which tax at 34% had been deducted. Grandchildren not liable to tax would recover the whole of the 34% tax, basic rate taxpayers would recover the difference and higher rate taxpayers would pay an extra 6%.

Tax treatment of dividends from 6 April 1999 to 5 April 2004

(3)   From 6 April 1999 dividend credits were reduced to 1/9th of the cash amount (10% of the tax credit inclusive figure) – this rate still applies now. Trust expenses are deducted from dividend income in priority to other sources of trust income. The dividend tax credits are not repayable. Thus a dividend of £80 carries a non-repayable credit of £8.89.

Grandchildren with a life interest (the first 25th birthday appears to have been in 2002 or thereabouts) were accordingly no longer able to recover the tax credits even if the total was within their personal allowance. Those liable at the basic rate still had no further tax to pay and those with income above the basic rate threshold were liable at the excess of the Schedule F (later dividend) upper rate of 32½% – or 22½% over the tax credit rate of 10%. Their net position at the end of the day was broadly unchanged by this new system from what it had been before 6 April 1999.

(4)   As far as dividends subject to accumulation (or distributable at discretion) were concerned, they became chargeable from 6 April 1999 at a special Schedule F (later dividend) trust rate of 25%. The trustees, similarly, were left with broadly the same net of tax income as previously prior to any distributions, ie:

	Pre-6 April 1999	*6 April 1999 to 5 April 2004*
	£	£
Dividend received	80.00	80.00
Tax credit	20.00	8.89
Trust income	100.00	88.89
Tax at 34%/25%	34.00	22.22
Net of tax income	66.00	66.67

However the fact that the dividend tax credit became non-repayable had an impact on the amount that could be distributed to beneficiaries without leaving the trustees with an additional liability – see **point 6** below – a problem which was only magnified by subsequent increases in the dividend trust rate (see **point 5** below).

Tax treatment of dividends from 6 April 2004

(5)   From 6 April 2004 the dividend trust rate for income subject to accumulation or to discretionary distribution was increased from 25% to 32½%; from 6 April 2010 this has been further increased to 42½. However, in 2005/06 a special trust standard rate band tax rate was introduced in relation to the first £500 of trust income (in 2005/06, rising to £1,000 from 2006/07) which would otherwise be chargeable to tax at the trust rate or the dividend trust rate trusts. Such income is instead chargeable to income tax at the basic rate or the dividend ordinary rate, depending on the nature of the income. Therefore, the first £500 or £1,000 of income held on discretionary or accumulation trusts will be charged at these rates.

	Pre-6 April 2004 as above	*2004/05 to 2009/10 inclusive*	*Post-6 April 2010*
	£	£	£
Dividend received	80.00	80.00	80.00
Tax credit	8.89	8.89	8.89
Trust income	88.89	88.89	88.89
Tax at 25%/32½%/42½%	22.22	28.89	37.78
Net of tax income	66.67	60.00	51.11

Grandchildren with a life interest continued to receive dividends with a non-repayable tax credit of 10% and, if higher rate taxpayers, to be liable to the dividend upper rate of 32½% (less tax credit of 10%). This remains the case since 6 April 2010, except that if their total income is in excess of £150,000 so that they become top rate taxpayers, the dividend additional rate of 42.5% will apply above that threshold (dividends being the top slice of income).

Effect on income available for distribution

(6)   Distributions out of the trust to grandchildren under 25 are now made net of 50% tax (34% from 1999/2000 to 2003/04 inclusive, 40% from 2004/05 to 2009/10 inclusive), and taxed as income of the

grandchildren as previously. Since 6 April 1999, however, the trustees cannot treat dividend credits as tax already paid in calculating how much of the 50%/40%/34% tax on a distribution has already been accounted for, since they may only include in the tax pool the excess of tax at the dividend trust rate of 42½%/32½%/25% over the 10% tax credit rate. The effect is that (before taking account of the standard rate band so far as it goes) the maximum distribution out of dividend income is now 50% (prior to 6 April 2010 – 60%, prior to 6 April 2004 – 66%) of the tax credit *exclusive* amount, eg:

	1999/2000 to 2003/04 inclusive £	2004/05 to 2009/10 inclusive £	2010/11 onwards £
Tax credit exclusive dividend income (net of trust expenses), say	1,800	1,800	1,800
Tax credit (1/9)	200	200	200
Trust gross income	2,000	2,000	2,000
Tax on dividend income (25%/32½%/42½)	500	650	850
Net income	1,500	1,350	1,150
Maximum gross payment to beneficiaries:			
Tax credit *exclusive* dividend	1,800	1,800	1,800
Tax thereon @ 34%/40%/50%	612	720	900
Distributable amount	1,188	1,080	900
Tax to be paid by trustees:			
Tax on gross income	500	650	850
Covered by tax credits	200	200	200
Payable by trustees on income	300	450	650
Tax on distributions	612	720	900
Further tax due from trustees	312	270	250

Although the trustees received £1,800 as income it is not possible to distribute that amount because of the tax due on income. In fact it is not normally possible to distribute all of the net income because of the additional tax due from the trustees on distribution, except so far as that amount may be covered by amounts brought forward within the tax pool. The effect is increased further to the extent that the dividends fall within the trustees' £1,000 standard rate band (see **explanatory note 1**): the (now) 50% liability on distributions would thus, since 6 April 2010, incur an additional £400 of tax on that £1,000, which would apart from that have suffered only the 10% dividend ordinary rate.

Because the non-repayable tax credit has already been taken into account in working out the tax payable by the trustees on distributions, the whole of the tax deducted from the distributions may be repaid to non-taxpaying beneficiaries. Thus if the full amount distributable in the above Example were in fact distributed to a beneficiary in whose hands it fell within his personal allowance, the amount he could recover would bring his total receipt back to the full £1,800 net dividend received by the trustees as follows:

	1999/2000 to 2003/04 inclusive £	2004/05 to 2009/10 inclusive £	2010/11 onwards £
Maximum amount distributable, and distributed, by trustees as above	1,188	1,080	900
Tax on distribution as above, recoverable by beneficiary	612	720	900
Gross income of beneficiary	1,800	1,800	1,800

Tax pool brought forward

(7)   The provisions in **point 6** from 6 April 1999 onwards may not apply where there is a tax pool brought forward (£650,000 at 6 April 1999 in the case of the Green grandchildren's trust, although this will have been increased by tax paid at the dividend trust rate (formerly Schedule F trust rate) on dividends received after that date as indicated in **point 6**). The whole of the brought forward figure, which largely represents dividend tax credits, was fully available to cover the tax on distributions to the beneficiaries. However, on the basis that roughly half of the dividends received each year has been distributed to beneficiaries, the pre-April 1999 tax pool will have been significantly absorbed by the additional tax chargeable on distributions compared to accumulated income. Conceivably, if dividends have been increasing over the years, the tax pool may even have been exhausted by now, with eleven tax years past since tax credits became non-repayable. The precise position can only be ascertained from a detailed year by year review since then. However, to the extent that a balance does still remain in the tax pool, it can be used to cover the 'further tax due from the trustees' identified in **point 6**, thus allowing the distribution of a greater amount of current or accumulated income. If a balance still remains in the tax pool when the last grandchild attains age 25, it becomes blocked and can no longer be used.

Although making an income distribution would use some of the residual tax pool brought forward, the benefit would depend on the tax position of the beneficiaries, since if the distribution was chargeable to higher rate tax in the hands of the grandchild, only a modest amount of tax would be repayable to them (the trustees' 50% liability less the beneficiary's 40% liability) – or nil in the unlikely event that the grandchild already had income in excess of £150,000 so that the whole of the distribution was liable in his hands at the 50% additional rate.

To the extent that trust income has been definitively accumulated so as to form part of the trust capital, it could no longer be distributed as income; thus, any distribution would be under a power to distribute capital (with inheritance tax rather than income tax implications), and no part of the income tax previously suffered could be recovered; nor, on the other hand, would any higher rate income tax be payable.

Capital gains if trust wound up

(8)   The Green plc shareholding is currently worth around £2 million, and may increase to over £5 million if the company is floated on the Stock Exchange. Its base cost for capital gains tax in 1988 was (850,000 less heldover gain 650,000 =) £200,000, so that there will be a substantial capital gain on disposal. Indexation allowance and taper relief were abolished in 2008 (as was the halving relief previously applicable where the person from whom a gain had been held over before 6 April 1988 – here the settlor – had acquired the asset before 31 March 1982), and the gain on any disposal after 22 June 2010 will be taxed at a flat rate of 28% unless it is possible to attract entrepreneurs' relief in respect of some part of the gain.

(9)   For a disposal to qualify for entrepreneurs' relief in respect of shares or securities held by trustees, a qualifying beneficiary – ie one who has an interest in possession in the assets disposed of, otherwise than for a fixed period (so in the present case limited to grandchildren over age 25) – must have been an officer or employee of the company throughout a period of one year ending not more than three years before the disposal and the company must have been both a trading company (or the holding company of a trading group) and the beneficiary's 'personal company' (with at least 5% of the ordinary share capital, or of the voting rights, held by him) for a corresponding period.

In the case the Green grandchildren's settlement, only two of the beneficiaries work for the company, and even if both of them have life interests their respective funds comprise less than 3.4% of the issued shares. Even if their respective funds were of more than 5%, however, life interest shares do not count towards making the company a beneficiary's personal company in any case; so unless one or other of those beneficiaries holds 5% of the company in his own right no entrepreneurs' relief will be available on a disposal of any part of the trustees' shareholding. On that basis the whole of the trustees' gain, on the deemed disposal that would result from a terminating the trust in respect of any of the shares, will be taxed at the 28% rate.

(10)   As explained in **point 11** below, any distribution of capital, except in the case of the grandchild(ren) who had already attained age 25 by 22 March 2006, would now incur an inheritance tax charge (even if this was at 0% on the figures eg as a result of business property relief), subject to one exception not relevant until early 2018, Holdover relief under TCGA 1992 s 260 could therefore be claimed in respect of the trustees' gains on those younger grandchildren's shares of the trust, so that the beneficiaries' acquisition costs would be reduced accordingly, provided the grandchildren are UK resident. As regards the proportion held for the benefit of any grandchild(ren) who were already 25 by 22 March 2006 (see **point 11(a)** below), holdover relief could similarly be claimed under TCGA 1992, s 165 and Schedule 7 providing the shares remained unquoted, or the trustees retained 25% or more of the voting rights; for this purpose the whole holding of the trustees can be counted, not merely the part in which life interests had vested before 22 March 2006.

Inheritance tax rules for Accumulation and Maintenance Settlements post-FA 2006

(11)   The inheritance tax treatment of the Green grandchildren's trust varies as between the shares of any grandchild(ren) who had already attained age 25 by 22 March 2006, and the remainder.

(a)   Any grandchild whose life interest had already vested (at age 25) by that date has an estate interest in possession which results in the relevant portion of the trust fund being treated for inheritance tax as if he was the absolute owner of it. To this extent, the winding up of the trust – resulting in the grandchild(ren) concerned becoming absolutely entitled to the fund in which they currently have an interest in possession – would entail no inheritance tax charge.

(b)   As regards the remaining shares the trust was still within the privileged rules for A&M settlements at 22 March 2006, when the inheritance tax rules for trusts were substantially altered, Interests in possession arising (on 25th birthdays) on or after that date are not estate interests in possession – neither the underlying capital nor the interest in possession itself counts as part of the beneficiary's estate for inheritance tax purposes – except to the extent (most unlikely in the circumstances) that the beneficiary is question met the definition in IHTA 1984 s 89 of a disabled person – not at the date his interest in possession arose, but at the date the shares were originally put into trust. Instead, the relevant share of the fund is within the relevant property regime from, at latest, the date the interest in possession arose.

(c)   However, a further feature of the 2006 changes was that A&M settlements in existence before 22 March 2006 lost their privileged status as such (to the extent that it had not already ceased on interests in possession arising) at the end of a transitional period on 6 April 2008.

(i)   To the extent that the trust provided by then for beneficiaries to become absolutely entitled to capital at age 25 instead of merely receiving life interests at that age, the trust became an age 18-to-25 trust within IHTA 1984 s 71D, with a more beneficial charging regime than that applicable under the relevant property regime (though in principle a charge, at a more lenient rate, would still be incurred when the beneficiary became absolutely entitled at 25). This was not the case in relation to the Green grandchildren's trust.

(ii)   Apart from that the trust became subject to the relevant property regime from 6 April 2008, to the extent that it had not already entered that regime when beneficiaries became entitled to interests in possession on or after 22 March 2006.

To the extent that the relevant property regime applies by virtue of **(b)** or **(c)** above, the settlement is now subject to the exit and ten-yearly charges regime. The cycle of ten-year anniversaries will be based on the date the trust was established in January 1988 rather than the date the trust property became 'relevant property' in April 2008 (or earlier 25th birthdays since 22 March 2006); a ten-yearly charge will thus have arisen in January 2008 in relation to any portion of the trust fund in which grandchildren had become entitled to life interests at age 25 on or after 22 March 2006, though the rate of tax on such charge will have been quite low since at least 32 quarter-years since the preceding ten-year anniversary (January 1998) had been completed before the property in question entered the relevant property regime.

An exit charge is not imposed in the three months following a ten-year anniversary (the next of which will not occur until January 2018); through a quirk of the legislation this would prevent a claim for capital gains tax holdover relief under TCGA 1992 s 260 in respect of distributions made in that three-month period, though relief under TCGA 1992 s 165 and Schedule 7 would still be available if the relevant conditions were satisfied at that time. (See **point 10** above.)

Explanatory Notes

Treatment of dividend income in discretionary trusts

(1)   The basic income tax treatment of discretionary trusts is that in respect of income which the trustees have the power to accumulate, or which may be distributed at their discretion, the trustees are liable to tax under ITA 2007 ss 479–481 at the dividend trust rate of 42½% on dividend income and at the 'trust rate' of 50% on other income. (These rates were increased by FA 2009 from 32.5% and 40% respectively with effect from the tax year 2010/2011.) The tax suffered by the trustees forms a tax pool (ITA 2007 ss 493–498 (replacing ICTA 1988 with effect from 6 April 2007)), which while it lasts is available to cover the tax on any distributions to the beneficiaries. Since 6 April 1999 not all of the tax charged to the trustees on grossed-up dividends goes into the tax pool, hence the reduced level of possible distribution as indicated in the Example; although the calculation is differently expressed in the legislation, the blocked amount has consistently been 10% of the grossed-up amount of the dividend, equating to the non-repayable tax credit on the dividend.

Under ITA 2007 s 491, however, the first £1,000 of relevant income (or less if there is more than one trust current with the same settlor), known as standard rate band, is not charged at the special trust tax rates, but will instead be charged at the basic rate. Therefore, if payments are received net of tax (for Example, building society interest) and the gross amount does not exceed the standard rate band, then the trustees will have no further tax to pay.

The standard rate band set out in ITA 2007 s 491 applies to trust income *net* of trust management expenses, and of other charges on income as well if there are any.

Although the management expenses are deducted from the trust income taxed at the lowest rate first, the standard rate band will apply in the order – basic rate income at 20% first, followed by dividends at 10%.

See **Examples 42, 47 and 48** for the details of this provision including the basis for abatement if the settlor had more than one trust still current. The standard rate band has applied since 6 April 2005, though its level in 2005/06 was £500 (without abatement provisions).

(2)   In this Example, once a grandchild reaches age 25 and becomes entitled to a life interest in the trust, his share of the trust income is taxable on him, whether it is received or retained within the trust. If there is unutilised tax within the pool of tax under ICTA 1988 s 687 when the last grandchild reaches age 25 the unused amount will be wasted, although this would not be a disadvantage to the extent that capital distributions were then made to grandchildren who would be liable to higher rate tax on income distributions. The inheritance tax charge on capital distributions would be at a relatively modest rate even if the shares held by the trustees were by then quoted shares, but would still represent an incentive to have utilised the tax pool in full in distributions to grandchildren who were not higher-rate taxpayers before it became unavailable.

Capital gains tax holdover relief and entrepreneurs' relief

(3)   There are two holdover reliefs available for capital gains tax, the business assets holdover relief of TCGA 1992 s 165 (see **Example 50 part a(d)** for the definition of business assets for this purpose) and the holdover relief of TCGA 1992 s 260 for gifts on which inheritance tax is chargeable – which includes a charge which works out at £0, but not an occasion where an exit charge is prevented by IHTA 1984, s 65(4) relating to distributions within three months after a ten-year anniversary (see **Example 64 explanatory note 3**). No inheritance tax charge arises if the beneficiary who becomes absolutely entitled had an estate interest in possession immediately beforehand – which would be the case for those beneficiaries who had reached age 25 before 22 March 2006; but so long as the shares remain unquoted, or the trustees retain 25% of the voting rights, the Green plc shares will be business assets for TCGA 1992 s 165 and attract hold-over relief under that provision instead.

(4)   Entrepreneurs' relief, set out in TCGA 1992 ss 169H to 169S, was introduced by FA 2008 s 9 and Sch 3, with effect for disposals on or after 6 April 2008, as limited compensation for the abolition of (in particular) business taper relief that took effect from the same date. The original provisions resulted in the first £1 million of gains arising on or in connection with disposals of the whole or part of a business (including, in certain circumstances, disposals of shares or securities) or of trust business assets ('qualifying business disposals') being charged to capital gains tax at an effective rate of 10% (4/9ths of the flat 18% rate then introduced). The relief was extended twice in 2010, first by doubling the limit to £2 million from 6 April 2010 (FA 2010 s 4); then (after the general election) by extending it to £5 million from 23 June 2010 (F(No 2)A 2010 Schedule 1 paragraph 5(2)). At the same time the 10% effective rate was converted to an actual rate, applying (so far as relief was available) in place of the new general capital gains tax rate of 28% (or 18% to the extent that income and gains of an individual fall within his basic rate band for income tax purposes).

A disposal by trustees will attract entrepreneurs' relief, as a disposal of trust business assets, when all three of the following conditions are met:

(a)   there is a disposal by trustees of assets which are part of the settled property of the settlement and are shares in or securities of a company, or interests in such shares or securities; or assets that have been used for the purposes of a business, or interests in such assets ('settlement business assets');

(b)   there is an individual in relation to a the settlement who has have an interest in possession (other than an interest in possession which has a fixed term) in the whole of the settled property of the settlement or in a part of the settled property that contains the settlement business assets (a 'qualifying beneficiary');

(c)   in relation to the disposal of settlement business assets a 'relevant condition' is satisfied. The nature of the relevant condition depends upon the nature of the assets disposed of:

(i)   In the case of shares in or securities of a company (or interests in such shares or securities), the company should have been the qualifying beneficiary's personal company, and the qualifying beneficiary must have been an officer or employee of the company, throughout a period of one year ending not more than three years before the disposal. To be the beneficiary's personal company, the beneficiary himself must hold 5% of the ordinary share capital or of the voting rights; the trustees' holding, even to the extent that he has an interest in possession in it, will not count towards the 5% threshold.

(ii)   In the case of assets (or interests in assets) that have been used for the purposes of a business, the relevant condition is that the qualifying beneficiary – not the trustees – has carried on the business throughout a period of one year ending not more than three years before the disposal and ceases to do so on the date of the disposal or within three years before then.

INDEX

References are to page numbers.